ASIAN DRAMA

An Inquiry Into the Poverty of Nations

PRINCIPAL ASSISTANTS

William J. Barber, Professor of Economics,
Wesleyan University, Middletown, Connecticut, U.S.A.

Altti Majava, Demographer, National Planning Office,
Helsinki, Finland

Alva Myrdal, Cabinet Member, Minister for
Disarmament, Stockholm, Sweden

Paul P. Streeten, Professor of Economics,
University of Sussex, Brighton, England

David Wightman, Reader in International Economic History,
University of Birmingham, England

George W. Wilson, Chairman, Department of Economics and Division of
Economic Research, Indiana University, Bloomington, Indiana, U.S.A.

A TWENTIETH CENTURY FUND STUDY

ASIAN DRAMA

An Inquiry Into the Poverty of Nations

by **GUNNAR MYRDAL**

VOLUME **I**

PANTHEON
A Division of Random House
NEW YORK

THE TWENTIETH CENTURY FUND

founded in 1919 and endowed by Edward A. Filene, is a nonprofit foundation which, through research and publication, seeks to throw light upon emerging issues of our times. The studies supported by the Fund are defined by its Board of Trustees and fall chiefly in the broad fields of economics, social problems and international affairs. The Fund attempts to ensure the scholarly quality of works appearing under its imprint; the Trustees and the staff, however, accord the author or authors complete freedom in the statement of opinions and the interpretation of facts.

First Printing

Published in New York in hard cover by the Twentieth Century Fund and in paper cover by Pantheon Books, a division of Random House, Inc. Published simultaneously in Toronto, Canada, by Random House of Canada Limited.

Printed in the United States of America
Library of Congress Catalog Card Number 67–19179

FOREWORD

IT HAS BEEN traditional for the Director of the Twentieth Century Fund to write a brief foreword to works completed under the Fund's auspices. Though circumstances have recently taken me from the post of Director, I was responsible for bringing to the Trustees more than a decade ago the first plan for this book. I have watched closely over its progress and changes through the years since then, up to the time when the last words of the manuscript were written and arrangements for final editing and publication were completed. Throughout this period – longer than Professor Myrdal or any of us anticipated – I suffered with the author through the discouragements which so large a task inevitably brings, and rejoiced with him as the end came into view. Visits to his headquarters in New Delhi, in London and in Stockholm are among the most vivid memories of these years; and Professor Myrdal's journeys to this country, when Fund business was combined with brief and revivifying reunions with American friends, always left a sense of excitement in their wake.

The substance of the book speaks for itself. It would be foolish to try to sum it up here. Suffice it to say that the argument goes against the grain of much contemporary thought, cuts deep, and moves at a level where differences of opinion are fundamental. Professor Myrdal began with a hopeful view of the possibilities for rational planning and ordered growth in the underdeveloped countries; in the course of his work he has come to a sombre realization of the difficulties they must surmount and the need for a reappraisal of the theories basic to their planning efforts. He is understandably reluctant to admit how largely thinking about the underdeveloped countries has been shaped and influenced by his own studies; yet unless one realizes this, the achievement of the present volume is not fully weighed. For Professor Myrdal had not only to move against accepted premises and assumptions; what was more difficult, he had to move against those premises which he had himself done so much to establish and to make seem self-evident. Burke says somewhere that there is no vested interest so powerful as the vested interest in an idea. When the idea is of one's own making, the efforts required to transcend it may be nothing less than heroic.

The world has changed rapidly since Professor Myrdal began this study in 1957. It would seem that we are all less naively hopeful about paper plans and the immediate benefits of economic aid than was once the case. The gulf separating the rich from the poor nations has come to be accepted as a tragic fact of international life – tragic not in the sense that we are excused for doing nothing about it, but that we must labor to obliterate it without hope of seeing our efforts crowned with rapid success or ourselves blessed with appreciation and gratitude. In such an atmosphere Professor Myrdal's book may be better received than he is inclined to expect. When men have learned not to be frustrated because their wishes are not immediately fulfilled, and not to be bitter because the world has proved tougher and more complex than they dreamed, then they may be in a mood to value truth very highly. It may be claimed for his book that it honestly seeks to find and assert truth – the kind of truth that does not pretend to be final or authoritative, but to fit the facts as they actually exist.

Being no longer on the staff of the Fund, I am free to say (as I know Professor Myrdal would want me to do) that the thousands of pages of the manuscript presented a formidable challenge to our editors. As chapter after chapter came in, several of them longer by themselves than many a published volume, the offices of the Fund were almost swamped. Nor was Professor Myrdal, on his side of the water, always the most patient of scholars! But there was a spirit in the enterprise which made all seem worthwhile, a spirit contributed, along with so much else, by the author. So it remains only to thank Professor Myrdal for undertaking the work in the first instance, and for laboring so long, and most of the time so cheerfully, to complete it. Mrs. Myrdal, in the midst of her own duties as Ambassador and Foreign Secretary, bore with us all, and lent her special knowledge and insight to important parts of the manuscript.

It is a pleasure to acknowledge the cooperation of the Institute for International Economic Studies, of Stockholm, in Professor Myrdal's study for the Twentieth Century Fund. The Institute, of which Gunnar Myrdal is the founder and director, began in 1961 to participate in the research and its financing. Thereafter, completion of the work was one of the major projects of the Institute as well as of the Fund.

AUGUST HECKSCHER

PREFACE

HABENT SUA FATA LIBELLI — books have their own destiny, even while they are being written and before they are published. Often, the simplest way of explaining what a book is about and what it aims to achieve is to tell why and how it came to be written.

After the Second World War I became increasingly interested in the economic problems of the underdeveloped countries. This was not in any way an extraordinary and original bent of mind; it followed closely the general reorientation of the social sciences in the post-war period on which I comment in Section 2 of the Prologue to this book. The same inclination manifested itself in the secretariat of the Economic Commission for Europe, which came into being in the spring of 1947 with myself at the head. Its work was to a considerable extent oriented toward the study of the development problems of the underdeveloped countries in Southern and Eastern Europe; it also investigated similar problems outside Europe in cooperation with the secretariats of the Economic Commissions for Asia and the Far East and for Latin America.

In connection with the E.C.E.'s particularly close cooperation with ECAFE and at the instigation of P. S. Lokanathan, who was then Executive Secretary of ECAFE, I made a six-weeks' tour of South Asia in the autumn of 1953, visiting Pakistan, India, Burma, Thailand, and Indonesia. I had consultations with my colleagues on the ECAFE staff in Bangkok, with government officials, and with other indigenous and foreign experts at the universities and in the field; as is my custom, I also visited industries and villages. In short, in the limited time available I tried in every way to familiarize myself with the economic, social, and political problems of the countries in the region. Since that visit I have never been free of an intense awareness of the momentous human drama of the desperate strivings for national consolidation and economic development in the South Asian countries. I decided then that as soon as I could free myself with good conscience from my duties with the E.C.E., I would return for a couple of years to these countries and devote myself to studying their problems of economic underdevelopment, development, and planning for development.

My own readings and writings during the next few years were almost exclusively directed toward preparing myself for this task,[1] and I made

[1] See, in particular, *An International Economy,* Harper, New York, 1956, and *Economic Theory and Under-developed Regions,* G. Duckworth & Co. Ltd., London, 1957 (published in the United States under the title *Rich Lands and Poor,* Harper, New York, 1957).

two more visits to the region. I also had the opportunity to make a similar tour of seven weeks in the adjacent region, which I then called the Near and Middle East but which I have now grown accustomed to calling by the more appropriate name of West Asia. There I met the same basic problems as in South Asia, though in a somewhat different political, social, and economic setting. In the spring of 1957, before I left the position I held with the E.C.E., my horizons were further enlarged by an exploratory visit of several weeks to the Soviet Central Asian Republics.[1] An eight-weeks' visit to Australia as Dayson Lecturer in the early autumn of 1957 gave me some idea of how Asian problems appear in the perspective of a continent that is geographically almost a part of Southeast Asia yet is very different and distant. From my earlier life and work I was, of course, intensely aware of the West European and East European perspective and the American as well. And so I felt, when in the late autumn of 1957 I became free to take up full-time work on the study that has resulted in the present book, that I had for a long time been circling around the task and was at least somewhat versed in the world setting of South Asia's economic problems. The next step was to tackle these problems directly, and to this end I spent the larger part of the next three academic years living and working in the region.

My intention was to write a general book focussed on actual conditions in South Asia, the prospects for development there, and the main policy alternatives facing the national governments. The attempt to do this, I felt, should not be deemed pretentious. Books and articles are continually being produced which are even more general in scope, as they concern the economic problems faced by all the underdeveloped countries in the world; indeed, I had myself been guilty of occasional contributions to this literature. The defense of these even more general studies has been — and I believe it is a fully valid one — that they provide a broad conspectus of what we know about these countries and their problems. That conspectus is needed for the guidance of practical policy in underdeveloped and developed countries; policy formation cannot wait until relatively complete information is available, but must be based on a provisional assessment of everything that is known in a general way. From a scientific point of view, a more essential function of studies following a generalizing approach is to provide a logically correlated system of questions to be answered by further detailed research, a "theory" in other words. In a sense, this study was designed to occupy a middle ground, slightly nearer the concrete facts than the most general literature on the development problems of underdeveloped countries. It was thought that by concentrating on the underde-

[1] The results of this visit, which I made in company with three members of the E.C.E.'s research staff, were published in the November, 1957, issue of the *Economic Bulletin for Europe,* Vol. 9, No. 3, under the title "Regional Economic Policy in the Soviet Union: The Case of Central Asia."

veloped countries in one region – which, though heterogeneous, are more similar than underdeveloped countries in widely separated parts of the world – one might hope to reach a somewhat deeper understanding of the common problems.

The foregoing paragraphs are an attempt to state and explain how the idea for the study took shape in the mind of the author. Meanwhile the Twentieth Century Fund, which had concentrated its work during the prewar years on major problems in the United States, had undertaken a few studies of other countries, and was beginning to enter into broad regional studies. As the plans of the Fund's Trustees for a study of South Asia agreed with my own ideas, the Fund undertook the study in its own program, as is its regular practice when supporting scholarly work, and appointed me director of the project. This relationship with the Fund continued after my return to Stockholm at the beginning of 1961, when the work remaining to be done on the study became a major part of the research program of the newly created Stockholm University Institute for International Economic Studies, of which I became the director. The Trustees and staff of the Fund have been extremely helpful in all respects, and were understanding when it turned out that the work on the book would take much longer than originally planned. In accordance with its rules and general practice, the Fund has not interfered with either the approach chosen or the conclusions reached and the manner of expressing them; responsibility for these matters was left entirely to me.

One preconception of mine deserves mention, as it determined my approach to the task. My personal journey through life and work, from early youth when my research interests were focussed on economic theory in a very narrow sense, had instilled in me an increasingly firm conviction that economic problems cannot be studied in isolation but only in their demographic, social, and political setting. Like all others who keep alive their interest in contemporary world history, I felt that crucially important things were happening in the region of South Asia. As I had been molded by my particular research experiences, I felt at the outset of the study that only by means of a broad institutional approach could I understand and explain the economic underdevelopment in the region, as well as what there is of economic development and planning for development. As my work proceeded and I saw how significant are levels and modes of living and attitudes and institutions in relation to underdevelopment and development in South Asia, I became even more convinced that such an approach was necessary to give realism and relevance to research. In general terms, the reasons for this orientation of my work – and my objections to the usual "modern approach" that is embodied in the structure of the plans and in the scientific and popular discussion of the economic problems of these countries – are spelled out in the Prologue; in specific terms they are developed in all of the chapters and in the methodological Appendices 1 to 8.

It is not altogether a pretentious metaphor when I describe my endeavor to apply an institutional approach in this study as an attempt to analyze the development problems of South Asia in the manner that Adam Smith studied England's development problems two hundred years ago. Smith, of course, never dealt with economic problems as purely "economic," and the same can be said in general of the whole classical school, including toward the end Karl Marx. John Kenneth Galbraith has stressed this aspect of the classicists' approach:

> The principles of good government, the inducements to individual performance, the role of popular enlightenment, the foundations of thrift, the effect of competition and of monopoly, the relation between social classes, the reasons why some people, notably the English, worked hard and others, notably the Irish, were idle, were all grist for their highly diversified mill. Anything that was deemed to have a bearing on economic advance came into the discussion. The only test was broad relevance to the questions: What made for economic progress? Or, on the other hand, what led to stagnation – to the much discussed stationary state?[1]

The classicists had "concerned themselves with the aggregate requirement of progress." From this vantage point, Galbraith sees "some serious shortcomings in the modern discussion" of the underdeveloped countries, and states: "We have given too little attention to inquiring whether [the things that contribute to economic development] are being employed in a context that is favorable to development."

But Adam Smith's England contained only about 7 million people, while the present study concerns a fourth of mankind; and the fact that there is a vast amount of literature relating to various aspects of the South Asian situation proved to be a mixed blessing. I frankly confess that I found my task much more difficult than I had expected. Although I have not spared myself, but have worked harder than ever before in my life, this book, with all its shortcomings, has taken me four times as long to produce as I thought it would.

The length is abominable. The question can, indeed, be raised why I did not break it up into five or six books on separate topics. But the central idea in the institutional approach is that history and politics, theories and ideologies, economic structures and levels, social stratification, agriculture and industry, population developments, health and education, and so on, must be studied not in isolation but in their mutual relationships. Incidentally, one consequence of this approach was that I found myself constantly laboring to adjust all of the several chapters; none was considered complete until the entire manuscript reached the final stage. As I realize that the interests of many readers will tend to be restricted to particular parts

[1] *Economic Development,* Harvard University Press, Cambridge, 1964, pp. 38–40.

of the study — the chapters on health and education, perhaps, or the methodological discussions in the Prologue, some of the appendices, and portions of certain chapters — I am happy to report that consideration is being given to making some of the more specialized material available in separate volumes, where references to other parts of the study will underline my basic conception that all problems in these countries are closely interrelated.

I met some difficulties besides those I inflicted upon myself by choosing to deal with a whole region and electing to view the economic problems in their total demographic, social, ideological, and political setting. One was the extremely frail basis for factual knowledge about the South Asian region, of which I was not fully aware when I began the study. Wherever I turned, I found that any statistics available had to be scrutinized most severely before being used; at best they were highly uncertain and not as specific as the analyst would desire. Most of the general figures so confidently quoted in the literature, such as those pertaining to trends in income, population, literacy, and school enrollment, proved to be no more than extremely crude guesses, often palpably wrong. To establish this was itself a time-consuming process. When, instead, I made my own more specific estimates on the basis of meager statistics — as, for instance, in regard to schooling — they were of necessity extremely tentative, often having as their main purpose to indicate more clearly the sort of data that should be produced by further research.

Worse still, as I worked on I became increasingly aware that many of the concepts and theories commonly used in analyzing the problems of the underdeveloped countries in South Asia broke down when criticized from the point of view of their logical consistency and their realism, that is, their adequacy to reality. To work my way through what I gradually came to view as severely biased preconceptions — many of which I had shared with most of my fellow economists — was again a slow and painful process. This analytical deficiency has had a crucial effect on the character of the study. It is not unrelated to the statistical deficiency, as the weakness of much of the data stems from the fact that inadequate concepts and theories provided the framework of categories used in their collection and analysis.

So the work went on far beyond any deadlines the Twentieth Century Fund and I had set for the study, which in my work life was a unique experience. And instead of producing the facile but, as I had hoped, still respectable book on the main development problems of South Asia I had set out to write, I found myself engaged in a study where the main concern was methodological — how to cleanse concepts and discard theories and then state problems in a logical and realistic way — and where the results were very often merely a demonstration of our ignorance and a clearer statement of what we do not know. It is in this way that the work on the study became to me personally a destiny, the course of which I had not foreseen or planned from the beginning. I sincerely believe that at the present stage an important contribution to the advance of knowledge about these countries is the negative act of destroying constructs that we have rapidly put together and exposing to criticism masses of more or less worthless statistics collected within the framework of these constructs, which we are using all too confidently. I believe this because these constructs and statistics now stand in the way of scientific progress.

The chapters in Part Two on the political problems and several chapters or sections in later parts, particularly, may seem to belong to the type of book I originally intended to write – and may to an extent serve the purpose of such a book – as they consist of generalizations about conditions in the several countries of the region which I believe are broadly valid. But, as I explain in Section 7 of the Prologue and Section 2 of Chapter 1, from a methodological point of view my main purpose in stating these generalizations, especially in fields outside the main focus of the study, is to set down logically and explicitly the ideas that have determined my approach to the more intensive study of some particular problems. In a sense, what I have reached for in this book, beyond mere criticism, is a tentative "theory," one that coordinates in a systematic manner a general conception of what is happening in the region of South Asia. I tried to make this theory realistic; more specifically, I tailored it to fit the facts, so far as I knew them.

"Theory" in this context means nothing more than a logically correlated system of questions addressed to the material. It is in the nature of this conception of theory – which will be further developed in the Prologue – that the author of a theory should not fear, but expect as a perfectly normal consequence of fresh research, that further insights into various components of the complex of social interrelationships about which he has tried to inform himself will invalidate his theory, perhaps in fundamental respects.

I would like to emphasize that I am deeply conscious of the fact that I have myself shared many of the ways of thought that I criticize in this book. This has, I hope, saved me from falling into a polemical mood. Also, it has made it subjectively easier to simplify the text. Thus I have not, except on a few occasions, found it necessary to quote extensively from the literature in order to exemplify the views I am criticizing. I have been more concerned with a main line of thought than with the variations on the theme by individual authors. In this connection I should stress that I am well aware that most of the elements of which my own approach is composed have found expression in the observations, qualifications, or reservations of other writers. If the book has any degree of originality, it is as a total composition and in the insistence upon following the basic institutional approach through to its consequences.

New primary research was never contemplated and could not have been carried out without a much bigger research apparatus than I had available; it could not in any case have been more than extremely spotty. As I was determined to achieve realism, i.e., adequacy to the facts, as well as logical consistency, I have naturally tried to delve as deeply into the many diversified and involved conditions in the several countries as time and ability permitted. But the scope of the study was so wide that the results have had to be presented on a rather abstract level and the treatment has had to be selective. Many very important problems – including, I realize, many that have been given primacy in the economic literature – could only be hinted at and their place in the system abstractly demarcated, as for instance those of taxation (Appendix 8, Section 8). Thus this book is not in any sense a survey.

The "theory" I have tried to formulate relates to the South Asian region, which is the only one I have kept under close observation. I have not in general felt it within my province to inquire in this study whether the theory, or any part of it, is valid for other underdeveloped regions in the world. To stress this limitation is felt to be the more imperative as I come to the conclusion that a major vehicle for introducing serious biases into research on South Asian problems has been the uncritical application of concepts and theories that have been developed in, and have validity for, another region or group of countries, viz. the rich Western or Communist countries.

Theory is always tentative and provisional. No publication is ever the final one (though reviewers occasionally say as much about a particular book), and undoubtedly there are differences in regard to how much is left open for further research. In this particular case I want to confess that never have I felt so far from being able to present something resembling the final truth about a matter. It is my conviction that in twenty or even ten years' time we shall have different approaches and use quite different concepts and theories from those we have been accustomed to using. This book aspires to do little more than speed up the reorientation of economic and social research on South Asia. In this situation my findings can only be suggestive and tentative, and I expect that they will soon be lost like the memory of a variation of a melody in a mighty fugue of thinking and research which will proceed and never reach a finale.

In working on this book I have been reminded of a friend of mine who long ago wrote a doctoral thesis on the fiscal problem as one of the collective satisfaction of individual needs, and in the preface told a story from the Icelandic Aesir sagas. Thor, the god of war and manly prowess of the pagan Scandinavians, paid a visit to the Giants in Utgård. While they were eating and drinking, the Giants teased Thor about his physical prowess and challenged him to lift a cat that lay purring in a corner of the hall of feasting. Irritated, Thor rose to toss the cat out of the window, but however much he exerted himself, he could only get the cat to stand on its legs. Finally, by using all his strength he succeeded in lifting it so that one of its feet was for a moment a hairsbreadth off the floor. When the exhausted Thor returned to the table, he found, however, the Giants upset and showing signs of fear. The saga explains that the Giants had distorted Thor's vision. What he had been challenged to lift was not any normal animal but the mythical Great World Serpent swaddling the earth seven times, its tail firmly gripped in its jaws. If in the beginning of this study I was naive like Thor, at the end I am humble. I shall be satisfied if I have succeeded in indicating the nature of the problems of underdevelopment, development, and planning for development in South Asia, stating more systematically the immense scope of our ignorance, and hinting at the most profitable areas for further research.

* * *

No book of this size and scope could have been written without the assistance of a great number of people. First of all, I am immensely indebted to the many scholars, journalists, government officials and other political figures, businessmen, and, not least, common people in the South Asian countries who generously made available to me the information and ideas they possessed about the region's development, past, present, and future. Any attempt to list all the South Asians and others knowledgeable about the region who helped me in this way would be futile. In writing the book I have also had much direct assistance, without which the analysis would have been less intensive in several chapters and the publication date even further delayed. On this point I can be more specific.

When in the autumn of 1957 I took up my work in New Delhi, I was accompanied by two senior colleagues from the Research Division of the secretariat of the E.C.E., Mogens and Ester Boserup. The study had been planned to take two and a half years, and the Boserups left me, as we had agreed, in the spring of 1960. Because my own views about the kind of book I wanted to write were at that time gradually changing, the text in its final version contains comparatively little of what Mr. and Mrs. Boserup produced during their term of duty. Nevertheless, the further work on what are now Chapters 22 and 26 on labor utilization in agriculture and agricultural policy could build on early drafts for several sections by Ester Boserup, and a large part of Chapter 10 on population and development of agricultural resources is in the main founded on a manuscript by Mogens Boserup; he also wrote the very first sketch of Chapter 27 on population prospects. In some other chapters of the book there are passages that go back to the early association of the Boserups with the study.

My own work during this period was devoted mainly to research on the historical, political, and ideological problems and the preparation of preliminary outlines and sketches for Parts Two and Four. I also began laboring, even then, on Appendix 2, where my gradually evolving institutional approach was to be presented in a systematic way.

In the spring and summer of 1960, while continuing to work on Appendix 2, I began sketching two methodologically crucial chapters, Chapter 19 on operational controls and Chapter 21 criticizing the use of the concepts and theories of unemployment and underemployment in the "modern approach." For more than a year I was assisted by Kamal Azfar and Michael Lipton, both newly graduated from Balliol College, Oxford, which in 1959 and again in 1960 gave me temporary working accommodations. For four months in the autumn of 1960 I was also joined by Shu-Chin Yang from the ECAFE secretariat.

Mr. Shu-Chin and particularly Mr. Azfar, whose collaboration extended over a longer time, collected much of the factual material that has gone into Chapters 17 on Asian socialism, 19 on operational controls, and Appendix 8 to that chapter. Mr. Lipton wrote the first draft of Appendix 10 on climate, and prepared an intensive analysis of national accounting in the South Asian countries, which has been incorporated in condensed form in Chapter 11 on national output and structure of the economy. Mr. Lipton's most difficult and time-consuming assignment was to carry out a lengthy comparative analysis of the development plans in the countries of the region, which Ester Boserup had begun; as explained in Appendix 4, it was not thought necessary to publish this analysis in the book. Both Mr. Azfar and Mr. Lipton were helpful in reading and criticizing what I was writing in the meantime; toward the end of their term on the project they also assisted Professors Wilson and Barber, who joined my staff at this time.

At the beginning of 1961 I had moved my workshop to Stockholm, where I had been appointed professor of international economics at my old university; I was released from all teaching duties in order to devote all of my time to directing the new Institute for International Economic Studies and completing the present study.

In February of 1961 I was joined by George W. Wilson, of Indiana University, Bloomington, Indiana, who not only spent several months at the Institute in 1961 and again in 1962 but also did some work on the study in Bloomington in those years and later. Professor Wilson's main task was to prepare Chapters 10 and 13 on economic realities in South Asia. Beyond Chapter 10, for much of which he had the draft written by Mogens Boserup, he found nothing on paper other than my very broad outlines. He was guided mainly by our continual discussion, orally and in writing, as drafts were gradually produced.

Except for Chapter 13, where I made extensive additions and amendments in preparing the final text, these chapters stand substantially as Professor Wilson left them. He had had some assistance on Chapter 11 from Mr. Lipton, and Altti Majava had worked on statistics relating to various elements of levels of living analyzed in Chapter 12, particularly those important to health. Professor Wilson contributed substantially to Chapter 14 (especially Section 6) on differences in initial situation, which I drafted. He also had a hand in preparing Appendix 10 on climate and an early draft of Chapter 27 on population prospects.

William J. Barber, of Wesleyan University in Middletown, Connecticut, joined the study in June of 1961 and remained with me in Stockholm until September of 1962. Professor Barber undertook the drafting of Part Five on problems of labor utilization, except the first three parts of Chapter 21 on "unemployment" and "underemployment" and Appendix 6 on the concept and theory of "underemployment," which I had drafted. In addition to some drafts, prepared by Ester Boserup, of parts of what are now Chapters 22 and 26, he had my sketches of drafts for particular parts of these and the other chapters in Part Five. When I produced the final text, my additions and amendments were extensive only in Chapters 25 and 26.

Meanwhile, besides continuing my work on Appendices 2 and 6, and beginning to work on other methodological appendices (Appendix 4 on the structure of development plans, Appendix 5 on "accounting prices," and Appendix 7 on inadequate approaches to the economic effects of population changes), I had set out to draft what is now the Prologue and the Introduction as well as Part Four, devoted to the main problems of ideologies and institutions in planning. I had also resumed work on the political problems, which I had begun while stationed in New Delhi and travelling a good deal in India and the other countries of the region.

In 1962 David Wightman, of Birmingham University, enlisted in our work and stayed in Stockholm from March until September; he gave a shorter summer term in 1963 and had some work left to do when he returned to Birmingham. Dr. Wightman's assignment was to take my drafts, and for some sections (particularly those now constituting Chapters 5, 8, and 9) my bare outlines, and produce a fuller and more definite draft of what would become Part Two on political problems. I then went over this draft, made my amendments and additions, organized it into chapters and sections, and wrote anew the sections covering more recent events.

It was natural that I also turned for assistance in my work to Paul Streeten, then Fellow of Balliol College, Oxford, who as translator and editor of some of my earlier studies on methodological problems[1] had earned my gratitude and come inside my way of thinking. Mr. Streeten

[1] *The Political Element in the Development of Economic Theory,* Routledge & Kegan Paul Ltd., London, 1953, and *Value in Social Theory, A Selection of Essays on Methodology,* Routledge & Kegan Paul Ltd., London, 1958.

spent parts of two summers – 1961 and 1962 – and a month in the summer of 1964 with the project staff in Stockholm. A major part of his time was devoted to developing and elaborating the criticism in Appendix 2, and in many other contexts in the book, of the type of model-thinking that characterizes the "modern approach." The core of this work is presented in Appendix 3 on economic models and their usefulness for planning in South Asia; it is so much his own that it is specifically designated as a contribution by him to this book. But besides this major personal contribution, Mr. Streeten read some other methodological parts of the book and helped to amplify and improve them. This work of his was particularly important for the final text of Appendix 2 (especially Part IV, Sections 23 and 24), Appendix 4 (especially Section 4), and Appendix 7 (especially Section 3).

Alva Myrdal has, of course, been closely associated with my work from the time of our early youth. At the beginning of this study she undertook to assist in preparing the chapters on health and education. After some groundwork by her, Altti Majava took over the responsibility for assembling information for the chapter on health, but Mrs. Myrdal remained with her task in regard to education till the very end of the study in the summer of 1967. As I wrote the chapters on education, Chapters 31–33, I had not only statistical material that had been prepared by her with Mr. Majava's assistance but also drafts and sketches of the text. She read and criticized the successive drafts and, ultimately, the final text.

In 1955 when Mrs. Myrdal was head of the Social Science Department of UNESCO – and well before economists were roused to their present interest in education (and, occasionally, health) – she gave five lectures in the Heath-Clark series at the School of Tropical Medicine, London University, on "Health and Education in Economic Development" which, because of the pressure of her other duties, were not published. I feel a husband's satisfaction that in our cooperation on the present book she has seen her thoughts on these subjects amplified and specified in the broader setting of the development problems in South Asia.

I owe a special debt of gratitude to my statistical assistant, Altti Majava of Helsinki University, who was engaged for the study in the spring of 1961 and stayed with it to the end. Over the years he has gained a comprehensive knowledge of all quantitative information from South Asia, and its deficiencies, and has perfected his analytical ability. Mr. Majava was responsible for the final form and content of all tables and charts in the book. He also wrote the final draft of Appendix 10 on climate and the next-to-final drafts of Chapter 27 on population prospects, Appendix 11 on migration, and Appendix 12 on Indian family planning.

Chapter 30 on health is founded on material collected and partly analyzed by Mr. Majava. He not only assisted Alva Myrdal in gathering and analyzing the statistical material on financial planning, literacy, and adult education in Chapter 32 and on the school system in Chapter 33, but also constructed, under my direction, the tables and charts in those two chapters.

All my collaborators aided me by reading and criticizing certain parts of the book other than those within their particular purview. Thus Professor Barber read through the bulky manuscript that was to become the Prologue and the Introduction and made helpful comments; he even did some preliminary editing.

Frank W. Notestein and his colleagues at the Population Council, New York City, read and criticized an earlier version of what are now Chapters 27 and 28 on population prospects and population policy. Eric H. Jacoby, the chief of the F.A.O. secretariat unit for land reform in Rome, read two consecutive drafts of Chapter 26 on agricultural policy, as did Horst Foelster of Göttingen University. Harold Lydall of Adelaide University read Sections 7 and 8 of Chapter 12 on levels of living and inequality, and Appendix 14. Tarlok Singh, who arrived as research fellow at the Stockholm Institute in June of 1967, read Chapters 26 and 31–33 in proofs and also certain other parts of the book; so did Ingvar Svennilson of Stockholm University. Vera Micheles Dean of New York University, New York City, read various chapters and appendices in galley proofs.

Elizabeth Blackert, chief editor of the Twentieth Century Fund, was responsible for the final editing, in which she was assisted by Ruth Rocker and Katharine A. Beyer. They and others who worked in various capacities with the manuscripts and proofs in New York City and Stockholm contributed greatly to the style in which the text now appears. They also helped me strengthen the argument in several places and weed out some mistakes that had eluded me. Esther I. Persson had the difficult assignment of preparing an index. I am particularly grateful to Mrs. Blackert for all the personal attention she gave to the book despite other demands upon her time.

To all my collaborators, to the critics mentioned, and to the editors, I remain in gratitude. Recognizing that the responsibility for the content of the book would have to remain my own, each contributed unstintingly toward helping me to realize my aims.

All outlines, drafts, proofs, staff memoranda, correspondence, and other documents relating to the study are deposited with the Royal Library in Stockholm, at its invitation, where they are open to the public.

GUNNAR MYRDAL

The Stockholm University Institute for
International Economic Studies
July 1, 1967

Outline of the Book

Volume I

Volume II

Volume III

Contents of Volume I

PART TWO: POLITICAL PROBLEMS

Tables in Volume I

CHAPTER 10

CHAPTER 11

Figures in Volume I

CHAPTER 5

CHAPTER 10

CHAPTER 12

PROLOGUE

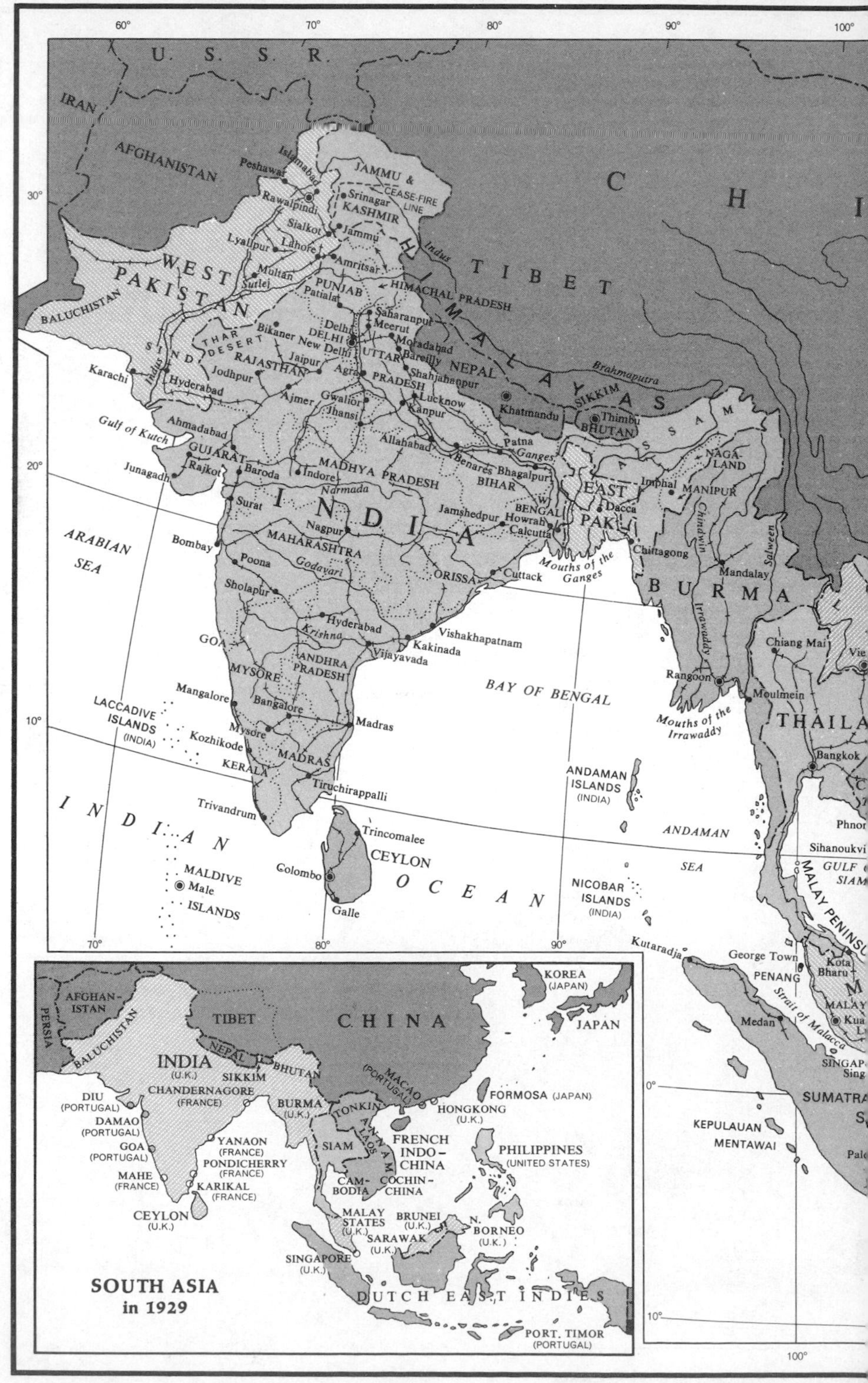

U. S. S. R.
IRAN
AFGHANISTAN
Peshawar
Islamabad
Rawalpindi
JAMMU &
KASHMIR
Srinagar
CEASE-FIRE LINE
Sialkot
Jammu
Lyallpur
Lahore
Amritsar
Multan
Sutlej
Indus
WEST PAKISTAN
BALUCHISTAN
PUNJAB
Patiala
HIMACHAL PRADESH
HIMALAYAS
TIBET
C H
Saharanpur
Meerut
Delhi
DELHI
New Delhi
Bikaner
Moradabad
Bareilly
UTTAR PRADESH
Shahjahanpur
NEPAL
Brahmaputra
THAR DESERT
SIND
RAJASTHAN
Jaipur
Agra
Jodhpur
Karachi
Hyderabad
Ajmer
Gwalior
Jhansi
Lucknow
Kanpur
Khatmandu
SIKKIM
Thimbu
BHUTAN
ASSAM
Gulf of Kutch
Ahmadabad
GUJARAT
Junagadh
Rajkot
Baroda
Indore
Allahabad
Benares
Patna
Ganges
Bhagalpur
BIHAR
NAGA-LAND
MADHYA PRADESH
Narmada
Imphal
MANIPUR
EAST PAK
Dacca
Surat
INDIA
Jamshedpur
BENGAL
Howrah
Calcutta
Chindwin
Salween
ARABIAN SEA
Bombay
Nagpur
MAHARASHTRA
Chittagong
Poona
Godavari
ORISSA
Cuttack
Mouths of the Ganges
Mandalay
BURMA
Sholapur
Hyderabad
Krishna
Vishakhapatnam
Kakinada
Irrawaddy
GOA
Vijayavada
Chiang Mai
ANDHRA PRADESH
MYSORE
Rangoon
Mangalore
BAY OF BENGAL
Moulmein
Bangalore
LACCADIVE ISLANDS (INDIA)
Mysore
Madras
Mouths of the Irrawaddy
Kozhikode
MADRAS
KERALA
Bangkok
ANDAMAN ISLANDS (INDIA)
Tiruchirappalli
INDIAN OCEAN
Trivandrum
Trincomalee
ANDAMAN SEA
CEYLON
Sihanoukville
MALDIVE ISLANDS
Male
Colombo
NICOBAR ISLANDS (INDIA)
Galle
MALAY PENINSULA
Kutaradja
George Town
PENANG
Kota Bharu
Medan
Strait of Malacca
SUMATRA
KEPULAUAN MENTAWAI
60°
70°
80°
90°
100°
30°
20°
10°
0°
AFGHAN-ISTAN
PERSIA
BALUCHISTAN
TIBET
CHINA
KOREA (JAPAN)
JAPAN
INDIA (U.K.)
NEPAL
SIKKIM
BHUTAN
CHANDERNAGORE (FRANCE)
MACAO (PORTUGAL)
DIU (PORTUGAL)
DAMAO (PORTUGAL)
BURMA (U.K.)
TONKIN
FORMOSA (JAPAN)
HONGKONG (U.K.)
YANAON (FRANCE)
GOA (PORTUGAL)
PONDICHERRY (FRANCE)
SIAM
LAOS
ANNAM
FRENCH INDO-CHINA
PHILIPPINES (UNITED STATES)
MAHE (FRANCE)
KARIKAL (FRANCE)
CAMBODIA
COCHIN-CHINA
CEYLON (U.K.)
MALAY STATES (U.K.)
BRUNEI (U.K.)
N. BORNEO (U.K.)
SARAWAK (U.K.)
SINGAPORE (U.K.)
SOUTH ASIA in 1929
DUTCH EAST INDIES
PORT. TIMOR (PORTUGAL)

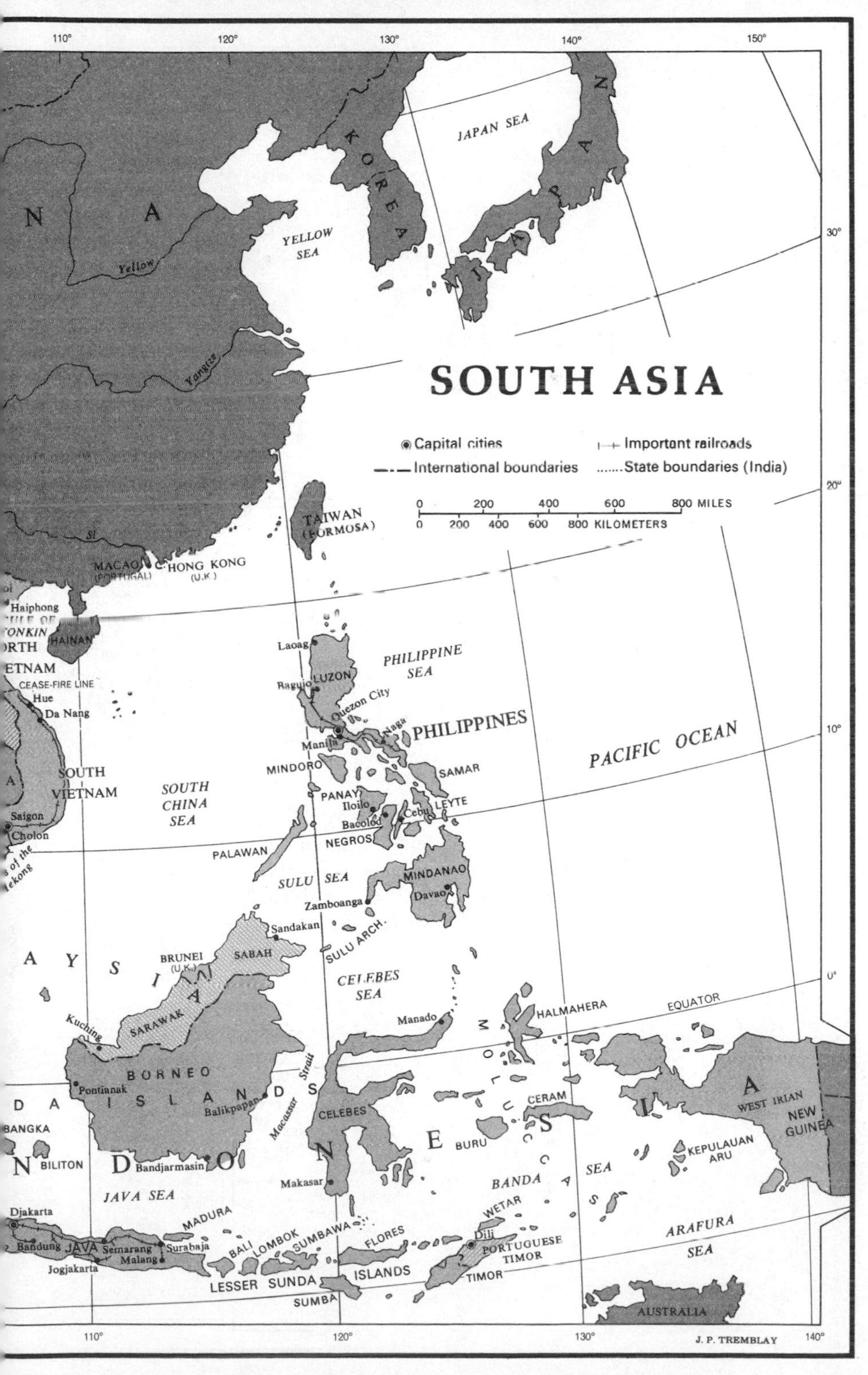
SOUTH ASIA
Capital cities
Important railroads
International boundaries
State boundaries (India)
0 200 400 600 800 MILES
0 200 400 600 800 KILOMETERS
JAPAN SEA
KOREA
JAPAN
YELLOW SEA
Yellow
Yangtze
Si
TAIWAN (FORMOSA)
MACAO (PORTUGAL)
HONG KONG (U.K.)
Haiphong
HAINAN
CEASE-FIRE LINE
Hue
Da Nang
SOUTH VIETNAM
Saigon
Cholon
SOUTH CHINA SEA
Laoag
LUZON
Baguio
Quezon City
Manila
Naga
PHILIPPINE SEA
PHILIPPINES
PACIFIC OCEAN
MINDORO
SAMAR
PANAY
Iloilo
Cebu
LEYTE
Bacolod
NEGROS
PALAWAN
SULU SEA
MINDANAO
Davao
Zamboanga
Sandakan
SULU ARCH.
BRUNEI (U.K.)
SABAH
CELEBES SEA
SARAWAK
Kuching
Manado
HALMAHERA
EQUATOR
BORNEO ISLAND
Pontianak
Balikpapan
Macassar Strait
CELEBES
CERAM
WEST IRIAN
NEW GUINEA
BANGKA
BURU
KEPULAUAN ARU
BILITON
Bandjarmasin
Makasar
BANDA SEA
JAVA SEA
Djakarta
MADURA
WETAR
Dili
ARAFURA SEA
Bandung
JAVA
Semarang
Surabaja
Malang
Jogjakarta
BALI
LOMBOK
SUMBAWA
FLORES
PORTUGUESE TIMOR
TIMOR
LESSER SUNDA ISLANDS
SUMBA
AUSTRALIA
INDONESIA
MOLUCCAS
110°
120°
130°
140°
150°
30°
20°
10°
0°
J. P. TREMBLAY

Prologue

THE BEAM IN OUR EYES

1 *A Plea for a Sociology of Knowledge*

Through the pursuit of social study, human beings and their interrelations in society, like other natural phenomena, are increasingly brought under scientific observation and analysis. What is scientific about this scrutiny and can justify its being called "social science" is its underlying assumption that the way an individual in a society feels, thinks, and acts is not a singular and haphazard phenomenon but one with definite causes and effects. Contained in this assumption is the idea that if we had complete knowledge, every state or change of mind and body could be fully explained and related to every other phenomenon in the world. We would know not only *how* people feel, think, and behave, but *why* they feel, think, and behave as they do, and *with what consequences* for themselves and for others. Without ever approaching such total knowledge, we attack our problems on that assumption and organize our findings accordingly, in terms of observed regularity and causal necessity.

Proceeding along these lines, the social sciences are now penetrating every corner of society and every phase of human life. Taboos are gradually being broken down. Their destruction in order to rationalize common sense has become a major aim of Western social science. We realize that all problems of living are complex; they cannot be fitted into the pigeonholes of our inherited academic disciplines, to be dealt with as economic, psychological, social, or political problems. Sometimes – for teaching purposes and for greater efficiency in research, through specialization – the old disciplines have been retained and even separated into sub-disciplines; however, we do not attach the same significance to these divisions as in earlier times. Today, for instance, no one would draw inferences about social reality from the concepts of economics alone, although this was done frequently two generations ago. To avoid a superficial and one-sided approach, the specialized social science disciplines cooperate in research. In addition, one discipline, sociology, focusses on the totality of social relations and takes special responsibility for those fields of social reality that are less closely scrutinized by the other disciplines. This development has been prominent in America for some time.

Thus we economists and other social scientists are now studying intensively how people behave, and how they are motivated and then conditioned both by their inherited constitution and by their environment. We are interested in the selective processes operating on the young as they find their way in life and are guided into different occupations. We are examining the formation of opinions and attitudes, especially decision-making by public administrators, business managers, employers and employees in the labor market, and political leaders and their followers. We are observing how people spend their leisure time, how they marry and pursue family life, how some become criminals, vagabonds, or prostitutes. In short, we are concerning ourselves with human behavior and motivations, in whatever profession, social class, or geographical location.

Only about the peculiar behavior of our own profession do we choose to remain naive. How we as scientists operate in seeking to establish knowledge is largely shielded from the searchlight of social study. But, surely, though we are seeking truth, we are not less conditioned by our mental make-up and the society in which we live and work than are other men. Social scientists are human; some, as we know well, are "all too human"; and they are part of a social system and a culture. Our research interests, the particular approach we choose, the course we follow in drawing inferences and organizing our findings, are not determined by facts and logic alone. We are not automatons like the electronic machines we increasingly use to master large masses of data. And yet, although literature and art have long been considered in relation to the psychology and the environment of their creators, our writings have not been.

Our lack of curiosity about our own peculiar behavior as researchers should be surprising. As a group we are certainly as interesting and important to the dynamics of the social system as are maladjusted girls, new immigrants, and other special groups in society that we are studying more and more intensively; we perhaps even rank with business managers, professional politicians, or creative artists. Our behavior can be easily ascertained from our writings. A deeper study would, of course, entail investigation of our personal history and our present inclinations as these are influenced by our relation to the class structure and our cultural and social milieu.

The desire to make money is naturally a strong determinant of the behavior of men in business and of all of us when we are acting in the "economic" sphere; so the desire to find truth affects the behavior of scientists and, indeed, of all men when they try to form a correct view of reality. As scientists we are not blind to the fact that in the economic sphere there are also other motives. No longer do we assume that in their economic pursuits people have the singlemindedness of the "economic man" of classical economic theory. Recognizing that even in their economic choices people are conditioned by their total mental make-up and, in particular, by the community in which they live, that they are motivated in a variety of ways as are all human beings in all their behavior, we are directing our attention more and more to the interplay of all these forces. But the "scientific man," thought to be conditioned by nothing except his desire to discover the true nature of things, is still commonly taken much for granted. No great effort is made to spell out that abstraction itself, and thereby give it a precise meaning, as the classical economists tried to do for the "economic man." The concept of the "scientific man" exists simply as an observed taboo.

It is clear, of course, that with few exceptions, we want to make scientific study as "pure" as possible, in the sense that it should render as accurate a picture of reality, when looked at from a particular viewpoint, as is attainable. Other influences, external to this objective, acting on our minds during scientific inquiry are irrational: they cause us to take a view that is biased in some direction. There are devices of logic by which we can attempt to purge our research of biases. But as part of the naiveté we retain about our own behavior in social study, those problems of the philosophy of knowledge, of the logic of social study, are usually kept in the shadow. We shall return to them in Sections 7 and 9.

Our main interest in this Prologue is in the sociology of knowledge, which is concerned with causation. The point is that we could better avoid biases, and could therefore expect more rapid progress in the social sciences, if we were a little less naive about ourselves and our motivations. A minimal desideratum is that we be always aware of the problem and attain some degree of sophistication about the operation of the personal and social conditioning of our research activity.[1] From this should rationally follow systematic inquiry into this important part of social reality. That would

[1] The American novelist, Richard Wright, who in his book *White Man Listen!* tried to deal with a problem in general terms, was conscious of the need to watch the way he was conditioned in his views: "I state that emotion here precedes the idea, that attitudes select the kind of ideas in question. . . . We are human; we are the slaves of our assumptions, of time and circumstances, we are the victims of our passions and illusions, and . . . our critics can ask of us . . : Have you taken your passions, your illusions, your time, and your circumstances into account? This is what I am attempting to do." (Richard Wright, *White Man Listen!*, Doubleday and Company, New York, 1957, p. 64.)

A social scientist should not be less humble and assume that he is purely "factual and objective." He cannot, in any case, escape valuations, as he needs explicit, or implicit, value premises even to ascertain the facts; see below in Section 9.

require the firmer establishment of a hitherto much neglected discipline: the sociology of knowledge.

These forces working on our minds, which cause irrationality if not recognized and controlled, are exceptionally strong and insidious in our approach to the problems of underdevelopment, development, and planning for development in the underdeveloped countries of South Asia. On this fact rests the defense for beginning our book with the general observations just made.

2 *The Spurt of Interest in the Problems of Underdeveloped Countries*

There was little scientific interest in the underdeveloped countries of South Asia, or elsewhere, almost until the Second World War. Since then a swelling flood of research has been devoted to their problems. Many of our resources in the social sciences are now employed in the study of underdeveloped countries. The tide is still rising, and we economists are riding the crest of the wave. Before the war the most intensive work in the underdeveloped world was done by the cultural anthropologists, sent out from centers of learning in the rich Western countries. They described for us, usually in static terms, the structure of institutions and attitudes by which people in those countries live, work, and survive. Now the lead is taken by economists, studying the dynamic problems of underdevelopment, development, and planning for development.

This tremendous re-direction of our work has not been an autonomous and spontaneous development of social science, but a result of vast political changes. Three changes, closely interrelated, stand out sharply: first, the rapid liquidation of the colonial power structure; second, the emergence of a craving for development in the underdeveloped countries themselves, or rather among those who think, speak, and act on their behalf; and, third, the international tensions, culminating in the cold war, that have made the fate of the underdeveloped countries a matter of foreign policy concern in the developed countries. So far as Western countries, scholars, and scholarly institutions are concerned, it is clear that the third cause has been foremost in arousing interest in the problems of the underdeveloped countries. In the underdeveloped countries themselves it is fairly well understood by their intellectuals – and has occasionally given rise to slightly cynical comments – that the readiness to give aid and, more fundamentally, the interest of both the West and the Soviet Union in their conditions and problems were largely due to the world tensions that give significance to their internal affairs abroad.

It should be remembered that the economic and social conditions of the

South Asian countries today are not very different from those existing before the disintegration of the colonial power system. The only major change has been the recent rapid acceleration in the rate of population increase. But the outburst of scientific interest in their economic problems preceded this acceleration, and, even more, our full awareness of it. On the whole, the masses in South Asia in pre-war times were as poor and their lives as miserable as they are now. Their poverty and misery did not, however, induce economists to take any great interest in their situation, let alone concentrate attention on the practical problems of how to engender development through economic planning and coordinated large-scale state intervention. Practical action along such lines was then not within the realm of political feasibility. Still less was there a feeling of urgency about such action.

The lack of interest among social scientists, particularly economists, in the extreme poverty and economic stagnation in the underdeveloped countries and in their problems of economic development was clearly a reflection of the existing world political situation. More specifically, this lack of interest reflected the character of the colonial regimes and their effect on us as well as on the subject peoples: these regimes were not such as to call forth large-scale research on economic underdevelopment by giving political importance to these problems.

What has happened in this field of study is, of course, a glaring indication of a much more general relationship. For social scientists it is a sobering and useful exercise in self-understanding to attempt to see clearly how the direction of our scientific exertions, particularly in economics, is conditioned by the society in which we live, and most directly by the political climate (which, in turn, is related to all other changes in society). Rarely, if ever, has the development of economics by its own force blazed the way to new perspectives. The cue to the continual reorientation of our work has normally come from the sphere of politics; responding to that cue, students turn to research on issues that have attained political importance. Theories are launched, data collected, and the literature on the "new" problems expands. By its cumulative results, this research activity, which mirrors the political strivings of the time, may eventually contribute to a rationalization of these strivings and even give them a different turn.

So it has always been. The major recastings of economic thought that we connect with the names of Adam Smith, Malthus, Ricardo, List, Marx, John Stuart Mill, Jevons and Walras, Wicksell and Keynes were all responses to changing political conditions and opportunities. Of these great scholars not only List and Marx but also Smith and Keynes, even, to an extent, John Stuart Mill, were aware of the political background of their contributions. The expanding volume of literature on development problems represents a more profound re-direction of economic science, indeed of all social science. A collective effort involving many workers, it cannot be ascribed to any one man or group of men. We are almost all participants in this revolutionary reorientation of research interests.

3 *Sources of Bias: The World Conflict*

To obtain a more sophisticated picture of research in the social sciences, we must first acknowledge that the changed world political situation is responsible for our shift of emphasis to the problems of the underdeveloped countries. Once we admit the importance of this influence, we must ask whether it does not affect the manner in which research is conducted as well as the field of research chosen. Although this shift of *field* represents a rational adjustment of our work to the needs of our society, we must suspect that the effect on the *approach* used in our research efforts may be to introduce irrational biases. The epistemological implications of the latter type of influence are quite different from those of the former. The merely selective – negative or positive – conditioning of the choice of research problems does not, in itself, invalidate the research that is done; the fact of such conditioning, however, should make us wary of less tangible influences on the content of our research.

One source of bias is the involvement of our society in the political changes referred to and the tensions they generate, along with our personal involvement. As mentioned above, the world political situation since the Second World War has been characterized by the almost complete liquidation of the colonial power system. The colonies have been replaced by independent nation-states in which influential groups are pressing, with varying success, for state planning to bring about economic development that would lift their countries out of stagnation and poverty. Concomitant with these two major changes has been another set of changes: the rise to power of the Soviet Union; the staggering gain in the size of territories and populations under Communist governments, especially the emergence of Communist China; and the ensuing cold war. To both sides in the world conflict the political allegiance – or at least the neutrality – of the underdeveloped countries has become a stake in the struggle for security and power. Concern is not restricted to the foreign policy of the underdeveloped countries. Their attempts at national consolidation and economic development have also become aspects of the cold war in the sense that the effectiveness, the speed, and, even more, the direction of their reforms have become politically important to the contending power blocs.

The current international political situation bristles with tensions and emotions of the most violent kind. Governments and nations feel their vital interests to be involved. And quite apart from any formal or informal pressures from the authorities or from public opinion, the individual scientist is himself usually deeply engaged in these momentous events. As an American, a European, or a national of one of the underdeveloped countries, he is bound to be anything but indifferent to the theoretical and practical findings of his research. This must have an influence on his inclinations in research and on how he presents his results to the public – unless he exercises the utmost care to avoid a biased view.

In the Communist countries, bias is massively and systematically incorporated in the approach to all social, economic, and political problems and has been hardened into a stale dogma. In these countries, scientific as well as literary writings are programmatically expected to contribute to the fight for Communism.[1] This limitation has virtually eliminated social science as we know it. It has stifled even that sophistication with which laymen approach social problems and which in democratic countries is continually fed by, and in turn stimulates, social research. Another sobering thought for social scientists is that there can be rapid economic development and flourishing progress in the natural sciences and in technology while the social sciences are represented by little more than a crude, teleological doctrine plus a highly developed economic technocracy.

The cramped situation of the social sciences in the Communist countries is explained, of course, by the absence of democracy. In order to exist and function, the social sciences more than other sciences require the freedom of thought and expression that we associate with democracy. At the same time, they themselves fulfill an essential function in a democracy and, on a level of highly trained rationality, they actually represent the democratic way of thinking and living. It is no accident that we may search in vain for important and original contributions by social scientists in the Communist countries to the scientific discussion of development problems in the poor countries.

Gradually, as the degree of personal security and independence is heightened, such contributions may and probably will be forthcoming. The trend toward greater freedom of expression seems sure to continue, as it is spurred by the rapid rise of educational levels in these countries, which is the real force behind de-Stalinization in its broad sense. There have been signs both in the Soviet Union and in some of the East European countries, though not as yet in poverty-stricken China, of greater willingness to allow objective research in the social sciences. Until now, however, the signifi-

[1] In Khrushchev's words: "The impact of the social sciences will increase steadily in the study of mankind's historical path to Communism . . . in moulding the materialist world outlook in people, in the education of the man of Communist society and in the struggle against bourgeois ideology. . . . Literature and art will play a big part in moulding the new man. By asserting Communist ideas and genuine humanism, literature and art instil in Soviet man the qualities of builders of the new world . . ." (Nikita S. Khrushchev, "Report on the Programme of the Communist Party of the Soviet Union," as delivered to the Twenty-second Congress of the C.P.S.U., *Soviet Weekly*, Supplement, October 18, 1961, p. 15.)

cant modern contribution to the scientific discussion of underdevelopment and development has come from students in the Western democracies and in the underdeveloped countries themselves, a very large part of it from the United States. It is in relation to these research efforts in the non-Communist world that the problem of biases is raised here.

This is not to say that bias arises in the perception of national interest only when it is raised to the pitch of cold war. It stems also from internal interests and pressures exerted by the dominant social strata. In retrospect we can see that even economic studies conducted during the long and carefree era of nineteenth-century liberalism were not free from biases.[1] The present world tension must be expected to be a powerful additional source of bias, particularly in the study of the underdeveloped countries.

4 *Political Strategy and Diplomacy in Research*

Impelled by the immense interests at stake, it is natural that the national authorities, the institutions sponsoring and financing research, and, indeed, public opinion in the West all press for studies of the problems of the underdeveloped countries. This clamor for research is entirely justified, as these problems are of increasing political importance to the Western countries themselves. But the studies are also expected to reach opportune conclusions and to appear in a form that is regarded as advantageous, or at least not disadvantageous, to national interests as these are officially and popularly understood. Such community pressure for opportunistic research operates in all Western countries, especially in the larger ones actively involved in the cold war. It operates also, though occasionally in a different direction, in the underdeveloped countries themselves. Their institutions and authorities and their educated class – whose views are commonly referred to as "public" opinion – are becoming more and more touchy about most questions dealt with in social study.

The most perceptible political influence on the research approach in Western countries to the problems of South Asian countries is the predominant role given to considerations of national power and international power relations. In a world full of perils to national security and survival, this tendency is understandable; it is often asserted to be a more realistic direction of social research. The implication is, however, that studies of the problems of underdeveloped countries are now undertaken, not with a

[1] Gunnar Myrdal, *The Political Element in the Development of Economic Theory,* Routledge and Kegan Paul, London, 1953; cf. two other works by the same author: *Economic Theory and Under-developed Regions,* Duckworth, London, 1957, Part II (in America: *Rich Lands and Poor,* Harper, New York, 1957); and *Value in Social Theory, A Selection of Essays on Methodology,* Paul Streeten, ed., Routledge and Kegan Paul, London, 1958.

view to the universal and timeless values that are our legacy from the Enlightenment, but with a view to the fortuitous and narrow political or, narrower still, military-strategic interests of one state or bloc of states. All sorts of studies are now justified by, or focussed on, their contribution to the "security" of Western countries. This officious accommodation by the scholarly profession to a new political "realism" in research often borders on the ridiculous. Even a respectable biologist's compilation of available research on the influence of climatic factors on organisms in the tropics may be introduced by and interspersed with glib and, understandably, inexpert reflections concerning the political effect on the "free world" of economic development there.

Often this is no more than a confession of faith by a troubled soul. At other times it may be intended to provide a mantle of respectability in an emotional environment dominated by non-professionals. Most of the time it turns out that the political or even the military-strategic interests of one's own country are taken to consist in the preservation of very general values. The "best interests of the United States," for instance, dictate the establishment and growth in the underdeveloped countries of what many people there themselves strive for: a stable and, where possible, democratic regime in a consolidated nation capable of economic development. This would be an interesting and, we believe, a broadly valid formulation of how American democracy evaluates the underdeveloped countries in the long run. Applied, as it frequently is, to a contemporary short-term perspective on American foreign policy at a time of fluid conflicts and tactical alliances, the proposition is less evidently valid in the policies pursued and is often clearly belied by them. In any case, it is difficult to see the relevance of this assumption about American society, or American interests, to the scientific study of an underdeveloped country's own experiences and problems. If, nevertheless, it *is* given relevance, the door is opened to all sorts of extraneous influences on research approaches, in other words, to biases.

A major source of bias in much economic research on poor countries is thus the endeavor to treat their internal problems from the point of view of the Western political and military interest in saving them from Communism. Sometimes this intention is stated, though not in the form of a reasoned presentation of specific value premises logically related to the definition of the concepts used.[1] More often it remains implicit in the approach, though the study is interspersed with suggestive formulations. This type of reasoning must often make the public and scholars in the underdeveloped countries suspicious and irritated, as they naturally want their problems analyzed from the point of view of their own interests and valuations. The taking of an outside view does not in itself constitute a fault in

[1] Chapter 2, Section 1.

the methodology of scientists, whose criterion of validity cannot be the acceptability of approaches and conclusions to the people concerned. What is important is that the practice usually goes hand in hand with a retreat from scientific standards, which permits the entrance of uncontrolled biases — and this, of course, gives substance to the suspicion and irritation in underdeveloped countries.

Consideration of Western political and military interests in saving the underdeveloped countries from Communism invites inhibitions, for instance, about observing and analyzing the shortcomings of political regimes in those countries — provided, let it be noted, that they are not friendly with the enemy in the cold war. An indication of such tortuous reasoning, which lends itself to opportunistic arrangement of the facts, is the use even in scholarly writings of labels like "the free world" or "the free Asian countries" to denote, not that people are free in the ordinary sense of the word, but the purely negative fact that a country's foreign policy is not aligned to that of the Communist bloc or blocs. This is not an innocent terminological matter; such practice hides shifts in the meaning of concepts. And, as the literature abundantly proves, this kind of reasoning tends to give strength by association to an assortment of loosely argued and inexplicitly stated value preferences even in matters of internal policy — economic policy in regard to foreign trade and exchange, public versus private enterprise, and so on.

This opportunistic approach to a research task is not necessarily, or even ordinarily, egoistic and hard-hearted in its conclusions. A study may have as its purpose to discover better based and politically appealing reasons for giving more generous aid to the underdeveloped countries. The political influences on Western social research do not usually encourage unkind treatment of underdeveloped countries — as long as they are not hopelessly lost to the enemy bloc. On the contrary, what national communities more or less overtly demand from their social scientists are essays in practical diplomacy pleading certain directions of external and internal policy and giving a more solid and scholarly foundation to such pleas. When, as often happens, social scientists resist having their work turned into diplomacy, the pressures on them may nevertheless force them to engage in research on particularly innocuous problems in an underdeveloped country that have less immediate connection with political issues. They become accustomed to bypass facts that raise awkward problems, to conceal them in technical terminology, or to treat them in an "understanding" and forgiving manner. These are also biases in research. Conditioning that results in omissions rather than commissions nonetheless erodes the basis for objective research. The scholar should not be made to speak with tongue in cheek.

These remarks are not intended to isolate the economic problems of underdeveloped countries from the ideological and power constellations of world politics. The cold war has, of course, considerable bearing on events in the underdeveloped countries of South Asia; and their political allegiance to a power bloc, or their neutrality, is worth studying. Most certainly, the drift of its economy and the social and economic policies it pursues can affect such a country's alignment in the cold war, though this problem is often oversimplified. An underdeveloped country that, for whatever reason, comes under Communist rule will apply Soviet methods of planning for economic development, and this will bring about a major change in the situation under study. In the same way a country's dependence on credits and gifts from the Western bloc may influence its internal policies and thereby affect the social reality we are studying. But to recognize these causal relations is not to say that the Western interest in winning the underdeveloped countries as allies or at least keeping them neutral is an appropriate value premise for the study of their development problems. If it *is* chosen as a value premise, it should be chosen openly and operate in a logical way that does not detract from scientific objectivity.[1] Diplomacy is essential to national policy, but it is disastrous when it dominates the work of social scientists.

The tendency to think and act in a diplomatic manner when dealing with the problems of the underdeveloped countries of South Asia has, in the new era of independence, become a counterpart to the "white man's burden" in colonial times. No one with any critical sense can be unaware of this trend. I can myself testify that British and American and other Western scholars confess and defend as a principle – when speaking "among ourselves," that is, among us who are from the rich and progressive countries – the necessity to "bend over backwards." Not only politicians but also scholars, in public appearances, will apologize for making even slightly derogatory remarks and suggest that as foreigners they should not venture to express a view on the matter. In the literature such discretion leads to the avoidance of certain problems and the deliberate understatement of negative findings. I have often heard writers explain that they did this in order not to hurt feelings. A Russian scholar addressing a South Asian audience is equally tactful now that the policy of the Soviet Union has become friendly to the "bourgeois-nationalist" regimes in the region.

I am here not arguing against diplomacy, except in scientific research. A scholar should work and express himself identically at home and in a foreign country. As a scientist he should, of course, have no loyalty other than that to the truth as he perceives it. When speaking in a wealthy, powerful country like the United States this is easy, as I know from experience. The situation is apparently felt to be different in the underdeveloped countries. But it should be understood that diplomacy of this kind is tantamount to condescension, while to speak frankly is to treat the nationals of these

[1] Chapter 2, Section 1.

countries as equals. If South Asians realized this, they should be offended by such diplomacy.

An example of how our thinking has become biased in this direction is the escape into terminology that is thought to be more diplomatic than the ordinary usage, as when one or another euphemism is preferred to "underdeveloped countries." For a discussion of the logical embarrassment into which such attempts lead, see Appendix 1, "Diplomacy by Terminology."

5 *Another Source of Bias: Transference of Western Concepts and Theories*

Another primary source of bias of special importance to the study of the underdeveloped countries of South Asia may appear to be more mechanical, a function merely of the rapidity with which we have undertaken massive research in a previously almost uncultivated field. As research must of necessity start from a theory, a set of analytical preconceptions,[1] it was tempting to use the tools that were forged in the West and that, in the main, served a useful purpose there,[2] without careful consideration of their suitability for South Asia. Thus a Western approach became incorporated into the mainstream of the discussion of development problems in South Asia, both within the region and outside it. Indeed, Western theoretical approaches have assumed the role of master models. For reasons we shall go into at considerable length in the body of the book, a Western approach must be regarded as a biased approach. Let us attempt to understand how this transfer came to pass.

Economic theorists, more than other social scientists, have long been disposed to arrive at general propositions and then postulate them as valid for every time, place, and culture. There is a tendency in contemporary economic theory to follow this path to the extreme. For such confidence in the constructs of economic reasoning, there is no empirical justification. But even apart from this recent tendency, we have inherited from classical economics a treasury of theories that are regularly posited with more general claims than they warrant. The very concepts used in their construction aspire to a universal applicability that they do not in fact possess. As long as their use is restricted to our part of the world this pretense of generality may do little harm. But when theories and concepts designed to fit the special conditions of the Western world – and thus containing the implicit

[1] Section 7 below.

[2] Throughout this book I am making the generous assumption that the Western approach is fairly adequate to Western conditions. This might be an overstatement. In any case, this is a book on South Asia, and I have not felt it to be my task to go into a critical analysis of the use of Western concepts and theories outside the region I am studying.

assumptions about social reality by which this fitting was accomplished — are used in the study of underdeveloped countries in South Asia, where they do *not* fit, the consequences are serious.

There is a conservatism of methodology in the social sciences, especially in economics, that undoubtedly has contributed to the adherence to familiar Western theories in the intensive study of underdeveloped countries. Economists operate to a great extent within a framework that developed early in close relationship with the Western philosophies of natural law and utilitarianism and the rationalistic psychology of hedonism. Only with time has this tradition been adapted to changing conditions, and then without much feeling of need for radical modifications. That economists work within a methodologically conservative tradition is usually not so apparent to the economists themselves, especially as the tradition affords them opportunity to display acumen and learning and, within limits, to be inventive, original, and controversial. Even the heretics remain bound by traditional thought in formulating their heresies.[1] As circumstances, particularly political ones, changed, there was room for a shifting of emphasis and approach. When theoretical innovations lagged far behind events, such adjustments sometimes took on the appearance of definite breaks, as in the so-called Keynesian "revolution." The new thoughts were soon integrated into the traditional mold, slightly modified to better suit the environment, the changes in which were themselves largely responsible for inspiring fresh thinking.

Occasionally a breakthrough established new lines of thought that contrasted more sharply with tradition. The most important challenge came, of course, from Marx and his followers. But Marx, at the base of his constructs, retained much of classical economic theory. And gradually economists remaining within the fold incorporated large parts of what was or seemed novel in Marx's approach, not least in regard to the problems of development, as we shall see. For both these reasons we should not be surprised to find that the biases operating on Western economists often tend to converge with those conditioning economists in the Communist countries. These assertions will be exemplified in various contexts in this book.

When we economists, working within this tenacious but variegated and flexible tradition of preconceptions that admittedly are not too badly fitted to our own conditions, suddenly turn our attention to countries with radically different conditions, the risk of fundamental error is exceedingly great.[2] This risk is heightened by the dearth of empirical data on social

[1] See Myrdal, *Economic Theory and Under-developed Regions*, pp. 129 ff.

[2] "One ever-present problem is the possibility that a conceptual scheme will imprison the observer, allowing him to see only what the scheme directs him to see and ruling out other interpretations of data. It is readily admitted that this danger is implicit in all a priori thinking." (Richard C. Snyder and Glenn D. Paige, "The United States Decision to Resist Aggression in Korea: The Application of an Analytic Scheme," in *Administrative Science Quarterly*, Vol. 3, No. 3, December, 1958, p. 358.)

realities in the underdeveloped countries of South Asia, which enables many biases to be perpetuated that might be questioned and corrected if concepts and theories could be exposed to the challenge of concrete facts. The problem is compounded by another consequence of the Western-biased approach. When new data are assembled, the conceptual categories used are inappropriate to the conditions existing: as, for example, when the underutilization of the labor force in the South Asian countries is analyzed according to Western concepts of unemployment, disguised unemployment, and underemployment. The resulting mountains of figures have either no meaning or a meaning other than that imputed to them. Empirical research then becomes faulty and shallow, and, more important in the present context, less valuable for testing the premises latent in the Western concepts that have guided the production of new statistics. The very fact that the researcher gets figures to play with tends to confirm his original, biased approach. Although it is the confrontation with the facts that ultimately will rectify our conceptual apparatus, initially the paucity and flimsiness of data in underdeveloped countries leave ample opportunity for biases, and the continuing collection of data under biased notions only postpones the day when reality can effectively challenge inherited preconceptions.

The danger of bias does not necessarily arise from the fact that students from the rich countries in the West inevitably face the problems of underdeveloped countries in South Asia as strangers. If anything, the outsider's view has advantages in social research. There are two ways of knowing a toothache: as a patient or as a dentist, and the latter is usually not the less objective. The white Southerner's conviction that he, and he alone, "knows" the American Negroes because of his close association with them has been proved erroneous. The stranger's view may be superficial, it is true, but superficiality is not the monopoly of strangers; it is a matter of the intensity and effectiveness of research. There is thus no necessary connection between superficiality and the extent of bias. Indeed, biases in research have no relation to superficiality *per se*. They emanate from the influences exerted by society, from our personal involvement in what we are studying, and from our tendency to apply approaches with which we are familiar to environments that are radically different. Biases can be present or absent as much when we are strangers to the country we are studying as when we are its nationals and as much when the research undertaken stretches over long periods and is conducted with a huge apparatus as when it is simply a journalist's attempt to put his impressions and reflections in order.

Nor are Western economists uniquely subject to the specific biases emanating from our methodological conservatism. Our confreres in the South Asian countries are afflicted as much, if not more, with them. Many have been trained at Western centers of learning or by teachers who acquired their training in the West. All have been thoroughly exposed to the great economic literature in the Western tradition. Familiarity with, and ability to work in accordance with, that tradition is apt to give them status at home. Their motivations for sharing in this bias are fairly independent of their political attitudes. Part of the explanation, as will be shown in the next section, is that application of the Western approach serves both conservative and radical needs for rationalization in the South Asian countries.

That the use of Western theories, models, and concepts in the study of economic problems in the South Asian countries is a cause of bias seriously distorting that study will be a main theme of this book. For the moment a few *obiter dicta* must suffice to outline this general criticism.

The concepts and the theory of unemployment and underemployment rest on assumptions about attitudes and institutions that, though fairly realistic in the developed countries, are unrealistic in the underdeveloped countries.

The neat division of income into two parts, consumption and saving, is realistic in Western societies where the general levels of income and a stratified system of income redistribution by social security policies and other means have largely abrogated any influence of consumption on productivity. This is not the case in the underdeveloped countries.

Marx's assumption, so widely adopted by Western economists, that the effects of industrialization and, indeed, of investment generally – in the final instance Marx's changes in the "modes of production" – spread quickly to other sectors of the economy and to institutions and attitudes, may be fairly realistic for Western countries, both now and when they started their rapid economic development. But as these "spread effects" are a function of the level of living and of the general culture, the assumption is not valid for most underdeveloped countries, particularly when the sectors of change are small in comparison with the total community. This should be obvious after many decades of colonial history during which the modern enterprises remained enclaves in a largely stagnating economy, but it is seldom given the recognition it deserves, either in economic analysis or in planning for development.

The lack of mobility and the imperfection of markets in underdeveloped countries rob the analytical method of aggregation of magnitudes – employment, savings, investment, and output – of much of its meaning. This conceptual difficulty is in addition to the statistical one already pointed out: that the data aggregated are frail and imperfect, partly because their categories are unrealistic.

The list could be made much longer, as will be seen in this book. Our main point is that while in the Western world an analysis in "economic" terms – markets and prices, employment and unemployment, consumption and savings, investment and output – that abstracts from modes and levels of living and from attitudes, institutions, and culture may make sense and lead to valid inferences, an analogous procedure plainly does not in underdeveloped countries. There one cannot make such abstractions; a realistic analysis must deal with the problems in terms that are attitudinal and institutional and take into account the very low levels of living and culture. The newest attempts to analyze education (and health) in terms of "investment in man" do not even state the problem in a rational way. The "non-economic" facts do not adjust smoothly to economic changes, but set up inhibitions and obstacles to them, so that often the "economic" terms cannot even be given a clear meaning. A practical corollary is the much greater need for coordination of planning in the "economic" and the "non-economic" fields.[1] Acknowledgment of this important difference is frequently made by way of qualifications and reservations. But the basic approach, not least in regard to the problems of economic planning, has remained a rather simple application of Western concepts and theories.

6 *The Western Approach Serves Deeper Inclinations to Bias*

The temptation to apply the Western approach was said above to be almost mechanical, a function of the speed with which research was begun in a nearly untouched field and our natural inclination to utilize research methods with which we were familiar. The urge to do so was the more impelling as no other kit of tools was available for bringing a semblance of order into the analysis of the complex conditions in South Asian countries. But the matter is not so uncomplicated. The appeal of the Western conceptual approach draws further strength from the fact that it is well fitted to the rationalization of opportunistic interests both in the developed Western countries and among the influential intellectual elite in the underdeveloped countries themselves.

Generally speaking, the Western approach abstracts from most of the conditions that are peculiar to the South Asian countries and are responsible for their underdevelopment and for the special difficulties they meet in developing. These conditions and difficulties are all of a type that South Asians and their foreign well-wishers must desire to forget. They were the features of the social structure that were prominent in the thoughts of the European colonial masters, both in their stereotypes and in their more sophisticated reasonings. Exaggerated emphasis on these impediments to development served their need for rationalization. It explained away their

[1] See Appendix 2, Section 19.

"For all practical purposes growth and development in the less developed parts of the world seem to depend rather upon the speed and efficiency with which given attitudes and institutions can be and actually are modified and changed. Viewed in its truly dynamic dimension the process of economic growth and development is and always has been a problem of political and socio-cultural change." (K. William Kapp, *Hindu Culture, Economic Development and Economic Planning in India,* Asia Publishing House, Bombay, 1963, p. 69.)

responsibility for the backwardness of colonial peoples and their failure to try to improve matters. Both the post-colonial ideologies and the ideologies of the liberation movements were deeply stamped by protest against that thinking.[1] And so the pendulum of biases swung from one extreme to the other. The intellectuals in these countries want to rationalize in the contrary sense, and it serves their needs to make the abstractions implied by Western economists. Genuine sympathy, in addition to reasons of diplomacy, brought Western economists under the same spell of opportunism. The fact that what they were applying was established theory, which had been successfully used in the Western countries, made the entrance of this systematic bias the easier.

It was an approach that appealed to both radicals and conservatives in South Asia. The radicals, partly under the impact of Marx's thinking, were prone to exaggerate the rapidity of adjustment of the entire social system to changes in the "economic" sphere; conservatives, averse to direct policy intervention in modes and levels of living, attitudes, and institutions, welcomed an approach that placed these matters in the shadow. Concerning the radicals, we must also remind ourselves of the similarities, particularly in basic concepts, between Marx's and Western economic theorizing. These have already been referred to and are illustrated in many contexts in the ensuing chapters.

There are also differences in approach, however, and it should be clear that certain elements of Marx's economic speculation often seem to fit situations in South Asia much more closely than those in the rich modern welfare states of the West: for instance, the apparent existence of a "reserve army" of idle, or largely idle, workers; the existence and the increase of a dispossessed proletariat; the often frank exploitation of workers by employers; and the big and widening gap between a few rich individuals or families and the masses of very poor people. It is remarkable that very little fresh analysis of the problems of the region in Marx's terms is forthcoming, while essays in the Western pattern are abundant. We thus often find at the universities in South Asia economists who are strongly anti-Western in their sympathies and politically far to the left, even avowed Communists or fellow-travellers, but who are yet eager and proud to place the emphasis of their teaching on the latest abstract and formal growth models developed at Cambridge or Yale, and whose ambition is to write articles resembling those in the Western journals and, hopefully, to publish them there.

In attempting to understand this bent of mind of the radicals we must take into account the virtual bombardment of massive Western research on the underdeveloped countries in recent times, while the literary output on their problems in Communist countries has been small, polite, but un-

[1] Chapter 21, Section 7 *et passim*.

inspiring. An additional factor is, however, that pursuit of Marx's particular approach referred to above would inevitably have led to a consideration of "non-economic" factors. The competitive strength of the Western approach is, at bottom, that its abstractions give an optimistic slant to the thinking about the development problems in the underdeveloped countries of the region.

Optimism, and therefore approaches that make optimism seem more realistic, is itself a natural urge for intellectuals in South Asia. That all planning in the region tends to err on the side of optimism is rather palpably clear.[1] The leaning toward diplomatic forbearance in the Western countries fits equally well with biases toward unwarranted optimism among their economists. In Western countries, especially America, optimism is even prized, as a foundation for enterprise and courage; it is almost part of the inherited cultural pattern – what George F. Kennan once called "the great American capacity for enthusiasm and self-hypnosis."[2] In the contest for souls, it is felt to be to the interest of the West that the underdeveloped countries outside the Communist sphere have development and be made to believe in it. In the West there is also a natural wish, and so a temptation to believe, that the underdeveloped countries in South Asia will come to follow policy lines similar to those of the Western countries, and that they will develop into national communities that are politically, socially, and economically like our own. For this reason, too, there is a normal tendency to use a Western approach in studying these countries, as to do so is to play down the initial differences and make such development appear more feasible.

The two main sources of bias in the Western countries thus strengthen each other in that their influences tend to converge. As we saw, the international power conflict and the tensions and emotions associated with it have influenced the study of the problems of the underdeveloped countries in South Asia in the general direction of diplomatic kindness and tolerance – again, provided that these countries are not on the wrong side in that conflict. Many of the conditions peculiar to these countries are highly undesirable; indeed, this is what is meant by their being underdeveloped.[3] Therefore, the other source of bias with which we dealt in the last section – the tendency to use the familiar theories and concepts that have been used successfully in the analysis of Western countries – exerts influences

[1] India's First Five Year Plan would seem to be an exception, as it underestimated the growth of output. But the surpassing of estimates was largely due to unexpectedly favorable monsoons and other accidents. The targets in regard to the policy measures actually making up the plan, and in particular the investments, were not met.

[2] In the Soviet Union uncritical optimism is programmatic, and realism, when it does not lead to optimistic conclusions, is considered a "bourgeois" deviation; this constitutes one of the many similarities in cultural situation between the United States and the Soviet Union.

[3] Appendix 2, Section 5.

in the same direction. For when using the Western approach one can more easily soften the bite of these peculiar and undesirable conditions.

We have wanted to stress the political urges behind these tendencies that affect research on underdeveloped countries in the region. But these tendencies have at their core a compassion that makes them almost irresistible. Quite aside from the cold war and the opportunistic tendencies to bias emerging from it, we of the West are by tradition disposed to be friendly to peoples in distress, once we begin to take an interest in their condition. And it is our earnest hope, apart from all selfish interests, that they will succeed in their development efforts. That we wish them to develop into national communities as similar to our own as possible is a natural ethnocentric impulse that would make itself felt in the calmest world situation. Perhaps it should be stressed again that the concern of the West about the possibility of Communist expansion in underdeveloped countries is also understandable, and from the viewpoint of our own interests valid. And these interests justify using our influence to stop it. Still less can one criticize the human sympathy that characterizes the Western attitude toward these countries.

Nevertheless, we must not let these understandable and genuine feelings influence our perception of the facts. It is the ethos of scientific inquiry that truth and blunt truth-speaking are wholesome and that illusions, including those inspired by charity and good will, are always damaging. Illusions handicap the pursuit of knowledge and they must obstruct efforts to make planning for development fully effective and successful. For this reason, the present book is intended to be undiplomatic. In our study we want to step outside the drama while we are working. We recognize no legitimate demand on the student to spare anybody's feelings. Facts should be stated coldly: understatements, as well as overstatements, represent biases.[1]

[1] In regard to issues that have been felt to be awkward and threatening — for instance, the Negro problem in America — biases toward forbearance and optimism have been quite general in the social sciences. A "balanced view" on such issues tends to be a view that soft-pedals difficulties and causes for worry. Understatements, though in principle just as damaging to the establishment of truth as overstatements, are considered more "objective" and certainly give more respectability. When working without explicit value premises, "the optimistic bias becomes strengthened, paradoxically enough, by the scientist's own critical sense and his demand for foolproof evidence. The burden of proof is upon those who assert that things are bad in our society; it is not the other way around. Unfortunate facts are usually more difficult to observe and ascertain, as so many of the persons in control have strong interests in hiding them. The scientist in his struggle to detect truth will be on his guard against making statements which are unwarranted. His very urge to objectivity will thus induce him to picture reality as more pleasant than it is." (Gunnar Myrdal, *An American Dilemma, The Negro Problem and Modern Democracy*, Harper, New York, 1944, p. 1039.)

"I have often observed that social scientists who are responsible for the publication of other authors' works or who utilize them in their own writings, when they apprehend biases, believe that these can be 'edited away,' by modifying certain expressions used or cutting out or revising certain practical conclusions drawn. Similarly, a general tendency toward understatement is observable in most social science literature. When

One more point should be mentioned before we leave this attempt to characterize briefly the forces tending to create biases in research on development problems in South Asia. As these biases engender an over-optimistic view of development prospects, they sometimes provide encouragement; but mainly they are apt to create undue complacency. In any case, a more realistic view makes it clear that *development requires increased efforts: speedier and more effective reforms in South Asia and greater concern in the West.*

7 *A Note on the Unavoidable A Priori*

Our criticism of the tendency to take the Western approach in studying the conditions and problems of the underdeveloped countries in South Asia should not be understood as a denial of the right to start out with a theoretical preconception about how things are or, indeed, of the necessity of doing so. Questions are necessarily prior to answers, and no answers are conceivable that are not answers to questions. A "purely factual" study – observation of a segment of social reality with no preconceptions – is not possible; it could only lead to a chaotic accumulation of meaningless impressions. Even the savage has his selective preconceptions by which he can organize, interpret, and give meaning to his experiences. On a fundamental level modern social science is no different from the magical thinking of primitive man. Scientific data – facts established by observation and classification – have no existence outside the framework of preconceptions. Generalizations about reality, and their organization within an abstract framework of presumed interrelations, precede specification and verification. They constitute "theory" in research.

In strict logic a non-theoretical approach in scientific work is thus impossible; and every theory contains the seed of an *a priori* thought. When this theory is stated explicitly, we can scrutinize its inner consistency. This immanent criticism does not take us beyond the sphere of abstract logical relationships; it conveys nothing about empirical reality. But it is also a first principle of science that facts are sovereign. Theory, therefore, must not only be subjected to immanent criticism for logical consistency but must constantly be measured against reality and adjusted accordingly.

The two processes go together. As we increase the volume of observa-

---

an author has set down something which he feels to be unfavorable about a social class or a region, he looks for something favorable to say in order to 'balance the picture.' A 'balanced view,' a colorless drawing, is considered to be more 'scientific.' Particularly in governmental investigations great care is usually taken to spare the readers. The deliberate attempt that is made in such reports not to offend anyone will often make them difficult to use for scientific purposes. This tendency is, of course, not only ineffective in mitigating biases, but, even worse, it is itself one of the main types of bias in research." (*Ibid.*, p. 1043.)

Concerning the general problem of bias, see the same work, pp. 1035–1045.

tional data to which we are led by our analytical preconceptions, our original theories are refitted in order to make sense of the data and explain them. This is the crux of all science: It always begins *a priori* but must constantly strive to find an empirical basis for knowledge and thus to become more adequate to the reality under study. This is also the reason why we can never achieve perfection – merely an approximate fitting of theory to facts. But there are differences in how close we can come to the facts. In the underdeveloped countries of South Asia, most of the crucial data are deficient in scope and reliability. Moreover, such data as exist are heavily prejudiced by inadequate preconceptions, and we must always be on guard against biases arising from this source.

Theory is thus no more than a correlated set of questions to the social reality under study. Theory always has its essential function in relation to research still to be carried out. As greater realism is approached, theory becomes better equipped to fulfill this function. "Pure" and unrestricted model-building *pro exercitio* may have its aesthetic or pedagogical value, but it is a diversion from serious research.

What must be emphasized is that *all knowledge, and all ignorance, tends to be opportunistic,*[1] and becomes the more so the less it is checked and reconditioned by solid research directed to the empirical facts. Through wide and arduous travelling, which seldom means taking the shortest route, students undoubtedly will be forced gradually to correct their preconceptions, however deeply rooted in opportunism these may be. Until the approach is better tailored to reality, the data fail to fall into place, the facts rebel, and the logic is strained. In the longer time perspective I see no reason for pessimism about the study of the underdeveloped countries in South Asia. Inherent in all honest research is a self-correcting, purifying force that in the end will affirm itself.

An interesting parallel comes to mind – namely, the history of research on inherited group differentials in aptitudes, especially intelligence. This to me has always stood as one of the great monuments to the ethos of truth-seeking and its intrinsic quality of leading, in the end, to truer knowledge. The psychologists who more than half a century ago set out to measure innate differences in intelligence between whites and Negroes, men and women, rich and poor, had no doubt that such differences existed and that they were pronounced. There is truth in the biblical saying that "he that seeketh, findeth"; but if a scientist seeks what isn't there he will find it only as long as empirical data are scanty and the logic is allowed to be forced. As the researchers amassed their observations and as they refined their tools for observation and analysis, they found what they had *not* been seeking and what, indeed, was contrary to their preconceptions: the differences disappeared, or at least could not be scientifically established.

We shall in time come to see a similar change in the approach to the

[1] Myrdal, *An American Dilemma*, pp. 40–42 *et passim.*

study of the underdeveloped countries in South Asia. The more we labor with these problems, the more evident will become the necessity to modify the analytical preconceptions that are now dominant. But this process of improvement can be speeded up if we help by scrutinizing our approaches for irrational influences that are working on our minds. This is why I have asked for greater interest in the sociology of knowledge. Such an inward turn of research interests would pay large dividends in more rapid scientific progress.

8 *A Plea for an Institutional Emphasis*

As we are far from satisfied with the conventional approach to the development problems in South Asia, it is incumbent upon us to sketch an alternative theory that can serve as an analytical framework for the conduct of this study.

We shall use as a starting point the incontrovertible fact that the basic social and economic structure of the countries of South Asia is radically different from that existing in advanced Western countries. Conditions in the rich Western countries today are such that, broadly speaking, the social matrix is permissive of economic development or, when not, becomes readily readjusted so as not to place much in the way of obstacles in its path. This is why an analysis in "economic" terms, abstracting from that social matrix, can produce valid and useful results. But that judgment cannot be accurately applied to South Asian conditions. Not only is the social and institutional structure different from the one that has evolved in Western countries, but, more important, the problem of development in South Asia is one calling for induced changes in that social and institutional structure, as it hinders economic development and as it does not change spontaneously, or, to any very large extent, in response to policies restricted to the "economic" sphere.

This view, of course, has been implicit in our criticism of the adequacy of Western conceptual approaches and it forms the essential preconception running through the body of this study. We do not preclude the possibility that, at a future date, the institutional structure of the South Asian countries may be such that some of the Western tools of analysis, at present woefully inadequate, will come into their own. Neither this possibility nor a defense sometimes offered for the current use of Western concepts – their potentiality for defining the targets these countries are seeking to hit – justifies the use of modern Western preconceptions now. The essential first step toward an understanding of the problems of the South Asian countries is to try to discover how they actually function and what mechanisms regulate their performance. Failure to root analysis firmly in these realities invites both distortions in research and faults in planning.

So our approach is broadly "institutional," and we plead for greatly intensified research efforts along these lines. We should remember that to be really fruitful this new approach cannot be restricted to the insertion of qualifications and reservations meant to take into account the things left out by conventional economic analysis along Western lines. As the very theories and concepts utilized in that analysis guide it away from those "non-economic" factors, what is needed is a different framework of theories and concepts that is more realistic for those societies.[1]

Building such a framework, however, is a very large order; it is understandable why it has not been met and why, perhaps, its demands will not be satisfied until much more solidly based empirical work has been done. In this situation even the negative accomplishment of demonstrating the inadequacy of our inherited economic theories and concepts, and thereby discovering that we know much less than we pretend to know, is worthwhile. But, of course, our goal is also the more ambitious one of replacing conventional theories and concepts by other, new ones better fitted to the reality of these countries. And we need not only to establish the mechanisms that can explain the unique properties of these economies but also to build an analytical structure fitted to the dynamic problems of development and planning for development.

In the latter respect the Western economic approach has an alluring appearance of superiority, as it provides a simple system permitting generalizations and, more particularly, one that can fit the needs of dynamic analysis in terms of planning for development. In addition to the influences of theoretical conservatism and of opportunistic interests of various types, as analyzed in Sections 4–6 above, these properties seem to provide more objective reasons for adhering to the Western approach and accounting for its lack of realism by means merely of qualifications and reservations. One might have expected the behavioral disciplines, particularly social anthropology and sociology, to provide the more broadly based system of theories and concepts needed for the scientific study of the problem of development. Unfortunately, they have not done so. The tradition of social anthropology has been to work in static terms, attempting to explain the structure and internal relations of societies in what we now call a state of stagnation or

[1] "We all agree that the basic requirement of any model is that it should be capable of explaining the characteristic features of the economic process as we find them in reality. It is no good starting off a model with the kind of abstraction which initially excludes the influence of forces which are mainly responsible for the behavior of the economic variables under investigation; and upon finding that the theory leads to results contrary to what we observe in reality, attributing this contrary movement to the compensating (or more than compensating) influence of residual factors that have been assumed away in the model. . . . Any theory must necessarily be based on abstractions; but the type of abstraction chosen cannot be decided in a vacuum: it must be appropriate to the characteristic features of the economic process as recorded by experience." (Nicholas Kaldor, "Capital Accumulation and Economic Growth," in *The Theory of Capital,* Macmillan & Co. Ltd., London, 1961, pp. 177–178.)

"low-level equilibrium." Much sociological research has remained within this tradition. It is, for instance, surprising how little attention has been devoted in village surveys to the effects of population increase on social stratification. And when studies in these disciplines are focussed on change, as they increasingly are, the emphasis is not often placed on development, much less on framing a more comprehensive system of theories and concepts suited to the needs of the planner.

For this there may seem to be an obvious explanation, that the factors abstracted from in the economic analysis – attitudes, institutions, modes and levels of living, and, broadly, culture – are so much more difficult to grasp in systematic analysis than are the so-called economic factors. They undoubtedly are. But if the view propounded in this book is correct, it simply follows that the problems of underdevelopment, development, and planning for development in South Asia are themselves exceedingly difficult and that they have yet to be mastered. An artificial restriction of "reality" to that which is seemingly easier to grasp misses the central point. For in the South Asian countries the "economic" facts cannot be studied in isolation from other social facts.

To the economists belongs the credit for spearheading the attack on the dynamic problems of underdevelopment, development, and planning for development. Economists have always been the cavalry of the social scientists and have enjoyed the status corresponding to this role. It is to us the politicians turn for advice; it is to us they listen. The doctrine of the preponderance of economic factors has been blamed on Marx. However, it was devised before his time and, as is obvious from national and international political debate, it is adhered to with few reservations by politicians in all countries. Economists dominate fact gathering and planning in every country, and when an international organization is set up, everyone agrees that it must have an economic research unit. For more than two hundred years economists have advised both those in power and those in opposition; some of us have been members of parliaments and governments. By comparison, the other social sciences have been "poor relations."

Our strength in all generations has been our singular sensitivity to the political needs of the time and our courage in offering theories that, though sufficiently complicated to flex our intellectual muscles and to impress the multitude, have been communicable in essence to the public and capable of suggesting solutions to practical, political problems. We have been a fighting church with a message, albeit one with much disputing among sects. When we turned decisively to the dynamic problems of underdeveloped economies after the Second World War, problems that were at the same time of great political significance, this was in keeping with our traditions. Our confreres in the other social sciences noted, as they often have, our impetuous sweep and occasionally warned us that we ought to consider certain matters excluded from our framework of analysis. Administrators and other men of practical affairs also went outside our framework when dealing with such issues as community uplift, educational advance, or land reform. But seldom, and never effectively, did either of those two groups, both of which were in closer touch with reality, formulate their skepticism as a challenge to our fundamental approach. And they had, in any case, no other system of theories and concepts to offer for tackling a problem as political and dynamic as that of development.

In this book we argue that there is a need not merely for qualifications and reservations, but for a fundamental change in approach. If we are correct, there is room for more interdisciplinary research, and we should welcome efforts by sociologists and others to improve our system of theories and concepts. The fact is, however, that a political and dynamic point of view is embedded in the tradition of economics, and less so in the other social sciences. As it is we economists who have inherited that viewpoint, the main hope must be that the economics profession will gradually turn to remodelling our framework of theories and concepts in the direction characterized above as institutional. Just as general philosophy failed to provide economics with a ready-made methodology, with the consequence that economists were left very much on their own to cleanse the metaphysical conception of value (a task they have far from accomplished), so the responsibility for working out a more realistic approach to the problems of underdevelopment, development, and planning for development must rest with economists. Despite the strivings for "cross fertilization" and interdisciplinary research, the barriers hampering transmission of ideas among our disciplines remain considerable. And the new approach must concentrate on the dynamic problem of development, an emphasis that does not come naturally to those brought up outside the tradition of economics.

Certainly we hope to gain support from the practitioners of behavioral research. With strong ideological influences and vested interests working to retain the Western approach of economic analysis, as shown in the foregoing sections, attempts to change it will meet resistance from a majority of both the producers and the consumers of economic research in South Asia, as well as in the West. If the present study, by placing the economic problems in their wider setting, can stimulate researchers in other disciplines to focus their work more directly on issues relevant to economic research, planning, and development, it will have made a contribution.

In the body of this book, we attempt to plot the course in which we believe further research efforts can most profitably be steered. The difficulties in formulating a satisfactory alternative theory of the processes of underdevelopment and development are immense. We are seriously handicapped by the dearth of relevant empirical data; many important matters that we would like to qualify have not yet been measured. The general pattern of preconceptions underlying our approach — namely, that the institutional environment of South Asian countries is radically different from the one familiar in the West and that "economic" facts cannot be dealt with in isolation – is, however, firmly grounded in observation of life in the region. In attempting to fill out an alternative theoretical scheme, one aim is naturally to develop a broad set of generalizations about conditions in the region and about the mechanism of causal relations between them. Ideally, we should like to support each of these generalizations with a solid body of empirical data. Unfortunately, given the present state of knowledge, this is rarely possible.

For this reason, many of the specific generalizations advanced stem from what Marshall once described as "staple general reasonings." While we are confident that this approach leads us closer to the essential realities of economic processes in South Asia than does one inspired by current analytical preconceptions in the West, we make no claim to infallibility in the substantive content of our generalizations. At this stage, the fundamental merit claimed for an alternative approach is not that it yields answers to the urgent development problems of South Asian countries, but that it raises the right questions.

We regard the generalizations making up our "theory" as highly tentative and often conjectural. Many will challenge them; it is healthy that they should. For an essential ingredient to progress toward an understanding of the complexities of the development process is the dialogue in which generalizations are advanced, challenged, and then modified and corrected. In this fashion, the sources of differing interpretations and conclusions can be isolated and inspected. This function of generalizations should be borne in mind by readers of this book. That the text is not splashed with question marks but, for convenience, is largely written in declarative form should not obscure the role and function of the generalizations contained in it.

A few remarks on what an institutional approach is *not* have their place at the end of this section. It is not an indulgence in "loose thinking," as some of the conventional economists would be apt to think; on the contrary, it imposes the demand that theories and concepts be logically consistent as well as adequate to reality. Anyone who reads this book, especially the methodological appendices, will find that considerable effort is devoted to clarifying the concepts used. Indeed, a major general criticism launched against the conventional approach of economists is that they have generally been very careless in their reasoning. Paradoxically enough, loose thinking is most often found when they have pretended to be strict and rigorous in their reasoning, but have not scrutinized it as they should by submitting it to transcendental and immanent criticism.

Neither can an institutional approach be characterized as reasoning in "qualitative" terms. If anything, his approach induces the institutional economist to press harder for research that can give quantitative precision to his theories and bring them to the empirical test. In our view, the idea that there is a sphere where "qualitative" reasoning can substitute for thinking in quantitative terms is mistaken. The goal must always be to quantify facts and the relationships between facts, and until we can measure them our knowledge has not proceeded far from the initial *a priori*. Moreover, the institutionalist, since he is basically more critical than the conventional economist, regularly finds the latter's claims to quantitative precision unwarranted, often on logical grounds.

Finally, the conventional economist, whose models we shall frequently have to criticize for loose thinking and unwarranted precision, should not conclude that the institutionalist is "adverse to models." Model-building is a universal method of scientific research, in the same way that quantifying knowledge is a necessary aim of research. As research proceeds, models can be made ever more useful tools in our work. Even if as yet we are in most respects far from the stage where algebraic master models for the whole economy, or large sections of it, have meaning, there are many specific relationships where, to the great advantage of further intensified empirical research, an algebraic statement of the problem can be useful. But to construct such models in the air, out of uncritically conceived concepts that are inadequate to reality and usually not logically consistent, and so pretend to knowledge when none has been established, does not represent scientific progress; it comes near to being an intellectual fraud.

9 *Valuations and Their Inevitability in Scientific Study*

This is the point when at last we have to raise the question of objectivity in research as a problem of logic.

In principle, it would seem easy to lay down the rules for objective research on the South Asian countries. The student should have no ulterior motives. He should confine himself to the search for truth and be as free as possible from both the pressures of tradition and of society around him and his own desires. More particularly, he should in his research have no intention of influencing the political attitudes of his readers, either inside or outside the countries whose conditions he is studying. His task is to provide factual information that will help them all reach greater rationality in following out their own interests and ideals, whatever those are. In his scientific work he should have no loyalties to any particular country or group of countries or any particular political ideology, whatever his own preferences. Indeed, he should have no loyalties at all except to the professional standards of truth-seeking.

These are laudable principles well worth expressing. But they do not solve the methodological problem of how to avoid biases. The problem of objectivity in research cannot be solved simply by attempting to eradicate valuations. Just as the fault with our general views is not that they are general but that often they are logically untenable and not adequate to reality, the fact that valuations are implied cannot be condemned as unscientific. On the contrary, every study of a social problem, however limited in scope, is and must be determined by valuations.[1] A "disinterested" social science has never existed and never will exist. For logical reasons, it is impossible. A view presupposes a viewpoint. Research, like every other rationally pursued activity, must have a direction. The viewpoint and the direction are determined by our interest in a matter. Valuations enter into the choice of approach, the selection of problems, the definition of concepts, and the gathering of data, and are by no means confined to the practical or political inferences drawn from theoretical findings.[2]

The value premises that actually and of necessity determine approaches in the social sciences can be hidden. The student himself may be unaware of them. In fact, most writings, particularly in economics, remain in large part simply ideological. Some two centuries ago, the modern social sciences branched off from the metaphysical philosophies of natural law and utilitarianism. As our heritage from these philosophies, we continue to attempt to "objectify" and "neutralize" the valuation viewpoints and the value-loaded concepts used in scientific analysis. Such attempts are, for instance, plainly visible in the so-called welfare economics, which has lately had a new efflorescence, but they are a much more general phenomenon. Throughout the history of social studies, the hiding of valuations has served to conceal the inquirer's wish to avoid facing real issues. As, for logical reasons, no one can approach a social problem and analyze it without valuations, the result of remaining unaware of these valuations by leaving them implicitly assumed is a concealed *non sequitur*, and thus a space for uncontrolled influences from the valuation sphere. I have seen few efforts in recent years by economists to reform themselves on this

[1] For substantiation of the views expressed in this section, see Myrdal, *Value in Social Theory, Essays on Methodology*, and earlier works cited therein. See also Myrdal, " 'Value-loaded' Concepts," in Hugo Hegeland, ed., *Money, Growth, and Methodology and Other Essays in Honor of Johan Åkerman*, Glerup, Lund, 1961, pp. 282 ff.

[2] The terms "theoretical" and "practical" (or "political") are used in this book as they are in the discipline of philosophy. The former word refers to thinking in terms of causes and effects, the latter words to thinking in terms of ends and means.

To stress the subjectivity of the valuation process we deliberately use the word "valuations" rather than "values" — except in the combination "value premises," where certain valuations have been defined and made explicit for use in research. The common use of the term "values" invites confusion between valuations in the subjective sense, the object of these valuations, and indeed the whole social setting of valuations. The use of the term "values" also usually contains a hidden value premise, that a "value" *eo ipso* is valuable in some objective sense; this implies a bias of the *"laissez-faire"* variety. See Myrdal, *An American Dilemma*, p. 1031.

Concerning the relations assumed between valuations and beliefs, see *ibid.*, Appendix 1.

score, least of all among those devoting themselves to abstract economic theory.[1]

Efforts to run away from the valuations are misdirected and foredoomed to be fruitless and damaging. The valuations are with us, even when they are driven underground, and they guide our work. When kept implicit and unconscious, they allow biases to enter. The only way in which we can strive for objectivity in theoretical analysis is to lift up the valuations into the full light, make them conscious and explicit, and permit them to determine the viewpoints, the approaches, and the concepts used. In the practical phases of a study the stated value premises should then, together with the data – established by theoretical analysis with the utilization of those same value premises – form the premises for all policy conclusions.

We have argued here for making the value premises explicit that research may be objective. But we also need to specify them for a broader purpose: clarity and conclusiveness in scientific reasoning. Here we touch on the main problem of the philosophy of knowledge. There is this relation between that problem and the problem of the sociology of knowledge, which has been the focus of interest in this Prologue: that the elucidation of our general views and the definition of our specific value premises are more obviously imperative, and at the same time are made easier, once we realize that we must not naively expect our ideas, even in scientific re-

[1] The situation is aptly described by Paul Halmos, who rightly stated that "all social science is 'action research' no matter how etherealized." See "Social Science and Social Change," *Ethics*, January, 1959, p. 108.

He continues a few pages later (p. 117): "One may expect that the efforts of social scientists aimed at 'immunising' their communication from injunctive-normative tendencies will continue. The esoteric, highly speculative and often incomprehensible conceptual systems, the frantic search for specially coined terms free from associated 'value-dross,' the tendency towards explicit neutralism and relativism and the pretence that scientific honesty and loyalty do not belong to a wider context of values – all these and some other aspirations will not stop the positive social sciences from their fact-moulding and object-altering function, a function which the non-social sciences do not possess. There is no way of escaping from the issue of moral responsibility in social science communication, and there is no way of lowering an 'iron curtain' between social science and moral philosophy."

And he quotes David Riesman: "Some social scientists have sought escape from terms which common usage has loaded with values, escape into manufactured symbolism so lacking in overtones as to avoid connotations of praise or blame. In the spirit of certain schools of logical positivism, they want to make only 'meaningful' statements and only purely denotative ones. But, in my opinion, the relation of social science to its subjects, who are also its audience, forbids any such easy undialectical answer to the problem of the researcher's ethical judgments. Terminological opacity will itself be taken as a judgment upon the world, perhaps a manipulative, frightened or unsympathetic one. . . . Literate peoples are going to read what is said about them, no matter how many verbal formulae are set up as barriers, and what they cannot understand they may aggressively misunderstand. Communication involves 'noise,' redundancy – and overtones." (David Riesman, *Individualism Reconsidered*, Free Press, Glencoe, Illinois, 1954, pp. 12–13.)

search, to be unconditioned by anything other than our urge to find the truth.

In Chapter 2 we shall follow up this train of thought by attempting to define the value premises applied in the present study.

10 *The Conception of Drama*

The title of the book, *Asian Drama,* was chosen in order to express the conception of events in South Asia held by the author at the beginning of his work and fortified in the course of study. Behind all the complexities and dissimilarities we sense a rather clear-cut set of conflicts and a common theme as in a drama. The action in this drama is speeding toward a climax. Tension is mounting: economically, socially, and politically.

To some degree all of us are participants in this drama. It is as if the stage, set for South Asia, were enlarged and drew onto itself the entire world, so that no one could be merely a spectator. The growing Western literature on the problems of the underdeveloped countries in South Asia since the Second World War, to which this book is another contribution, is due to a heightened awareness of our stake in the dramatic happenings in these countries. As was pointed out in Section 2 the spurt of interest of the social sciences in their problems is not a spontaneous widening and deepening of research, but is politically determined. Despite the increased interest in South Asian problems in other parts of the world, the leading figures in this drama are the people of South Asia themselves, above all their educated class. The participation of outsiders through research, provision of financial aid, and other means is a sideshow of rather small importance to the final outcome.

This drama has its unity in a set of inner conflicts operating on people's minds: between their high-pitched aspirations and the bitter experience of a harsh reality; between the desire for change and improvement and mental reservations and inhibitions about accepting the consequences and paying the price. Such conflicts are a part of human life in all times and places; but in the countries under study, they have an exceptional, mounting intensity and assume a unique form.

Urged on by aspirations but curbed by material conditions and their own inhibitions, articulate individuals and groups in all these countries continually take decisions with the objective of resolving or accommodating the conflicts. The drama gains its fast pace from the terrific strength of the forces creating the conflicts. The lofty aspirations of the leading actors are separated by a wide gap from the abysmal reality – including the unreadiness of leaders, followers, and the more inert masses to accept the consequences of attempting to attain these aspirations. And that gap is widening. The movement of the drama is intensified as, through time, aspirations are inflated further by almost everything that is printed and preached and demonstrated, be it planned or not, while positive achievements lag. Meanwhile populations are increasing at an ever faster pace, making the realization of aspirations still more difficult.

This conception of the problems in South Asia is not a mere artifice but an image that comes naturally to an observer of the present life of these nations. No one who listens to the public proclamations, reads the papers, talks to people in various walks of life, watches the moves and countermoves in private and public affairs, compares pretensions with reality and declared aspirations with achievements, appraises the efforts and the fulfillments, contemplates the extraordinary disparities, discrepancies, and outright contradictions woven into that half-intentional or unintentional confusion present in almost everything that meets the eye, can fail to sense a fateful constellation of explosive potentialities for extremely rapid change and stubbornly formidable external difficulties and internal obstacles and inhibitions to change. One cannot escape feeling that what one is observing is precisely the unfolding of a drama in the classic sense. It is exceptionally intense, as well as immense in its involvement of hundreds of millions of people, but through its complexities and dissimilarities, as through a classical drama, runs an essentially simple theme.

Indeed, the whole public discussion, whenever it transcends the particulars, runs in terms of a momentous drama. Even debates on particular issues are readily cast in terms of a country's destiny. Wrapped up in the dramatic conception of the life of these nations is also the recognition, shared at bottom even by those who assert the opposite, that the outcome is anything but certain. The student knows, of course, that at some future date a backward glance will be taken, and today's choices will then seem necessary under the circumstances. For this is the way history is explained; everything that happened had its causes and exerted further effects in unending sequence.

In the classic conception of drama — as in the theoretical phase of a scientific study — the will of the actors was confined in the shackles of determinism. The outcome at the final curtain was predetermined by the opening up of the drama in the first act, accounting for all the conditions and causes of later developments. The protagonist carried his ultimate fate in his soul, while he was groping for his destiny. In life, while the drama is still unfolding — as in the practical phase of a study, when policy inferences are drawn from value premises as well as from premises based on empirical evidence — the will is instead assumed to be free, within limits, to choose between alternative courses of action. History, then, is not taken to be predetermined, but within the power of man to shape. And the drama thus conceived is not necessarily tragedy.

Part One

INTRODUCTION

Chapter 1

SCOPE AND DIRECTION OF THE STUDY

1 *The Regional Approach*

The regional approach has no intrinsic justification. There are no mystical qualities in geographical proximity that make neighboring nations a "unit" in any real sense, culturally, politically, or economically. In the specific case of the South Asian countries many circumstances have combined to make their present-day mutual relations feeble. Economic planning and, indeed, all economic policies in the countries under investigation have a rather narrow nationalist horizon, and in recent years the trend has been toward a reduction in the scale of their economic inter-relationships.[1]

With the important exception of the studies carried out by the Economic Commission for Asia and the Far East, most economic research on South Asian problems has been "national" rather than "regional" in extent. For practical reasons, much of the voluminous literature on the plans and on evaluations of plan fulfillment has been confined to the problems of individual countries. Moreover, most research projects initiated abroad have been adjusted to this pattern in order to ensure maximum cooperation by national governments and research organizations and to enhance the immediate practical value of the research results. These reasons are admittedly valid. But the preoccupation of research with single countries has

[1] Chapter 13, Sections 4 and 6.

left a wide gap in the analysis of the more general problems that confront all South Asian countries. This study, embracing the whole region in its frame of reference, is thus partly justified by its attempt to draw analytical comparisons among the countries of South Asia. These countries display enough similarities in basic conditions to make comparisons relevant, and enough differences to make comparisons rewarding for an analysis of the main causal relations.

The regional approach was originally chosen for another reason as well: It was thought that regional cooperation might come to play a larger role in the struggle of these countries for economic development. This possibility was duly emphasized in the background work on their trade and exchange relations and in the analysis of their general problems of economic planning. However, the results indicate that, realistically, the scope for regional cooperation may be very narrow even in the future.[1]

In reporting our findings, we have attempted to follow the general practice of presenting the main facts for all the countries of the region, as defined below, in connection with each of the problems taken up for discussion. Paucity of reliable materials has, however, severely restricted our ability to make comprehensive comparisons in most cases. Thus discussion must often center on one or a few countries, or even districts of a country, that display features of particular interest or where the available material is more satisfactory. As our main concern is analytical rather than merely descriptive, we have not felt obligated to produce exhaustive factual details or to spread the discussion uniformly among the several countries of South Asia.

India, because of its huge population and its political importance in both South Asia and the world, looms much larger in the study than do the other countries. In addition, statistical and other materials are far more abundant and better organized there. India, furthermore, has the most advanced political and administrative machinery in South Asia, and most of the problems dealt with in this book have been discussed there much longer and at a higher level of sophistication than elsewhere. India's three Five Year Plans represent the most serious attempt at economic planning in South Asia, or in any underdeveloped country outside the Soviet orbit. To say that this book is mainly about India with numerous and systematic attempts at comparisons with other countries in South Asia would not be far from the mark.

India's neighbors, Pakistan, Ceylon, and to some extent Burma, have also been given rather close attention. Because of a dearth of material, Afghanistan and Nepal – and Sikkim and Bhutan – have not been considered. In Southeast Asia, Indonesia is a big country of great importance, and we have tried to keep its problems within the focus of our study, though we

[1] Chapter 13, Section 15.

have been unable to treat them as thoroughly as we would have wished. For Thailand, the Federation of Malaya,[1] and the Philippines, available material, at least in certain respects, has been richer. The problems of Singapore are so unusual that it has mostly been left outside the main focus. We reluctantly abandoned the original intention of encompassing the countries that emerged after the collapse of the French Indo-Chinese colonial empire – North and South Vietnam, Laos, and Cambodia – as some of them are primitive and all are in flux. Occasionally we have touched on the last three of these when information of interest was available.

All of West Asia and Iran have been excluded from the region studied, as have Japan, Formosa, the two Koreas, China, Hong Kong, the Soviet Union's North Asian republics, the Portuguese territories, the three British dependencies, and West Irian.

Thus in this study "South Asia," or "the region," takes in Pakistan, India, Ceylon, Burma, Malaya, Thailand, Indonesia, and the Philippines, and sometimes South Vietnam, Cambodia, and Laos as well. The subregion "Southeast Asia" excludes India, Pakistan, and Ceylon. The expressions "the Western countries" or "the Western world" refer in this study to the highly developed countries in Northwestern and West Central Europe (but not Eastern and Southern Europe), to the United States, and to those British Dominions populated by people of European stock, that is, Canada, Australia, and New Zealand; the latter are sometimes referred to as "the white dominions." South Africa is an anomaly and is not included in the classification.

Comparisons with the outside world have generally been restricted to Western Europe. This procedure is to an extent rational because most of South Asia until recently was dominated politically by countries in Western Europe and that domination had profound commercial, social, and cultural influences. In fact, the countries of South Asia have long felt the impact of that political relationship and its influences in all other spheres of life, and they continue to do so in large measure. Comparisons with the Communist world, especially the Soviet Union and China, and with Japan, would admittedly be relevant to a discussion of South Asian development and planning for development. When the writer has not pursued this line, his honest excuse is that while he knows the Western countries reasonably well, his knowledge of these other parts of the world is scanty.

In correcting the proofs of the book an attempt was made to carry the narrative to the beginning of 1966; no events later than that are taken into account, though sometimes more recent literature is discussed.

[1] The main work on this book was carried out before the formation of the Malaysian Federation. As we have not studied conditions in North Borneo and Sarawak – the two territories that, initially together with Singapore, were added to the Federation of Malaya – we shall in general refer to the latter political entity.

2 *The Broader Setting*

The central concern of this study is with the problems of economic underdevelopment, development, and planning for development. But it is false to imagine that economic analysis unaided can probe exhaustively into these matters. In reality, as we have taken pains to point out in the Prologue, there are no exclusively "economic" problems; there are simply problems, so that distinctions between "economic" and "non-economic" factors are, at best, artificial. The very act of clarifying what we should mean by "economic" problems or "economic" factors implies an analysis that includes all the "non-economic" determinants. The only worthwhile demarcation — and the only one that is fully tenable logically — is between relevant and less relevant factors, and the line of demarcation will vary with the characteristics of the environment under study.

Abstraction from part of the complexity of the real world does, of course, have its uses in scientific analysis. But the scope for useful abstraction is far narrower under South Asian conditions than in the economic and social environment of the West. Especially when problems are viewed from a dynamic and policy perspective, a host of factors conventionally excluded from contemporary economic analysis in Western countries have a powerful influence in a South Asian environment — which means that attempts to isolate purely economic factors there are much more dangerous for the validity and relevance of the analysis.[1] All the consequences the writer draws from this methodological position may not now be universally accepted. But as a general proposition, the need to account for more than "economic" factors when studying the processes of economic underdevelopment, development, and planning for development is a commonplace in the literature on these problems. An attempt to view those economic processes systematically in their broader setting should thus not be a radical methodological innovation.

It is also worth noting that attempts in the region to formulate plans for economic development often include programs for policy action extending over the entire field of social relations. These encompass not only programs for investment in physical facilities and for mobilizing resources through savings, taxation, and foreign loans and grants, but also policies directed toward population control, health, education, vocational and professional training, general civic culture, improvement in administration and self-government, intensification of voluntary cooperation in various fields, higher levels of social security and social conditions generally, protection and uplift of depressed classes, and so on. This inclusiveness in the general layout of planning stands in rather sharp contrast to the tendency to end up by laying the main stress in both research and planning on the

[1] Prologue, Sections 5, 6, 8; Appendix 2, Sections 19, 20.

"economic" factors, conceived in terms of the Western concepts of markets and prices, employment, savings, investment, and output.[1]

In the practical field, the inclusiveness, in principle, of planning in the region is a recognition of general interdependence among the factors involved in a process of social change. To engender and accelerate development, induced changes in *all* social conditions and relations must be assumed to be instrumental or even to play a strategic role in the cumulative causation of a development process. In Appendix 2 an attempt is made to elucidate the nature of those wider relationships within the whole social fabric of an underdeveloped country and thus give a tentative foundation to a general social theory of economic underdevelopment, development, and planning for development in the region.

While these convictions have determined the approach to the problems dealt with in this study, we cannot pretend to have come far toward formulating a completely general framework of analysis. In attempting to view the "economic" facts in their relation to all other social facts, we have been brought into contact with a wide range of problems and with a rapidly swelling literature. Despite its volume, much of this literature leaves us in great uncertainty, partly because we cannot master it, partly because its coverage is so spotty, and partly because the questions posed are often not directly relevant to the central concern of our study. *Essentially this remains a study of major economic problems in South Asia, though one that maintains a constant awareness of the broader setting of these issues.* Although we have been obliged to work under severe practical limitations, we have attempted to point out clearly and systematically the position within the broader set of social relations of the economic problems analyzed.

In its more intensive discussions the study is directed to the dynamics of the forces presently at play, chiefly their significance for the future. Wherever feasible – for instance, in Chapter 27 where we deal with population developments – we try to project trends. Alternative policies are also considered – as in the concluding sections of Chapter 26 on agricultural policies in regard to land ownership and tenancy. We are thus not primarily interested in the history behind the current situation and trends, though we must often make historical generalizations and include selected material of a historical kind in order to explain present conditions. We realize that the lack of historical depth in our approach restricts our understanding of the social reality we are investigating. This again is due solely to the practical limitations of time, research facilities, and technical competence.

Having stated these qualifications, we must add that the economic situations and trends in the several countries in the region are so immensely variegated and complex, and the data so weak, that a study of the magnitude

[1] Concerning these general points, see the Prologue, Section 5; Appendix 2, Sections 19–21; and Appendix 4. See also Chapter 15, Section 1.

of the present one cannot aspire to a high degree of intensity, much less to encyclopedic comprehensiveness, even in the economic field. We have consciously directed our inquiry toward analysis, toward the clarification of problems. The difficulties inherent in such an approach are, however, staggering. Even a map encompassing a huge territory should be correct. We have tried to steep ourselves in the empirical details thoroughly enough to prevent our going astray when seeking answers to relevant questions about broad interrelationships and trends. But many of the essential facts are elusive and unrecorded, and on many points the empirical evidence is contradictory.

The scope and focus of our study have prevented our undertaking new primary research. We have, of course, tried to avail ourselves of the findings of earlier detailed studies in the many fields included in our wide terms of reference. For our purposes, however, much of this material is deficient. Therefore we have often drawn inferences that are only indicative or suggestive and that, at times, have been based on our own impressions from looking at things and talking to people. The conclusions reached and the supportive reasoning are thus highly conjectural, as we shall often have occasion to remind the reader. It remains a worthwhile scientific task to state clearly what is not known but *should* be known in order to understand what is happening. Indeed, one of the main purposes of this book is to indicate gaps in knowledge and to spell out at some length a system of rational hypotheses for further research; and this can be done only by conjectural reasoning.

We are thus caught in a dilemma. We are seeking knowledge; this search must involve details that are not observed in a comprehensive way. Concurrently, because we insist on the general interdependence of all social factors, the scope of what should be studied is enlarged. The inevitable result is that considerable space in this book is allotted to such generalizing judgments, which are presented without the support of conclusive evidence.

3 *Dissimilarities in a Framework of Broad Similarities*

The countries with which we are concerned have proximity in space. All are located within the tropical, or subtropical, zone, though there are significant differences in climate among and even within the countries.

In each, the populations are "colored" or, as this expression has gone out of fashion in South Asia, "non-white." Although this fact is now usually played down, both in these countries and abroad, it gives an important undertone to most of their thinking about themselves and about their relations with the rest of the world. It is notable that their protests against colonialism regularly include the word "racialism."

But perhaps the strongest thread that binds these countries is the historical experience they have shared and its subsequent effects on their view of political problems and processes. All save one are ex-colonies. The periods of colonial rule, though of varying length, were of such duration and intensity as to leave a definite imprint on almost every aspect of their existence. Thailand, the sole exception, lived in the shadow of colonialism and its destiny too was molded by colonial intervention.

The recent liberation of these countries has been of tremendous importance to their entire national life. The process by which national independence was achieved differed radically from country to country, with major and probably lasting consequences for both their internal conditions and their relations with the outside world.

All these countries and nations owe their geographical definition and, indeed, their understanding of their own nationhood to the colonial era. Thus far only the partition of imperial India calls for qualification of this generalization. When now, as politically independent entities, they struggle for national consolidation within their boundaries, the relative strength of centripetal and centrifugal forces varies considerably from country to country.

Liberation came as a result of a world development in which these peoples played a secondary role. But in all these countries it is true that independence was in the end brought about by members of the small, articulate elite groups within the educated class – "educated" in the special sense the term has in South Asia, comprising only a small percentage of the total population. These elite groups now have the responsibility of consolidating the new nation-states. Among them, however, there were and are differing degrees of cohesion and internal unity behind the drive for consolidation.

Generally speaking, politics in its broadest sense – including all strivings for power and for changing or preserving economic, social, and cultural relations – increasingly absorbed the interest of the educated elite in all these countries as the hour of independence approached, and it has continued to do so. This interest has been diffused to at least some layers of society below the educated class, though to a varying degree in the different countries.

The fight for independence gave importance to politics and a high status to politicians. Their subsequent ascendancy to power and the exploitative use they have often made of it – or are suspected of having made of it – have tended to deflate this status and make it appear shoddy. But few people, even below the "elite" class, lack views on how things should and, particularly, should not be – even when they are frustrated, confused, apathetic, or cynical about their prospects for influencing conditions. Especially in the big urban agglomerations, people can readily be aroused to participate in public demonstrations that are something more than anarchic mob riots.

The idea of a self-regulating and self-reforming community is spreading, though it is not always or even ordinarily envisaged as a national community. For many generations history has evolved at a slow pace in these countries and in many ways it continues to evolve slowly even now. Of course, conditions were also far from static in colonial times; but with political control in the hands of foreign and, on the whole, authoritarian regimes, many social and economic relations became frozen. With the termination of colonial rule the realization that people can shape their own destiny, and have the responsibility to do so, has brought all relationships within society into challenge.

This fluid state has often been characterized as a "revolution of rising expectations." That the change in attitude has thus far mainly affected the educated class and scarcely touched the lower strata does not make it less important in countries where that class is dominant. These aspirations are bound to rise over time, and to spread to an ever larger part of the population. In a political sense, the aspirations now paramount have been formulated in terms of the modern democratic welfare state of the rich Western countries. In fact, they have their roots in the era of the Enlightenment that inspired the American and French revolutions. One of the ironies of history is that these ideas and ideals were brought to the countries of South Asia mainly by colonialism, which thereby unwillingly, and unwittingly, destroyed its own foundation.

Initially all these countries attempted to build their constitutional and civic structure on the lines of parliamentary democracy, based on free elections and adult suffrage for men and women, and on an extensive list of civil liberties. This was another influence from the peculiar but very real contact through colonialism with the newly democratic Western nations. In none of the South Asian countries has the experiment with ultra-modern political democracy been anything like a complete success; many of them have come under authoritarian rule of one shade or another, and this movement may still be in the ascendancy.

The ideals in regard to social and economic relations within these countries, adopted from the ultra-modern welfare state, had developed gradually in the rich, progressive nations of the Western world and began to be realized only during the past generation. Therefore it is natural that, particularly in this respect, a wide gap exists between aspirations and accomplishments.

There is a similarity in the basic economic conditions of the South Asian countries. All are very poor and, in general, the largest are the poorest. Social and economic inequalities are extreme, and are usually most pronounced in the poorest countries. All have endured a long period of stagnation in regard to the larger part of their economies, and in most of South Asia levels of living of the masses are either lower or not substantially higher today than they were before the Second World War. There are considerable differences among the individual countries, but the phenomena of poverty and inequality are universal.

All the new nations in South Asia are now pledged to the promotion of economic development through the planned and coordinated efforts of governments. Only a few, however, have come far in this direction. Even India has been unable to register a rate of progress comparable to that in the Western countries, either now or in earlier stages of their economic development.

The obstacles to rapid economic expansion are formidable and their significance must not be minimized. In the main they are rooted in the inefficiency, rigidity, and inequality of the established institutions and attitudes, and in the economic and social power relations embodied in this framework of institutions and attitudes. Again there are differences in degree among the several countries, but the point is that there is a fundamental difference in kind that distinguishes the economic environment of South Asia from that familiar in advanced Western economies.

These are sweeping generalizations, and this book will be concerned with expanding and documenting them and analyzing their implications. They are set out here in skeletal form because of their importance in determining the approach to the problem of underdevelopment and planning for development selected for this study.

Chapter 2

THE VALUE PREMISES CHOSEN

In Section 9 of the Prologue we discussed the need to make explicit the value premises applied in a social study, for both logical clarity of the conceptual apparatus utilized in research and the avoidance of hidden valuations that lead to biases – that is, for the sake of relevance, effectiveness, and objectivity of research. All social study, even on the theoretical level where facts and causal relations are ascertained, is policy-directed, in the sense that it assumes a particular direction of social change to be desirable.

Ideally, sets of alternative value premises should be used; however, this usually presents a complication too great to contend with. It is true that by stating one set of value premises we not only inform the reader of the valuations implicit in a study but also make it easier for him to substitute another set. But the value premises used in the study do not lose their strategic advantage; it was that set that steered the interests and determined the approaches, the statement of problems, and the definition of concepts.

This is one reason why the student should feel bound not to select his value premises arbitrarily. They should be chosen because they are both *relevant*, in that they reflect actual valuations held by people who are concerned with the problems being studied, and *significant*, in that these people are influential in molding public policy.[1]

[1] For a fuller presentation and justification of these views on the methodological value problem see the writer's *Value in Social Theory* (American ed.), Harper &

1 *The Logical Feasibility of External Value Premises*

It would be perfectly feasible to carry out a quite objective scientific study of the problems of underdevelopment, development, and planning for development in the countries of South Asia from the point of view of Western or American political and military interests in the region, or from the viewpoint of those same interests on the part of the Communist countries, or some of them. Such an approach, however, should spell out these interests, clarifying their role as value premises in determining the direction of study. With the cards thus placed on the table, such a study could not be censured on methodological grounds.

From it could be also inferred the practical steps that should be taken by the outside country or countries concerned, in their own interest. Of course, the choice of steps is considerably narrowed by the political independence of the countries of South Asia; their policies cannot simply be bent at will, even though they are economically so very dependent on the policies of the developed countries. The choice is further narrowed if we exclude outright compulsion or threat of compulsion, fraud, corruption of individuals and groups, and other practices condemned by the ethos of Western civilization. Yet, barring such irregular practices, the policies of outside states can alter the conditions under which the South Asian countries exist and form their national policies, and can thus be influential, for instance, in keeping certain groups in power; they can even change the valuations held by these and other groups.

In the final instance, external policies must be shown to coincide, after the induced conditioning, with the valuations that actually are, or rather have been made to become, relevant and significant in the countries of South Asia. These other valuations thus become important for the rational consideration of the outside policy measures to be recommended as practical conclusions from a study undertaken from the valuational angle of the foreign country or bloc of countries. Such a coincidence cannot be casually assumed. It must be demonstrated by scientific analysis of the valuations and power relations, and their dynamics, that in such a study are conceived of as objects of foreign policy conditioning. Such an analysis has to be carried out, not from the viewpoint of the set of valuations, of ideals and interests, of the foreign observer, but from the viewpoint of those valuations that have relevance and significance in the countries of South Asia. In this specific sense the valuational angle of the South Asian countries themselves is more basic, even in a study pursued primarily from the valuational angle of the interests of a foreign country or bloc of countries.

Brothers, New York, 1959, particularly pp. 157 ff. These pages are reproduced from Appendix 2, "Facts and Valuations," in *An American Dilemma, The Negro Problem and Modern Democracy,* Harper, New York, 1944, pp. 1035 ff.

In the present study we have attempted to look at problems in the countries of South Asia as they appear from the point of view of the interests and ideals, norms and goals that are relevant and significant in these countries themselves. The interests of foreign countries are left out of consideration entirely, so far as the value premises are concerned.

2 *The Difficulties in, and Necessity of, Identifying Valuations in South Asia*

The task of specifying the relevant and significant value premises anchored on the valuations actually held by the peoples in the several countries of the region is an immensely difficult and challenging one – far more so than are similar exercises in Western countries. The three main reasons for this will here be stated in summary form; they will be elaborated in later chapters, especially in Part Four where we study ideologies thoroughly.

One reason is ignorance of how people in different occupations, social and economic strata, and locations really feel, the intensity and tenacity of their feelings, and the extent to which they can be influenced by policy measures aimed, directly or indirectly, at changing them. There are great lacunae in our knowledge of such matters in Western countries; what is ascertained about the public's valuations is often only vague and uncertain. But the difference between what we know about these valuations in a Western country and in any one of the countries of South Asia is, of course, very considerable. Research into public opinion has gone much deeper in the Western countries.[1] The use of such research methods for this purpose in South Asia is hampered at the start by our ignorance of how to classify people there, the actual size of the various groups we want to define, and, indeed, of the elementary facts of population size, age distribution, and vocational distribution.[2]

Moreover, in the Western countries a wealth of knowledge can be ac-

[1] A main criticism of opinion research is the common failure to distinguish between beliefs and valuations and between "personal" and "political" opinions. On this problem see *An American Dilemma,* Appendix 10, Sections 2 and 3; cf. also the Introduction and Appendix 1. Opinion research has not changed in these respects as much as one could have hoped since that work was written.

[2] "Another difficulty is the infrequency or absence of any of the more formal methods of assessing public opinion and relating it to social and political structure which are becoming more common and useful in the West. Progress toward careful assessment of Eastern public opinion is hampered by the simple absence of census data and other sociological information necessary to describe a population accurately enough to permit respectable sampling or reliable interpretation of the results of observation." (Charles A. H. Thomson, "Western Influence and Asian Opinion," in *Nationalism and Progress in Free Asia,* Philip W. Thayer, ed., The Johns Hopkins Press, Baltimore, 1956, p. 335.)

quired indirectly. With the far greater mass participation in public life in a Western country – through elections to representative assemblies at various levels, through organizations for the promotion of common interests and ideals, and through reflections of the public mind in the press – the valuations of people in all stations of life are constantly manifested in a manner amenable to study. There is also a large literature on the social and emotional history of various movements and of changes in people's attitudes induced by political and other means, counterparts of which are almost entirely lacking in the countries of South Asia.

A second cause of difficulty is the fluid, uncertain, and, from an egalitarian point of view, biased character of the processes by which public policies are decided in South Asia. Apart from the educated class, "citizen" participation is low throughout the region, though not uniformly so in the various countries. The rigid and inegalitarian social stratification and, in particular, the social monopolies of property and education result in inequalities in power, whatever the constitutions prescribe. Real influence is therefore more narrowly held than in Western countries.

By itself, this might seem to simplify the problem of discovering the relevant and significant valuations in the South Asian countries, as we could focus our study on the small groups that hold most of the power. To some extent such a focus is undoubtedly possible and important; but the precise facts of this restriction of participation in power are difficult to assess. It is also uncertain how much and how rapidly the spread of elementary education and other impulses from within these countries and from the outside world will change the situation. Moreover, every government in the region, whatever its actual degree of "democracy," has to consider the desires of the broad masses of people and what they will tolerate. This is true even where power is in the hands of the military. The masses may be "passive" in regard to the collective processes of policy formation, but their passivity includes more or less resistance to the effectuation of policies. And every regime must reckon with the possibility that those inert masses will be roused to activity. Non-participation thus constitutes a vast problem containing much uncertainty and much that is not known.

But there is a third severe obstacle to laying bare the actual valuations of peoples in these countries and the selection of those valuations that are relevant and significant: their immense heterogeneity. In the course of the Great Awakening, aspirations, interests, and ideals have been exploding in discrete sections of societies that are culturally and economically ill-prepared to assimilate them systematically. One effect of the inverted and telescoped historical sequence of social and economic development in the countries of the region is that people in the various layers of society live very different kinds of lives and consequently have very different outlooks toward their world. Indeed, most individuals, apart from those entirely isolated by backwardness and stagnation, harbor within themselves sharply conflicting valuations.

In Western countries such differences also exist, but through a long process of national consolidation, or of what in India is called "emotional integration," these differences have tended to diminish. The modern democratic welfare states developed in the West during the past half century have a high degree of "created harmony" of interests and ideals.[1] It has thus become possible to study problems in the Western countries on the basis of a fairly explicit national creed that determines people's long-range strivings, if not always their daily conduct of life. This is true even when the problem concerns such departures from the creed as discrimination in America against Negroes and, particularly in earlier times, against Jews and immigrant groups. In the most advanced nations of Northwest Europe, the national ethos is seldom so explicitly formulated, mainly because it enjoys an even less questioned allegiance on the part of almost all citizens. The situation in the South Asian countries is, of course, utterly dissimilar. In none of them is the degree of national consolidation and "emotional integration" comparable to that in the Western countries, either now or when they were on the eve of their industrial revolutions.

The fundamental difficulties in identifying relevant and significant value premises do not relieve the student of the methodological necessity of attempting to discover them. On the contrary, the heterogeneity of actual valuations in South Asian countries and the magnitude of our ignorance about them and about the actual power relations make it the more essential to insist on clearly stated value premises. In Western countries, with their greater national consolidation and "emotional integration," it would be more reasonable to expect that the value premises used in a study, even if left implicit, would be likely to correspond broadly to commonly shared valuations. This is not a valid defense for leaving valuations hidden in implicit assumptions in studies referring only to Western countries.[2] But the core of "knowns" is sufficiently solid that less stringent methodological procedures are apt to have less disastrous effects on the clarity, effectiveness, and objectivity of research than in studies of South Asia.[3]

Most important is that those value premises that have actually determined the approach in a study be made explicit and permitted to fulfill their function. Whatever these value premises are, and however they were reached, this is what methodological clarity demands in the first place. It

[1] Gunnar Myrdal, *Beyond the Welfare State,* Yale University Press, New Haven, 1960, pp. 72–77 *et passim.*

[2] This is the argument in the writer's contributions referred to in footnote 1, p. 32.

[3] Gunnar Myrdal, "'Value-loaded' Concepts" in Hugo Hegeland, ed., *Money, Growth, and Methodology and Other Essays in Honor of Johan Åkerman,* Glerup, Lund, 1961, pp. 275–276.

should be clear from the foregoing that considerable doubt remains whether the value premises chosen *are* relevant and significant. Of this doubt the reader as well as the author should remain conscious.

3 *The Set of Value Premises Selected for This Study: The Modernization Ideals*

Among all the heterogeneous and conflicting valuations that exist in the countries of the region, we have deliberately selected the new ones directed toward "modernization"; they are specified in the next section. These valuations, which for brevity we label "the modernization ideals," were impressed on the nations of South Asia in the Great Awakening following independence, though people there had been gradually conditioned to them by influences from the Western world during colonial times, and more recently by influences from the Soviet Union. They have become the "official creed," almost a national religion, and are one of the powerful strands of the "new nationalism."[1]

Even before independence, the modernization ideals were prominent in the programs of the liberation movements. Later they were often inscribed in the new constitutions. They now appear as the declared main goals in the development plans with which all the countries of the region are equipped and in the introductions to reports by public commissions and committees considering questions of major reform. The programs and general pronouncements of the various political parties regularly adhere to them, or at least avoid contradicting them. They are reiterated in speeches, in leading articles in the press, and in the textbooks for schools and universities. They have, indeed, infiltrated the vocabulary of public discussion. In choosing these ideals as the value premises for our study we are, in a sense, taking these nations, or rather those who speak for them, at their word.

Although the relative homogeneity of this system of valuations is evident, there are differences among the countries in the region and among groups in a single country. The modernization ideals are expressed more clearly and are less confused with other valuations of the traditional type in India, Pakistan, Ceylon, and the Philippines than in Indonesia and Burma. In particular, emphasis on the several elements of the creed varies. In terms of the conventional Western axis of conservatism-radicalism, Pakistan, the Federation of Malaya, Thailand, and the Philippines give a more conservative slant to the modernization ideals, while the official creed of India, Ceylon, Burma, and Indonesia tends to be more radical. There are also movements in time along this axis. At least until recently, Ceylon and,

[1] See in Part Four, and see Appendix 9.

perhaps, Indonesia have moved toward the left, as has Burma, which for a time had tended toward the right. On the whole, India is still moving toward the left in public declarations, though hardly in practical politics.

Viewed in the light of prevailing conditions, however, the creed is radical throughout the South Asian countries, for even modest realization of the ideals would drastically change their economic, social, and political conditions. In fact, when abstractly presented – and very general pronouncements are much more common in South Asia than in the West – the modernization ideals are there ordinarily stated with a more radical flair. On this point there is an interesting parallel with the era of Enlightenment in the Western countries, when radical ideals – notably, but not exclusively, concerning equality – were commonly expressed more uncompromisingly in the literature than at present, although their society was much further from the realization of these ideals than is ours.[1]

As a matter of fact, it turns out that this official creed of the South Asian countries is composed mainly of the ideals long cherished in the Western world as the heritage of the Enlightenment and more recently realized to a large extent in the "created harmony" of the welfare state. These valuations have a long-standing association with thinking in the social sciences, particularly economics, though always with serious opportune compromises and even deviations, and without the methodological clarity of being stated as value premises.[2]

We have noted the relative heterogeneity of the official creed among countries and among groups of intellectuals within the countries. On the general level of valuations, where this creed exists, the ideals are also somewhat vague and indeterminate; at times, moreover, they are internally inconsistent. These logical deficiencies are part of the reality that must be faced; they cannot be disposed of by conceptual tricks that tidy the argument.[3] They indicate that the valuation viewpoint is not really a point but rather a limited space within which the key concepts are often blurred at the edges.

The modernization ideals are mainly the ideology of the politically alert, articulate, and active part of the population – particularly the intellectual elite. The judgments that follow refer to the opinions of these groups. Though their members are trying to spread their ideology to the whole educated class and to the masses of the population, their success in accom-

[1] Gunnar Myrdal, *Economic Theory and Under-developed Regions,* Duckworth, London, 1957, p. 112 *et passim.*

[2] See the works quoted in footnote 1, p. 12, particularly Myrdal, *Economic Theory and Under-developed Regions,* Part II, "Economic Inequalities, the Public Conscience and Economic Theory."

[3] "These conflicts cannot be concealed by such blanket terms as 'maximum welfare.' The main aims of economic policy have to be listed, their compatibility investigated, and where incompatibility remains, preferences have to be stated." (Paul Streeten, *Economic Integration, Aspects and Problems,* Sythoff, Leyden, 1961, p. 17.)

plishing this should not be exaggerated. The inclinations of the broader strata of the population, as yet only partially touched by the Great Awakening, greatly influence the prospects for initiating and implementing policies that conform to the modernization ideals. At least the masses can resist and create obstacles.

And we should also be aware that the modernization ideals have to compete with conflicting valuations. Even politically alert and active members of the educated class are often of two minds and engage in awkward and frustrating mental compromises. Although such conflicts are characteristic of ideologies of this nature,[1] in South Asia they are magnified by the vast distance between ideals and reality.

It should be stressed that endowing the modernization ideals with the technical function of serving as value premises for our study does not, in itself, say more about actual valuations and power relations in the countries under study than that these ideals are relevant because they are present among these actual valuations and that they have that significance of being held, or at least expressed, by social strata which exert most of the political power. Still less does this choice imply any *a priori* assumption that events must go in the direction of the realization of those ideals.[2] It means simply that we are looking at conditions and events from the point of view of the stated value premises, and that we are defining our concepts in terms of that viewpoint.

Naturally, the choice of this set of value premises would be more fully justified if our study were to indicate that their realization represented the trend of the future. This finding did not emerge. But one of the convictions we hold as a result of our investigation is that, particularly in view of the accelerating population increase, rapid strides toward the realization of the modernization ideals must be made in order to avoid increasing misery and social upheaval. They all have a rationale, as we shall point out in Part Four. This is what gives our set of value premises, or rather a study of the countries in the region undertaken from that angle, practical importance.[3] We should also bear in mind that, in one sense, they have all passed

[1] This is a main viewpoint in the writer's *An American Dilemma,* stated in the first section of the Introduction, p. lxix.

[2] The contrast to the writer's study of the Negro problem in America comes readily to mind. Not only were the set of value premises in that study, the "American Creed," much more firmly rooted in actually existing and powerful valuations in the whole population, but those valuations were so strong that – after study – they also stood out as determining the trend in the past and for the future. See *ibid.,* p. 23 *et passim.*

[3] The writer must in honesty add that the distinct aura of Enlightenment surrounding the modernization ideals in South Asia is congenial to him and to his collaborators, who are conservative in their moral allegiances and are personally deeply attached to those inherited radical ideals. Undoubtedly, this attitude made it easier to work with, and stick to, this set of value premises. As instrumental in this study they were not, however, selected on that personal ground, but rather for their relevance and significance in South Asia. The sympathy of the writer and his collaborators for those ideals may have been psychologically favorable to the conduct of the study but has in principle to be considered as accidental and logically irrelevant.

the point of no return. The modernization ideals are in effect in South Asia, at least to the extent of preventing these countries from reverting to their traditional undisturbed status. "Countries may never succeed in becoming modern, but they can never return to a traditional society or polity. A state which, however minimally, advances toward modernity . . . has irreversibly turned its back on the traditional oligarchic alternative."[1]

4 *Summary Specification of the Modernization Ideals*

In abstract form the modernization ideals making up the official creed in these countries have been given expression to an extraordinary degree. In various contexts, but mainly in Part Four, we shall examine the details of these ideals, their relation to other valuations held within the region, how they have come to play their role in the region, and what their effects are and can be expected to be in the future. We shall there stress that the role they now play in South Asian countries represents a significant difference in "initial conditions" as compared with the Western countries in their early stages of development. At this point in the argument, a condensed statement of the modernization ideals must suffice. It should be noted that many of these ideals overlap and, indeed, that they are regularly interdependent and mutually reinforcing, though occasionally conflicting.

a. *Rationality.* It is regularly assumed in public debate that policies should be founded on rational considerations. It is also taken for granted and often stressed that such a course represents a break with tradition. Superstitious beliefs and illogical reasoning should be eradicated.[2] This valuation is occasionally expressed explicitly, as in the statement that the nation is now entering the "scientific era."

An important element in this valuation is the need to apply modern technology in order to increase productivity, but it has been given a much broader interpretation embracing all economic and social relations.[3] His-

[1] Edward Shils, "The Military in the Political Development of the New States," in *The Role of the Military in Underdeveloped Countries*, John J. Johnson, ed., Princeton University Press, Princeton, N. J., 1962, pp. 60–61. See Postscript, Section 2.

[2] The following is a typical statement: "The new way of life is only possible through a deliberate cultivation of the scientific attitude that removes the deadwood of superstition, kills the fanaticism of the mind and kindles a new spirit of inquiry, analysis and objectivity. A mental revolution is necessary." (L. S. Chandrakaut, "Problems of Technological Change," *Yojana*, October 1, 1961, p. 73.)

[3] "But we have to deal with age-old practices, ways of thought, ways of action. We have got to get out of many of these traditional ways of thinking, traditional ways of acting, traditional ways of production, traditional ways of distribution and traditional ways of consumption. We have got to get out of all that into what might be called more modern ways of doing so. What is society in the so-called advanced countries like today? It is a scientific and technological society. It employs new techniques, whether it is in the farm or in the factory or in transport. The test of a country's advance is how far it is utilizing modern techniques. Modern technique is not a matter of just getting a tool and using it. Modern technique follows modern thinking. You can't get hold of a

tory, tradition, and indigenous attitudes and institutions are taken into account, in principle, only on the rational grounds that it is practical for the attainment of specific objectives to do so. No one publicly defends views while acknowledging them to be irrational.[1]

In the first instance, the quest for rationality implies that opinions about policies should be logically valid inferences rooted as deeply as possible in knowledge of the relevant facts. A corollary to this is that opinions, though founded on valuations of both goals and means, should form a logically coherent system. Another corollary is that, though logically the value premises are a volitional and *a priori* element in scientific study, the quest for rationality means that they nevertheless become dependent, to an extent, on the outcome of that study.

b. *Development and Planning for Development.* The desire for development and planning for development flows directly from the quest for rationality and represents in the economic and social field the all-embracing and comprehensive expression of the modernization ideals. Development means improvement of the host of undesirable conditions in the social system that have perpetuated a state of underdevelopment. Planning is the search for a rationally coordinated system of policy measures that can bring about development.[2]

c. *Rise of Productivity.* Higher output per head of the population or of the labor force is a commonly shared goal of development planning. It is generally assumed to be achieved primarily by improved techniques and increased capital intensity in all branches of production and by an improvement in what we shall call the modes of production.[3] These are in turn dependent on raised levels of living, improved attitudes and institutions, national consolidation, and, in fact, on the realization of all the other value premises listed below.

Output per head of the population or of the labor force can, with certain reservations, be taken as an indication of the level of underdevelopment, and the rate of upward change of that output as an indication of development.[4] But it can never serve as a satisfactory definition of these

---

modern tool and have an ancient mind. It won't work. We have 400 million people in India, very fine people, very capable people, very intelligent people, but people who have functioned for ages past in certain ruts of thought and action. Take our peasant; it is a matter of amazement and shame to me that any peasant should go about today with a plough which was used in Vedic times. There has been no change since then. It should have been a museum piece; yet the fact is, it is there. It astonishes me." (Jawaharlal Nehru, "Strategy of the Third Plan," in *Problems in the Third Plan: A Critical Miscellany,* Ministry of Information and Broadcasting, Government of India, 1961, p. 46.)

[1] Chapter 3, Section 2.

[2] Chapter 15, Section 1; and Appendix 2.

[3] Appendix 2, Part II.

[4] Appendix 2, Section 7.

concepts. As we proceed with our list of the modernization ideals, we shall note that changes in other conditions are important, not simply as instrumental in raising productivity but as goals in themselves,[1] and that the goals may sometimes conflict.

d. *Rise of Levels of Living.* That this valuation is commonly accepted is not surprising in view of the extremely low levels of living of the masses in South Asia, especially in the bigger and poorer countries.[2] Indeed, a main reason for desiring a rise in output per head is that it could raise levels of living.

It is commonly believed, however, that substantial improvements in levels of living must be postponed for some time to come in order to permit capital accumulation and even higher productivity and levels of living in the future. This need would assume a partial conflict, at least in the short run, between higher consumption and higher production. But there is also a positive relationship between these conditions to which we shall often call attention – that improved levels of living are a pre-condition for higher labor input and efficiency and, generally, for changes in abilities and attitudes that are favorable to rising productivity. This interdependence between productivity and levels of living is much stronger in the countries of South Asia than in Western countries, though the relationship is mostly obscured by application of the Western approach in the economic analysis of South Asian development problems.[3]

e. *Social and Economic Equalization.* In all the countries of South Asia the ideal that social and economic stratification should be changed in order to promote equality in status, opportunities, wealth, incomes, and levels of living is commonly accepted in public discussion of the goals for planning and for policies generally. In India, Ceylon, Burma, and Indonesia, this ideal has, on the general level of valuations, been carried to the point of a widespread acceptance of such radical policy formulas as "a socialistic pattern of society" and the "classless society." In the other countries – Pakistan, Thailand, the Federation of Malaya, and the Philippines – such extreme formulations of the egalitarian ideal are seldom granted the official imprint, though greater equality is given an important place in all statements of policy goals. Indeed, development is usually interpreted as creating the conditions for raising levels of income and living for the masses.[4]

Social and economic conditions are generally, though in varying degree, far from the realization of this ideal.[5] Recent changes have in fact probably tended to increase inequality, particularly in economic levels. Moreover,

[1] Appendix 2, Section 7 *et passim.*

[2] Chapter 12, Sections 2–6.

[3] Appendix 2, Section 21; and Chapter 21.

[4] Chapter 15, Section 1; and Chapter 16.

[5] Chapter 12, Sections 7 and 8.

specific policies, motivated by the equalization ideal, have often not been carried out, or else have benefitted people other than those at the bottom of the social and economic hierarchy.[1] Occasionally, non-realization of the equalization ideal has been excused, in a vague way, by references to the priority of raising output;[2] this explanation would imply a conflict between the ideals under *c* and *e*. But the opposite can be and sometimes is argued: in the conditions prevailing in South Asia, greater equality is a pre-condition for speeding up production and development.[3]

f. *Improved Institutions and Attitudes.* In general, it is held that social and economic institutions and attitudes should be changed, in order to: increase labor efficiency and diligence, effective competition, mobility, and enterprise; permit greater equality of opportunities; make possible higher productivity and well-being; and generally promote development. It is even quite common in all the countries of the region to discuss these desired changes as a social, as well as an economic, "revolution" and to proclaim that such a revolution is necessary for development.

In regard to institutions, perhaps the easiest way to illustrate the prevalent valuations contained in the modernization ideals is to picture the kind of national community implied in reasonings about the need for a social revolution and in the motivation for specific reform proposals. What is envisaged is a united and integrated national community within which there is solidarity and "free competition" in a much wider sense than the term implies in economic analysis. In such a national community the barriers of caste, color, religion, ethnic origin, culture, language, and provincial loyalties would be broken down, and property and education would not be so unequally distributed as to represent social monopolies. A nation with marked social and economic equality, high social as well as spatial mobility, and firm allegiance of the whole population to the national community is visualized. The desire for such a "modernization" of institutions is most clearly expressed in India,[4] where the barriers to free competition in this wider sense are strongest and most pervasive. The ideal is shared,

[1] Chapter 16, Sections 6–8, *et passim* throughout the book.

[2] Chapter 16, Section 3.

[3] Chapter 16, Section 3.

[4] "Let us be clear about our national objective. We aim at a strong, free and democratic India where every citizen has an equal place and full opportunity of growth and service, where present-day inequalities in wealth and status have ceased to be, where our vital impulses are directed to creative and co-operative endeavour. In such an India communalism, separatism, isolation, untouchability, bigotry, and exploitation of man by man have no place, and while religion is free, it is not allowed to interfere with the political and economic aspects of a nation's life." (Nehru's Convocation Address, Allahabad 'Varsity, December 13, 1947.)

In his *The Discovery of India* (4th ed., Meridian Books Ltd., London, 1956, p. 534), Nehru had already pleaded for a "functional organization of society" where "merit is the only criterion and opportunity is thrown open to everybody."

however, in the whole region, though in Ceylon and Southeast Asia with considerable reservation in regard to foreign ethnic groups.

The modern welfare state in the rich Western countries is, of course, much closer to the realization of this ideal, as are, at lower but rising levels of living, the Communist countries. From the valuation perspective of national consolidation, South Asian countries are all much more amorphous and splintered. The ideal system is viewed as a unified and integrated nation-state, branching out into smaller communities bound together by loyalties to the nation-state. In reality, however, the social and political framework is traversed by lines of interests and allegiances to other types of communities that do not fit into the ideal order but are inimical to it. Although these narrower communities for the most part have no formal existence in a constitutional legal sense, they greatly influence how people feel and think and what they are prepared to do or not do. Many of the proposed and partially enacted reforms of the institutional system – land reforms, tenancy legislation, attempts in India to break up the caste divisions, etc. – should be viewed in this broader perspective, as attempts to eradicate social monopolies and barriers against free competition in the pursuit of happiness, considered inimical to national consolidation, to equalization, and to advances in productivity and levels of living.

Attitudes, in turn, are understood to be supported by and at the same time to uphold established institutions. In regard to attitudes, the general ideal of a social revolution is commonly referred to as the creation of the "new man" or the "modern man," the "citizen of the new state," the "man in the era of science," the "industrial man," and so on. What is implied is illustrated below, though the list should not be regarded as complete, nor should the individual items be viewed as independent of one another:

(1) efficiency;
(2) diligence;
(3) orderliness;
(4) punctuality;
(5) frugality;
(6) scrupulous honesty (which pays in the long run and is a condition for raising efficiency in all social and economic relations);
(7) rationality in decisions on action (liberation from reliance on static customs, from group allegiances and favoritism, from superstitious beliefs and prejudices, approaching the rationally calculating "economic man" of Western liberal ideology);
(8) preparedness for change (for experimentation along new lines, and for moving around spatially, economically, socially);
(9) alertness to opportunities as they arise in a changing world;
(10) energetic enterprise;
(11) integrity and self-reliance;

(12) cooperativeness (not limiting but redirecting egoistic striving in a socially beneficial channel; acceptance of responsibility for the welfare of the community and the nation);

(13) willingness to take the long view (and to forego short-term profiteering; subordination of speculation to investment and of commerce and finance to production, etc.).

The desirability of changing attitudes, though accepted at a very general level, is usually played down in public debate.[1] Least of all does discussion take the form of demands for specific policy measures aimed directly at changing attitudes. Attitudinal changes are glossed over even in the formulation of educational policies.[2]

There are several explanations why a frontal attack on attitudes is avoided. First, it would wound national pride. The educated themselves, including the intellectual elite, are aware of the failure to live up to ideals in this respect. Even more important is the separation of this group from the masses. Conscious of the wide gap between their modes and levels of living, culture, and all circumstances of their life and work and those of the villagers and urban slum dwellers, the intellectual elite compensate for their alienation by romanticizing the plight of the masses. The demand for more efficient labor performance and greater enterprise is often countered by protests that the peasants are rational, intelligent, hard-working, and zealous.[3]

Another important determinant of such thinking is that it developed during the fight for liberation as a protest against colonial theories and stereotypes.[4] Europeans in colonial times typically described the "natives" of these countries as superstitious, lazy, careless, unenterprising, and merely survival-minded. These derogatory views were part of the rationalization of the prerogatives they took to themselves and were able to retain as a super-caste.

[1] Gandhi upbraided his people for wrong attitudes toward life and work much more frankly than have his followers. Occasionally, however, an Indian intellectual does not mince the subject but speaks out: "The young Indian must come round to a rational and objective view of material advancement. He must be able and willing to tear himself away from his family ties; flout customs and traditions; put economic welfare before cow worship; think in terms of farm and factory output rather than in terms of gold and silver ornaments; spend on tools and training rather than on temples and ceremonials; work with the low caste rather than starve with the high caste; think of the future rather than of the past; concentrate on material gains rather than dwell on *Kismet* (destiny). These are extremely difficult changes to envisage in the Hindu social structure and ideas. But they seem unavoidable." (D. K. Rangnekar, *Poverty and Capital Development in India,* Oxford University Press, London, 1958, p. 81.)

[2] Chapters 32–33.

[3] This tendency toward romantic pastoralism when viewing subordinate social strata is familiar from European history. It was particularly prominent in the eighteenth century, when the social system in Europe was somewhat closer to a surviving feudal order while the intellectuals were becoming radical in their philosophy.

[4] Chapter 21, Section 7.

It is obvious, moreover, that the attitudes that are thought to need changing are a function of the low levels of living and culture, and that these levels can only slowly be elevated. These attitudes are also fortified by the institutions in which they are molded and which they help to preserve. Together, the modes and levels of living, the attitudes, and the institutions form a complex social system that is difficult to change, particularly as all these countries are reluctant to apply compulsion.[1] In curious juxtaposition to this awareness of the complexity of the problem is the over-optimism, nurtured by Marx's thinking but largely taken over by Western economists – mostly only as an implicit assumption, revealed by immanent criticism – that economic development and, in particular, industrialization will automatically change both institutions and attitudes.[2] The escape from thinking or doing much about institutions and attitudes is made easier by the application in economic analysis and planning of the Western approach, which ordinarily takes into account solely the "economic" factors. Because it serves vested interests in the *status quo,* this approach appeals to the conservatives at the same time that it permits the radicals to be optimistic.[3]

To sum up: among the articulate groups there is unanimous support, on a very general plane, for changing institutions and attitudes, but there is also much escapism, particularly in regard to specific issues.

g. *National Consolidation.* Ideally, national consolidation means a national system of government, courts, and administration that is effective, cohesive, and internally united in purpose and action, with unchallenged authority over all regions and groups within the boundaries of the state. Consolidation is thus a pre-condition both for the preservation of the state as a going concern and for its efficient functioning as a matrix for the effective formation and execution of national policies, that is, for planning. National consolidation in this sense does not necessarily imply a highly centralized government.[4]

India comes closest to the goal of national consolidation in a restricted sense. Although its population is fragmented into particularist groups, the country as a whole has been relatively free of open rebellions. It is obvious that a still higher degree of national consolidation is needed, and, to support it, more "emotional integration" – which is to say changed attitudes among the people and, to make that possible, reform of the whole institu-

[1] Chapter 18, Sections 13 and 14; see below under *k.*

[2] See Prologue, Section 5; Appendix 2, Section 20.

[3] Prologue, Section 6.

[4] India, Pakistan, the Federation of Malaya, and Burma have federal systems of government, though much power is concentrated at the center. All the countries in South Asia are with varying success trying to build up more local self-government (see below under *j*). A federal system and, more generally, a certain independence of political units below the national level can be justified as being practical for good and effective government, even if it is often utilized for separatist aims.

tional system.[1] In its wider sense, national consolidation as an ideal thus coincides with the ideal of changed attitudes and institutions.

Throughout South Asia the idea of national consolidation, even in a narrow sense, is still being contested. In every country there are groups of people who want to dissociate themselves from the existing national entity; they demand autonomy or at least more independence than is compatible with a reasonable degree of national consolidation. Aside from such movements there are divisions of culture, religion, caste, and economic interests that work against national consolidation. In Ceylon and Southeast Asia, these divisions follow the lines of visible and recognized differences in ethnic origin. However, the ideal of national consolidation enjoys common allegiance among the intellectual elite, apart from those involved in separatist movements.

h. *National Independence.* This ideal is firmly adhered to and, of all the ideals, is given the most explicit expression. National independence, like a reasonable degree of national consolidation, holds a key position among the modernization ideals. Together the two are pre-conditions for planning, that is, the effective formation and execution of national policies aimed at realizing development and all that development includes.

In one sense, even the rebellions constitute no exception to the general urge for national independence. South Asian rebel groups are not shifting their allegiance to a foreign country, but are fighting for an autonomous existence. The ideal of independent nationhood – though not always associated with the boundaries demarcated on the attainment of independence – has been disseminated more successfully throughout the lower strata than has any other modernization ideal. The "new nationalism" is commented on further in Appendix 9.

i. *Political Democracy, in a Narrow Sense.* All the countries of South Asia began their independent existence by declaring their ambition to become democratic nation-states; they gave themselves constitutions, or began to work on constitutions, patterned on those recently evolved in Western countries, with representative assemblies founded on free elections and universal suffrage. They also attempted to establish legal guarantees for civil liberties and to give these a very inclusive interpretation. As these ambitions were thwarted in some countries in the region and their full realization curtailed or endangered in all of them, certain alternative ideals such as "guided democracy," conceived to be more compatible with the "genius" of the country, were substituted for the original Western ideals.

[1] "In India, the first essential is the maintenance of the unity of country, not merely a political unity but a unity of mind and heart, which discards the narrow urges which separate and disunite, and which breaks down the barriers which are raised in the name of religion or between State and State or in any other form." (Nehru's broadcast speech, December 31, 1952, "The Future Beckons to Us.")

Enough has been retained of the ideals of democracy and civil liberties, however, to support a common assumption that the national regime should not only be in accord with the interests of the people, as understood by those in power, but should be willingly accepted by the great majority, and that it should permit general freedom of thought and action, even if it engages in some suppression of public opposition.[1]

Yet it may be doubted whether this ideal of political democracy – with political power based on free elections and with freedom of assembly, press, and other civil liberties – should be given weight in formulating the modernization ideals. This is not because the ideal is at present not very fully met, and may not be met in the future: value premises represent merely an angle from which actual conditions are viewed and need not be "realistic" in that sense; many of those stated above are not. But experience has shown that, unlike the other value premises, this ideal is not essential to a system comprising all the other modernization ideals. National independence, national consolidation, changes in institutions and attitudes, equalization, rise of productivity, rise and redirection of consumption, and, more generally, planning for development can be attained by an authoritarian regime bent on their realization. On the other hand, the substitution of an authoritarian regime for a more democratic one gives no assurance that policies will be directed toward the realization of those ideals, or that, if so directed, they will be more effective.[2]

Granted that political democracy is not essential to a coherent system of value premises corresponding to the modernization ideals, it should be noted that as an abstract ideal it is sincerely adhered to by many, perhaps most, of the intellectual elite in those countries of the region where even the outer forms of democracy and full civil liberties have been sacrificed.

j. *Democracy at the Grass Roots.* Somewhat independent of the political forms and the power basis of a national government is the degree to which it is desired that responsibility for their own affairs be delegated to local and sectional communities and accepted by the people in those smaller communities. This ideal of local and sectional self-government and cooperation has much in common with the ideal of changed institutions and attitudes.

Under the actual circumstances in South Asia today, an oriental despotism of the type that existed in most parts of the region in pre-colonial

[1] Chapter 16, Part II.

This is also a common assumption in the Communist countries–many of which, incidentally, have equipped themselves with constitutions largely molded after the modern Western pattern, however un-Western the practices of the regime.

[2] The writer may be permitted the observation that few things in the outcome of this study have been more disturbing to him, in view of his own personal valuations, than the conclusion that political democracy is not a necessary element in the modernization ideals.

times, and to some extent in a few of the princely states during the colonial era, is clearly no longer possible.[1] It could only be sustained when population growth was still effectively curbed by the intermittent appearance of Malthusian checks – famines, epidemics, and wars – and when the masses of people were cut off from the larger society, especially from the rest of the world. The old-fashioned despotism was able to confine itself to preserving and protecting its power, to sanctioning a measure of internal peace, and to extorting tribute for the expenses of a court and an aristocracy, for wars, and for limited public works. South Asian governments nowadays must strive for economic development, and successful development presupposes a rather high degree of popular acceptance of the development goals. All effective governments, whether democratically based or authoritarian, must enforce some measure of social discipline through compulsion; but even an authoritarian regime cannot record major achievements unless it can somehow mobilize acceptance, participation, and cooperation among the people. Even the poorest and least articulate layers of society have considerable potential for resisting and obstructing measures intended to coerce them. As Nehru observed: "Nobody, not even the greatest autocrat or tyrant, can force vast numbers of people to do this or that."[2]

Thus it should not be surprising that this ideal, referred to in South Asia as "decentralization" or "democratic planning," which is directed toward the creation of conditions for popular cooperation and joint responsibility in local and sectional communities within the nation, is – on the general level – a more widely accepted valuation than any of the modernization ideals other than the quest for independence. But, as we shall find in Chapter 18, no country in the region has progressed very far toward its realization. A number of serious and closely related obstacles stand in the way: deficiencies in government and administration; social and economic inequalities; and, in general, vested interests in the *status quo*, and the traditions of a stagnant society.

k. *Social Discipline versus "Democratic Planning."* These countries are all "soft states,"[3] both in that policies decided on are often not enforced, if they are enacted at all, and in that the authorities, even when framing policies, are reluctant to place obligations on people. This reluctance, which derives from the economic, social, and political structure of the South Asian countries as they have emerged under the impact of colonialism and the fight for independence, is then excused and, indeed, idealized. By "democratic planning" is meant not only, and not even primarily, that poli-

[1] This has repeatedly been pointed out, particularly by K. M. Panikkar: ". . . it is fairly certain that even if democratic institutions in Asia . . . get metamorphosed into something quite different from their original shape and focus, or do not develop in the spirit of genuine vigour, the principles of 'Oriental despotism' will not come back." (K. M. Panikkar, *Asia and Western Dominance,* Allen and Unwin Ltd., London, 1953, p. 499.)

[2] Nehru, "Strategy of the Third Plan," *Problems in the Third Plan,* p. 43.

[3] Chapter 18, Sections 13 and 14.

cies should be decided on by democratic political procedures (under *i* above) and that they should, as far as possible, be implemented with the cooperation and shared responsibility of local and sectional communities (under *j* above). More specifically, it is implied that policies should not require compulsion, and this is often held to be a fundamental difference from the practice in Communist countries. The abstention from compulsion has thus been permitted to masquerade as part of the modernization ideals.

This problem will confront us often in the chapters that follow. For the present let it be said that this particular interpretation of the ideal of democratic planning is not among the value premises of this study. On the contrary, our investigation has convinced us that the success of planning for development requires a readiness to place obligations on people in *all* social strata to a much greater extent than is now done in any of the South Asian countries. It requires, in addition, rigorous enforcement of obligations, in which compulsion plays a strategic role. This value premise runs parallel to, and is partly identical with, the quest for national consolidation (under *g* above) and, in particular, effective government. It would not in principle conflict with the ideal of political democracy, which only concerns the manner in which policies are decided upon.

We cannot claim that this ideal of a more disciplined nation is shared by a large number of people, even among the intellectual elite in South Asia. It is another example of how our study has forced us to choose a value premise that is not widely accepted, in order that the system of value premises may be coherent and in accord with the primary quests for rationality and planning for development.

If this value premise does not conflict in principle with the ideal of democracy, it often does so in practice. Conflict arises when the modernization ideals do not have – and, with the means available in a democratic setting, cannot be made to have – enough force to induce people, including the intellectual elite, to voluntarily undertake diligent efforts toward their realization and to cast aside conflicting valuations.[1] This very serious problem should not be concealed. Under present South Asian conditions development cannot be achieved without much more social discipline than the prevailing interpretation of democracy in the region permits. An authoritarian regime may be better equipped to enforce social discipline, though its existence is no guarantee of this accomplishment.

1. *Derived Value Premises.* We have noted that the modernization

[1] Western aid is commonly argued in terms of making such efforts possible. For example: "Most underdeveloped countries today are determined to achieve higher standards of living and the events of the last twenty years have injected into their bodies politic the dynamics of economic and social change. Our task is to help these countries to attain their economic goals within a political and social framework that remains democratic." (Benjamin Higgins, *Economic Development,* W. W. Norton Co., New York, 1959, p. 438.) The point is that with or without foreign aid – the importance of which should not be overrated – the task may be impossible to effectuate.

ideals cannot be entirely independent and *a priori;* they are partly dependent on the outcome of the study for which they serve as value premises. This is a corollary to the general quest for rationality and planning (under *a* and *b* above). In one sense all of the modernization ideals are contained in, and derived from, the ideal of rationality and planning – though usually not entirely, as they mostly have an independent and not only an instrumental importance. It follows that as we take up concrete problems many value premises that are more specific will come into discussion.

We may illustrate by referring to the ideal of spreading birth control among the masses. Only a few South Asian governments – primarily India but later also Pakistan and, more tentatively, Ceylon – openly supported the spread of birth control among the masses until recently, and no government was willing, or able, to apply policy measures so effectively as to have any great influence on population prospects.[1] Behind this fact is much diversity and uncertainty about the valuations surrounding the population issue, even among the intellectual elite, in all the countries of the region. Yet population increase severely hampers the rise of output per head and development in general.[2] As the rate of population increase in South Asia is very high and rising rapidly, and as this rapid population increase is not likely to be abated spontaneously,[3] the logic of the situation forcefully demands the choice of this value premise. This conclusion is now becoming accepted in all the countries of the South Asian region.

Redirection of consumption in order to raise productivity must also be a value premise. While, as already stated, changes in levels of living (under *d* above) have little importance for productivity in the Western countries within practical limits, the opposite is true in the countries of South Asia, particularly in the poorest of them. There are, however, differences in the effects on productivity of a rise in levels of living according to the economic strata and the particular item of consumption in which the rise occurs. Generally speaking, the productivity effects of a rise in consumption should be greatest in the lowest economic strata and in the items of food intake, health care, and education. As productivity is very low everywhere, with depressing effects on the levels of living of the masses, these differentials in the productivity effects of changes in consumption should be observed and policy measures directed in favor of those strata and those items where a rise in consumption has the greatest productivity effects. Such a redirection of consumption would be in the interest of the general well-being and culture. In large part, though not entirely, this ideal runs parallel to the equalization ideal (under *e*) or is, rather, an expression of it; it gains support from the productivity ideal (under *c*). Although those

[1] Chapter 28, Sections 8 and 14.
[2] Chapter 28, Part I.
[3] Chapter 27.

differentials have not been in the focus of public awareness, it seems likely that, on an abstract and general level at least, this value premise would find wide acceptance among the intellectual elite. Its greater practical realization in specific policy fields would, however, encounter vested interests and other inhibitions and obstacles.

The presence of these hindrances does not fully explain why the reallocation of the nation's consumption has been given so little consideration in planning. Another part of the explanation is the application of the Western approach to planning. The whole conceptual apparatus, of income, consumption, savings, and investment, assumes the absence of productivity effects of consumption.[1] That this approach in turn serves to accommodate opportunistic interests was pointed out in the Prologue, Section 6.

With the same type of motivation, we have been brought to adopt a number of other derived value premises – for instance, that non-discriminatory controls are preferable to discriminatory ones,[2] and that popular education and the spread of literacy should have a leading role in education and reform.[3] We have also accepted the value premise that everything within practical limits should be done to improve health conditions and prevent premature death, independent of the consequences for fertility and mortality. This latter value premise is not derived; it stands as a moral imperative.[4]

[1] Appendix 2, Section 21 *et passim*.

[2] Chapter 19, Section 1.

[3] Chapter 32, Section 3.

[4] Chapter 28, Section 9; Chapter 29, Section 2.

Chapter 3

THE WIDER FIELD OF VALUATIONS

1 *Relation of the Modernization Ideals to Other Existing Valuations*

In the preceding chapter we endeavored to make explicit the set of value premises used in this study. We categorized them as the modernization ideals. They overlap in part and are generally interrelated, for two reasons: first, all conditions in a social system are causally interrelated[1] and, second, since all the more specific value premises should satisfy the first premise of rationality, they have to form a logically coherent system. As they all have an independent value and not only an instrumental one, the modernization ideals, though usually mutually supporting, occasionally conflict with each other. The system can be worked out, verified, and specified by analysis; but, except for the primary quest for rationality, these ideals are all somewhat indeterminate and vague. This fact should not be concealed by any conceptual tricks. It does not, however, seriously decrease their usefulness as value premises for scientific study of the problems. Generally speaking, their fuller realization is remote. In using the modernization ideals as value premises in our study we are simply assuming the desirability of bringing society closer to these ideals and the undesirability of a lapse backward.

[1] Appendix 2, Section 5 *et passim*.

The indeterminate and vague nature of the system of modernization ideals on the general level, which we have chosen for the technical purpose of stating the value premises for the present study, allows for differing views even in a discussion carried on within the framework of those ideals. Opinions differ, for example, as to the causal relationship between a rise in production and equalization and the relative importance of these two goals, and about the state's role in industrial production and the policy measures that should be applied. So long as the rationality ideal is accepted by the participants, this discussion turns very largely on what the facts are; but there are also various shades of valuations concerning both means and ends in planning for development. Communism, "the socialist pattern of society," "free enterprise," etc., are loose expressions for positions taken in this discussion, all with their own connotations of valuations. In the present study this discussion as well as actual policy trends will be treated in their common setting of the more general modernization ideals.

Outside the sphere of the modernization ideals are all the other relevant and significant valuations that should be accounted for in order to put our chosen value premises into perspective.[1] We shall try to consider other valuations in this chapter; the difficulties in doing so have been discussed in Chapter 2, Section 2. We shall find that not all of these other valuations conflict with the modernization ideals: some actually give support to them; some are neutral; and some are ambivalent and can be used both for and against attempts to realize these ideals.

Insofar as these other valuations clash with the modernization ideals, from the point of view of their effect on planning for development they act as *inhibitions* when held by members of government and by those who participate in shaping and carrying out government policies. They account for the hesitancy and the half-heartedness in making and executing plans. When present only among the majority of the people who are not active participants in policy formation and execution, these conflicting valuations act as *obstacles*. As such, they occupy in principle the same position in the analysis as do other obstacles — for example, climatic difficulties or a downturn in the demand for a country's export commodities. They must either be overcome by policy measures that constitute a rational plan or be circumvented, if planning as an expression of the modernization ideals is to forge ahead. The conflicting valuations can, of course, be both inhibitions and obstacles simultaneously, and they very often are. Planning and plan implementation are themselves instruments to break down inhibitions and obstacles.[2]

The dividing line between an active in-group and a passive out-group in regard to the formation and execution of policies — and thus the distinc-

[1] They have importance for planning; see Appendix 2, Section 13.

[2] See Appendix 2, Section 17.

tion between valuations as inhibitions or obstacles when they are not both – is vague throughout South Asia. In every country, to some extent, the government is dependent on acceptance of its policies by the people. This is true not only in countries like India or Ceylon where the government seeks its power basis in general elections but also in more authoritarian countries like Burma or Pakistan. On the other hand, in every country that has reached some degree of national consolidation, there is a government and an administration, and generally these depend more heavily on certain groups than on all other people. In the existing circumstances, as we said in Chapter 2 (Section 2), political power is much more concentrated in South Asia than in Western countries; it is held by a small, politically active and articulate group, most of whom belong to the educated class. The distinction in this study between "inhibitions" and "obstacles" is a somewhat simplifying, abstract model though we believe it represents a realistic approach.[1] It envisages a government and its entourage as the active subject in planning, and the rest of the people as the relatively passive objects of the policies emerging from planning. That the model does not encompass the complex reality in its entirety should be borne in mind.

The modernization ideals are all, in a sense, alien to the region, since they stem from foreign influences.[2] But they have come to be indigenous in the sense that they have been adopted and shaped by the intellectual elite, who, in turn, have endeavored to diffuse them throughout the population. The other valuations, held by the mass of people and in large part also by the intellectual elite, are mainly "traditional": they are part of an inherited culture long identified with a stagnating society. Related to this is another distinction. While the modernization ideals, both individually and as a system of valuations, are dynamic and interventionist, requiring changes through public policy,[3] all the traditional valuations, including those on the most intellectualized level, are static. Even when they are of such a nature as to lend support to the modernization ideals, they themselves are not the driving force. The static character of the traditional valuations is obvious when they appear as inhibitions and obstacles.

In all the South Asian countries the modernization ideals are so firmly fixed among the articulate elite that rationality and planning for development are the recognized precepts for policy-making, however unsuccessful the planning efforts are in practice. Even those traditionalists who oppose these ideals have not managed to produce a reactionary "plan" of their own; for this would necessitate organizing their valuations on the

[1] Appendix 2, Sections 12–13; Appendix 3, Section 8.
[2] See in Part Four.
[3] Chapter 15, Section 1.

principles of rationality.[1] Put another way, the impact of the modernization ideals has already placed the traditional valuations under the serious "inhibition" of being difficult to express in policy terms.[2]

As traditional valuations, unlike the modernization ideals, are ordinarily not subordinated to the rationality ideal – except on that "higher" level where they do not conflict with the modernization ideals – they cannot be synoptically classified. Many of them lead a shadow life, which is real although obscured from the analytical observer thinking in terms of a logical system. Frequently, they are not verbalized at all, let alone comprehensively articulated in public debate. It would thus serve little purpose to attempt an inventory of all the relevant and significant traditional valuations. Some of them, to be sure, find expression in the statements and writings of the articulate and literate, but the evidence afforded by these sources is, at best, only partial.

2 *Traditional Attitudes on the "Higher" Level*

At one level – that of the intellectual elite – some traditional valuations are articulated and thus available for inspection even if not for systemization. Although a few intellectuals are, or feel that they are, completely Westernized and secularized, most observe the prescribed rites of their inherited religion and are cognizant of the broad lines of its theology. They have a knowledge of their country's history, its architectural treasures, its literature and philosophy, music, drama, and dance, and its fine crafts, all of which have positive connotations and add to the richness of life. Their attachment to their nation's history, religion, and culture provides more than mere pleasure; it is a psychological necessity, the more so because of the long subjugation of these peoples and the shocked awareness of eco-

[1] "What weakens the Hindu parties in their political efforts is their failure to have a clear-cut political program for returning to the old order; theirs is to a large extent a kind of rear-guard action, aiming to prevent the passage of government legislation affecting the Hindu social structure, to minimize the use of English in the educational system, and more positively, to fight for the passage of legislation banning cow slaughter. (Support for such legislation has increasingly become a symbol of one's identification with the Hindu faith.)" (Myron Weiner, "Some Hypotheses on the Politics of Modernization in India," in *Leadership and Political Institutions in India,* Richard L. Park and Irene Tinker, eds., Princeton University Press, Princeton, New Jersey, 1959, p. 21.)

[2] Only in India have the traditional valuations emerged as a body of doctrine that posits a set of alternative guidelines to the direction of social change: Gandhi's political philosophy. But Gandhi's philosophy was dynamic and demanded radical change. At bottom he accepted most of the modernization ideals, though he succeeded in associating them emotionally with traditional views. This explains why many of his followers found it easy to become apostles of modernization and development, a role made easier by the many ambiguities in his policy prescriptions. The various aspects of Gandhi's political philosophy will be discussed in Part Four and in most chapters of this study.

nomic and social backwardness following upon acceptance of the modernization ideals. Just as an individual, during a crisis that demands a reappraisal of his way of life, needs to establish himself as a continuous personality, with a past and a defined relationship to his social and cultural environment, so the most enlightened intellectuals in these countries feel compelled to identify themselves with their nation.

Nehru described this involvement:

> Yet the past is ever with us and all that we are and that we have comes from the past. We are its products and we live immersed in it. Not to understand it and feel it as something living within us is not to understand the present. To combine it with the present and extend it to the future, to break from it where it cannot be so united, to make all this the pulsating and vibrating material for thought and action – that is life.[1]

And again,

> The rising middle classes . . . wanted some cultural roots to cling on to, something that gave them assurance of their own worth, something that would reduce the sense of frustration and humiliation that foreign conquest and rule had produced . . . The past of India, with all its cultural variety and greatness, was a common heritage of all the Indian people, Hindu, Moslem, Christian, and others, and their ancestors had helped to build it.[2]

[1] Jawaharlal Nehru, *The Discovery of India*, 4th ed., Meridian Books Ltd., London, 1956, pp. 6–7.

[2] *Ibid.*, p. 343.

The very title of Nehru's book, *The Discovery of India*, testifies to this search for identification. Nehru tells (p. 36) how this discovery "produced a sensation of pride in me as well as that of shame, for I was ashamed of much that I saw around me, of superstitious practices, of outworn ideas, and, above all, our subject and poverty-stricken state. As I grew up and became engaged in activities which . . . promised to lead to India's freedom, I became obsessed with the thought of India. What was this India that possessed me and beckoned to me continually, urging me to action so that we might realize some vague but deeply-felt desire of our hearts? The initial urge came to me, I suppose, through pride, both individual and national, and the desire, common to all men, to resist another's domination and have freedom to live the life of our choice."

And farther on (p. 522): "India must break with much of her past and not allow it to dominate the present. Our lives are encumbered with the dead wood of this past; all that is dead and has served its purpose has to go. But that does not mean a break with, or a forgetting of, the vital and life-giving in that past. We can never forget the ideals that have moved our race, the dreams of the Indian people through the ages, the wisdom of the ancients, the buoyant energy and love of life and nature of our forefathers, their spirit of curiosity and mental adventure, the daring of their thought, their splendid achievements in literature, art and culture, their love of truth and beauty and freedom, the basic values that they set up, their understanding of life's mysterious ways, their toleration of ways other than theirs, their capacity to absorb other peoples and their cultural accomplishments, to synthesize them and develop a varied and mixed culture; nor can we forget the myriad experiences which have built up our ancient race and lie embedded in our subconscious minds. We will never forget them or cease to take pride in that noble heritage of ours. If India forgets them she will no longer remain India and much that has made her our joy and pride will cease to be."

Or, in his address to the United States Congress, October 13, 1949, after pointing out

In South Asia, it is commonly assumed that a nation must identify itself with the past even while breaking away in new directions. As the then Vice President, later President of India, Professor Radhakrishnan, put it, in speaking to a meeting of state governors: "To survive, we need a revolution in our thoughts and outlook. From the altar of the past we should take the living fire and not the dead ashes. Let us remember the past, be alive to the present, and create the future with courage in our hearts and faith in ourselves."[1] Implied in this search for historical moorings and identification with inherited culture is a sense of national pride in them: "It is essential to awaken a sense of pride in our past and re-inforce the faith of the people in what India achieved in the past and what, by dint of intelligent effort, they could achieve in the future."[2]

Awareness of *history* and search for national identity do not in themselves endanger or even compromise allegiance to the modernization ideals, especially on a high intellectual plane. The fact that India and many other South Asian countries had advanced cultures at a time when the now rich and powerful Western countries were uninhabited, or were inhabited by barbarians who left no monuments or records, can be used to build up national pride. It also has an ornamental and ceremonial value that can be appropriated by the new governments.

Memories of the more recent colonial regimes and the process of gaining independence are, naturally, an important element in the consciousness of the politically alert. Insofar as the colonial period appears dark in retrospect, planning and development stand out as means for summoning energies and realizing hitherto unused opportunities. The colonial period is thus ordinarily viewed as a long stretch of time during which people were denied the chance to develop to the full extent of their capacities. The favorable aspects of the colonial system can be looked on as a foreshadowing of the urge for development along national and independent lines.

---

that the drafters of the Indian constitution had been greatly influenced by the American constitution: "Yet it is true that India's voice is somewhat different; it is the voice of the old world of Asia. It is the voice of an ancient civilization, distinctive, vital, which at the same time has renewed itself and learnt much from [America] and the other countries of the West. It is, therefore, both old and new. It has its roots deep in the past, but it also has the dynamic urges of today."

We quote Nehru rather extensively on this point, as we shall on others, for the reason that as an intellectual leader he imbibed the Western ideals very deeply, while as an active politician he was constantly occupied in trying to fit them into a national setting. Thus, and by his honesty and exquisite intelligence, he is an ideal type in Max Weber's meaning, setting forth in high relief what other intellectual leaders and most of the intellectual elite in the region feel and think with less lucidity and insight.

[1] Quoted in Romesh Tapar, "Wiffle Woffle in High Places," *The Economic Weekly*, November 4, 1961, p. 1683.

[2] Congress Planning Sub-Committee, *Report of the Ooty Seminar*, May 30–June 5, 1959, All India Congress Committee, New Delhi, 1959, p. 44.

Knowledge of pre-colonial history is usually so shaky that it lends itself even better to a rationalization of the modernization ideals. Idealization of past periods makes the modernization ideals appear both more urgent and more homespun.[1] In India, for example, there is a rich mythology about the ancient village as a perfect democracy with a rational cooperative organization of production and community life, where caste observance was less rigid and degrading and women enjoyed a higher status.[2] Virtually any cause can find sanction in "history," and the Indian mythology has its counterparts in other South Asian countries, especially Burma and Indonesia. Whether the "golden age myth" is founded on historical fact or is merely an imaginative interpretation is not of immediate consequence; as long as it renders a picture in accord with the modernization ideals, it can be used in their support. Of course, the opposing valuations can be supported by a different interpretation of the facts (or assumptions) about the glory and superiority of the past. Awareness of the past can provide a mantle for a reformer and planner like Nehru, but it can also be exploited by those who wish to clip his wings.[3]

[1] On this point Nehru quotes Aurobindo Ghose: "If an ancient Indian of the time of the Upanishad, of the Buddha, or the later classical age were to be set down in modern India . . . he would see his race clinging to forms and shells and rags of the past and missing nine-tenths of its nobler meaning . . . he would be amazed by the extent of the mental poverty, the immobility, the static repetition, the cessation of science, the long sterility of art, the comparative feebleness of the creative intuition." (Nehru, *Discovery of India*, p. 85.)

[2] About the secure position of women in ancient India, see S. N. Vyas, "Position of Women in Ancient India," *Social Welfare*, 3 (9), December, 1956, Delhi, pp. 36–37. See also Rattan Lal Khanna, *Panchayat Raj in India*, English Book Shop, Chandigarh, 1956.

"Incessantly, Indian women pointed out that their enslavement did not exist in the Vedic time of early Indian history, before the advent of the Christian Era. Indian historical evidence shows that there were many learned women and capable women rulers of this early period. It seems likely that child marriage was not practised at that time, and that widow-marriage was allowed.

"Marriage for girls was not compulsory during the Vedic period. Some women used to remain unmarried throughout their lives, in order to carry on their spiritual work. This tradition continued later on in Buddhist periods. Famous were the Buddhist welfare nuns, who lived in the convents." (Hurustiati Subdranio, "The Changing Social Position of Women in the East," *Eastern and Western World*, W. van Hoeve Ltd., The Hague, Bandung, 1953, p. 116.)

"Many Indians still refer to the old Vedic laws, in order to improve the conditions of women and other subjugated groups. They point out that the recently drafted Hindu Code Bill contains the essence of these ancient laws; only they should be interpreted apart from customs and usage, which came into existence at a later date. Women of the peasant and working classes have always enjoyed a greater freedom than high-ranking sisters, for whom 'purdah' and the veil have been regarded as the insignia of respectability." (*Ibid.*, p. 117.)

[3] Whether the intellectuals in South Asia have a special interest in ancient history, and what role a consciousness of this history plays in their attitudes toward current problems, is a moot point, worthy of empirical study. The illiterate masses are apparently static and backward-looking, but that they look so far into the past is questionable. One wonders what they feel and think about the monuments they often have in

The same can be said of *religion* in its more lofty meaning.[1] The basic doctrines of the old religions in the region – Hinduism, Islam, and Buddhism – are not necessarily inimical to modernization. For example, Islamic and, less explicitly, Buddhist doctrines are advanced to support reforms along the lines of the modernization ideals.[2] The modern constitution worked out for Pakistan prior to the 1958 military putsch was given a generally Islamic façade, as was the First Plan, though the rules laid down in the constitution and the policies prescribed in the plan were hardly influenced by it.[3] Much of the detailed work on the First and Second Plans was directed by American experts, who evidently had no difficulty in adjusting to the Moslem façade. That the Islamic character of the Pakistan republic was, especially in the beginning, played down by the military regime reflected the more secular views of those taking power, and their greater independence of the mullahs.[4] The slight reversion to stress on religion that later took place did not by itself necessitate any change in the regime's position on the modernization ideals.

---

the fields. The educated elite are in large measure engaged in accommodating to a contemporary situation in flux, and their interest in ancient history is perhaps slight. But there are always some who have an interest in history and cultivate it. They are furnishing the material needed for the alternative purposes referred to in the text. In comparing African intellectuals with those from South Asia, particularly those from India, one sometimes gets the impression that the former, because they do not carry the same pretensions of ancient history, religion, and philosophy, more easily accept the experimental and practical approach to life, and that they resemble ordinary farmers' boys who have made good in America or Sweden.

Memories of the recent colonial regimes and the process of gaining independence are, of course, more commonly present in the minds of the intellectuals. The question is how they are molded to suit present interests. Again there is need for empirical research to establish the facts. The outsider's impression is that while specific events in the recent past are rapidly receding from interest, a gradual stereotyping has taken place. In all probability these stereotyped beliefs and valuations will be vastly more significant in forming people's outlooks than is pre-colonial history, because the former ruling nations are still important partners in the outside relations of the South Asian countries.

[1] As Nehru pointed out: "Science today challenges the old concept of religion. But if religion deals not with dogmas and ceremonials, but rather with the higher things of life, there would be no conflict with science or *inter se* between religions." (Jawaharlal Nehru, *India Today and Tomorrow*, Azad Memorial Lectures, Indian Council for Cultural Relations, New Delhi, 1959, p. 32.)

[2] Attention is focussed mainly on the egalitarian ideals, but Islam, in particular, is used to support other modernization ideals as well. In Indonesia the first Sarakit Islam Congress in 1916 strongly criticized the improvidence and negligence of the Indonesians. "At the second Congress in 1917 it was stated that religion commands people to exert themselves in approved professions, such as agriculture, handicrafts, trade, etc., and strictly forbids laziness, idleness, resignation to poverty, and living off the charity of others. 'Religion prescribes all the people to acquire knowledge and to practise the sciences.'" (W. F. Wertheim, *Indonesian Society in Transition*, W. van Hoeve Ltd., The Hague, Bandung, 1956, p. 212 *et passim.*)

[3] See Chapter 8, Section 1.

[4] Chapter 8, Section 8.

In Burma, likewise, these ideals have been explained as an outgrowth of the teachings of Buddha. In fact, even more specialized views – on free enterprise or socialism, "Marxism" or "non-Marxism," and so on – have been held to be in conformity with Buddhism.[1] The greater syncretism and confusion in most Burmese pronouncements should not be attributed to Buddhism, but to other causes – the personality of U Nu, which is so different from that of the Indian and Pakistani leaders; the delayed development of higher education in Burma and the low standards of its university; the small number of Burmese trained for, and accepted in, higher positions in the British civil service; the upheavals and ideological adjustments due to the Japanese occupation; and the burdens placed on the intellectual leaders by the insurrections.

Much the same is true in the other South Asian countries. W. F. Wertheim makes this point about Indonesia: "As the claim for land distribution, springing from a desire to own a piece of ground of one's own, is quite reconcilable with Islamic teachings, it may well be, that the struggle between Left and Right in Indonesia will begin with a fight between Islam and . . . Islam!"[2]

Since independence and the death of Gandhi, less stress has been laid on the religious foundation of policies in India. But whenever references to religion are made on the abstract level, those who defend the moderniza-

[1] Particularly in the earlier years of Burma's independence, "Marxism" was rather commonly explained to be in full conformity with Buddhism. "Marxist theory is not antagonistic to Buddhist philosophy. The two are, frankly speaking, not merely similar: in fact they are the same in concept." (U Ba Swe, *The Burmese Revolution*, Union of Burma, Information Dept., Rangoon, 1952, p. 7.)

Later it became the fashion to stress that "democratic socialism" followed Buddhist lines. Meanwhile the Communists are careful not to attack religion. Frank Trager gives an amusing example of this:

"However much Marxism in the West was atheistic and anticlerical, and however personally secular the Marxists may have been, in Southeast Asia they carefully, except during the 'third period,' concealed or otherwise tempered classic doctrine on this point. The views put forth by Asian Communist leaders, such as Tan Malaka, at the Fourth Comintern Congress generally governed Communist tactics in Southeast Asia. More than most, Tan Malaka was keenly aware of the role of religion in a traditional society. Accordingly, Communist propaganda was designed to take into account this element. Schricke quotes one of the propaganda leaflets used in Sumatra. By any standard an extremely skillful job, the leaflet attempted to show that 'religion, *adat* and prosperity' were one with Communism, and quoted directly from the Koran. The government and the capitalists were dubbed *Kafir*, or unbelievers. The word 'capitalist' was translated into the local language as equivalent to the money-grubbing unbeliever, *Kapisetali*, 'the skinflint *par excellence*, the tax-demanding government.'

"When, much later, anticlericalism crept into the writing of one leading Burmese Communist, a storm broke loose and he had to be publicly disciplined. Though some Burmese leaders attempted to reconcile 'Marxist theory and Buddhist Philosophy,' more recently U Nu, in distinguishing Socialism from 'Marxism' and in equating the latter with Communism, indicated that to identify Marxism with Buddhism was 'ill-considered and unfounded.'" (Frank N. Trager, ed., *Marxism in Southeast Asia*, Stanford University Press, Stanford, 1960, p. 260.)

[2] *Indonesian Society in Transition*, p. 227.

tion ideals can usually manage to quote the scriptures in support of them.[1] Islam and Buddhism can provide support for one of the modernization ideals in particular: egalitarian reforms. Hinduism is unique among the great religions in having no central core of egalitarian doctrine that asserts the fundamental equality of all human beings. This aspect of Hinduism is generally played down in India, though Hindu scriptures are sometimes strained to support even this modernization ideal.[2] Hinduism can also become identified with rationalism and social reform,[3] as can purified Buddhism.[4] On the other hand, religion, like history, can be used by the opponents of all or some of the modernization ideals for their own purposes; as is said in the West, "the devil can cite scripture."

In South Asia the ancient *philosophies* and their more modern versions are regularly of the *Welt-und-Lebensanschauungen* variety and are closely related or identical to the religious doctrines on the "higher" level. They are almost systematically inconsistent in the definition of concepts and, like the religious doctrines, are held together by means other than simple logic. In regard to the issues raised by the modernization ideals they share the flexibility and ambivalence of the religious doctrines.

The higher forms of *esthetic expression,* such as sagas and poetry, drama, music, dance, and the finer crafts, represent, of course, national assets, and their preservation, promotion, and dissemination to broader strata of the population are natural goals for rational planning. In South Asia, as in the rest of the world, these efforts often require public support. To the extent that such goals are incorporated in planned policies,[5] and

[1] In Section 7 below, we shall return to this subject and to the conflict between the "pure" doctrines extracted from the ancient scriptures and the popular version of Hinduism today.

[2] "Work without aiming at personal profit and with an eye only to the welfare of the community is the way of life taught in the Bhagavad-Gita. It lays emphasis on the equal dignity and sacredness of all labour that falls to one's lot, and on honest effort with detachment and without agitation over results. Indeed, the Gita lays down in a unique manner the socialist doctrine in terms of religion." (C. Rajagopalachari, *Vedanta the Basic Culture of India,* Hindustan Times, New Delhi, 1946, p. 5.)

[3] "In India there is a religious philosophy as old as civilisation itself which, strange as the claim may seem to outsiders, is remarkably consistent with science. Out of that religious philosophy has been evolved a code of ethics which can be a firm spiritual basis for a juster social and economic organisation. It is remarkable that the evolutionary hypotheses and the rule of law as men of science know it were anticipated in Hinduism." (*Ibid.,* pp. 3f.)

[4] "Buddha had the courage to attack popular religions, superstition, ceremonial, and priestcraft, and all the vested interests that clung to them. He condemned also the metaphysical and theological outlook, miracles, revelations, and dealings with the supernatural. His appeal was to logic, reason, and experience; his emphasis was on ethics, and his method was one of psychological analysis, a psychology without a soul. His whole approach comes like the breath of the fresh wind from the mountain after the stale air of metaphysical speculation." (Nehru, *Discovery of India,* p. 109.)

[5] In Communist countries artistic strivings are usually strongly supported. As these pursuits require social investments or socially organized activity, and are often thwarted by the competitive demands of a free-enterprise economy, Communist countries are as a rule more successful in developing "national culture."

are, or become, cherished, they enhance the appeal of the modernization ideals. In no way are they intrinsically hostile to these ideals.

It should be noted that in the neutral, or rather ambivalent, value attached to history, religion, and other elements of the inherited national culture, South Asian societies are no different from those anywhere else. As we know, in all Western countries this type of association has been used both for and against the ideals we have selected as our value premises. From history are adduced arguments for radical change as well as for conservatism. Support from religious doctrines has been sought by those fighting for egalitarian reforms as well as by those who admonish the poor to be contented. If in the advanced welfare state the reform arguments have gradually become more prominent, this is a reflection of the general trend of opinions, and of social and political change. The elements of inherited folk culture, and of upper-class and even court culture, have inspired both education methods and industrial design and progressive forces generally; occasionally, however, they have been used to support resistance to industrialization and the spread of machines. The South Asian situation is much the same in principle.

3 *Valuations in Regard to the Indigenous Languages*

Rich in metaphors relating to ancient times and suited to the recounting of sagas and myths, the indigenous languages are understandably cherished, particularly after the long period of political domination by foreigners, who seldom were interested in their preservation and enrichment.[1] Thus, in principle, the value attached to them is no different from that attached to other elements in the inherited culture. However, there are some special complications in connection with the use of indigenous languages, and the problem is of considerable practical importance.

It should first be noted that furtherance of the modernization ideals requires the extended use of the indigenous languages. No real "emotional integration" of the new nations and therefore no secure national consolidation[2] is possible as long as the members of the tiny upper class in charge of administration, law enforcement, and modernized business and industry communicate in a European language and the masses speak only their native tongue. An elected assembly must be narrowly selective on a class basis rather than truly representative as long as law or custom decrees that the language of debate be foreign. The people cannot be brought to accept responsibility for their own local and provincial affairs and community cooperation – the "democratic planning"[3] so essential for develop-

[1] See, however, Chapter 31, p. 1638, footnote 1, on the active interest of European scholars in the history of the old cultures and in their languages.

[2] See under *g*, Chapter 2, Section 4.

[3] See under *j*, Chapter 2, Section 4; and see Chapter 18.

ment – unless they can deal with an administration that does its speaking and planning in their language. The alternative would be virtual extinction of the indigenous language and wholesale adoption of a European tongue, ordinarily English. Not only would such a policy be resisted on national and cultural grounds; it would be a practical impossibility, even in the Philippines where the literacy rate is high and English is taught from the primary grades to the university level, and certainly in the other countries of the region.[1]

On rational grounds, therefore, increased use of the indigenous language must be part of the planning in all South Asian countries, both in the conduct of ordinary affairs and in businesses, governmental bodies, and, of course, schools and universities. The language will have to be developed to serve these purposes, and dialects will have to be standardized. In this process problems will arise. Some rationalist language reformers will concentrate on making the language as easy and as serviceable as possible, by sticking to common usage and by borrowing freely from other languages, beginning with that of the former metropolitan country. Others will attempt to "purify" the language – in India and Pakistan by "Sanskritizing" or "Persianizing" it – and will sometimes produce an artificial idiom hardly more intelligible to common people than the foreign tongue. Rationalism, of course, dictates the former course. Purification is a costly process, especially for the peoples of South Asia who already have to contend with poverty and the many other obstacles to their rapid development. In deciding to give a wider and eventually an exclusive place to the indigenous language the South Asian countries are following in the steps of many European countries – all of them, in fact, if we take into account their breakaway, after the Middle Ages, from the dominance of Latin in the church, the law courts, diplomacy, and the universities. The European countries also experienced difficulties and controversies in developing and standardizing a national language. The only difference is that the South Asian countries cannot afford a process that takes centuries; they need much quicker results.[2]

If we leave the thorny question of script for later consideration, the main problem is that of accelerating the use of the indigenous language. In some South Asian countries the broad issue is rather uncomplicated and the process is well under way. Burma and Thailand are perfecting their na-

[1] Chapter 32, Section 4; Chapter 33, Sections 3, 4, 6.

[2] The closest parallel is, perhaps, Finland. When, after being split off from the wider Swedish community, it began a hundred years ago to develop a national Finnish language out of a number of local dialects with little written literature, the country comprised only 1.7 million people. Finland has succeeded in that effort, though the material and cultural costs were considerable. In retrospect there was clearly no other way to achieve national consolidation, as about five-sixths of the people did not speak Swedish, the language of the commercial and administrative upper class at that time, or Russian, the other official language of the Grand Duchy of Finland before Finnish gained that status, under an 1863 law, in 1883.

tional languages and getting them accepted and used in the representative assemblies, courts, administration, schools, and universities; although part of the trouble the Burmese government has had in enforcing its authority and gaining the loyalty of the people in outer regions stems from the language issue. In Indonesia there are many local languages and dialects, but Bahasa Indonesia (developed from Coastal Malay with a liberal admixture of Sanskrit, Arabic, Dutch, and English words) should in time prevail as the national language, provided Indonesia can master other disruptive political forces. In the Philippines, Tagalog is becoming more generally understood and may become the national language, though there is still resistance to it in regions where other dialects are spoken.

In Ceylon, however, the difference in language aggravates the struggle between the Singhalese majority and the Tamils. In Pakistan, Urdu was designated as the national language after partition; it was spoken mainly in West Pakistan but was nevertheless foreign to most of the inhabitants of that zone. In East Pakistan, Bengali is the common idiom and the language difference became a serious element in East Pakistani grievances against dominance and exploitation by the other half of the country.[1] The East Pakistanis were not satisfied even when the constitution finally adopted both Bengali and Urdu as national languages; English is the official language.

In Malaya, the almost equal division of the population between Malays, on one hand, and Chinese and Indians on the other, did not prevent the establishment of Malay as the national language. Possibly the Chinese and the Indians will in time be forced to acquire a working knowledge of Malay, but this will not keep them from communicating among themselves in their own language. As the Chinese dominate Malayan business and have a large majority in nearby Singapore, a very important part of the country's economic life will continue to be carried on outside the national language.

The language situation in India is especially complicated and hazardous for national consolidation and development. The Indian National Congress began even under British rule to divide the country into linguistic units; this was, indeed, necessary in order to get the fullest possible backing in the fight against the British. By repeated decisions it was also prescribed in the Congress program that independent India should be divided into states demarcated on language lines.[2] The Indian constitution designated fourteen official languages for administrative and educational purposes, including Sanskrit but not English. Among these languages Hindi in Devanagri script was to become the official Union language in 1965. Until then, and while knowledge of Hindi was spreading, both Hindi and English were to have official sanction as Union languages.

[1] Chapter 8, Section 3.

[2] The necessity for reorganizing the British provinces on the basis of language was in principle often recognized by the British from the beginning of the century.

Through a chain of decisions, marked by much strife and some bloodshed, a structure of linguistic states has come into existence, and the process may not yet be at an end. On the whole, this reorganization is a drastic simplification and rationalization achieved by suppression of the princely states and many of the arbitrary provincial boundaries of British times.[1] Many of these states have a population the size of the larger European countries.

The constitutional prescription that Hindi should become the Union language within fifteen years after independence has met, however, with greater difficulties in execution. For one thing, Hindi is admittedly less highly developed than, for instance, Bengali, Tamil, or Marathi. Furthermore, the split of the syncretized Hindustani into Hindi, Urdu, and Punjabi has produced a much smaller language in terms of popular usage. The Indian philologists who have devoted their efforts to improving Hindi have usually been purists, eager to cleanse it of foreign words, and to enrich it by adding words from Sanskrit. As a result Hindi has tended to become an increasingly strange language even to the people who live in the area that is officially supposed to be Hindi-speaking.[2] Even more important, however, is the resistance in the southern states where the official languages are Dravidian. Understandably people in these states feel that the efforts to make Hindi the all-Indian language provide an undue advantage to the northerners. This cannot be cancelled by the pious advice offered by Nehru and other appeasers: that the northerners should learn a southern language in exchange. The advice is seldom followed; nor would it effect a substantial change as, in any case, no southern language is privileged to be the Union language. These feelings of resentment, shared by people in West Bengal, present a serious barrier to the spread of Hindi since education is a prerogative of the states.

[1] Chapter 7, Section 2.

[2] All this was contrary to Gandhi's intentions. He wanted, instead, to unify and standardize Hindustani to include Urdu, Punjabi, and, if possible, other minor languages; he favored the study of additional Indian languages in order to strengthen the unity of the country. Nehru's ideas were along the same lines, and he particularly opposed the purist tendencies in the development of Hindi: ". . . an effort must be made to discourage the extreme tendencies and develop a middle literary language, on the lines of the spoken language in common use. With mass education this will inevitably take place. At present the small middle-class groups, that are supposed to be the arbiters of literary taste and style, are terribly narrow-minded and conservative, each in its own way. They cling to antique forms that have no life in them and have few contacts with their own masses or with world literature. . . . I would personally like to encourage Hindustani to adapt and assimilate many words from English and other foreign languages. This is necessary, as we lack modern terms, and it is better to have well-known words rather than to evolve new and difficult words from the Sanskrit or Persian or Arabic. Purists object to the use of foreign words, but I think they make a great mistake, for the way to enrich our language is to make it flexible and capable of assimilating words and ideas from other languages." (Jawaharlal Nehru, *An Autobiography*, The Bodley Head, London, 1953 ed., pp. 454–456.)

As a result of all this, the time is still far distant when India will have a Union language in effective use. In practice, English is the language of the higher courts, the Union administration, to a large extent that of the state administrations, and that of the Indian Parliament. It is also used by educated people generally when they gather together, particularly when they are from different parts of India.[1] English is still, in a sense, the cementing force in this huge country, as it is in Pakistan. Many of the intellectual elite, and not only those in the southern and western states outside the Hindustan tradition, conclude that English should be preserved indefinitely as the *de facto* national language. Meanwhile the state languages are developing rapidly, and their use in the press, state assemblies, administration, and universities is gradually expanding. Many more youths are now learning English, but only as a second or third language, and standards are continually sinking. One writer has observed that "As a result, all ten languages [i.e., excluding Sanskrit and Urdu, Punjabi and Kashmiri], not Hindi alone, are emerging as alternatives to English."[2]

Looked at from the point of view of the modernization ideals, which are the value premises of this study, the improvement and effective utilization of the state languages is not only desirable but necessary. The isolation of a small intellectual elite – defined and held together by mastery of a foreign language that can never become the popular idiom in any part of India – must be broken, and the masses brought into active participation. But there can be no real national consolidation and responsible participa-

[1] In the autumn of 1961 an all-India National Integration Conference was called together. "It was a large gathering of distinguished persons from different walks of life, political, social, economic and educational." (*Yojana,* October 15, 1961, p. 2.) The conference language was generally English – even in the discussion about whether and when and how to implement the constitutional prescription that Hindi should become the national language. The official organ of the Planning Commission, quoted above, commented as follows: "Fourteen years after Independence it looks as though the change-over is to be a prolonged and painful one, for even the first steps do not seem to have been taken. . . . It is obvious that in some subtle ways English and English ways of thought and feeling overpower us in our national affairs of the greatest importance. We persist in clinging to them almost unconsciously; such is their enchantment." (*Ibid.,* pp. 15–29.)

"The irony of the situation is that nothing more happened beyond this professed adoption of Hindi as our National Language. The Congress leaders went on making their publications in English, pouring forth their orations in English, drafting their resolutions in English, carrying on their debates in English and even conducting their informal *tête à têtes* in English. The espousal of Hindi by the Congress at this stage strikes one as a conjugal alliance without its consummation!

"And this state of affairs, it appears, would have carried on indefinitely. The Congress had its hands full with the struggle for Independence. And it was fantastic, anyway, to think of the Congress leaders, most of them the product of English universities, [willing] to give up the foreign language and switch over to Hindi. Therefore, it appeared that the newly-born babe of Hindi had been given an unobtrusive burial at its very birth." (T. S. Bawa, *Nehru's India,* Freeland Publication Private Ltd., New Delhi, 1956, pp. 160–161.)

[2] Selig S. Harrison, "The Challenge to Indian Nationalism," *Foreign Affairs,* Vol. 34, No. 4, July, 1956, p. 623.

tion in local and sectional self-government and in cooperatives if admin istration, representative assemblies, law courts, and schools continue to employ a language the masses do not understand. Gandhi fully recognized this crucial need; his promotion of the idea of a federal system and demarcation of states along linguistic lines was more than just a tactic to join all forces in the fight against the British.[1]

However, the development of the state languages implies a threat to the Union. Without an all-Indian language, understood by everyone, or at least by all who are taught in schools, it is difficult to see how the Union can be kept together. Present trends would seem to imply a gradual break-up of the relative unity and mobility of personnel in administration, courts, universities, and the professions.[2] The prospect of counteracting these trends by general and prompt acceptance of Hindi as a second language seems slight. Neither is continued reliance on English as a unifying upper-class language a permanent solution, since it is socially restrictive and does not meet the need for national consolidation and popular participation. As long as the debates in the Union Parliament, for instance, are conducted in English, national politics must remain a class monopoly estranged from the people. In the absence of an all-Indian language it would, indeed, be more appropriate to let everyone speak his own language and to have simultaneous translation, as in international organizations. As it is, all planning and policy-making under the Union government in New Delhi, as well as negotiations with state governments, are carried on in a language unknown to most of the people whose interest and cooperation are sought. Aside from the class problem – which is so important for national consolidation and popular participation – it would be strange if popular feelings in a newly liberated country were to permit the continuation of this system over the long run.

In the absence of a generally accepted all-Indian language as a unifying

[1] "It is evident that unless we advance this cause, we shall not be able to remove the growing intellectual and cultural gulf between our men and women and between the classes and the masses. It is also equally certain that the vernacular medium alone can stimulate originality in thought in the largest number of persons." (*Young India*, April 21, 1920.)

"Our love of the English language in preference to our own mother tongue has caused a deep chasm between the educated and the politically-minded classes and the masses. The languages of India have suffered impoverishment. We flounder when we make the vain attempt to express abstruse thought in the mother tongue. There are no equivalents for scientific terms. The result has been disastrous. The masses remain cut off from the modern mind. We are too near our own times correctly to measure the disservice caused to India by this neglect of its great languages. It is easy enough to understand that, unless we undo the mischief, the mass mind must remain imprisoned." (*Constructive Programme*, Navajivan Press, Ahmedabad, 1944, p. 16.)

[2] "It is . . . necessary to emphasise that the growth of these languages led to an integration of linguist nationalities in India, to the emphasis on the fissiparous tendencies of particularism, so that, moved by their pride in their language, the Gujeratis, the Marathas and the Kanarese, for example, began to feel different from each other in a way they had never done before." (K. M. Panikkar, *A Survey of Indian History*, Asia Publishing House, Bombay, 1954, p. 222.)

force, the Union's division into states along linguistic lines invites and strengthens the tendencies toward narrow sectionalism, inimical to national consolidation.[1] These centrifugal tendencies are magnified in India by their correlation with caste. It is not only that the caste structure is broadly regional and encompassed within the language boundaries; the existence and functioning of linguistically defined states adds opportunities for, and intensifies, conflicts between castes.[2] The constant appeals by national leaders rightly condemn "casteism, provincialism, and linguism." It is through these that attachment to one's own language, which is natural and could be consistent with the realization of the modernization ideals, comes into severe conflict with those ideals.

The language problem is complicated by differences in scripts. Such differences are less frequent, of course, in those countries that have or are on the way to having only one national language. Indonesia and the Philippines have simplified matters by adopting the Roman script for their national language, thereby enabling students to have English as a second language without learning a new script. In India not only are there a large number of indigenous languages, but most of them have their own scripts and a high cultural value is commonly attached not only to the languages but also to the traditional ways of writing them. In many parts of the country the public schools have to require the children to learn three languages; this places a heavy burden on the curriculum, but, under the circumstance explained above, can be justified on rational grounds. The burden is increased when children must be taught three scripts – the script of the state language, that of Hindi, which is supposed to become the national language, and the Roman script for English.[3] Teaching of other subjects has to be curtailed.[4] Another cost of this policy is the necessity for

[1] The Linguistic Provinces Commission, appointed by India's Constituent Assembly in 1948, warned that its inquiry "has in some ways been an eye-opener for us. The work of 60 years of the Indian National Congress was standing before us, face to face with centuries-old India of narrow loyalties, petty jealousies and ignorant prejudices engaged in a mortal conflict, and we were simply horrified to see how thin was the ice upon which we were skating. Some of the ablest men in the country came before us and confidently and emphatically stated that language in this country stood for and represented culture, race, history, individuality, and finally a sub-nation." (Harrison, "The Challenge to Indian Nationalism," *Foreign Affairs*, p. 621.)

[2] Chapter 7, Section 5.

[3] Not to mention a fourth language, another state language, as proposed by Gandhi, Nehru, and others. The situation is similar in Pakistan, where both Urdu and Bengali are now national languages. The *Overseas Hindustan Times*, of New Delhi, carried the following notice (on December 7, 1961): "Mr. Zabir Hussain, Pakistan's Minister for Home Affairs, said last week that the Government had asked experts to examine the possibility of evolving a common script of various Pakistani languages, especially Urdu and Bengali. He told newsmen at Larkana that a common script would foster greater unity among the people. He also made a plea for a simplification of the language, used by the Radio and the Press."

[4] Chapter 33, Sections 3, 4, and 6.

specially constructed typewriters, and many Indian scripts are not easily adjusted to typewriting. Moreover, the use of different scripts makes it all the harder for people who have learned only one or two languages to learn a second or a third.

Many national leaders in India, beginning with Gandhi and including the former and the present Presidents, have proposed the use of a single script for all the Indian languages, but this proposal has not met acceptance. It would certainly decrease the costs just described, but would not eliminate them. For knowledge of English is commonly agreed to be necessary for all students above the elementary level, and English cannot very well be written in any of the Indian scripts. Students must learn the Roman script in order to read the foreign literature; at the advanced level the literature in the Indian languages is meager and difficult to keep up to date. From the viewpoint of our value premises, the ideal solution would be to accept the Roman script for all languages, as has been done in Indonesia and the Philippines. Some intellectuals in India stress that this is an obviously needed modernization;[1] they would place scripts, if not languages, among things not deserving of emotional attachment. Thus Humayan Kabir, cabinet minister recently in charge of the Ministry of Scientific Research and Cultural Affairs in India, has argued that script "has no relation whatever to any language or to any alphabet . . . Any alphabet can be written in any script, provided the alphabet has the symbols for the necessary sounds. If it has not, such sounds may be added and visual symbols invented or adopted to represent them. The only basis on which to prefer a script should therefore be clarity, legibility and capacity for easy manual and mechanical manipulation."[2] He prefaced this declaration by pointing out that the languages of India have been written in different scripts throughout history.

But such arguments do not have much influence on those who are attached to a particular script. There is, of course, no difficulty in integrating a cultural preference of this kind in otherwise rational reasoning and in planning. However, the costs in terms of lost opportunities of an educational policy requiring different scripts for different languages must then

[1] It is often pointed out "that the single script for India is absolutely necessary and that the South will accept none other than the Roman or Indo-Roman." (Nomesk Thapa, "Sins and Sinners," *The Economic Weekly*, October 7, 1961, p. 1553.)

This is also the position of many intellectuals in West Bengal. It is open to doubt, however, whether even in these non-Hindi parts of India, this solution would be accepted, if the proposal were put to a decision. That it would meet fierce resistance in the Hindi parts of India is certain: so long as the constitution prescribes that the national language is Hindi in Devanagri script, they are *beati possidentes*.

"National integration does demand a certain degree of conformity in the interest of functional efficiency. Here the emphasis is not on meaningless 'codes' and 'pledges' but on matters such as a common script which is as important as a common currency or common weights and measures." (*Ibid.*)

[2] Humayan Kabir, "Language, Alphabet and Script," *Studies in Education and Culture*, pp. 208–209.

be accounted for. A similar calculation could be made for the costs of having to learn the several languages in the first place. But the national cost of the language issue in India is very different and much larger than the opportunity costs of having to learn more languages and scripts. It adds its load of irrationality and emotion to all other divisive forces in the new nation.

When on January 26, 1965, in accordance with the constitution and the Official Languages Act of 1963, Hindi was declared the official language of India, serious riots broke out in Madras and spread to other non-Hindi-speaking states. After long and acrimonious negotiations, the government was pressed to accept an amendment to the act, giving the force of law to Nehru's promise that English would continue to be an associate language as long as the non-Hindi-speaking people wanted it. At the same time the decision to have a tri-lingual basis for education – implying that Hindi states should teach a southern language in exchange for the teaching of Hindi in non-Hindi-speaking states – was confirmed, though without much hope that it would be carried into practice more effectively than before. The language issue has, in short, been left where it was, except that even more bad feeling has been generated. As one Indian weekly commented on the outburst of rioting early in 1965: "The painful logic of the language issue is such that the fanatics are easily able to force those who normally think and act rationally to yield to local and necessarily narrow sentiment."[1]

4 *The Hindu Taboo on Cow Slaughter and Similar Valuations of a Specific Type*

There are other specific traditional valuations that are widely held and articulated systematically enough to be easily observable. Sometimes they are given the force of constitutional prescript or law. Since they are specific they cannot remain flexible, indifferent, or ambivalent as can the "higher" valuations dealt with in Section 2. They must often conflict with the modernization ideals, and thus represent inhibitions and obstacles to planning for development.

From a practical point of view the most important of these valuations is the Hindu taboo on killing animals, epitomized in the ban on cow slaughter. India is estimated to have more than half as many cattle as human beings and, in fact, one-fourth of all the cattle in the world. Many of them are useless, or destructive since even wandering and half-starved animals eat something; almost all have a very low productivity. The cattle stock has recently been increasing; and there is a real danger that the number of unserviceable and unproductive cattle will increase even faster with control

[1] *Link*, February 21, 1965, p. 1.

of local famines and improved treatment of cattle diseases, particularly if the taboo should be strengthened by new and better enforced laws. This problem of cattle increase offers a somber parallel to the population explosion, which we shall discuss in Chapter 27. The religious taboo that places the life of cattle on a par with that of human beings finds expression in legislation throughout the country. In Chapter 26 (Section 7) we shall consider how this taboo affects productivity in agriculture; here we are interested in its valuative aspect.

The British, believing in non-interference in social and religious matters, had followed a *laissez-faire* policy, though they defended Moslem practices and, toward the end of the colonial era, even tried out, with the support of Indian representative assemblies, cautious legislation against the taboo on cow slaughter. Independence and the upsurge of Hindu nationalism gave the ardent supporters of traditional valuations an opportunity to strengthen the hold of this taboo. They succeeded in inscribing in the Indian constitution a Directive Principle (Article 48) instructing the states, as responsible for agricultural policy, both to endeavor to organize agriculture and animal husbandry on scientific lines and to prohibit the slaughter of milk and draft cattle. With the general backing of this Directive Principle, laws against slaughter of cattle have been enacted in a number of states and there is constant propaganda for such legislation in other states. The Indian Planning Commission commented dryly on the situation created by this Directive Principle and the ideological and emotional force behind it:

> Famines and epidemics having been largely brought under control, there is a tendency for the number of surplus cattle to increase even in the ordinary course and this trend will become more marked owing to action taken in recent years to place a total ban on slaughter of cattle. Proposals for bans on the slaughter of cattle derive from a widely prevalent sentiment which has found expression in the Constitution and must inevitably also enter into national planning. . . . But in giving effect to this Directive Principle care has to be taken to see that conditions are not created which may defeat the very objective which the Constitution seeks to achieve.[1]

For the time being it seems impossible to effect a fundamental change in Indian legislation, or to test the strength of the taboo among ordinary people by offering economic incentives, through taxation and/or subsidies, for the slaughter of useless cattle. The only recourse is to circumvent the taboo. One proposal in the First Five Year Plan was to set aside special areas (Gosadans) where cattle could be left to die – possibly, cynics said, with some assistance from the tigers. But this scheme, continued in the Third Plan, is costly and has made little progress.[2] Another proposal has

[1] India, Government of, Planning Commission, *Second Five Year Plan*, New Delhi, 1956, p. 282.

[2] Chapter 26, Section 7.

been "birth control" through castration of bullocks. But that runs into the difficulty of lack of enough people qualified to perform castrations, and is limited also by a widespread popular taboo against their performance.[1] Since a cow must drop a calf each year if she is to produce milk steadily, it also would mean that still fewer cows would be in milk.[2]

In the circumstances, it is understandable that the designers of the Second Plan concluded on what sounds like a note of despair. "States should take a realistic view of the fodder resources available and the extent to which they can get the cooperation of voluntary organisations to bear the main responsibility for maintaining unserviceable and unproductive cattle with a measure of assistance from the Government and general support from the people."[3] The Third Plan abstained from any general judgment on the problem of cattle numbers apart from emphasizing its "seriousness"; it proposed an increase in the number of Gosadans and a large-scale program of castration of scrub bullocks.[4] The simple fact is, of course, that it is impossible to plan a rational policy for husbandry in India, if cattle cannot be selectively killed to the extent and at the age that is most advantageous economically. In asking for both rational husbandry and a ban on cow slaughter the Directive Principle is self-contradictory.

For India, with its large and growing number of cattle, many of which are surplus, and with so many other adverse conditions that keep the rural masses in poverty and backwardness, the ban on cow slaughter represents a very serious complex of inhibitions and obstacles to planning. Nehru, always adhering strictly to rationality, bluntly came out against this religious taboo on several occasions;[5] however, he did not find it feasible to make a major issue of it and demand a revocation of the ban on cow slaughter in the Directive Principles. It is known that he frequently fought for his view in the cabinet and with members of the state governments.

[1] The Third Draft Plan seemed to place its main hope in birth control, though it noted some difficulties: "The most effective way of checking the further multiplication of useless and inefficient cattle is . . . the castration of scrub and uncertified bulls commonly used in the villages. An all India scheme of Mass Castration for the sterilisation of undesirable males has been incorporated in the Third Five Year Plan. Its success will, however, depend on the active participation of the public and the availability of the requisite number of Burdisso castrators." (India, Government of, Planning Commission, *Third Five Year Plan, Draft Report*, New Delhi, May, 1961, pp. XX–7.)

[2] One writer estimates that at present only one-third of the adult cows are in milk, and that if birth control were adopted, "not even one-tenth of the cows could be kept in milk and it would be impossible economically to maintain such a herd of cows." (V. M. Dandekar, "Problem of Numbers in Cattle Development," *The Economic Weekly*, Annual Number, February, 1964, pp. 351–352.)

[3] India, Government of, *Second Five Year Plan*, p. 283.

[4] India, Government of, Planning Commission, *Third Five Year Plan*, New Delhi, 1961, pp. 348–349. See Chapter 26, Section 7.

[5] In a speech in his own constituency during the next-to-last election campaign, he dared to say that he saw no difference between a cow and a horse, and added that in India the cow is maltreated while kept holy. Louis Fischer reported:

"He has, for example, defeated a bill introduced in Parliament by Hindu extremists which would have banned the killing of any cow. Arguing against the measure, Mr.

Many intellectuals express views similar to Nehru's in private conversation but avoid taking a public stand, either because they do not dare or because they consider the situation hopeless.[1] Many more, and not only those who abhor cow slaughter, make valiant attempts to justify the taboo as economically advantageous, or at least compatible with rational husbandry. Numerous articles and books have been written in support of this opportune rationalization. Like other elements of irrationality in reasoning, it is damaging to logical thinking in general. It should also be noted that in India the taboo is often used to back up nationalist aggressions against the Moslem minority, which does not share in it. Not a few of the riots and fights between Hindus and Moslems have been touched off by incidents arising from their contrary views on cow slaughter.

In Ceylon and the other Buddhist countries there are like sentiments against slaughtering cattle, or killing any animal – broader sentiments that are also present in India. In regard to cattle, however, the taboo is not as damaging as in India, because the surplus cattle population is not as great. The numbers are kept down in part because the people in these countries, unlike the Indians, are averse to breeding animals in captivity, but principally because almost all Buddhists eat meat. The taboo mainly results in a kind of division of labor, with the actual killing left to foreigners – in Southeast Asia often to Indians – and to low-caste groups. There is, consequently, no general tendency to legislate a ban on cow slaughter.

The Moslems in Pakistan, Indonesia, Malaya, and elsewhere consider pigs unclean and have a strong aversion to eating pork.[2] This certainly in-

---

Nehru, according to an Associated Press report from New Delhi dated April 2, 1955, called the idea 'most silly. We are totally opposed to it,' he exclaimed. 'We stand or fall by it.'

" 'Shame, shame,' cried the obscurantist Hindus.

" 'I don't get excited over any animal,' the Prime Minister retorted, 'not even the cow.'

"It takes courage to make such a statement in India, and it is political dynamite. Hindu sentiment and religion are deeply opposed to ending a cow's life, even if its existence robs young cows of necessary pasture and fodder." (Louis Fischer, *This Is Our World,* Jonathan Cape Ltd., London, 1956, p. 470.)

Gandhi's support of the ban on cow slaughter is one of the few points where he deviated from the modernization ideals.

[1] The writer has seldom seen such a large exhibition of portraits of Gandhi as when he visited the Indian Veterinary Institute. It seems that veterinarians, because they are suspected of unconventional views on cow slaughter, are in particular need of a protective front.

[2] In the Soviet republic of Uzbekistan the farmers are almost all Uzbeks, who are Moslems; a large number of non-Moslem Russians work in industry and administration and live in the cities. The Uzbeks, as Moslems, don't eat pork, but since the Russians do, pig breeding is a profitable occupation. When visiting Uzbekistan the writer found that the collective farms had usually solved the problem in the following way: In a distant corner of the farms, far away from the houses where the farmers lived and worked, there were establishments for breeding pigs, the pork being sold in the cities. The breeding, feeding, and slaughtering of the pigs and the transporting of the meat were done by hired Russian workers, under the supervision of an Uzbek, who kept at a safe distance from the pigs.

terferes with the efficiency of peasant farming as the breeding of pigs is often an ideal supplement to raising crops; it also seems to improve health conditions since pigs are scavengers. But again this taboo is not as serious a deviation from rational planning as is the Indian taboo against cow slaughter. As it is the breeding and eating of pigs and not the killing of them that is disliked, and as this aversion rests on a doctrine that pigs are unclean and not that they are sacred, this taboo does not demand a legislative ban; its non-observance by people of other creeds is not felt to be a crime.

The conflict between articulated specific traditional valuations and the modernization ideals can be expressed in terms of the costs to the latter through lost opportunities. In the case of the ban on cow slaughter in India, these costs are very high, though never calculated. Other specific traditional valuations that are articulated appear to be fairly inconsequential for the modernization ideals. Some may be entirely in accord with planning. For example, the Directive Principle in the Indian constitution that the states should prohibit the manufacture and sale of alcoholic beverages may be rational, if the prohibition could be enforced and did not merely encourage disobedience of law and corruption of administrators. The remarkable thing about most traditional valuations of the specific type, however, is the infrequency with which they have been articulated in public discussion. Still less frequently have they been given sanction by constitutions and laws or have they overtly motivated public policies. With some few exceptions, of which the Indian ban on cow slaughter and the positions on the language question are the most important practically, the modernization ideals have reigned supreme in public discussion and overt public policy-making.

An example of formal repudiation of a traditional valuation is that of caste and caste observance in India. Although caste permeates Indian life, and although in private conversation many intellectuals are prepared to defend it as a useful institution, it is condemned in the constitution and by virtually everyone who speaks publicly or writes on the issue. Idealization of the caste system as it is supposed to have operated in the mythological past has its obvious emotional background in a different, and more "realistic," attitude toward it on the part of many of the intellectual elite, who come mainly from the higher and privileged castes.

5 *The "Asian Values"*

So far, we have dealt with verbalized valuations, made explicit by the small intellectual elite. They may be supported by similar feelings in the inarticulate broader strata, but about this we do not know much. That the two specific valuations dealt with in Sections 3 and 4 – in regard to indigenous languages and cow slaughter – have at least some popular backing is apparent. The valuations on the "higher" level, discussed in Section 2, seem to be restricted to the educated class, yet they are certainly not unimportant, as this class holds such a disproportionate share of the political power in South Asia. But an examination that confines itself to what is verbalized and explicit can convey only an inkling of the social significance of traditional attitudes and beliefs, some of which are very important inhibitions and obstacles to development. What is needed is intensive empirical investigation of these attitudes and beliefs in different strata of the population and their influence on behavior. At present, solid knowledge about this highly relevant matter is scanty. Our discussion must therefore be largely restricted to the statement of open problems and the formulation of reasonable hypotheses for further research.

Before taking up that discussion, in the next section, we need to dispose of a presumed short cut by way of generalizations about "Asian values," or the "values" of one or another of the religions or nationalities of the region. There is a large literature expounding this general theme, and many more works refer to these values in explanation of behavior. According to this view, people of one religion, one country, or of the entire region – meaning, usually, all Asia – have the same fundamental cultural and personality traits and world outlook: they share certain basic modes of thinking, feeling, and acting. These traits are supposed to emanate from their history and religion[1] – an explanation that recalls the attitudes discussed in Section 2.

Insofar as there are considerable and systematic differences in conditions among the several South Asian countries, there is undoubtedly something to the concept of a "national character." The same may be said of religions. And as the differences in conditions are much more pronounced between these countries as a whole and the Western world, there is room also for the concept of the "Asian" – or "South Asian" – mind. But these terms are not suitable for scientific use. They have been contaminated by being made to serve – in South Asia as in the Western world – specula-

[1] "Vedanta is the tap-root of Indian culture in the past as well as now. Whatever courage, heroism, self-sacrifice or greatness was shown by men and women in India, was all derived from Vedanta, the philosophy of the Vedas. Even now Vedanta is the living spirit and genius of the people of India. However much foreign civilisation or new aspirations may affect us, the main source has not decayed. The lives of the rich and the poor, of the leisured classes and the peasants and labourers, of Indus, Mussalmans and Christians, of the illiterate and the learned, of the honest and the dishonest, are sweetened alike by the pervasive fragrance of Indian philosophy. Vedanta is the basic culture of India." (C. Rajagopalachari, *Vedanta the Basic Culture of India,* pp. 7–8.)

Similar statements about the unity of culture among South Asians, directly related to history, religion, and ancient philosophy, abound. A Western scholar with a similar message is F. S. C. Northrop. See his *The Taming of the Nations,* Macmillan, New York, 1952.

tive, nationalist, aggressive, or apologetic ideologies. For convenience we shall refer to these values as "Asian values"; in criticizing them we have in mind South Asian, or more specifically Indian, conditions. These alleged cultural and personality traits all turn out to claim a special wisdom and, particularly, a superior moral status. In any case, they are flattering to the collective ego and, at the very least, excuse the shortcomings that exist in material conditions. This is the element of valuation in the belief in common traits. The "genius" of a country or of Asia – an expression with wide currency in the region – is understood to embrace all these characteristics.

For our purpose a summary of some of the most common attributions will suffice. No distinctions among the several countries in the region are acknowledged, since much the same traits are alleged to characterize them all. A central claim is that people in Asia are more spiritual and less materialistic than Westerners. They are other-worldly, selfless, and disposed to disregard wealth and material comfort. They sustain poverty with equanimity and even see positive virtues in it. They have a special respect for learning and a capacity for contemplation and meditation. Their intellectual strength lies in intuition more than in reason and hard calculation. In current affairs their main criterion is the moral worth of a person or a policy, and they are apt to censure expediency and opportunism in politics. With spiritual concerns and personal salvation paramount, the external world takes on an illusory and transient aspect. The attitude toward the environment tends to be timeless, formless, and therefore carefree and even fatalistic. The ideal is alleged to be detachment, withdrawal, if not renunciation and asceticism. This bent of mind, it is said, gives Asians serenity and the capacity to endure extreme physical suffering. They are pictured as tolerant, non-aggressive, and non-militant in their social relations and their international politics. They are said to dislike definitive legal principles and to prefer to settle conflicts by mutual agreement rather than by formal procedures; to regard status as more important than contracts; to desire peace with their neighbors and the world, and peace in their souls.

Stereotypes like these abound in the literature, and allegations of common traits are injected into almost all public pronouncements about Asian countries and their problems and policies. On a par with the modernization ideals they have, in fact, infiltrated the vocabulary of public discussion. Even those intellectual leaders who have questioned their accuracy in general or specific terms (see below) often refer to these "Asian values" in addressing their countrymen, as do visiting statesmen and scholars from the West.

An important field of study would be to cull from the literature and the public debate such statements about Asian cultural and personality traits, analyze them critically, in historical perspective and in their present political, social, and economic setting, and check by opinion surveys and other means the extent to which they coincide with the actual attitudes and behavior of people in different countries and different social and economic strata. As to the realism of the stereotypes, we shall offer here only a few broad observations.

The most cursory examination reveals that the alleged cultural and personality traits bear little resemblance to reality – as little as their counterparts in the Western world (see below). For instance, the charity and tolerance often attributed to the Indians is in direct contradiction to the extreme intolerance bred by rigid social stratification[1] and the callousness toward those in a lower social stratum[2] that is found among the most cultivated Indians and soon adopted by Westerners who live in India for any length of time.[3] That India's foreign relations have sometimes seemed to reflect tolerance is explained by national interests and the accident of Nehru's leadership.[4] In dealing with particular issues, especially with neighboring countries, Indians are generally felt to be haughty and intolerant; this is the consensus in South Asia and often also in the Western countries.

Non-violence, under Gandhi's intelligent leadership, was a broadly successful political tactic of the Indian liberation movement, as it has been for many other groups opposing organized social power, including workers in Western countries in the early stages of trade unionism when their struggle for collective bargaining rights was suppressed by the police and the military. To Gandhi personally, and to many of his followers, the principle of non-violence was undoubtedly a strong moral imperative, related to his philosophy of life and his religion. But non-violence is certainly not a national trait in India, as demonstrated by the Hindu-Moslem strife at

[1] Chapter 16, Sections 6–9.

[2] Arthur Koestler observes this, though, following convention, he promptly takes it as another, but different, expression of the Asian values; the Oriental attitude to the sick and the poor is notoriously indifferent, because caste, rank, wealth, and health are preordained by the laws of Karma. "Welfare work in the slums and care of the poor in general was, and still is, a monopoly of the Christian missions in Asia. Gandhi's crusade for the Untouchables and Vinoba's crusade for the landless are modern developments under Western influence – Gandhi himself acknowledged that he was inspired by Christianity, Tolstoy, Ruskin and Thoreau." (Arthur Koestler, *The Lotus and the Robot,* Macmillan, New York, 1961, p. 280.)

The explanation may sooner be found in the social relations that develop in a very poor country. See below and in Chapter 16.

[3] "This [individual-to-individual] callousness is . . . so strong in the country that it is the greatest danger for a foreigner living in India, for it is a frighteningly easy thing to find it creeping into one's own soul." (A. M. Rosenthal, "The Future in Retrospect, Mother India Thirty Years After," *Foreign Affairs,* Vol. 35, No. 4, July 1957, p. 623.)

This contaminating pattern of being crude and exploitative, while feeling guiltless, is one that all thoughtful Westerners become aware of and often touch on in conversation. Chapter 16, Section 6.

[4] Chapter 7, Section 2.

the time of partition and the conflicts of various types in India today.[1] Buddhism, in particular, is supposed to cultivate non-violent attitudes. But the incidence of recorded crimes of violence in the Buddhist countries of South Asia is among the world's highest, and in Burma the rebellions since independence fail to testify to a particularly tolerant and non-violent national character. Former premier U Nu often referred to "the evil tradition of wresting power by force" in Burma: "Burmese history is full of instances where a king is overthrown by a contender by force and who in turn is similarly ousted by a still more forceful rival. Except for the glorious periods of Anawrata, Bayinnaung and Alaungpaya, Burma has been a battlefield for warring states, each cutting one another's throat."[2]

Similar conclusions can be drawn about all the other stereotyped pretensions to a national or regional personality. The widely accepted idea that Asians are bent on settling disputes peacefully and by mutual agreement, without resort to legal procedures, is refuted by the popularity of litigation in all South Asian countries once there is access to the courts.[3] And the idea that, in the conduct of political life, they are preoccupied with moral issues to the exclusion of expediency and personal advantage is, of course, repudiated by the facts, as will be discussed in Chapters 16 and 20. That status means more than contract is generally true, but this is not uniquely Asian; it is characteristic of all societies that have long stagnated at low levels, especially when the social stratification is rigid and inegalitarian.

Against the claim that people in Asia are peculiarly spiritual and non-materialistic must be placed the common observation of a propensity for

[1] As one of India's foremost journalists has pointed out: "In the ten years of independence there have been more police firings on workers, students and other demonstrators, admittedly obstreperous, than there were in the ten comparatively quiescent years between 1932 and 1942 when the British *raj* held sway. . . . Of non-violence . . . there is therefore little evidence inside India – which is not to say that a state of turmoil persists (it does not) but that authority as represented by those in charge of law and order is more trigger-happy in independent than it was in British-ruled India." (Frank Moraes, "Gandhi Ten Years After," *Foreign Affairs,* Vol. 36, No. 2, January, 1958, pp. 257–258.)

[2] Hugh Tinker, *The Union of Burma,* Oxford University Press, London, 1959, p. 384, quoting U Nu, *Towards Peace and Democracy.*

[3] About Ceylon it is reported: "The inordinate desire of the Sinhalese for litigation is pursued with undying zeal throughout life and cases where men have ruined themselves on account of this vicious habit are legion. Win or lose the result is inevitable. It entails ruin from which one seldom escapes when one has commenced. Every little misunderstanding has to be settled in the Courts. The frivolity can hardly be imagined. Murders have been committed over an olive and whole fortunes have been lost in litigating over a tiny bit of land. Unfortunately, the prevailing legal system provides ample scope and no little facility for going to Courts. The peasant enjoys the novelty of it. He is boastful of his association with reputed lawyers in town. He gets a lot of fun by his visit to town. All the while he himself pays prohibitive sums to be humiliated in Courts and inconvenienced in public." (N. D. Wijesekera, *The People of Ceylon,* M. D. Gunasena & Co. Ltd., Colombo, 1949, p. 179.)

narrow materialism in all social strata – which is not surprising considering the general poverty and the strains of caste and social inequality. The great respect for learning in India, regularly referred to even by Nehru, tallies poorly with the low social and economic status accorded the village teacher and, increasingly, the college professor. Asceticism and the renunciation of material pleasures, often idealized as the "simple peasant life," is a typical example of making virtue out of necessity in very poor countries. Outward austerity, even on the part of those who could afford luxury, was propagated and observed by Gandhi, and was certainly in agreement with his personal ideals. Clearly, however, the continued observance of simple, folksy dress, for instance, which has become almost a uniform for popular leaders, is more a symbolic rite and a political device than a sign of a basic attitude.[1]

If these remarks – based on personal observation and on comments of journalists and others who do not pretend to write as professional social scientists – seem deprecating and unfriendly, that impression is unwarranted. They seem so only in juxtaposition to the completely unrealistic views commonly expounded as a defensive cover. When, later, we turn to the causes of these stereotyped views about cultural and personality traits of the people of Asia, their opportunism should be noted. An hypothesis for further research should be that their appearance and spread in the South Asian countries is ideological and acquires its driving force from the complex emotions we call nationalism. To indulge in this type of wishful thinking offers a particular temptation for the intellectuals in these countries, which were so long under Western political dominance and are now trying against heavy odds to rise out of their underdeveloped status by applying ideals and ideas largely borrowed from the Western world.

The fact that during colonial times the Europeans in South Asia generally ascribed to themselves traits superior to those of the natives partly accounts for the strength and tenacity of the myth of the "Asian values" during the fight for independence and since. The acceptance of these values is very much in the nature of a protest against the colonizers' opinions of the natives – and against the views Westerners are still suspected of harboring.[2] To acquiesce in the ideology of the Asian values is, of

[1] Frank Moraes, in the previously quoted article, says: "In the Mahatma's immediate entourage which adopted this repressive habit of life, these complexes and contradictions were abundantly manifest. They were by no means confined to an inner circle, for on the outer fringes there also popped up a series of minor Mahatmas who sought to mold themselves in their Master's image. Flaunting their outward austerity as a sign of inward grace, not a few of these individuals came to regard themselves as representing the authentic voice of the Mahatma. More than anything else this trend has been responsible for the slightly shop-soiled hypocrisy which characterizes some Congress circles, and detracts from the intrinsic virtue of much of what the Mahatma taught." ("Gandhi Ten Years After," *Foreign Affairs,* pp. 258–259.)

[2] However, this protest is often expressed – and often simultaneously – by the contrary ideology, that conditions and attitudes in South Asia are identical to those in the West. Chapter 21, Section 7.

course, easy for Westerners, who are in a position of strength and have, moreover, in the difficult period since the Second World War, felt a need for diplomacy.[1] This tendency may be observed in the conduct by UNESCO of world-wide conferences on how to reconcile the Asian values with those of the West.

In keeping with the psychology of biased ideologies, most Western writers, like their confreres in South Asia, do not consciously present false views to credulous readers, but, in perfectly good faith, deceive themselves. At the very least, they avoid questioning the reality of the "Asian values"; for this reason we have been unable to cite any work on that subject. The absence of critical study of their realism is rather surprising in view of the importance of these values in the literature and in public debate. Another opportune interest in the Western countries served by the "Asian values" is the belief that they provide immunity against Communism.[2] This view is never closely reasoned; it would be extremely shaky even if the "Asian values" should correspond to reality.

A nationalist ideology that ascribes wisdom, higher morality, and other flattering or apologetic traits to one's own people has, as we well know, its counterparts in the West. However, except in Germany under the Nazi regime, the myth of national superiority, or of the superiority of the West or of Christian civilization, was never allowed to reign unchallenged. It is perhaps even more remarkable that in the South Asian countries, where conditions so forcefully invite a compensating and protest ideology, so many intellectuals, particularly in India, have seen through this type of wishful thinking and have sharply criticized the attempts to present their own peoples as better than others. Nehru early took the lead:

[1] See the Prologue, Sections 4 and 6.

[2] An example of this unwarranted generalization, based on the Indian variant of the "Asian values," is the following passage:

"In India, Hinduism is still a tremendously strong tradition; if Indian society is reformed of its archaic excesses, Hinduism itself – or its basic concepts – may be strengthened because they will be less assailable. From the earliest days of Indian history Hindus have been concerned about the state of the individual human soul and have been hungry for individual salvation. In the course of centuries they have constructed sweeping metaphysical doctrines, some of which had as their base the belief that the world was in a sense illusory and that salvation was to be found by withdrawal, others the idea that salvation was to be found by action in the world. But whichever doctrine was accepted the emphasis was on personal salvation; each man had to live his own life and determine his fate by his own decisions; the drama of the individual human soul was, morally and metaphysically, of infinitely more importance than the vicissitudes of empires and the fate of mankind in the mass; these were but the setting, tremendously spectacular though they might be, for the personal drama. The great images of traditional Hindu thought – the images of the sadhu meditating on the mountain-side, of the Brahmin living in the world but without attachment to the world, of the warrior who fights because it is the predestined duty of his life, and all these and other castes by their different means striving to find salvation and peace – still live powerfully in the Hindu mind. While they do so it will be difficult to enclose India within a Communist straitjacket." (Guy Wint, *Spotlight on Asia*, Penguin Books, Middlesex, U. K., 1955, p. 213.)

A country under foreign domination seeks escape from the present in dreams of a vanished age, and finds consolation in visions of past greatness. That is a foolish and dangerous pastime in which many of us indulge. An equally questionable practice for us in India is to imagine that we are still spiritually great though we have come down in the world in other respects. Spiritual or any other greatness cannot be founded on lack of freedom and opportunity, or on starvation and misery. Many western writers have encouraged the notion that Indians are other-wordly. I suppose the poor and unfortunate in every country become to some extent other-wordly, unless they become revolutionaries, for this world is evidently not meant for them. So also subject peoples.[1]

Repeatedly he comes back to this theme: "I won't put it that way, that Indians are 'more spiritual.' I would say that a static society talks more about so-called spirituality."[2]

To Nehru, many of the alleged virtues attached to the ideology of the Asian values were, in fact, not virtues at all. Thus he occasionally spoke out against the idealization of poverty in terms of asceticism, differing with Gandhi on this point:

Nor do I appreciate in the least the idealisation of the 'simple peasant life.' I have almost a horror of it, and instead of submitting to it myself I want to drag out even the peasantry from it, not to urbanisation, but to the spread of urban cultural facilities to rural areas. Far from this life giving me true happiness, it would be almost as bad as imprisonment for me. . . . What is there in the 'Man with the Hoe' to idealise over? Crushed and exploited for innumerable generations he is only little removed from the animals who keep him company.[3]

Personally I dislike the praise of poverty and suffering. I do not think they are at all desirable, and they ought to be abolished. Nor do I appreciate the ascetic life as a social ideal, though it may suit individuals. I understand and appreciate simplicity, equality, self-control, but not the mortification of the flesh.[4]

Nehru was particularly outspoken in his criticism of the mythology of the Asian or Indian values, but several other Indian intellectual leaders have endorsed similar views and continue to express the same criticism.[5]

[1] *The Discovery of India*, p. 69.

[2] Tibor Mende, *Conversations with Mr. Nehru*, Secker & Warburg Ltd., London, 1956, p. 118.

[3] Nehru, *An Autobiography*, p. 511.

[4] *Ibid.*, p. 510.

[5] An Indian author, examining the impact of foreign study on Indian students, observes: "The contention of the superior spirituality of India has, of course, for a long time been the stock in trade of Indian critics of the West and its impact on India and the argument has been shared by Western critics of the West and admirers of India. The fact was that most of the Indian students [abroad] admitted that they wanted a foreign degree for quite secular reasons. For some, no doubt, their spirituality was an intellectual conviction, but for many it was merely an unthoughtout cliché. To some extent, it is a result of the feeling of national inferiority, a defence mechanism, against

In other South Asian countries there is seldom the same clarity of thought and speech. And so strong is the force of this nationalist ideology that even those who criticize it in general – including Nehru himself – cannot avoid, when facing a local audience, a tone of reverence toward one or another of the "Asian values" – the tradition of tolerance and non-violence, the inherited respect for learning, the spiritualism. In consequence, these myths are given some reinforcement, even by those who would like to dispel them.

A problem about which we know very little is whether and to what extent this ideology, which typically is a creation of the intellectual elite, has penetrated to the masses, and what changes it has undergone in the process. For the intellectuals it undoubtedly represents an attempt to identify with the masses, but there is no assurance of their response. A second problem, and the most important one in the present context, is whether and to what extent this ideology supports or conflicts with the modernization ideals chosen as the value premises for this study. The very fact that it is so often acclaimed by those who stand for the modernization ideals and is utilized for their propagation would indicate that this ideology has a high degree of flexibility, just as do the references on the "higher" level to history, religion, and inherited culture.[1] It undoubtedly is very flexible. But as it is irrational – in that it contains a false conception of reality – it must make for less rational study of goals and means of planning for development, and may even be presented in opposition to the modernization ideals. We find, for instance, that the alleged Asian (or Indian, etc.) acceptance of poverty, and interest in spiritual rather than material matters, is occasionally invoked as an argument against planning for development, the implication being that planning is an outflow of Western materialism. More often, this ideology is used to support a go-slow attitude toward planning or, what amounts to much the same thing, irrational compromises in framing public policies. The weaknesses of the "soft state" – the reluctance or inability to put people under obligations, to enforce obligations, or to apply effective measures against corruption, and so on – can be explained away or defended as expressions of Asian (or Indian, etc.) tolerance.

In the absence of empirical studies, we have very little organized information about these relationships.

---

the superiority of the West in earthly things and a sort of apology for Indian poverty. Professor Shils, I think, is right to suggest that the 'sense of national inferiority underlies the clichés in praise of India, which Indian intellectuals often put forward in public and which seldom find expression in private conversations – which are much more observable in Indian intellectuals abroad than in Indian intellectuals in India.'" (Amar Kumar Singh, "The Impact of Foreign Study: The Indian Experience," *Minerva*, Vol. I, No. 1, London, 1962, p. 47.)

[1] Section 2.

6 *Valuations on the Deeper, Everyday Level: The Problem*

If we are to do more than scratch the surface, we need to examine all the mental inclinations that determine the behavior of the peoples in South Asia. For that wider category we shall use the commonly accepted term "attitudes," meaning the totality of the beliefs and valuations[1] that cause behavior to be what it is. These are the attitudes behind all inarticulateness and all protective and rationalizing precautions, attitudes that have been molded by a long spiritual and material history and that are causally related to levels and modes of living and working and to the entire framework of institutions. As indicated in the preceding section, they are not meaningfully and accurately depicted by myths of the "Asian values" type, but this is not to imply that people's attitudes do not differ systematically, or that the differences do not influence their readiness to accept, and to permit the realization of, the modernization ideals. Attitudes such as these necessarily vary with geographical area and with the social and economic strata in each region and, indeed, in each village.[2]

To ascertain by scientific inquiry these attitudes on the deeper level of actual living patterns and determine their relations to the modernization ideals is, of course, particularly difficult in countries where the masses are illiterate, live within narrow confines, and have little conception of the state that is the matrix for the national policies of which they are the object. The effective attitudes among the intellectual elite or the whole of the educated class certainly cannot be considered representative, especially in South Asia with its sharp social and cultural divisions. Moreover, in these articulate strata, too, many attitudes are shielded from outside observation and often from full subjective awareness. One function of the generalizing rationalizations of the "Asian values" type is to conceal the true nature of people's attitudes from others and from themselves.

The need for scientific inquiry into actual and effective attitudes comes to the foreground in any realistic study of the problems of underdevelop-

[1] On the relation between beliefs and valuations, see Myrdal, *An American Dilemma*, Harper, New York, 1944, Appendix 1.

[2] "It is clear . . . that there is no uniformity yet in the prevailing value systems which determine not only a community's pattern of production and consumption, of farm management, marketing and even housing, but also its primary attitudes and wants. These vary greatly from one community to the next, within groups in the same region and even locality otherwise enjoying in all respects equal resources and opportunities.

"In the absence of common valuations, a uniform response to common incentives and stimuli cannot be expected. On the other hand, variations in the value system can make all the difference to the extent of success or failure of a development scheme independently of the material and natural resources. They can also defeat the central purpose of many of the reforms, policies and programmes – such as, for instance, the land reforms – which are centrally framed for universal and uniform application to all rural communities throughout the country." (Kusum Nair, *Blossoms in the Dust*, Duckworth & Co. Ltd., London, 1961, p. 191. See also the many examples given in her book.)

ment, development, and planning for development in the South Asian countries. We shall in this book be deeply involved in such an inquiry, as, for instance, in our study of labor utilization in Part Five. In the almost complete absence of intensive empirical inquiries aimed at revealing these attitudes, knowledge is scanty and uncertain; we cannot go much beyond formulating reasonable hypotheses for further research. Such research has to be specialized in particular sectors and strata of the national communities and particular types of behavior. But there is also room for a more general approach to these problems.

In both respects, some leads for research can be given. To begin with, research should be factual. It should not start out with the stereotypes illustrated in the preceding section. Neither are the traditional valuations or the "higher" level dealt with in Section 2 of much aid. History certainly becomes important, not as a source of generalizing rationalizations, but rather as the long sequence of ramifying causation that has culminated in present conditions. Myths and sagas are known and recited even among the illiterate villagers, and a common treasure of folklore does help bind together those who share in them; otherwise, their influence on attitudes toward the political, social, and economic issues posed by the modernization ideals should not be exaggerated.

Religion is, of course, crucial, but not the interpretation of old scriptures and the lofty philosophies and theologies developed over centuries of speculation. It is, indeed, amazing how much Western, as well as South Asian, writers think they are saying about the peoples in the region when they refer loosely to the impact of Hinduism, Buddhism, or Islam, which they think of as general concepts and often as intellectualized and abstruse. Religion should be studied for what it really is: a ritualized and stratified complex of highly emotional beliefs and valuations that give the sanction of sacredness, taboo, and immutability to inherited institutional arrangements, modes of living, and attitudes.

7 *The Role of Religion*

Understood in this realistic and comprehensive sense, religion usually acts as a tremendous force for social inertia. The writer knows of no instance in present-day South Asia where religion has induced social change. Least of all does it foster realization of the modernization ideals – though, of course, appeals to religious principles on the "higher" level can be used for, as well as against, those ideals, while cruder religious conceptions can be exploited to incite people to resistance or to demonstrations, riots, and lynchings. From a planning point of view, this inertia related to religion, like other obstacles, must be overcome by policies for inducing changes, formulated in a plan for development. But the religiously sanctioned beliefs and valuations not only act as obstacles among the people to getting the plan accepted and effectuated but also as inhibitions in the planners themselves insofar as they share them, or are afraid to counteract them.

Among the masses, these traditional beliefs that with their related valuations have religious sanction are normally irrational, for they are superstitious and imply a mystical rather than a logical way of thinking. Religious conceptions to that degree irrational have not commonly been held in the West for centuries. To a considerably lesser extent, irrational beliefs sanctioned by religion are also present among the educated class, including its intellectual elite. Even Islam and Buddhism, which at the rarefied "higher" level are so rational and free from iconism and magic, have, in the forms in which they actually influence life and social relations, become demonological and permeated by taboos, magic, and mysticism. In particular, social and economic stratification is accorded the sanction of religion. The attitudes, institutions, and modes of living and working that make up and are reflected in this stratification do constitute very real inhibitions and obstacles to planning and the execution of plans. Considerable differences exist among the countries of the region, but in general the inherited stratification implies low social and spatial mobility, little free competition in its wider sense, and great inequalities. This system of social relations is the product of history and is strongly supported by custom in traditional society; religious beliefs and valuations furnish the emotional support. It is evidence of the stability and strength of this social and economic stratification that it is not commonly challenged by the underprivileged and exploited lower strata but is generally considered by them to be natural and right – a fate ordained by the gods and the whole paraphernalia of supernatural forces. It is this feeling, for instance, that restrains the untouchables in India from pressing into the temples and using the wells of the higher castes.

In India, K. M. Panikkar was one of many enlightened Hindus who have tried to strip institutions such as caste and the subordinate status of women of their religious protection by stressing that Hinduism, as expressed by the scriptures since ancient times, does not sanction them; he concluded that "every kind of custom however poisonous, came to be tolerated and received sanction under the cover of [Hindu] religion."[1] Primary among the modernization ideals is the quest for rationality; hence efforts to realize these ideals conflict with religion, not necessarily or even ordinarily on the "higher" level, but religion as it exists among the people. Even aside from the factor of inertia, implying that the social and economic *status quo* has religious sanction, the permeation of religion, as it is commonly experienced, by irrational views and illogical thinking is inimical to the spread of

[1] K. M. Panikkar, *Hindu Society at Cross Roads*, Asia Publishing House, Bombay, 1955, p. 40.

the modernization ideals and to their realization by planning for development and the effectuating of plans.

An important problem for research is whether, to what extent, and how fast, secularization is diminishing the force of this source of social inertia and irrationality, as a result of the spread of the modernization ideals and of planning and other social and economic changes.[1] Probably, secularization varies in amount and speed both for different social groups and for the several countries in South Asia.[2] It should be noted that from the point of view of the modernization ideals what is needed is merely the eradication of the ballast of irrational beliefs and related valuations. As pointed out in Section 2, no religion on the "higher" level need be in conflict with the modernization ideals. But as religion is part and parcel of the whole complex of people's beliefs and valuations, their modes of living and work-

[1] See below in the next section.

[2] W. Norman Brown asserts that secularization all over the Indian peninsula had proceeded fast even in British times and that "With both Hindus and Muslims religion and magic are contracting into narrower and more sharply defined boundaries . . . Within the cities Brahmans are called upon less frequently for prayers and ceremonies in times of illness and misfortune. Brahmans add that in the cities witchcraft has come to hold fewer terrors for the populace, magicians are less patronized, and their own antidotes are less in demand. Muslims say that charm workers have fewer customers . . . urban temples and shrines seemed less frequented than in 1922 or 1928 or 1935." The observations he records are, however, qualified by the statement that they all refer to cities and towns: "There is no reason to think that any great change has taken place in the villages." (*The United States and India and Pakistan,* Oxford University Press, Oxford, 1955, pp. 50–51.)

An eminent Indian sociologist, M. N. Srinivas, states in the same vein: "Indians are still, by and large, a religious people, but large areas of life are becoming secularised." Contrary to Brown, he holds, however, that "pilgrimages have become more popular than ever before," and that the "demand for the services of the Brahmin priest is increasing among castes which hitherto did not resort to him." (M. N. Srinivas, "Changing Attitudes in India Today," *Yojana,* October 1, 1961, pp. 27–28.) As he attributes the former change to the development of communications and the latter to the "Sanskritization," meaning the imitating in lower castes of the rituals, customs, and way of life of the Brahmans, there need not be a contradiction implied.

The general question whether, how fast, and with what differences for the several countries and social and economic strata a secularization is taking place in South Asia, has not been made an object of scientific research. An example of the type of generalizing judgment that needs to be tested by empirical research, and that in this case relates broadly to "ancient civilizations," is an article by A. Vanistendael, "Thinking about Asia," in *World Justice,* Vol. I (1959–1960), No. 1, September, 1959, p. 73:

"There are the ancient rites and old customs, to be sure, but these are mere gestures and customs. The political leaders and the intellectuals no longer believe in the absolute secret value of these rites and traditions. Do the young ones still believe in them with all the strength which is necessary for a favorable evolution? Again, I very much doubt it. The intellectuals whom I met are certainly very much permeated with Western ideas. Do they still consider themselves as Orientals differing from us in other ways over and above the opposition existing between them and us as whites, as Europeans, as Americans? Have they not become a rather sceptical group, a group of agnostics, who are forced to follow the current of customs and traditions, of social pressures the importance whereof is very rapidly increasing?"

ing, and their institutions, it needs to be reformed in order to break down inhibitions and obstacles to development.[1]

In India, from the beginning of the nineteenth century a series of religious reformers tried to modernize Hinduism.[2] They were under obvious Western influence and can indeed be regarded as harbingers of the spread of the modernization ideals. Their immediate appeal was to the intellectual elite; their message did not directly reach the masses. And, like other reformers in the same line, they evoked reaction. Gandhi himself was in this great line of religious reformers. By being sympathetic to a purified version of the old beliefs and, in particular, by identifying his message with Indian nationalism in the struggle for independence and coordinating these beliefs with his policy lines in this struggle, he appealed also to strata other than the intellectual elite.

Although recognizing that their basic approach was determined by Western influences, these reformers were able to find support for their ideals in the Hindu scripture from the ancient time of the Vedas; this, indeed, became their chief message.[3] They could also point to an ancient

[1] "The fight against such customs leads directly to the reform of religion. It is significant that every movement for religious reform in free society has been against traditionalism. The breakdown of religious *tabus*, priestly influence and of social practices having a religious sanction has been the noticeable characteristic of the establishment of liberal political institutions on a traditional society. Even in Islamic societies, there has been a notable trend against such institutions as polygamy, seclusion of women and similar customs. The purifying of religion and the revival of the great religions of the East have gone side by side with the development of liberal ideas in society." (K. M. Panikkar, *Afro-Asian States and Their Problems,* Allen & Unwin Ltd., London, 1959, pp. 94–95.)

[2] K. M. Panikkar, *Asia and Western Dominance,* Allen & Unwin Ltd., London, 1955, pp. 321ff. *et passim.*

[3] "As a religion Brahmo Samaj was based firmly on the Vedanta of genuine Hindu tradition, but its outlook on life was neither Christian nor Hindu, but European, and derived its inspiration from the intellectual movements of the eighteenth century.

"Thus it may be said that as early as 1820 India had come into the direct current of European thought and had begun to participate in the ideal. Its social message was Westernization, to purge Hinduism of the customs and superstitions with which it was overlaid, to raise the status of women, to bridge the yawning gulf between popular and higher Hinduism, to fight relentlessly against caste, social taboo, polygamy and other well entrenched abuses. To the educated Hindu, who felt unsettled in mind by the attack of the missionaries, the Brahmo Samaj provided the way out." (K. M. Panikkar, *Asia and Western Dominance,* p. 321.)

"This seemed all the more the right path since the Vedas gave no authority to the usages and superstitions that had come to be accepted by the masses as Hinduism. There was no sanction in the Vedas for caste, for the prohibition of the marriage of widows, for untouchability, for the taboo on food and the other characteristics of popular Hinduism which had been seized upon by the missionaries in their campaign and were being widely rejected by Hindu intellegentsia." (*Ibid.,* p. 323.)

"Ram Mohan Roy and his followers, petitioning for the abolition of *Suttee,* for education in English, for greater freedom for women, though they quote from Hindu scriptures in justification of their reforms, are really thinking in terms of Rousseau, watered down to meet Indian conditions. European inspiration of the Asian reform movements of the first half of the nineteenth century cannot be denied." (*Ibid.,* p. 484).

ideological lineage of reformers including Buddha. The present-day social reformers in India who, like Panikkar, attach interest to religion, follow this method of attempting to show that pure Hinduism in its original form did not sanction the popular prejudices and social arrangements they now want to change. Occasionally they express themselves as if the Hindu religion had no connection with attitudes, customs, and institutions, and maintain that they are out to reform not religion but society;[1] this may be good tactics, but it is bad sociology. Religion as a social fact cannot be identified with, and has, indeed, very little relation to, the religion on the "higher" level that they want to preserve.

A remarkable situation has gradually come about in South Asia. First, practically no one is attacking religion.[2] Even the Communists do not take

[1] This was Gandhi's position. "Caste has nothing to do with religion," he said. "It is harmful both to spiritual and national growth." Later Panikkar made himself the principal protagonist for this view:

"The major difficulty of Hinduism which had made it a wild jungle growth of widely varying customs, usages and superstitions was lack of a machinery of reform and unification. The institutions of Hinduism, which in a large measure got identified with the religion itself, were the results of certain historical factors. They were upheld by law and not by religion. Vivekananda put the point well when he wrote: 'Beginning from Buddha down to Ram Mohan Roy, everyone made the mistake of holding caste to be a religious institution . . . But in spite of all the ravings of the priests, caste is simply a crystallized social institution, which after doing its service is now filling the atmosphere of India with stench.' " (*Ibid.*, p. 327.)

"Among the more enlightened Hindus themselves, at one time this view gained wide acceptance. Most of the reform movements of the last century were, it would be remembered, directed against orthodox Hinduism. They proceeded on the assumption that what was necessary was a purification of the Hindu Religion. The Brahmo Samaj, the Arya Samaj and other similar movements, which were started with the laudable object of reforming Hindu society confused the main issue and organised themselves on the basis of a reform of religion. This basic misconception had two very significant results. It aroused the dormant powers of the Hindu religion which called forth from its ancient armoury all its weapons to defend its institutions, right or wrong. Practices which had authority neither in religion nor in tradition, came to be regarded as fundamental. Even the self-immolation of widows, which was never widely prevalent and which certainly had no sanction in religion found its defenders at one time. Secondly, it made even the internal reorganisation of Hindu society difficult as reformers came to be identified with the thought and practice of other religions." (Panikkar, *Hindu Society at Cross Roads*, p. 1.)

"It is a religion giving sustenance to every aspect of human life, and the modification of laws or the abolition of customs will no more adversely affect the religion of Hinduism than the discarding of old and dirty clothes and wearing of clean and new ones affect a man." (*Ibid.*, p. 88.)

"The attack on religion has definitely failed now. Even the most ardent workers in the mission field do not have any longer the hope of converting India to Christianity. Equally decisive has been the failure of movements from inside which aimed at a large-scale reform of religious ideas. Hindu religion has emerged triumphant from the struggle and today does not feel her supremacy challenged from any side. But the problem of the Hindu social organisation has remained materially unchanged except that it has now come to be recognised that its solution does not lie through the machinery of religion. It is the Hindu society that has to be basically reorganised and not the Hindu religion." (*Ibid.*, p. 2.)

[2] Nehru was almost alone in publicly admitting agnosticism, though he did not make an issue of it. He had stated in his autobiography, however: "The spectacle of what is called religion, or at any rate organized religion, in India and elsewhere, has filled me

a stand against religion in any of the South Asian countries.[1] In spite of its obvious relevance for all those who want to modernize South Asian society, Marx's declaration that religion is the opium of the people is never quoted. What is insisted on in India and constantly preached by those intellectual leaders who support the modernization ideals is that religion should be relegated to private life; it should not influence those in public life. While occasionally a bow is made to religion in the abstract as a force for creating good citizens – which from their point of view must be contrary to truth, if popular religion is meant – the secular character of the state, public institutions, education, politics, and business is constantly stressed. Any division of people according to religious creed is branded as "communalism" and put on a par with "casteism, provincialism, and linguism" as a danger to national consolidation. This position cannot be shared, of course, by the leaders of the communal political parties; yet even they mostly play down the religious issue publicly and use it in an almost underhanded way. The official views, which are a legacy of the liberation movement, do not prevent all political parties, including the Communist Party, from exploiting religious communalism for their own purposes in elections, despite public condemnation of such maneuvers.

The situation is, of course, different in Pakistan, because it was created as an independent state for the Moslems; its Islamic character at first was, however, played down by the military regime that took power in autumn 1958. In Ceylon, the dominant Singhalese group identifies itself openly with Buddhism, while the Tamil minority stresses its Hinduism. In Indonesia, one of the five guiding principles is "belief in God," which to the Moslem majority implies that Indonesia is basically an Islamic country, though this is not much stressed. In Burma, Buddhism was by gradual steps made the state religion; nevertheless, as in all the other countries, religious freedom is an accepted principle. In both Indonesia and Burma there has been what may be called a religious revival. In Indonesia, though not in Burma, this is a reversal of earlier tendencies toward religious skepticism among the intellectuals.

Secondly, there are now very few organized attempts at religious reformation in any South Asian country. In India, there is a definite retreat from the nineteenth century movements to purify Hinduism; a hands-off attitude is observed by the intellectual elite, who do not even carry forward Gandhi's criticism of the filth in the temples and of all the supersti-

with horror." (*An Autobiography,* p. 374.) In his last will and testament he wrote: "I wish to declare with all earnestness that I do not want any religious ceremonies performed for me after my death. I do not believe in any such ceremonies and to submit to them, even as a matter of form, would be hypocrisy and an attempt to delude ourselves and others." (*Indian and Foreign Review,* June 15, 1964, p. 4.) On this point his will was not respected.

[1] Section 2.

tions connected with popular religion.[1] To the progressive rationalists among the intellectual elite in India who are working for modernization, avoidance of any interference with religion, even in its most irrational manifestations, and the relegation of it to private life is the way to achieve progress: let sleeping dogs lie.

These tactics undoubtedly have some pragmatic basis. Important legislative reforms – for instance in regard to family legislation – are being carried out, and support for them is found in the "higher" forms of religion now prevalent among the intellectual elite, while silence is preserved about the fact that popular religion is different. The hope is that through these and other reforms, and through education, religious reformation will take place without a frontal attack. In fact, this ideological and political process started under British rule.[2] There are, however, the urgent problems of whether "communalism" can be eradicated; whether the reform legislation will be observed in practice; whether, more generally, people will change in the way development requires; and whether all these changes will happen rapidly enough, without a deliberate reformation of popular religion that would drive out superstitious beliefs and elevate in their place the cherished rites, philosophical thoughts, and general moral precepts accepted by most of the intellectuals. But there may well be no basis for a reformation of religion, in which case a choice of this alternative to the present tactical policy of the intellectual elite in India could bring about a violent reaction that would spell disaster for all the efforts toward modernization and development.

By characterizing popular religion as a force of inertia and irrationality that sanctifies the whole system of life and work, attitudes and institutions, we are, in fact, stressing an important aspect of underdevelopment,[3]

[1] Gandhi was in many ways more courageous than later popular leaders; he also upbraided the people for disorderliness and laziness.

[2] "The unifying doctrine was the Vedanta, but the abstract conceptions of this philosophical approach could only appeal to the elite. Popular Hinduism continued in the old way, sectarian, devotional and based on daily rituals. But it also underwent extraordinary changes. The gnarled branches of this ancient tree either fell away by themselves or were chopped off by legislative action promoted by the reformers. Child marriage, which many Hindu communities considered as an essential part of their religion, was abolished by law through the insistence of popular agitation. The remarriage of widows was permitted. Social disabilities based on caste vanished by themselves, and the occupational basis of caste-communities was weakened. Temples were thrown open to the untouchables, and in the most orthodox province of Madras, Hindu religious endowments were placed under the control of public bodies. The movement for the regeneration of the depressed classes assumed a national character, and their participation in social and political life became a major factor in the last days of British rule. Popular Hinduism had a more vigorous life than it ever had in the immediately preceding times, but it had in the course of a hundred years changed its character and temper, though it had kept much of its form." (Panikkar, *Asia and Western Dominance,* p. 326.) This account may have an element of truth, though it displays exaggerated optimism on every single point.

[3] Appendix 2, Section 5.

namely, the resistance of that system to planned, induced changes along the lines of the modernization ideals. This wider definition of popular religion by the social scientist is defensible on the ground that any narrower definition is arbitrary and does violence to reality.

It should be noted, however, that not all elements of that system are necessarily irrational from the point of view of the modernization ideals. Some beliefs and practices undoubtedly represent a pragmatic accommodation to actual conditions and are in accord with rational considerations in planning. For example, the ritual washing of the body observed by some castes in India and by groups in other South Asian countries can certainly be a health-protecting custom. It can also be a basis for attempting to educate people to more hygienic habits. Likewise, the vegetarian diet, observed by many in the higher and middle castes in India, particularly in the South, and increasingly by some lower castes, has a justification in terms of planning in a country as poor as India where climate makes the preservation of animal food so difficult and where vegetable crops can be grown that are high in protein and vitamins and cheaper than animal food. Often the positive valuations attached to various elements of the inherited culture in the broad sense of the word are irrelevant from the point of view of the modernization ideals.[1] This is true of dress, for instance. An old custom is often based on utilitarian considerations that justify it from a modernization point of view. We now realize that this is true of many of the inherited customs in the construction of buildings.

Other traditional attitudes related to religious beliefs and valuations are not inimical to rational planning in the present stage of development in South Asian countries. Thus, as long as there is so great a scarcity of trained doctors and nurses prepared to serve in the villages, the popular emotional attachment to indigenous systems of medicine is harmless, or even advantageous, especially if public policy is directed to improving the

[1] This is, essentially, what Kingsley Davis means in the following passage:
"First, from any standpoint as fundamental as that which we are pursuing, much of so-called cultural change is irrelevant, because it has little to do with the kinds of national requirements just described. Important social changes may occur while countless cultural elements remain stable. For instance, neither the Russian language nor the Russian tea-drinking habit changes much despite the whole Communist revolution in Russia. Conversely, cultural changes may occur with no significant national or social consequences. Whether women wear skirts or pants, whether they believe in one god or three, smoke pipes or cigarettes, or prefer cubistic to representational art, it is hardly of significance to a nation. Only when such cultural traits take on some kind of national significance may their change become relevant. Then they are important for what they mean not in economic or technological context, but in a ritual or emotional context in which case it is the national or international context that makes them important, not the traits themselves. For this reason, when we approach the subject of change from the standpoint of a systematic discipline – political science, sociology, or economics – we are not faced with the encyclopedic task of talking about the endless variety of 'cultural change.' Our interest lies specifically in *social* change, and with criteria of relevance plainly in view." (Kingsley Davis, *Identification of Fundamental Social Changes which Condition Inter-Nation Relations*, 1958, roneod.)

training of the practitioners of these ancient arts of medicine. Furthermore, it has been found that the use of modern medicines and, in particular, inoculation, does not arouse much resistance, for the masses rapidly incorporate the new medications into their old magical way of thinking about illnesses and their cure.

Relatively innocuous too is the belief in astrology and horoscopes, often entertained even by intellectuals. In all South Asian countries one meets politicians, businessmen, doctors, engineers, and experts of every kind who are rational and effective in their particular vocation but hold such beliefs and conduct their private affairs accordingly. And it is never made a public issue. Even when politicians are occasionally moved to arrange public events in accordance with the advice of astrologers, this usually does not greatly upset rational planning. Among the lower strata these beliefs are cruder and probably more important in their life and work, though not too consequential. Nevertheless, a considerable increase in general well-being, productivity, and savings would result if people in all strata spent less money on weddings, funerals, and other social events, to which custom and tradition, usually with some religious sanction, commit them.[1] Unnecessary family expenditure for social — or, rather, status — purposes is paralleled by extravagance in official functions in all South Asian countries.

As a whole, however, this combination of attitudes, institutions, and customary modes of living and working, sanctioned by popular religion, creates a tremendous weight of social and political inertia, which planning for development must try to lift. And the irrational elements in people's thinking about themselves and society erect a wall of confusion that makes the very idea of planning difficult to disseminate rapidly and effectively. After all the diligent efforts to popularize the Indian development plans, one wonders how much has taken hold in the minds of villagers and slum dwellers, and how this thinking in terms of planning, if transmitted, has been molded by the transference. Among the educated and the intellectuals the irrationality inherent in traditional thinking undoubtedly con-

[1] "Still greater effort is involved when a change in what may be called social mores is required. An instance is the reduction of expenditure on social events or religious ceremonies. If this were achieved on a large scale, a substantial contribution to capital formation might be made in many rural areas. It is obvious that such an advance depends entirely on educative effort in the widest sense of the term. There have been isolated cases of success in this type of effort in India. For example, among one large semi-aboriginal tribe the alcohol-drink habit was almost eradicated in one area through the efforts of an indigenous social and religious leader. For sustained progress over a wide area, however, the emergence of local leadership alone cannot be depended upon. Success can be achieved only by a national movement conducted on a moral or spiritual plane such as to attract and inspire local leadership everywhere. A beginning in many directions in this wider field can be made only by a wide national movement which may or may not be directly sponsored by the State. Obviously, political, social and religious leaders would all have to come together in such efforts." (D. R. Gadgil, *Economic Policy and Development,* A Collection of Writings, Gokhale Institute of Politics and Economics, Sangam Press Ltd., Poona, 1955, p. 148.)

tributes to the relative lack of interest in facts and straight reasoning from facts that has been commonly observed as a regional characteristic.

A most important general problem for investigation is whether whatever attitudes, institutions, and modes of living and working should prove to be peculiarly South Asian are primarily a function of South Asian poverty and low levels of living, including poor educational facilities. For instance, the survival-mindedness of the people, their unresponsiveness to opportunities for betterment, and their scorn of manual labor, especially work for an employer, may result, directly or indirectly, from long ages of hopeless poverty. The fact that they are not very different, at least in the type, from those that prevailed in pre-industrial Europe, and that were widely discussed in the Mercantilist literature, rather supports this view.[1] The inegalitarian social stratification, in particular, may partly be a result of stagnation in poverty. We shall comment on these behavioral peculiarities in other parts of the book. The intensity and stale forms they have acquired in South Asia may be due to the much lower economic levels that have long been the rule in most of the South Asian countries and to the absence until independence of a functioning and self-reforming national community.

In any case, it is completely contrary to scientific principles to follow the easy, speculative approach of explaining the peculiarities in attitudes, institutions, and modes of living and working by reference to broad concepts of Hinduism, Buddhism, or Islam, or to personality or cultural traits such as abstention, spiritualism, lack of materialism, and other allegedly "Asian values." And it is not accidental that these broad generalizations can so easily be shown to be unrealistic. It should rather be an hypothesis for further study that people in this region are not inherently different from people elsewhere, but that they live and have lived for a long time under conditions very different from those in the Western world, and that this has left its mark upon their bodies and minds.[2] Religion has, then, become the emotional container of this whole way of life and work and by its sanction has rendered it rigid and resistant to change.

8 *The Dynamics of Social Change*

This research on attitudes in their total social setting needs to be pursued within the framework of social change. Almost nothing is known

[1] Chapter 21, Section 3.

[2] "Europe and Asia are divided chiefly by time. Between them lie barriers still more effective than oceans – the Industrial Revolution, the growth of modern science, and the evolution of modern parliamentary government. The antithesis of East and West refers ultimately to the consciousness of different stages of political and economic development; it distinguishes a world which has already experienced those metamorphoses from a world which, for the most part, has yet to undergo them." (John M. Steadman, "The Myths of Asia," *The American Scholar*, Spring, 1961, p. 175.)

about how all that is continually happening in South Asia affects the attitudes of different groups and strata. Some happenings are in the stream of events that are not directed by the governments; some are planned as intentionally induced changes; ideally, planning should control all the changes taking place and direct them so that they are most favorable for development. These changes will be commented on in detail in the appropriate chapters. A condensed and therefore superficial enumeration of some of the most important categories of influences must suffice for the present.

The creation in colonial times of an educated class and an intellectual elite implied a gradual enlargement of a very tiny group of people who, through education and by their contacts, received ideological impulses from the Western world, and later also from the Soviet Union. Over the decades their minds reflected the major world events with a selection, relative emphasis, and interpretation that were molded by their special situation and differed in various strata and in the several countries. It was in this way that the modernization ideals spread and became integrated in the "new nationalism," which, however, also contained other ingredients. Newspapers made their appearance; they enjoyed, in spite of occasional attempts at suppression, a large degree of freedom, often more than they do today. The liberation movements, which were strong in India, Burma, and Indonesia but weak in Malaya and Ceylon, opened possibilities for spreading nationalism in some measure and in some form to the broader strata. Occupation of Southeast Asia by the Japanese in the Second World War stirred up conditions for almost all people in that area, as did their forced departure, and, in Indonesia, the warfare against the Dutch and finally the rebellions there and in Burma. The partition of British India into two countries was, of course, a traumatic experience for the population in the whole subcontinent, especially its northern parts.

In the economic and social field, the colonial governments had generally followed a *laissez-faire* policy, but the foreign business enterprises, the accomplishments in the field of expanding public activities, particularly in transport, and the pursuance of other policies implied changes of conditions, ordinarily in the direction of greater mobility and monetization of markets. Urbanization was proceeding. Legislation was used against some traditional abuses. Immigration of Indians and Chinese to Ceylon and the Southeast Asian countries was encouraged. Generally, with all its shortcomings, the colonial period provided these countries with more "development" than they had ever had, though not always in the direction that now seems desirable.

The winning of independence, the coming to power of independent national governments of new would-be nation-states, and the regular routines of political activities, including elections, implied in themselves big changes, which in some measure touched the broader strata of the populations. So did the spread of the ideals of planning, welfare, and democracy.

Many of the new governments instituted legislation aimed at greater equality or against the interests of the foreign groups in the population. Quite generally, moves were made to increase the health and educational facilities more rapidly. The spread of communications, particularly radio and film, was a common experience, as were improvements in transportation facilities: airplanes were flying in the sky. Urbanization was given a new spurt. New industries were promoted. In agriculture attempts were made, with varying success, to raise productivity through agricultural extension, community development and cooperation, and, more generally, to uplift the rural population.

To this should be added the effects of the new international relations that developed after independence at the peculiar juncture of world politics in the post-war era. To the intellectual elite, especially its higher strata, the new experience of sending and receiving diplomats and the policies pursued through these channels and in the international assemblies were of considerable importance. The large number of technical assistance experts sent by individual nations or through the international organizations and distributed throughout all the South Asian countries had their "demonstration effects" even outside each one's special mission.

The various impulses mentioned are not abating, but are bound to accelerate. What they signify is uncertain. The assertions frequently made in the literature about their effects on people's attitudes must for the time being remain unsubstantiated. These range from assertions that attitudes are in rapid flux to statements that these impulses are not of much import and that people remain fairly unchanged in their attitudes, particularly in the rural districts.

In our list of new impulses we did not mention the population explosion in recent years, which constitutes by far the most important social change in South Asia, overshadowing everything else that has happened. Contrary to most of the other changes, its general effect has been to delay economic and social advance for the masses of people and to solidify all institutions and attitudes.

A common assertion in much of the literature is one variant or another of the statement that what we are seeing is a "revolution of rising expectations." Even if for the time being this meant a widening gap between aspirations and realizations, it would not be a bad thing from the point of view of the modernization ideals, and is apparently not so considered by those in the intellectual elite who are pushing planning for development. They know that complacency among the masses is a main enemy of development, and that only by rousing the people from apathy to aspire after something better can they hope to overcome the strong forces of resistance. But they must also know that if actual trends do not somewhat keep pace, the results would then be increased strains on their political systems. The relative stability of a country's development process should thus be considered as consisting in a delicate blending of rising expectations sufficient to press and permit development with enough complacency to prevent political explosion.

The concept of "rising expectations" is, however, rather loose and borders on meaninglessness unless it is quantified. The prefixed substantive "revolution" suggests that the changes in attitudes are great and proceeding fast. In the present context only one preliminary remark need be added. Without doubt, the idea of the rising expectations as a revolutionary movement among the masses is in large part a false rationalization. It reflects the Western observer's and the indigenous intellectual's feeling of how he would react if he had to live in the dire poverty of the masses, and his bad conscience when confronted by this extreme inequality. Among other things, the radical tone of most South Asian political proclamations is difficult to understand unless it is assumed that in them speak the members of a privileged class, who wish to identify themselves with their nation and, despite the great social distance, are aware of the misery of the broader strata. It represents how they themselves would react if they had to live under similar circumstances.[1] The actual feelings of the masses must be ascertained, however, by studying the attitudes of these people with a minimum of sentimentality and preconceived ideas; this is not done to any large extent.[2] We need only note here that in none of the South Asian countries has a political regime been unseated by means of a popular revolt.[3]

When this problem of social change is, instead, viewed from the practical angle, the attitudes and institutions and the modes of living and working should be studied as the objects for intentional planning, that is, for rationally coordinated policy measures, inducing changes that go in the direction of development. One fundamental question then becomes whether it is more difficult to cause a big and rapid change in that direction than a small and gradual one. This is in another and more appropriate sense the problem of revolution versus evolution, posed as a policy choice.[4] Through our study we have grown more and more convinced of the realism of the hypothesis that *often it is not more difficult, but easier, to cause a big change rapidly than a small change gradually*. This problem is related to another one: what policy means are felt to be available for carrying out reforms. The bigger and more rapid change ordinarily must be attained by resolutely altering the institutions within which people live and work, instead of trying, by direct or indirect means, to induce changes in attitudes while leaving institutions to adjust themselves to the changed attitudes. But institutions can ordinarily be changed only by resort to what

[1] Chapter 16, Section 13.

[2] Kusum Nair, *Blossoms in the Dust,* Chapter XXIV *et passim.*

[3] Chapter 16, Section 12.

[4] Appendix 2, Sections 19–20.

in the region is called compulsion – putting obligations on people and supporting them by force.

On a general level, the public debate in the countries of South Asia is filled with pronouncements that a social and economic revolution is needed. A study of their actual conditions can hardly avoid strengthening this view. In particular, the recent and continuing very rapid rise in the rate of population increase must make radical changes seem necessary to avoid a much too slow advance or even a disastrous decrease in economic levels. But in practice the policies resorted to are piecemeal and gradualist, often to the extreme. All these countries remain "soft states" – as defined under *k* in Chapter 2, Section 4 – much more so, in fact, than the Western world, with its inherited legalism and recently won political democracy.[1] The results of their policies are also most often disappointing, as we shall find in the course of this study.

The adherence to the gradualist approach to this extent and in this manner in spite of the common recognition of the need for revolutionary change must, of course, be explained by the social situation in these countries, especially the innumerable inhibitions and obstacles that rational planning meets. There are always strong interests opposing changes, particularly of institutions, and particularly those institutions that relate to property and the stale and inegalitarian social stratification; these are traditional and so are protected by religious sanction. As we must constantly bear in mind, the intellectual elite who, on one hand, are the vehicles for the modernization ideals, on the other hand, largely belong and/or have numerous ties to the privileged groups that have vested interests in the institutional *status quo*, at least in the shorter view.

Many other things support the over-gradualist approach. The historical development in the Western countries was on the whole one of social evolution. With this fact the intellectuals in South Asia are familiar through their Westernized education and contacts. The fundamental differences in initial conditions[2] fade from their thoughts more easily by the common use of the Western approach in research and planning. Western students of South Asia are biased by their own background in favor of a gradualist approach. They as well as their South Asian confreres are also aware that the introduction of sudden changes has often caused disruption, demoralization, and rootlessness. The history of early English industrialization and its serious social effects was widely publicized by Marx and before him by contemporary English students of social conditions. The general thesis has been confirmed by anthropological and sociological studies of isolated and stagnant communities upon which modern Western culture has intruded. It is mostly forgotten, however, that these disrup-

[1] Chapter 18, Sections 13–14.

[2] Chapter 14.

tions are all examples of the effects of change under *laissez faire*, or at least in the absence of adequate planning to avoid them.

When faced with the realities of the "soft state," Western students are, moreover, apt to play down their observations for reasons of diplomacy. For economists, in particular, this tendency is abetted by their Western approach, which – except for some general qualifications and reservations injected in their analysis – implies an abstraction from those types of social facts that represent resistance to change: modes of living, attitudes, and institutions. The indigenous students are under strong Western influence in their thinking; moreover, on this particular point, their national pride encourages this approach. Insofar as the social realities are taken into account, they tend but to offer another reason for a very gradualist approach. The South Asian countries are regarded as unable to master, administratively and otherwise, a policy of more rapid induced change – except by relying on totalitarian and monolithic methods. "Democratic planning," with reliance on persuasion, is thus rationalized, to defend the avoidance of radical reforms through changing the institutions – to which mostly those with an interest in the *status quo* would, of course, not voluntarily agree, even after ever so much persuasion. Although the idea of "democratic planning" is stretched to exclude many social controls that have been resorted to freely and successfully in the Western democracies, it usually is sympathetically received in the Western world – by social scientists as well as others – because it is associated with resistance to Communism; this association tends to emasculate criticism.[1]

And so the South Asian planners remain in their paradoxical position: on a general and non-committal level they freely and almost passionately proclaim the need for radical social and economic change, whereas in planning their policies they tread most warily in order not to disrupt the traditional social order. And when they do legislate radical institutional reforms – for instance in taxation or in regard to property rights in the villages – they permit the laws to contain loopholes of all sorts and even let them remain unenforced. This contradiction is intellectualized in two opposing views, simultaneously held, on what planning for development really requires in the way of social change. On the one hand, it is propounded that social change must be radical and go very deep. On the other hand, it is stressed that it must proceed with the utmost caution, upsetting the inherited traditional social setting as little as possible.

This internal contradiction is usually bridged by an over-optimistic assumption about the magnitude and rapidity of the spread effects from

[1] Chapter 18, Section 13.

It is apparent, though, that even Western students of a conservative leaning, who cannot be suspected of any Communist sympathies, have begun to ask themselves whether a social revolution is not necessary in order to set the South Asian countries firmly on the road to progress. See below in Chapter 16, Section 18.

development spurts in industry – a confidence, as we point out elsewhere,[1] that is rooted in Marx's thinking but is widely shared by Western and South Asian economists and all other planners. The general assumption is slipped in without evidence that it is realistic; it is, in fact, most often left implicit. It does not agree well with South Asia's historical experience. And it is certainly not in accord with what little we know about attitudes, institutions, and levels and modes of living and working in the region.

9 *The Role of the "New Nationalism"*

As rationality is the first among the modernization ideals, they are all logically interrelated and can intellectually be contained within the ideal of planning for development. Thus, as soon as policies are discussed in terms of ends and means, the modernization ideals gain a strategic advantage over the traditional valuations, for these can be presented, not in the dynamic terms of planning, but only in the static terms of permitting or resisting change.[2]

Emotionally the traditional valuations are contained in religion, in the wider sense of people's actual experience of sanction given to existing modes of living and working, attitudes and institutions. This sanction – irrational or a-rational, that is, outside the sphere of rationality – is what gives the traditional valuations their strength to act often as inhibitions and obstacles to planning for development. The corresponding emotional container of the competing modernization ideals, or, as these ideals are dynamic, the vehicle for them, is nationalism. Some of the modernization ideals directly need nationalist emotions in order to be grasped. People must have a conception of the nation as a whole and attach positive valuations to this idea before they can feel that national independence and national consolidation[3] are goals worth striving for and that all the other modernization ideals can only be realized in the setting of an independent and consolidated nation-state. Part of their emotional appeal stems from the expectation that as these ideals begin to be realized the nation-state will become stronger, more united, and better consolidated. Nationalism, therefore, is commonly seen as a force for good by all those in the intellectual elite who are bent on planning policies aimed at development. To them, fostering nationalism will provide the means of breaking down inhibitions and obstacles.

Like the modernization ideals, nationalism in South Asia, in the main, has spread rather recently under influences from abroad, mainly from Europe. These influences were negative as well as positive. In South Asia,

[1] Prologue, Section 6; Appendix 2, Section 20; and Chapter 24, Section 7.

[2] See above in Section 1.

[3] See under *g* and *h* in Chapter 2, Section 4.

where the primary national goal had to be liberation from colonial bonds, nationalism was alloyed with resentment against the Western countries and the former metropolitan country in particular, though in this respect there is much ambivalence. As in Europe, nationalism began in the higher, though not usually in the highest, social strata, but sought identification with the common people, and it seems to be the one valuation in line with the modernization ideals that has with some success been disseminated in the broader strata, changing, it is true, in filtering downward.

In spite of its association with romanticism, nationalism in Europe tended to be secular and rational; it was often tinged with anti-clericalism. To serve in South Asia as the emotional vehicle for the spread of the modernization ideals, which are also imported from the Western world, it would need to have the same character, and it often does with a limited group of Westernized intellectuals. More generally, however, nationalism in South Asia became associated with religion. In the educated class where religion often has been purified and raised to what we have called the "higher" level, this does not substantially diminish the ability of the new nationalism to be the emotional carrier of the modernization ideals. But when the new nationalism spreads to broader strata, where religion is of the type described in Section 7 above, its chance of serving this purpose is seriously impaired, even in regard to its primary function of keeping the new nation-state united.

The essential dissimilarity is due to the historical fact that the development of nationalism, which in Europe spanned centuries and proceeded step by step, in South Asia is violently telescoped and then becomes confused and chaotic, as events and situations tumble over each other with no orderliness of historical precedence. In Europe the strong independent state with a fairly effective government and a common pattern of law enforcement and observance preceded nationalism, and both preceded democracy. The states in South Asia were created anew, partly as an effect of rising nationalism. And they were immediately given a ready-made democratic ideology, if not much democratic reality. The practical problems in South Asia are: how to consolidate and strengthen the newly created states brought into existence by the collapse of the colonial power system under the onslaught of nationalism; how, at the same time, to make governments in these new, not very advanced, states stable and effective; and how to do all this in the turmoil of nationalism with some degree of democracy from the beginning and attempts at what we have called democracy at the grass roots.[1]

It is, then, not only a telescoping in the sense that the changes are concentrated in a shorter time span, but there is also a break in the order in which the changes occur. What could in Europe unfold gradually and proceed as a grand symphony with one movement following the other in

[1] See under *j* in Chapter 2, Section 4.

thematic sequence[1] is by destiny syncopated in South Asia into almost a cacophony. Little wonder that Western observers often confess confusion about this new nationalism. And less wonder that South Asian writers, who exaggerate at least as much the analogy that is evidenced by use of the same term for the two phenomena and are under an inner compulsion to seek and convey a meaning and a telos to the life of their nation, are usually no more successful in analyzing it for us.[2]

There certainly is a melody of progressive and rational ideas in the new nationalism in South Asia, soaring above the tumult of noises. And, as we shall shortly discuss, almost everything there depends on whether this melody will be able to ring out loudly enough to become the main theme. This is the nationalism that appeals to unity and condemns all internal, spatial, religious, and social particularisms. It stands for rationalism against superstitious beliefs, and expresses the will to modernize society and to achieve economic development. But this is not the sole component of South Asian nationalism, and in many countries and at many junctures not even the dominant one.

For it is also a brand of nationalism when the East Bengalis are agitated by what they regard as the inferior status afforded their language and their region in Pakistan; or when Dravidians in Madras demonstrate against North India, against the higher status given the Hindi language and the power and privileges of the Brahmans, and when occasionally they go so far as to burn the flag and the constitution of the Indian Union; or when Sikhs march in protest against the Gurdwara Act and in support of a separate Sikh state in Punjab; or when loyalties of caste, religion, and language dominate elections in India; or when in Ceylon the Singhalese rise and demand the only true citizenship of the island; or when the Tamils then stand up against the Singhalese; or when the Karens or the Shans in Burma fight against the national government; or when everywhere in Southeast Asia protection for "nationals" against the "foreign group" is demanded;

[1] We are, of course, speaking relatively and abstracting from the wars and the frequent suppressions of national minority groups and also from reactionary throwbacks as under Nazism in Germany.

[2] Nehru, with his usual intellectual honesty, explained his bewilderment in a speech to a Scandinavian audience:

"Now it is in the minds of men, hundreds and millions in Asia, that changes have taken place and are taking place. . . . It is difficult for you to understand. It is difficult for me to understand, much more so to persons coming from afar, but the main point is that something has happened, and it had to happen. You cannot keep a whole continent bottled up. The bottling up process is ended, and great forces have come out, and they have to make changes. They are making changes. Changes are happening. What direction those changes will take depends on so many factors, primarily of course on those very people, those very countries. Secondarily, on what other countries do or do not do; also, of course, if there is peace or war in the world.

"So I want you to appreciate this. I myself am a seeker after this, and I try to understand what is happening in my own country. I know something about my country, but I do not understand it even now fully, much less do I understand the other countries of Asia." (Information Service of India, Stockholm, *Nehru in Scandinavia,* 1958, pp. 36–37.)

or when those groups then resist.[1] It is nationalism, though it distracts from and distorts the wider nationalism that is represented by what we called the melody of progress and rationalism.

It is, of course, totally unrealistic to study the new nationalism in South Asia except as a composite of a great variety of collectivist emotions that have emerged in the long historical process, some of which are not directed to unifying and strengthening the nation, defined as all the people who live within the state boundaries. Even those feelings that come closest to such an all-embracing nationalism often contain traces of separateness and exclusiveness directed at some group of people within their boundaries. But the most important thing is that so many of those feelings, and so many of the strongest ones, are not focussed on the new nation-state and its development, but conflict with that type of nationalism and consequently are inimical to national consolidation and to planning for development.

Realistic studies of attitudes in their over-all social setting must be focussed also on that aspect of social reality which is represented by this new nationalism in the South Asian countries. The remarks in this section and in Appendix 9 on the new nationalism in South Asia are made for the primary purpose of spelling out reasonable hypotheses for these studies. It is apparent that they should start out from a dynamic conception of a complex of diverse emotional pressures for change working in a framework of strong inhibitions and obstacles; these pressures will take different courses, depending on how they are channelled. South Asian nationalism harbors conflicts that must rage within the minds of the individuals themselves. Even though one of its sources has been precisely the influence of nationalism in Europe, this new nationalism in South Asia has a very different historical determination from that of the emerging nationalism in Europe long ago. Important problems are: how the stream of ideas from that source joined with the urges from traditional society, especially inherited religious and other attitudes of an anti-rational and separatist nature; how it was tainted by all sorts of aggressive impulses, some of them directed against the Western world and some against neighbor countries or groups within the particular country; how it then resulted in inner conflicts; how nationalism differs in different countries, different areas within a country, different ethnic groups, different social and economic strata, and different generations; how ideas are diffused from one group to another and how they tend to change in transference.

The main practical problem from the point of view of the modernization ideals that are the value premises of this study is whether and how

[1] ". . . the separate regional patriotisms within India represent just as authentic expressions of nationalist spirit as the broader pan-Indian ideal. Independence offered the opportunity for each region to assert its own interests in the name of the golden age that each can summon forth from the millennia of Indian history." (Harrison, "The Challenge to Indian Nationalism," *Foreign Affairs*, p. 622.)

this complex of emotions can be controlled in the interests of national consolidation, rationalism, planning and coordination of national policies for development. In these long-stagnant countries, the dynamic nationalism of various sorts represents a flood of intense emotions that, unlike the traditional valuations generally, are not necessarily indifferent to the modernization ideals or bent on preserving the *status quo*. If this flood could be harnessed to produce energy for reform, national planning for development and induced changes would be more feasible and more successful. From the point of view of the value premises selected for this study, this must be the new nationalism's functional role.

In all the South Asian countries there are leaders and groups in the intellectual elite who are aware of the need to harness the nationalist emotions in a productive system of channels, consolidating and strengthening the new nations, making possible more effective government, and rendering national policy more feasible and successful. The urge must be to counteract the feelings of exclusiveness, separateness, and particularism and convert them into allegiance to the entire entity of peoples living within the new state's boundary. Such a more inclusive nationalism then becomes a force for progress – not for reaction, as it now so often is in Western countries. It becomes a vehicle for rationalism and for the ideals of planning, equality, social welfare, and perhaps democracy. We know that a channelling and redirection of emotions often occurs without the causal mechanism of this psychological process being fully exposed. As a practical act this is being attempted on a large scale in South Asia, and Gandhi and Nehru were only the most outstanding of the leaders in these efforts. How far such efforts will be successful is uncertain, but they are an essential phase of the drama that is unfolding in these countries, and will determine its outcome.[1]

[1] This redirection and consolidation of the mixed complex of emotions in the new nationalism into a productive ideological channel is what Kingsley Davis has in mind in the following passage:

"Under these circumstances, how is a program of rapid industrialization to be accomplished? How are poor people to be induced to keep limiting their consumption when they see shiploads of goods coming into the country and bales of money coming from the government printing presses? How are they to be induced to give up their time-honored but inefficient customs, beliefs, and techniques? How are those who hold a high stake in the old order to be liquidated or compensated without interfering with the purpose for which they are being dispossessed? How are the popular demands for equality, democracy, social security, full employment to be contained? Presumably the only way is through the sway of a dominant but new and appropriate ideology, which displaces the concern with individual wants to some higher and more collective level. To assume that the motivation to achieve economic development is itself 'economic' is a contradiction in terms. The motivation must lie outside of and above the economic if industrial development in an agrarian country is actually to take place.

"At present there are two dominant motivational systems that seem to be capable of justifying the authority necessary to enforce the sacrifices. They are communism and nationalism. Both of course have implications for international relations, but . . . neither in itself can be described as 'economic' . . . Suffice it to say at this point that the requirement of cohesion within a nation is not some sort of idle abstraction dreamed

10 *Asian Nationalism*

Nationalism is fundamentally a feeling of solidarity with a group of people. As we have seen, this group can be, and in South Asia very often is, smaller than the entire population within a state's boundaries, but it can also transcend them. It is worth considering briefly how far the new nationalism in South Asia includes feelings of unity with other peoples in the region, or in all Asia, or poor peoples all over the world – who are also mostly colored and also have recently won independence or are in the course of winning it.

The early existence of such solidarity would seem natural, because of the resentment against the rich Western countries marking nationalism in South Asia.[1] Such a wider solidarity is often expounded by South Asian writers.[2] Western writers testify that they have observed signs of it.[3] The reality of that wider nationalism, encompassing Asia or the entire world of colored people who have been or still are under colonial rule, is indi-

---

up by the sociologist. It is an absolute essential of rapid industrialization in any contemporary underdeveloped agrarian country. The contrary point of view – which actually is the dominant though seldom articulated point of view – is a major cause of false predictions in international affairs." (Davis, *Identification of Fundamental Social Changes which Condition Inter-Nation Relations.*)

Of course, communism and nationalism are not mutually exclusive but may go together.

[1] "Pan-Asian sentiment has been the result of anti-European sentiment – not its cause." (Steadman, "The Myth of Asia," *The American Scholar*, p. 173.)

"If nationalism developed directly by resistance and indirectly by the recovery of historical sense and pride in cultural achievement as a result of Western contact, the sense of Asianism is exclusively the counterpart of the solidarity of European feeling. Before the end of the nineteenth century there was no such feeling as Asianism. But in the beginning of this century we find the great Japanese artist Okakura Kakuzo opening a book with the startling declaration 'Asia is one.' Undoubtedly there is much that is common in the tradition of non-Islamic Asia, in religious approach, social organization, art, and so on. . . .

"The idea that there is no common social or spiritual background for an attitude of Asianism to develop is . . . not wholly correct. In any case, if it did not exist, the common experience of a hundred years has created a political background. All the Asian countries have had to go through the same suffering, fight the same battles and meet the same enemy. The evolution towards political freedom has been, generally speaking, on parallel lines. The racial arrogance of the Europeans, their assumed attitude of intellectual and moral superiority, and even the religious propaganda to which all the Asians were subjected, gave rise to a common political outlook in the Asia of the twentieth century. Books like the *Futurism of Young Asia* by the Indian Socialist, Benoy Kumar Sarkar were indicative of this change of attitude." (Panikkar, *Asia and Western Dominance*, pp. 493, 494.)

[2] Sir John Kotelawala, *An Asian Prime Minister's Story*, G. G. Harrap & Co. Ltd., London, 1956, p. 172.

[3] Thus Louis Fischer says: "I was astounded when I first went to India in 1942, how often the Russo-Japanese War of 1904–5 came up in conversation. It was the first time a coloured people defeated a white country, and Indians said it had stimulated their nationalism. On subsequent study trips to the Orient I noted deliberate efforts to weld the consciousness of colour with the protest against poverty and the dislike of Western imperialism into an Asian mood, a sense of Asianhood. It is coupled with an

cated by the wide use of the terms "colonialism" and "racialism," usually together, and by a uniform stand taken in the United Nations and elsewhere on issues relating to the liberation of the last vestiges of colonial empire. Even those South Asian countries that have military alliances with the United States and the former colonial powers seldom deviate from this unity.

These attitudes, however, do not seem to penetrate much beyond the level of general principles and the position taken on the struggle of other peoples who are still under the colonial yoke. There can be a shared common resentment against the West without much positive solidarity among these nations themselves. It is notable that the Bandung Conference and other similar encounters have never managed to produce more than rather platitudinal and non-committal resolutions in regard to economic cooperation between the participant governments. The regional cooperation in the United Nations Economic Commission for Asia and the Far East has not really come to grips with concrete questions of cooperation,[1] and the fault was not only that of the non-Asian members. In none of the South Asian countries today is such cooperation a live political issue. From a practical standpoint Asian nationalism is hardly more than a phantom, and it is regularly catered to only by a select group in the intellectual elite.[2]

This is not difficult to understand. The colonial power system involved a peculiar organization of the dependent people's outward contacts. On the one hand, their relations with the metropolitan country were forcibly stimulated; on the other, their mutual relations were not developed, not even very much within individual empires. This was, to begin with, true of their commercial relations.[3] But it was equally true in regard to political, social, educational, and broadly cultural matters. When the South Asian countries now emerge as independent nation-states, they bear, as we shall find, deep imprints of the pattern of international relationships established

---

attempt to make Africa a sentimental peninsula of Asia. This Pan-Asia, if achieved on an emotional or political or any level, would by its very nature constitute a bloc of brown, black, and yellow races antagonistic to the white West. The prospect presents the world with a subtle problem transcending in importance most of the tasks that now occupy overburdened foreign offices and state departments.

"'Asia is one by its culture and art,' said C. Rajagopalachari, then India's Minister of Education, at a conference on Asiatic Art and Culture in Calcutta, in January, 1947." (*This Is Our World,* p. 140.)

[1] David Wightman, *Toward Economic Cooperation in Asia, The United Nations Economic Commission for Asia and the Far East,* Yale University Press, New Haven and London, 1963. See Chapter 13, Section 15.

[2] As Louis Fischer aptly puts it, the unity of Asia "is a myth, and those who speak in its name are spinning fantasies. The desire to unify Asia politically is the pursuit of an abstraction." He adds that it is "a type of endeavor in which, alas, quite a few Indians gladly indulge." (*This Is Our World,* p. 145.)

[3] "By its very nature . . . western influence, which was largely confined to commercial exploitation by a number of rival interests, national or otherwise, continued with the passage of time to wrench even farther apart the disjointed and artificial units

in colonial times. Least of all, of course, were the colonial powers interested in promoting a consolidation of feelings of unity in the region. The liberation movements, as they got under way, provided a reason not to encourage such feelings. There was little contact among the liberation movements in the several countries, even if the achievements of the Indian National Congress — as of the Kuomintang revolution — were admired widely in South Asia. After independence both the close relations with the former metropolitan countries and the isolation from the neighboring countries were preserved, and in some respects intensified. In commerce, for example, dependence on Western countries has increased, while intraregional trade has decreased.[1] A factor contributing to the persistence of the pattern is that planning in the several South Asian countries has been narrowly nationalist and usually pursued even without much knowledge of what was being done in the neighboring countries.

The heritage from the colonial era has resulted in situations and developments in individual countries that are bound to create animosity toward, and conflict with, other countries in the region. Leaving aside the strained relations between India and Pakistan, the presence of Indians in Burma and the departure of most of them during and after the Japanese occupation did not contribute to warm feelings between India and Burma. Generally speaking, the presence of large Indian and Chinese communities in Ceylon and Southeast Asia has resulted in a narrow nationalist outlook among the majority populations in these countries; their treatment has not endeared these countries either to India or to China. After independence, the Western countries' eagerness to involve as many countries as possible in military alliances, while India, Ceylon, Burma, and Indonesia preserved various and changing sorts of neutrality in the cold war, has further undermined what basis there was for regional solidarity. From the other side, China has figured differently — and changeably — depending on many factors: the position of a particular country in the cold war, whether or not it has a large Chinese minority, and China's policy toward this minority and in regard to boundary disputes.

---

which it had established for its own purposes." (W. Gordon East and O. H. K. Spate, eds., *The Changing Map of Asia,* 2nd ed., Methuen & Co. Ltd., London, 1953, p. 223.)

"In the years prior to 1942 there had developed, apart from the limited measures of co-operation inaugurated by the world economic crisis, only superficially important links between the several territories. Economically, like the republics of South America, they faced the world, turning their backs to one another; their indigenous subsistence economies were self-contained, and in respect of commercial products the political units were competitive rather than complementary. The simple radial or even more skeletal rail networks, draining each country's wealth out through one or two large ports and, excepting the link between Siam and Malaya (which in any case originated in a German project designed to oust British influence from southern Siam), completely unconnected with one another, epitomize this fragmentation." (*Ibid.*, p. 222.)

[1] Chapter 13, Sections 6 and 12.

Part Two

POLITICAL PROBLEMS

Chapter 4

THE COMING OF INDEPENDENCE

1 *The World Perspective*

Portentous changes have occurred in recent years in the way people's lives have been organized and directed through national communities and in the political interrelationships of those communities. One fateful change was, of course, the spectacular rise of the Soviet Union to great power status and its westward encroachment on Eastern and Central Europe. Future historians, however, are likely to see an event of still greater consequence in the emergence of China, under the enforced discipline of a Communist regime, from economic stagnation and generations of political impotence and anarchy. Another political mutation of comparable importance was the liquidation of the European colonial power system in South Asia after the Second World War. Within the space of a little more than a decade, nearly 600 million people in South Asia were liberated from colonial rule. As in the case of the other changes mentioned, the significance of this event was not confined to the region in which it occurred. It is clear that, as the process of South Asian liberation gathered momentum, it powerfully stimulated nationalist aspirations in West Asia and Africa. The process of emancipation is not yet complete, but there is no doubt that in a few years' time all colonial peoples will be politically independent. Political independence in the newly liberated countries brought in its train a desire for freedom from foreign economic domination; where this urge has not been satisfied, a chorus of protest has risen from intellectuals craving more radical policies. In this respect the trend of events in South Asia has also sharpened the ambitions of countries only formally independent, especially those in Latin America.

Meanwhile, the economic development of Western countries, including the former rulers of South Asia, has been proceeding faster and more steadily than it did in the troubled period between the two world wars. Indeed, with the major exceptions of Britain and the United States, the national product of Western countries has been rising at least as fast and as steadily as it did in the half century before the First World War, when the colonial power system was reaching the ultimate limits of its geographical expansion. This rapid economic growth bluntly contradicts the belief that the critics of imperialism, following the theories of Hobhouse, Hilferding, Luxemburg, and Lenin, and the supporters of imperialism shared in common, particularly in Britain and even in recent decades, namely, that a metropolitan country was bound to suffer a decline in its standard of living if it lost its empire. Certainly today it never occurs to anyone to ascribe the relative economic stagnation of Britain or the United States in recent years to the loss of colonial possessions.

The historical coincidence of these three momentous trends of change has broadly determined the present-day pattern of international relationships. More particularly, it has fashioned the international setting within which the economic problems of the now independent states of South Asia have acquired political importance in the world. One obvious feature of this setting was the trend toward a polarization of international relationships within the magnetic field created by tension and rivalry between the Communist bloc and most of the Western powers. That not all interstate relationships have become polarized in this way is due partly to developing uncertainties and differences within these two major power blocs, but more to the attractions of a policy of non-alignment for a number of the newly independent countries.

It may well be that the magnetic power field established by the cold war is now gradually disintegrating under the impact of the growing split between China and the Soviet Union, and the interest the latter shares with the United States in avoiding direct military confrontations that could escalate into nuclear war. At any rate, the division of the world between Communist and non-Communist forces is beginning to be regarded as less significant than that between rich white peoples and poor colored peoples. What is particularly disturbing about present trends in international affairs is that the gap between the level of economic development of the Western countries and that of most countries of Asia, Africa, and Latin America has been steadily widening for some considerable period of time; the pattern of economic development in the Soviet Union and the East European Communist countries is more similar to that of the Western countries. It must be a matter for grave concern that this represents a contrast between the living conditions and the economic prospects of most of the world's white population, on the one hand, and most of the world's colored population, on the other.

A main purpose of this book is to offer an intensive analysis of the reasons for this dramatic contrast between development in South Asia and development in Western and East European countries. All the new governments in the South Asian countries are committed to the idea of overcoming the mass poverty of their peoples through the instrumentality of state policies coordinated by state planning. The existence among the politically articulate in these countries of an urge to achieve economic development by means of modernization is the main determinant of the viewpoint and approach adopted throughout the present study. The value premises implied in this viewpoint are worked out in more specific terms in Chapter 2. One of them, which in a sense embraces all, is the quest for state planning. It is therefore appropriate to begin our analysis of the problems involved by considering in Part Two the nature of the states that are required to play so central a role in the economic development of South Asia. How did these states come into being? How were they affected by the legacy of colonial rule, and what kinds of social forces have since determined their character and their actions?

2 *The Catalytic Force of the World Wars*

The dissolution of the colonial power system in South Asia after the Second World War was rapid and had the character of a political revolution. In strict chronological sequence the Philippines in 1946 was the first to achieve full political independence. But that event was not a sudden or unexpected occurrence; it had been scheduled by the United States more than ten years previously.

The first major breach in the walls of colonial domination came with the peaceful ending of British rule in India in 1947 and the creation of the Union of India and the Republic of Pakistan as successor states. Political independence for Burma and Ceylon followed in 1948. Since the Dutch and French attempted to reimpose their rule over their territories by force, Indonesia did not achieve full independence until 1949, and the constituent parts of the French Indo-Chinese Union until 1954. The Federation of Malaya did not become an independent state until 1957, owing to the relatively slow development of national political consciousness and British military intervention to put down a Communist rebellion. Singapore remained under full British rule until 1959 when it was granted self-government. Four years later it was merged with Malaya and the two remaining British dependencies, Sarawak and British North Borneo, or Sabah as it is now called, to form the Federation of Malaysia. Thailand had managed to maintain its formal independence by virtue of its position as a buffer state between the frontiers of British and French imperialism although it had had to make occasional territorial concessions to the two imperial powers and its economy had become dominated by foreign interests. A few small enclaves of colonial rule, such as Dutch New Guinea (if it should be reckoned in the region) and some tiny possessions of France and Portugal in India, remained after the principal nations of South Asia had acquired their independence. But by conquest, negotiation, or international settlement, these irritants to South Asian self-respect have now all been annulled, with the exception of the diminutive half-island of Portuguese Timor in the Indonesian archipelago and the British protectorate of Brunei on the island of Borneo. The manner in which colonial rule was finally lifted from the region, which we shall examine more closely in Sections 6–12, was to have a decisive influence on the political character and problems of the successor states.

Except on the part of the Soviet Union and, in some degree, the United States,[1] the liberation of colonial peoples was not an explicit war aim of the belligerent countries during the Second World War. Nevertheless, when that struggle was over, the colonial powers found themselves unable to prevent a political avalanche that led to the independence of colonies all over the world. This avalanche was unleashed by the liberation of the South Asian countries. In order to understand why the Second World War had this profound effect we need first to look a little closer into the vagaries of that war as it was fought and experienced in South Asia.

The Japanese military conquest of all the Southeast Asian colonies dealt a number of decisive blows to the prestige basis of the established colonial power structure. Just as naval supremacy had made possible the European conquest of Asia, so superior Asian naval strength – that is, Japanese – ultimately undermined the military basis of European imperialism in the region. The handwriting had been on the wall ever since the Japanese victory over Russia in 1905. It is no coincidence that after that event the forces of nationalism took on a more militant form in various parts of South Asia.[2] From that time onwards it became increasingly clear

[1] See below in Section 4.

[2] In a letter to his daughter, dated November 22, 1932, Nehru wrote: "Early in the twentieth century an event occurred which had a great effect on the mind of Asia. This was the defeat of Tsarist Russia by Japan. . . . I remember well how excited I used to get when news came of the Japanese victories." In another letter to his daughter, on December 7, 1932, he described the Japanese triumph as "a great pick-me-up for Asia." (Frank Moraes, *Jawaharlal Nehru, A Biography,* Macmillan, New York, 1956, p. 27. See also Jawaharlal Nehru, *Glimpses of World History,* Lindsay Drummond, London, 1939.)

that the European colonies were vulnerable to a determined Japanese assault. When that assault came, the complete and sudden capitulation of the colonial rulers in Southeast Asia destroyed their prestige and mystique insofar as these attributes rested on superior strength.

Many nationalists in South Asian countries took pride in the Japanese military victories against the West.[1] Thus when the Japanese swept through Southeast Asia they initially encountered a not unsympathetic political climate,[2] except in the Philippines. Impervious to the anti-Japanese propaganda of the Western powers,[3] many leading nationalist politicians openly collaborated with their new rulers. It is true that the arrogant, highhanded, and often brutal methods of the Japanese brought disillusion and eventual resistance, but the Japanese must be credited with creating indigenous military forces, accelerating the political organization of local nationalist movements, and providing greater administrative experience and opportunities to persons previously denied positions of responsibility by their European masters. During the interlude of the Japanese occupation, therefore, many nationalist leaders, particularly

[1] After remarking how rapidly the British colonial empire crumbled before the advancing Japanese armies, Nehru, writing in prison toward the end of the war, asked: "Was this proud structure then just a house of cards with no foundations or inner strength? Inevitably, comparisons were made with China's long resistance to Japanese aggression in spite of her lack of almost everything required for modern war. China went up in people's estimation, and though Japan was not liked, there was a feeling of satisfaction at the collapse of old-established European colonial powers before the armed strength of an Asiatic power. That racial, Oriental-Asiatic, feeling was evident on the British side also. Defeat and disaster were bitter enough but the fact that an Oriental and Asiatic power had triumphed over them added to the bitterness and humiliation. An Englishman occupying a high position said that he would have preferred it if the *Prince of Wales* and the *Repulse* had been sunk by the Germans instead of the yellow Japanese." (Jawaharlal Nehru, *The Discovery of India,* Meridian Books, London, 1956, p. 458.) It may be added that many Dutchmen would probably have preferred the Germans, instead of the Japanese, to have occupied the East Indies.

[2] The widespread unpopularity of the local Chinese populations also contributed to the welcome the Japanese received as liberators. In Malaya, where Chinese were extremely numerous, the situation was more complicated: the Japanese were certainly not welcomed by the Chinese, but the Malays were friendly.

[3] Thakin Nu, later to become, as U Nu, the Prime Minister of Burma, describes the reaction of his fellow Burmese nationalists to this propaganda as follows: "The Japanese seemed to be the only eastern people that could hold its own against the West, and we came to look confidently to Japan for leadership. So people made excuses for the Japanese. There was probably some reason for what they did; the various charges might not be true, and in any case it was only to Japan that we could look for freedom from western rule. So Burmans were very reluctant to believe anti-Japanese propaganda. They told U Ba Cho to stop preaching when he insisted on the evils of Japanese fascism, and they laughed at Thakin So and Than Tun as unpractical, academic. And, as it was the westerners who were most active in exposing Japanese fascism, many people believed that these men had been bribed by western imperialists and capitalists whose real object was to prevent eastern islands from obtaining independence." (Thakin Nu, *Burma under the Japanese,* Macmillan, London, 1954, pp. 1–2.)

in the Netherlands East Indies and Burma, suddenly acquired greater status and power within their own societies.[1] Naturally enough, they were not prepared to abdicate when the European colonial rulers returned after the defeat and withdrawal of the Japanese.

While the war strengthened the forces of South Asian nationalism, it severely weakened the metropolitan countries. What is most important, it drained Britain of the means and the will to maintain its authority over the Indian subcontinent against the uncompromising determination of a well-organized nationalist movement to achieve complete political independence. By their early withdrawal from most of their colonial empire in South Asia,[2] the British established a precedent that made it more difficult for the Dutch and the French to retain power in their colonies. And so the worldwide avalanche gathered momentum.

The wholesale liquidation of the colonial power system thus came about as a result of the Second World War. Before we go deeper into an analysis of the causal factors involved, it is important to point out that the First World War had marked a decisive turning point in the development of colonialism in South Asia as elsewhere in the world. We should recall that it was in the four or five decades preceding that war that the colonial power system, which had evolved over more than four centuries, enjoyed its greatest expansion and consolidation. The war itself marked the end of the era of "new imperialism" and set limits to the further expansion of colonial dominions. K. M. Panikkar is probably right when he expresses the opinion that it was only the outbreak of the First World War, which he significantly calls "the European Civil War," that prevented the French and the British from consummating – after a long series of mutually agreed infringements, the last in 1909 – the final division of Siam between themselves. It was the approach of that war rather than the feeble beginning of the Chinese national revolution, says Panikkar, that stopped the great powers from partitioning all of China into colonies or at least spheres of influence.[3] It is never possible to ascertain positively what would have happened if a major development had not occurred, but there is much that makes this view credible.[4] In any case, the advance of colonialism that had been a trend since the 1870's was brought to a stop.

[1] In Indo-China, the Japanese left internal administration and security in the hands of the (Vichy) French until the closing stages of the war. Had the Japanese taken over from the French somewhat earlier, they might well have left behind them in Vietnam an even more effective national liberation movement.

In Thailand everyone, from the king down – except, to some extent, the Chinese minority – collaborated.

[2] For reasons already alluded to and discussed more fully in Section 10, the British did return to Malaya, without intending to stay longer than necessary to establish order.

[3] K. M. Panikkar, *Asia and Western Dominance* (third impression), Allen & Unwin Ltd., London, 1953, pp. 227, 259 *et passim*.

[4] John Strachey, *The End of Empire*, Gollancz, London, 1959, p. 127.

One important factor that made the First World War a turning point in the development of colonialism was undoubtedly the relative weakening, economically, politically, and militarily, of the main colonial powers. Before the First World War began, the European colonial rulers never doubted the permanency of their empires; by the time it had ended, most of them realized that this could no longer be an axiom of colonial policy.

3 *Deeper Causes*

While it is correct to impute the final dissolution of colonial power to the catalytic agency of the Second World War, and to observe how the relative weakening of the colonial powers in Western Europe after the First World War contributed to putting an end to the era of colonial expansion, such a momentous political transformation would hardly have occurred unless the situation had become ripe for radical change. In historical perspective it is clear that a much longer and more complex chain of events had been undermining the foundations of the colonial power system. It is probably no exaggeration to say that almost all of the major developments in world history during the present century, and in some cases even earlier, served to feed and strengthen the forces working toward its ultimate dissolution.

In the first place, the imperial powers themselves had created an educated class to provide administrative and professional services in the colonies. This class, and particularly an upper stratum steeped in Western ideology, was, in the main, not the product of economic development but of legal, administrative, and educational structures built up in order to rule and advance the colonies according to the interests and ideals of the metropolitan countries. Such an indigenous elite had been growing for a longer time and was quantitatively and qualitatively stronger in British India, Ceylon, and the Philippines than elsewhere, but was nowhere entirely absent. Particularly in the period between the two world wars, many of the colonial governments began to share their power by permitting members of this elite to qualify as administrators of relatively high rank and by setting up consultative assemblies with appointed and/or elected members. When welfare became a concern of the policy-makers the indigenous elite were called on to assume more responsibility for their own people. As this elite grew, they came to press for more posts for their kind and for more responsibility at higher levels. The most important observation that can be made about this development in the present context is that it introduced a trend which was antithetical to colonial rule.

Although many of the indigenous intellectual elite found their immediate economic and social interests converging with those of the colonial governments that had awarded them status and high incomes, their educational experience had exposed them to Western ideals of justice, liberty, and equality of opportunity. In the Western countries themselves these ideals could not be reconciled with colonialism any more than with the harsh political, social, and economic inequalities remaining at home. In the colonies members of this Westernized elite used these concepts to give political definition to the new nationalism,[1] and they directed the liberation movements that emerged as a result.[2] They had been equipped with European ideals to fight European rule.[3]

Colonial rebels were never without allies in the metropolitan countries in Europe, although their influence varied during the period under review. After the 1870's, when colonialism was again expanding, the illusion grew that the welfare and greatness of a country were proportionate to the size of the territory controlled. In the minds of many in the British ruling class, for instance, the extension of empire gradually replaced free trade as the basis of power, wealth, and influence. From the simple slogan "trade follows the flag" a direct connection was drawn between the expansion of empire and the improvement of the living standards of the British people. The notion that it was the mission of the white man, his manifest destiny, to implant civilization among the colored "barbarians" of the world provided moral justification for colonial ventures. The doctrine of a "white man's burden," which is as old as imperialism, acquired something of the quality of a faith. At best it was equated with service; but

[1] Appendix 9.

[2] This was a gradual development and there were great differences in the manner in which it proceeded in the several colonies. The general pattern is well described by Fatma Mansur: "The process of westernization follows in general the same trends, with the following characteristics: as far as the reaction to Western ideas goes, there seems to be at first a re-examination of the indigenous culture, in the light of new knowledge. There follow attempts at establishing a *modus vivendi* where objectives are limited, and where political life is seen as a matter of participation, not as the struggle for supreme political power. Finally, a rejection of Western political power. The first period is characterized mainly by intellectual activity, the second by the beginnings of political action, both these periods involving a small group of people, those traditionally associated with the ruling groups. The third period marks the enrolment of the masses for the final effort of gaining independence." (Fatma Mansur, *Process of Independence,* W. J. H. Sprott, ed., London, 1962, p. 53.)

[3] The leaders of the national liberation movements were thus essentially European in character. In passing, we may note two important consequences of this fact. First, the ideological principles they applied against their colonial masters also represented a challenge to the power structures in the indigenous societies involved. Native politicians had either to follow through with radical policies at home or engage in embarrassing and frustrating compromises. Much of this book will deal with this problem, which is paramount in the discussion not only of political organization but of development and planning for development. Secondly, on attaining power, the new governing elites often became almost as remote from the masses as the colonial rulers had been.

more frequently it became subservient to the play of uncontrolled economic forces.[1]

The emotional appeal of imperialism never completely stilled the British conscience, however. Liberal thinkers throughout the nineteenth century argued that democracy was incompatible with the maintenance of authoritarian rule over foreign peoples.[2] To think imperially was to think in terms of restrictive and protective measures, in defiance of the revealed truths of classical economics. Thus when the British government took over responsibility for India from the East India Company in 1858, many politicians were conscious of saddling Britain with a heavy burden. In the first seventy years of the nineteenth century, enlightened British liberals looked forward to the day when India would stand on its own feet.[3] Even in the heyday of colonialism British radicals continued to protest that self-proclaimed imperialists, however honorable their motives, would place *faits accomplis* before the country and commit blunders of incalculable consequence. The danger, they felt, was all the greater because British foreign policy still remained a stronghold of the aristocracy, while that related and persuasive lobby, the British officer class, also had a vested interest in imperial expansion.

It took the humiliation of the Boer War to teach the British government what it would cost to hold an empire by force.[4] However, this fact did not escape Gandhi, the supreme tactician of the Indian liberation movement. He saw what some perceptive British thinkers had much earlier recognized, namely, that Britain could not long continue to rule India except with the cooperation of many sections of its population.[5] Once that coop-

[1] This point is well argued in J. S. Furnivall, *Colonial Policy and Practice,* Cambridge University Press, London, 1957, p. 289 *et passim.*

[2] "The government of a people by itself has a meaning and a reality," wrote John Stuart Mill, "but such a thing as government by one people over another, does not and cannot exist. One people may keep another as a warren or preserve for its own use, a place to make money in, a human cattle farm, to be worked for the profit of its inhabitants; but if the good of the governed is the proper business of a government, it is utterly impossible that a people should directly attend to it." (John Stuart Mill, *Considerations on Representative Government,* 1st ed., 1861; quoted in Strachey, *The End of Empire,* p. 72.)

An earlier example was Bentham, who thought colonies created artificial markets, endangered peace, and cost a lot of money. He perceived that they also gave employment and therefore a vested interest to the ruling class, which the latter disguised behind all manner of high-sounding arguments. James Mill and many others followed the same line.

[3] "India, with its government by dictation, based on its Army, remained as a perpetual challenge to the English liberal conscience." (A. P. Thornton, *The Imperial Idea and Its Enemies,* Macmillan, London, 1959, p. 218.)

[4] *Ibid.,* p. 106.

[5] In a famous series of lectures delivered in 1881 and published in 1883, J. R. Seeley, Regius Professor of Modern History at Cambridge University and an apostle of imperial unity, questioned the wisdom of acquiring India. Having acquired it, the

eration was withdrawn, the foundations of British authority in India would crumble. Furthermore, the Indian nationalist leaders were able to exploit the aversion of the British liberal conscience to methods used by the local colonial rulers in combatting Indian non-cooperation.

These ideological currents in Britain were present in weaker form in Holland and even in France. While imperialist expansion ran its course, the West European countries, including the imperial ones, were on the way to becoming political democracies with universal suffrage. That development reached a climax at the end of the First World War, when various restrictions on the right to vote were generally abolished. Although people in the lower income brackets often proved receptive to jingoist slogans, most of them had little direct interest in colonial exploitation, and this fact tended to undermine the domestic political basis for imperialist ventures. Parallel to this shift in political power in the metropolitan countries, and clearly related to it, was the emergence of the welfare state. This development began around the turn of the century, gathered momentum after the First World War, and came into full flowering after the Second World War. It signified the acceptance by the government of responsibility for the underprivileged members of the community. As concern for social welfare mounted on the domestic front, it became an increasingly heavy moral burden to stand for a system of government in the colonies that was in contradiction to this philosophy.

4 *Mounting Pressures*

The ideology of the "new imperialism" had been seriously undermined when the First World War broke out. This war speeded up the process

---

British must govern it he said, but only until an Indian nationalism arose, and not a moment longer.

"We could subdue the mutiny of 1857, formidable as it was, because it spread through only a part of the army, because the people did not actively sympathise with it, and because it was possible to find native Indian races who would fight on our side. But the moment a mutiny is but threatened, which shall be no mere mutiny, but the expression of a universal feeling of nationality, at that moment all hope is at an end, as all desire ought to be at an end, of preserving our Empire. For we are not really conquerors of India, and we cannot rule her as conquerors; if we undertook to do so, it is not necessary to inquire whether we could succeed, for we should assuredly be ruined financially by the mere attempt." (J. R. Seeley, *The Expansion of England,* Macmillan, London, 1883, pp. 227–228 and 234.)

It is interesting to note that Seeley did not expect a popular insurrection in India, and for reasons that are often overlooked even today: "I find great populations cowering in abject misery for centuries together, but they do not rise in rebellion; no, if they cannot live they die, and if they can only just live, then they just live, their sensibilities dulled and their very wishes crushed out by want. A population that rebels is a population that is looking up, that has begun to hope and to feel its strength." (*Ibid.,* pp. 233–234.)

in many more ways than by the weakening of the colonial powers, referred to in Section 2.

For one thing, the war gave South Asian intellectuals reason to challenge the morals and, indeed, the sanity of the Western nations. How could Europeans justify imperialism as a civilizing mission and uphold their claims to superiority over colored peoples after indulging in such wholesale carnage? This thought must have come with a great sense of release to many in the colonies. Moreover, South Asian soldiers and laborers had been pressed into service in the Allied war effort. Thus men from broader strata than the intellectual elite were directly exposed to the ferment of ideas and ideals that activated political and social life in the metropolitan countries during that period. More particularly, they had a chance to see people from these countries not as superior beings, but as struggling and frustrated mortals.[1]

Britain and France actually appealed to their colonial subjects for moral support to "save democracy," an irony too obvious to miss,[2] unless it meant that the subjects were to share in the benefits of democratic freedom. That particular issue came to the fore when the principle of national self-determination, included among the Fourteen Points President Wilson enunciated as a basis for a peace settlement, was elevated to the status of an Allied war aim. However cynical the secret, and not too secret, thoughts of the West European politicians, they had to fall in with the Allied propaganda line. The Asian elite greeted the Fourteen Points as a doctrine of liberation, and, despite their naiveté, their claim to self-government became morally irresistible.[3]

[1] "In order to satisfy the increasingly urgent need for manpower, the colonial states began enticing thousands of young men from Asian and African territories into service as soldiers or set them to work as laborers behind the lines. There those men saw the European no longer as sahib or tuan; they saw him in the mud of the trenches, they saw him as a prisoner, bereft of his halo as a superior creature. The First World War deprived the European of still another portion of the prestige he had previously enjoyed in the eyes of Asia." (Djambatan N.V., *A World on the Move*, Djambatan, Amsterdam, Institute of Pacific Relations, New York, 1956, p. 90.)

[2] As Panikkar points out, articulate opinion in South Asia tended to sympathize with Germany rather than with the Allies, mainly because Germany had no record of colonial conquest in the region and was allied to Turkey, the leading Moslem power. See Panikkar, *Asia and Western Dominance*, p. 261 *et passim*.

[3] "Whatever [the] effect [of Wilson's statement] was on the suppressed nationalities of Europe, in Asia it was acclaimed as a doctrine of liberation. As every Allied Power hastened to declare its faith in the new formula of Wilson (and it was soon raised to the position of an accepted 'war aim' in the propaganda campaign against the Germans), the colonial Powers found it difficult to oppose openly or resist publicly the claims of Asian nations based on this formula. It became difficult to proclaim self-determination of peoples as a great ideal for the establishment of which Asian peoples should co-operate with Europeans and fight and lose their lives in distant battlefields, but which, however excellent, could not be applied to themselves. Self-government for colonial countries had thus to be accepted, and the claim to it could no longer be brushed aside as premature or stigmatized as sedition." (*Ibid.*, p. 263.)

Speaking on January 5, 1918 about colonial possessions, Lloyd George declared:

That much, in principle, the British conceded in the case of India. In 1917, in the Montagu Declaration, Britain, for the first time, formally committed itself to "the gradual development of self-government with a view to the progressive realisation of responsible government in India as an integral part of the British Empire." It added, however, that progress toward that goal would depend on "the extent to which it is found that confidence may be reposed in their [i.e., the Indians'] sense of responsibility," a qualification that seemed to make government in India accountable to the British Parliament rather than the Indian people. All the same, the implications of the declaration were not lost on the intellectual elites of other colonial territories in South Asia. Nor did South Asian nationalists fail to note that Ireland won home rule from the British because it was no longer practical politics in Britain to hold it by superior military force.[1]

Along with secret diplomacy and balance of power politics, the First World War discredited the emotional appeal of imperialism within the domestic confines of the European colonial powers. Certainly, when that conflict ended, there was no popular support for further costly extensions of empire. To European radicals, whose influence was rapidly growing because of the democratization of political power, colonial possessions were a disreputable preserve for aristocratic and plutocratic adventurers. This group felt a sympathy for and an identification with colonial peoples as the victims, along with the European masses, of capitalist exploitation. They saw the liberation of colonial peoples as part of their own struggle against the upper-class state. It was mainly from these radicals and the political tradition they represented that Western-educated South Asians derived their own ideological outlook.

Toward the end of the war, events in Russia dealt a series of blows to the European colonial power system and gave moral support to South Asian nationalists in a variety of ways. In the first place, the Soviet Union vigorously denounced imperialism and supported the nationalists' demands for political independence. Secondly, it preached a doctrine of social justice based on the equality of all, regardless of sex, race, color, or class. The assumption of white supremacy implicit in colonial rule was peculiarly vulnerable to this attack.[2] Later the Soviet Union's success in

---

"The general principle of national self-determination is . . . as applicable in their case as in those of occupied European territories." (*A History of the Peace Conference of Paris,* H. N. V. Temperly, ed., Oxford University Press, London, 1920, Vol. II, p. 227.)

[1] Percival Spear, *India, A Modern History,* University of Michigan Press, Ann Arbor, 1961, pp. 342–343.

[2] It is worth noting that the tsarist empire had expanded by incorporating non-European peoples into the class structure of Russian society. This process of assimilation gave it a very different character from that of the empires of Britain, the Netherlands, and, only to a slightly lesser extent, France.

transforming a backward country into an industrial power through state planning, and reports of economic progress in Soviet Central Asia, would inspire Westernized Asians to add the idea of planned economic development to the purely political aspiration of freedom from foreign domination. Sensitive Asian nationalists like Nehru were not unaware of the harsh realities and stale dogmatism of Communist rule; but to them it was more important that the Soviet Union was a great anti-imperialist power and sided with their own political cause. The mere existence of such a revolutionary ideological center was a threat to the European colonial power system long before the Soviet Union was strong enough to have much of a voice in the international concert.

There is another significant point to be made about the impact of the Russian Revolution, and Communism in particular, and that is that it was most marked in those regions where the regenerative and constructive role of colonialism, in the sense of educating the intellectual elite in the powers and responsibilities of governments, had been least developed. It is no coincidence that it was in these colonial territories where effective nationalist movements emerged only after the Russian Revolution that the Communist Party became a major force. In the case of India, which had experienced a hundred years of British reforms, the direct inspiration from Russian Communism was relatively minor. The stubborn refusal of the French and Dutch to make even moderate political concessions to the nationalists' demands ensured that the liberation struggles of Indo-China and the Netherlands East Indies would come under greater Communist influence than those of India.[1]

The emergence of the United States as a world power was yet another force destined to weaken the European colonial power system. During the First World War, it was American initiative that made the principle of national self-determination an Allied war aim. Similiarly, it was American influence that helped to put an end to imperialist competition for special trading privileges in China: the United States was on the same side as the Soviet Union, which declared null and void the unequal treaties that tsarist Russia had forced on China. Finally, the war so altered the world distribution of sea power that effective naval protection for the South Asian territories of the European colonial powers was dependent on the United States. But the United States withdrew into isolation after 1918 and did not again exert serious pressure against the continuation of the European colonial power system until the Second World War, though American distrust and dislike of European colonialism increased during

[1] As Nehru once pointed out: "The tendency of Asian nationalist movements to follow the leadership of the Communist party is dependent on the degree to which their deep-rooted anti-colonial impulse is ignored by the Western powers." (Quoted in Moraes, *Jawaharlal Nehru,* p. 45.)

the inter-war period.[1] In the case of Indonesian independence, in particular, the attitude of the United States was to prove decisive after the Second World War.

It is true, of course, that by annexing the last remaining parts of the Spanish overseas empire, including the Philippines, after the Spanish-American War of 1898, the United States had itself become a colonial power. Toward the end of the last century a number of influential Americans, particularly members of the upper classes of the northeastern states, became convinced that it was the destiny of Anglo-Saxons to inherit the earth. This notion, with its racial overtones, found political expression in the bellicose preaching of Theodore Roosevelt. There was, however, considerable opposition in the United States to the annexation of the Philippines. Many Americans regarded it as a perversion of the Declaration of Independence. Others managed to rationalize it as a means of liberating people from the grip of a decadent, aristocratic, and Catholic European power. As it turned out, this phase of imperialist self-assertiveness in American history was short-lived and never seriously deflected the long-standing, anti-colonial tradition of the country. Shortly before the United States entered the First World War, the Philippines was promised independence once a stable government had been established there.

Although the First World War ruled out the permanency of empire as an axiom of colonial policy, for reasons already indicated, the expectations South Asian nationalists entertained of a speedy progress toward self-government were not realized. They quickly discovered that it was only in Europe that the principle of national self-determination was to be practically applied. The British government's somewhat tardy and reluctant moves toward its declared objective of ultimate self-government for India cast doubts in the minds of Indian nationalists about its honesty of purpose. As for the French and Dutch, they were not only far more intransigent about conceding constitutional advances to their colonial territories; they did not even formally accept the ultimate objective of independence. Not surprisingly, therefore, French and Dutch colonial rule in

[1] The interplay in Britain between the forces boring from within and the criticism coming from the United States is well described by Northcote Parkinson: "Behind this process was the realisation in Britain that a democracy has no right to govern an empire. British voters could not logically deny to the Hindoos the political privileges they claimed for themselves. When, moreover, the British forgot the weakness of their moral position the Americans were always quick to remind them of it; being in fact (as it happened) less sensitive about American imperialism than British. As a background, therefore, to British foreign policy was the weakening of the Empire generally and the steady deterioration of the position in the Far East; due in part to American pressure but also in part to the moral sentiments of the British voters whose sentiments joined happily with their preference, for the money saved on warships could be (and was) spent on social benefits for themselves." (E. Northcote Parkinson, *The Evolution of Political Thought,* University of London Press, London, 1958, pp. 245–246.)

the inter-war period was characterized by more severe and more frequent measures of repression than British rule in India – though it must also be said that the British had good reason to be grateful for Gandhi's policy of non-violence. Only Ceylon and the Philippines proceeded fairly rapidly along the path to self-government through peaceful negotiation.

It was during and immediately after the Second World War that all the forces and pressures that had been gradually weakening the European colonial power system came together to effect its final collapse. Of crucial importance was the position taken by the United States. Once brought out of its isolation, it immediately began to exert pressure against the continuation of European colonialism. The Atlantic Charter drafted by Churchill and Roosevelt in 1941 as a declaration of Allied war aims stated that the Allies "respected the right of all peoples to choose the form of government under which they will live and they wish to see sovereign rights and self-government restored to those who had been forcibly deprived of them." The American leaders made it plain that they expected this principle to be applied to the European colonial dependencies.[1] Thus Roosevelt favored an international trusteeship for Indo-China[2] and pressed Britain to take immediate steps to grant India independence.

The European colonial powers did not take kindly to American idealism at the expense of their empires.[3] Churchill especially was not prepared to listen to Roosevelt on the subject of the British empire, and he subse-

[1] In May, 1942, Sumner Welles said: "As a result of this war we must assure the sovereign equality of the peoples the world over. Our victory must bring in its train liberation for all peoples. The age of imperialism is ended. The right of people for freedom must be recognized." (Quoted in P. S. Gerbrandy, *Indonesia,* Hutchinson, London, 1950, p. 58.)

[2] In January, 1944, Roosevelt wrote to Cordell Hull: "France has had the country – thirty million inhabitants – for nearly one hundred years, and the people are worse off than they were at the beginning. . . . France has milked it for one hundred years. The people of Indochina are entitled to something better than that." (Ellen J. Hammer, *The Struggle for Indochina,* Stanford University Press, Stanford, 1954, pp. 42–43.)

It might be added that both Stalin and Chiang Kai-shek, but not Churchill, appeared to support the idea of an international trusteeship for Indo-China.

[3] Even so liberal a journal as *The Economist* (September 16, 1944) in good imperialist tradition characterized the stake of Britain, France, and Holland in the Far East as a "necessity of greatness and wealth." After noting the American assumption that the European powers would not resume their sovereignty over colonial territories, the article continued: "Since this attitude exists and is even backed by some of the most widely distributed American journals and newspapers, it is time that the future intentions of the British, French and Dutch were frankly and fully explained. Since none of them has any intention of abandoning its colonial empire, but on the contrary, regards the restoration of Malaya to the British, the East Indies to the Dutch and French Indochina to the French as an essential part of the destruction of Japan's co-prosperity sphere, it would be inviting the worst sort of misunderstanding, and even accusations of bad faith, if the three nations allowed any doubt in the matter to continue in the mind of their American ally."

quently exempted it from the provisions and scope of the Atlantic Charter.[1] The Americans for their part feared that after the war their power might be used, or appear to be used, to prop up a tottering British empire. Like Stalin, they grew suspicious that Churchill was fighting the war to resurrect and reassert British imperial power. Pressure from the international community, but especially the United States and the Soviet Union, was a factor a much weakened Britain could not easily ignore, but in the end the issue was resolved by the compulsion of events, as we shall see in Section 7.

5 *Economic Aspects of Colonialism*

Looking back on the period that encompassed the decline and fall of colonialism, it is surprising how little public discussion there was of the economic advantages and costs of having a colonial empire.[2] Instead, the issue was debated in terms of world power, national honor, civilizing missions, political and legal principles and, toward the end, military and political realities. There had been much more interest in the economic aspects of the subject in the early nineteenth century, when informed opinion was often critical of the idea that it was economically advantageous to have colonies. The glib and never closely argued contention during the era of the "new imperialism," that empire was a bread and butter issue for the people,[3] had gradually been toned down as the public came to re-

[1] In the summer of 1941 Churchill is widely alleged to have remarked: "I have not become His Majesty's First Minister to preside over the liquidation of the British Empire." (Quoted from Michael Brecher, *Nehru, A Political Biography*, Oxford University Press, London, 1959, p. 282.)

[2] Except in Holland; see Section 11 below.

[3] Cecil Rhodes, that ardent exponent and practitioner of imperialism, explained the connection as follows: "In order to save the 40 million inhabitants of the United Kingdom from a bloody civil war, our colonial statesmen must acquire new lands for settling the surplus population of this country, to provide new markets for the goods produced in factories and mines. The Empire, as I have always said, is a bread and butter question. If you want to avoid civil war, you must become Imperialists." (Quoted in John Strachey, "The Great Awakening," *Encounter*, Pamphlet No. 5, 1961, p. 9.)

Later on, Churchill became a leading exponent of much the same view. In fact, the notion of a direct connection between the possession of empire and the standard of living in Britain influenced the thinking of a few less conservative minds in British public life, particularly in the less intellectual Trades Union wing of the Labour Party, right down to the end of the Second World War. Thus, in defending the Labour Government's intervention in Greece in 1946 to prevent a possible Communist threat to the Mediterranean lines of communication with the empire, Bevin told the House of Commons: "I am not prepared to sacrifice the British Empire, because I know that if the British Empire fell . . . it would mean the standard of life of our constituents would fall considerably." (Quoted in Michael Barratt Brown, *After Imperialism*, Heinemann, London, 1963, p. 294.)

Dutch imperialists feared, with somewhat better reason, as we shall see, that the loss of Indonesia would have dire consequences for the Netherlands.

alize that it was, at least in Britain, a rationalization of the considerable tribute the relatively few derived from colonial power. The fact that Britain, France, and Holland became far more prosperous after they lost their colonies[1] has finally laid to rest the imperialist argument about the economic advantages of colonizing as far as the public debate in the Western countries is concerned.

There has been a surprising lack of interest in colonialism among economists. The few articles and books that have been published do not provide a very intensive analysis of this phenomenon. Whether colonies were economically advantageous or not is still an open question calling for research that now must be of an historical nature. Any future investigator will have to remember that one effect of a gathering liberation movement in a colony was an increase in the costs of maintaining colonial rule. And while these costs had to be carried by the whole nation – insofar as the colony was not made to pay them to the full – the profits went to restricted groups of nationals who had settled there and to shareholders or other interested parties in the metropolitan country. As long as the groups who had vested interests in colonialism were able – sometimes, as in France, by illegitimate means – to influence the press and legislators, they could determine policy. However, the general trend toward broadening the franchise, which began at the turn of the century and gathered momentum after the First World War, gave political power to broad masses of people who had little or no economic stake in the colonies. Furthermore, the costs of policing the colonies and providing some measure of welfare for their inhabitants rose, and became – or threatened to become – charges on the national budgets of the metropolitan countries. The difficulties of persuading a financially disinterested electorate that these expenditures were justified must have weakened the determination of the metropolitan governments to hold on to their colonial dominions.

Leaving aside the issue of distribution, it is probably true that in the case of Britain the colonies were never, after the first period of crude exploitation, very profitable. Free trade and investment in the areas of white settlement in the New World, not colonialism, laid the basis for rising economic levels in Britain in the latter part of the nineteenth century.[2] It is even probable, indeed, that the impoverishment of indigenous eco-

[1] Communist theoreticians – who consistently argued along the same line as the imperialists, though stressing the element of colonial exploitation more – explained this outcome by maintaining that whatever the outward changes in political control, the imperialist exploitation of native peoples, in fact, continues. In other words, nothing essential has changed in the imperialist relationship. (See, e.g., R. F. Palme Dutt, *The Crisis of Britain and the British Empire*, Lawrence and Wishart, London, 1953.) The Soviet Union and Communist parties the world over denounced the liquidation of colonial rule as a trick to hand over the façade of power to the lackeys of imperialism. But this line of reasoning ignores the all-important fact that the former colonial territories can now formulate their own policies.

[2] For a recent restatement of the historical evidence against the theories of Hobson and Lenin (and Cecil Rhodes, Churchill, and Bevin), see Brown, *After Imperialism*.

nomic enterprise in India, which resulted from the particular brand of *laissez-faire* policies adopted there,[1] worked in the long run to the disadvantage of the British economy insofar as it set strict limits on the expansion of India's demand for Britain's goods.[2] In the East Indies, where the Dutch had invested much larger sums, not only relatively but absolutely, and put into operation a much more carefully thought out system of exploitation, colonialism may have been a more profitable venture. Also, a relatively large number of Dutchmen, at home and abroad, were involved in administering the colony and making a living out of it.

After the Second World War, British military and civilian authorities must have realized that holding on to India – and Burma – would require deploying there a large army and police force, the cost of which could not have been extracted from the colony, and keeping an increasing number of Indian and Burmese patriots in prison. Ceylon was calmer, but even there a liberation movement was likely to arise, particularly if a tide of unrest developed in India. Sooner or later the financial as well as the moral burden of colonial rule would have become overwhelming. It must also have been evident to the British that they would have a better chance to protect their enterprises and capital assets and to expatriate capital if they settled the independence issue amicably. Although, as we said, there was little open discussion of British interests in rational terms, these considerations were certainly important to the policy choice after the Second World War.[3] The British were cool and rational rather than generous and idealistic in giving up their South Asian colonies. In a sense, too, they did not give them up voluntarily, but because they felt they had no other reasonable choice. The French and Dutch acted differently because they did not see their own interests with as much intuitive intelligence. In pointing out the influence of enlightened self-interest on British policy, we do not wish to belittle the fact that the trend toward greater political democracy and a welfare state at home had softened the ideological ground for colonialism. But since France and Holland also embraced the ideals of welfare democracy, that factor alone apparently was not strong enough to determine policy.

There is another question that must puzzle the historian. How could the metropolitan countries so lightheartedly carry the moral burden of being accountable for the destiny of millions and hundreds of millions of destitute people on the other side of the oceans? It is hard now to imagine any form of national glory, still less of profit, to be derived from such a

[1] Chapter 10, Section 8 *et passim*.

[2] "The tragedy is that the failure to develop India was a great loss for Great Britain as well as for India; a richer India would have been even a better customer, a better supplier, and a firmer basis of Empire." (Maurice and Taya Zinkin, *Britain and India*, Chatto & Windus, London, 1964, p. 67.)

[3] A high military officer informed the writer that, in the final stage of the war, he had had the task of preparing an analysis of what it would cost in military and police forces to hold India and how many Indian subjects would have to be retained in prison.

responsibility that could make the prospect an inviting one. The truth is that people grow accustomed to all manner of situations, however daunting, particularly when they are far removed in distance and in social standing from those who are in distress.

6 *The Transfer of Power: The Philippines*

There were important differences in the nature of the forces that determined the final transfer of power from any one metropolitan country to any one colonial territory. Since these differences were to have profound and probably lasting consequences for the new states in South Asia, some attention must now be given to the circumstances under which individual countries came into existence.

The discomfiture many Americans felt at the annexation of the Philippines[1] was not assuaged when in consequence of this policy the United States had to suppress for over two years a Filipino rebellion against the Spanish, in the course of which the revolutionaries had declared an independent republic and adopted a democratic and liberal constitution. Soon after, however, American policy was firmly committed to the ultimate goal of Philippine independence.[2] The whole political tradition of American democracy stressed the legitimacy of government only with the consent of the governed. Moreover, the United States had always disclaimed territorial ambitions, though its business interests were not slow to derive the maximum benefits from sharing in the privileges granted to the European colonial powers.

A legislative assembly was established in 1907 and the local civil service was increasingly staffed by Filipinos. Great emphasis was placed on improvement of health conditions,[3] and on expansion of educational opportunities; the proportion of literacy in the population rose to one of the highest levels in the entire region.[4] Shortly before the United States entered the First World War, President Wilson confirmed his country's intention of granting independence to the Philippines. In the early 1930's it was formally decided that the colony should have political independence after a ten-year transition period of nearly complete self-government. The Philippines was authorized to give itself a constitution through an elected assembly and a popular referendum. The constitution of 1935 was modelled closely on that of the United States, except that it provided for a unitary rather than a federal state and gave the Philippines' President

[1] The Senate ratified the treaty of annexation of the Philippines by only the bare two-thirds majority required by the United States Constitution.

[2] It is worth noting that the United States never established a Colonial Office or appointed a Colonial Secretary within its executive system.

[3] Chapter 30, Section 3.

[4] Chapter 31, Section 3; Chapter 32, Section 4.

more power in relation to the other organs of government than the American President enjoys. The Philippines' constitution antedated its formal independence, which, as the Americans had promised, arrived on July 4, 1946.

If the United States had prepared the Philippines for political independence rather better than the European colonial powers had prepared their dependencies, the same cannot be said of its achievements in the economic sphere. American policy did little to modify the Spanish heritage of large landholdings, the high proportion of sharecropping, and the wealth and influence of the Catholic Church.

In fact, the situation worsened in some respects. Thus American investment in, and free trade with, the Philippines stimulated the colony's dependence on the export of a few agricultural products – sugar, cocoanuts, and abaca – and led to an increase in the number of absentee landlords. The percentage of Filipino farmers who were tenants doubled between 1900 and 1935. Much of the foreign (meaning overwhelmingly American) investment in the Philippines was tied to its export industries; of such industry as developed, a significant part was foreign-controlled. In general it may be said that economic development under American influence merely reinforced the economic and political power of wealthy businessmen and hereditary landlords, whose interest in preserving their privileged position was hardly compatible with the democratization of Filipino society. Yet it was to this class that political power was increasingly transferred from the 1930's onwards, and the results were what might be expected. "Political bosses" effectively controlled the votes of those who were enfranchised by virtue of their literacy qualifications; corruption was widespread and shameless; and these conditions were bluntly disclosed by an extraordinarily free press, which was another product of American dominance.

At the American end of the economic relationship it was no coincidence that among the most enthusiastic supporters of independence for the islands were senators from states affected by competition from Philippine sugar. American investors in the Cuban and Puerto Rican sugar industries, and American trade unions fearful of the immigration of cheap labor from the Philippines, joined in pressing for action that would end the free entry of Philippine goods[1] and workers. After the political connection had been severed, American business interests that had a stake in the Philippine economy were able to secure important safeguards and privileged treatment in return for substantial American assistance to the Philippines for post-war rehabilitation and recovery.

[1] The decision to grant independence after a ten-year transitional period was made conditional on the progressive liability of Philippine sugar to ordinary customs duty on entering the United States, so that by the time of independence the full rate would be charged.

There had been little need for a liberation movement in the colony, as on that score the Americans collaborated wholeheartedly. The Philippines did not have to be pushed into independence like Malaya (Section 10); rather, it achieved independence with even less effort than Ceylon (Section 9). As we shall note in Chapter 9 (Section 12), political developments followed a conservative trend, not only in colonial times but also after independence. One reason was undoubtedly that, in the absence of a need to form a liberation movement and to seek support against the imperial power among the lower strata, no comprehensive program of social and economic reform, to be carried out when the country was free, was ever worked out. This demarcates a similarity with Malaya and Ceylon, but a dissimilarity with India (Section 7). The almost frictionless cooperation with the United States in ending political dependence, and the interest shown by the Filipinos in retaining rather close economic relations with the former metropolitan country, implied that there were few urges to the radical nationalism so prominent in Burma and Indonesia (Sections 8 and 11). In the Second World War the Japanese were not welcome in the Philippines. The Filipinos still take pride in the way they fought with the American forces against the Japanese.

The manner in which the Philippines achieved liberation from colonial domination, and the generous economic aid the United States has since given the islands, indicate that independence did not cause any break in established commercial, cultural, and political ties with the mother country. Emotionally and ideologically, most of the articulate classes in the Philippines were probably more attached to the United States immediately after independence arrived than they had been in the colonial era. However, occasionally, and particularly in more recent years, there has been some rift within the elite, a fact we shall note in Section 12 of Chapter 9.

7 *India and Pakistan*

The granting of independence to the Philippines was a predictable event, and did not represent a major breach in colonial domination of South Asia. If only because of the reverberations it had in other colonial territories, the early withdrawal of the British from what is now India and Pakistan was a much more dramatic event.

As already mentioned, the British in 1917 explicitly declared self government to be the ultimate objective of their dominion over India.[1] Their

[1] The British tried to satisfy Indian ambitions in other ways too. Thus Lloyd George nominated two Indian members to the War Cabinet in London. India was also invited to the Imperial Conferences, the membership of which, till then, had been confined to the self-governing members of the Commonwealth. Finally, India was given a seat at the Paris Peace Conference after the war.

negotiations and struggles with the Indian liberation movement in the period between the two world wars really concerned the speed, manner, and relative completeness with which that objective should be realized. It is a commentary on the way the British conducted this contest of wills that by the end of the Second World War they no longer were in a position to negotiate from strength. The unexpectedly rapid defeat of Japan removed the justification for keeping substantial British forces in India and thus brought about a drastic reduction in the physical means of enforcing British authority in a country aflame with revolt. It is highly doubtful that a war-weary British public would have countenanced their use for the large-scale coercion of a resolute opposition in any case.[1] In Britain, Churchill and his party were heavily defeated in the British general elections by the Labour Party, which had long been pledged to a speedy settlement of the question of Indian independence.

Unfortunately, when the Attlee government approved the task of withdrawing quickly and gracefully, it no longer had the power of British prestige to bridge the gulf that had opened up between the Indian National Congress and the Muslim League because of the latter's insistence on partition.[2] Faced with mounting communal strife and the danger of a widespread breakdown in law and order, the Attlee government could only try to galvanize the Indian leaders into reaching a speedy settlement of their differences by the expedient of setting a deadline for the British withdrawal. Sir Stafford Cripps, who with Attlee was most responsible for the Labour government's policy on this issue (Bevin seems to have played a more passive role), put the alternatives to the House of Commons with a clarity that makes his statement worth quoting in full:

What then were the alternatives which faced us? Those alternatives were fundamentally two . . .: first we could attempt to strengthen British control in India on the basis of an expanded personnel in the Secretary of State's services and a considerable reinforcement of the British troops, both of which would have been required, so that we should be in a position to maintain for as long as might be necessary our administrative responsibility while awaiting an agreement amongst the Indian communities. Such a policy would entail a definite decision that we should remain in India for at least 15 to 20 years, because for any substantially shorter period we should not be able to reorganize the Services on a stable and sound basis. . . . The second alternative was, we could accept the fact that the first alternative was not possible, and make a further attempt to persuade the Indians to come together, while at the same time warning them

[1] Lieutenant General Sir Francis Tuker, the G.O.C. Eastern Command in India at the time, has written: "Ultimately we found that this garrison commitment was more than the industrial needs of our impoverished country could stand. That was another very strong reason for our leaving India and leaving it quickly." (Lt. Gen. Sir Francis Tuker, *While Memory Serves,* Cassel & Co., London, 1950, p. 518.)

[2] The deeper historical causes of the partition of British India in 1947 and its implications for the successor states of Pakistan and India are discussed in Chapter 6.

that there was a limit of time during which we were prepared to maintain our responsibility while awaiting their agreement. One thing that was, I think, quite obviously impossible was to decide to continue our responsibility indefinitely and, indeed, against our own wishes, into a period when we had not the power to carry it out. These were the alternatives, and the only alternatives, that were open to us. . . .

The first alternative we had no hesitation in putting aside. It would be contrary to all we have said, and to the policy of this country, to prolong our stay in India for more than a decade against the wishes of the Indians. . . . It would be politically impractical from a national, and international point of view, and would raise the most bitter animosity of all parties in India against us. Even if we had been prepared to make available the extra troops that would be required to deal with the opposition by the Indian people over that period of years, it is certain that the people of this country — short as we are of manpower as we all know — would not have consented to the prolonged stationing of large bodies of British troops in India, for a purpose which was not consistent with our expressed desire that India should achieve self-government at as early a date as possible.[1]

The decision clearly indicated that the initiative for effecting the transfer of British power in India had passed to the Indians themselves. The British government was no more than a go-between trying to reconcile two opposing forces.[2]

The British Conservative politicians, and Churchill especially, denounced the decision as unconditional surrender, an unjustifiable gamble, and an abnegation of British responsibilities. They claimed to be committed to Indian self-government, but to the very last their minds dwelt on obstacles that would seem to relegate it to the distant future. From their statements it is reasonable to infer that had a Conservative government been in power in Britain, it might have attached conditions to Indian independence that would have led to delays and more unrest and ill-feeling in India. Attlee defended the British withdrawal as the fulfillment

[1] House of Commons Debates, March 5, 1947, *Hansard,* Vol. 434, cols. 503 to 505.

[2] "What Nehru and his colleagues did not sufficiently appreciate was that the British Government, while willing to accept a constitution agreed to by the major political parties in India, was unwilling to impose one. The British view was honest and logical, for if they imposed a constitution they would have to stay in order to implement it. And they wanted to withdraw — and withdraw gracefully. Hence the onus of devising a constitution for free India devolved on the Indians." (Moraes, *Jawaharlal Nehru,* p. 318.)

Some years after the heat of controversy surrounding the manner of the British withdrawal had died down, Attlee recorded the following comment on the decision to set a deadline: "I'd come to the conclusion from my own experience of Indians that there was a great deal of happiness for them in asking for everything, and putting down everything that was wrong in India to British rule, then sitting pretty. I thought that most of them were not really keen on responsibility. They would talk, and talk and talk, and as long as they could put the responsibility on us they would continue to quarrel among themselves. Therefore I concluded the thing to do was to bring them right up against it and make them see they'd got to face the situation themselves." (Francis Williams, *A Prime Minister Remembers,* Heinemann, London, 1961, p. 208.)

of a British imperial mission as envisaged by Victorian statesmen like Macaulay. Of course, a divided India was a somber reflection on the way that mission, if such it can be called, had been carried out. But in helping to consummate the process of independence without further delay, the British Labour government can fairly be credited with recognizing and accepting a political necessity.[1] It is surprising at first sight that the British decision to quit India generated so little public rancor, much less the sort of deep divisions that prevented the French and Dutch from taking a rational view of their own self-interests in South Asia. Outside of the relatively muted protests of a much weakened Conservative Party, British opinion generally supported the decision. The political forces that stood full square for welfare democracy at home and abroad had achieved a moment of fulfillment.

Because of its decision to relinquish its political hold in the area, Britain was able to preserve all its financial, industrial, and commercial positions in India and Pakistan practically intact.[2] It also maintained much of its political and cultural influence in these two countries, as witness the fact that both countries chose to remain in the Commonwealth. Britain after the war was not in a position to give generous financial aid to its former colonies, as the United States did to the Philippines. But the large reserves of gold and foreign exchange accumulated by the colonial governments served the newly independent countries as a financial buffer for many years. Also, Britain initiated the Colombo Plan to coordinate modest bilateral aid projects, and in this way confirmed its role as a friendly helper and advisor. On the whole, Britain successfully showed itself to the peoples in the former colonies as a country with which it was wise to preserve good relations.

With the departure of the British, a few tiny French and Portuguese settlements, of which Portuguese Goa was the most important, were the only parts of the Indian subcontinent remaining under foreign rule. After a period of procrastination the French negotiated the transfer of their settlements to India, though it was not until 1962 that the French National Assembly finally ratified the agreement. Indians frequently cited this precedent in an effort to persuade the Portuguese to relinquish Goa, but the Portuguese adamantly maintained that this territory was an in-

[1] "I am aware of no other important instance of imperial authorities recognizing such a necessity when they encountered it. It was Frederick Engels who cited the Hegelian maxim that freedom was the recognition of necessity. If so, the British Government's recognition of the necessity of Indian independence in 1947 was one of the most truly free acts in history." (Strachey, *The End of Empire*, p. 197.)

[2] Britain accomplished this without insisting on any formal recognition of those positions from the successor states. Maurice and Taya Zinkin are correct when they refer to Britain's "refusal to do anything to protect those interests which really were specifically British. No protection was obtained for British interests." (*Britain and India*, p. 121.)

tegral part of Portugal itself. After counselling patience and peaceful negotiations for a number of years, Nehru, toward the end of 1961, capitulated to a fabricated campaign to seize Goa by force. At the same time India seized the smaller Portuguese settlements of Daman and Diu. It does not require much insight to see the advantages to the ruling party of generating public excitement in this way on the eve of the Indian general election of 1962.[1] The move also served as a useful demonstration to the Afro-Asian bloc that India had lost none of its fidelity to anti-colonial causes since achieving its own independence. India's resort to force over the issue of Goa met with a bad reception in the West. It was called an act of aggression, and as such it tarnished the image of Nehru as a man of peace. However, articulate Indian opinion held that the existence of a colonial relic on the subcontinent constituted a permanent aggression against Indian territory.[2] Other newly liberated nations in the region tended to share this view of colonial holdings as permanent aggressions against which it was perfectly legitimate to resort to force when circumstances allowed. But toward the actual boundaries they inherited from their former colonial rulers they adopted a rigidly legalistic attitude of "what we have we hold." In the next chapter we shall return to this double standard of thinking about territorial questions.

The achievement of political independence on the Indian subcontinent was the decisive impulse that set in motion a wave-like movement of emancipation from colonial rule all over South Asia – and beyond it into West Asia and Africa. For one thing, nationalist movements in a number of other colonial territories had long derived inspiration from the Indian liberation struggle and had come to regard the constitutional advances conceded to India as a yardstick by which to judge their own progress toward self-government. Once India achieved independence, other British colonial territories, especially, could feel hopeful that they were in striking distance of this goal. They were not disappointed. Political independence for Burma and Ceylon quickly followed that for the Indian subcontinent, and Malaya was pushed in the same direction by British policy itself. But the circumstances under which power was transferred were markedly different in each case. Burma and Ceylon afford a particularly striking contrast in this respect. The former was propelled into independence by revolutionary ferment; the latter achieved it as the logical culmination of a more gradual process of maturation.

[1] At his first press conference after the invasion of Goa, Nehru told the newsmen present that "nothing in the 14 years of independence has excited and thrilled the people of India as the liberation of Goa." (*New York Herald Tribune,* European Edition, December 29, 1961.)

[2] "No aggression has been committed because we have regarded Goa ever since 1947 as our rightful territory, we not having inherited any of Britain's treaties or understandings with Portugal. To drive out the intruder who is in illegal occupation of part of our territory is not aggression." (*Link,* December 24, 1961.)

8 *Burma*

Certain elements in the experience of Burma under colonial rule help to explain the rather unusual manner in which it acquired its independence, as compared with other British colonial territories. Until 1937, Burma was ruled as a subordinate and relatively backward province of British India. Indeed, the large number of Indians engaged in local commerce and industry – Indians together with British and Chinese nationals virtually controlled the modern and quasi-modern sectors of the economy – made Burma as much an Indian as a British colony. Rangoon, for instance, was mainly an Indian city. Indians predominated in most of the public services and professions. Few Burmese succeeded in entering the Indian Civil Service and not many were admitted to institutions of higher learning.[1] The colony did not even have its own army. Not surprisingly, therefore, Burmese nationalism came to be focussed on freedom from all alien domination and not just British colonial rule.

Western institutions by no means blanketed the countryside, and where they existed they made less of an impression than in other British colonial dependencies. The rule of law and a rudimentary form of parliamentary representation were more of a surface veneer, and corruption within the administration was more widespread than in other British territories in South Asia. This was not unrelated to the fact that Burma did not develop a significant Western-educated upper class steeped in Western liberal ideology and capable of assuming political power. As Burma moved nearer to self-government before the Second World War, the political initiative passed to a relatively unsophisticated group of revolutionary idealists with a confused ideology and a marked taste for direct political action rather than peaceful parliamentary processes. Certain political advances had been conceded in the wake of the constitutional progress India had achieved. When formally separated from India in 1937, Burma acquired a system of cabinet government responsible to a parliament, but not a parliament responsible to a united people. Since little had been done to develop the nation-building functions of government, this step tended if anything to exacerbate communal and sectional antipathies. Nor did it appease the intense nationalist feelings of the younger group of political leaders, mainly ex-university students fired with revolutionary zeal, who were eventually to bring about political independence.

The Japanese occupation during the Second World War destroyed the foundations of colonial power in the territory. The Japanese helped

[1] Out of 138 students graduating from Rangoon University in 1937, only 60 were Burmese; of the 128 licentiates from the Medical School, only 39 were Burmese; and of the 20 who graduated from the Government Technical Institute, only 4 were Burmese. (Hugh Tinker, *Union of Burma,* 2nd ed., Oxford University Press, London, 1959, p. 151.)

Burma to acquire its first national army; many Burmese officials received sudden and unexpected promotions to senior positions in the administrative services; and the country was granted formal independence. Burmese nationalists soon realized the hollowness of their new status, and toward the end of the war they turned against the Japanese occupiers. During that period more than one kind of underground movement came into being; a pattern of split and anarchic resistance to authority developed that has continued right down to the present day. However, upon the defeat of Japan, the British recognized the Anti-Fascist People's Freedom League – the only nationwide resistance rally that had been formed – as genuinely representative of post-war popular opinion in Burma and promised it full self-government. In an increasingly explosive situation marked by militant demonstrations, strikes, the recruiting of private armies, and near anarchy it was the Burmese nationalist leaders who, in fact, dictated the timing and terms of the country's political independence. As in India, Britain did not have the physical means to re-establish its authority. The Attlee government decided not to resist the demands of the Burmese nationalists, and in so doing reduced the risk that the liberation movement would come wholly under the control of Burmese Communists. In June, 1947, Britain agreed to grant full political independence to Burma within a year.

As if to underline the revolutionary break with the past and advertise its independence, the new government dismissed all non-Burmese officials immediately and left the Commonwealth. Despite this, Britain did its best to remain respectfully friendly; its big business interests accommodated themselves to the large-scale nationalization program instituted by the new regime and tried to work in cooperation with government officials. However, this policy met with very limited success. Thus the manner in which Burma acquired its political freedom led to the severance of practically all relations with Britain. It also left a legacy of schisms and violence that was to plague the new state when it attempted to establish its authority and achieve national consolidation (Chapter 9, Part II).

9 *Ceylon*

Political independence came to Ceylon in a totally different manner than it did to Burma. In the case of Ceylon there was no Japanese occupation, no revolutionary ferment, and no sudden break with the past. The colony did not even experience the sort of liberation struggle the Indian National Congress organized. There was no civil disobedience or noncooperation and no imprisonment of national leaders. As there was no struggle in Ceylon, neither was there the usual concomitant of a struggle: the hardening of national solidarity through national sacrifice. Ceylon emerged from colonial rule through a process of peaceful negotiation, but, as we shall see in Chapter 9 (Part I), this was not an altogether unmixed blessing.

An essential element in the explanation of the unique way in which Ceylon achieved political independence is the fact that the process of Westernization had gone further there than in other colonial territories. To start with, Ceylon had experienced nearly four hundred and fifty years of colonial rule, first under the Portuguese, then the Dutch, and finally the British. From schools founded and run by Christian missions – and in the British era more and more modelled on British lines, even to the extent in some cases of emulating English public schools – there emerged a thoroughly Anglicized upper class with generally conservative political leanings. These Ceylonese were so much like their colonial masters in outlook, manners, and social habits that they were often called "brown sahibs," and negotiations between them and the British were almost in the nature of dealings between gentlemen of the same club. After the First World War this elite group formed a Ceylonese National Congress, which it hoped would grow in strength like its Indian prototype. But it collapsed a few years before the country achieved independence. During the period of British rule Ceylonese leaders felt no inclination to make any radical or egalitarian appeals for public support and nationalism struck no roots among the masses. It is no wonder, then, that the British felt that such men could safely be entrusted with ever larger installments of political responsibility.

In 1912 "educated," i.e., English-educated, male Ceylonese were allowed to elect a representative to the Governor's Legislative Council. By the early 1920's the Ceylonese had acquired an elected majority on this Council, though a number of the seats were based on the separate representation of religious and ethnic groups, and the franchise was restricted by fairly stringent property and literacy qualifications. Ceylonese leaders did not appear to be aiming at political independence at this stage. They did, however, press for a larger share of executive power, the more rapid Ceylonization of the civil service, and more opportunity and state support for indigenous enterprise. As regards the first two demands, they could feel well satisfied with the concessions made in the 1930's. By the outbreak of the Second World War the Ceylonese had attained a predominance in the civil service that the indigenous elements in other colonies might well have envied. In 1931 a new constitution had given Ceylon unprecedented scope for legislative initiative in domestic affairs and had created virtually a cabinet system of government.

More striking still, the British Labour government at that time decreed universal suffrage for men and women in Ceylon and abolished communal representation, a step not popular with the minority community of Ceylonese Tamils. It is remarkable that the former action came only three years after voting rights for men and women in Britain itself had been put on the same basis. It was indicative of the oligarchic character and outlook of the Ceylonese National Congress that it was against such an extensive broadening of the franchise. This was the main reason why the British Labour government acted as it did: it wanted to strengthen the hand of the lower classes in their dealings with the ruling class. In Ceylon's first general election in 1931 a little over half the potential electorate registered and voted. Thus Ceylon experienced the processes of parliamentary democracy and a large measure of internal self-government for a longer period than any other colonial territory in South Asia and had, in addition, the unique distinction of serving its political apprenticeship under conditions of universal suffrage for almost two decades.

During the Second World War Ceylon's political leaders refrained from demanding outright political independence and, unlike the Indian nationalist leaders, gave unstinting support to the British war effort. It was only the election of a Labour government in Britain and its recognition of Indian political independence that prompted them to demand their freedom. The British had no misgivings about granting them full independence and did so on February 4, 1948. Very few constitutional changes were required to bring this about. The new state not only remained in the Commonwealth but retained the British Crown as its Head of State; its first two Governors General were also British. Finally, with an eye to their own internal security, Ceylon's leaders gladly permitted Britain to keep its military base on the island.

The manner of Ceylon's advance to independence was not without ominous implications for the future. In the first place, somewhat complicated provisions in the 1931 constitution had prevented the integration of executive initiatives into a coherent government policy and inhibited the development of political parties. The resolution of all issues had depended on shifting coalitions of rival personalities and factions. Ceylon's political apprenticeship tended, in other words, to encourage a diffusion of responsibility rather than a concentration on the problems of government. But perhaps Ceylon's difficulties stemmed more from the fact that the ruling upper class was less homogeneous than it seemed at first sight, and that under that class there were fissures related to ethnic origin, language, and religion. The absence of any radical Singhalese nationalism before the achievement of political independence goes a long way to explain the relatively painless emergence of Ceylon from colonial rule. Developments since independence will be dealt with in Part I of Chapter 9.

10 *Malaya*

The last sizeable colonial territory in South Asia to acquire its independence was Malaya. The fact that this event did not take place until 1957, or nearly a decade after the other South Asian colonies had become independent, suggests that some special forces were at work to delay the final transfer of British power. A comparison with Ceylon is particularly pertinent. Like Ceylon, Malaya was ethnically a plural society but, unlike Ceylon, or, indeed, any other territory in the region, it harbored immigrant groups – principally Chinese and Indian – that in the aggregate outnumbered the indigenous population.[1] Moreover, the process of Westernization had not, to the same extent as in Ceylon, built a bridge between the different communities in the form of an English-educated upper class with many opportunities and interests in common, on whom the British could devolve increasingly larger installments of political responsibility.

These features of colonial Malaya inhibited the growth of any national solidarity or independence movement. National consciousness developed, in fact, along communal lines; only the indigenous population took Malaya itself as the focus of its loyalty. The Malays and the Chinese disliked each other, and both looked down on the Indians. Each community lived, so to speak, in a separate social compartment and the antipathy each felt for the others was heightened by religious sentiment. In addition, each of the three communities was divided within itself by distinctions based on economic and social position or, in the Indian case, caste and religion (some of the Indians were Moslems). The situation was further aggravated by the fact that the Malays were economically by far the weakest community; on the whole they were in the majority only in the less developed parts of the country where subsistence farming was the main occupation. The modern and quasi-modern sectors of the Malayan economy were dominated by the Chinese and, to a lesser extent, the Indians (apart from British interests). In these circumstances substantial progress toward self-government would almost certainly have meant handing over political power to a Chinese community whose patriotism was centered more on their own community and on China than on Malaya.

Before the Second World War there was a marked lack of interest in self-government for the colony, except on the part of a handful of English-educated Malays. The Chinese and Indians were content with a regime that safeguarded their economic interests; the Malays did not want British rule to end until they were in a better position, socially, economically, and politically, to hold their own against the Chinese. Feeling a special

[1] Out of a population of nearly 2.7 million in 1911, the Malays formed 51 percent, the Chinese 33 percent, and Indians 11 percent. By 1931 the Malay share of a larger total had fallen to 44.7 percent and the Chinese and Indian shares had risen to 39 and 14.2 percent respectively. By 1947, when the total population was 5.8 million, the Malay share had fallen to 43.3 percent. The Chinese share had by then risen to 44.9 percent but the Indian had fallen back to about the same proportion as in 1911. See Lennox A. Mills, *Malaya: A Political and Economic Appraisal,* University of Minnesota Press, Minneapolis, 1958, p. 13.

responsibility for the indigenous and economically weaker community, the British reserved land for the Malays, paid particular attention to advancing their education, and recruited them for the civil service while largely excluding Indians and Chinese from this employment. Another factor that held back constitutional advance before the war was the extremely cumbersome way in which the country was governed. There were actually eleven separate governments: one for the Straits Settlements of Penang, Malacca, and Singapore; one for each of the four constituent states of the Federated Malay States, in addition to their federal government; and five for each of the unfederated states, where the legal rights of sovereignty still rested with the sultans. Any significant advance toward democratic self-government clearly required a drastic simplification of this inefficient structure.

Since no nationalist movement to speak of had emerged and little political progress had been achieved before the Second World War, the Japanese occupation had less revolutionary effects on Malaya than on other South Asian territories. The Japanese never promised Malaya independence. Its substantial Chinese population was enough to ensure the Japanese a less sympathetic reception than they got in Burma, for instance, or Indonesia. The only serious resistance to their occupation came, in fact, from the Chinese and was usually Communist-led; the Malays were willing to collaborate. With this background in mind, it is not particularly surprising that the British were welcomed back to Malaya after the war. Nevertheless, with the movement toward political independence gathering momentum all over the region, a restoration of the political *status quo* in Malaya was hardly feasible. Therefore the British tried, albeit belatedly, to create a basic national unity that would enable the country to proceed rapidly toward self-government.

Britain attempted at first to form the disparate parts of the country into a Malayan Union under a strong central government. But the plan was vigorously opposed by the Malays, under the leadership of English-educated aristocrats – partly because it deprived the sultans of their legal sovereignty, but mainly because it aimed at equal citizenship rights for the Chinese and Indian populations. The Malays regarded the latter proposal as a threat to political privileges, which they felt were necessary to keep political control of the country from passing to the Chinese.[1] The fact that the British plainly intended to push the country toward self-government galvanized the Malays into political action in defense of their special privileges. Out of this agitation came the United Malay National Organization (U.M.N.O.), the leading Malay political party. Its leaders were largely aristocrats, many of whom were government officials, and

[1] In the beginning the British felt a certain sympathy toward the Chinese who had not been collaborators during the war; this sympathy vanished rapidly because of the Communist insurrection; see below.

its main political plank was simply Malaya for the Malays. It was from this group that the demand for self-government came in the early 1950's. The fear that a politically dominant Malay community in an independent Malaya might threaten the economic interests of other ethnic groups prompted the wealthier sections of the Chinese and Indian communities to form their own political organizations. In other words, the prospective departure of the British stirred Malaya into political consciousness, but along communal lines. All attempts to form non-communal political parties failed.

Another significant development that took place in Malaya after the Second World War was the outbreak of a Communist insurrection, organized and supported mainly by local Chinese. Large British forces were deployed to contain and defeat an armed revolt that seriously disturbed the normal life of the territory for a number of years. This rebellion provided a strong additional motive for pushing the country as rapidly as possible toward self-government, since the Communists claimed to be fighting for freedom from colonial rule. It had the further consequence of worsening relations between the two major communities since the Malays alone gave wholehearted support to the British effort to crush the rebels. The attitude of the larger part of the Chinese community was conditioned less by the aim of the Communists than by their prospects of success. This apparent desire to be on the winning side was resented by the Malays.

Having failed in their attempt to impose the basis of a united nationalism, the British in 1948 negotiated with the Malay political leaders – including the sultans, who had regained their legal sovereignty – the formation of a new Federation of Malaya to exclude Singapore with its overwhelmingly Chinese population. The principle of a strong central government was retained, though as it worked out, considerable power was exercised by the constituent states. Of vital importance to the Malays was the fact that the new constitution made it somewhat more difficult for the Chinese and Indians to acquire federal citizenship than the British had originally intended. The Chinese community naturally disliked qualifications for citizenship that favored the Malays,[1] and resentment against such discrimination was one of the principal impulses behind the formation of a Chinese communal party.

Having done much to stimulate political consciousness in the first place, British policy itself became increasingly subject to pressures from the communal associations that had resulted. The constitution of 1948 did not provide for parliamentary democracy, and the Malays, in order to combat the Communists' claim to represent the true nationalism of the

[1] It has been estimated that in 1949 only 375,000 of the 1,952,682 Chinese residents of the Federation were federal citizens.

country, were forced to press for rapid progress in that direction. Their leaders were aware, however, that unless they made some effort to surmount communal antagonisms, it would be difficult to obtain substantial concessions from the British. Accordingly, the three communal political parties joined in an alliance and through this marriage of convenience, as it may fairly be called, completely dominated the federal Legislative Council after the first federal elections in 1955 and demanded and secured full self-government two years later. Thus within the space of two years Malaya had proceeded from a government with a nominated legislature under the control of the British Colonial Office to parliamentary democracy and political independence. Its political apprenticeship had been both brief and forced. In their anxiety to present a united front to the British, Malaya's political leaders had shelved rather than resolved the real issues dividing the two major communities, and of these the most troublesome was the question of federal citizenship. In their negotiations with the British and the Chinese, the Malay leaders had conceded qualifications for federal citizenship that enabled the bulk of the Chinese in Malaya to acquire this status by the time of independence. However, the Chinese were not accorded equal attributes of citizenship as their leaders had demanded.

In other ways also the Malays asserted their claim to special privilege. Although English could continue to be used for official purposes for ten years, Malay was made the only national language of the new state. Although complete freedom of worship was guaranteed, Islam became the state religion. Most important, a "reasonable proportion" of lands, public service positions, permits to engage in business and trade, educational scholarships and assistance, and "such similar privileges accorded by the government" were to be reserved for Malays. In short, the transition to full independence was managed so that the Malays retained the bulk of the political power in the new state even though the Chinese were in general the more economically advanced and better educated community. This left open the question whether the Malays would advance economically and socially more rapidly than the Chinese would grow impatient with the political discrimination they suffered.

The aristocratic Malay political leaders and the wealthier Chinese and Indian political leaders were united in a hearty dislike of radical economic and social change. This conservative upper-class alliance opposed the nationalization of foreign enterprise and sought to attract private foreign capital. It kept Malaya within the Commonwealth and firmly aligned with the West in world affairs. It welcomed the continued presence of British forces, because this served to keep down radical movements. In fact, though the conservative ruling class of Malaya talked the language of parliamentary democracy, it expected and received from the masses the sort of passive obedience and loyalty that are customarily found in a highly inegalitarian society. How things developed in independent Malaya will be discussed in Section 11 of Chapter 9.

11 *Indonesia*

We now turn to the way political independence was achieved in the last two areas under review, the Netherlands East Indies and French Indo-China. Unlike the other colonial territories in South Asia, these colonies had to fight for their freedom. There was no voluntary transfer of power by either Holland or France; it had to be wrested from them by armed rebellion, and the colonial wars that resulted became the object of international concern.

To take first the Netherlands East Indies, Dutch colonial policy was very different from Britain's, in that the Dutch were more inclined to govern indirectly through hereditary local leaders. The rationale of this policy was that it softened the impact of Western domination by leaving the people nominally under their own rulers, laws, and customs. But it was also a simpler and cheaper method of economic exploitation than the system of direct rule the British applied to most of their territories. The choice of system was not fortuitously determined. As Furnivall has pointed out,[1] it was to a large extent influenced by the nature of the economic stake of the colonial ruler. When a colony was valued mainly for its products and its supply of cheap labor, as was the Netherlands East Indies, a system of indirect rule was often the simplest method of gaining economic control of its resources at the lowest possible cost. But when a dependency was valued more as a market, or when there were a considerable number of European enterprises besides plantations, Western laws and procedures had to be imposed and a system of direct rule served the purpose more effectively. Of course, most colonial dependencies came to be exploited in both ways and the distinction between indirect and direct methods of colonial rule became somewhat blurred. Thus the Dutch instituted direct rule over those parts of the East Indies that came to be dominated by Dutch business interests. Similarly, the British resorted to indirect rule in the princely states in India and the feudal outer provinces in Burma. Nevertheless, a difference did persist and the two distinct styles of colonial government had rather different implications from the standpoint of political advancement.

The system of direct rule involved the implantation of Western principles and institutions of government in a colony and the adaptation of colonial society to Western modes of behavior. In contrast, the Dutch

[1] J. S. Furnivall, *Colonial Policy and Practice*, Cambridge University Press, London, 1957, Chapter VIII *et passim.*

system of indirect rule was designed to disturb traditional society as little as possible. Naturally, the former system required a larger number of "natives" educated along Western lines to implement it than did the latter system. Even when a demand for Western-trained indigenous officials developed under the "ethical policy" that motivated the last phase of Dutch colonial rule, it amounted to little more than a call for subordinate clerks.[1] A substantial Westernized upper class did not emerge as a by-product of Dutch rule. For this reason the British system was more consonant with, and a better preparation for, ultimate self-government than the Dutch system. However, the Dutch were not concerned with any such eventuality; on the contrary, they never seriously doubted the permanency of their own reign.[2]

The type of colonial rule favored by the Dutch had other distinctive consequences for the East Indies. The aim of recognizing and preserving diverse cultural and ethnic traditions meant, in practice, an even more pronounced policy of divide and rule than is natural in every colonial regime. It did nothing to break down the compartmentalization of Indonesian society or to promote social cohesion. It impeded the formation of a national outlook and relegated the indigenous population to positions of permanent inferiority. The Dutch authorities, under the sway of an "ethical policy" dating from the beginning of the present century, hoped to promote welfare in the colony beyond that which would accrue from the development of Western enterprise. But higher production was more than counter-balanced by population growth, so that by the outbreak of the Second World War the people of Java, who accounted for about two-thirds of the total population of the colony, were probably worse off than they had been forty years earlier. The Dutch government may have regarded its subjects with paternal benevolence, but it did little to curb the power and cupidity of the foreign economic interests that dominated the colonial economy. Neither did it eliminate the discrimination against indigenous people that existed in social life as well as in government and business.

On the other hand, certain aspects of Dutch colonial rule redounded to the advantage of the colony. First, it prevented an undue concentration of land ownership or, more specifically, the wholesale appropriation of land by aliens. Consequently, tenancy was less widespread in the East Indies than elsewhere in South Asia. Also, there was less disorganization

[1] J. M. van der Kroef, *Indonesia in the Modern World,* Vol. I, Masa Baru Ltd., Bandung, 1954, p. 16. See Chapter 31, Section 3.

[2] In 1936 the Dutch Governor General of Indonesia remarked: "We have ruled here for 300 years with the whip and the club and we shall be doing it in another 300 years." (Quoted in Herbert Feith, "Indonesia," in George McTurnan Kahin, ed., *Governments and Politics in Southeast Asia,* Cornell University Press, Ithaca, 1959, p. 168.)

of the traditional village society than in Burma, for instance.[1] Secondly, the Dutch relied largely on indigenous rather than foreign labor for their plantations; "Oriental aliens" therefore formed a smaller proportion of the total population of the East Indies than they did in Ceylon and in the other countries of Southeast Asia, except for the Philippines. Chinese immigrants, who were by far the largest foreign ethnic group, numbered well over two million of a total population of some ninety million before the Second World War, but they were mostly commercial middlemen. It should be pointed out, however, that including Eurasians there was a relatively large European element in the economy. It is also worth noting that, despite a highly centralized administration based on Java, the East Indies under Dutch rule was well administered in comparison with other colonial territories. Corruption was virtually unknown in the administrative and judicial services of Java, for instance, whereas it was rampant in the system of direct rule the British imposed on Burma.[2]

It was in their refusal to permit any significant advance toward responsible government that the Dutch, together with the French, stood out in comparison with the British as the guardians of a reactionary imperialism. In 1922 Holland recognized the East Indies as an integral part of the Netherlands and dropped the appellation "colony." But this did not imply a weakening of the government's stand against greater autonomy for the territory, and by the outbreak of the Second World War the Netherlands East Indies had failed to achieve any substantial beginning of parliamentary government. Holland's stubborn refusal to accede to the moderate demands of indigenous nationalists, as well as its practice of reserving even the less elevated positions in the colonial administration to Dutch and Eurasian residents, drove the forces of nationalism into conspiratorial channels and militant agitation.

Using their religion as a symbol of social unity, Moslem Javanese merchants before the First World War organized the first significant political expression of national sentiment as a reaction against the economic activities of the Chinese and European business classes and their favored treatment by the government. In the 1920's Dutch authority was menaced mainly by Communist-led agitations. But when, toward the end of that decade, a non-Communist and non-Islamic Indonesian Nationalist Party was formed under the Westernized leadership of men like Sukarno and Hatta, the Dutch outlawed the organization and exiled its leaders. Under these conditions it was difficult for a single nationalist movement to develop out of the various regional, communal, ideological, and political forces that existed in the colony, though some coalescing did take place shortly before the outbreak of the Second World War.

[1] Chapter 18, Section 5.

[2] Chapter 18, Section 5; Chapter 20, Section 3.

During that war, with the Germans occupying Holland and the Japanese occupying the East Indies, the Dutch government-in-exile made the Indonesian nationalists a vague promise of greater autonomy within the Dutch kingdom at the conclusion of hostilities. But by then Dutch colonial thinking had become quite divorced from realities in the colony. The swift surrender to Japan destroyed the last vestiges of Dutch prestige in the East Indies. The Japanese interned nearly all the Dutch and many of the Eurasian residents of the colony, and released the government's political prisoners. Nationalist leaders advanced rapidly within the local administration and received Japanese support in the formation of a volunteer army. In addition, they were promised self-government by the conquerors. As it happened, Sukarno and Hatta proclaimed an independent Republic of Indonesia two days after the Japanese surrender. Within a remarkably short time, this entity had acquired a temporary constitution and was being governed by a cabinet responsible to a president. After the war the Dutch were only able to return to the territory with the help of the British forces that had received the Japanese surrender. This fact advertised their weakness and the alien nature of their rule.[1] Nevertheless, they returned determined to regain control rather than deal with the newly established republic, which they regarded as a Japanese creation.[2] While strongly advised by the United States and Britain to negotiate a settlement, they pursued a strategy designed to destroy the Republic and did not scruple to resort to open warfare to gain their ends.

Indonesia's fight for political independence was regarded by many, including liberal Western commentators,[3] as a struggle between capitalist colonial economic interests and the prevailing socialist ideology of its nationalist leaders. Certainly the Dutch had a huge economic stake in the colony. Leading Dutch economists reckoned that it provided 16 percent of the national income of Holland; some much higher estimates were made.[4] Whether these calculations pointed in the right direction or not,

[1] Prominent Dutch conservative politicians subsequently blamed Britain for failing to facilitate the speedy return of the Dutch colonial authorities, thereby enabling the revolutionaries to strengthen their position.

[2] In the view of Gerbrandy, the Dutch wartime Prime Minister, Sukarno and Hatta were simply agents of an insidious Japanese plan to make an Asian satellite out of the East Indies. The Republic "is a delayed time-bomb to ensure that although the Japanese lost the war they will win the peace." (P. S. Gerbrandy, *Indonesia,* Hutchinson, London, 1950, p. 68.)

[3] See, for example, "Indonesia – the Real Issues," *The Economist,* July 26, 1947, pp. 157–158.

[4] The lower figure is given in H. B. D. Derksen and J. Tinbergen, "Calculations About the Economic Significance of the Netherlands Indies for the Netherlands," Netherlands Information Bureau, New York, 1947. See also Arthur S. Keller, "Netherlands India as a Paying Proposition," *Far Eastern Survey,* Vol. IX, No. 2, June 17, 1940. This article supports the view that the withdrawal of the Dutch, "or even the curbing of their interests on a large scale," would be "a crushing blow to the economic life of the mother country." East and Spate – quoting the article in *The Economist*

many Dutchmen believed that their country would be impoverished if it relinquished its sovereignty over Indonesia.[1] It is true that colonial investments meant more to Holland than they did to Britain, for example,[2] especially since the Dutch were anxious to use their colony to recoup their war losses, which were much greater than those of any other West European country aside from Germany. Moreover, the sizeable Dutch element in the colony engaged in administration, production, and trade, even at the lower echelons, formed a broader vested interest in colonialism than was to be found in British dependencies. But there was more than commercial and financial concern behind Holland's resolution to preserve its dominance over the East Indies. The treatment meted out to the Dutch by the Japanese during their occupation of the colony had been deeply humiliating to the national pride; Holland's determination to reassert itself in the area must have been related to this fact. The Dutch, in addition, were honestly convinced that the indigenous people in the East Indies lacked the necessary qualities for self-government and that utter confusion and misery would ensue if they were left to rule themselves. Partly because of this attitude, the Dutch had done very little to prepare their subjects for independence. In turn the East Indians' lack of schooling in the art of government gave substance to the Dutch contention that a continuation of Dutch rule would be in the interests of the indigenous people.

Eventually, in the face of pressure within the United Nations and a threat by the United States to suspend its share of aid under the Marshall Plan, the Dutch were forced to withdraw. At the close of 1949, sovereign power was transferred to the Republic of the United States of Indonesia, a political federation of all the Indonesian territories. It was linked to Holland through a Netherlands-Indonesian Union whose titular head was the Dutch Crown. Under the terms of the final settlement, Indonesia accepted the greater part of the debts to Holland that had been contracted by the Dutch on behalf of the Netherlands East Indies, and private

---

referred to in the preceding footnote – estimate that "the loss of all economic interests in Indonesia would reduce the standard of living in Holland by some 30% to 35%." (W. Gordon East and O. H. K. Spate, eds., *The Changing Map of Asia,* 2nd ed., Methuen, London, 1953, p. 229.)

[1] "A nation which has an historic maritime destiny, deprived of the estates overseas in which its peoples have staked their fortunes, must suffer decline. In our case these estates, fashioned by history, are the East Indies. . . . If the bonds which attach the Netherlands to the Indies are severed there will be a permanent reduction in the national income of the Netherlands which will lead to the country's pauperization." (Gerbrandy, *Indonesia,* pp. 26–27.)

[2] Probably less than 5 percent was added each year to the British national income from overseas investments during the 1930's, and only about one-fifth of this came from investments in colonial territories, including India. Of course, what was taken out formed a much more significant proportion of the national income of the colonial territories themselves.

Dutch economic interests and property were safeguarded. These were important concessions from the Indonesian side. The Dutch continued to dominate Indonesia's foreign commerce and, to a very large extent, its plantation industry; they also retained important advisory posts in the administration. Having succeeded fairly well in maintaining their dominating position in the area's economy, the Dutch then placed in jeopardy, and finally lost, their huge stakes in Indonesia over the issue of West New Guinea, or West Irian as the Indonesians now call it. Under the terms of the agreement that transferred sovereignty to an independent Indonesian state, the political status of West New Guinea was to be determined by a new conference between the Dutch and Indonesian governments, to be called within one year. But the Dutch subsequently declined to negotiate the issue. They argued that since West New Guinea was ethnically, linguistically, and religiously different from Indonesia and far more primitive, bringing it into the modern world was a task for experienced colonial administrators. The only reason the Indonesians could put forward for possessing this territory was that it had formed part of the Netherlands East Indies.[1] Nevertheless, there were reasons to be suspicious of Dutch solicitude for a territory they had hitherto neglected – indeed, more so than the Australians on the other side of the boundary that crossed the island. For one thing, West New Guinea had become a convenient haven for refugees, including ex-colonial officials who were die-hard opponents of Indonesian nationalism.[2] These expatriates, who were mainly Eurasian, clearly hoped to benefit from the expected failure of the new state to win the loyalty of its outer islands; they did not, for instance, hide their sympathy for the rebellion of the mainly Christian population of the South Moluccas between 1950 and 1956. It might be added that it was the Christian communities in the extreme eastern parts of the Indonesian archipelago that had provided the Dutch with the bulk of their native colonial army. In Holland public opinion was such that only by insisting on the retention of West New Guinea could the Dutch government win the necessary votes in Parliament for ratification of the agreement transferring full sovereignty to Indonesia.

It was this obstinate refusal of the Dutch to relinquish West New Guinea – together, of course, with many more deep-seated grievances – that persuaded the Indonesians to abrogate the Netherlands-Indonesian Union, then to repudiate the public debt of the former Netherlands In-

[1] Chapter 5, Section 3.

[2] As Gerbrandy put it in 1950: "We can provide in New Guinea a haven for those who wish to live in conditions of safety and tolerance if the stresses within the Indonesian Republic become too severe." (*Indonesia,* p. 185; cf. p. 190.)

"Since many believed that the Djakarta government would never be able to win the loyalties of the outer territories, it was felt that New Guinea might provide a base from which to save something from the wreckage, if the new Indonesia eventually disintegrated." (Charles A. Fisher, *South-East Asia,* Methuen, London, 1964, p. 395.)

dies to the Netherlands, and, finally, to expropriate all Dutch property and compel large numbers of Dutch residents to leave the country. All this involved no small economic loss to Indonesia as well as to the Netherlands.[1] The later severance of diplomatic relations merely served to symbolize the complete rupture of all ties between the two countries, as did, with more permanent effects, the systematic substitution of English for Dutch as a foreign language in institutes of higher education.

Holland's throwing away of its immense economic power and influence in Indonesia for so barren a territory as West New Guinea must surely be regarded as one of the most astonishing national follies of recent times. It is in line, however, with the lack of generosity and imagination that marked the course of Dutch dealings with the Indonesians after the war. It is difficult not to relate this policy to the rigid social ethics of self-sufficiency and self-righteousness that are often thought to derive from a Calvinistic heritage. As one Dutch writer aptly remarked: "There hangs an aura of stodgy burgherdom about the Dutch national character which Dutch policy-makers in the Indies only rarely seem to be able to surmount."[2] As a further explanation, we must remember that the fight over West New Guinea served as an outlet for accumulated mistrust and resentment. The war for power on the mainland had left a legacy of bitterness on both sides. Turning to more recent history, the Indonesians felt that the Dutch had used the dominant position they preserved in their former colony in a ruthless and crudely selfish way. The owners and managers of the big Dutch plantations, in particular, showed a great unwillingness to adjust to a new role in the now independent country. They generally gave the impression that they were more interested in reaping quick profits to take out of Indonesia than in building up the countryside for sustained cultivation. The Dutch, who proudly remembered the efficient and honest government they had afforded the people of the territory, viewed the confusion and corruption in the Indonesian administration with misgivings and did not leave the Indonesians unaware of their attitude. As is only human, they did not ascribe much of the blame for this situation to their own failure to prepare their subjects in the East Indies for self-government.

In the event, the resilient Dutch economy took the blow in its stride. Holland is still among the more prosperous countries of Western Europe; indeed, in retrospect, it provides perhaps the clearest example available of the combination of a rising standard of living with the dissolution of empire. As for West New Guinea, it became increasingly

[1] The Dutch investment stake in Indonesia in 1940 has been estimated at $1.3 billion. (See Herbert Feith, "Indonesia," in Kahin, ed., *Governments and Politics in Southeast Asia,* p. 166.)

[2] Van der Kroef, *Indonesia in the Modern World,* Vol. 1, p. 45.
Gerbrandy's book provides revealing illustrations of this aspect of Dutch character.

evident that, in the face of mounting war threats from Indonesia and the absence of any support from the West, and especially the United States, the Dutch did not have the power to hold on to the territory. Through the good offices of the United Nations – and the United States – its peaceful transfer to Indonesia was negotiated in 1962 and carried out the following year. The final irony of this protracted conflict is that by any rational calculation of costs and benefits, West New Guinea itself can only be regarded as a long-term liability to any country that assumes responsibility for its administration and welfare.[1] But national prestige is rarely assessed on a rational basis.

12 *French Indo-China*

Indo-China is the other area in South Asia where the former colonial ruler withdrew only after a bloody struggle had made independence such a broad question that it had to be settled by international agreement. But in the case of Indo-China, unlike that of Indonesia, the issue had become badly infected with cold-war politics, a virus that has blighted the search for stability in the entire Southeast Asian region in recent years.

There were certain broad similarities between French and Dutch colonial rule. The French, like the Dutch, did not envisage the ultimate separation of their colony from the mother country, but rather its assimilation into a wider French community. The rationalization of their colonial purpose was to subject their dependencies to the influence and opportunities of French civilization so that in the course of time their inhabitants would become capable of acquiring French citizenship. This was the highest reward, the badge of elite status that was held out to ambitious "natives." In fact, however, very few Indo-Chinese ever achieved the necessary qualifications or were given the opportunity to do so. Without this status even an educated Vietnamese was made to feel socially inferior, a second-class citizen in his own country.

The point was brought home to him in another way. The population of Indo-China, or more especially that of the provinces of Cochin-China, Annam, and Tonkin, which were later divided between South and North Vietnam, came to contain, like the Netherlands East Indies, a relatively large European element. The Vietnamese were generally excluded from the modern sectors of their economy as well as from higher posts in the government. Banking, mining, large-scale manufacturing industry, and rubber production were jealously guarded French preserves, while most of the rice mills, sugar refineries, saw mills, and most of the internal trade of the country were firmly in Chinese hands. The French colonial regime

[1] The Dutch reportedly subsidized the territory at the rate of $30 million a year. (*New York Times*, August 21, 1962.)

maintained a monopoly on the sale of salt, opium, and alcohol. In addition, French settlers, usually of peasant stock and with a background of service in the lower ranks of the French army, acquired large amounts of land in Tonkin and Cochin-China. Also, Frenchmen of lower-class origin, but constituting part of what is called the "middle class" in Indo-China and the region as a whole, occupied positions in government and business that the British in their colonial territories considered beneath them, and thus blocked the way for local people whose education fitted them only for relatively subordinate or routine tasks.[1] From this type of colonial domination the emergence of a substantial Westernized upper class was hardly to be expected.

The social structure of Vietnamese society, traditionally based on land ownership, remained essentially unchanged under French rule. In Tonkin and Annam the dominant pattern was that of small, fragmented peasant holdings. However, many peasants suffered from so oppressive a burden of indebtedness that they came to own their land in name only or lost it altogether. Usury was an important factor working against the economic independence of the peasants. By contrast, Cochin-China contained many large estates, the bulk of them held by absentee French and Vietnamese landlords and cultivated by sharecroppers. During the colonial era thousands of Tonkinese were transferred to the rubber plantations of the South, where they worked and lived more or less as peons. If anything, French rule widened the gulf between the rich and the impoverished in Vietnamese rural society, thereby providing a ready-made situation for Communist activists to exploit.[2] Laos and Cambodia were largely primitive peasant societies with an upper class of noble landlords and princely families. Under colonial domination, however, the economies of these areas came increasingly under the control of the Chinese and Vietnamese as well as of the French. Much of their administration, too, came into the hands of the French and Vietnamese. Here, as elsewhere in Indo-China, French authority was deliberately buttressed by exploiting particularist tendencies and fomenting regional and personal rivalries.

The Vietnamese were by far the most numerous and most cultured of the Indo-Chinese peoples and it was from them, with their age-long tradition of opposition to Chinese invaders, that early resistance to French rule emerged. At first it took the form of a reactionary revolt by mandarins

[1] "The proportion of French officials to Indochinese was higher than that of European officials to the people of any other Southeast Asia dependent area." (Hammer, *The Struggle for Indochina*, p. 73.) The Netherlands East Indies came nearest to the Indo-Chinese situation: Eurasians included, the Dutch colony probably surpassed the French.

[2] Despite the cold-war element of international politics, the present civil war in South Vietnam has much of the character of a violent struggle between an impoverished rural peasantry and a rich, privileged upper class of largely absentee landlords, mostly urban.

of the old order concerned only with driving out the French,[1] but under the stimulus of the Russian and Kuomintang revolutions a new generation of Vietnamese nationalists emerged after the First World War. Like the Dutch in the East Indies, the French intransigently discouraged even moderate nationalists, and then wreaked terrible vengeance on the innocent and guilty alike when violent agitation and conspiratorial activity became the customary mode of political expression. The Vietnamese were denied various liberties, including the right to organize political parties and trade unions and the right to travel in certain parts of the country without official permission. The predictable consequence of this stern policy of repression was to leave the underground Communist Party in the forefront of the Vietnamese struggle for independence. The French were thus able to claim, as they eagerly did, that in fighting Vietnamese nationalism they were in fact fighting a war against Communism.[2]

With the fall of France in 1940 the French community in Indo-China supported the Vichy regime, and tamely capitulated to the Japanese demand for military control of the whole peninsula. The Japanese responded by leaving the internal administration and security of the colony in French hands. In return for complete subservience, the French community was spared the harsh internment the Dutch suffered in Indonesia and was allowed to preserve the illusion that French sovereignty over Indo-China was intact. However, French collaboration with the Japanese made it easier for Vietnamese nationalists to organize and lead a broad-based liberation movement – the Viet Minh, as it came to be called – with a notably moderate political, social, and economic program. The Viet Minh formed the only effective resistance to the Japanese occupation. With the help of Kuomintang China, it gained *de facto* control of large parts of rural Tonkin.

Two further developments put the Viet Minh in a position to proclaim an independent republic of Vietnam when the Japanese surrendered. In the closing stages of the war, when the French colonials opportunistically switched their support to de Gaulle and the Allied cause, the Japanese replaced French administrations in Vietnam, Laos, and Cambodia with puppet regimes. This action disrupted the structure of established order and clearly advertised the Viet Minh as the only genuine and effective nationalist movement in the country. The Viet Minh was further

[1] Long before the arrival of the French the Vietnamese had adopted the Chinese system of a hierarchical mandarin bureaucracy, membership in which conferred an elite status. Any impulses to social change were readily suppressed by this self-perpetuating elite. The French to some extent camouflaged their colonial rule over Annam by attempting to govern through the mandarinate though in practice French officials retained effective political control. Most of the rest of Indo-China was governed more directly by the French.

[2] At the same time the French let a few Vietnamese come to Paris as students, thereby providing a schooling for revolutionary intellectual leaders.

assisted by the fact that Chinese forces received the Japanese surrender in the north and thereby blocked the way to a swift resumption of French authority. In the south, where British forces arrived to receive the Japanese surrender, the French were able to regain political control.[1] Compelled to acknowledge the existence of the new Democratic Republic of Vietnam, the French determined to neutralize its influence by surrounding it with puppet regimes and then destroy it by direct military attack. The Dutch, it will be remembered, adopted the same tactics in their dealings with the Republic of Indonesia. Unlike the case of Indonesia, however, that of Indo-China did not immediately become an international issue. The United States was not aroused by the French colonial war in Indo-China until a Communist regime came to power in China in 1949. Before then it did not feel that it had an important stake in Indo-China. The Soviet Union seemed unconcerned; it did not bother to bring the issue before the United Nations.

Nor was there in the beginning any organized opposition to the war in France itself. Gaullists and Vichyites were agreed that French sovereignty had to be re-established. Apart from some workingmen and a few intellectuals, the people of France were firmly wedded to a grandiose conception of national *gloire*, the more so because of the deep humiliations their country had suffered during the Second World War. They wished to retain the illusion that France was still a great power, and the possession of an overseas empire was regarded as a prerequisite for such status. The French version of the ideology of the "white man's burden"—France's *mission civilisatrice*—served as an extraordinarily effective blinder to a rational perception of national interests and political and military facts.[2] Not even the French Communist Party, which participated in the post-war coalition government of France until May, 1947, took a stand in defense of Vietnamese independence.[3] In fact, as the largest political party in the country, it opportunistically appealed to French nationalist sentiment in the hope of winning power. It was only after their expulsion from the government that the French Communists became the major organized opposition in France to the colonial war in Indo-China. The broad-based sentiment in France in favor of retaining French colonial dominions was ruthlessly promoted by the tiny minority who had vested interests in Indo-China. Financial scandals toward the end of the war in Indo-China revealed that members of this group had succeeded in corrupting not only newspapers but some leading politicians as well.

[1] It is perhaps worth noting in passing that the southern region accounted for the bulk of French capital invested in Indo-China.

[2] On August 27, 1946 General de Gaulle declared: "United with the overseas territories which she opened to civilization, France is a great power. Without these territories she would be in danger of no longer being one." (Hammer, *The Struggle for Indochina*, p. 190.)

[3] A directive ordering military operations against the Viet Minh was countersigned by the Communist Vice Premier of France, Maurice Thorez.

Looking further back, it is apparent that, except for those with a direct business or financial stake and those connected with colonial administration, very few Frenchmen were ever well informed about their empire or much interested in it. The popular assumption, if anything, was that territories like Indo-China were friendly and grateful to France. Wilsonian idealism, the democratic welfare state, and the radical anti-imperialist attack from the left were less well developed in France than in Britain. It is not so surprising, therefore, that the Vietnamese determination to achieve independence was neither expected nor really understood. With the Communist Party – which was discredited in 1947 – as the only outlet for French political opposition to the war,[1] French policy in Indo-China was increasingly made by French colonials on the spot. With their petty bourgeois background and Bonapartist outlook, they ensured that control of the Viet Minh liberation struggle would overtly pass into the hands of the Communists. When a Communist regime took over in China as well, the United States accepted the French view that Communism was the real issue at stake. By 1954, Americans were paying about 80 percent of the cost of the French military effort in Indo-China.

Only the defeat of the French and the threat of direct big-power involvement brought the conflict and French colonial rule to an end. By an international settlement negotiated in Geneva in 1954, it was decided to establish a military demarcation line at the seventeenth parallel, but to hold general elections within two years under international supervision in order to bring into being a united country. Laos and Cambodia were recognized as sovereign states; they achieved their political independence as a by-product of what was in effect the Vietnamese liberation struggle. Developments after 1954 will be discussed further in Chapter 5 (Section 13) and Chapter 9 (Sections 14–16).

13 *Concluding Remarks*

In retrospect, it is difficult to avoid the conclusion that the dissolution of colonial rule in South Asia was inevitable. Certainly, once the movement had been given momentum by the withdrawal of Britain from the

[1] The Indo-China war, like the later colonial wars in North Africa, was a boon to the Communist Party in France. In the setting of post-war France, voting for the Communist Party became a natural action for any Frenchman who was against the protracted war in Indo-China, and for a long time the only means whereby he could give political expression to such a view. This should not be forgotten when evaluating the remarkably high percentage of votes for the Communists in the post-war elections in France, although there were many other factors involved. Since Communist votes in the parliament were counted when confidence in the government was questioned, even though after 1947 no government felt it possible to include Communists among its supporters, the French policy toward Indo-China, and later toward the North African colonies, bears part of the responsibility for the collapse of parliamentary democracy in France.

Indian subcontinent, South Asian nationalists in other territories could well feel that "there is a tide in the affairs of men, which, taken at the flood, leads on to fortune." Only the Dutch and French, with their own special notions of national prestige and their relative inability to comprehend their true economic interests, the nature of real power relations, and the incongruity of democracy at home and imperial rule abroad, attempted to stem the tide. In both cases their efforts to reassert their supremacy were humiliatingly swept aside by the compulsion of events and at no small cost to their financial and commercial stake in the region, to say nothing of their influence and goodwill in South Asia and the world at large. By yielding readily to nationalists' demands for independence, Britain, by contrast, not only preserved its economic stake in its former dependencies, but earned their good will and respect as well. This was confirmed by the decision of all save Burma to remain within the Commonwealth. The United States even more purposively ended its colonial venture in the Philippines, while managing to preserve its political and economic assets.

In the colonies, the arrival of independence was a traumatic experience and one that justifies the common description of it as a political revolution. The force and character of its impact varied greatly between different parts of the region according to the colonial policies pursued, the duration of colonial rule, and the manner of its passing. It was most profoundly felt in those territories where the transfer of power was least smooth and peaceful and where the participation of indigenous people in the processes of government had been least encouraged. By what looks like an accident of history, though, as we have shown, there is a close causal relationship, these conditions coexisted in the same territories, with the result that Burma, Indonesia, and the successor states of Indo-China were more handicapped in assuming the responsibilities of independence than were other new states in the region, even taking into account the painful consequences for India and Pakistan of partition (Chapter 6).

All of the new states had to face the fact that independence did not automatically bring about a condition of national consolidation. Part of the legacy of colonialism worked in that direction, but very apparently independence released powerful forces working in the opposite direction. The resulting struggle of the new states to weld their peoples into national communities will form the basic theme of Chapters 7, 8, and 9. Each new state faced the more immediate task of asserting its authority over its territorial inheritance. How individual territorial inheritances came to be determined, and the problems of spatial definition they presented to the new states, will be taken up in the next two chapters.

Chapter 5

THE FRONTIERS OF INDEPENDENCE

In this chapter we shall survey the frontier problems of the South Asian countries against the historical background of events in colonial times.

A number of broadly common impulses and features can be discerned in the expansion, gradual decline, and eventual dissolution of colonial rule and, as will be argued later in many contexts, in their continuing political, social, and economic impact on South Asia. But how particular colonial empires were founded and their boundaries drawn was more fortuitously determined. Generally speaking, the present political map of South Asia is the outcome of the historical interplay of imperial policies and rivalries in the colonial era. In founding their empires, the European colonial powers accorded no more respect to older political entities and their boundaries than suited their interests as they conceived them.

1 *The Advance of Colonial Rule*

The buccaneering merchants of the British East India Company, who were the instrument of British imperialism until after the Indian Mutiny, first gained political control over Bengal and then gradually acquired a dominating influence over lesser states. They were helped in this process by a developing class of Hindu capitalists with a stake in foreign trade and an ingrained hatred of Moslem rule. The quest for cheap supplies, potential markets, and profits from intra-regional trade in Asia, together with the fear of intervention by European rivals, provided the driving impulses behind the extension of British rule on the Indian subcontinent. One step led to another as the British pushed on in search of durable frontiers behind which to consolidate their gains. By the middle of the nineteenth century the frontiers of their direct or indirect rule corresponded, with few exceptions, to the natural boundaries of the subcontinent.

One exception was the Himalayan kingdom of Nepal. After an unsuccessful war against the British in 1814–15, Nepal came under the tutelage of Britain, but otherwise was left to its own devices. However, as a source of Gurkha recruits for the Indian army, it became a valuable auxiliary to British rule in India. In the northeast somewhat impetuous actions on the part of the Burmese gave pretext for an extension of British authority beyond the natural confines of India. Following their conquest of Arakan and Assam, the Burmese threatened to invade Bengal in 1824 in order to subdue local rebels who were constantly crossing the border between British and Burmese jurisdiction. The British reacted by launching a seaborne invasion of southern Burma. Their gain of portions of Burmese territory, including Arakan and Assam, marked the first stage in the subjection of the whole of Burma to British rule.

The search for a secure and stable frontier in the northwest met with less immediate success. The Iranian plateau had long been regarded as the key to the security of northern India, for it was through this region that successive invasion armies had marched. Consequently, even before Russia replaced France after the Napoleonic Wars as the strongest power in Europe and began to expand into Central Asia, the British saw in Russian imperialism a threat to their supremacy in India that could only be countered by bringing Afghanistan under British control. This would also placate Ranjit Singh, the powerful ruler of the Sikhs, an old enemy of Afghanistan but a friend whom Britain valued since his kingdom bordered on British India. However, Britain's efforts in this direction ended in disaster in 1814 when the Afghans successfully revolted against the ruler the British had forcibly imposed on them.

By way of compensation for this humiliation, the British occupied Sind and then annexed the Punjab when the Sikhs turned against them after the death of Ranjit Singh. They thereby extended their dominion over the entire Indian subcontinent. About two-thirds of the area had been acquired by conquest; the remainder had been acquired by negotiations that left local rulers nominally in charge. Having subdued the Sikhs, the British detached Kashmir from their kingdom and handed it over under their paramountcy to a friendly hill-raja named Gulab Singh, who had wrested the plateau of Ladakh from a dynasty of Tibetan origin with their encouragement a few years earlier.[1] It was a dispute over the legal ownership of the northeastern corner of Ladakh that began the present frontier troubles between India and China, which we shall discuss in Sections 6–9.[2]

Although their first attempt to make Afghanistan a reliable buffer between Russia and India had failed miserably, the British did not abandon this aim. By diplomatic pressure and armed intervention, they eventually succeeded in bringing that country under British suzerainty.[3] The Russians then agreed that Afghanistan lay outside their sphere of influence and the British undertook not to annex or occupy it so long as it accepted their political control. Reducing Afghanistan to the status of a buffer state did not, however, guarantee a peaceful frontier between Afghanistan and British India. The principal source of friction was the unruly Pathan tribes who inhabited the inhospitable hill country between the Indus and Kabul. For a short while in the eighteenth century these tribes had formed part of a single Afghan empire. When dynastic strife brought about the collapse of this entity, the Sikhs under Ranjit Singh extended their dominion over the Pathans living between the Indus and the Peshawar Valley. The subjugation of the Sikhs by the British brought this territory under British rule.

[1] In a book entitled *Gulab Singh* (Martin Hopkinson, London, 1930), which he wrote in his youth and republished more than twenty years later, K. M. Panikkar tells the story of this exploit and reproduces a translation of the peace treaty in which the Tibetan and Chinese authorities accepted the loss of Ladakh. Panikkar has reservations about the brutal and sometimes treacherous way Gulab Singh acquired the territory, but his final judgment is full of national pride: "He is the only ruler in India's long history who could be said to have extended the geographical boundaries of India. His conquest and annexation of Ladak . . . is an achievement which writes his name for ever in the history of India. No previous Indian ruler, not even Samaudra Gupta or Akbar, had even dreamed of invading Tibet." (K. M. Panikkar, *The Founding of the Kashmir State: A Biography of Maharajah Gulab Singh,* Allen & Unwin Ltd., London, 1953, p. 151.)

In 1959 the writer asked Panikkar whether he had eulogized Gulab Singh at the request of, or to please, the Maharaja of Kashmir and Jammu, since he was serving as Divan at the latter's court when the book was written. The answer was: "Not at all. The inspiration was entirely patriotic pride."

[2] In Panikkar's view, "The plateau of Ladak does not belong geographically to India." (Panikkar, *Gulab Singh,* p. 74.)

[3] At about the time of the second British invasion of Afghanistan in 1878, Sir Alfred Lyall, the then Foreign Secretary of the Government of India, summed up the predicament of the Amir of Afghanistan in the following stanza:

"Shall I stretch my right hand to the Indus
 that England may fill it with gold?
Shall my left beckon aid from the Oxus? The
 Russian blows hot and blows cold.
The Afghan is but grist in their mill, and the
 waters are moving it fast,
Let the stone be the upper or nether, it grinds
 him to powder at last."

(Quoted in Sir Percy Sykes, *Sir Mortimer Durand,* Cassell & Co. Ltd., London, 1926, p. 151.)

Replacing England with the United States would give these lines a recognizable relevance to the cold war situation in which Afghanistan finds itself today.

Nevertheless, the Amirate of Afghanistan never ceased to claim all the Pathans as its people and the trans-Indus region as part of its realm. Pathan unity became the aim, and sometimes the obsession, of successive Afghan rulers. Some British colonial administrators recognized the unsatisfactory character of the northwestern limits of India. For instance, Sir John Lawrence, the ruler of the Punjab at the time of the Indian Mutiny, favored the restoration of the trans-Indus territory to Afghanistan. He believed this would strengthen British relations with the Afghans and in no way weaken the defenses of India, for, as a contemporary wrote: "The natural and impregnable boundary of our Empire is the Indus."[1] By contrast, the then Governor General felt it was essential to "Hold on to Peshawar to the last."

In the event, the British neither pushed on to incorporate all of the Pathan people within British India nor withdrew to the Indus. The line between Afghan and British authority over the Pathans remained blurred and unsettled. To remove the sources of strain inherent in this situation, the British got Afghanistan to agree in 1893 to define the frontier between their two territories. The frontier they established was named the Durand Line, after Sir Mortimer Durand, the principal British negotiator, and it was this frontier that Pakistan later inherited. Ethnically, economically, and strategically the Durand Line was and is a thoroughly irrational boundary. Although both parties agreed not to interfere in tribal areas outside their jurisdiction, the Afghans continued to exert an influence over the tribes on the British side through bribes, the encouragement of holy wars, and the provision of a refuge against punitive reprisals. The British tried to bring these Pathans under greater control,[2] but their authority over them remained tenuous to the end.[3] A peaceful frontier, in any case, presupposed greater control over the tribes on the other side of the Durand Line. Tribal affairs were so interconnected with the internal politics of Afghanistan that it is doubtful whether the government could have exercised more control in this area even if it had wished to do so. The ending of British suzerainty over Afghanistan in 1921 did not materially alter this situation.

To the British in the nineteenth century, the defensive frontiers of the Indian subcontinent extended well beyond the limits of the territories they

[1] Quoted in Sir William Kerr Tytler, *Afghanistan, A Study of Political Developments in Central and Southern Asia*, 2nd ed., Oxford University Press, London, 1953, p. 130.

[2] Sir Mortimer Durand is quoted as saying: "The tribes are brave enough no doubt, and the country is difficult, but the power of the rupee and of roads and railways is very great." (Sir Percy Sykes, *Sir Mortimer Durand*, Cassell & Co. Ltd., London, 1926, p. 221.)

[3] In the northwest frontier region "the tribes were still treated like tigers in a national park. They could kill what deer they liked in the park; they risked a bullet if they came outside and took the village cattle. That had been the position in 1900 and it was still a fair description in 1947." (Philip Woodruff, *The Men Who Ruled India: The Guardians*, Jonathan Cape, London, 1954, p. 291.)

administered. In the last quarter of the century, particularly, British newspapers and governments were quick to sense Russian intrigue in every tribal disturbance on the northwest frontier. To the British army officer in India the Cossack was the established enemy. The British middle-class investor in India wanted his countrymen to believe that the defense of that colony's northwest frontier was essential to the security of Britain itself.[1] This fear of Russian influence came to lend an entirely new significance to India's neighbors in the minds of its British rulers. That celebrated viceroy, the imperious Lord Curzon, expressed this attitude, as follows:

> India is like a fortress, with the vast moat of the sea on two of her faces, and with mountains for her walls on the remainder; but beyond these walls, which are sometimes of by no means insuperable height and admit of being easily penetrated, extends a glacis of varying breadth and dimension. We do not want to occupy it, but we also cannot afford to see it occupied by our foes. We are quite content to let it remain in the hands of our allies and friends, but if rivals and unfriendly influences creep up to it and lodge themselves right under our walls, we are compelled to intervene, because a danger would thereby grow up that one day might menace our security. That is the secret of the whole position in Arabia, Persia, Afghanistan, Tibet, and as far eastwards as Siam. He would be a short-sighted commander who merely manned his ramparts in India and did not look beyond.[2]

In a way reminiscent of latter-day cold war politicians, the British tried, therefore, to control or restrict the relations of neighboring states with rival imperial powers.

That British trading interests commonly supported, if they did not actually determine, this policy was clearly shown in the case of Tibet. Toward the end of the eighteenth century, Tibet closed its doors to foreigners and in the following century all attempts to open them for trade were unsuccessful. The Tibetans were under the nominal political protection of China and themselves claimed a special influence and position in Ladakh, Sikkim, Bhutan, and other areas south of the Himalayas where they had religious, commercial, and ethnic affinities with the local populations. This situation gave rise to not a few anomalies and ambiguities in the Himalayan border territories; but so long as Tibet itself remained isolated from foreign influences, these had little or no significance for the security of India. The British were anxious to gain access to the Tibetan market, especially for the Bengal tea planters,[3] but the Chinese refused to grant them any concessions. Although it was becoming obvious that China had no

[1] Leland Hamilton Jenks, *The Migration of British Capital to 1875,* Jonathan Cape, London, 1938, p. 232.

[2] Quoted in Guy Wint, *The British in Asia,* Faber & Faber, London, 1947, p. 24.

[3] Tea was one of the few commodities that could be carried through the mountains and there was a considerable market for it in Tibet, which China normally supplied.

power to enforce agreements it negotiated on behalf of Tibet, the Dalai Lama continued to shelter behind its suzerainty to avoid direct dealings with the British. A suspected Russian intrigue at Lhasa, the Tibetan capital, gave Curzon the pretext needed for settling the issue by force. In 1904 a British expedition invaded the country and secured the trading rights and extraterritorial privileges sought by British nationals. Panikkar called the episode "the high-water mark of the 'Empire State' in India."[1] Having opened the Tibetan door to its traders, Britain closed it to Russia a few years later when both countries formally agreed to recognize Chinese suzerain rights in Tibet and to refrain from sending diplomatic representatives to Lhasa. (In the view of the Chinese this agreement did not settle the status of Tibet, for they claimed not only suzerainty but sovereignty over the territory.)

The northern frontier of India was further secured when the British established a protectorate over Sikkim and took over the foreign relations of Bhutan. As a by-product of these diplomatic arrangements and under British pressure, the Tibetans agreed in 1914 to settle upon a boundary for a substantial section of the frontier between Tibet and India. This line became known as the McMahon Line, after Sir Henry McMahon, the principal British representative in the negotiations. Although a Chinese representative initialled the convention incorporating this agreement, the Chinese government refused to ratify it, primarily because it was dissatisfied with the settlement simultaneously suggested for the boundary between China and Tibet. The British promptly entered into a formal agreement with Tibet itself, but it was ominous, as events were later to prove, that China never accepted the validity of this agreement. It took the British over twenty years to show the McMahon Line on their maps, and it was never marked off on the ground.[2] Tibetan officials continued to make expeditions south of it to collect taxes from the tribal peoples who inhabited India's northeast frontier region. But so long as no strong power dominated Tibet, this situation did not threaten the security of India.

Not surprisingly, young Indian nationalists in the pre-independence era felt that Britain sought to push its dominion outward and establish a ring of buffer states around the subcontinent simply to reinforce its imperial rule in India.[3] Except for frequent assertions of non-responsibility for this

[1] K. M. Panikkar, *Asia and Western Dominance,* Allen & Unwin Ltd., London, 1953, p. 162. India had been designated an empire in 1876.

[2] "In those laissez-faire days, with no political problems ahead, we were content just to leave it undefined." (Lord Birdwood commenting on Sir Olaf Caroe's paper "The Geography and Ethnics of India's Northern Frontiers," *Geographical Journal,* Vol. CXVII, Part 3, September, 1960, p. 309.)

[3] In 1921 the All India Congress Committee passed a resolution designed to reassure neighboring states:

"1. that the present Government of India in no way represents Indian opinion and that their policy has been traditionally guided by considerations more of holding India in subjection than of protecting her borders;

and of good will toward all other victims of British imperialism, educated Indians, with the notable exception of Nehru, paid little or no attention to India's relations with neighboring states, the internal fight for independence being all engrossing. But once independence was achieved India felt forced to look at its frontiers and even, as we shall see, to practice buffer state diplomacy. The British could afford to be somewhat complacent about the lack of precision in the boundaries they established, because they had the strength to deal with external challenges and their neighbor to the north was weak. Independent India was not to prove so fortunate.

The imperial structure Britain erected in India was an "Empire State"; from it the authority of British officialdom, in partnership with Indian traders and laborers, radiated to all parts of Asia. It was from India that the British organized the annexation of Lower Burma in 1852 in order to satisfy their trading interests. Upper Burma was seized in 1886 to prevent the growth there of French influence (from Indo-China), which might threaten the security of Lower Burma. An additional motive was provided by commercial interests seeking a trade route to southern China. Burma became a province of India and was directly administered from there, with the assistance of Indian officials and clerks, until after the turn of the century. The administrative connection with India was not formally severed, in fact, until just before the Second World War. Economically, too, Burma became as much a colony of India as of Britain. The Chinese accepted the extension of British influence to their southern boundaries in return for British recognition that Tibet lay within their suzerainty (or even sovereignty). The line between Chinese and British jurisdiction in areas where Tibet did not serve as a buffer was, however, extremely blurred and agreements on it proved difficult to reach or, if reached, to implement, not least because the physical features of the disputed areas had not been adequately surveyed and mapped. In the absence of an agreed line of demarcation, the British arbitrarily extended their administrative control over Burma into disputed terrain and China was too weak to oppose this practice by force. Consequently, when the British left Burma in 1948 some hundreds of miles of Burma's frontier with China had still to be properly delineated.

Imperial appetites and rivalries also reshaped the political map of the

---

"2. that India as a self-governing country can have nothing to fear from the neighbouring states or any state as her people have no designs upon them . . . and

"3. that the people of India regard most treaties entered into with the Imperial Government by neighbouring states as mainly designed by the latter to perpetuate the exploitation of India by the Imperial Power, and would therefore urge the States having no ill will against the people of India, and having no desire to injure her interests, to refrain from entering into any treaty with the Imperial Power."

(Quoted in N. V. Rajkumar, ed., *The Background of India's Foreign Policy,* All India Congress Committee, New Delhi, 1952, p. 44.)

rest of Southeast Asia. When France occupied Holland during the Napoleonic Wars, the British took over Dutch colonial possessions in South Asia to prevent their falling under French control. On the conclusion of these wars, and as part of its policy of restoring a balance of power in Europe, Britain returned Holland's East Indian possessions. It did not, however, return Ceylon, which remained under British rule. Following the British acquisition of a trading base at Singapore in 1819, Britain and Holland agreed that henceforth the Malayan peninsula would be within the British sphere of influence while the Indonesian archipelago would be the special province of the Dutch. Free at last from the intrusions of commercial rivals, the Dutch proceeded to extend their control over the islands in what was coming to be called the Netherlands Indies – though it would not be complete until well into the twentieth century – and began a systematic program of exploitation. Their rule did not encompass all of Borneo island. A British adventurer acquired Sarawak in 1841 and several decades later North Borneo and Brunei came under British protection. The boundaries between Dutch Borneo and its neighbors were agreed on by Britain and Holland in the early part of the present century.

The fact that the Malayan peninsula was reserved for British commercial interests did not immediately bring the whole of it under the formal political protection of Britain. Only when warfare between opposed Chinese mining communities and disorders occasioned by dynastic struggles threatened the prospects for British trade and capital investment did Britain decide to assume political power in the area. The fact that the pace of imperial rivalry was quickening throughout the world also had a bearing on this decision. The Malayan rulers surrendered their independence peaceably, by treaty, and British authorities never established policies and administrative procedures that were uniform throughout the peninsula. This probably accounts in part for the comparatively slow awakening of national political consciousness in Malaya.[1]

At about the same time that the British were consolidating their hold over Lower Burma, the French were establishing a foothold in Indo-China and extending their protection over Cambodia. Every move by Britain and France in their penetration inland from the coastal areas of Southeast Asia heightened the sense of rivalry between them. As already mentioned, it was suspicion of French intentions in the area that led the British to conquer Upper Burma. Like Britain, France was looking for a tradesman's entrance to southern China, and so in the same decade it forcibly established a protectorate over the northern Indo-China territories of Annam and Tonkin. Not long afterward these territories were combined with Cambodia to form a French Indo-Chinese Union, to which was later added the French protectorate of Laos.

[1] Chapter 4, Section 10.

Thailand escaped the fate of Indo-China primarily because Britain was determined to keep it as a buffer state between British and French colonial possessions. Britain no more wished to share a frontier with France in Southeast Asia than with Russia to the northwest. Another reason why Thailand's formal independence was not further encroached on in the era of expanding colonialism was the willingness of its rulers to bring its system of law and order into line with Western practice. Later the First World War put a stop to further imperialist ventures.[1] The Thai rulers were shrewd enough to declare war on Germany in 1917, thereby assuring themselves a place beside the Allies at the Paris Peace Conference. Thailand, nevertheless, had to pay for its freedom from colonial rule by ceding territory to Malaya and Indo-China and granting extraterritorial privileges to Britain, France, and the United States. Also, it did not avoid the heavy dependence on Western and Chinese enterprise and capital that characterized neighboring colonial economies. Nationalism in Thailand, insofar as it existed, thus became focussed not on political independence, but on freedom from the non-Siamese groups and interests that so largely controlled its economy.

2 *The Fortuitous Character of Colonial Dominions*

Broadly speaking, the newly independent states in South Asia owed their territorial make-up – and, as we shall find, the definition of their nationhood – to colonial arrangements which had come about as a consequence of the rivalry between the West European countries that thrust themselves upon the region in the scramble for empire.[2] The outline in the last section of the way in which European imperial powers shaped and reshaped the political map of South Asia is sufficient to show that the main structure of the administrative units they established was not founded on any historical necessity.

Consider first those territories that preserved their political independence. We have just seen how Siam's status was conditioned by the rivalry between the French and the British until the First World War put a stop to further colonial expansion. It is perfectly reasonable to suppose that if the Burmese rulers had shown as much ability to adjust to circumstances as the Siamese, Burma might also have remained independent.[3] The border states of Nepal, Sikkim, and Bhutan retained their independence,

[1] Chapter 4, Section 2.

[2] East and Spate speak of "the disjointed and artificial units" that Western influence "had established for its own purposes." (W. Gordon East and O. H. K. Spate, eds., *The Changing Map of Asia*, 2nd ed., Methuen, London, 1953, p. 223.)

[3] "If Burma could have held fast to her independence to the end of the precarious 19th century, she might have gained her admission into the family of nations." (Maung Maung, *Burma in the Family of Nations*, Djumbatan Ltd., Amsterdam, 1956, p. 2.)

though under conditions not unlike those imposed on the princely states in India, mainly because the British had little to gain either commercially or politically by assuming sovereignty over them. The fact that Afghanistan was not adjoined to British India or Russian Turkistan – or divided between Britain and Russia – can hardly be explained by the stiff resistance the Afghans put up against intruders. Although that undoubtedly played a role, the interest of Britain and Russia in preserving an independent state between their respective territories was a more important factor.

In the case of the main colonial empires, it is even more apparent that historical determinism played no part in the evolution of administrative entities in South Asia. If Britain had not restored Holland's East Indian possessions after the Napoleonic Wars, the territories on both sides of the Malacca Straits would have been ruled by a single colonial power and we might now have a large Malayan state in Southeast Asia, encompassing not only the hundred million people in what is now Indonesia but also the ten million recently brought together in the Malaysian Federation.[1] Or some parts of the East Indies, particularly Sumatra or a portion of it, could well have become politically aligned with neighboring Singapore and Malaya instead of with Java. This is no more difficult to imagine than that with a retouch of history there would have been no boundary, or a different boundary, between the United States and Canada, or that Belgium would not have been created as a state in the 1830's, but would have remained part of Holland or been absorbed by France or divided between these two powers. Likewise, just as Scandinavia through an accumulation of historical accidents came to be divided into several states, so under certain circumstances could the much larger and more heterogeneous Indian subcontinent have been divided into several smaller political units with more cultural and linguistic homogeneity than present-day India or Pakistan. On the other hand, had Britain decided to promote a closer relationship among its territories in South Asia, Ceylon and Burma might have been cast in the same mold as India.[2] In particular, if the British had adopted a different policy in India it might not have been necessary to partition the subcontinent when British rule ended. That, at any rate, as one easily discovers, is still the inner conviction of a good many Indian and Pakistani intellectuals, though it is seldom expressed and is perhaps less ardently believed now that partition is an established fact. Even with-

[1] Section 11; Chapter 9, Section 11.

[2] Indian intellectuals occasionally had a vision of some such broader unity or even a still broader one. For example: "I have no doubt that in any future order Ceylon and India must hang together. My own picture of the future is a federation which includes China and India, Burma and Ceylon, Afghanistan and possibly other countries." (Jawaharlal Nehru, *An Autobiography*, The Bodley Head, London, 1953, p. 608. The quotation is taken from the chapter "Five Years Later" that was added in the 1942 and subsequent editions.)

out assuming a different British policy, it does not require much imagination to see how chance events could have shaped the feelings and behavior of the leading personalities involved in the struggle for independence and thereby changed the course of history.[1]

Reflections about what might have happened under different circumstances are, of course, "unhistorical." For the social scientist, however, they are legitimate and even important. They arm one against the temptation to rationalize an existing situation by giving it teleological significance. We are all prone to find historical necessity and even rationality in political arrangements, and especially political entities, that actually emerged out of an accumulation of chance events.[2] But when this has been said, it remains true that the *status quo* always has significance, and the longer it has been in existence and become hallowed by time, the greater that significance will seem to be.

3 *The Importance of Faits Accomplis*

All the newly independent states had compelling reasons for clinging to the *status quo* as regards their territorial inheritances. Once the transfer of sovereignty had been effected, each new state had to establish its authority over the whole of its territory and it became a matter of national pride or prestige to avoid divisions in what had previously been administered as a single unit. Indeed, since the appeal to nationalism presupposed a clear conception of what the nation meant in terms of area and population, many a new constitution included a general description of the area under its rule. We shall see later that the nationalist appeal was not sufficient to prevent the development of serious internal splits and rebellions. Nor was the sanctity of the territorial legacy of colonial rule always accepted on both sides of every national boundary line. But the first and almost instinctive reaction of every new government was to hold fast to the territory bequeathed to it. What the former colonial power had ruled, the new state must also rule.

The strength of this feeling was strikingly exemplified in Indonesia's persistent claim to Dutch New Guinea or West Irian, a rather distant territory quite unlike the rest of Indonesia. As one easily discovered in contact with Indonesians, this demand was morally and emotionally founded on the fortuitous historical fact that West New Guinea had been administered

[1] See the next chapter.

[2] Appendix 2, Section 3, particularly footnote 1 on page 1848.

As was indicated at the beginning of this chapter, broad trends with an implication of historical necessity can be discerned in some events in South Asia's past. This theme is developed in Chapter 4, Sections 2 and 3, and elsewhere in this book.

by the Dutch as part of a single colony, the Netherlands East Indies.[1] Had the western part of the island of New Guinea originally been a German colony and thus come under Australian trusteeship after the First World War like the eastern part, it is difficult to believe the Indonesians would have been so adamant about possessing it.

By contrast, India's determination to remove the French and Portuguese from their precarious footholds on the subcontinent implied a demand for slightly more than its territorial inheritance from Britain. In fact, India and other Asian states have tended to apply a double standard of judgment to territorial questions. They regard colonial possessions within their borders as "permanent aggressions," which they are prepared to deal with forcibly when it is to their advantage and within their power to do so. But they are quite legalistic when it comes to justifying their own inherited frontiers against neighboring states, even though these boundaries took little or no account of ethnic, cultural, or linguistic criteria and for large stretches were not even carefully defined. These contrasting approaches are clearly illustrated by India's seizure of Goa and by its stand against Chinese claims on its northern boundary. Not surprisingly, this dichotomy of attitude has earned the new states a good deal of opprobrium in the West. Western critics note that while South Asian governments denounce colonialism and all its works, they have formed an intense emotional attachment to one of the most important legacies of colonialism, namely, their own territorial definitions. Apparently, the root of nationalism that is fixed in the possession of a particular piece of territory is particularly strong among South Asians. The very integrity of the new state is felt to be dependent on the maintenance of the *status quo*. In some instances this feeling has been consecrated by legislation infringing on free discussion of boundary questions.[2]

A major exception to the rule that the spatial and political definitions of

[1] "The General Assembly has been told by the distinguished delegate of the Kingdom of the Netherlands that Indonesia sustains a territorial claim to West Irian. Mr. President, that is not true. Indonesia is not sustaining any territorial claim. Indonesia is declaring the right of the Indonesian people to be sovereign and independent within all the territory formerly covered by the Netherlands East Indies. . . . We are sustaining a national claim, and that national claim is the right of our nation to be united and independent." (Dr. Subandrio, Minister of Foreign Affairs of the Republic of Indonesia, in a speech to the United Nations General Assembly, October 6, 1960, *Indonesian News and Economic Bulletin,* November 15, 1960.)

Note that the nation is defined as the people who lived in the former colony of the Netherlands East Indies.

[2] Under the Pakistan Penal Code (Amendment Act) of 1950, for example, it became a criminal offense to condemn the creation of Pakistan or to advocate the curtailment of its sovereignty. Similarly, Section 2 of the Indian Criminal Law Amendment Act of 1961 states that "whoever by words either written or spoken, or by signs, or by visible representation or otherwise, questions the territorial integrity or frontiers of India in a manner which is, or is likely to be, prejudicial to the interests or safety or security of India, shall be punishable with imprisonment for a term which may extend to three years, or with fine or both."

the new states were handed down to them by the colonial powers is, of course, the case of Pakistan and India. It is not a clear-cut exception, however, for, apart from Kashmir, the main line of division between India and Pakistan, and even the principles on which it was drawn, were worked out and accepted under British guardianship (the "Mountbatten Award" of 1947). On the other hand, since both sides participated in the search for a solution to the problem of Moslem disaffection, it cannot be said to have been bequeathed to them by Britain. As partition has exercised a crucial influence on the course of political events in the two countries since independence, a special treatment of it is reserved for Chapter 6. The separation of the Federation of Malaya from Singapore may seem like another violation of our general proposition regarding the continuation of political entities in South Asia. But the government of Singapore had never been integrated with the Malay states so far as British rule was concerned.[1] Nor is the division of Vietnam an exception; like East and West Germany or North and South Korea, it represents a temporary position in the cold war and one that neither protagonist regards as satisfactory.[2] An exception can be made, however, for the more recent inclusion of Singapore, Sarawak, and North Borneo in the Federation of Malaysia; these territories became free of colonial rule only through incorporation.[3]

4 *Enlargement and Unification of Political Entities*

In most cases, colonial domination resulted in the creation of larger political entities than those which existed in pre-colonial times. It also brought a measure of internal consolidation to these new entities.

British India is a striking case in point. The conception of kingdoms under an emperor existed in India long before the arrival of the first European adventurers. Conquest and dominion were prominent elements in the kingly ideal during both the Hindu and the Mogul periods of Indian history. In the dynastic struggles for paramountcy, some rulers succeeded in extending their authority over large portions of the subcontinent. From time to time, Indian rulers even achieved a measure of control over trade routes and strongholds far outside the present-day frontiers of India and Pakistan. Some of these ancient empires, like Asoka's or Akbar's, may have exerted unifying influences over large portions of the Indian subcontinent no less intensive than those of the Roman Empire around the Mediterranean or those of the emperors who attained supra-national dominance in Western and Central Europe during the Middle Ages. But while the vision may have inspired many an Indian ruler and his entourage, not

[1] Chapter 4, Section 10.
[2] Chapter 4, Section 12; Section 13 below; Chapter 9, Section 16.
[3] Section 11.

even the greatest of the Mogul emperors achieved the political unification of the entire subcontinent. By the beginning of the eighteenth century the Mogul empire was visibly disintegrating. War-lordism and struggles for territorial ascendancy among the succession states completed its demise. Just as dissension among the Hindu kingdoms in an earlier period had made them vulnerable to Moslem conquest, so the breakdown of Mogul authority enabled the British to gain a foothold and then expand their authority in the subcontinent. In the main, the lack of unity in India was a condition for, rather than a consequence of, conquest and colonization.

In India, and in Pakistan as well, it is now generally recognized that not only the unification of British India but also the measure of political integration that made possible the creation of two independent states was the result of the last hundred years and more of British rule. The process of unification, and the change-over of colonial rule from crude commercial and fiscal exploitation, had started even before the British government, after the Great Mutiny, took over direct responsibility for India from the East India Company, and continued unfinished to the end of imperial rule. In one of his justly famous American articles on India, published in the early 1850's, Karl Marx depicted rather accurately what was happening and was going to happen.

> The political unity of India, more consolidated, and extending farther than it ever did under the Great Moguls, was the first condition of its regeneration. That unity, imposed by the British sword, will now be strengthened and perpetuated by the electric telegraph. The native army, organised and trained by the British drill-Sergeant, was the sine qua non of Indian self-emancipation, and of India ceasing to be the prey of the first foreign intruder. The free press, introduced for the first time into Asiatic society, and managed principally by the common offspring of Hindoo and Europeans, is a new and powerful agent of reconstruction. The Zemindars and Ryotwar themselves, abominable as they are, involve two distinct forms of private property in land – the great desideratum of Asiatic society. From the Indian natives, reluctantly and sparingly educated at Calcutta, under English superintendence, a fresh class is springing up, endowed with the requirements for government and imbued with European science. Steam has brought India into regular and rapid communication with Europe, has connected its chief ports with those of the whole Southeastern ocean, and has revindicated it from the isolated position which was the prime law of its stagnation.

Marx felt that British industrialists

> have discovered that the transformation of India into a reproducing country has become of vital importance to them, and that, to that end, it is necessary, above all, to fit her with means of irrigation and of internal communication. They intend now drawing a net of railroads over India and they will do it.[1]

[1] "The Future Results of British Rule in India," *New York Daily Tribune,* August 8, 1853.

As usual, Marx overestimated the magnitude and, in particular, the rapidity of the pending changes. He exaggerated the effectiveness of railroads in bringing about industrialization in India, and also the power of spurts of industrialization to induce changes in attitudes and institutions.[1] Nevertheless, he showed remarkable clairvoyance. In hindsight, one century later, we can complete Marx's list of major changes that worked toward political unity, bearing in mind that these innovations were interrelated. In spite of the leeway given to the princely states, which encompassed a third of India, a unified penal code and a fairly comprehensive system of civil law were gradually established. An efficient and well-regulated civil service was also created, which came to include indigenous personnel even at relatively high levels. The creation of an educated class, at which Marx hinted, and the emergence of an intellectual elite came in time to assume greater significance than Marx could have foreseen. Of special importance was the fact that this upper stratum was educated in English and thus acquired a common language.[2]

Similar induced changes operated in other colonial regions in South Asia and there, too, they fostered political unity. It can unreservedly be stated that the conception of the Indonesian archipelago as a nation state is the result of Holland's hegemony in the area and its attempts to tie the islands together politically, administratively, and, to an extent, economically. Despite the perilous road the territory has travelled since the Dutch were driven away by the Japanese during the Second World War, a political climate has been evolving wherein an appeal to Indonesian national unity strikes a chord. Such a concept had no reality in the minds of the pre-colonial rulers of these islands. Much the same process took place in the Philippines and in the states of continental Southeast Asia, though the latter remained smaller and internally less unified for reasons we shall discuss later.

[1] Chapter 10, Section 8 *et passim*.
This reveals the systematic bias present in Marx's belief in rapid spread effects. This view, based on his idea of "modes of production" as a primary determinant of social and cultural change, has been taken over, most often innocently, uncritically, and only implicitly, by contemporary economists in the West and, of course, South Asia. We criticize it in various contexts; see especially Appendix 2, Section 20, and Chapter 24, Section 9.

[2] Panikkar reflects that a different pattern of education would have made a vast difference in India's development: "Had the new education been through the Indian languages, the emphasis of the movement would have been different from province to province, according to the development, flexibility and character of the language used. . . . There would have been no 'master plan' of change and, instead of the Hindu community being unified, it would have split into as many different units as there are languages in India, and would have repeated the pattern of Europe with its conglomeration of mutually hostile units within the same Christian community. From this development India was saved by the common medium of education which Macaulay introduced into India." (K. M. Panikkar, *Asia and Western Dominance*, p. 332.) Cf. Chapter 31, Sections 3 and 4.

5 *Pakistan's Border with Afghanistan*

Some of the new countries in South Asia inherited boundaries from colonial times that are clear and not contested. Ceylon is an island and has no frontier problems. The idea that occasionally emerges in Tamil agitation in southern India that northern Ceylon should belong to a new independent "Tamil-land" elicits no response in New Delhi. Indeed, India has largely ignored even the treatment accorded the Ceylonese and Indian Tamils in Ceylon.[1] Like Ceylon, the Philippines has no problem regarding its territorial domain; its recent claim to North Borneo is obviously concocted and when future history is written it should not require more than a footnote to record this as a passing curiosity. As the West Irian question was not a boundary question, and is in any event now settled, Indonesia would be in the same comfortable situation, except for its conflict with the Federation of Malaysia, with which we shall deal in Section 12.

With the major exception of the partition of British India, as we pointed out in the preceding section, problems of national boundaries did not seem to be very important to the continental South Asian countries either, when they first became independent. As successor states to the European colonies, they took over border lines that had remained unchanged since the First World War. Their paramount concern was to establish their authority within their inherited boundaries and to consolidate their gains. But states outside the region whose territorial integrity had been encroached on by the colonial powers were not always prepared to regard existing frontier lines as fixed and unalterable.

Pakistan, which fell heir to the consequences of British policy in the northwest frontier region of the Indian subcontinent, was among the first of the new states to be reminded of this fact. As was mentioned earlier, the boundary between Afghanistan and British India, the Durand Line, was less a frontier proper than a definition of the limits of Afghan and British suzerainty over the Pathan tribes. It was in any case a thoroughly irrational demarcation, doomed to be perpetually troublesome. More important for Pakistan, it in no way weakened Afghanistan's ambition to unite all the Pathan people within a single Afghan state.

During the last decade of British rule in India, the political leaders of

[1] Chapter 9, Section 2.

India has consistently declined to become involved in defending Indian minorities abroad. It has advised them to identify themselves with the national cause in the country in which they are living, and made it clear that they will have to rely on their own resources. This policy was adhered to, on the whole, even when the independent government in Burma began to drive out the remaining Indian merchants, bankers, and small industrialists after having virtually confiscated their property (see Chapter 9, Part II, and Chapter 17, Section 12). Since there are substantial Indian minorities in many countries all over the world, and these are often maltreated, a different policy would have led to numerous conflicts without India being in a position to exert much effective pressure on offending nations.

India's North-West Frontier Province maintained an alliance with the Indian National Congress and favored unity with India. They were discredited when, in 1947, the Pathans voted to unite with Pakistan instead.[1] Afghanistan thereupon stepped in with a proposal for an independent Paktunistan for all Pushto-speaking people.[2] Considering the trouble the British had in trying to govern the northwest frontier region, it might be argued that Pakistan would have found it easier in the long run to consolidate its holdings without the inclusion of the Pathan territory. But such a confession of weakness at the outset could well have precipitated even more disintegration than actually occurred.[3] At any rate, Pakistan rejected Afghanistan's proposition and relations between the two countries have been strained ever since.[4]

Neither Pakistan nor Afghanistan abandoned its efforts to achieve dominance in the area of the frontier. Agents of both sides have continued to play the traditional game of winning over the tribesmen with rupees and rifles. On occasion Pakistan has intimidated rebellious tribes with the sort of force that earned the British no little opprobrium in the past. At the same time it has tried to provide them with more facilities for overcoming their economic backwardness and isolation. For its part, Afghanistan has played on the Pathan fear of Punjabi domination within the new state of Pakistan, especially when, in 1955, the various subdivisions of its western wing were merged into a single administrative and political unit.[5]

To complicate matters further, the Soviet Union sympathized with the Paktunistan campaign,[6] the United States has had a military alliance with

[1] Had the ballot included the alternative of an independent Pathan state, the Pathan tribes might, as the Congress leader Maulana Abul Kalam Azad argued, have preferred this destiny to unity with Pakistan. On the other hand, independence sentiment could well have been swamped by the wave of Moslem solidarity that followed the Punjab massacres at the time of partition and the manner in which the Hindu ruler of predominantly Moslem Kashmir opted for joining India. At any rate, neither Mountbatten, the British Viceroy, nor Jinnah, the leader of the Muslim League, was prepared to include an independent Pathan state among the choices open to the North-West Frontier Province. (Maulana Abul Kalam Azad, *India Wins Freedom,* Orient Longmans, Calcutta, 1959, p. 195.)

[2] Pathan is the Indianized form of Paktun. There is some ambiguity about Afghanistan's conception of Paktunistan. For one thing, not all Pathans speak Pushto; for another, Paktunistan appears to encompass frontier tribes that are not Pathan. Its geographical limits seem, in fact, to be based on memories of the Afghan empire as it existed in the eighteenth century.

[3] East and Spate, *The Changing Map of Asia,* p. 159 *et passim.*

[4] Afghanistan cast the only vote against the admission of Pakistan to the United Nations.

[5] Chapter 8, Section 3.

[6] The position taken by the Soviet Union seems natural in view of its interest in Afghanistan and Pakistan's political bonds with the United States. The fear Pakistanis sometimes express in private conversation, that the Soviet Union has designs on West Pakistan, had its origin in colonial times; see Section 1 above. Occasionally such a fear is expressed also by Western writers: "For whatever happens in north-western India,

Pakistan since 1952, and both have vigorously wooed Afghanistan with aid. Any interruption of Afghanistan's trade across Pakistan adversely affects American aid shipments, and this became very apparent in 1961 when diplomatic and trade relations between the two disputants were severed after Pakistan closed down the Afghan consulates at Quetta and Peshawar for allegedly engaging in subversive activities among the frontier tribesmen. Although the United States pressed for a settlement, it was not until the middle of 1963 that the border was reopened and diplomatic relations were resumed.[1] Afghanistan has not openly disavowed the cause of Paktunistan.[2] The fact that President Ayub Khan is a Pathan and a number of Pathans are included in his government has probably helped to diminish the appeal of Paktunistan inside Pakistan itself. But in the long run only the full administrative, political, and economic integration of Pakistan's Pathan tribes into the rest of Pakistan is likely to bring permanent peace and stability to that country's border with Afghanistan.

6 *Troubles Brewing on India's Northern Boundaries*

The frontier between India and Tibet also became a trouble spot after the British relinquished their authority in India. We noticed in Section 1 that in the course of opening Tibet to trade and making it a buffer state against Russian influence, the British sought to fix the limits of Tibetan authority on the Himalayan frontier with India. However, the agreement reached on this issue did not resolve all the ambiguities in the situation; neither was it ever recognized by China. Furthermore, the Chinese never renounced their claim that Tibet was an integral part of China: they were simply too weak to enforce it. Therefore, the situation along India's north-

---

there is one great factor in the political development of Central Asia which is likely to increase in importance as time passes. Great areas in Russian territories across the Oxus are being developed and to some extent industrialized. This process will in time lead to a demand for access to the sea, for a port through which Russian merchandise can be exported to the markets of the world, and through which imports may enter Central Asia. There is one port to which access can easily be obtained from the Russian frontier in Central Asia, and only one, the port of Karachi." (W. K. Fraser-Tytler, *Afghanistan*, p. 300.)

The Soviet Union would gain a considerable advantage if it could turn Afghanistan into a Russian satellite. That has not happened. The Soviet Union, like the United States, has moved with great caution on this cold-war frontier.

[1] The departure from office of the Afghan premier, Sardar Mohammam Daud, who had deeply committed himself to the cause of Paktunistan, doubtless facilitated this rapprochement.

[2] As late as 1965, in the general debate of the United Nations Assembly, the Afghan delegate referred to the issue as one involving a population much larger than that of Kashmir, which had been deprived of the right of self-determination, though he "hoped that the issue would be solved peacefully." (*Indiagram*, October 16, 1965, issued by Information Service of India, Stockholm.)

Figure 5–1

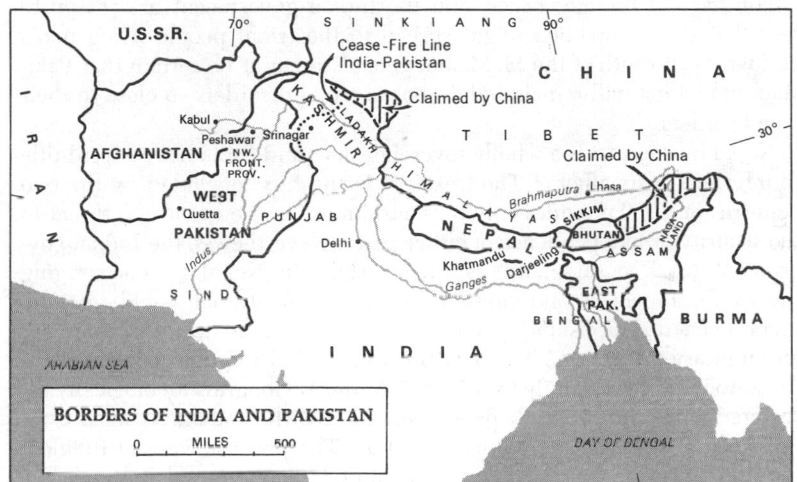

BORDERS OF INDIA AND PAKISTAN

ern frontier was bound to change when a strong government arose in China and British power was withdrawn from the subcontinent.

Even before India attained formal independence, it had received and rejected a protest from the Chinese Kuomintang government about the activities of Indian government officials in the Assam tribal areas south of the McMahon Line. Very shortly after this, Tibet asked for the "return" of what it called "Tibetan territory," extending from Assam to Ladakh and specifically including such areas as Sikkim and Darjeeling. In reply the new Indian government sought and obtained an assurance from Tibet that it would continue to honor the arrangements that had been worked out with the British.

Although naturally disinclined to admit the parallel, India continued the buffer state policies the British had applied to the small kingdoms bordering the Himalayas. Sikkim was declared an Indian protectorate in 1949 and a treaty concluded with Bhutan the same year obliged that state to accept Indian "guidance" on foreign affairs and defense. The Indian government never doubted that it should maintain the control the British had established over these states; the only question was the form such control should take. When the Chinese arrived on the northern frontiers of Sikkim and Bhutan, the Indians felt that the wisdom of their decision to continue the British policy had been confirmed. In another strategic area of the country, the corner bordering on East Pakistan and Tibet, the Indian government has been waging a long-drawn-out war against a separatist rebellion among the Naga tribes, which apparently seek much the same relationship with India as that enjoyed by Bhutan and Sikkim.

The concession of separate statehood for Nagaland within the Indian Union has not brought peace, and the Indian government has reason to fear that the disaffection might spread to the tribal people living north and west just south of the McMahon Line. Nor can it be certain that Pakistan and China will remain indifferent to tribal disorders so close to their own frontiers.

Nepal by contrast is a wholly sovereign state and India has no legal title to interfere in its affairs.[1] The treaty of friendship concluded by the two countries in 1950 provides only for consultation in the event of a threat to the security or independence of either party. Nevertheless, the Indian government tried to safeguard its special stake in Nepal by encouraging the establishment of a representative government that could institute much needed reforms and would look to India for advice, economic aid, and military protection.[2] The overthrow in 1950 of the century-old rule of the autocratic Rana family by a Nepali National Congress ideologically associated with, and probably partly financed by, the Indian National Congress was a welcome step in that direction. The promise was not fulfilled, for after a brief and turbulent experiment in parliamentary democracy, the King of Nepal in 1960 dismissed his pro-Indian ministry, arrested its leaders, banned all political activity, and reimposed direct rule. The Indian government did not conceal its disapproval of these actions.

Through the years, Nepali nationalism has become increasingly tinged with anti-Indian sentiment. Articulate Nepalis resented the interference of Indian civilian and military advisers, the penetration of Indian capital, Indian control over their foreign trade and tariff policies, and the generally patronizing attitude Indians exhibited toward them. A more recent source of estrangement has been the safe haven and moral support India has given to the emigré opponents of the present autocratic monarchy in Nepal. India's influence in Nepal was further undermined when the latter established diplomatic relations with other countries, notably the Soviet Union, the United States, and China, and began to be wooed by them with aid. Signs that Nepal intended to follow a policy of non-alignment in regard to India and China particularly disconcerted Indian opinion. In 1961 Nepal signed an agreement with China settling the hitherto undelimited borders between them. In the following year these two countries reached an agreement concerning the construction of a road linking Lhasa with Khatmandu. Equally disturbing, from the Indian point of view, is the fact that landlocked Nepal has recently been cultivating closer relations with Pakistan in order to reduce its dependence on India for channels of

[1] Britain recognized Nepal's independence in 1923.

[2] As Nehru stated on December 6, 1950: "India had . . . a stake in assuring that nothing went wrong in Nepal and that the Himalayan barrier was not crossed or weakened, because that would be a risk to India's as well as Nepal's security." (Girihal Jain, *India Meets China in Nepal,* Asia Publishing House, Bombay, 1959, pp. 23–24.) China could be the only possible intruder across "the Himalayan barrier" at this time.

international communication and foreign trade. India's attempt to mold the political evolution of Nepal in its own image and to establish some kind of *de facto* protectorate over it has thus suffered some sharp rebuffs. This appears to have made India more sensitive to Nepalese feelings and less inclined to take the friendship of its small northern neighbor for granted.

7 *The Beginnings of India's Border Conflict with China*

The backwash effects of Indian independence on Nepal and other northwestern border areas would not have made India uneasy about the security of its Himalayan frontier but for one new factor: the presence from 1949 on of a unified and militarily strong China on the other side. This is a situation the British never had to face and it has given rise to a bitter and protracted border conflict. Since the conflict made a deep impression on the Indian public and had repercussions in the political and economic sphere, its origins and character deserve some detailed attention.

In 1950 Chinese forces marched into Tibet to "liberate" it from "imperialist intrigue" and its antiquated theocratic "feudalism." Even the Kuomintang government on Formosa considered that this was a purely Chinese affair[1] and accordingly it joined the Soviet Union, India, and others in blocking a Tibetan appeal to the United Nations. Stripped of its ideological purpose, the new Chinese government's attitude toward Tibet was as much a legacy from the past as India's. But whereas Britain had had the strength to impose its views on China, which in any event was disunited and feeble under the tutelage of the rival great powers, independent India was weak economically and militarily and in no position to face down a united and strong China. It could only counsel the Chinese to settle their relations with Tibet peacefully and deplore their resort to military force. The Chinese government offended the Indians by replying that their mild protest in the last regard had been "affected by foreign influences hostile to China in Tibet." Although the subsequent Chinese involvement in the Korean War inclined Indians to believe that the peace of the region was more threatened by events in Korea than by events in Tibet, Nehru felt constrained to warn China that India would resist any transgression of its northern frontier with Tibet.[2]

It was on a rather different basis that India rested its hopes for tranquil-

[1] It differed from the Chinese Communist government only in that it regarded Tibet as an integral part of the fictitious Republic of China rather than the People's Republic of China. The British and the Americans also regarded Tibet as part of China.

[2] "The McMahon Line is our boundary, map or no map. We will not allow anybody to come across that boundary." (Nehru to the Indian Parliament, November 20, 1950, *India-China Border Problem,* Bureau of Parliamentary Research, Congress Party in Parliament, Woovin Press, New Delhi, 1960, p. 4.)

lity along the roughly 2,000 miles of frontier it now shared with China. In a trade agreement concluded with China in 1954 India renegotiated the basis of its relationship with Tibet. It recognized, in effect, Chinese sovereignty over Tibet and renounced all the extraterritorial privileges in Tibet it had inherited from the British. In addition, the two signatories agreed in the preamble to the trade treaty to base their relations on Panch Shila, or the five principles of co-existence, one of which was respect for each other's territorial integrity and sovereignty.[1] The doctrine of Panch Shila gave moral expression to India's policy of non-alignment in world affairs; it was India's answer to the approach to international relations epitomized by security pacts and military alliances.[2] Its principles gained wide currency in India, where they were thought to reflect the traditional background and temper of a people reared on the precepts of Buddhism and Hinduism and the teachings of Gandhi.[3] Nehru himself was, of course, aware of the dynamics of power politics in world affairs; but, as one of his biographers has remarked, "the most compelling experience in his life was the struggle for freedom by non-violent means. He assumes, therefore, that

[1] The other four were: mutual non-aggression, non-interference in each other's internal affairs, equality and mutual benefit, and peaceful co-existence.

[2] India concluded Panch Shila agreements with Cambodia, Ceylon, Egypt, Indonesia, Poland, the Soviet Union, and Yugoslavia, among others.

[3] "The doctrine of *panchshila* might claim to be as old as the Buddha whose precepts of peace were enshrined in the rock edicts of Asoka and echoed more than two thousand years later in Gandhi's teachings. Through the thought of these three teachers runs the recurring theme of means and ends. Buddha taught that through the Noble Eightfold Path – right views, right intention, right speech, right action, right livelihood, right effort, right mindfulness, right concentration – lay the road to nirvana wherein he who attains nirvana attains all knowledge of the truths and is emancipated. Good means make for good ends, Gandhi constantly preached." (Frank Moraes, *Jawaharlal Nehru, A Biography,* Macmillan, New York, 1956, p. 442.)

India's political philosophy has not always been non-violent, however, and its pacificism in world affairs may more credibly be traced to other influences, as the following quotation suggests:

"The Indian Ocean and the high Himalayas have effectively isolated India and barred easy movement from without. This has made the Indian mind largely isolationist. Indian isolationism has been accentuated by three other characteristics – wholly Indian. Indian society has always been continental; until recent times there has been little mobility of movement even from region to region. India's vast spaces have the effect of imprisoning the minds of her people; little interest is evinced beyond the vast internal horizons. The outer geographical framework of India was permanently fixed by nature; at times the expansionist ambitions of an outsider may have resulted in the nibbling of small fringes of territory in the northwest or the northeast regions of India. Such temporary shiftings of frontier in the remotest parts were inconsequential events in India's long history. The energy of everyone – indigene or the foreigner – was fully extended in reaching up to the limits set by geography and there was no need to look at India's neighbours with greed or envy or covet any part of a neighbour's territory. India's pacific intentions were mainly dictated by this, apart from any philosophical detachment. Thirdly, Hinduism as a religion is exclusively confined to its own territorial limits and has no extra-territorial affiliations unlike Christianity and Islam. Hinduism has been responsible for political incapacity and pragmatic indifference to the existence of neighbours." (C. S. Venkatacher, *Geographical Realities of India,* Far Eastern Economist Pamphlet, No. 34, 1955, p. 40.)

this technique of political action can also serve to mitigate world tensions."[1]

It is clear that the Indian policy of non-alignment and Panch Shila was based on a realistic appreciation of national self-interest. India hoped to create a network of international relationships that would minimize the need for heavy defense expenditures.[2] Thus the Panch Shila agreement with China was thought to commit the Chinese to certain principles of international conduct that would ensure the security of India's northern frontier.[3] It erected a moral barrier against aggression that relied for its support on the opprobrium that would attach to any violation of its principles – the assumption being, of course, that China would not risk alienating Asian opinion in this way. In the competitive situations fashioned by the cold war this policy brought India prestige and supplied its intellectual elite with an important source of national pride. The Panch Shila agreement with China, Nehru's assurances that all was well,[4] and a certain traditional belief in the impregnability of the Himalayan barrier[5] gave the Indians confidence in the security of their northern frontier in the years immediately following the Chinese occupation of Tibet.

Yet soon after the conclusion of their Panch Shila agreement with India, the Chinese published maps showing large stretches of Indian territory as part of China and reports reached the Indian government of Chinese infringements on its northern frontier. The Chinese explained to Nehru that the maps were old Kuomintang ones, which they had not yet revised, and that, while the McMahon Line established by "British imperialism" was not fair, they would recognize it for all practical purposes as the boundary of China with India. Nevertheless, reports of Chinese intrusions continued

[1] Michael Brecher, *Nehru: A Political Biography,* Oxford University Press, London, 1959, p. 562.

[2] "We want at least 10 or 15 years of peace in order to be able to develop our resources." (Jawaharlal Nehru, "Independence and After," March 22, 1949, in *Speeches,* Government of India, Delhi, 1949–1958, Vol. 1, p. 258.)

[3] As Nehru reminded his countrymen: "If we have to think of any policy that we may have to pursue in regard to the Chinese State we have to remember that we have a frontier of roughly 2,000 miles with them and we are neighbours today, tomorrow and in the future." (*India News,* March 21, 1952, p. 96.)

"If India did not pursue a policy of friendship with China, many Indians feel, it would find it harder to retain its posture of non-alignment with any grouping of major powers. More important the country would then be saddled with defense commitments far more extensive than the present security arrangements along its northern frontiers in Nepal." (Phillips Talbot and S. L. Poplai, *India and America, A Study of Their Relations,* Council on Foreign Relations, New York, 1958, p. 135.)

[4] "I see absolutely no danger – external danger – to India from communism or any other source." (Nehru in a B.B.C. interview, June 12, 1953 and quoted in J. C. Kundra, *Indian Foreign Policy 1947–1954, A Study of Relations with the Western Bloc,* J. B. Wolters, Groningen, Netherlands, 1955, p. 69, f.n. 2.)

[5] In Panikkar's view the Himalayan barrier had fostered in Hindus "a false sense of security, a Maginot-line mentality." (K. M. Panikkar, "The Himalayas and Indian Defense," *India Quarterly,* Vol. III, No. 2, 1947, p. 135.)

and China's official maps remained unaltered. The impression left by later events is that the Chinese had not at this time completed the surveys of the frontier areas that they had begun after occupying Tibet, and consequently had little first-hand knowledge of the actual extent of the claims shown on old Chinese maps.

It also came out later that between March 1956 and October 1957 the Chinese had constructed a motor road linking Sinkiang with Tibet across the desolate and virtually uninhabited Aksai Chin salient of northern Ladakh.[1] In October, 1958, an official Indian protest against this transgression of their territory was dismissed by China as an interference with Chinese sovereignty. Nehru subsequently stated that the Indian government knew nothing about the existence of the Sinkiang-Tibet highway across the Aksai Chin area until the summer of 1958.[2] This appeared to indicate, as the Chinese were quick to point out, the absence of any effective Indian jurisdiction over an area claimed to be legally Indian. But when officials of the two countries came together in 1960 to examine the evidence supporting their respective boundary claims, the Indian side presented records of military patrols carried out in the Aksai Chin salient from 1951 to 1958 to prove that they maintained effective control in the area.[3] On this evidence it is scarcely credible that the Indians had neither come across the numerous Chinese soldiers, surveyors, and laborers who were engaged for more than three years in planning and constructing the Sinkiang-Tibet highway nor heard about their activities from the Ladakhis who visited the area every year for pasture and salt.

Nehru seemed genuinely shocked to have learned so late of the highway's existence. The obvious inference, in the words of one shrewd commentator, is

> that knowledge of what was going on was kept from Mr. Nehru by persons in high position more strongly, or more recklessly, committed than he was to winning the favour of China. Such persons were to be found among those most directly concerned with the contest with Pakistan in Kashmir, that is to say, in the Kashmir State Government and in the Indian Defence Ministry.[4]

[1] This was the route followed by the Chinese forces when they moved into western Tibet in 1950.

[2] From an Indian patrol "we learnt that there was a part of this road in Indian territory. This was a year ago, roundabout the end of September last year [1958] when we knew with some definiteness that there was this road which had crossed our territory in Aksai Chin." (Nehru to the Indian Parliament, November 25, 1959, from *India-China Border Problem.*)

[3] India, Government of, *Report of the Officials of the Governments of India and the People's Republic of China on the Boundary Dispute,* Ministry of External Affairs, 1961, p. 143.

[4] G. F. Hudson, "The Aksai Chin," *St. Anthony's Papers,* No. 14, Far Eastern Affairs, No. 3, Chatto & Windus, London, 1962, pp. 20–21.

Krishna Menon, the then Indian Defense Minister, was the most prominent official to be suspected. To turn a blind eye to China's construction of a road across a remote, worthless, and strategically indefensible slice of Indian territory may well have struck those in the Indian government who knew about it all along, as a very small price to pay for Chinese friendship or neutrality in the event of a military showdown with Pakistan over Kashmir. The strategy misfired only when the Chinese formally claimed the territory as their own.

This episode has been discussed at some length for two reasons. In the first place, the Aksai Chin salient constitutes the hard core of China's frontier demands on India. Secondly, the disclosure of the apparently furtive and deceitful way in which the Chinese had built the Sinkiang-Tibet highway – in what to Indians appeared to be a clear violation of the principles of Panch Shila – so aroused and offended the articulate layers of Indian society as to make it impossible for the Indian government to negotiate an immediate frontier settlement that would, through outright cession or permanent lease, leave China in control of the Aksai Chin salient in return for its formal endorsement of the McMahon Line.[1]

The outbreak of widespread rebellion in Tibet in the early part of 1959 also contributed to the developing border tension between India and China. The Dalai Lama and tens of thousands of Tibetans sought refuge in India from Chinese retribution and some border clashes with Indian patrols probably resulted from Chinese efforts to block the escape routes through the Himalayas. Indian feeling ran high against the Chinese and much sympathy was expressed for the Tibetans and the "God-King" Dalai Lama. On the Chinese side, the way the Dalai Lama was allowed to hold press conferences in India, at which he appealed for United Nations action and claimed to be the only true governor of Tibet, strengthened Chinese suspicions that the rebellion was being directed from Indian soil.[2]

[1] It was not until the Indian government published a white paper on September 8, 1959, containing documents bearing on Sino-Indian relations since 1954, that the articulate Indian public became fully aware of and aroused by the Chinese frontier intrusions and the notes exchanged about them.

In the first public phase of the Sino-Indian border dispute Nehru was still prepared to regard the Aksai Chin area as a separate issue. On September 12, 1959 he told the Indian Parliament: "The place, Aksai Chin area, is in our maps undoubtedly. But I distinguish it completely from other areas. It is a matter of argument as to what part belongs to us and what part belongs to somebody else. This has nothing to do with the McMahon Line. It has nothing to do with anything else. That particular area stands by itself. It has been in the challenge all the time. . . . I cannot say what parts of it may not belong to us and what parts may. The point is, there has never been any delimitation in that area and it has been a challenged area – bits of it; I cannot say which bit is and which not." (*India-China Border Problem*, p. 73.)

[2] Nehru was clearly embarrassed by the impression that India was giving sanctuary to a government and not simply a number of individual refugees. On September 10, 1959 he warned the Dalai Lama not to claim any relation between Tibetan sovereignty

The Chinese regarded the Tibetan refugees who fled to the Lamaist Buddhist centers in the northern borderlands of India as actual or potential subversive agents and felt that it was necessary to demarcate effectively, and seal, the border with India in order to negate their influence.[1]

The border affrays that followed in the wake of the Tibetan uprising and the official disclosure of the Sinkiang-Tibet highway across the Aksai Chin area put an end to private diplomatic exchanges between India and China about their frontier dispute. What replaced them was more in the nature of a public debate through diplomatic channels. From this the Indian public learned that China not only repudiated the "illegal" McMahon Line, but laid claim to some 50,000 square miles of territory lying south of it and in Ladakh as well. In 1960, officials from the two governments met to examine all the evidence in support of their opposing claims, but no conclusions were reached and what Nehru called "the game of military chess" on the frontier continued with the opposing forces maneuvering for position and occasionally clashing.

The Indian argument for its inherited frontier line is better documented than the Chinese brief for a different alignment;[2] but in neither case can the evidence be regarded as conclusive. Each side has used ambiguous definitions; appealed to maps, travellers' accounts, historical traditions, and legends of uncertain foundation; and cited treaties of doubtful legality or open to varied interpretations. Each side could easily justify its position by going back into history to the point most favorable to its cause. Despite this, it is evident that whereas the Indians have presented a legal case, the Chinese have put forward a political one. The Chinese contend that the whole dispute, and the McMahon Line in particular, is a legacy of British "imperialist aggression." It follows that to claim, as the Indians do, that the McMahon Line is legally valid is to defend British imperialism. Thus while China is anxious to right the wrongs and humiliations inflicted by colonialism, the Indians, so the Chinese argue, are only concerned with profiting from them; this puts India firmly in the imperialist camp.[3] India

---

and the McMahon Line. (H. E. Richardson, *Tibet and Its History,* Oxford University Press, Toronto, 1962, p. 231.) But on Indian soil in March, 1963, the Dalai Lama publicly proclaimed a new constitution for "free Tibet."

[1] Chou En-lai's letter to Nehru, September 8, 1959, *Documents on the Sino-Indian Boundary Question,* Foreign Language Press, Peking, 1960, p. 12.

[2] See, for example, India, Government of, *Report of the Officials,* p. 30.

[3] "China and India are both countries which were long subjected to imperialist aggression. This common experience should have naturally caused China and India to hold an identical view of the above-said historical background and to adopt an attitude of mutual sympathy, mutual understanding and fairness and reasonableness in dealing with the boundary question. The Chinese Government originally thought the Indian Government would take such an attitude. Unexpectedly to the Chinese Government, however, the Indian Government demanded that the Chinese Government give formal recognition to the conditions created by the application of the British policy of aggression against China's Tibet region as the foundation for the

has either evaded this argument by asserting that its present boundary lines were established before British rule,[1] which is doubtful, or faced up to it by replying that states must often take boundaries as they find them, since in the final analysis all boundaries are the outcome of conquest at some time in the past.[2] In the Indian view, the anti-imperialist argument is a counsel of confusion and chaos since it logically calls for a reconsideration of all territorial limits, including those of China itself.

India has chosen to appeal to international law to justify the frontiers fixed by an imperial policy the Indian Congress movement denounced in its younger days.[3] It readily disavowed the extraterritorial privileges it inherited in Tibet as a disreputable legacy of British imperialism, but refuses to acknowledge that the McMahon Line is also one of the sins of the same imperialism. The Chinese themselves, however, are in no small degree responsible for the rigidity of the Indian position. Their arbitrary actions on the frontier so aroused Indian nationalism as to leave the In-

---

settlement of the Sino-Indian boundary question." (Chou En-lai's letter to Nehru, September 8, 1959, *Documents on the Sino-Indian Boundary Question*, p. 2.)

How can the Indian Government "claim the boundary line which Britain unlawfully created through aggression against Tibet and which even includes areas to which British authority had not extended as the traditional customary boundary line . . . ? If this assertion is maintained, the inevitable conclusion to be derived would be that the British colonialists were most fair minded while oppressed China was full of undisguised ambitions; that the powerful British imperialism was, for the past one hundred years and more, invariably upholding the traditional Sino-Indian boundary, while the weak China was ceaselessly encroaching upon British territory! The Chinese Government believes that no one would accept this conclusion." (Chou En-lai's letter to Nehru, December 26, 1959, *ibid.*, pp. 54–55.)

Despite the language used by Chou En-lai, his attitude toward the McMahon Line is more traditional and nationalist than ideological. A confirmation of this came from the Chinese refugee government on Formosa when, at the height of the Chinese assault on India's northern border in October, 1962, it protested to the United States about the latter's recognition of the McMahon Line as the international boundary between India and China.

[1] See, for example, the Indian Government Note to the Chinese Government, April 30, 1962, quoted in *Overseas Hindustan Times*, May 10, 1962.

[2] ". . . all great States have been built up by conquest, violent conquest, and if you apply the theory, the Chinese State was not born complete in itself when civilization began." (Nehru to the Indian Parliament, September 12, 1959, *India-China Border Problem*, p. 74.)

[3] The Indian government has even been driven to find arguments to justify the treaty-making powers of Tibet at the time the McMahon Line was negotiated, although neither Britain nor any other country ever recognized Tibet as a separate and fully sovereign national state.

It is also significant that in referring to the changed conditions that made the plebiscite that India and Pakistan agreed to hold in Kashmir no longer appropriate, Krishna Menon, India's spokesman in the United Nations, invoked the doctrine of *rebus sic stantibus:* "It is a well established principle of international law that a treaty ceases to be binding when the basic conditions upon which it has been founded have essentially changed. . . . No international tribunal has so far rejected the validity of this doctrine. Otherwise we would not have a dynamic international society." (Quoted in *Link*, May 13, 1962.)

dian government little room to negotiate a settlement based on a realistic appraisal of national self-interest. India's apparent stubbornness, in turn, provoked the Chinese into applying more forceful pressure to bring the Indians to the bargaining table. What began as a number of minor frontier disputes of no great practical importance thus became, by a process of cumulative causation, a major border conflict of far-reaching consequence.

To underline India's obduracy and isolate it diplomatically, the Chinese point to their friendly and conciliatory border agreements with Burma (1960), Nepal (1961), Mongolia (1962), Pakistan (1963), and Afghanistan (1963). The agreement with Pakistan concerning the border between Sinkiang and Pakistan-occupied Kashmir particularly incensed Indian opinion. In the first place, China, unlike the Soviet Union and its allies, now refused to support India's claim to sovereignty over the whole of Kashmir,[1] and consequently denied India's competence to discuss the boundary between Pakistan-occupied Kashmir and Sinkiang. Pakistan for its part naturally welcomed the Chinese acknowledgment that Kashmir was disputed territory. Secondly, Pakistan and China agreed that the 300-mile frontier between the two areas in question had never been formally delineated and demarcated, an admission that came perilously near to giving India's case away. The Pakistanis did not bother to conceal their delight at the hurt this agreement inflicted on India; but they also had other reasons. Undemarcated frontiers, as the Indians know better than anyone else, can be perpetual sources of trouble. Faced with unfriendly neighbors in India and Afghanistan, Pakistan understandably wished to reduce the risk of conflict with China. Fortunately, it was able to enter into negotiations free from the rhetorical commitments to which the Indian government has tied itself since 1959.

There is nothing in the agreement that is inconsistent with Pakistan's alliances, and India's interests are safeguarded by the inclusion of a provision for fresh negotiations once the dispute over Kashmir is settled. Pakistan lost no territory it actually controlled and gained some that had been under Chinese jurisdiction. Nevertheless, the Indian government and press bitterly criticized it for surrendering some 21,000 square miles of Kashmir, a criticism no doubt intended to convince Asian and Western opinion that India is not being stubborn with China over trifling bits of territory. In fact, what Pakistan is alleged to have surrendered was no more than a claim on a map. With more skillful diplomacy India might well have reached a similar settlement with China. The border agreement with Burma will be commented on in Section 9.

[1] This was apparently a somewhat new position on the part of China, motivated by the brewing conflict with India. The writer is informed that before the outbreak of that conflict the Chinese government had let it be known through diplomatic channels that it would not tolerate Kashmir's joining with Pakistan, which China considered a satellite of its enemy, the United States.

8 *India's Undeclared War with China and Its Aftermath*

As it was, by the middle of 1962 the Chinese, according to India, had occupied over 12,000 square miles of Indian territory and showed no signs of abating their pressure. In October of that year Nehru ordered the Indian army to go on the offensive,[1] and the Chinese countered swiftly with a large-scale invasion of the northeastern frontier area at several points and further advances in Ladakh.[2] Neither side formally declared war or risked all-out war by throwing its air forces into the contest. The two countries did not even break off diplomatic relations. Handicapped by the terrain (which favored an attacker from the north), inadequately equipped and supplied, and, as commonly alleged in India, badly led, the Indian army proved no match for the Chinese forces. Having decisively demonstrated their military superiority, the Chinese suddenly halted their lightning advance, unilaterally declared a cease-fire, and withdrew to their own side of the McMahon Line on condition that the Indian army make no attempt to reoccupy the territory they had vacated. This left them still in control of the Aksai Chin salient in Ladakh and put the onus for continuing the hostilities on India. The Indian public was offered a variety of reassuring reasons for the sudden Chinese withdrawal. It was said to be due to Russian pressure, a reluctance to alienate Asian opinion, a failure to gauge the speed and scale of Western assistance to India, the unity and solidarity of Indian resistance, and, more credibly, the obvious difficulties of extended supply lines during a Himalayan winter. Some Indian commentators managed to interpret the Chinese withdrawal as a Chinese defeat.

Acceptance of the situation created by the withdrawal of the Chinese formed the basis, broadly speaking, of the truce terms drawn up at Colombo by a small group of non-aligned states led by Ceylon. With some misgivings, India accepted these proposals in detail and demanded that China do likewise before negotiations were resumed. The Chinese, however, have accepted them only in principle and not in detail. Their sticking point has been the proposal that they allow Indian civilian posts on their side of the line they established in Ladakh. The presence of Indians behind the Chinese claim line would be a symbolic affirmation of India's

[1] When the Indian offensive was scheduled, the Western press carried obviously inspired articles playing up the efficiency of the Indian army and its role in upholding the great traditions of the British era, and depreciating the fighting strength of the Chinese.

[2] The United States Ambassador to India at the time, Professor John Kenneth Galbraith, is reported to have commented on the situation as follows: "During the preceding summer, there had been evidence of increasing pressure and support from various sources in India for military action to move the Chinese out of the area which they claimed. In light of this, one can imagine the Chinese coming up with the notion of a major military demonstration to show the Indians that this kind of military policy had no future." (American Academy of Arts and Sciences, *Bulletin,* January, 1965, pp. 2–3.)

right to the larger area of Aksai Chin. At the beginning of 1966 there is still no formal settlement and none in sight.

The tactical deadlock over conditions for a resumption of official talks does not alter the fact that the Chinese are in possession of what they evidently wanted all along. Whatever other aims have motivated their actions, their primary objective throughout the dispute has been possession of the Aksai Chin salient with its strategic highway between Sinkiang and Tibet.[1] Their concentrated assault on the northeast frontier area of India was mainly a punitive expedition to convince the Indians that they had no choice but to concede Aksai Chin in Ladakh in return for formal Chinese recognition of the McMahon Line in the former region. In Ladakh, China has imposed a *de facto* border settlement that the Indians can hardly hope to upset by force, and one that appears not altogether unreasonable considering that the Aksai Chin area was virtually uninhabited and of no practical value to India.

China's actions placed the Indian government in a difficult position. In the face of intense anti-Chinese feeling at home, it could not add national humiliation to military defeat by conceding the Chinese territorial gains in Ladakh; nor could it hope to redeem its pledge to clear the Chinese from Indian soil and avenge the national honor by engaging in further battle. The face-saving Colombo proposals provided a respite from this problem, but the government still had to contend with the domestic repercussions of the conflict. Articulate Indians felt that the doctrine of Panch Shila had failed in its purpose with regard to China, and they demanded a credible military deterrent to take its place. That demand could not be met, however, without additional defense expenditures and considerable military assistance from abroad. The national effort required to support the former drew attention to the deficiencies of government policy, performance, and leadership at home. The decision to secure foreign military aid raised doubts abroad and at home about the traditional Indian policy of non-alignment.

The Indian government continues to proclaim the necessity for non-alignment in world affairs, but the collapse of its China policy has dissipated the moral and emotional climate surrounding this concept. Nehru put the seal of finality on public disillusionment when he told his countrymen: "We were getting out of touch with reality in the modern world. We were living in an artificial atmosphere of our own creation."[2] The admission did not fail to produce wry comments from Western countries long

[1] This has been a strategic aspiration of Chinese military commanders since 1911, when the Tibetans took advantage of revolutionary disorders in China to drive the Chinese garrisons from their country and declare themselves independent. Cf. Hudson, "The Aksai Chin," *St. Anthony's Papers*.

[2] *The Guardian*, October 26, 1962.

irked by Indian moral preaching. Western governments responded readily to Nehru's urgent appeal for assistance at the height of the crisis, though it soon became apparent that they expected India in return to make an earnest effort to settle its Kashmir dispute with Pakistan. None of them, however, showed much inclination to kindle a major war between India and China. The Soviet Union had even less of a desire to see the border flare-up develop into a full-scale conflict. Nehru appreciated the difficult position of the Soviet Union and tried to play down the cold war aspect of the struggle by emphasizing that India was opposing China and not Communism. Nevertheless, the Indian public was disappointed by the lack of more effective Russian support for its cause.

The non-aligned countries seemed more concerned with preventing the conflict from spreading than with its merits and causes, an attitude India itself had often adopted in the past. This was the more natural because their notion of non-alignment had largely been equated with Afro-Asian solidarity against Western colonialism and the white racialism they usually associated with it. It is also true that the other non-aligned states in South Asia had never liked India's assumption that it had a natural and self-evident right to lead their cause. The crisis brought home to thoughtful Indians as never before their unpopularity in the region.[1] No South Asian state offered to help them when China attacked. Indeed, when the Chinese blamed the border flare-up on Indian intransigence and pointed to their frontier settlements with Burma, Nepal, Afghanistan, and Pakistan to prove their contention,[2] the other non-aligned countries adopted a neutral attitude toward the Indian cause. This was something China doubtless had reckoned on but that India had not expected.

The meaning of non-alignment became further confused when the Western powers agreed to provide India with an "air umbrella" – a description the Indian government dislikes – to guard against the possibility of more serious Chinese attacks. To preserve the posture of non-

[1] "It is no use looking through the blinkers: it would be sheer lunacy to believe in what our newspapers print about how much we are loved in South Asia and how much our standpoint is appreciated by all and sundry. The sad fact is that we present the image of a loquacious, overbearing breed who have been too long used to having their own way." (*Economic Weekly*, Bombay, June 1, 1963, p. 871.)

"If the present difficulties are still to do some good to the country and the nation, it should then at least persuade the Indians to accept a few simple truths, for example, that arrogance is no substitute for literacy, that moral attitudinising is not the same thing as morality, that oration is not creation, and that humility is the noblest of all attributes." (*Economic Weekly*, Annual Number, February, 1963, p. 116.)

[2] "The Premier said that in the past five years China has settled boundary problems with Burma, Nepal, Mongolia, Pakistan, Afghanistan, etc. This is an outstanding achievement in our foreign relations." The relations with India constituted an exception, for which China was not responsible. "We are for peaceful settlement of the Sino-Indian border issue through negotiations, but if India is determined not to have negotiations – no matter, we can wait." (Premier Chou En-lai's Report on the Work of the Government (Summary), delivered at the First Session of the Third National People's Congress, *Chinese News Bulletin*, Stockholm, January 5, 1965, p. 23.)

alignment it became essential for India to obtain military assistance from the Soviet Union as well. Since the Western powers do not seek a military alliance with India, and are satisfied with its policy of non-alignment, military aid from the Soviet Union would not be unwelcome from a Western point of view. However, it seems unlikely that the supply of military equipment from these various sources will be sufficient to satisfy India's needs. In the first place it cannot be assumed that because of their quarrels with the Chinese over doctrinal and other issues, the Russians will be willing to make a very substantial contribution to India's military build-up against China. For their part, the Western powers are likely to be less than generous because they do not want to compromise Indian non-alignment too much in the eyes of the Russians. Nor, by the same token, do they wish to alienate Pakistan still further, their decision to strengthen Indian defenses having met with a hostile reception there. Therefore, the Indian posture in world affairs depends to a large extent on the way the Western powers and the Soviet Union read one another's intentions. To sum up, the need to rearm has left India without an independent and secure basis for its policy of non-alignment.[1] Certainly its prestige and its ability to influence world opinion have decreased,[2] and it has had to exercise more care in formulating domestic and foreign policies. India, in other words, is less carefree and independent than it was before its difficulties with China.

A glance at the political map of the subcontinent shows that the task of devising effective defenses for India's northern boundary would be less difficult and costly if it were undertaken jointly with Pakistan. But such

[1] The meaning of Indian non-alignment certainly acquired a new dimension in 1963 when, without realizing its political implications, the Indian government agreed to accept a powerful broadcasting transmitter from the United States on condition that the Voice of America, the very embodiment of cold war commitment, be allowed some use of it for daily broadcasts to South Asia. As it happened, this agreement caused such a political outcry inside and outside Parliament that it had to be abrogated.

[2] The following reflections by the former United States Ambassador to India, John Kenneth Galbraith, deserve attention:

"As a result of this episode [the collapse of its armed forces under the Chinese onslaught in 1962] there has . . . been a radical change in Indian foreign policy. . . . The formal commitment to nonalignment has, of course, continued, and the United States has been very careful in the last two years not to force the Indians into any position where they would have to disavow their past policies. But, as Nehru once said, it is not entirely easy to be nonaligned against an invader. India as a result of the Chinese attack has had to be much more considerate toward its friends. It recognizes that safety against a Chinese attack depends greatly on American and British support; thus the prospect of alienating the Americans is not nearly so inviting now as it was when the risk of an attack was not considered imminent. . . .

"This greater caution has inevitably resulted in a considerable loss of influence. The Indians in the future will be a good deal more popular [presumably in the United States] but a good deal less powerful. It would be interesting to speculate whether the Chinese had anticipated that a possible consequence of their attack would be the weakening of India's influence in world affairs." (American Academy of Arts and Sciences, *Bulletin*, January, 1965, pp. 3–4.)

cooperation would be unthinkable without a prior settlement of the Kashmir dispute, a problem that is rooted in the very conditions that produced the two states, as we shall see in the next chapter.[1] Without settled agreements with Pakistan and China, India will, at best, have to live with merely a *de facto* truce on practically all its boundaries, except those fronting the oceans. Forced to rely pretty much on its own resources, India after 1962 continually had to increase its defense expenditure. Admittedly, it is still not devoting a greater share of its national income to military purposes than is common in some other underdeveloped countries in South Asia, not least in Pakistan. But the added burden came at a time when India's Third Five Year Plan was running into severe difficulties because of strains in precisely those sectors of the economy which are essential to defense. Moreover, increased defense spending was bound to worsen India's already acute foreign exchange shortage (Chapter 7, Section 4).

China must have noticed how its pressure and probings along the border stirred up dissension inside India, discredited the authority of the government at home and abroad, and played havoc with its economic plans. In the context of the competition between the Indian and Chinese roads to modernization that is commonly said to exist and is emphatically advertised in the West, especially in the United States, these effects were useful additional gains for China that can hardly have failed to influence its approach to the dispute. The repercussions of the conflict have added to the political difficulties the Indian government has experienced at home. But, paradoxically enough, these difficulties have given the Indian government a reason for wanting to publicize and stress the state of tension along the northern border. The sudden, large-scale Chinese assault in October, 1962, produced spontaneous affirmations and demonstrations of national solidarity and purpose in India.[2] The upsurge of patriotic

[1] On October 31, 1961 the *Times* (London) reported from Delhi: "At the time of the Chinese suppression of the revolt in Tibet in 1959, senior Indian and Pakistan officers took the view that the differences between their countries over Kashmir should be dropped, as China was the real danger. On both sides there were those who favoured the signing of a defence pact. The Indian Government, however, considered that the differences with China would be settled by negotiations."

Had the accidents of history been other than what they were, Kashmir would now belong to Pakistan. In that case, ironically enough, Pakistan, not India, would have been required to cede the Aksai Chin salient of Ladakh to China. Indians now tend to say that the Western powers should support their control over Kashmir since this territory is essential to their defense against China. As Nehru put it: "Remember that at present Srinagar offers the only way to reach Ladakh, and all our campaigns against China depend on the Kashmir Valley." (*Overseas Hindustan Times,* December 27, 1962.) Later he termed as "outrageous and unthinkable" any idea that the defense of Ladakh should be handed over to Pakistan. (*Hindustan Times,* June 20, 1963.)

[2] Only rarely does anyone in India – other than the disreputed and now mostly imprisoned leaders of the pro-Chinese wing of the Communist Party – express the view that Indian policy in its conflict with the Chinese may not have been a hundred percent right. One exception is K. P. S. Menon, who, in an article, "The Nehru Technique in

fervor so affected its leaders that some of them, including Nehru himself, began to extol the therapeutic effects of war on a flaccid and divided society. The new mood did not long survive the cessation of hostilities, however. In the period of anticlimactic uncertainty that followed, disillusionment and discontent became the order of the day and both the government and the Congress Party attracted critical comment. Faced with internal dissension and the need to spur on aid from abroad, it was tempting for the Indian leadership to maintain the atmosphere of imminent external danger by repeated warnings and protests about the Chinese military build-up in Tibet. The Indian government may genuinely fear that the Chinese will again attack south of the McMahon Line on the northeastern frontier, though no one has put forward any convincing reason why they should do so. In any event, it has reason enough on the home front for sustaining a sort of controlled combustion against China.

Fostering national consolidation by playing up external dangers to territorial integrity has been a common technique of governments in South Asia as elsewhere. But, except in relation to Pakistan, it is not one the Indian government has heretofore employed. A consequence of its border conflict with China has been to give luster to this expedient.[1]

Diplomacy" (*Link*, May 30, 1965, p. 24), states: "Undoubtedly the blame for the present deplorable situation rests on China. Yet, it is up to us to search our hearts and see whether we, too, have not, by any acts of omission or commission, aggravated the situation; whether, for instance, public opinion, as expressed in Parliament, did not, in its righteous frenzy of indignation against China, tie the hands of the Government overmuch and left the Government with little room for manoeuvring on critical occasions."

[1] The text of this chapter was completed early in 1965. Events later in the year have not substantially changed India's relations with China, or their repercussions on India's international posture as described in this section. The Soviet Union, however, has shown a somewhat greater generosity in assisting India with military equipment. After the border agreement between China and Pakistan, and still more after the gradual deterioration in India-Pakistan relations following Nehru's death, there had been a conspicuous rapprochement between Pakistan and China, demonstrated by an exchange of visits of top officials and by various agreements, among them one calling for the opening of a direct airline between Karachi and Peking. When, beginning in the spring of 1965, military clashes broke out between India and Pakistan, amounting in the end to a virtual, though undeclared, war (Chapter 6, Section 8), China emphatically took Pakistan's side, declaring India to be the aggressor. There were incidents at China's borders with India and its buffer state Sikkim, and mutual recriminations between China and India, which, however, left their positions the same as before the conflict. The understanding between Pakistan and China, inspired by their having a common adversary, obviously placed India at a further disadvantage. On the other hand, India was able to point to it, and to the danger of China's involvement in the conflict with Pakistan, for the purpose of winning sympathy in the Western countries for its cause. Whether that cooperation between Pakistan and China will develop into a firm and durable joint policy seems doubtful, considering both the dissimilarities in the political structure of the two countries and Pakistan's dependence for development, and, indeed, for feeding its people, on assistance from the West, particularly the United States. In the last instance everything will, of course, depend on whether India and Pakistan can reach a settlement or, at least, a *modus vivendi* on the Kashmir issue (Chapter 6, Sections 7 and 8).

9 *The Settlement of Burma's Boundary with China*

Still another border dispute directly involving China should be discussed. We mentioned earlier that some hundreds of miles of Burma's frontier with China still awaited formal agreement and demarcation when Burma achieved independence in 1948. With the departure of the British from Burma the Chinese Kuomintang government immediately indicated its interest in reaching a settlement, and when it fell from power Burma quickly made an approach to the Communist regime. It was, indeed, the first country to accord diplomatic recognition to the new government in China. The government did not at first respond, apparently because it was too preoccupied with domestic affairs. The situation grew threatening for Burma when fleeing Kuomintang troops established themselves on Burmese territory and refused to be disarmed. In conducting operations against them, Burmese forces ran into Chinese Communist troops and some minor clashes occurred. This military game of hide and seek took place along a boundary that had never been formally posted and was extremely difficult to police. In addition, official Chinese maps showed large portions of Burmese territory as part of China. The Chinese government declared that it did not recognize frontier lines "imposed" by the British and implied that Burmese forces had moved into areas belonging to China. As in the case of India, articulate opinion in Burma grew alarmed once the facts about Chinese intrusions, particularly those in the northern part of the country, became public knowledge.

Having repudiated all previous agreements, the Chinese then offered to negotiate the whole frontier, except for a few village tracts, on the basis of the boundary the British had established. In short, they abandoned the large claims implied by their maps. In this light, the initial repudiation of colonial arrangements appeared to be largely a matter of morally redressing the humiliations of the past. Agreement in detail was finally reached in 1960. Except for the transfer to China of a tiny portion of territory and a suspended judgment on the western extremity of its boundary, whose exact location could not be determined until the Sino-Indian border dispute was settled, Burma secured formal Chinese recognition of its inherited frontier claims, and these were given precision. The agreed boundary has since been formally demarcated on the ground. It is interesting to note that the Chinese accepted the Burmese portion of the McMahon Line, but called it the "traditional customary" line. In both countries the border agreement was hailed as a triumph for the five Panch Shila principles of co-existence.[1] Be that as it may, Burma was sensible to seek a

[1] Chou En-lai described it as "a brilliant model for the Asian peoples to live together on friendly terms and a good example of the settlement of boundary questions and other disputes between Asian countries." (*Burma Weekly Bulletin*, October 13, 1960, quoted by Daphne E. Whittam, "The Sino-Burmese Boundary Treaty," *Pacific Affairs*, Vol. 34, No. 1, 1961, p. 175.)

speedy settlement in view of the size and strength of its neighbor and its own internal schisms and weaknesses. In the circumstances it had good reason to feel well satisfied with the bargain it made.

China's approach to the dispute was noteworthy also in that it desisted from exploiting the presence of Kuomintang troops on Burmese soil, or the divided loyalties of tribal peoples, such as the Kachins, living on both sides of the border, or the existence of rebels who called themselves "Communists," to enforce much larger territorial claims than those actually presented. An ill-defined and undemarcated frontier could have provided a cloak of legality for such a policy. It is reasonable to infer from this that China's conciliatory attitude was dictated by broader considerations and it is not difficult to surmise that keeping Burma free of cold war commitments was one of them. From the Chinese standpoint, the agreement served to keep Burma's foreign policy from falling under Western influences, a development that might have led to the further American encirclement of China.

10 *Southeast Asia's Border Problems*

In their first indulgence in foreign affairs it was natural for the new states in South Asia to strike global attitudes, especially against colonialism and white "racialism." The feeling of solidarity they experienced and demonstrated extended to the new states in West Asia (except Israel) and Africa and to Communist China, which to them had the appearance of another underdeveloped country that had thrown off the yoke of imperialism and now steered a course toward national consolidation and planned economic development.[1] This trend reached its high-water mark in the Bandung Conference of 1955.[2]

[1] "For most Indians the events of 1948–9 represented the rebirth of a united China after a lengthy period of disorder, something to be welcomed as part of the decline of Western colonial influence all over Asia. A sense of Asian solidarity takes precedence over divergent ideologies and social, economic and political systems. Moreover, Nehru is genuinely convinced that Chinese nationalism is a far more potent force in Chinese policy than Communism, that Chinese civilization is too old and too deeply rooted to succumb to Marxist dogma; or, to put it in other terms, that the Chinese Communists will adapt Marxism to suit Chinese needs and traditions.

"Closely related is the belief that China is not inextricably tied to the Soviet Union, that the Western policy of 'containing' the Peking regime is forcing it to complete dependence on Moscow and that acceptance of Communist China by the West would inevitably weaken the tie with Russia." (Brecher, *Nehru: A Political Biography,* p. 590.)

[2] The critical attitudes toward China, after the revolution in 1949, of the Philippines, Malaya, Thailand, and, in the beginning, even Ceylon and, particularly, Pakistan, which in different ways and degrees were aligned with the Western cause, were at that time rather muted; their occasional assertions that the anti-imperialist protest should also be directed against Communist imperialism were addressed to the Soviet Union, which was not represented at the Bandung Conference, and this remained a rather

By then it was already clear, however, that as colonial boundaries had been drawn there was plenty of scope for frontier troubles between neighboring states, particularly in Southeast Asia. Furthermore, old enmities and antagonisms that had been heightened by problems of national consolidation and cold war diplomacy tended to focus on boundary issues. It was not so much the frontiers themselves that mattered as what could be gained by threatening or disputing them. For centuries before the arrival of European colonists the area was the scene of an almost uninterrupted struggle for territorial ascendancy, in which the kingdoms of Burma, Siam, Cambodia, and Annam (Vietnam) were the leading protagonists. Most of the new states of Southeast Asia, and Thailand as well, can thus look back to periods when their territorial limits far exceeded their present boundaries. On top of this, the frontiers traced by colonial rule were ill-conceived in relation to the topographical, ethnographic, and historical realities of the area.[1]

Fervent Thai nationalists, for example, are quite aware that the present-day boundaries of their nation would have extended much farther but for concessions Siam had had to make to the imperial appetites of Britain and France. They also know that the territorial residue left them bears little relation to ethnic or linguistic criteria. There are ethnic affinities between people living in parts of Thailand and neighboring Burma and Cambodia. In the northeast section of the country the people speak much the same language as the Laotians across the border of the Mekong River. Since this section is also the poorest and most isolated part of Thailand, it is not surprising that the government in Bangkok is highly sensitive to political trends in Laos and the danger that politically hostile elements there will foment separatist feelings in northeast Thailand. Although Thailand ceded territory to Malaya in 1909, Thailand's southern provinces contain a large Malay population and also a substantial Chinese minority. After the Second World War an active Malay separatist movement in the area was dealt with by a combination of social improvement and po-

---

shallow ideological talking point only, as the Soviet Union was not involved anywhere in South Asia, except that it had switched its support from the Kuomintang to the victorious Communist government in China, a move that could not very well be characterized as Russian imperialism.

[1] "Basically the cause of . . . instability [in Southeast Asia] is the demographic immaturity of the area in which, since geographical position has made it a zone of passage, no lasting adjustment has yet been reached between land and state. To the political geographer the parallel with the Balkans is depressingly obvious. And both the historian who remembers that the Second Balkan War followed swiftly on the heels of the First, and the psychologist who recognizes the violence with which temporarily transferred hatreds may return to their original objects, will surely join the geographer in suggesting that the present phase of comparative friendliness among the peoples of Southeast Asia may be merely the prelude to a renewal of strife, should the Europeans completely withdraw from the area." (East and Spate, *The Changing Map of Asia*, p. 236.)

lice repression. It received no official encouragement from Malaya because the British government there needed Thailand's cooperation to put down Communist rebels in this borderland. But frontier troubles could develop here if the Pan-Malayan Islamic Party of independent Malaya, whose electoral stronghold lies in Kelantan, bordering on the southern provinces of Thailand, should acquire significant standing in Malayan politics.

Thailand's relations with Cambodia have rarely been free of threats, plots, irritating border incidents, and abusive propaganda. The enmity between the two countries has deep roots. Fear of domination by the more vigorous Siamese or Vietnamese had existed in Cambodia since its Khmer empire collapsed in the fourteenth century, and probably only the intervention of France in the last century saved this country from final extinction. Since the departure of the French, the principal causes of tension between Cambodia on the one hand and Thailand and South Vietnam on the other have been their different political alignments and involvements in the cold war between the Communist nations and the West. Because Cambodia has recognized China and follows a policy of non-alignment, recently bent more emphatically toward friendship with China and hostility toward the United States, the staunchly anti-Communist regimes of Thailand and South Vietnam regard it as a menace to their own political security. Thailand belongs to a Western defense alliance, while only a heavy and direct American involvement has so far prevented a Communist victory in the civil war being waged in South Vietnam.

In these circumstances all three states have tended to magnify real or imagined border incidents into deeply laid plots against their very existence. Although some of the intrusions complained about have probably been due to the lack of effective government control, especially in cases where the frontier is relatively inaccessible and not clearly demarcated, political leaders have found it more expedient to exploit them for diplomatic and political purposes than to obviate them through sensible border agreements. By such political alchemy a dispute over the ownership of a ruined temple on the frontier between Thailand and Cambodia, which few had ever heard of, much less seen, is transformed into a struggle over a priceless national shrine and becomes a reason for breaking off diplomatic relations.[1] The arrival in Cambodia of a public figure from China is the occasion for abusive press and radio campaigns in Thailand and sometimes public demonstrations as well. The Cambodian govern-

[1] "We shall not hesitate to give our blood and our lives, even sacrificing our neutrality" to possess it, declared Prince Sihanouk, the Prime Minister of Cambodia, according to the *New York Times,* International Edition, July 4, 1962. In 1962 the International Court at the Hague ruled that the temple was on Cambodian territory. On hearing the verdict, Marshal Sarit, the Prime Minister of Thailand, said, "We speak with tears"; and in the Thai cabinet "many ministers wept." (*New York Times,* June 25, 1962.)

ment, for its part, rallies national feeling against the allegedly aggressive designs of Thailand and South Vietnam and, behind them, the United States. But for real protection against harassment from these sources, Cambodia has relied, in effect, on the restraining influence of the United States, which naturally does not want to give Cambodia cause to appeal for Russian or Chinese support. In the last resort, Cambodia has protected its territorial integrity by a policy of non-alignment that is often indistinguishable from political blackmail.

11 *The Formation of Greater Malaysia*

Fundamental differences in response to cold war pressures have also strained relations between Malaya and neighboring Indonesia. Whereas Malaya, under a conservative government, refused to recognize China and has followed an avowedly pro-Western foreign policy, Indonesia, under radically inclined leaders, recognized China and has been a fervent advocate of non-alignment in world affairs. A similar contrast is apparent in domestic policy. Malaya has clamped down hard on Communists at home, while Indonesia has harbored the region's largest Communist Party. The link between Communism and local Chinese minorities has been important for both countries, but in different ways. The Malayan government has had to disclaim any suggestion that its anti-Communist policies are directed at its substantial Chinese population, while Sukarno has had to deny that his maltreatment of the relatively small Chinese population of Indonesia is anti-Communist.[1] Only a notable degree of mutual trust and tolerance could have prevented estrangement between such dissimilar neighbors. Far from being cordial, however, their relations have frequently been punctuated by diplomatic snubs and instances of public abuse. One symptom, as well as one cause, of their mutual antipathy was Malaya's ill-concealed sympathy for the rebellion that broke out in Sumatra against Sukarno in 1957 – an attitude that led it to grant political asylum to a number of the rebel leaders. But it was not until the formation of the Federation of Malaysia in 1963 that the two regimes confronted each other in a state of acute tension along a common land frontier. We shall return to this conflict in the next section, after having studied the forces that brought about the larger federation.

The idea of merging the independent Federation of Malaya with the British colonies of Singapore, Sarawak, and North Borneo and the British protectorate of Brunei, to form a new Federation of Malaysia, or a Greater Malaysia, as it has been called, was first publicly proposed by the Malayan Prime Minister, Tunku Abdul Rahman, in May, 1961. For some

[1] This is how the Indonesian situation looked before internal political upheaval was precipitated by an abortive coup on September 30, 1965; see Chapter 9, Section 10.

years before this, Singapore, with its large Chinese population, radically minded government, powerful and active trade unions, and difficult student problems, had looked to be a thoroughly undesirable partner to the conservative, Malay-dominated government of newly independent Malaya. But when threats of defections and election setbacks seriously undermined the authority of the moderately socialist ruling party in Singapore, Tunku Abdul Rahman became convinced that an early merger, which would place internal security firmly in the hands of a federal government, was the only way to prevent pro-Communist groups from gaining political control of the colony. As it was, the ruling party in Singapore succeeded in holding power only by imprisoning the leftists who were its most dangerous political opponents. From the standpoint of Malaya it was important, too, to arrange the merger before Singapore achieved full control over its own internal and external affairs. In Singapore it had long been generally assumed that the economic future of the island lay in a complete merger with the mainland; but this concern made no impression on the Malayan government until it perceived that Singapore might exert a more disturbing political influence outside than inside a Malayan federation.

It was concern for national security rather than economic advantage that eventually forced Malaya's hand.[1] The Malayan government was then faced with a difficult exercise in communal arithmetic. Malaya itself is a plural society in which the Chinese comprise more than 40 percent of the population and are stronger economically and more dynamic than the Malays, who constitute about the same proportion of the population. Malay predominance is, however, built into the political structure of the federation and the Chinese are discriminated against in government service and education.[2] If Singapore were to join the federation, the Chinese would outnumber the Malays and all other ethnic groups and would thereby threaten the Malay hold on political power. The answer was to bring in the mainly non-Chinese populations of Brunei, Sarawak, and North Borneo as a counterweight to the Chinese. It so happens that the excess of Chinese over non-Chinese in Singapore almost equals the excess of non-Chinese over Chinese in Brunei, Sarawak, and North Borneo.

The solution implied no similarly neat political equation; for although the principal opposition to Malaysia in Sarawak and North Borneo has come from predominantly Chinese political groups, it cannot be assumed that the indigenous populations of these principalities will always support the pro-Malay federal government. But including them did at least make

[1] As the Malayan Minister of the Interior put it: "We must do something to prevent the Communists from dominating this country. That is why, today, we are discussing this question of merger." (*The World Today*, Royal Institute of International Affairs, London, Vol. 18, No. 5, May, 1962, p. 196.)

[2] Chapter 4, Section 10; Chapter 9, Section 11.

the merger with Singapore more palatable politically in Malaya itself. Probably Tunku Abdul Rahman was also anxious to bring the small populations of these remaining British dependencies into the Malayan fold because independence, which the pressure of anti-colonial sentiment was bringing nearer, would leave them ill-equipped to combat Communist and Indonesian subversion.

For the British government the idea of Greater Malaysia had the obvious attraction of enabling it to divest itself of its last possessions in Asia in a way that would deny pro-Communist elements the chance of fomenting and leading national liberation movements in them. At the same time Britain had to avoid the appearance of arranging a shotgun marriage at the expense of dependent peoples whose political and constitutional evolution lagged well behind that of the populations of Malaya and Singapore. A joint Anglo-Malayan commission accordingly conducted a democratic test of opinion in Sarawak and North Borneo and reported in 1962 that the majority of the people polled were in favor of Malaysia, provided a number of special interests were adequately safeguarded. A referendum in Singapore also produced a verdict clearly in favor of Malaysia on conditions that best safeguarded its special interests.[1]

In the event, the formation of Malaysia did not rid Britain of all its colonial responsibilities in the region, for after approving the idea in principle, the Sultan of Brunei refused to join. Apparently the terms of membership, particularly in regard to his rank among the other titular rulers in the federation and the disposition of his oil revenues, proved to be unacceptable to him. Ironically enough, the leading political party in Brunei, the People's Party, which had won all the available elected seats in the legislative council, was also against the merger and staged a coup against the sultan to prevent him from taking the territory into Malaysia. "We want history to say," the leader of the party declared, "it was our sweat and struggle, and not Malaysia, which gave Brunei independence."[2] Although British forces quickly suppressed the revolt against the sultan, it is difficult to believe that the politically anachronistic regime of this tiny territory has any assured future. Malaysia may be the poorer without the oil revenues of Brunei, but it was politically simpler to establish the larger federation without Brunei with its peculiar form of government.

It would be wrong to infer from the prominence given to the need to establish a firm bulwark against Communist pressures that this is the only common interest Malaysia was designed to serve. All of the constituent territories form a single currency area and share the same *lingua franca*, Malay; they also have similar systems of law and administration. All of

[1] The Singapore referendum did not permit the electors to opt out of Malaysia in principle, but only to choose between alternative conditions of membership.

[2] *The Guardian,* December 10, 1962.

them should benefit in varying degrees from the larger internal market created by the new federation. Singapore has an obvious interest in being inside the tariff walls of Malaya, and it is difficult to see how the tiny territories of Sarawak and North Borneo could have had an economically or politically viable future on their own. Federal aid for the economic development of Sarawak and Sabah was guaranteed when the federation was established, and there was some hard bargaining concerning the size of Singapore's contribution to these development funds. On the other hand, the large disparities in political and economic development among the partners, their geographical separation, and the differences in the size and ethnic composition of their populations are likely to give rise to serious internal stresses and strains. Political federation is under any conditions a difficult concept to establish and put into practice. None of the constituent territories of Malaysia can boast any marked degree of consolidation, and joining them together will not make unification any easier to achieve.[1]

Singapore retained a relatively large degree of financial autonomy and was fairly free to develop its own labor, education, health, and social security policies, its own citizenship laws, its entrepôt status, and so on. In return, it adopted Malay as its official language. More important, it accepted far fewer seats in the federal Parliament than it was entitled to by virtue of its population. All Singapore citizens automatically became "nationals" of the federation, but were not eligible to vote in federal elections unless they qualified under the more restrictive citizenship laws of the federation. Special concessions were also made to Sabah and Sarawak. Thus they retained control of immigration and deportation though this is normally a federal matter. Since Moslems are far from predominant in these territories and Christianity is fairly influential, they have not adopted Islam as their official religion. English continues to serve as the primary medium of education and the official language for government communications. The indigenous populations enjoy special privileges, such as preferential quotas for government jobs and scholarships and the exclusive right to own land in large areas. Both territories were given more seats in the federal Parliament than their populations warrant. In these various ways the pattern of ethnic discrimination established in the constitution of the Federation of Malaya[2] was continued and elaborated when the Federation of Malaysia was brought into being.

In Part III of Chapter 9, which focusses on Southeast Asia, we shall examine the Malaysian Federation and its problems more analytically, and take note of Singapore's separation from the federation during 1965. See Section 11 of Chapter 9.

[1] See Chapter 9, Section 11, for further discussion of the problems of consolidating the Federation of Malaysia.

[2] Chapter 4, Section 10.

12 *The Indonesian "Confrontation"*

In the long run Malaysia's prospects of surviving depend on its ability to contain and overcome the strong centrifugal elements that have been built into its structure. However, the immediate danger came from the enmity of Indonesia and, to a lesser extent, that of the Philippines. Both the Philippines and Indonesia opposed the formation of Malaysia, though for very different reasons, and both refused to recognize the existence of the new state.

The Philippines introduced an unexpected complication into the negotiations on the proposed Malaysian Federation by formally laying claim to North Borneo, and it was the rejection of this claim that lay behind its refusal to accept Malaysia. North Borneo once belonged to the Sultan of Sulu, from whose legal heirs the Philippines derives its title to the territory. The contention hinges on whether the present sultan's forebear ceded or merely leased the area to the private interests from whom the British government later acquired it. This is clearly one of those recondite issues that appeal to international lawyers. What is surprising about the claim is that, though formally presented, it was not pressed until sixteen years after the Philippines achieved independence, and then in connection with North Borneo's becoming independent from Britain. Considering the Asian view of colonial possessions as permanent aggressions, an earlier submission might have won it somewhat more understanding and sympathy. The Philippine government could hardly feel comfortable about pursuing its case against a friendly and staunchly anti-Communist Asian neighbor. It would probably never have put forward the claim in the first place but for the sudden and fortuitously successful pressure exerted by the Moslem minority faction in Philippine politics.

As a counter to the idea of Malaysia the Philippines proposed the creation of a confederation to include itself in company with Malaya and Indonesia, and all three countries agreed in principle to set up consultative machinery, under the name of Maphilindo, for regular discussions on problems of common concern.[1] What sort of policies they hoped to pursue or develop in common was far from clear and it may well be that each of them saw in Maphilindo simply a means of postponing or avoiding a diplomatic showdown over the different issues raised by the projected formation of Malaysia. In time the whole idea was buried under the mounting campaign the Philippines and Indonesia waged against Malaya's apparent determination to establish the new state with all possible speed no matter what they thought. The Philippines has not so far

[1] This was only the latest of several abortive attempts to join various countries in Southeast Asia into a union of some sort; the desirability of such an organization had, as a matter of fact, been widely discussed among the Allies during the closing stages of the Second World War and had been pressed by the United States.

threatened Malaysia and if some face-saving formula can be found for disposing of its claim to North Borneo, the cause of its refusal to recognize the new federation will also disappear.

Indonesian opposition was more complex in origin and bitter in spirit. It was also more serious, since Indonesia shares a common frontier with Malaysia. Indonesia has never openly avowed any ambition to unite North Borneo with Indonesia Borneo or Kalimintan,[1] though Sukarno is reported to have entertained some such aspiration.[2] Since the Anglo-Dutch colonial boundary in Borneo island separated intimately connected ethnic groups, inclusion of these groups within a single political entity would not be without justification. That most of the articulate strata of the indigenous population of North Borneo (or Sabah) opted to join Malaysia was less a reflection of their warm feelings for Malaya than a sign of their fear of Indonesia.

At the outset of the negotiations over Malaysia the Indonesian government publicly denounced British colonial rule over North Borneo and explicitly welcomed the possibility that this territory would merge with Malaya. But at this time it was still engaged in the final stages of its campaign for West Irian. Once that was over, Indonesia began to accuse Malaya of "neo-colonialism," meaning the perpetuation of colonial domination by methods other than direct political rule. In Indonesia's view, Britain was handing over its colonial dependencies to its pro-Western Malayan confederates in return for the right to maintain military installations in the area. The government of Tunku Abdul Rahman was simply a disguised form of colonial rule. If logic was on Indonesia's side, it should have long ago denounced the Philippines, which is studded with American military bases and belongs to a Western defense pact, as an "imperialist puppet," instead of accepting it as a somewhat incongruous ally in the struggle against Malaysia. Then again, the continued presence of British military forces on Borneo island is hardly a valid cause for Indonesian excitement. It is strange, too, that Indonesia's solicitude for the self-determination of dependent peoples has not so far been directed at the Australian trusteeship territory of New Guinea.

Both Indonesia and the Philippines questioned the degree of support the idea of Malaysia enjoyed in the British Borneo territories. But when, at the request of all concerned, the Secretary General of the United Nations made an independent assessment of public feeling in these territories and reported that the majority of the voters wished to achieve political independence through the proposed federation, the Indonesians called into question the way the assessment had been conducted.

[1] See p. 186, footnote 1. Even Indonesia's threat to "crush Malaysia" is but a pledge to split it into its component parts and expel the British from their military bases. Such a move would, however, leave the individual members at the mercy of Indonesia.

[2] *Far Eastern Economic Review*, April 3, 1962, p. 443.

From long experience Sukarno knew how quickly and thoroughly a display of vociferous anti-colonialism could arouse the national fervor of his countrymen. Anti-imperialist invective has enabled him to shine on the international stage and win easy popularity at home. It kept alive the spirit of the "Indonesian Revolution" when the reality of Indonesian nationhood was much less apparent. It also served to express his pique at real or imagined rebuffs from abroad[1] and to cover up difficulties and mismanagement at home. Some observers saw his anti-colonialism as an expedient whereby Sukarno maintained his balance between the army and the Indonesian Communist Party.[2] Thus it is possible that Indonesia's campaign against Malaysia was designed to deflect the aspiration of Indonesian Communists for a more prominent role in the government, while giving the army more stature in relation to the Communist Party. The success of a policy of flexible diplomacy combined with threats and unconventional military actions on a limited scale in the case of West Irian may have influenced Sukarno's Malaysian policy.[3] As in that earlier contest he succeeded in winning the sympathy of the Afro-Asian bloc, so he must have seen a fair prospect of isolating Malaya as "a conservative community presided over by reactionary sultans and ruled by a feudal aristocracy in league with Chinese millionaires,"[4] protected by British troops.[5] Sukarno was, of course, aware that Indonesia carries considerable weight in the region because of its one hundred million population and the fact that it is now one of the most heavily armed countries in the world. Also, Sukarno may simply not have relished the thought of sharing a common land frontier with a government so antipathetic to all he stands for as that of Tunku Abdul Rahman. Through invidious comparisons, this might even have encouraged dissident elements within his own badly integrated and much poorer state. Perhaps, too, he saw himself as the architect of a grander design for uniting all the Malay-speaking peoples,[6] with Maphilindo as the first step, in which case Rahman may have seemed a dangerous rival for that role. Besides, Sukarno may have felt that neither Malaya nor Britain consulted him sufficiently about Malaysia and were deter-

[1] Undoubtedly the positions taken and the language used by the Prime Minister of Malaya, Tunku Abdul Rahman, have often been less than friendly and diplomatic.

[2] Chapter 9, Part II.

[3] George Modelski, *Indonesia and Her Neighbors,* Policy Memorandum No. 30, Center of International Studies, Princeton University, Princeton, 1964, mimeographed, p. 6 *et passim.*

[4] *Ibid.*, p. 15.

[5] At least, Afro-Asian friendly neutrality was a fair prospect; Ceylon denied military transit facilities to parties in the Malaysian conflict, and Malaysia was at first not invited to be represented at a second Bandung conference scheduled to meet in Algiers in 1965, which could not be held because of internal upheaval in Algeria.

[6] Sukarno has described Indonesia as the second biggest power of the future and he renamed the part of the Indian Ocean in which the islands of Indonesia are scattered the Indonesian Ocean.

mined to establish it regardless of his opposition. Whatever the motives at work, once Malaysia was an accomplished fact Sukarno embarked on a policy of "confrontation" – a word that appears to cover all types of intrusion and sabotage short of war. Diplomatic and trade relations with the new federation were severed, troops moved to the borders of Sarawak and Sabah, small guerrilla bands landed or dropped on the Malayan mainland, and anti-British demonstrations were staged in Indonesia. In addition there are enough Malaysian dissidents,[1] to say nothing of the thousands of Indonesian immigrant workers in Sarawak and Sabah and the so-called "freedom fighters" who were infiltrated across their frontiers, to give Indonesia footholds for fomenting trouble from within.

Open warfare must have seemed more risky as, unlike Holland when the ownership of West Irian was in question, Malaysia could count on the support of Britain, Australia, New Zealand, and, if it should come to a showdown, in all certainty the United States. In physical terms, then, the Indonesian confrontation policy seemed unlikely to amount to more than the encouragement of rebellious activities inside Malaysia, and the maintenance of a general state of tension along the borders, dramatized by sporadic frontier incidents.[2] It might manifest itself on the highly charged industrial labor front in Singapore. In economic terms the severance of trade relations probably hurt Indonesia more than Malaya. Indeed, it is indicative of the way Sukarno relied on emotional heroics rather than constructive achievements to maintain his position that he was willing to break off trade relations with Malaysia despite the adverse effects of this move on the balance of payments, foreign exchange reserves, and financial stability of the Indonesian economy.[3] Naturally, his countrymen were told that the confrontation policy would strengthen Indonesia economically. For Malaysia the break meant some disruption of trade and a sharp increase in defense burdens to the detriment of development and welfare projects. In the long run, as already argued, the more serious threats to its existence will probably be internal rather than external, even though, as in

[1] Among many Malays Sukarno has a mystique similar to that of Nasser among the Arabs. There is a sizeable minority of Indonesians settled on the coast of the mainland near Sumatra and many Malays are descendants of Indonesians who came to Malaya from the outer islands during the last fifty years. Not all of these can be considered completely reliable, but Indonesian sympathizers recently were able to influence the policy of the (opposition) Pan-Malayan Islamic Party. In the urban areas many radicals are for Sukarno because of his "socialism."

[2] "You can imagine what will happen if we have a common land frontier with the Federation that is hostile towards us. The possibility of physical conflict would be difficult to avoid. I do not mean war, but incidents . . . incidents of physical conflict." (Dr. Subandrio, the Indonesian Foreign Minister, *The Times* (London), February 12, 1963.)

[3] Chapter 9, Section 10.

the case of the other new states in the region, internal difficulties are aggravated by external ones.[1]

This section brings the history of the Indonesian "confrontation" up to the spring of 1965. How the violent change in the internal political situation in Indonesia since the autumn of that year will affect Indonesia's relations with her neighbors is uncertain; see Chapter 9 (Section 10).

13 *The Long Shadow of China*

The new government that came to power in China in 1949 felt at first the same urge as the South Asian successor states to concentrate on consolidating its rule internally while leaving boundary questions as a *cura posterior*. When at a later date the government began to take interest in these questions, it developed that all the states in South Asia having a common frontier with China had border problems to settle with their big neighbor. To understand the nature of these problems and the way they have been raised and in large part solved, we need to take a look at the history of China.

For the several thousand years of its existence before the colonial era, China was, in a sense, a boundless country. In some measure, this is explained by the geographical character of the frontier regions: they were, for the most part, very thinly populated mountainous areas, as in the direction of British India, Burma, and most of Russia. Because of this and the hugeness of its empire and its high level of culture, China became self-centered to an extreme degree and insolent to foreigners; it never acquired practice in the conduct of normal diplomatic relations with neighboring sovereign states.[2] From China proper, which was a territory defined differently in different historical epochs according to the strength and consolidation of the country, Chinese influence stretched out in all directions and expressed itself in the acquisition of suzerain rights. These rights also varied through time, both in regard to the territory encompassed and the intensity of Chinese dominance. From a Chinese point of view, these rights were felt to be justified not only by considerations of national security but also by the fact that China's civilization was clearly

[1] Early in 1965, Indonesia left the United Nations and some of its specialized agencies as a protest against Malaysia's becoming a permanent member of the Security Council. Sukarno was keeping all doors open, however, by hinting that this move might be only temporary and by declaring Indonesia willing to negotiate under the auspices of the United Nations or Afro-Asian powers.

[2] In view of this circumstance and the importance of integrating China into a world with ever closer international relations, the foolishness of the United States policy of keeping China outside the United Nations and denying it an apprenticeship in diplomacy is glaringly apparent. More recently the international isolation of China has been intensified by the break between it and the Soviet Union.

superior to that of these tributary areas. This system did not encourage or necessitate the fixing of definite boundaries in all directions; rather it resulted in large territories being left as frontier regions within China's recognized sphere of influence. It was a system that, as we have seen, the British also often followed toward the north, though Britain and the other colonial powers in South Asia felt compelling reasons to establish explicitly the boundaries between their own colonial empires. This was another element in China's boundlessness. Still another was its relative indifference to nations outside the territories where it cared to exert suzerainty; even India was in this category, not to speak of faraway Europe and, later, the United States.

China's attitude toward boundary questions and international affairs generally has, as a result, been given a somewhat different twist by its more recent history. Under the increasingly ineffective rule of the Manchus, China was for more than a century unable to resist the encroachments of European colonial powers, including tsarist Russia,[1] on its suzerain rights abroad and its territorial integrity at home; these encroachments were especially numerous and ruthless during the era of the "new imperialism" after the 1870's. But except for the many occasions when local or central authorities succumbed to a feeling of utter helplessness, or were simply bribed, the Chinese government did not accept the frontiers imposed on it as valid and permanent. When the Chinese revolution in 1911 and the establishment of the Republic of China were followed by further infringements on Chinese rights – British attempts to loosen Tibet's traditional ties to China and the establishment of the McMahon Line, without Chinese consent, the conversion of Outer Mongolia into a Russian satellite, Japan's intrusions in Manchuria, etc. – the outrage to Chinese nationalism demanded a moral and political expiation of the sins of colonial frontier policies. On this point the present Communist government of China follows the line established by staunch nationalist leaders like Sun Yat-sen and Chiang Kai-shek. And we have seen that the territorial demands it has raised have always had the support of the Chinese exile government on Formosa.

Against this background, it is no wonder that, in the beginning, the new states in South Asia felt that free China, under the present government even more than the Kuomintang government, was similar to them in that it had come into being in the fight for, and in the end as a result of, the liquidation of Western – and in China's case also tsarist Russian – imperialism, and had national grievances to set right. Indeed, this view

[1] It is entirely in line with the Chinese government's general policy, as founded on the traditional ambitions of all Chinese nationalists, that the Soviet Union has not been exempted from demands for a boundary resettlement. We do not imply by this that the recent ideological and political conflict between the two great Communist powers has not influenced both the timing and the manner of China's raising this issue.

was correct, and it is a sad commentary on how the Western nations succumb to their own propaganda that their opposition to Communism led them to lose sight of this fundamental historical fact. When the United States failed to recognize the government that took over after the Communist revolution, maintaining the fiction that China continued to be ruled by the exile Kuomintang government on Formosa, and maneuvered China's exclusion from the United Nations,[1] its lead was not followed by all of its allies in South Asia.[2]

Again, with China's background in mind – and it is a living tradition with the Mandarin class of Chinese – it should not surprise us that in the negotiations leading up to its border agreements China requested a recognition that the boundary lines drawn up by the colonial powers without its effective participation, and often against its protests, were invalid. What should surprise us is the fact that when that moral and ideological basis had been established, China was prepared to agree to boundaries with its southern neighbors that are reasonable and do not imply nationalist expansion. It did not press its demands to the maximum of what it could legally and militarily insist on.[3] Surprisingly often China accepted

[1] The writer has criticized United States policy on this score in *Challenge to Affluence,* Pantheon, New York, 1963, Chapter 9.

[2] Pakistan took the same line as India and the other neutralist countries in South Asia regarding diplomatic relations and the proper party to represent China in the United Nations. India did not change its position even after its border conflict with China developed into an undeclared war.

[3] A recent comment in an Australian periodical is worth quoting at some length: "It seems clear from the recent history of Chinese frontier policy that China would, other factors being equal, prefer to create a buffer than to assert ancient territorial claims. In the Sino-Burmese Boundary Treaty of 1960 the Chinese surrendered claims over much of the upper Irrawaddy valley, claims to which both Manchus and Republic had adhered, in return for a settled border with very minor adjustments. The same can be seen in the Sino-Nepalese boundary agreement of 1962, in which the Outer Protectorate status of Nepal was surrendered by China in return for an agreed frontier which did not depart radically from that which Nepal claimed. In the Sino-Pakistan Boundary Agreement of 1963, likewise, the Chinese made a significant abandonment of past claims in return for a workable boundary. In this instance they gave up, albeit tacitly, their argument to some kind of suzerainty over the State of Hunza which now forms part of Pakistan. . . . It could be argued that in the cases of Burma, Nepal and Pakistan, given the extent of the claims which China could have raised had she wished, the Chinese have given rather more than they received."

The author feels that the unsettled boundary conflict with India is partly "due to a mishandling of the problem by Indian diplomats" but more fundamentally to "the basic unsuitability of India as a Chinese buffer state." To qualify as a "buffer state" a country should, in his terms, be "unlikely either to attack China or to serve as bases for any power hostile to China." He concludes:

"There is no evidence that the Chinese have any intention of undertaking the physical occupation of this buffer belt between the Burmese Himalayas and the Gulf of Tonkin, or, for that matter, that they intend to take these states under some form of Chinese colonial rule. So long as they have been 'neutralised,' that is to say effectively denied to the influence of the West, the Chinese are probably content; and, in turn, this probably means that the Chinese will continue to tolerate Western influence in the states beyond the buffer, Thailand, Cambodia and South Vietnam, so long as it

the "imperialist legacy." (India's pride prevented it from acknowledging inherited sin and it has consequently been punished in a wasteful border war with China.) A third reflection is the equally hopeful one that China, as part of its modernization drive – and to please the underdeveloped new countries in South Asia and elsewhere – is now for the first time in its long history prepared to negotiate and establish definite and demarcated border lines around its empire, which would thus no longer be boundless as in ancient times.

Against this sanguine perspective – from the South Asian point of view – it can be argued that agreement on formal boundaries will not prevent China from exerting pressure on its weaker neighbors to follow foreign and domestic policies that coincide with its interests. In fact, no great power has ever abstained entirely from doing this, though both the methods employed and the intensity of the pressure brought to bear have varied; and it would be foolhardy to expect that China would establish an exception in world history. Independence always is a relative thing for small weak countries bordering on great ones, especially when the former are not protected by an age-old tradition of statehood. Nevertheless, the existence of definite and demarcated boundaries should strengthen a nation's ability to maintain control of its internal and even external policies. The degree of independence enjoyed by China's neighbors will depend on how well these countries succeed in achieving national consolidation and development, on the environment created by international politics, and, of course, on China's own fate.

It is generally assumed that China has a special interest in Southeast Asia. For this there are several reasons. Southeast Asia opens up toward China without the extreme natural deterrent of the Himalayan border region farther to the west, and must, when viewed from China, seem un-

---

does not threaten the 'neutrality' of the buffer itself. It may well be argued that Chinese interest in the South Vietnamese crisis lies very largely in the fact that its solution in a way acceptable to Washington does contain a very real threat to the 'neutral' status of the Hanoi Government."

Even Pakistan can be regarded as a buffer state in this sense: "Both Pakistan and Afghanistan have, in the 1960s, adopted postures of 'neutrality' towards China which, so long as they are not departed from, will ensure a tranquil frontier. This 'neutrality,' it should be noted, does not seem to imply the necessity for anything like a Communist regime. Pakistan at present is ruled by a military oligarchy far removed from the Marxist ideal, and Afghanistan is a monarchy with many medieval features. The point is that, as at present constituted, neither State is likely to permit its territory to be used as a base for measures directed towards embarrassing the Chinese Government. In this sense it may perhaps be argued that both Pakistan and Afghanistan, for the time being at least, are filling the role of Chinese buffers." (Alastair Lamb, "China's Land Borders," *Australia's Neighbours* (Melbourne), September-October, 1964, pp. 3–4.) It would seem, however, that India even more than Pakistan could have qualified as a "buffer state" within this frame of reference.

derpopulated and over-rich in land and resources.[1] Add to this what East and Spate call the "demographic immaturity" of the populations in Southeast Asia, made worse by the inheritance of carelessly drawn linear boundaries, which are "traced for the most part through completely unknown country" and which "in addition to catastrophically arresting indigenous politico-geographical evolution . . . proved to be singularly ill-conceived in relation to both topographical and ethnographical realities."[2] Finally, it is notable that all Southeast Asian countries contain large Chinese minorities who are unassimilated and discriminated against. The sincerity of the allegiance of these aliens to the new states is felt to be in doubt. The indigenous ruling elites tend to look upon them as a sort of Trojan horse that China might use to subvert the political order and endanger their independence.[3] Naturally, this fear becomes more justified the more they are discriminated against. Actually, of course, many Chinese who suffer this discrimination take the attitude that if China has a powerful government, whatever its ideology, persons of Chinese origin will be more respected abroad.

The last point is important as the first Chinese Republic in 1912, following old-established Chinese law, based citizenship on the principle of *jus sanguinis,* making all Chinese abroad and their descendants Chinese citizens. The Kuomintang government on Formosa has never given up this principle. The Communist regime, in the friendly climate created at the Bandung Conference, seemed more prepared to allow Chinese who had settled abroad to choose between retaining Chinese nationality and opting for that of the country in which they lived. If followed out, this policy along with China's willingness to fix definite boundaries without insisting on large-scale expansion, would be another act of modernization working toward peaceful co-existence with independent states in Southeast Asia. In the case of Indonesia – despite an interval of high tension when the Chinese merchants and moneylenders were driven out of the villages in 1961–63 – the Chinese government observed a hands-off policy in regard to the interests of the Chinese minority; in fact, after the Bandung meeting, it signed treaties with Indonesia and with Burma, relinquishing the

[1] It is, indeed, something of an historical riddle why the Chinese pressure against Southeast Asia has been restricted to the occasional acquisition of suzerainty rights and a trickle of Chinese immigration. Why did not the Chinese swarm over Southeast Asia in great masses and incorporate the territory into the Chinese empire hundreds or thousands of years ago? The deadliness of the malaria-infested jungles might be the answer, but there was malaria in South China as well.

[2] East and Spate, *The Changing Map of Asia,* p. 199.

[3] Americans frequently find justification for the refusal of their government to accord diplomatic recognition to China's government, or to permit it to take the Chinese seat in the United Nations, in the argument that such action would tend to strengthen the feelings of attachment and, hence, of loyalty of the overseas Chinese to their motherland.

principle of *jus sanguinis.*[1] Whether the Chinese government will really apply the same principle, so intrinsically in disagreement with the traditional Chinese nationalism that otherwise has informed its policies, in its dealings with less friendly countries in Southeast Asia must seem doubtful.[2]

Taking all these things into consideration, the prospect that Southeast Asia might be swarmed over by the Chinese at a propitious time cannot be discarded offhand. If Southeast Asians, for understandable reasons, often find it inopportune to express their fear in too clear a text, except in private conversation, Western writers who have discussed the matter are less inhibited. Thus Chester Bowles, an American liberal statesman who has twice served as ambassador to New Delhi, and who has occasionally questioned the wisdom of keeping China outside the United Nations, sees the possibility of Chinese expansion into Southeast Asia "with its wealth of under-populated, food-rich countryside, as well as the great reserves of oil, tin, rubber and other resources which China badly needs." Speaking for the United States, he concludes: "Our objective must be to create a military, political and economic barrier sufficient to discourage any such attempt."[3]

Unfortunately for Washington, French policy in Indo-China in colonial times, but, more particularly, after the Second World War, and Dutch policy in what was the Netherlands Indies very much worsened conditions in the region and decreased the likelihood that the United States can make these countries strong bulwarks against both Communism and Chinese pressure.[4] For Dutch post-war policy, the United States is not responsible; indeed, it did its best to counteract it after the war. However, the United States, after an initial period of disinterest, supported the French colonial war in Indo-China, although it was unable to prevent the ultimate collapse of French authority in the area. A considerable and gradually increasing part of Indo-China came under Communist rule or came to lean toward Communism, but this was not the result of any action by China; it was a reaction to French colonial policy. Another large part of Southeast Asia, Indonesia, had, as a similar legacy from colonialism, the strongest Communist Party in South Asia, and was increasingly taking an anti-Western position, a concomitant of its conflict with the Federation of Malaysia.

[1] There is a clause in the treaty, however, making it possible for them to regain Chinese nationality if they should wish to do so.

[2] The Chinese constitution drawn up in 1953 contained a provision enabling the overseas Chinese communities to be represented in the National People's Congress.

[3] Chester Bowles, "The 'China Problem' Reconsidered," *Foreign Affairs,* April, 1960, p. 483.

Many writers believe that the Chinese threat is not limited to Southeast Asia. "The aim – hegemony [over Southern Asia] – has been constant since 1949, but the techniques and tactics have varied." (Michael Brecher, *The New States of Asia,* Oxford University Press, London, 1963, p. 163.)

[4] Chapter 4, Sections 11 and 12.

In the division of responsibility within the Western bloc, the United States has for the time being left the defense of Malaysia[1] to the British (and the Australians and New Zealanders). It has tried to placate the Indonesians with economic aid and even military equipment, and it helped them to wrest West New Guinea from the Dutch. In Indo-China, or rather the part of it that by 1954 was not already lost beyond remedy, the United States shouldered the role of helper and protector in order to prevent a further drift of peoples and territories into the Communist sphere. In Laos the United States policy was unsuccessful almost from the beginning; despite considerable assistance, including military support, the country had to be given over to a "neutral" government in 1962, and this regime has not restored order or hindered the Communist advance.[2]

Initially, United States military and economic aid to South Vietnam – which against the intention of the Geneva settlement was established as a separate state – scored some moderate gains, mainly in helping to consolidate the truncated new state and settle refugees. It did not, however, succeed in promoting the economic development of South Vietnam so that it would be less dependent on large-scale foreign aid. Since economic aid went mainly to pay for consumption goods, the cost to the United States, quite apart from military aid, remained very high.[3] More recently, a full-scale civil war has developed in South Vietnam and the National Liberation Front (the Viet Cong, as it was called in the United States in the propaganda war), which has been supported from the northern part of Vietnam, was gradually winning ground in spite of an impressive build-up of the military forces of the South Vietnam government. With decreasing support from the people, the South Vietnamese leadership has had to rule by ever more authoritarian methods, and though there were a series of coups, none of them produced a stable government. By 1965 the country was in flame and confusion despite the deployment there of an increasing American military force, which was more and more impelled to exceed its role as an advisory group.

The gradually increasing involvement of the United States in the war in Vietnam began immediately after the Geneva settlement of the French colonial war in Indo-China in 1954. It was inaugurated by President Eisenhower in an attempt to follow out the position he had taken against the Truman government during the election campaign in 1952, to wit: "If there must be war there [in Asia], let it be Asians against Asians, with our support on the side of freedom."[4] That policy has broken down. The United

[1] Section 12 above.

[2] Chapter 9, Section 15.

[3] The total cost till the end of 1964 – before the "escalation" – has been calculated at considerably over $3 billion.

[4] *U. S. News and World Report,* October 31, 1952, p. 18.

"Mr. Dulles indicated that a key feature of the Administration's Far East strategy was a long range program for disengaging Western military forces by replacing them

States has "escalated" its military commitment in the war and is now weighing the possibility of engaging its own military forces in a large-scale attack on North Vietnam – and eventually China, if it comes out in support of the latter country – and doing this without the operational base of a stable government and a loyal following among a united people in South Vietnam. The other two alternatives are to get out or to take a defensive position, holding on to what they now control, without waging a major war; the latter choice might only delay the need to get out. Withdrawal would signify the final failure of American policy in Indo-China.[1]

The most tragic aspect of the situation – from a Western point of view – is that the strength of Communism in the nationalist movement in Indo-China was created, first, by the character of France's policy during decades of colonial rule and, second, by its imperialist intransigency after the Second World War. De Gaulle – who instigated the latter phase of French policy – has advised France's American ally to appeal for the "neutralization" of South Vietnam and the whole of Indo-China and, indeed, all Southeast Asia, and, by implication, to withdraw its military forces. By drawing such lessons from France's defeat in Indo-China and its later defeat in North Africa, de Gaulle undoubtedly succeeded in restoring France's posture in these regions and in the world. But this courageous and rational political retreat and his recommendation to the United States to act in the same way have not been accompanied by any recognition on de Gaulle's part of earlier French responsibility for the situations created in Indo-China. France's new posture must, therefore, be felt by thoughtful and informed Americans as salt in the wound.

Again, we have to recall that there is no such thing as historical necessity. Had different policies been pursued, there might today be an altogether different situation in former French Indo-China. Judging the present situation, it is feasible, as we have shown, to lay bare and analyze the play of economic and political forces against the background of history. But what the future, even the near future, holds as a result of the opera-

---

with Asian troops." ("The News of the Week in Review," *New York Times*, February 22, 1953, p. 1.)

In the election campaign, this program had been developed by Eisenhower as a counter to Truman's Korean policy: "The new program, it is understood, is contemplated as an extension of President Eisenhower's announcement during the election campaign that more of the Korean battleline should be manned by South Korean troops, with Asians thus fighting Asians." (T. J. Hamilton, "U. S. Plans to Arm Asians for Defense in Long Range Aim," *New York Times*, February 7, 1953, p. 1.) While redefining the inherited principle of "containment," it remained an important element in Republican foreign policy, together with "instantaneous retaliation" and "brinkmanship."

[1] Internal developments in South Vietnam as a separate state will be discussed in Chapter 9, Section 16, where military developments during 1965 will also be commented on.

tion of these forces, and human actions and reactions on all sides, cannot be scientifically established. One negative inference may be drawn, namely, that as things have been permitted to develop, China's relations with Southeast Asia can no longer be regarded as a simple matter of boundary disputes, the problem on which we have focussed our main attention in this chapter. This outcome was not necessary, but it is now a fact.

Chapter 6

PARTITION OF IMPERIAL INDIA AND ITS AFTERMATH

1 *The Basis of Pakistan's Statehood*

The partition of the Indian subcontinent on the withdrawal of the British raj is the most important exception to the general rule that the new states of South Asia accepted the configuration of political entities established by imperial conquest and rivalry and took their definition of nationhood from this legacy. During the last few years of British rule a small but resolute group of men in the All India Muslim League, headed by Mohammed Ali Jinnah, successfully mobilized mass support for the idea of an independent Moslem homeland, or Pakistan. This idea took root and flourished mainly because of the religious split between Moslems and Hindus and the communal conflicts stirred up by extremists in both groups. When the danger of civil war and anarchy appeared imminent, the leadership of the Indian National Congress, which included several outstanding Moslem personalities, felt compelled against its better judgment to accept partition as the price of a rapid and peaceful settlement of the independence issue. To the very end, some Congress leaders, including Gandhi and Maulana Abul Kalam Azad, dissociated themselves in principle from the idea of partition.

The communal excitements and disorders that preceded and followed partition were largely confined, as indeed was the whole struggle for Moslem independence, to the northern part of British India. It is a fact, seldom given enough emphasis, that Moslems and Hindus in southern India did not participate very actively in these dramatic and portentous happenings.[1] The two groups continued to live rather peacefully together here, and some of the Congress leaders from the South were among the first to break the front of Congress resistance to the Moslem demand for partition. The leaders of the untouchable castes in India, though most of them remained loyal to the Congress, could not have had the same zeal for resisting partition, or, rather, resisting the theme of the Moslem movement: freedom from Hindu domination.[2]

No country in South Asia has so little historical individuality as Pakistan.[3] It cannot claim descent from the Mogul empires, which represented not nation-states but loosely knit entities wherein a Moslem ruler and aristocracy dominated a mixed population, few of whom were ever converted to Islam. The demand for Pakistan as a separate homeland for nearly one-quarter of the population of British India was instead a kind of Moslem zionism – the more so since before partition there were no large areas exclusively inhabited by Moslems. It rested on the assertion that Hinduism and Islam were not merely different religions but that the two peoples were distinct nations as well. This "two-nation doctrine" had been vaguely propounded by Moslem leaders toward the end of the nineteenth century; it subsequently gained currency whenever cooperation with the Hindu majority became difficult. Thus, following the rejection of separate

[1] Nor for that matter had southern India been much involved in the Indian Mutiny of 1857. Perhaps there is an even longer thread of historical continuity, for those who at various times in Indian history sought to unify the peoples on the subcontinent began by first organizing a land power in the northwest. They were never wholly successful, primarily because of their failure to solve the problem of maintaining lines of communication between the North and South. Consequently, the peoples of the peninsular South often remained almost as distant and strange to the northerners as did foreigners. Britain reversed this long tradition and successfully united the country by starting out from the peninsular South. Cf. C. S. Venkatacher, *Geographical Realities of India,* Far Eastern Economist Pamphlet, No. 34, New Delhi, 1955.

Turning to modern history, interest in the Kashmir conflict has in recent years been visibly less intense in southern and eastern India than in the northwest section of the country; similarly, there has been less concern in East than in West Pakistan.

[2] "From the depressed Castes' point of view, Muslims or British or almost anyone would have been better as rulers than upper-caste Hindus." (W. Norman Brown, *The United States and India and Pakistan,* Oxford University Press, Calcutta, edition for India, Burma, and Ceylon, 1953, p. 136.)

The Indian Communist Party in its first congress, in the spring of 1943, came out in favor of partition.

[3] Even the name Pakistan is an artificial construction, made up from the initial letters of the provinces of Punjab, Afghania (the North-West Frontier Province), Kashmir, and Sind and the Persian word *stan,* meaning country. As *pak* in Persian-Urdu means pure, by a convenient coincidence the whole word signifies "land of the pure." Its parentage is usually attributed to a pamphlet *Now or Never,* signed and published by Choudhary Rehmat Ali and three other Cambridge students in 1933.

communal electorates by Congress leaders, Sir Muhammad Iqbal, in his presidential address to the Muslim League in 1930, put forward the idea of a separate Moslem homeland in northwest India, but one that would remain "within the body politic of India."[1] Not until the late 1930's did Iqbal suggest: "Why should not the Moslems of North-West India *and Bengal* be considered as a nation *entitled to self-determination* just as other nations in India and outside India are?"[2] Jinnah anticipated this line of reasoning. After participating in the abortive London conference of 1930–32 he remarked: "In the face of danger the Hindu sentiment, the Hindu mind, the Hindu attitude led me to the conclusion that there was no hope of unity."[3] In 1934 he declared in more definite terms: "We are a nation with our own distinctive culture and civilization, language and literature, art and architecture, names and nomenclature, sense of value and proportion, legal laws and moral codes, custom and calendar, history and tradition, aptitude and ambition; in short, we have our own distinctive outlook on life. By all canons of international law we are a nation."[4] As an avowed political objective, however, the demand for Pakistan was not adopted by the Muslim League until its meeting in Lahore in 1940, only seven years before partition. If this stand was intended to be a bargaining position, as some believed, Jinnah pursued the goal of Pakistan with such calculated logic, skill, and determination that in the end no independence settlement was possible without partition.[5]

This is not to imply that partition was inevitable once the Muslim League formally adopted an independent Pakistan state as its political program.[6] No historical explanation of partition can ignore the play of chance events on the feelings and actions of the dominant figures involved. In this connection the personalities and individual contributions of Jinnah and Gandhi were all-important. Nor can we overlook the cardinal mistakes in policy and tactics made by all parties concerned during the last decade of British rule. Until too late the Congress leadership refused to take the pretensions of the League seriously and the British complacently waited

[1] *Struggle for Independence 1857–1947,* Pakistan Publications, Karachi, 1958, Appendix IV, p. 17.

[2] Letter to Jinnah, June 21, 1937, in *ibid.,* Appendix V, p. 35. Italics added.

[3] *Ibid.,* p. 64.

[4] *Ibid.*

[5] Indians believe that Jinnah made up his mind seriously to seek independence for a new Moslem state only at the last moment. Maulana Abul Kalam Azad, according to his posthumously published memoirs, written by Humayun Kabir, a friend and close associate, held the opinion that "Till perhaps the very end Pakistan was for Jinnah a bargaining counter, but in fighting for Pakistan, he had overreached himself." (Maulana Abul Kalam Azad, *India Wins Freedom,* Orient Longmans, Calcutta, 1959, p. 83.)

[6] Naturally, the view that it was not inevitable is more often expressed in India. In an interview conducted by an American scholar, Nehru stated: "The partition of India became inevitable, I should say, in less than a year before it occurred. It wasn't inevitable till the last year." (Michael Brecher, *The New States of Asia,* Oxford University Press, New York, 1963, p. 195.)

on events.[1] In the end, Jinnah could not accept any sort of attachment to an all-Indian union in lieu of an independent Pakistan state. A closer look at Indian history will help to make the position of Jinnah and the Muslim League more intelligible.

2 *The Deeper Roots of Partition*

With the arrival of British rule in India, Moslems gradually lost the positions of power and influence they had enjoyed under the Moguls. The substitution of English for Persian as the official language of government and the introduction of English law diminished their role in the public services. No large Moslem urban upper and middle class existed because its functions had been effectively and willingly performed by Hindus. And later it was the Hindus who responded more eagerly and quickly to the educational opportunities created by British rule. Consequently, the growing class of officials, clerks, and professional and business people was recruited largely from this community.

The disparate social and economic advancement of the two main communities in the nineteenth century had a geographical dimension, too, in that areas with a predominantly Moslem population remained more backward and poorer than the rest. Thus the thriving commercial center of Calcutta was in the western part of Bengal, while Karachi in Sind was a small and insignificant port, where in any case Hindus predominated. Sind as a whole was a poor outlying territory ruled from Bombay, whereas the barrenness of the North-West Frontier Province is legendary. As for the Punjab, the scene of the worst atrocities that were to follow partition, the relative position of the two communities there has been described as follows:

> In that province most of the commercial, industrial and banking establishments were controlled by Hindus. In none of them was any Muslim employed except in a menial capacity as a coolie or watchman or as an artisan. Well-paid posts and positions of profit were not open to outsiders, but were filled on the basis of family, caste and other similar connections according to the deeply-embedded habits and traditions of Hindu society.[2]

[1] Immediately following the statement quoted in the preceding footnote, Nehru declared: "I don't think that preceding the war they [the British] had any clear ideas about partition or, indeed, wanted it. But obviously throughout that period, and long before, the British Government's policy, as the policy of any such governing authority in a colonial territory, was to weaken the national movement. And the major way of weakening it was to play up the Muslim League and other dissident elements. . . . I think now, looking back, that Partition could have been stopped if the British Government's policy had been different, about a year or, say, eighteen months before the partition." (*Ibid.*)

[2] Penderel Moon, *Divide and Quit*, Chatto & Windus, London, 1961, p. 288.

Only the big landlords among the Moslems flourished, and they were mainly in Bengal, Bihar, Orissa, and the United Provinces. When, late in the day, Moslems began to evince an interest in the public services and business and professional occupations, it was this landlord class from which most of them originated or to which, if successful, they became related by marriage. With Hindus already entrenched, however, Moslems remained underrepresented in the growing urban upper class – which in Asia is usually called the "middle class" – and felt discriminated against by both the Hindus and the British. This feeling was probably keenest with respect to the administrative services of the central government.[1] In addition, Moslem producers of cotton and jute alleged that the commercial policy of maintaining high tariffs and encouraging industry, which was introduced toward the end of the colonial era and supported by the Congress movement, operated against their interests and in favor of Hindu mill owners and capitalists.[2] The relatively small number of Moslem capitalists, merchants, and bankers saw in the creation of Pakistan the prospect of less fierce competition and greater profits. Even before partition the Muslim League passed resolutions urging Moslems to consume goods manufactured or sold by Moslems. Pakistan as a political program thus whetted the appetites of the ambitious. Moslems in humbler circumstances also felt that their lot would improve if they could escape from Hindu oppression.[3]

It is not surprising that a Moslem society dominated by large landowners could not identify itself enthusiastically and wholeheartedly with the liberalist opposition to British rule the Congress movement initially expressed and developed. The Hindu nationalism subsequently fostered by religious revivalists like Tilak was, of course, inimical to every Moslem ambition and inevitably tended to widen the gulf between the two communities. After the First World War, however, the Congress movement under

[1] Hindus with long memories would in their turn recall the discrimination and persecution their forebears had often suffered under the Moguls.

[2] "It has been reported that when the Cotton Bill was being discussed in the Central Assembly, Jinnah did not realize the conflict of interests between Hindu mill owners and Muslim producers of cotton and supported a high tariff policy which was in favour of the cotton manufacturing interests of Bombay and Ahmedabad. Sikander Hyat [the Muslim premier of the Punjab] rushed to Delhi to impress upon the Quaid-i-Azam [Jinnah] that as leader of the Muslims he should support the interests of Muslim cotton growers and not the mill owners. When Jinnah was informed of this, he was quite disturbed and asked Sikander Hyat to assure the *zamindars* of Punjab that such a mistake would not occur again." (Khalid Bin Sayeed, *Pakistan, The Formative Phase,* Pakistan Publishing House, Karachi, 1960, p. 97.)

[3] "To the Muslim masses this [partition] held out an ill-defined but alluring prospect of looting Hindus. With greater clarity of vision, ambitious politicians and civil servants, as also some professional men, perceived that under a Muslim Raj, with the crippling if not the elimination of Hindu competition, they could rise to positions of power and affluence unattainable in a single mixed Hindu-Muslim State." (Penderel Moon, *Divide and Quit,* p. 22.)

Gandhi's saintly but politically astute leadership began to preach the unity and equality of all religions. To unite Moslems and Hindus in common cause against the British, Gandhi seized upon the dismay that traditionalist Moslems felt at the defeat and dismemberment of the Ottoman Empire in West Asia by the West European powers and their treatment of Persia and Afghanistan as playthings of international politics.[1] Many Moslems joined the Congress and for a time Jinnah became one of its leading figures. Indeed, at the end of the First World War Jinnah dismissed the threat of Hindu domination as a bogey designed to undermine the unity of the struggle for independence from Britain.

But the honeymoon between Hindus and Moslems did not last for long. In the Congress itself, as in society at large, Moslems found themselves in the minority and out of place. Despite its broad-minded leaders and secularist resolutions, the Congress was basically Hindu in outlook. To win the popular backing necessary, as he thought, to bring pressure on the British to quit India, Gandhi had to appeal to the masses in an idiom they could readily understand, which meant in religious terms. He achieved some degree of success in northern India but only at the expense of alienating the Moslems, for his religious appeal was heavily spiced with Hindu symbolism. With all his tolerance he could not but offend faithful Moslems by his emphatic support of cow protection and idol worship.[2] With a Hindu's preference for ideals rather than reality, Gandhi believed that the Congress, and he especially, being broad-minded, tolerant, and moral, could and did represent everyone. Yet under the cloak of its sophisticated leadership, most Congress supporters were crudely indifferent, if not hostile, to Moslem interests.[3] Therefore, the more successful the Congress was in appealing to the masses, the more it became, in Moslem eyes, an essentially Hindu organization. It was thus Gandhi more than anyone

[1] Moslems also resented Britain's declared policy of establishing a Jewish homeland in Palestine at the expense of the Arabs.

[2] Of this aspect of Gandhi, Frank Moraes has written:

"The result of his teaching, with its strong bias against modern civilization and culture and its simultaneous stress on the need for political independence, was to create a sort of intellectual schizophrenia, a split approach to political and economic problems. Gandhi regarded himself as primarily an Indian, but his political appeal was largely religious and mainly Hindu. . . . One unfortunate result of the Mahatma's attempt to give politics a religious hue was gradually to antagonize the Moslems and to deepen their suspicion that his politics was steeped in Hinduism. It was ironic, since Gandhi was no religious conservative and in reality sought to secularize Hinduism." (Frank Moraes, *India Today*, Macmillan, New York, 1960, pp. 72–73.)

Where Gandhi was a spokesman for reform, he occasionally used as an argument the Moslem dislike of Hindu tradition: "You cannot finally solve the Hindu-Muslim problem until you have removed the stain of untouchability by non-violent means. The Muslims will then cease to regard us as unbelievers." (Priyaranjan Sen, *Mahatma Gandhi's Sayings*, selected by the author, Orient Book Company, Calcutta, 2nd ed., 1948, pp. 24, 25.)

[3] "Many a Congressman was a communalist under his national cloak." (Jawaharlal Nehru, *An Autobiography*, The Bodley Head, London, 1953, p. 136.)

else who helped to transform Jinnah from a keen Indian nationalist into the architect of Pakistan.

An additional reason for the growing estrangement of Moslem leaders from the Congress movement was its increasing commitment, under the influence of Nehru and other left-wing intellectuals, to radical policy declarations. Hindu capitalists, anxious to end British competition and willing, therefore, to support the Congress movement financially, hoped – not without good reason as it proved – that this emerging radicalism need not be taken too literally. The dominant landed interests of the Muslim League, whom Hindu intellectuals regarded as the relics of an outworn feudalism, detested this ideological trend in the Congress.[1] As it turned out, with partition many Moslem landlords found themselves and their vast estates on the wrong side of the boundary. Even so, most were able to transfer much of their wealth to Pakistan where they were unmolested, while independent India, on the other hand, enacted the zamindar reform.[2] From the standpoint of their own economic interests, therefore, this class had little reason, even in retrospect, to regret the fact of partition.

In the fateful conjunction of forces making for partition, in which religious,[3] cultural, social, economic, and political elements interacted, British policy played a decisive role. Almost to the end of the nineteenth century the British distrusted the Moslem upper stratum as the former governing class, representative of an older India, whose violent, conservative revolt against Western influences lay at the heart of the Indian Mutiny. Hindus

[1] With their simple "Marxism," the more radical intellectual leaders in the Congress believed that their program of social and agrarian reform would induce the Moslem masses to disown their leaders.

[2] Chapter 7, Section 2; Chapter 26, Section 13.

[3] The religious element should not be minimized. Although over the centuries Hinduism and Islam have borrowed rites, customs, and even – at a higher level – ideas, or rather, doctrines, from each other, the difference between them is very wide. It is certainly much wider than that between Roman Catholicism and Protestantism, for instance, in whose name a number of cruel European wars were fought. Islam contains many ideas and customs repugnant to Hindus and the reverse is true. Cow slaughter to the Hindus and idol worship to the Moslems are good instances in point.

Under the influence of "Marxism" there has been a tendency to minimize the religious element in the forces making for partition. Nehru often expressed this bias: "The new development of communalism had little to do with religious differences. These admittedly could be adjusted. It was a political conflict between those who wanted a free, united and democratic India and certain reactionary and feudal elements who, under the guise of religion, wanted to preserve their special interests. Religion, as practised and exploited in this way by its votaries of different creeds, seemed to me a curse and a barrier to all progress, social and individual. Religion, which was supposed to encourage spirituality and brotherly feeling, became the fountain head of hatred, narrowness and meanness, and the lowest materialism." (Nehru, *An Autobiography,* p. 606.)

The first sentence of this quotation is an exaggeration. Yet it is clear that religion can easily be used to provide a highly emotionalized and sanctified rationalization for actions that are selfishly motivated. It is the "passivity" of religion, its "meaninglessness," that makes it a handy tool for those who want to use it, for whatever purpose. See Chapter 3, Section 7.

were regarded with more approval because they responded more readily to Western influences (Britain did not in the beginning grasp the political significance of the emerging Westernized Hindu "middle class"). Indeed, the practice of favoring the Hindus over the Moslems was often regarded by British officials of this period as a basic feature of British policy. But when educated Hindus, with a growing sense of unity and determination, stood up against the continuation of British rule, a trend coincident with the rise of the Congress movement, British administrators began to favor Moslem interests instead. At the same time, Moslem leaders like Sir Sayyed Ahmad Khan saw in loyalty to the British the best protection for Moslems against Hindu domination. By the end of British rule in India the majority of British civil servants there were emotionally pro-Moslem.[1] Moslems were now welcome in the Indian Civil Service and in the schools preparing for such a career; however, relatively few availed themselves of these opportunities, partly because of the tradition of being on the outside and partly, and more decisively, because of the economic and social structure of the Moslem community with its much smaller urban "middle class."

This type of colonial policy, often labelled "divide and rule," could not only be rationalized but sincerely supported, as a matter of defending the weaker party or ensuring fair play for the underdog.[2] It was manifested in the division of administrative areas according to the majority religion and in the creation of separate representation, electorates, and reserved quotas for particular communities,[3] that was extended with every constitutional

[1] Leonard Mosley, *The Last Days of the British Raj*, Harcourt, Brace & World, New York, 1961, pp. 15–16.

[2] The thesis that the "divide and rule" policy of the British was responsible for partition is more acceptable to Indians than to Pakistanis, since by implication it detracts from Jinnah's achievements and the claim of Moslems to constitute a separate nation.

[3] This was British policy elsewhere in their colonial empire as well. T. H. Silcock, a most competent British observer with apologetic but liberal leanings, explains:

"We here encounter one of the curiosities of the British system of colonial development which has often led to our being considered hypocritical in our attitude to development. We have been accused of a policy of divide and rule in most of the territories in which we have exercised control, and we almost invariably leave behind difficult problems of integration, such as the Hindu-Muslim problem in India, because of this basic attitude. I refer to our basic attitude of separate obligation to almost any group which feels itself to be different, provided its interest does not conflict too strongly with the basic purpose for which power was secured in the first instance." (T. H. Silcock, *The Commonwealth Economy in Southeast Asia*, Duke University Press, Durham, N. C., 1959, p. 77.)

"If it is convenient and will cause minimum political strife to govern through an existing sultan, even if his territory is hopelessly inadequate for a modern state, he will become the unit through which rule is exercised and his advisers, although they are British, will become a vested interest and will preserve the sultan's position against the requirements of any wider unit to the limit of their powers. Moreover, this does not apply only to territorial units. The Chinese of the Straits Settlements were administered through their own community leaders, and this policy, which fostered a system of bidding for leadership within the community, has helped to perpetuate the communal pattern in modern Malaya." (*Ibid.*, p. 79.)

advance and found its ultimate expression in the constitution handed down by the British under the Government of India Act of 1935.[1] So deeply did the consequences of this policy infect the body politic that neither India nor Pakistan has yet eradicated them. The system of separate electorates and representatives for particular communities ensured, as K. M. Panikkar has pointed out, that "there could be a Hindu-Muslim alliance but no united national movement."[2] Admittedly, joint electorates would not necessarily have led Hindus and Moslems to adopt a national view, or to regard one another with tolerance. But the more the Moslems were singled out for special treatment, the more conscious they became of their minority status. Consequently, national politics became increasingly poisoned by communal loyalties.

So long as the British monopolized all political power there was little for Hindus and Moslems to quarrel over. Only when political power began to be transferred, albeit slowly and reluctantly, did rivalry between them become really acute. The dangers this portended might have been lessened if, once the goal of self-government had been proclaimed, political power had been handed over to a central Hindu-Moslem government before appeals to the masses could seriously damage the delicate fabric of communal life in India. It is understandable, however, that Britain, which had mostly conservative governments during the inter-war period, did not want to have a more rapid constitutional advance, especially in view of the rising militancy of the Congress movement.[3] In any event, when the British determined upon a prompt withdrawal they no longer had the authority to heal the rift between the two communities.[4] They "could only

[1] The partition of Bengal in 1905, which irked the Hindus but pleased the Moslems, since they became the majority in one of the parts, played a crucial role in this development. Although the decision was rescinded in 1911, it introduced the idea of partition on a larger scale as a possibility.

[2] *A Survey of Indian History*, Asia Publishing House, Bombay, 1954, p. 227.

[3] Frank Moraes speculates about what might have happened if Gandhi had not changed the character of the Congress movement: would India have been awarded responsible government more rapidly, like Ceylon? And, what is more pertinent in the present context, would that have prevented partition? It should be stressed that Moraes' thoughts are not representative of the views of Indian intellectuals, most of whom would consider them almost sacrilegious.

"Swaraj and swadeshi were ideals long before the Mahatma lighted on the Indian scene, and had the British-created middle class continued the battle for freedom on modern lines India, like Japan, might have staged its own Meiji revolution. Before Gandhi came, the internal battle for political leadership was waged between the liberal moderates such as Gokhale, Surendranath Bannerjea, and Phirozeshah Mehta and the militant revolutionaries represented by Tilak, Lala Lajpat Rai, and Aurobindo Ghose. Had the British Government responded with rapid constitutional reforms, the hands of the liberal moderates would have been strengthened and the transition to political freedom accelerated. Indeed, independence might have come earlier had not Gandhi intervened." (Frank Moraes, *India Today*, p. 78.)

[4] In the minds of some Congress leaders there lingers the suspicion that in the independence negotiations Britain was really applying its old policy of splitting India.

"In trying to explain why the Labour Government changed its attitude, I came to the painful conclusion that its action was governed more by consideration of British

argue and persuade; they could no longer command."[1] Partition was the end product of the unification of the subcontinent under British rule, a fact for which British policy itself must bear a heavy burden of responsibility.

One of the wisest American analysts of what happened, W. Norman Brown, makes the following division of responsibility:

> The immediate responsibility for the tragedies at the time of partition must be laid to Hindu-Muslim communal antipathy fomented by the Muslim League, the Hindu Mahasabha, and many individuals not belonging to either organization but animated by the communal spirit. But Indian National Congress shortsightedness and Muslim League intransigence had set the stage, while the British, by their political policies for fifty years, had augmented the communal mistrust. At the last moment the British were also unequal to the double demand of abrogating power and at the same time protecting those who had been subject to it.[2]

3 *Initial Consequences*

Partition involved a major surgical operation on the body politic of the India Britain had ruled directly and indirectly, and much blood flowed in the process. Two large chunks of territory, one in the West and the other in the East, were cut off to form the new state of Pakistan. Three provinces, Sind, Baluchistan, and the North-West Frontier Province, and three-fifths of the population of the Punjab were detached to form West Pakistan. Two-thirds of Bengal and parts of Assam (where, as in the Punjab, something less than 60 percent of the population were Moslem) went to form East Pakistan. Of a Moslem population that in undivided India approached 100 million, less than one-quarter were in West Pakistan and less than one-third in East Pakistan. Over 40 million Moslems remained in independent India, where they constituted more than 10 percent of the population; in East Pakistan, Hindus were between a fourth and a fifth of

---

than Indian interests. The Labour Party had always sympathized with Congress and its leaders and had many times openly declared that the Muslim League was a reactionary body. Its surrender to the demands of the Muslim League was in my opinion due more to its anxiety to safeguard British interests than to its desire to please the Muslim League. If a united India had become free according to the Cabinet Mission Plan, there was little chance that Britain could retain her position in the economic and industrial life of India. The partition of India, in which the Muslim majority provinces formed a separate and independent State, would, on the other hand, give Britain a foothold in India. A State dominated by the Muslim League would offer a permanent sphere of influence to the British. This was also bound to influence the attitude of India. With a British base in Pakistan, India would have to pay far greater attention to British interests than she might otherwise do." (Maulana Abul Kalam Azad, *India Wins Freedom,* pp. 191–192.)

[1] Percival Spear, *India, A Modern History,* University of Michigan Press, Ann Arbor, 1961, p. 415.

[2] Brown, *The United States and India and Pakistan,* p. 143.

the population. None of this was accomplished without a considerable amount of forced migration, plunder, persecution, and mass murder by frenzied mobs of Moslems, Hindus, and Sikhs. The cost in lives alone is a matter of guesswork: estimates range from 200,000 or under to one million. Communal fury and systematic butchery on that scale had not been experienced since the Indian Mutiny. Such mob violence presents a mystifying contrast to the general passivity of the masses in these poverty-stricken countries.

When the documents creating Pakistan were signed, the popular upheavals had already begun and were rapidly gathering momentum. Nevertheless, it must be assumed that none of the parties responsible for partition — the Moslem leaders who demanded it, the Congress leaders who stubbornly resisted it to the last, or the British who arranged it — foresaw the scale of human suffering it was to produce.[1] The most blighted area was the Punjab. That a similar holocaust did not overtake Bengal was due mainly to Gandhi's courage and moral exhortations. In general, officials complacently relied on the forces of law and order. But both Indian and Pakistani soldiers became so infected by communal fever that few were in a "fit mental state to take strong action against rioters,"[2] especially when they were co-religionists. British troops, unwilling and probably unable to distinguish Hindu from Moslem, might have helped to prevent the Punjab holocaust; but the Congress leaders made it clear that their use was politically impossible.

Within six months of independence, partition created at least 10 million refugees and possibly many more; in fact, it was responsible for the most extensive and miserable uprooting of human beings in modern history.[3] Moslem refugees probably outnumbered Hindu refugees; but even if they were equal in number, the burden on Pakistan, with its much smaller population, far exceeded that on India; in Pakistan almost 10 percent of the population were said to be refugees. Hindu extremists hoped that Pakistan would be brought to collapse by the influx of Moslems and the withdrawal of Hindu property and services. Among the lowest and highest strata of all communities the notion rapidly spread that all the property of the

[1] A principal participant in the negotiations admits: "It is true that the situation was full of fear and foreboding; but we had not expected to be so quickly and so thoroughly disillusioned." (V. P. Menon, *The Transfer of Power in India*, Orient Longmans, Calcutta, 1957, pp. 417–418.)

[2] *Ibid.*, p. 420.

Penderel Moon goes further: "All the while the military had to be held in check and kept within their proper bounds; for potentially they were by far the most dangerous sources of anarchy." (*Divide and Quit*, p. 154.)

[3] It is a revealing commentary on how the United Nations was directed by the Western powers in its earlier years that its refugee organization was concerned almost exclusively with European refugees. A separate organization was set up for Arab refugees from Palestine. There was never much concern for refugees in other parts of Asia; unless their governments helped them they had to look after themselves.

evacuees belonged to the territory they were leaving, or, alternatively, that the evacuees could be made to pay for the privilege of taking some of their belongings with them. On both sides many irregularities were committed by unscrupulous officials and political bosses. In the end, while the Moslems lost the most lives, the Hindus and Sikhs lost the most property.

The princely states posed some special problems. To prevent the danger of a still greater fragmentation of the subcontinent, the Indian army was used to ensure the adherence to India of pockets of territory with Moslem rulers though overwhelmingly Hindu populations. Thus when the Moslem prince of Junagadh decided to join Pakistan, India marched in troops and organized a plebiscite, which produced a declaration in favor of union with India. The Moslem ruler of Hyderabad, who wanted separate dominion status, was also brought into the union by what the Indian government officially described as "a police action." Even if the means of incorporating these territories were of doubtful legality, the result was consistent with the general spirit of the agreement on partition, and it also made political sense, since they were not contiguous with Pakistan and their populations were predominantly Hindu.

Kashmir, on the contrary, had almost all of its transport connections with Pakistan and had a predominantly Moslem population. The decision of the Hindu ruler of Kashmir and Jammu to affiliate with India (the final and formal access was preceded by a tribal invasion of Kashmir from the North-West Frontier Province, after which India insisted he had to take this step so that India could come to his assistance) brought Indian and Pakistani troops into armed conflict. A cease-fire line was negotiated in 1949 and supervised by United Nations observers, but no settlement was reached. The Kashmir issue has continued to poison all relations between India and Pakistan since partition; in 1965 it led to open warfare between the two countries. To these later developments we shall return in Sections 7 and 8.

4 *Economic Effects of Partition*

Partition involved dismemberment of an interdependent economy, and while both countries were hurt by their separation from the whole, Pakistan suffered more by this than India. True, India lost relatively more land, a fact that may have contributed in a minor way to its subsequent insufficiency in food production, but it retained the lion's share of the subcontinent's mineral resources, modern industry, ports, money and capital markets, and experienced entrepreneurs, together with virtually all the research and technical institutions that had been developed before independence. Relative to its population Pakistan also received a much smaller share of the higher civil servants, clerks, and army officers of British India, as Moslems had been underrepresented in these positions (Section 2) and as a number of Moslems so placed opted for India; almost no Hindus, Sikhs, Persians, or Christians in these groups, it may be added, opted for Pakistan.[1] Since India obtained the capital city, the central offices, and the Secretariat of British India, Pakistan had to improvise in these respects. It is true that the territories forming Pakistan produced important quantities of raw materials such as jute, cotton, wool, hides, and skins. The fact that after partition the industries that purchased these commodities were located in India gave a boost to the development of manufacturing, especially textile manufacturing, in Pakistan. Policies aimed at a diversified economic development of a united India could have contributed more to economic expansion than this hothouse growth. Pakistanis can argue, however, that an undivided India dominated by Hindus would never have pursued such policies in a manner fair to the Moslems.

When partition was still only a possibility the view was often expressed, particularly on the Congress side, that whatever the ultimate political settlement, organized cooperation would be necessary to avoid damage to common interests.[2] But so preoccupied were Hindu leaders with resisting partition to the bitter end and Moslem leaders with achieving Pakistan regardless of the consequences that when the final break came, quickly and in hideous circumstances, no preparations had been made to mitigate its harmful economic effects.[3] Even as Lord Radcliffe was dividing the Pun-

[1] Pakistan, for example, initially had hardly any civil servants with sufficient status and experience to direct its new ministries. "In the entire Interim Government of India on the eve of Partition, there was not one Muslim officer of the rank of Secretary. There were only four officers of the rank of Joint Secretaries." (Khalid Bin Sayeed, *Pakistan, The Formative Phase,* p. 391 and Appendix I.)

[2] See, for example, Jawaharlal Nehru, *The Discovery of India,* Meridian Books, London, 1956, pp. 546–547.

[3] It is rumored in India that at the time of partition some Indian economists in the Congress camp tried to get a hearing for practical suggestions on future economic policy. Reflecting the views of these students of the problem, C. N. Vakil writes in one of the early comments on the economic effects of partition:

"*Large economic gains may be secured in the long run, if each country formulates and executes economic plans on the assumption of the existence of harmonious relationship with the other. On the other hand, a policy in either country, which is based on the lack of response from the other, will drive the economic systems, which were made complementary by nature, towards self-sufficiency at high cost.*

"The plans for industrial development in both the countries can be undertaken either on the assumption of cooperation from the other or on the assumption of non-cooperation or no response from the other. Nature has made both India and Pakistan complementary in the economic field. If either country plans on the basis of self-sufficiency the pace and pattern of industrial development will be different from what it would be if complementary economy were to be assumed. The maintenance of a certain degree of economic cooperation between India and Pakistan will certainly result in large gains to both the economies. It will avoid the diversion of resources in area, capital, foreign exchange, raw materials and man-power, which would necessarily have to take place (and has been taking place), if each country tries to do without the other. There is a large scope for mutual assistance by way of exchange of technical personnel. The transport systems in both the countries will gain substantial advantages

jab, Jinnah and Nehru rebuked him for suggesting they operate its water system as a joint venture.[1] The political relations between India and Pakistan, resulting from partition and the way it was carried out, have not, of course, made it any easier to mend this unfortunate economic rift.

5 *Political Consequences*

India can undoubtedly claim as one of the advantages of partition that it was able to establish a stronger central government than would have been possible in an undivided India. No solution of the independence issue that prevented partition could have avoided, in the interests of predominantly Moslem areas, the creation of strong states and a weak federal center. It gradually dawned on many of the Congress leaders that this was too high a price to pay for unity. For one thing, it would have greatly limited the scope for central economic planning, especially as Moslem leaders had grown accustomed to think in terms of erecting defenses against Hindu domination in the larger unit. Moreover, among the upper strata of Moslems who chose Pakistan were many who, if not bent on playing up communal feelings, were rigidly opposed to the Congress's reform program. As this program became the policy of the new Indian government, it can be said that against any regrets for the lost unity of British India may be set the greater direction and purpose independent India acquired in consequence.

Another advantage India reaped from partition is that the very fight against it and the misery it caused have more firmly rooted the determination of the government and its intellectual supporters to develop the coun-

by the atmosphere of cooperation. The large amounts that are being spent on defence and refugees can be diverted for nation-building activities. The psychological atmosphere of fear and uncertainty that has engulfed the border areas will vanish and normal economic life will be resumed. In many ways the national wealth of both countries will tend to increase if both of them cooperate. The economic conjuncture will then be more suitable for the flow of foreign capital." (C. N. Vakil, *Economic Consequences of Divided India*, Vora & Co., Bombay, 1950, p. 46.)

The arguments for economic cooperation are, of course, valid even today. For instance, Professor Fritz Baade (. . . *denn sie sollen satt werden*, Gerhard Stalling Verlag, Hamburg, 1964, p. 126) has recently pointed out the advantages that would accrue to both countries if they could cooperate in the regulation of the Brahmaputra River.

[1] "Jinnah told him to get on with his job and inferred that he would rather have Pakistan deserts than fertile fields watered by courtesy of Hindus. Nehru curtly informed him that what India did with India's rivers was India's affair." (Leonard Mosley, *The Last Days of the British Raj*, p. 199.)

It was not until 1960, after long and painstaking mediation by the World Bank and considerable financial underwriting from the Western powers, that India and Pakistan signed an agreement for sharing the waters of the Indus basin. Even so, organized cooperation for their joint exploitation would have been a more economical solution.

try as a secular nation-state. In particular, this experience reinforced the stand taken by Nehru and most of the older Congress leaders against the divisive, and therefore reprehensible, influences of religious communalism on a society whose unity was already strained by many other centrifugal forces. The assassination of Gandhi by a Hindu fanatic in January, 1948 tragically underlined the consequences of inflaming religious passions.[1] On the other hand, many enlightened Hindus freely admit in private discussion to a sense of spiritual loss in not having a stronger Moslem intelligentsia in independent India. In line with the Gandhi tradition of syncretism and tolerance, they would have welcomed the continued influence on Hindu society, permeated by magic, superstition, and rigid caste mores as it is, of the sort of rationalism and egalitarianism to which, in its higher manifestations, Islam aspires. Pakistanis, for their part, can claim that only by getting a homeland in which they had a secure majority could Moslems free themselves from their wholly negative strivings against Hindu domination and have a chance to devote themselves to the task of nation-building.

Within the two countries, relations between Hindus and Moslems have undoubtedly improved as compared with the decade preceding independence, partly because of the sense of guilt both parties feel over the ugly aftermath of partition. In India and Pakistan, Hindu-Moslem tension is now only one of the forces, and not a major one at that, hampering national consolidation. Nevertheless, among members of the minority religious group in each country there still persist uncomfortable memories, disquiet, and a sense of split allegiance to the state they have made their home. They commonly feel discriminated against and are, in fact, frequently restricted in their opportunities. One symptom of this is the steady stream of Moslems moving from India to Pakistan and of Hindus moving in the opposite direction. In Pakistan the sense of injustice is particularly strong among those Hindus who have been deprived of their former privileged positions as members of the upper class of landlords, merchants, and moneylenders. In India a strong sense of injury is also commonly to be found among Moslems of the upper and middle classes. Intelligent Moslems concede that the reality behind this feeling is probably exaggerated because much of the prejudice Moslems meet with in India is similar to that suffered by anyone who does not belong to the "right" caste. Nevertheless, Moslems persist in seeing an extra dose of discrimination reserved for them alone. Even when they have little to complain of, they frequently entertain indeterminate fears for the future, especially now that that staunch supporter of non-discrimination, Nehru, is no more. They fear that in the long run India will be dominated by fanatical Hindu reactionaries – an

[1] "The Mahatma was even more powerful in death than in life. The policy of revenge was abandoned. The Hindu extremists were discredited." (Percival Spear, *India, A Modern History*, p. 424.)

anxiety, it may be noted, not altogether absent from the minds of many liberal Indian intellectuals. So far as the lower classes are concerned, the occasional rioting against Moslems in India and Hindus in Pakistan and the continuing arrival in Calcutta of refugees from East Pakistan tend to nourish communal resentments and anxieties within both countries.

But on the level of principle the issue has been settled. Pakistan, like India, has, on the whole, been given a pronounced secular character. The Koran does not permit unjust treatment of strangers and there is a band in the national flag supposedly representing the Hindu minority.[1] India should have even less difficulty than Pakistan in granting equal treatment to its minority groups, for since partition its leaders, with few exceptions, have strenuously rejected the two-nation ideology of Jinnah and the Muslim League. All the same, Indo-Pakistan relations are bound to have a profound influence on the interests and fears of the minority community in each country for some time to come. Under these circumstances it was a deeply satisfying experience for both countries that deteriorating relations between them and even the outbreak of open warfare in 1965 (Section 8) were not followed by communal outbreaks in either India or Pakistan.

So far as preparedness for independent nationhood was concerned, India had one enormous advantage over Pakistan. From the independence movement it had gained many outstanding political leaders, each with a national standing and following. Moreover, within the Indian National Congress the fundamental principle of government by discussion, with its correlatives of cooperation and discipline, had been established. Pakistan had far fewer leaders of similar caliber and less of a tradition of discussion among them. Jinnah not only became the permanent President of the Muslim League; he converted his position into a virtual dictatorship. This was symbolized in the title Quaid-i-Azam, "Great Leader," conferred on him when the League formally decided that he alone was entitled to speak for the "Muslim nation."[2] Fortuitous circumstances subsequently highlighted the disadvantages inherent in this type of leadership, for Jinnah died only

[1] In a major policy statement to the Pakistan National Assembly on August 11, 1947, Jinnah emphasized the equal rights of all citizens. "You will find," he said, "that in course of time Hindus would cease to be Hindus and Muslims would cease to be Muslims, not in the religious sense, because that is the personal faith of each individual, but in the political sense as citizens of the State." (Quoted in Khalid Bin Sayeed, *Pakistan, The Formative Phase*, p. 273.)

[2] This matter of title reveals a good deal of difference between the Congress movement and the Muslim League. While the latter was aristocratic and authoritarian in leadership, the former, though dominated by intellectuals and businessmen, appealed to the masses. Instead of "Great Leader," the courtesy title Gandhi acquired was Mahatma, the "Great Souled," and his public image was that of a saintly man who, with warmth, humor, kindliness, and wisdom, preserved unity in action between leaders of many minds and sought the devotion of the common man in the villages. He was also affectionately called Bapu or Bapuji, "Father"; after his death this became his official status.

one year after Pakistan was founded, and his right-hand man, Liaquat Ali Khan, on whom his mantle fell, was assassinated three years later.

In India the Congress kept together after independence and preserved its popular following and, particularly in the beginning, a remarkable degree of centralized direction. It thus remained an effective political machine. As such it ruled, and still rules, from the center and in most of the states. This has given a stability to government in India that Pakistan has not enjoyed. Shortly after independence the Muslim League split apart and became simply one of a number of contesting political parties, all loosely organized even at the top and with little popular following or, indeed, much reality, outside the legislative assemblies. This contrast stems from a basic difference in attitude between the Congress and the League. In the last phase of British rule the former not only constructed an effective political organization, but also formulated a program of economic and social reform to be implemented on the arrival of independence. It even sponsored preliminary attempts at economic planning. To Gandhi and the other Congress leaders it was essential to proclaim a program of reform in order to give purpose and direction to the struggle against the British. Embodied in countless Congress resolutions and gradually given substance and perspective in the literature of the nationalist movement, this program gave the Indian government after independence a momentum it could not otherwise have easily acquired. Jinnah and the Muslim League, on the other hand, concentrated on the one supreme, but negative, aim of drawing a firm boundary line against the Hindus. The following they won was interested not in better things for the masses but in communal vindication.[1] The League never formulated, or felt compelled to formulate, an

[1] Some of the League leaders, though hardly Jinnah himself, occasionally thought that mass support should be sought through a social and economic program.

In a letter to Jinnah dated May 28, 1937, Muhammad Iqbal wrote:

"I have no doubt that you fully realise the gravity of the situation as far as Muslim India is concerned. The League will have to finally decide whether it will remain a body representing the upper classes of Indian Muslims or Muslim masses who have so far, with good reason, taken no interest in it. Personally I believe that a political organisation which gives no promise of improving the lot of the average Muslims cannot attract our masses.

"Under the new constitution the higher posts go to the sons of upper classes; the smaller ones go to the friends or relatives of the ministers. In other matters too our political institutions have never thought of improving the lot of Muslims generally. The problem of bread is becoming more and more acute. . . . The question, therefore, is: how is it possible to solve the problem of Muslim poverty? And the whole future of the League depends on the League's activity to solve this question. If the League can give no such promises, I am sure, the Muslim masses will remain indifferent to it as before. Happily there is a solution in the enforcement of the Law of Islam and its further development in the light of modern ideas. After a long and careful study of Islamic Law, I have come to the conclusion that if this system of Law is properly understood and applied, at least the right to subsistence is secured to everybody. . . . For Islam the acceptance of social democracy in some suitable form and consistent with the legal principles of Islam is not a revolution but a return to the original purity of Islam." (Quoted in *Struggle for Independence,* Appendix V, pp. 33–34.)

(*Footnote continued on following page*)

economic and social program of its own in order to rally Moslems to its banner. The existence of a Congress program made it difficult for the Moslem leaders to draw one up without seeming to copy the Congress. To this inhibition was added the natural lack of interest in reform of the landlord class who controlled the League. Although revolutionary in tactics, the League remained basically defensive and conservative in aim.[1] No thought was given to the goals an independent Pakistan should pursue.[2] Its leaders fixed their attention on devising safeguards for minority interests rather than on formulating rules for the government and administration of an independent state. This ideological background is essential to an understanding of the very different way in which India and Pakistan took up the challenge of independence, a story we shall relate in the next two chapters.

Disregarding Kashmir for the moment and all the lesser boundary disputes, partition is now an established fact and generally accepted in form and spirit by both countries. It is true that one still finds people, especially in India, who think it an undesirable fact and privately state that view. There are also many Indians who still doubt that Pakistan can hold together and who believe, in particular, that East Pakistan will break away from West Pakistan. But, conscious of their own difficult road to national consolidation, intelligent Indians now generally regard this prospect, not as an opportunity for India to extend its realm, but as a threat, possibly a dire one, to the stability of their own society and the region as a whole. In Pakistan, on the other hand, there is still a widespread fear that India has

---

Liaquat Ali Khan, after partition, spoke in the same vein: "For us there is only one 'ism' – Islamic Socialism, which in a nutshell means that every person in this land has equal rights to be provided with food, shelter, clothing, education and medical facilities. Countries which cannot ensure these for their people can never progress. The economic programme drawn up some 1,350 years back [he means in the lifetime of the Prophet] is still best for us. . . . In adopting any reform, the whole matter will be carefully considered in the light of the Shariat, and before adopting the reform all possible care will be taken to ensure that it is not in any way against any of these sacred laws." (Speech in Lahore in August, 1949, *Pakistan News,* September 4, 1949, quoted from Richard Symonds, *The Making of Pakistan,* Faber & Faber, London, 1950, p. 178.)

[1] In this particular respect the campaign for Pakistan was similar to the secession of the southern states in the American Civil War.

[2] Occasionally, though very rarely, a prominent Pakistani will today complain of the Muslim League's lack of a program when Pakistan was created. Thus in his *Presidential Address* to the thirteenth All Pakistan Science Conference, in Dacca in January, 1961, Professor Abdus Salam, speaking of the need for a national resolve "to crash through the poverty barrier" (pp. 3–5), said: "Our independence in 1947 could have provided us with the necessary stimulus. Unhappily this was not the case. Our independence did not – definitely did not – coincide with the emergence of a political class which made economic growth the centre piece of state policy. I can still recall the interminable arguments, conducted in private and public, in the early years of Pakistan, about its ideology. Never in these discussions did I hear the mention of total eradication of poverty as one of the primary ideological functions of our new state."

not really accepted the fact of partition.[1] Indeed, it is plainly noticeable that Pakistan continues to be both fascinated and repelled by the great neighbor from whom it broke loose.

6 *Consequences for Pakistan's Foreign Policy Orientation*

Coming on top of the mutual recriminations between Muslim League and Congress leaders that preceded independence, partition left a legacy of contention about various sectors of the boundaries, the control of the Indus basin waters, the disposal of refugee properties, the steady stream of new refugees and of alleged "infiltrators," particularly Pakistanis into Assam and Kashmir – all of which embittered relations between India and Pakistan from the outset. Every border incident or related happening has been used by the press and politicians of each side to arouse feelings of national solidarity and stir resentment against the allegedly aggressive intentions of the other. It is also clear that politicians on both sides have exploited this antagonism for their own selfish purposes at home. The fact that each of these two extremely poor countries spent during the 1950's half or more of its central government revenues on armaments is also attributable to partition.[2] Their mutual animosity disturbs international relations in the region as a whole. It has, for instance, been a crucial obstacle to the development of economic cooperation among the South Asian countries. This has been plainly evident in the work and proceedings of ECAFE, where Indian support of any major initiative has usually constituted a sufficient reason for Pakistan to adopt a negative position.[3]

India, being the larger country and having in its possession the major part of Kashmir, the chief bone of contention, could take this legacy of partition somewhat more calmly than Pakistan. From the beginning, Pakistan's whole foreign policy orientation was determined by its hostile relations with India. Pakistan felt an urgent need to seek friends and funds everywhere in order to bolster its position vis-à-vis India. Its most important moves were its alliance in 1954 with the United States[4] and its

[1] In an interview Nehru gave to a *Washington Post* correspondent at the end of 1962, he stressed the historic ties between India and Pakistan and added: "A confederation remains our ultimate goal, though if we say it, they [Pakistanis] are alarmed and say we want to swallow them up." (*Overseas Hindustan Times*, Dec. 27, 1962.)

[2] This was before India's border war with China; of course, in the case of Pakistan the effects of this conflict on the military budget were only indirect.

[3] David Wightman, *Toward Economic Cooperation in Asia*, Yale University Press for the Carnegie Endowment for International Peace, 1963, especially Chapters 14 and 16.

[4] This policy line goes back to the time of partition. An American journalist reports a conversation with Jinnah soon thereafter:

"'America needs Pakistan more than Pakistan needs America,' was Jinnah's reply. . . . He leaned toward me, dropping his voice to a confidential note. 'Russia,' confided

adherence to the two Western sponsored and supported military blocs, CENTO in the west and SEATO in the east of Asia. One incidental by-product of these moves was that they helped Nehru maintain the firm and, for long, almost unanimous support of the articulate strata in India for his policy of non-alignment. At the same time American military aid to Pakistan contributed to Indian antagonism toward Pakistan, just as American aid to uncommitted India – which, after the commencement of India's border conflict with China, included military equipment – caused bad blood toward India in Pakistan.

That Pakistan sought the moral and political support of other Moslem countries was natural. The unity of purpose and outlook of the Moslem world became a cherished illusion of Pakistani politicians and newspapers. However, India has the third largest Moslem population in the world, and Pakistanis tend to be regarded in other Moslem countries as "Indian" Moslems.[1] Against the gain in Moslem solidarity represented by Pakistan's association with Iran and Turkey in CENTO must also be set the divisive effects of its boundary troubles with Afghanistan,[2] whose ruling circles are especially wont to stress that India is one of the great Moslem countries. Moreover, Egypt, Indonesia, and several other Moslem countries opposed to Western policies sympathized more with non-aligned India than with a Pakistan aligned with the West. Nationalism among Moslems, it seems, does not rest primarily on religion.

From about the beginning of the 1960's there were widespread and increasingly strong feelings in Pakistan that its alliance with the Western powers and pursuit of Moslem solidarity had not yielded much in the way of support for its claim to Kashmir. Dissatisfaction with the results of these policies helps explain Pakistan's rapprochement to China when the latter came into boundary conflict with India (Chapter 5, Sections 7 and 8); this rapprochement was not due solely to the fact that Pakistan and China now had a common enemy in India. At the same time, Pakistan made intensive efforts to win sympathy for its cause in the wider and largely non-aligned Afro-Asian community of new nations and to normalize its relations with the Soviet Union, which had come out in support of India on the Kashmir issue.

Mr. Jinnah, 'is not so very far away.' . . . 'America is now awakened,' he said with a satisfied smile. Since the United States was now bolstering up Greece and Turkey, she should be much more interested in pouring money and arms into Pakistan. 'If Russia walks in here,' he concluded, 'the whole world is menaced.'

"In the weeks to come I was to hear the Quaid-i-Azam's thesis echoed by government officials throughout Pakistan. 'Surely America will build up our army,' they would say to me. 'Surely America will give us loans to keep Russia from walking in.' " (Margaret Bourke-White, *Halfway to Freedom,* Simon & Schuster, New York, 1949, pp. 92–93.)

[1] This attitude is particularly noticeable in Arab West Asia, as any traveller there can testify.

[2] Chapter 5, Section 5.

An official document called "President Ayub's Manifesto Undertakings," appearing in the spring of 1965, prior to the military clashes with India which we shall discuss in Section 8, summed up the history of Pakistan's foreign policy as follows:

> Broadly speaking, Pakistan's foreign policy has passed through three main phases since 1947 – (1) the romantic phase marked by an unrealistic advocacy of Muslim world unity, (2) the phase of alignment with Anglo-Saxon Powers, and (3) the post-1962 phase of building an independent, though not necessarily neutral, image of Pakistan in special relationship with the Afro-Asian region.[1]

This document went on to stress, among other things: non-alignment in the cold war; the "search for a new relationship with Soviet Russia"; the evolution of Pakistan's relations with Iran and Turkey "not necessarily attached to the CENTO apron-strings"; and "a sympathetic but realistic – and not romantic – posture toward the Arab causes." The relation to the Kashmir issue was emphasized by crediting the Ayub regime with having "pulled the Kashmir dispute out of the quagmire into which it was thrust."

7 *Positions on the Kashmir Issue*

In the complex of conflicts between India and Pakistan that were the legacy of partition, the Kashmir issue was not only the most important one; it became the driving force behind all other issues.

Broadly speaking, Pakistan has invoked the principle of self-determination for which Junagadh provided a precedent, while India early agreed to a plebiscite in theory but has refused to proceed with one until Pakistan purges itself of "aggression" by vacating the smaller part of Kashmir which its troops "illegally" occupied. Pakistan's acceptance of American military aid and its adherence to Western-sponsored defense pacts hardened India's attitude toward a settlement, especially since the Soviet Union[2] declared its support of the Indian position.

Formally, India stands on the legal rights it claimed from the Kashmir ruler's pledge of allegiance in 1947. But behind the legal argument, and more privately expressed, are more cogent reasons for India's intransigence. To allow Kashmir to "secede" – for so the Indians see it – would be the first fatal step toward the "Balkanization of India."[3] More im-

[1] Quoted from *Pakistan News*, Embassy of Pakistan, Stockholm, March 23, 1965, p. 12.

[2] And, at that time more *sub rosa*, Communist China; see footnote 1, p. 202 above; for recent changes in China's position, see Chapter 5, Section 8.

[3] To this, Jayaprakash Narayan, who in recent years has become an outspoken critic of his countrymen's self-delusions, has pertinently replied: "The assumption behind the argument is that the states of India are held together by force and not by the sentiment of a common nationality. It is an assumption that makes a mockery of the Indian nation and a tyrant of the Indian state." (*The Times*, London, April 29, 1964.) His stand

portant, Indian leaders have made Kashmir the linchpin of their secular experiment. To the older Congress leaders of northern India especially, the accession of this predominantly Moslem province represented a welcome defeat for the hated two-nation doctrine of the Muslim League and a decisive vindication of their own secular ideology.[1] To allow a plebiscite in Kashmir – if the alternatives were so easily equated with religious adherence – so Indians argue, would be to risk the rise of communal tension all over the subcontinent and the collapse of India's secular ideals. The contention is not self-evidently insincere or erroneous. But it can fairly be pointed out that Punjab and Bengal were divided on grounds of religious differences, that the Hindu majorities in Junagadh and Hyderabad were part of the justification for bringing those territories into India, and that, while the Kashmir issue continues to poison Indo-Pakistan relations, the risk of communal tension exists in any case.

On a more opportunistic level Indians maintain that a plebiscite would be impractical anyway since the Indian-occupied parts of Kashmir have been integrated into India;[2] it would also be unnecessary as elections have been held. It is true that the special privileges enjoyed by Kashmir for a number of years, including the right to a separate constitution, have gradually been whittled down to bring it into closer conformity with the rest of the Indian Union. But to assume, as Indians do, that this process can withdraw Kashmir from the arena of dispute is unreal. Furthermore, India cannot dissociate itself from the fact that Indian-occupied Kashmir has

---

on the Kashmir issue, however, has been very exceptional. In India as in Pakistan there has continually been a "closing of ranks," not uncommon in countries brought into an international conflict. Loyalty to the national cause has extended not only to support on the principal issue, but to support of every move made by one's own country.

[1] As Nehru said: "You may consider it legally or otherwise, the accession [of Kashmir] to India. But Pakistan has no right at all unless they say that Kashmir has 75 or 70 per cent Moslem population, and therefore it should go to Pakistan. Now, we have never acknowledged that the division of India was on the basis of Hindu or Moslem or any religion. If we did, where would we be? After the partition, we have got 40 million Moslems in India. We do not treat them as citizens of Pakistan but as citizens of India. They are in every village, we cannot divide every village on the basis of religion. It is an out-of-date, medieval notion." (Information Service of India, Stockholm, *Nehru in Scandinavia,* 1958, p. 30.)

"According to the Pakistani argument, the forty million Moslems in India are in some way or other not suited for Indian nationality and should go to Pakistan. India would go to pieces, and India would cease to be a nation. It would just go into little bits of religious groups here and there." (*Ibid.,* p. 72.)

In rebuttal, Pakistanis are quick to point out that in the case of Junagadh and Hyderabad it was the principle of self-determination, not secularism, that India forcibly applied. The main difference, however, is that whereas Junagadh and Hyderabad are completely surrounded by Hindu territory, Kashmir constitutes a border between Hindu and Moslem territory, though all its principal transport outlets were to Pakistan.

[2] "Kashmir has become an integral part of India by the internationally accepted practices of law and democracy." (Sardar Singh, *The Times,* London, December 28, 1962.)

been badly and corruptly governed,[1] and that the elections had been less than free; that Pakistan itself was even worse in both respects was, however, evident.

Indian discussion of Kashmir was for many years imbued with the comfortable belief that the Kashmiris themselves would more and more adjust themselves and not complicate the dispute by asserting their own will in the matter. That this was just an illusion has in recent years become more apparent, particularly after the release in 1964 of Sheik Abdullah, who, except for a brief interval, had been kept in prison since 1953.[2] As any visitor can testify, intense feelings do, in fact, exist in the Kashmir Valley, the geographical heart of the disputed territory, though this does not necessarily mean that the people there have a strong desire for union with Pakistan.

Although both India and Pakistan have declined to discuss the Kashmir issue except in terms of whether the territory should belong to one or the other of them, from a friendly outsider's point of view a feasible solution would seem to be for Pakistan to hold those parts of the province it now occupies and for India to retain the predominantly Hindu area of Jammu; the Kashmir Valley could then exist as an independent political entity, possibly under the trusteeship of the United Nations or guaranteed by some jointly agreed arrangement, as Lord Birdwood, among others, suggested long ago.[3] Such a settlement would not guarantee good relations between India and Pakistan, since many other subjects of contention are involved, but it would help to normalize these relations by healing the most serious wound of partition and so make other settlements easier to reach.

India's border conflict with China gave a new dimension and an increased urgency to a settlement of the Kashmir dispute. It is known that the United States and Britain urged India and Pakistan to move in this direction, and even tried to make such a move a condition for assisting India with military equipment. Particularly in Pakistan, but also in India, these appeals were not entirely unheeded.[4] However, the two countries were brought no closer to a settlement, as their positions had become irreconcilable. This outcome was probably in some measure responsible

[1] The misrule of Kashmir attracted increasing public attention in India from the beginning of the 1960's, and in 1964 the government of Bakshi Ghulam Mohammed was liquidated.

[2] In 1965 he was arrested again and "restricted in his movements" to a locality outside Kashmir.

[3] Lord Birdwood, *Two Nations and Kashmir,* Robert Hale Ltd., London, 1956.

The thought of such a settlement was expressed right up to the outbreak of war in the autumn of 1965 by exceptionally independent Indian intellectuals; see, for instance, B. G. Verghese, "Indo-Pakistan Relations," *Conspectus,* Vol. I, No. 2, Second Quarter, 1965, pp. 18–19.

[4] Chapter 5, Section 8.

for Pakistan's rapprochement to China, which in its turn hardened India's attitude toward Pakistan in all respects, including the Kashmir conflict.

Nehru was, of course, fully aware that with China as an enemy of his country the Kashmir conflict was calamitous, and that only he had the status necessary to lead India toward a more flexible position on Kashmir. There have been reports that Nehru, in the last months of his life, knowing he would soon die, made a desperate attempt to reach a settlement with Pakistan. An American journalist, Richard Critchfield, who was on the scene, gives an account of fairly advanced negotiations, involving, besides Nehru, Sheik Abdullah, the Kashmir Prime Minister, G. M. Sadiq, and President Ayub Khan of Pakistan, on "the creation of an internally autonomous Kashmir, with India and Pakistan forming a confederation, guaranteed by the United Nations for its joint defense."[1] What precisely Nehru's proposal was, and why in the end it was turned down by Ayub Khan, must be left for future historians to ascertain.[2] It may be surmised that the most important reason for the failure of this attempt at reconciliation was Nehru's death; no one else in India was strong enough to negotiate such a settlement – a fact that was, of course, recognized not only there but also in Pakistan.

Thereafter, the Kashmir conflict was continually aggravated, and relations between the two countries deteriorated. Toward the end of 1964, constitutional provisions making it possible for the President of India under certain conditions to assume direct rule over a state were extended to Kashmir. The Pakistan government protested this decision to the Security Council of the United Nations, and there were demonstrations in Kashmir. In the spring of 1965, the Kashmir Legislative Assembly passed a constitutional amendment bill adjusting the titles of the head of the state and the first minister to conform with the nomenclature in the Indian states. In April, 1965, an armed conflict was flaring up over the Rann of Kutch, a desolate marsh area on the Sind border. Each party complained

[1] Richard Critchfield, "Background to Conflict," *The Reporter,* November 4, 1965, pp. 28ff.

"By the time Nehru, near the end of his life, made his dramatic moves for a rapprochement, public opinion in both countries had already hardened along new and seemingly impenetrable battle lines. Evidence has accumulated since his death to indicate that the Kashmir settlement envisaged by Nehru presupposed a larger Indo-Pakistan accommodation based on confederal relations between the two countries." (Selig S. Harrison, "Troubled India and Her Neighbors," *Foreign Affairs,* January, 1965, pp. 321–322.)

[2] According to Critchfield, when, four days after Nehru's fatal stroke, President Ayub publicly rejected the confederation proposal, this "was partly prompted by the announcement in Washington of a new five-year arms-aid program to India." (Critchfield, "Background to Conflict.") Harrison maintains that Nehru's proposal "was rejected by Ayub out of fear that even a limited confederation with adequate safeguards would imply separate status for East Pakistan in the new grouping. Indeed, the mere rumor that confederation was in the wind touched off backstage demands on the part of East Pakistan for separate treatment in any negotiations." (Harrison, "Troubled India and Her Neighbors.")

that the other used military equipment from the United States. After mediation by the British Prime Minister, an agreement was reached for a cease-fire and the modalities of a later definite settlement. The conflict, however, left in its wake tension and even more bitterness on both sides, as did several other incidents involving the two countries.

8 *The September War over Kashmir*

In August, 1965, India complained of massive infiltration into Kashmir by disguised military personnel from the Pakistan side of the cease-fire line. As tension mounted, fighting broke out between regular army units and there were transgressions of the armistice line from both sides. Kashmir experienced demonstrations and riots, though not on a very large scale; they were put down by Indian security personnel, and a number of opposition leaders were arrested. Then on September 1, Pakistani troops attacked the Chamb sector in the border region between Kashmir and Jammu, threatening to cut India's only road connection with Kashmir, whereupon Indian troops invaded Pakistan's section of Punjab. The two countries were now engaged in full-fledged, if undeclared, war – though the fighting was confined to rather small fronts, since destruction of enemy fighting power, not occupation of territory outside Kashmir, was the main objective. As both the Soviet Union and the Western powers were interested in ending the fighting, the United Nations was able to persuade the combatants to accept a cease-fire on September 23. However, this cease-fire was not fully respected.

So matters rest uneasily at the beginning of 1966. Both governments have accepted an invitation by the Soviet Union to meet in Tashkent, with Soviet officials as mediators. The Pakistanis demand a settlement of the Kashmir conflict once and for all, while the Indians contend that as far as Kashmir is concerned, there is nothing to discuss – Kashmir belongs in India. Both countries feel they were victorious in the brief war. In India it undid, to an extent, the humiliation of the Chinese frontier conflict. The war and the cease-fire also preserved the *status quo* in Kashmir. In Pakistan, too, there was much exhilaration about the prowess and accomplishments of the nation's troops, and a popular conviction that they could have won, had they fought longer. The question raised by Khan's opponents is why he agreed to the cease-fire.

In determining in retrospect how the conflagration originated, it is difficult to overlook the existence, then and now, of widespread dissatisfaction in Kashmir and the fact that Pakistan had an interest in fomenting it. Nehru's death and a number of other circumstances, including Shastri's need, at least initially, to avoid any serious risk of compromising

India's traditional policy line on Kashmir, nullified Nehru's desperate attempt in his last months to reach a settlement of the Kashmir issue. Meanwhile the Indians continued, step by step, to integrate Kashmir ever closer into the Indian Union. From the Pakistani point of view, there was a clear danger that the outside world would regard the Kashmir issue as a settled matter – settled according to India's interests. From the initial "infiltration" of Pakistanis into Kashmir, the conflict then escalated, by a series of moves and countermoves, to outright war. When it was rather quickly stopped and a cease-fire agreed upon, one reason given was the fear by both governments of a full-scale, prolonged war.[1] Both governments – mindful of the experience of partition – deemed the unleashing of popular feelings and perhaps uncontrolled political forces a greater risk than acceptance of a cease-fire that gave neither side complete and secure control of Kashmir. But with emotions running as high as they were in both countries, it is fair to conclude that the cease-fire was primarily the result of pressure exerted by the Western countries – and condoned more or less explicitly by the Soviet Union – through the suspension of both military and civilian aid and the threat of withholding aid in the future. Neither India nor Pakistan can survive and develop in peace, much less wage war, without large-scale foreign aid. Whether realization of this fact, which was highlighted by the September war, will inspire a serious attempt by these two countries to end the conflict over Kashmir, and come to terms on other issues between them that have disastrously interfered with their internal development, cannot now be known.

One very encouraging sign should be noted. The fear, so often expressed, that an armed conflict between India and Pakistan over Kashmir would immediately set off communal violence in both countries proved to be vastly exaggerated.

[1] The London *Times* reported on October 28, 1965: "When asked last week why Pakistan had not fought on, one senior officer replied: 'A fight to the finish would have become a people's war – societies change that way, you know.' "

Chapter 7

INDIA

This chapter and the two following are intended to give a preview of how the new states in South Asia started out. Many problems touched on in these chapters on individual countries and groups of countries will be discussed more fully later in the book under topical headings. What will concern us principally in this conspectus is the political problem of national consolidation. Our approach to this is not that of the historian – though the facts must be accurately noted and related to their antecedents – but of the social scientist who searches for the broad causal relationships and tries to discover the mechanism of societal change. It may be said at the beginning that the South Asian states differ more in their political development than in all other respects. There are, indeed, almost as many mechanisms of causation in operation as there are countries. Nevertheless, there are also some basic similarities, and these are equally important to detect. In Parts II and III of Chapter 16 we shall return to the problem of politics in South Asia, but from an ideological point of view.

Our value premises are, as throughout this study, the modernization ideals, motivated as specified in Chapter 2.

1 *The Bases for National Consolidation*

In India in recent years there has been lively and increasing discussion of the need for "emotional integration." This is a healthy sign, for it indicates that Indian leaders are aware of the paramount importance of a higher degree of national consolidation if the state is to be viable and to develop economically.

For several reasons, the problem is different for India than for most other South Asian countries – more difficult in some respects, but easier in others. In the first place, India has territorial unity, and its national frontiers, except with Pakistan, can broadly be considered natural frontiers.[1] Like Pakistan, but unlike Ceylon and the countries of Southeast Asia, it has no ethnic minorities of foreign origin. Apart from its tribal areas, India has a deeply rooted cultural tradition, which is shared by most of its people and also in large part by the people of Pakistan. Yet this cultural heritage was never translated into a widespread consciousness of nationhood until the nationalist movement of the present century. Even now a sense of alienation continues to prevail among the nearly 50 million Moslems living in India: in spite of the secular nature of the new state, Moslems have not yet become emotionally integrated with the rest of the nation.[2] Quite aside from this special problem, India is still very far from being an integrated and consolidated nation, despite its initial advantages and the highly successful functioning of its government immediately after independence. The main obstacle is, of course, the wide social and economic cleavages among its people and the accompanying inequalities of welfare and opportunity. This inegalitarian structure of society is especially detrimental to progress in India because economic levels are generally pitifully low and the poverty of its masses is debilitating and degrading.

The sheer size of the country contributes to the difficulty of national consolidation. It is, first of all, too big to be effectively governed as a unitary state: New Delhi can never be more than the apex of a huge administrative pyramid. A federal system with considerable power delegated to the constituent states is a practical necessity in a country of this size. Moreover, because of the diversity of languages, it is difficult to envisage for India a federal structure other than the present one, based on a linguistic demarcation of state boundaries. But once institutionalized in this way, provincial patriotism tends to neutralize the consolidation of the nation-state. Centrifugal forces have been further strengthened by the fact that social stratifications in Indian society, especially its caste system,

[1] This does not, of course, imply a judgment as to the Himalayan frontier, over which India and China are in dispute; see Chapter 5, especially Sections 6–8.

The term "natural frontier" relates to the facts of physical geography; historical, ethnic, religious, and natural boundaries often do not follow the same lines. Thus the border regions in the north of India are empty or are sparsely inhabited by tribal peoples of primarily Mongolian origin whose culture and religion derive from Tibet and China. The integration of these peoples into the Indian nation, or even the extension of effective administration to some of these areas, was begun in earnest only after Indian independence from Britain, and then primarily as a defense against Chinese encroachment.

There are, in addition, tribal peoples in many interior regions of India, numbering some 30 or 40 million, nearly a tenth of the nation's population.

[2] Chapter 6, Section 3.

are rather closely contained within the entities defined by linguistic boundaries. Each state or region of India has its own caste structure. However, there are in bigness some important compensations as well. First, given the prevailing poverty, it is only the bigness of the country that makes possible a sizeable national market. Even if India is economically small compared with the advanced countries – having less total monetized demand for non-food products than, say, Norway – its national market is still much larger than that of any other country in South Asia. This advantage, together with its resources of coal and iron ore, has made it possible for India to have proportionately more industry and a larger class of modern or quasi-modern entrepreneurs. In addition, its sizeable market has made possible a type of planning for economic development that in turn helps to bind the country together.

Then too, despite its greater poverty and higher rate of illiteracy than any other country of the region save Pakistan, India because it is big has been able to produce an intellectual elite of considerable size and competence and to develop a tradition of public debate on national issues. If we assume that only about 1 percent of the Indian population has an effective knowledge of English,[1] the language of national communication and debate, India would nevertheless have as large a population base for such an elite as that of Denmark (where the entire population can be reckoned as constituting such a base). The active intellectual elite rising up from this base has fostered enlightened ideas along the lines of the modernization ideology, and has given India a group of competent senior civil servants with a national orientation.

Another fact not to be overlooked is the immense advantages for national consolidation derived from India's independence movement. As we noted in Chapter 6 (Section 5), the differences between the Indian National Congress and the Muslim League largely account for the dissimilar beginnings of independent rule in India and Pakistan. To begin with, the Congress, much more than the League, was a political machine with nation-wide ramifications. Secondly, though both had strong central direction, the leadership of the Congress was collective, not dictatorial like that of the League. As the unchallenged tactician of the Congress, Gandhi did not merely tolerate but actively encouraged the emergence of many kinds of national and provincial leaders, and induced them to cooperate with one another through collective discussion. In the fight for independence from Britain there were no spoils to divide; on the contrary, the passive resistance policy of the Congress involved heavy personal sacrifices. Shared sacrifice in opposition to a common adversary – at first

[1] Chapter 32, Section 4.

the British and later the Muslim League as well – and the commanding presence of Gandhi, made for unified leadership despite considerable differences of opinion about the policies an independent India should follow. By the time independence was achieved, a tradition of disciplined political cooperation and collective responsibility had been firmly established within the Congress leadership. Instead of disintegrating into factions after independence, as the Muslim League did soon after Jinnah's death, the Congress was able to supply initial momentum to the new government.

Furthermore, the Indian government, in contrast to Pakistan's, had a definite policy program to implement. Through continuous discussion over the years, the Congress movement had committed itself in solemn resolutions to a program of economic and social reform in line with the modernization ideology. It had even made a start in pre-independence times toward formulating the ideas and machinery for economic planning. As we noted earlier in this connection, the big landlords never dominated the Congress as they did the League. Much of the power of the Congress and almost all of its financial support came, and still come, from the professional, industrial, and commercial upper classes in the modern or quasi-modern sectors of the Indian economy.[1] Although not markedly progressive in their economic and social outlook, these groups were far different in spirit from the feudal landlord class. If their support of the Congress was inspired by obvious self-interest in ejecting the British, they nevertheless acquired a receptivity to progressive ideas through their association with the Congress movement and through the influence of the British radicals who espoused the Indian struggle for freedom. Before independence large sections of the Indian business community had already accepted the principle of government economic planning, for instance. Nor was the composure of the industrial and commercial classes ruffled by Gandhi's palpably honest, if fuzzy, social conceptions,[2] which combined emphatic demands for improving the conditions of the masses with the idea of a trusteeship by the wealthy for the benefit of the poor and opposition to the use of violence, or even legislation, to bring about conditions of greater equality. This co-mingling of revolutionary views on economic and social questions with a solicitude for the vested interests of the Indian upper classes – including even those of the feudal princes and absentee landlords – was among Gandhi's more subtle ideological achievements. If his campaign against untouchability and his demands for greater social

[1] "Though Gandhiji was able to bring the broad masses of the people into the movement, basically, it remained the movement of the middle classes, which never gave up control over the Congress organisation." (Jayaprakash Narayan, *Towards a New Society,* Office for Asian Affairs, Congress for Cultural Freedom, New Delhi, 1958, pp. 110–111.) The term "middle classes" as used in South Asia actually refers to the upper classes, though not to the very top strata.

[2] Chapter 16, Section 5 *et passim.*

and economic equality had significance for the lower classes, or at least their leaders, the upper classes viewed the Mahatma's preachings with equanimity. His defense, in effect, of existing social and economic privileges reassured the upper classes[1] without affronting a lower-class leadership that had identified itself with his views on non-violence as a moral principle of social action.

Meanwhile, with the support and sometimes the inspiration of Nehru, the radical intellectuals in the Congress worked steadily to get their ever more advanced resolutions accepted, sometimes in the face of Gandhi's opposition or, at best, his seemingly amused tolerance.[2] Although these radical intellectuals were often related to landlords, industrialists, merchants, or financiers, many of them had little property themselves; at least property was not the basis of their social status. Mainly members of the liberal professions, they formed an elite within the elite. Their reaction to practical issues was rather detached, particularly when, as in pre-independence times, their ideals could not immediately affect the outcome. Although they were able, with some difficulty, to subsume their ideas about the necessity for a social and economic revolution in India under Gandhi's general teaching, the real source of their inspiration was the European radical tradition, mainly the British, but also Russian Communism. The industrial and commercial classes acquiesced in the radical commitments secured from the Congress by this intellectual elite, in part because they believed – quite rightly as events proved – that there was a vast separation between resolutions and their implementation. The Indian political pattern of bold radicalism in principle but extreme conservatism in practice, to which we shall often refer in this book (particularly in Part Four), was already well established before independence. The acceptance of radical programs was also furthered by the widespread assumption that the Indian masses, whose support was thought to be essential to the success of the freedom struggle, must be deeply dissatisfied with their lot.[3]

Whatever the explanation, with the departure of the British, the Indian National Congress had an agreed program for independent India – a program, moreover, that in relation to existing conditions was progressive,

[1] "The propertied classes felt safe in his hands as well as pleasantly and not too rigorously Hindu. . . . Thousands of congressmen felt in the thirties that independence was well worth a fast and a spinning wheel." (Percival Spear, *India, A Modern History*, University of Michigan Press, Ann Arbor, 1961, p. 361.)

[2] The relationship between the Indian radical intellectuals and the Mahatma is beautifully highlighted in Nehru's correspondence with Gandhi and in his books, *The Discovery of India* and *An Autobiography*.

[3] This assumption is still strong in the minds of the Indian upper classes – and, it may be added, of almost all Western observers as well. We shall take up the question of its validity in Chapter 16, Section 9, and in other contexts.

indeed radical, in outlook. The fact that the Congress was not simply a political machine for the achievement of independence from Britain but a movement with far-reaching aims gave the new Indian government a firmness of purpose and direction that was of inestimable value. While India, like Pakistan, inherited virtually one-party rule from pre-independence times, the traditions of the Congress, unlike those of the Muslim League, permitted a wide range of discussion and even political opposition. The socialists who broke away from the Congress, or the Communists, Hindu communalists, and other groups who organized their own national and local political parties, were not regarded by the ruling party as political traitors. In Pakistan, as we shall see, loyalty to the new state was often equated with political support of the Muslim League.[1] The Congress was therefore much better fitted than the League – or any other South Asian political organization – to provide the parliamentary basis for effective government.

In the civil administration, the army, and the police force, the new India inherited the efficient instrument of power which the British had devised for ruling the country. Since the "Indianization" of these services was already far along by the time the British left, India began its independence with a larger proportion of competent and experienced officials than any other South Asian country save the Philippines and Ceylon.[2] During the prolonged struggle for independence Congress leaders had often bitterly assailed the Indian Civil Service, not least its Indian members, and had promised fundamental reforms and drastic changes in personnel.[3] In the end, however, the new state took over the whole structure of public services almost intact and also, with few exceptions, their administrative personnel. The main explanation offered was the urgency of stabilizing the new political order, though the gradual and undramatic transfer of power by the British also contributed to the preservation of existing services. It is not surprising, however, that members of the ruling party often exhibit ambivalent feelings toward public administrators.

With the power of the national government resting firmly on a very

[1] This did not prevent its rapid dissolution; see Chapter 8, Sections 2–4.

[2] Their ranks were augmented by some of the (fewer) Moslem officials who opted for India at the time of partition. See Chapter 6, Section 5.

[3] See, for instance, Jawaharlal Nehru, *An Autobiography*, The Bodley Head, London, 1953, pp. 417ff. and 439ff.; and his *The Discovery of India*, 4th ed., Meridian Books Ltd., London, 1956, pp. 382ff.

"Of one thing I am quite sure, that no new order can be built up in India so long as the spirit of the I.C.S. [Indian Civil Service] pervades our administration and our public services. . . . Therefore it seems to me quite essential that the I.C.S. and similar services must disappear completely, as such, before we can start real work on a new order. Individual members of these services, if they are willing and competent for the new job, will be welcome, but only on new conditions. It is quite inconceivable that they will get the absurdly high salaries and allowances that are paid to them today." (Nehru, *An Autobiography*, p. 445.) See also *The Discovery of India*, pp. 377–378.

strong Congress Party, which was initially under the strict discipline of its central leadership, and with men of high quality and prestige in ministerial office in the national government and often in the newly formed states as well, administration could be properly subordinated to ministerial direction. Individual civil servants exerted an important influence on policy formation, and friction sometimes occurred between politicians and administrators, but India nonetheless avoided the politicizing of administration that took place in Pakistan after independence.[1] The Indian army, moreover, remained outside politics to a degree unique in South Asia.

The subordination of officials to ministerial direction happened to conform to theory and practice as developed in Britain itself, though less to the experience in pre-independent India; there, far removed from the parliament and government of Britain, officials from the Viceroy down assumed the role of rulers and guardians. Indian members of the Indian Civil Service, including those at the highest level, had seldom been able to identify themselves wholeheartedly with that colonial ideology, but experience with district administration and its paternalistic traditions instilled in them the habit of taking responsibility and even initiative, albeit on a narrow front – a training that was to prove invaluable to the new state. The preservation of the inherited structure of administration, while firm political command of it was being assumed, was indispensable to the effective establishment of government authority in the first difficult years of independence, and it was an accomplishment of crucial political importance. This makes it possible to discuss, as we shall do, the evolution of Indian policy in terms of politicians and their following in various strata of the population.

Naturally, civil servants in India, as in Britain, have exerted political influence, individually and as part of the governing elite. But for the most part this has been, again as in Britain, a regulating and stabilizing influence that has worked against radical departures from the *status quo* – in other words, a conservative force. The salary levels fixed by the British were scaled down, but not to the extent frequently advocated before independence. The hierarchical structure of the civil service, with its wide social as well as salary differentials between the higher and lower levels, was likewise retained. Indeed, one of the striking features of the administrative structure the British erected and the Indians inherited is its compatibility with the caste system. With the administrative machinery saturated by caste, it is small wonder that complaints are often heard about the aloofness of Indian officials in their dealings with the public and about their exaggerated notions of personal status.[2] Civil servants are

[1] See Chapter 8, Section 4.

[2] Chapter 16, Section 6; Chapter 18, Section 12.

"We have often been told that the reconstruction of the country requires close cooperation between the officials and the people and the former should be the friends

also criticized for their lack of dynamism. The administrative habits and procedures evolved to preserve law and order under a colonial ruler are inadequate, it is pointed out, for a state that wishes to induce rapid development through planning. But in the first years of independence it was precisely the re-establishment of law and order that was most urgently required. On the other hand, the conservative direction subsequently taken by Indian political development, which we shall discuss later, coincided with the inclinations of most civil servants, even though its primary cause lay elsewhere.

2 *The Successful Beginnings of Independence*

By any standard of comparison, the beginnings of independence in India were remarkably successful. Even if India's situation immediately following independence and partition was less desperate than Pakistan's[1] – the country that at once invites comparison – its capacity for political survival was nevertheless put to a severe test. While in the process of assuming power, the new government had to cope with one internal crisis after another. Following the bloodletting, looting, and mass migrations that accompanied partition, law and order had to be restored and machinery had to be organized to deal with the millions of refugees from Pakistan and the property of Moslems who departed from India. As was related in Chapter 6 (Section 3), fighting broke out with Pakistan over Kashmir (fortunately it was soon halted by a cease-fire arranged through the United Nations), and the accession of Junagadh and Hyderabad to India also involved the use of force. The Communists, who during the Stalin era interpreted independence to suit their own purposes and sought to foment rebellions in India as in most countries of South Asia, also met with quick and stern reprisals. Four states of the Indian Union outlawed the Communist Party and thousands of Communists were placed in detention. It was not only the maintenance of law and order that severely taxed the new government. Chronic shortages of food and other essentials, an overburdened transport system, the economic dislocations of partition, and the need for economic controls to cope with shortages and inflation, were among the emergencies demanding immediate attention. These problems, however, were tackled in a way that, on the whole, inspired confidence in the new government.

---

and the guides of the latter. But the official relation with the people is that of the old bureaucracy. They appear to be the agents of power and people are afraid of them. Yet the people are asked to give their cooperation." (From a speech in Parliament, delivered on February 16, 1958 by Acharya J. B. Kripalani on the President's Address; roneod.)

[1] Chapter 6, Sections 3 and 4; Chapter 8, Section 1.

In foreign relations the government formulated a policy consonant with what were thought to be India's national interest and ideals. On the one hand, the government decided that India should remain in the Commonwealth, though as a republic, thereby obviating the danger of isolation at a time of grave crises at home and mounting tensions abroad. On the other hand, it decided that India should not be aligned with either of the two power blocs engaged in the cold war. This policy was worked out under Nehru's close personal supervision; indeed, until his last years, foreign policy was virtually his private monopoly. Non-alignment did not preclude India from taking an independent stand on world issues. As a result, in the intensely competitive situations created by the cold war, this poor, almost powerless country rapidly gained world prestige and the semblance of big power status. This was apparent to those in the educated class who had any inkling of world affairs or were even slightly acquainted with Nehru's pronouncements on government policy. If they frequently exaggerated the weight of their country in world affairs and particularly the permanency of it, this is not surprising; for, after centuries of colonial domination, this sense of power flattered the national ego. When ties with the Soviet Union became close after the death of Stalin, even the Indian Communists had no choice but to support Nehru's popular foreign policy.

One of the earliest important domestic political achievements of the new government was the dethroning of well over five hundred princely rulers and the integration of their states into the Indian Union. With the transfer of British power, India and Pakistan did not automatically gain supremacy over the princely rulers; the princes in effect had the choice of joining India or Pakistan or of asserting their political independence. As the Congress leadership was not prepared to countenance India's political fragmentation, it used all its resources of diplomacy, cajolery, and legalized bribery to persuade the princely states contiguous to Indian territory to join the Indian Union. By 1950 most of the former princely territories had been integrated into the new pattern of Indian states and were soon placed under representative state assemblies, mostly for the first time. Except in the case of Junagadh, Hyderabad, and Kashmir, this absorption was peaceful. Very generous financial settlements were awarded the princes in the form of guaranteed privy purses for their lifetime.[1] They retained their titles and many privileges, such as the right to fly their own flags and to receive military honors, and, more important, their

[1] The value of the privy purses amounted in total to Rs. 58 million annually. The individual amounts received depended on the average annual income of the princes before their accession and varied from Rs. 5 million for the Nizam of Hyderabad to under Rs. 50,000 for lesser rulers. The privy purses were guaranteed by the constitution and exempt from taxation. For the details of the settlement, see V. P. Menon, *The Story of the Integration of the Indian States*, Longmans, Green, Calcutta, 1956, Chap. XXV.

exemption from customs duties and various taxes – all of which was in contradiction to the structure and spirit of the new state. The considerate treatment of these relics of feudal power and privilege aroused little controversy at the time[1] and is seldom questioned today even by Indian radicals. The usual explanation offered is that the lapse of British paramountcy over the princes put them in a strong bargaining position. Their strength was more apparent than real, however. The despotism of most and their support of the British during the war had isolated them from the mainstream of developments in India; moreover, they were incapable of united action. But their subjects did manifest strong feelings of allegiance to them, and even today it seems that feudal bonds in the former princely areas die hard.[2] A more realistic explanation of India's generosity toward the princes is that, in the conditions then prevailing, it was deemed of the utmost importance to achieve stability and order as rapidly and with as little friction and conflict as possible.

The liquidation of the princely states necessarily entailed a wholesale rationalization of the country's administrative and legal system. For one thing, India gained more territory and population through the integration of these states than it lost through partition. More important, under the British the princes were for the most part semi-autonomous rulers, operating independently in such fields as economic and fiscal policy, administration, communications, banking, and company and commercial laws. The integration of the states into the Union was thus essential to national consolidation.

With princely rule brought to an end, it was possible to construct a new political framework for the country as a whole. An elaborate constitution, perhaps the lengthiest ever recorded, was drafted in just under three years and became operative at the beginning of 1950. While strikingly similar to the 1935 constitution, it also incorporates ideas derived from the United States, other Commonwealth countries, Europe, and even the Soviet Union (on social matters). This document was certainly not put together hastily or by simply applying textbook models with the help of foreign constitutional advisers, as was the case in many other South Asian countries, but emerged after careful deliberation in the Constituent Assembly (consisting of the rump parliament from the British time); on most matters there was substantial accord, in part because many of the principles had so long been advocated by the Congress movement

[1] In fact, as Margaret Bourke-White has pointed out, the "self-sacrifice" and "remarkable patriotism" of the princes were extolled in the Indian press. "Under such headlines as 'Dawn of a New Era' and 'Rulers' Sacrifice,' tribute was paid to their 'voluntary transfer of power to the people'!" (Margaret Bourke-White, *Halfway to Freedom*, Simon & Schuster, New York, 1949, p. 213.)

[2] In the 1962 general election, for example, the largest majority of votes in the country was received by the Maharani of Jaipur.

as to seem almost axiomatic. There was no question, for instance, that India should be a secular state, free of religious discrimination, and so the new constitution abolished the separate communal electorates that had existed since 1909.[1] Thus the constitution denies, by simply ignoring, the obnoxious two-nation doctrine of the Muslim League. It was also accepted with little debate that India should have a parliamentary democracy and cabinet government, a federal structure, adult suffrage, and written guarantees of fundamental rights. The ready acceptance of these principles and, in particular, the continued adherence to them in India are the more remarkable in view of the widespread repudiation of parliamentary democracy in the rest of South Asia and the growing skepticism of many foreign experts about its suitability or desirability for underdeveloped countries.

The federal features of the constitution are modelled on those provided, but never implemented, under the Government of India Act of 1935. Some experts have argued that because of the extensive formal powers granted to the central government, India is not a genuine political federation: that it is a unitary state with subsidiary federal features rather than a federal state with subsidiary unitary features. If, indeed, the central government has betrayed weakness in its dealings with the states, this is not because it lacks formal constitutional authority. Parliament by a simple majority can abolish existing states, alter their territorial jurisdiction, or create new states. The President can take over the administration of any state in which parliamentary government has broken down or whenever national security is threatened by war, external aggression, or internal disturbance.[2] In addition, the Upper House of Parliament by a two-thirds vote may assume the prerogatives assigned to the states under the constitution, or decide that the central government should legislate on matters otherwise reserved to the states.[3] The President has the final power of review over state legislation if the state governor, whom he appoints, withholds legislation for presidential approval. Where state law is in conflict with federal law, the latter takes precedence. Finally, Parliament by a simple majority can amend most of the provisions of the constitution without consulting the states. The central government can and does wield other powers, not specified in the constitution. It can, for example, exert pres-

[1] Certain sections of the population, notably the scheduled classes (untouchables) and the backward scheduled tribes, were given reserved seats for a limited period, but these have not been voted for on a separate electoral roll.

[2] During the first twelve years of the constitution the President invoked these emergency powers on six occasions when constitutional government broke down in some of the states.

[3] Such legislation was voted in 1951 when central action was thought essential to deal with an acute food shortage. These powers of the Upper House are not quite as formidable as they seem, for the voting power of the smaller states is proportionately greater in that chamber than in the Lower House.

sure through its grants and subsidies to the states and by withholding a state's share of the central tax revenues. Another strong central influence, and one that was not envisaged in the constitution, is that exercised by the Planning Commission. This extra-constitutional body acts more like the secretariat of a central economic cabinet, but without any defined relationship to the statutory forms of government. It represents perhaps the clearest indication of how the formal powers of the central government have been augmented in practice by the policies of the single party in power since the beginning of independence.

Yet, strongly centralized as initiating power may seem to be in the Indian Union, the individual states are not without important means of resistance to central authority. The constitution gives the states exclusive powers of legislation in such crucial fields as agriculture, education, and the regulation of public health and welfare. Land reform, for instance, is reserved to the states because it was thought that the variety and complexity of land systems in India would make it impossible to legislate for the country as a whole. Again, while the financial power of the center is undeniably strong, the constitution gives the states control over what is the largest potential source of additional public revenue, namely, all forms of agricultural taxation. Land revenue, taxes on agricultural income, and even succession and estate duties on agricultural land are all specifically assigned to the states. The exclusion of agricultural income from the taxation powers of the Union government has proved to be a serious limitation on the national development effort.[1] It has enabled the dominant political lobby in most of the states, the rural upper strata, to keep their margin of prosperity beyond the reach of the central government.[2] It is no exaggeration to say that most matters directly affecting everyday life are the responsibility of the states. This situation prompted an American public administration expert to observe: "No other large and important national government, I believe, is so dependent as India on theoretically subordinate but actually rather distinct units responsible to a different political control, for so much of the administration of what are

[1] Appendix 8, Section 8.

[2] "Approximately 45 per cent of India's national income is derived from agriculture; yet land taxation takes less than one per cent of the gross value of agricultural output. In 1959/60 land revenue accounted for only 6.5 per cent of the country's total tax revenue, which was a lower proportion than before the Second World War." See Ayodhya Singh, "Land and Agricultural Taxes," *The Economic Weekly*, Vol. XIII, January 21, 1961, p. 21.

On September 14, 1963 this same journal pointed out that while an agricultural income tax was in force in all but three states, its meaning varied so widely that as much as 55 percent of the total cropped area of the country still lay outside the scope of the tax. The revenue from this tax tends, in fact, to be concentrated in those states where plantation agriculture is important, such as Assam, Kerala, and Madras. But only in Assam does it make a significant contribution to the total revenue of the state, namely, 15 percent.

recognized as national programmes of great importance to the nation."[1] From the standpoint of economic development what is particularly noteworthy about the Indian constitutional framework is less the initiating powers of the Union government than the vitiating powers of the constituent states, inasmuch as the central government is largely dependent on the states for the implementation of its national development programs and other basic policy decisions. This pattern of decentralization is in part the consequence of the practical difficulties of central control in so large a country. It has been a major source of weakness in policies concerning land reform, food distribution, and education, among others.

With the adoption of the constitution, India proceeded to organize its first general election, in 1952, on the basis of full adult suffrage. Elaborate preparations were necessary, both because of the sheer size of the electorate and because much less than 20 percent of the adult population was literate. Over 170 million people were eligible to vote, more than five times as many as under the 1935 Act. Withal, this feat was managed effectively and honestly. Approximately 50 percent of the electorate actually voted. The ruling Congress Party gained an overwhelming victory in Parliament and a working majority in all but four of the states. More important perhaps, the election was fought and won with less coercion, fraud, and other illegal practices than often characterize the elections of much more developed countries.

The process of forming a new Indian polity was complicated by the problem of linguistic diversity. Political decentralization and adult suffrage heightened regional pressures for reorganizing the Indian Union into states that clearly corresponded with the main language divisions of the country. The Congress had been pledged to the linguistic demarcation of state boundaries ever since the early 1920's when, in order to get its message across to the masses, it reorganized its own structure into linguistic party units.[2] In at least fifteen of the twenty-eight states of the Union after independence more than 75 percent of the people spoke a single dominant language.[3] The proponents of linguistic patriotism agitated, sometimes violently, especially in the South, for the creation of additional states along linguistic lines. After resisting their pressure for six years, for fear that centrifugal forces would gain at the expense of national unity, the central government yielded in 1953 to the demand for a separate state of Andra for the Telegu-speaking people of northern Madras. This opened the gate to other demands and, following the report in 1956 of the States Reorganization Commission, a more comprehensive solution

[1] Paul H. Appleby, *Public Administration in India: Report of a Survey,* Government of India, Delhi, 1957, p. 22.

[2] Chapter 3, Section 3.

[3] Norman D. Palmer, *The Indian Political System,* Allen & Unwin Ltd., London, 1961, p. 106.

of the problem was attempted. In effect, the government acceded to nearly all the major linguistic pressures. The Indian Union was reorganized into fourteen states, each of which had a clearly dominant language except Greater Bombay, which was a bilingual state, and Punjab, where the principal languages were, however, all associated with Hindi. Agitations and violence in Greater Bombay later led to its bifurcation into the states of Gujarat and Maharashtra. Probably no less drastic solution was feasible in a country as large and diversified as India, which was trying at the same time to form and operate a democratic system. The problem was in fact solved with relatively little friction and in short order. It is also true, however, that the pressures exerted for this solution cloaked the ambitions of dominant social groups for a share in the spoils of power and political patronage. The rural upper strata, seeking avenues of political, social, and economic advancement, used the transformation of state boundaries as a means of elevating themselves to a position of majority control. Linguistic patriotism, in short, was symptomatic of a gradual shifting of political power to the states and to these upper strata. This shift in the balance of power and its implications for the national development effort will be discussed in Section 5.

Much the same considerations have bedevilled a solution of the national language problem. The constitution declared originally that Hindi would replace English as the official language of the Indian Union after fifteen years.[1] But the non-Hindi southern regions of the country and also the eastern ones, particularly Bengal, showed a marked reluctance, if not active resistance, to learning Hindi.[2] At the root of this particular controversy lies the resentment of southerners against the alleged hold of northerners on the nation's political and economic affairs. The Congress leadership, for instance, was drawn predominantly from northern India, and southern Indians were underrepresented in the cabinets of Nehru, especially in comparison with the states of Uttar Pradesh, Gujarat, and Maharashtra.

Another feudal legacy attacked by the new government, along with the autocratic princely states, was the system of zamindar landlords, who together with the other rent-collecting intermediaries dominated nearly 45 percent of rural India. As with other aspects of land and tenancy reform in India, the central government and the Planning Commission could only outline and recommend broad principles to be followed, since the consti-

[1] According to the late B. R. Ambedkar, Union Law Minister at the time, no other article of the constitution aroused so much opposition in the Congress meeting that considered the draft constitution. After a prolonged argument and deadlock it accepted Hindi as the national language by a majority of one vote. See Selig S. Harrison, *India: The Most Dangerous Decades*, Princeton University Press, Princeton, N. J., 1960, p. 282.

[2] The language problem is discussed from the valuation standpoint in Chapter 3, Section 3.

tution gives exclusive legislative power in this field to the states. The zamindari reform also took time because of legal and financial complications. The financial compensation was often fixed at a high level, particularly in those states where many zamindars were affected or where they had powerful political support;[1] and the states were not allowed easy payment through interest-bearing bonds or annuities. Nor was the reform as radical in effect as in spirit. For one thing, legal loopholes permitted wholesale eviction of tenants and a resumption of land for "personal cultivation." Nevertheless, the zamindari reform was carried out more thoroughly and with less delay than the land and tenancy reforms directed at changing the social, economic, and political position of the peasant landlord class in the village hierarchy.[2]

To these major initiatives in the first phase of independence should be added the official launching of a large-scale community development program in 1952 and the agricultural extension service in 1953.[3] A number of important research institutions were also established and attempts were made to give new vigor to those inherited from the British. The whole apparatus of legislation and administration was directed toward policy changes in many fields, though not to the extent of disrupting, by intent or effect, the existing social and economic order; we shall come back to this qualification in the next section. Frank Moraes, Nehru's Indian biographer, gives a fair evaluation of this early period when he says:

> To have merged the princely states, redrawn the map of India, resettled and rehabilitated some eight million refugees, and restored a sense of unity and consolidation in the country within the space of five years was by any yardstick an impressive achievement. In the same period India drafted its Constitution, held its first general elections, and launched its First Five Year Plan. In those early years the dedicated zeal of the government carried the country forward at a pace which no one could have visualized when independence came.[4]

The Indian government's attempts to bring about social and economic change were consolidated as a political program based on organized planning within the machinery of government. Continuing the British tradition of making conscientious surveys of social and economic conditions,

[1] Precise estimates of the amount of compensation paid to the zamindars are hard to obtain. One reckoning puts the total at about Rs. 6,600 million. The basis and amount of compensation varied greatly between the states, as did the number of years over which the compensation was payable. See M. L. Dantwala, "Financial Implications of Land Reform: Zamindari Abolition," *Indian Journal of Agricultural Economics*, Vol. XVII, No. 4, October–December, 1962, p. 2.

[2] Chapter 26, Sections 12–17.

[3] Chapter 18, and Chapter 26, Sections 18–19.

[4] Frank Moraes, *India Today*, Macmillan, New York, 1960, p. 161.

Nehru himself, looking back on that early period, made a similar evaluation. See Michael Brecher, *The New States of Asia*, Oxford University Press, New York, 1963, pp. 197–198.

the Planning Commission generated ancillary bodies empowered to investigate and make recommendations on almost every aspect of Indian life. Above all, it became an established part of the planning process to carry out periodic appraisals of plan fulfillment. India was the first country in South Asia, and for a long time the only one, to follow this practice.

The First Five Year Plan, which ran from 1951 to 1956, was described by some as less a plan proper than the addition of a number of desirable public investment projects to those already under way; in other words, a program of public works. But it also formulated basic social and economic objectives in accordance with the modernization ideology. Special attention was paid to agriculture and related activities such as irrigation and flood control. On balance the plan was a success, or at least was commonly felt to have been a success. The over-all rise in the national income and in income per head[1] exceeded expectations. Industrial production as a whole showed a good rate of increase; only in iron and steel output was progress disappointing. Transportation, however, remained a serious bottleneck. Primarily because of delays in getting some projects started – a reflection of the scarcity of managerial and administrative skill – the investment targets were not achieved. The agricultural production targets, on the other hand, were generally surpassed because of exceptionally good monsoons during 1953–54 and 1954–55. This fortuitous circumstance gave the planners a deceptively favorable basis on which to formulate the targets of the Second Plan. In addition, India started its independence with considerable reserves of foreign exchange in the form of the sterling balances that had been accumulated from British wartime expenditure in the country.

By the time the Second Plan was being prepared, India, or rather its intellectual elite, wore an air of optimism and confidence that anyone who visited the country at that time will recall. It was in this mood that the country held its second general election during the spring of 1957. Nearly 200 million people were eligible to vote this time and roughly 60 percent of the electorate did so. The Congress won about 75 percent of the seats in the federal Lower House and was returned to power in all but one state. The Communists won Kerala and gained some striking electoral victories in West Bengal and Greater Bombay; these were the direct fruits of their successful exploitation of regional patriotism and caste interests. Disquieting from the standpoint of national consolidation was the discovery that political forces essentially local or regional in outlook had won more seats in the state assemblies and the federal Lower House than any national party opposed to the Congress Party, and that the Congress Party itself was coming more and more under the domination of those forces, particularly in the states.

[1] The difficulties of defining these Western concepts in the South Asian circumstances and of using them to measure economic development will be discussed in Chapter 11, Section 1.

The inception of the Second Five Year Plan in 1956 and the 1957 general election conveniently demarcate the end of the first phase of independence. If developments became steadily less reassuring thereafter, this was due as much to underlying political forces already at work in Indian society as to fortuitous circumstances not then foreseeable.

3 *The Postponement of the Social and Economic Revolution*

Few countries in recent times began their independence with such high ideals and such exalted leadership as India. Those who had been in the forefront of the struggle for independence stepped into political office as members of Parliament or the state assemblies and some achieved ministerial status, with the leaders at the center naturally holding more sway over policy than those in the states. The official political creed of the new government was derived, as we have indicated, from the progressive commitments of the Congress. Yet the more conservative element in the Congress gained an initial advantage from the imperative need, in the face of so many urgent problems, to stabilize the new political order.

In contrast to the poverty-stricken Indian masses, the national political leaders were all members of the privileged upper class, and their new positions of responsibility and power rapidly invested them with still greater privileges. Many who had borne heavy burdens of personal sacrifice in the independence struggle saw in their own advancement a symbol of the national political revolution.[1] For the Indian members of the civil service, the police, and the army, independence likewise brought rapid advancement, especially since the departing British had clustered in the upper ranks of these professions.

Under British rule the European sections of Indian cities – called in India the "civil lines" – had also housed a few Indians, either senior officials or simply men of wealth. Not surprisingly, the arrival of independence saw an influx of Indian office-holders into these privileged enclaves of the British raj. In New Delhi, the lavish palace of the former Viceroys, which Gandhi wanted to turn into a hospital for the poor, became the residence of the Indian President. Nehru, as Prime Minister, moved into the

[1] Foreseeing their avidity for the fruits of office after their years of sacrifice and suffering, Gandhi advised members of the Congress movement to withdraw from politics and concentrate on social work once independence was achieved. He believed that those entering politics after independence should do so on their own merits, and not by capitalizing on the prestige of the Congress. To the alleged suggestion of friends that he become the first Governor General of India, Gandhi is supposed to have replied that his acceptance of office in the new state would be tantamount to denying all the principles for which he stood. See Myron Weiner, *Party Politics in India*, Princeton University Press, Princeton, 1957, p. 257.

The Congress had functioned as a party in pre-independence times, both at the center and in the provinces. To have followed Gandhi's advice would thus have meant the break-up of an already functioning political organization and would have created a vacuum of uncertainty at a time when there was need for stable government.

sumptuous residence of the former British Commander-in-Chief. The state governors were also housed palatially and were given a civilian and military staff whose functions were mainly ceremonial and social.[1] There was also a pronounced tendency to have cabinets that were larger than necessary and to indulge in the luxury of two state assemblies instead of one.[2] The right to ride in big cars marked with flags was eagerly sought as a symbol of authority, and the official trips of governors and ministers were conducted with pomp and protocol.[3] Elaborate diplomatic social functions served as another mark of status. Members of the federal and state assemblies sought as eagerly to acquire privileges and status.

Although trivial in themselves, these manifestations tended to widen the gulf between rulers and ruled and to divert official attention from the urgent need for fundamental reforms in Indian society. At the same time such resplendence emphasized the new government's role as the successor to the British raj; it also encouraged the view that political independence had done little more than displace a foreign with a native privileged group. This aping of British pomp was sharply criticized by many of the "old guard," Jayaprakash Narayan, Vinoba Bhave, and others who carried on Gandhi's political teaching and kept conspicuously aloof from the perquisites of power. They occasionally even denied the suitability of a parliamentary system of government for India; for democracy to them meant, not mere majority rule or representation, much less the pursuit of personal power, but service and sacrifice. Frequent and outspoken censure came also from those who had little hope of garnering the rewards of office and particularly from those who stood in direct opposition to the Congress Party.[4] To some extent the two streams of criticism merged into

[1] Several persons with inside knowledge told this writer that at the time of independence Lord Mountbatten, the last Viceroy and first Governor General of India, strongly advised the new Indian government to take over all the pomp and splendor of the British raj as a means of preserving authority when the British withdrew.

[2] In 1956 seven states, of which all but one were in former provinces of northern India, had a second chamber. By 1962 the number had risen to ten. (Cf. M. V. Pylee, *India's Constitution,* Asia Publishing House, London, 1962, p. 242.) The second chambers of the states have a less important functional role than the Upper House of Parliament, but are useful providers of patronage for the ruling party.

[3] "The general pattern of public life in India is a stultifying spectacle of ministerial tours and appendages, of *bhashanas and udhaghatanas,* of commissions and committees, of inquiries and reports, of debates and seminars, of missions and deputations, of *sammelanas and akademies;* in short, of an endless pageant of dignitaries dashing up and down the countryside." (T. S. Bawa, *Nehru's India,* Freeland Publication Private Ltd., New Delhi, 1956, p. 22.)

Such ostentation is characteristic throughout South Asia.

[4] "Let me make my meaning clear about this pomp and show indulged in by high functionaries. I object to it (1) because it is imperial in conception, designed by the foreign masters, who, thank God, are no more to impress the people with the might of the British Empire; (2) because it is outlandish, not in accord with our past and especially with our recent traditions. Its niceties are not understood even by those who indulge in it. It neither appeals to our imagination nor to our feelings; (3) be-

one, the more the new ruling elite jettisoned Gandhi's economic and political ideals, especially as the opponents of the Congress Party could always use the memory of Gandhi as a stick with which to beat the government. Sour comments on standards of public morality appeared with increasing frequency in the Indian press. Nehru himself now and then spoke out against the ostentatious display and assertion of authority, but not too vehemently.[1]

In all of this, however, one underlying factor must be borne in mind. Because of the narrow social base of the elite and the absence of any pressure from the masses,[2] the leaders were under no compulsion to govern vigorously and disinterestedly. Another important reason why the commitment of the Congress movement to fundamental social and economic revolution was placed in cold storage immediately after independence has already been mentioned. India's acute problems, outlined at the beginning of the last section, made it seem imperative to avoid issues that might threaten the unity of the articulate upper strata. The urgency of achieving order and stability induced most leaders to shelve ideological commitments and acquiesce in postponing the implementation of the full Congress program. This was the position taken by Nehru, for example, in defending the government's industrial policy, which made sweeping concessions to private interests. In April, 1948, he told the Constituent Assembly: "After all that has happened in the course of the last seven or eight months, one has to be very careful of the steps one takes so as not to injure the existing structure too much. There has been destruction and injury enough, and certainly I confess to this House that I am not brave and gallant enough to go about destroying any more."[3]

---

cause it is undemocratic; (4) because it is too costly for a poor country whose masses are living at a bare minimum and often less; (5) because it keeps before our people wrong values and standards of life and conduct." (J. B. Kripalani, *Pomp and Poverty*, A Praja Socialist Publication, 1957, p. 10.)

[1] In pre-independence times, by contrast, Nehru had harshly criticized the British for "the display of imperial pomp and splendour." (Nehru, *The Discovery of India*, p. 57.)

[2] In spite of Gandhi's appeal to the masses, the fact is that the liberation movement was an upper-class protest movement. "Nowhere was it a movement starting from the bottom, an upsurge of social protest caused either by the sufferings or the awakened conscience of the masses," says Panikkar. He continues: "It was not the desire for progress or for betterment that was originally at the root of Asian revival. It was the determination to resist the foreigner who was pressing his attack in all directions, political, social, economic and religious. It was the desire for national strength and not for revolutionary changes that was the main motivation of the changes in Asian communities. . . . It was only because it was felt without an adjustment of social relations the strength necessary to resist Europe would not be available, that the reorganization of society was considered urgent and was accepted without serious protest even by vested interests." (K. M. Panikkar, *Asia and Western Dominance*, Allen & Unwin Ltd., London, 1953, p. 315.)

[3] Quoted in Michael Brecher, *Nehru, A Political Biography*, Oxford University Press, London, 1959, p. 512.

A few zealous members of the Congress defected to the Communist Party and many others left to form new left-wing parties. But on the whole, the bonds of loyalty forged in pre-independence times held fast. Gandhi's notion of a trusteeship by the wealthy in behalf of the poor, and his insistence on reform through persuasion, reconciled many to a gradualist approach to change. The successful working of parliamentary government in the first few years of independence and India's rising prestige abroad also strengthened their general support for moderation in domestic policy. The major determinants of the trend, however, were the upper-class basis of Indian political life and the priority given to immediate problems arising out of independence and partition.

At the same time Congress leaders like Nehru continued to espouse progressive principles. The modernization ideals were, and still are, proclaimed as a sort of state religion.[1] They were embodied in the preamble to the Indian constitution and specified in Part IV as directive principles of state policy,[2] largely at Nehru's insistence. Although these principles are not legally enforceable,[3] the state is duty-bound to apply them in making laws. The Congress Party also continued to strengthen its own commitment to radical policies; at its 1955 session, for instance, it postulated as its fundamental aim the creation of a "socialistic pattern of society."[4]

Thus the combination of radicalism in principle and conservatism in practice, the signs of which were already apparent in the Congress before independence, was quickly woven into the fabric of Indian politics. Social legislation pointed the direction in which society should travel, but left the pace indeterminate. Many of these laws were intentionally permissive. In banning dowries, child marriages, and untouchability, the government did not vigorously seek to enforce its legislation. Not even the prohibition clause of the constitution, embodying the stern Gandhian injunction to abstain from alcoholic beverages, was widely carried out.[5] Laws that were compulsory were either not enforced at all or were not enforced according to their spirit and intention. As the Indian Planning Commission observed:

[1] Section 6 below, *et passim.*

[2] Chapter 2, Section 3; Chapter 16, Section 2 *et passim.*

[3] Regarding Article 37, the Planning Commission commented: "The non-justiciability clause only provides that the infant State shall not be immediately called upon to account for not fulfilling the new obligations laid upon it. A State just awaking to freedom, with its many pre-occupations, might be crushed under the burden unless it was free to decide the order, the time, the pace and the mode of fulfilling them." (India, Government of, Planning Commission, *Social Legislation, Its Role in Social Welfare,* New Delhi, 1956, pp. 348–349.)

[4] Chapter 17, Section 7.

[5] At the beginning of 1964 only three of India's then sixteen states were totally dry, and the trend was clearly toward greater relaxation, partly because the laws were not strictly enforced.

There is a vast difference between putting the law on the Statute Book and seeing that it is actually carried out. Most legislation in the social field is only permissive. The Legislature passes a law; it is left to the Executive to bring it into operation, by notification, on a future date. The notification is often-times conditional upon the setting up of a prescribed machinery. This again is left to the Executive. In the absence of any specific obligation cast on it, the Executive follows the line of least resistance and omits to take any action. Thus statutes passed remain practically vetoed by Executive inaction. Public interest in a problem is lulled as soon as the law is passed. Surely, the passing of a law is not an end in itself. The Executive should be required to report it to the Legislature wherever it fails to take action within a prescribed period after the passing of an Act. A Committee of the Legislature should be required to go into the reasons and recommend further action. Even permissive laws should become compulsory after an interval of time.[1]

The dichotomy between ideals and reality, and even between enacted legislation and implementation, should be seen against the background that India, like the other South Asian countries, is a "soft state."[2] There is an unwillingness among the rulers to impose obligations on the governed and a corresponding unwillingness on their part to obey rules laid down by democratic procedures. The tendency is to use the carrot, not the stick. The level of social discipline is low compared with all Western countries – not to mention Communist countries. In India the "soft state" is often rationalized and even extolled by associating it with the Gandhian ideal that social reforms should be brought about by a change of heart, not by compulsion and violence. The Congress movement under Gandhi had used non-violent resistance to authority as a main tactic in the fight for liberation and Gandhi had developed a philosophy based on that tactic. The hold of this philosophy was strengthened, of course, when it was misapplied for the purpose of safeguarding vested interests.

The belief that ideals are important but that their realization must await a change of heart became the basis for rationalizing the discrepancy between precept and practice. That Nehru and other Westernized intellectuals for whom this thinking was not entirely convincing nevertheless acquiesced in it, did not indicate dishonesty or even self-deception. They were eager to get the modernization ideals firmly established in principle even though for various reasons, including the need to preserve Congress unity, they saw little chance of quickly putting them into practice. In compromising with the forces of conservatism they were merely postponing, so they believed, the social and economic revolution necessary to make India a modern and progressive country. The principal weakness of their position, as we shall elaborate in Section 5, has been that in the meantime

[1] *Social Legislation*, p. 348.

[2] This point is developed further in Chapter 2, Section 4 (under *k*); Chapter 18, Sections 13–14; Chapter 19, Sections 3–4; Appendix 2, Section 20 *et passim*.

the shifting power base of Indian politics has strengthened not merely conservative but often reactionary forces, thereby making the realization of the modernization ideals ever more difficult. Resistance has been given a chance to build up against many reforms that might have been pushed through in the first flush of independence. The postponement of the promised social and economic revolution, which was to follow India's political revolution, is thus in danger of becoming permanent. Even the political revolution became less of a reality than the ideological leaders expected. Behind its impressive parliamentary façade, India is still very far from being controlled by the majority of its people, or even from having its policies devised so as to be in the interest of the masses.

These political and ideological developments need to be viewed in the light of the country's economic and social conditions. India was and continues to be one of the poorest countries in the world. Where the average income is so low, economic inequalities inflict particular hardship on the masses. There has as yet been no important rise in average income, and inequality is generally assumed to have increased.[1] The inequities have been solidified by the rigid social stratification, of which the institution of caste is the most significant manifestation.[2] The caste system is probably stronger today than it was at the time when India became independent. And this in turn is largely the result of the operation in a very poor and inegalitarian society of the political processes themselves.[3]

The persistence of the caste structure in Indian society provides a striking example of the divergence of precept and practice. Caste was outlawed in the constitution, and a bill unanimously adopted by Parliament in 1955 made the practice of untouchability a criminal offense. A number of policy measures have since been legislated to aid the "backward classes." Yet nothing very much has changed.[4] Caste is so deeply entrenched in India's traditions that it cannot be eradicated except by drastic surgery; and for this there has been no serious political pressure. As a result, caste is coming more and more to be tacitly accepted and privately condoned. Were Gandhi alive he would tramp the countryside as he did before independence, trying by his moral authority to exorcise untouchability. The political and intellectual leaders of the Congress, though continuing to publicly condemn "casteism," together with "communalism," "provincialism," and "lingualism," and all the other forces that fragment national life, do so in an unconvincing manner; they suggest no specific, practical measures for its abolishment.[5] Politicians of all parties

[1] Chapter 11, Section 2; Chapter 12, Sections 7–8; Chapter 16, Section 6 *et passim*.

[2] Chapter 16, Section 8.

[3] Section 5 below and Chapter 16, Section 9.

[4] Chapter 16, Section 8.

[5] A prominent Indian sociologist has stated: "I am not trying to be cynical but I cannot help wondering how many of those who have of late started publicly speaking

in their election campaigns patently cater to caste sensitivities.[1] In this connection it should be remembered that, in spite of Gandhi's exertions, the independence movement did not penetrate deeply into the social setting of rural India. Universal suffrage has since compelled the politicians to come to terms with the dominant elements in that setting, the rural elite of landowners, merchants, and moneylenders. This implies, in the first place, condoning caste.

The Congress Party is not alone in pampering caste consciousness. Even the Communists do not seriously challenge it.[2] On the contrary, they have championed politically strategic caste lobbies, including at times the anti-social and anti-nationalist interests of village landowners. The Indian Communists are in truth a thoroughly disruptive element in the body politic, for the very reason that they unscrupulously exploit particularist tendencies. In turn, they have themselves been infected by the forces of disintegration, and, even if they wanted, are unable to function as a unifying force capable of transcending barriers.

Having said this much about caste, we would emphasize that it is only one element in the complex texture of social and economic particularism and inequality in Indian society. It is nevertheless crucial, in that it ties together all the other elements into a rigid structure. We shall often have occasion in this book to return to problems of inequality. In the present context we are interested in their harmful consequences not only for economic development but also for national consolidation. If the wellsprings of Indian development efforts seem now to be drying up, the explanation must in large part be traced to the inability or unwillingness to reform the social and economic structure of the country.

---

in favour of a casteless and classless society really mean what they say. . . . Most of us – not only our politicians but our intellectuals as well – are bamboozled into agreeing with something merely because we are afraid to be mistaken for being 'reactionary.' Even discussion of the subject is taboo. In the case of caste this disease has proceeded so far that there is great danger that our talk and policy will leave reality far behind. Secondly, coupled with the widespread fear of being dubbed a reactionary, there is also a shrewd if somewhat cynical appreciation of facts. I know that what I say may seem a contradiction but it really is not so. Agreeing to progressive resolutions satisfies our consciences and assures us of our worldly prospects, while at the same time our sense of facts tells us that nothing serious is going to be done by anyone, and that caste will continue to remain what it is. The best of both the worlds are secured by taking such a course." (M. N. Srinivas, *Caste in Modern India and Other Essays*, Asia Publishing House, New Delhi, 1962, p. 71.)

[1] "We say," Nehru chided them after the 1957 general election, "we are against communalism, casteism, provincialism and all that. And yet you know well enough how poisoned we are to the very core. . . . Which of us, I or you, is completely free of this?" (*New York Times*, June 2, 1957, quoted in Harrison, *India: The Most Dangerous Decades*, p. 286.)

[2] "I shall never forget the day," writes Taya Zinkin, "I visited the leader of the Communist Party of Kerala. . . . He had observed all the caste and sub-caste ritual reserved for such occasions. . . . His explanation was lame: He did not want to shock his caste fellows whose political support he could not afford to lose." (Taya Zinkin, *Caste Today*, Oxford University Press for the Institute of Race Relations, London, 1962, p. 22.)

Thus we see in independent India the operation of a political mechanism that has progressively inhibited national consolidation and economic development. The main elements have been as follows:

(1) India started out with a majority party, the Indian National Congress, that was fairly cohesive as a political machine, had a program in line with the modernization ideals, and was led by, and at first dominated by, men of considerable integrity and national purpose. This initial set of circumstances gave momentum to national consolidation and development, and continues to be a force in that direction.[1]

(2) At the beginning, high priority was given to establishing authority in the new state and solving the pressing problems arising out of independence and partition. The successful accomplishment of these tasks was another force that gave momentum to national consolidation and development.

(3) At the same time, however, it provided a rationalization for not utilizing this momentum to begin carrying out the promised large-scale reforms in the social and economic fields and for acquiescing in the suspension of the Congress program.

(4) Another explanation was the fact that India was a "soft state" and had become increasingly so during the fight for liberation; this acted both as an inhibition among the leaders and as an obstacle among the people.

(5) The upper-class status of those who stepped into power disposed them to abstain from taking policy measures that would contravene the interests of privileged groups. In addition, the Congress Party was probably increasingly dependent on the few rich in commerce, finance, and industry for financial support.

(6) The operation of the political forces under 3–5 was enhanced by the rigid social and economic stratification that has kept the masses of people poor, ignorant, and passive.

(7) The operation of the Western democratic processes meanwhile strengthened the power of conservative and even reactionary groups who lack the vision of a more egalitarian society that the first generation of Congress leaders possessed, even if they failed to live up to their ideals.[2]

(8) The absence of effective social and economic reforms hampers both national consolidation and economic development and thereby also strengthens the forces under 4–7 that put inhibitions and obstacles in the path of economic and social reforms. These different forces all act according to a pattern of circular causation that has cumulative effects.[3]

A similar political mechanism is to be found in all the countries of South Asia, though there are important differences in its operation, and con-

[1] See Section 7 below and Part Four of the book, where we discuss the spread and the effects of the modernization ideology.

[2] This point, in particular, will be developed further in Section 5.

[3] Appendix 2, Part II.

sequently in political developments, because of variations from country to country in the forces listed. Before going any further into the mechanism of causation in India, let us see what actually happened there after the first decade of independence – in which period the Indian rulers, by their skill and good fortune, were able to achieve the political successes discussed in Section 2.

4 *Mounting Difficulties*

From about the time of the second general election in 1957, economic and political developments in India gradually became less reassuring. To start with, the Second Five Year Plan, for the years 1956–60, soon ran into difficulties. The public investment program fell below its targets, though in some directions, particularly in the field of consumption goods, private investments began to exceed what was allowed for. The false hopes for early self-sufficiency in food aroused by the increase in agricultural production during the First Plan[1] were dashed. A disappointing harvest in 1957–58 necessitated large grain imports and underlined the still precarious dependence of agriculture on monsoon rains. Toward the middle of the plan period, a foreign exchange crisis developed for a number of reasons: the need for increased food imports; expanded imports for defense in response to Pakistan's rearmament with the aid of the United States; a general bungling of the exchange controls of private imports; and the rise in prices of imports and a consequent worsening of the terms of trade. To check the alarming depletion of its foreign exchange reserves, the government was forced to impose drastic licensing controls, scale down its planned development expenditures, stiffen the central budget, and resort to hastily improvised foreign credits, mostly of the "aid" variety. A better harvest in 1958–59 eased the food situation, though dependence on ever larger grain imports to feed the population had by then become an established trend. The job-creation targets were not met, and the rate of population growth, as it turned out, had been very seriously underestimated. National product per head, which was to have shown a modest rate of growth during the plan period, appeared to have risen much less than expected.

In the Third Five Year Plan, which began in 1961, the planners tried to rectify their neglect of agriculture under the preceding plan and aimed at self-sufficiency in food-grains by the mid-1960's. The Third Plan posited a substantial rise in national income and income per head, but increased

[1] An Indian economist engaged in the early preparation of the Second Five Year Plan told the writer that the agricultural problem was on the way to being solved, and that agricultural production would increase rapidly without much extra encouragement.

the country's dependence on foreign grants and loans. Progress during the first half of the Third Plan was, however, well below expectations. National income grew at only about half the target rate, and income per head may even have fallen slightly; the later years of the plan showed no substantial change in that trend. The additional employment generated again fell short of the target, and unemployment among the educated in particular continued to increase.[1]

The principal cause of this shortfall was the poor performance of agriculture. Throughout the first half of the Third Plan agricultural output was at best stagnant. With population growing at an accelerating rate, the goal of self-sufficiency in food-grains had to be moved forward to a distant and uncertain future. In addition to the vagaries of the monsoon rains, there was a serious failure on the part of the states to implement programs and projects for raising agricultural output. Significantly, no chief minister in the states had assumed the agricultural portfolio in his government. Most of them apparently did not even share the view of the Planning Commission that programs of land reform were crucial and had by no means been completed or fully implemented.[2] It is certainly true that land reform legislation has been administered in ways that generally frustrated its spirit and intention. At any rate, rural stagnation is proving much more stubborn than was assumed.

Stagnation in agricultural production in the face of rapid population increase inevitably led to an upward pressure on food prices, which rose sharply.[3] The consequent privation suffered by the poorer class in rural and urban areas, whose levels of living were very low, often reached the stage of starvation or near starvation. In 1964, public agitation, rioting, and looting of grain stores broke out in many parts of the country. Predictably, the food shortage was laid to hoarding by landlords and grain dealers, even by the government and its Congress supporters.[4] Hoarding

[1] The generalizations in this and the following paragraph will be substantiated in later chapters. About agricultural production, see Chapter 26, Section 2.

[2] *Overseas Hindustan Times,* November 14, 1963.

[3] *The Economic Weekly* (October 31, 1964, p. 1733) reports: "Food prices began to move up in April 1963, after the seasonal downturn in the early months of the year, and have continued to rise ever since . . . The rise since March 1963 has been almost 50 per cent."

[4] The following quotation from *The Economic Weekly* (July, 1964, p. 1187) is typical: "Investigations made by experienced political workers in Andhra, Tamilnad and Kerala bring one inevitably to the conclusion that the present hyperinflation is essentially the result of the grip on food supplies of the large landholders and the bigger wholesale traders, who often enough is simply the same Janus-headed individual or are pretty close relatives. These gentry have the ability to secure adequate credit both from scheduled banks and the cooperative credit institutions which have, in most places, come completely under their control. In addition, of course, they are themselves either moneylenders or, again, are closely related to moneylenders. Finally,

undoubtedly occurred; but the main cause of the shortage was a serious imbalance between food supply and the demands of a rapidly growing population. There was simply not enough food available.

The measures hesitatingly taken by the government to meet the emergency proved inadequate. Food imports and deliveries under the U. S. surplus food disposal program (P.L. 480) were increased; yet even this contribution – small in relation to total needs – strained India's internal distribution network and its inadequate port and railway facilities. Efforts to move food from surplus to deficit areas were resisted by states with surpluses. Frequent government promises to take firm action against food speculators, even to nationalize the wholesale trade in food grains, did not materialize, largely because the speculators themselves exert considerable political power.[1] From time to time the government promised a "firm price policy for the whole country" and talked vaguely about price fixing accompanied by food rationing. It set up a Foodgrain Trading Corporation, but then delayed the start of its operations and failed to stipulate its directives. The need for long-term agricultural policy was also debated. The state governments, however, showed a marked reluctance to accept any political responsibility for the remedial measures proposed.[2] Indeed, the emergency starkly exposed the inability of the central government to force its will and judgment on the separate states. In the process confidence in the central government was undermined.

The better crop in 1964–65 – which did not, however, halt the rise

---

there is the 'black money' about which the Finance Minister has been so eloquent but also about which he has been too eloquently inactive."

"The major factor [leading to a food crisis] . . . appeared to be speculative withholding from markets of both wheat and rice supplies." (United Nations, ECAFE, *Economic Survey of Asia and the Far East 1964*, Bangkok, 1965, p. 161.)

The official *Indian and Foreign Review* (Vol. 3, No. 5, December, 1965, p. 8) makes the same assertion in more polite language: ". . . surplus stocks got into the hands of traders and more progressive cultivators and the stocks did not come to the market."

[1] "The extent to which the wholesale traders and the larger landlords control the State, district and village level Congress party machine should on no account be underestimated. . . . Somehow any touching of their interests, any prodding of them to give up their familiar avocations appears almost like treason or even suicide to very influential sectors of Congress leadership at the State and grass-roots level." (*The Economic Weekly*, July, 1964, pp. 1187–1188.)

[2] See, for instance, M. J. K. Thavaraj, "Foodgrains: The Case for Rationing," *The Economic Weekly*, October 3, 1964, pp. 1599ff.; also the articles, "Postponed Again," October 31, 1964, pp. 1733f.; and "Food Policy Sell Out," November 21, 1964, pp. 1829f. The last article concludes: "In sum, the State Chief Ministers have written the epitaph on the hopes that, moved by the mass privations caused by the food shortage of these last two years, the Government might at last work out a rational long-term food policy necessary for sustaining a high-level of development expenditure without the prospect of a spectacular rise in agricultural production. Between the reluctance of the surplus States to share their bounty and the callous unwillingness of the deficit States to take on the commitment to feed their people and, not the least, Subramaniam's [the Minister of Agriculture] political ineffectiveness there has been a sellout of food policy."

in food prices – was apparently accepted as a reason for not taking firm central action and as an excuse for the delaying tactics of the surplus states and the resistance of the substantial agriculturalists, the money-lenders, and the grain dealers, who did the hoarding. But a disastrous failure of the June–October monsoon brought the autumn crop in 1965 down to a very low level; and with the continuing severe drought the prospects for the spring crops in 1966 are gloomy. It is generally recognized that India faces the worst food crisis in man's memory. As the months pass, estimates of the food shortage for the coming year mount; as of the beginning of 1966 the most recent official estimate is 16 million tons of food-grain,[1] and still higher figures are quoted, approaching 20 percent of normal (substandard) consumption in India. Although government stocks are being tapped, serious hunger riots have occurred. The national government, whose stockpiles are dwindling, is now prepared to resort to rationing, particularly in the big cities, and to compulsory procurement of stocks of food-grains in private hands. This depends, however, on co-operation from the surplus states. The fact that several of these states have also had a bad crop makes them even more reluctant to commit themselves to sharing their supplies with the rest of the country, lest they run short themselves. The government has begun to set up "relief camps" in Rajastan and Gujarat in western India, the areas hardest hit by the crop failure. Other states hard hit are Madhya Pradesh, Maharashtra, Andhra Pradesh and Mysore; Kerala, which normally imports half the grain it consumes, is, of course, in a particularly dangerous situation, if the government cannot procure grain from states that are better off.

United States food deliveries under P.L. 480 had risen to 6 million tons – about a sixth of total production in the United States – during India's relatively good crop year 1964–65. Since June, when the last agreement on these deliveries ran out, they have been maintained on the same scale but have been made only on a month-to-month basis; Washington has not disguised the fact that this change was made in order to force India to face up to its need for a long-range and more effective agricultural policy.[2] The Indian government has been pressing for a rise in American deliveries, assured for a longer period, and has also requested food aid from other Western countries.

But food surpluses in the United States and elsewhere are not inexhaustible, particularly now that the Soviet Union and China have entered the market as deficit countries. Moreover, there are problems in getting more grain to India, both in mobilizing increased shipping facilities, be-

[1] *Indian and Foreign Review*, Vol. 3, No. 5, December, 1965, p. 8.

[2] In India many believe that the U. S. motive in this action, and, later, in its suspension of financial aid when war broke out between India and Pakistan (see below and in Chapter 6, Section 8), has been to force India to make concessions on Kashmir. In consequence, many Indians take the unrealistic view that India should solve its food problem without foreign aid.

cause of the escalation of the Vietnam war, and in handling the requisite shipments at India's inadequate ports and railway depots. Finally, there is the question of how effectively India can manage the internal distribution of its own and foreign food-grains. This depends largely on whether the national government can win wholehearted cooperation from the states. When Shastri called on the upper strata of his country to observe "supperless Mondays" he observed that the purpose of this abstention was not only to conserve wheat and rice but, primarily, to build up national unity and discipline. Beyond all immediate measures to deal with the present emergency lies the larger need for far-reaching reforms in Indian agriculture. With India's population of almost half a billion increasing by some twelve million a year, the lag in food production is not a passing problem.

Agriculture has not been the only lagging sector. Industrial production has been running well below the expected average annual growth rate for the plan period, owing in part to a series of interlocking shortfalls in the public sector. The estimated cost and completion dates of a number of major projects have proved overly optimistic. Excess capacity has tended to grow in the private sector, partly because of bottlenecks and cutbacks in imports of raw materials and components. The planners miscalculated foreign aid requirements, with the result that by the end of 1962 foreign exchange reserves were already lower than they had ever been. Then came the Chinese assault on the Himalayan frontier and the consequent decision to roughly double Indian defense expenditure;[1] it was later increased even more. This sharpened the foreign exchange crisis and proved especially burdensome to those sectors of the economy already behind in meeting targets. The government felt compelled to seek still more assistance from abroad, mostly from the West. But the increased dependence on foreign grants and credits, not only for defense and for development expenditures but for feeding the rapidly growing population, heightened the government's sensitivity to Western criticism. Various parts of the plan were rephased, and to finance a much larger defense expenditure in an already inflationary setting the central budget for 1963–64 introduced tax increases. The new tax burdens were heaped for the most part on those sections of the population least able to bear them. War with Pakistan in the fall of 1965 not only brought major dislocations and costs but was followed by a suspension of aid from the West.

Midway through the Third Plan it was already clear that it would fall short of its important objectives by a large margin; later developments in most respects implied a further decrease in the expectations for plan fulfillment. The Fourth Plan will begin at a considerably lower industrial, as well as agricultural, base than was originally envisaged; as it was taking shape, it had to be drastically reconsidered. At the beginning of 1966 there

[1] Chapter 5, Section 8.

is doubt whether India will be able to decide upon a fourth five year plan or will have to be satisfied with emergency planning for one year at a time. There is more talk about increased "self-reliance" as a cure for the alarming economic situation.[1] Although in many sectors ingenuity is shown in finding substitutes for foreign spare parts and raw materials, the fact is that India is more than ever dependent on foreign aid, and less sure of getting it, while the economic situation is worsening in all respects. This has political consequences. "The rising prices, the fall in the tempo of growth, the labour discontent, the rise of food disturbances, and the demoralisation in planning, all this cannot be brushed aside by any Government."[2]

It should not, of course, be inferred from these shortcomings of plan fulfillment that the five year plans have achieved little. On the contrary, the level and diversification of industrial production, the exploitation of minerals, the development of power supplies, irrigation, and land reclamation schemes show that much has, in fact, been accomplished. But measured against what needs to be done in order to make a dent in the problem of poverty in a country whose population is increasing so rapidly, and simply to prevent greater misery, these achievements appear insubstantial. It has come to be acknowledged more and more in public debate that the gains of economic progress, so far as there have been any, have not been of benefit to the mass of very poor people. Various evaluation studies, of land reform, community development, cooperative farming, and of other government policies aimed at improving the lot of the poorer strata, show that government assistance has been channelled to the not-so-poor. The root of the trouble lies in the inegalitarian social and economic structure of rural India and, particularly, in the increasing power of what in India is called the "rural elite." But the phenomenon is not confined to rural India. Thus the redistributional purposes of direct taxation have been largely nullified by cleverly conceived exceptions, widespread fraud and evasion, and administrative inefficiency and corruption;[3] whereas indirect taxes, which fall most onerously on the poor, have been raised continually.

[1] An entire issue of the official journal of the Planning Commission, *Yojana* (Vol. IX, No. 20, October 10, 1965), was a special "self-reliance" number.

[2] D. K. Rangnekar, "Nehruism and the Second Plan," *The Economic Weekly*, Vol. XVI, July, 1964, p. 1242. For later developments see Postscript, Section 1.

[3] Appendix 8, Part III; Chapter 20, Section 3.

The following expresses a commonly shared view: "For over a decade Government have permitted a colossal evasion of tax payments. In addition to bidding resources away from plan projects and in addition to feeding smuggling and black marketing, it has had another very unfortunate repercussion viz. a far reaching withering of morals. They say it openly in industry and trade now that there is almost nothing and nobody that money cannot buy. In the face of the most shameless and impudent profiteering that is rampant in every facet of economic life, we cannot any longer look labour and the lower salaried classes in the face and ask for their best efforts and sacrifice for this generation and the next." (*The Economic Weekly*, Vol. XVI, No. 8, February 22, 1964, p. 409.)

Corruption and nepotism among politicians and officials are freely discussed and are generally assumed to be on the increase.[1] The central government has admitted the existence of corruption in the administration on a fairly large scale.[2] Whether corruption is actually increasing is, of course, hard to determine; but that people believe that it is, and feel that little is being done about it, is in itself damaging.[3] The political life of the nation has been tarnished as well. Indian newspapers regale their readers with stories of political intrigue and factional fights for power within the Congress, especially in the states, or between the government and the party wings of the Congress. Small wonder that intellectuals in India display a growing cynicism toward a course of politics shot through with caste and particularism, in which mediocre men band together to keep other mediocre men out of office.

Political conservatives, on the other hand, have taken heart from these developments. They no longer feel the need to acquiesce unreservedly in the modernization ideals and they foresee opportunities for outright opposition. In 1959, a nation-wide conservative political party, the Swatantra Party, came into being for the first time in India. It supports private initiative in all social and economic activities and opposes, among other things, cooperative farming, land ceilings, state trading, nationalization, economic controls, the government's taxation policy, the welfare state, and socialism. The party's leadership is a curious alliance of maharajahs, former zamindars, businessmen, retired officials, and disgruntled politicians from other parties. Its appeal is principally to independent peasant proprietors, craftsmen, shopkeepers, and professional men, and its main electoral support comes from the rural areas of northern India. It emerged from its first general election, in 1962, as the chief opposition group in four of the states. Yet even the Swatantra Party dare not stray very far from the modernization ideals. Nor has it seriously deflected general support for the Congress Party by the business community, which knows only too well that government practices are much less of a threat to them than Congress resolutions suggest. In the opinion of some observers of the Indian political scene, the most significant influence of conservative groups like the Swatantra Party has been to strengthen conservative elements within the Congress Party itself.

The Congress Party has to some extent always functioned as an umbrella under which many, and often conflicting, pressures co-existed, from obscurantists seeking to revive a polity of self-sufficient villages to vocif-

[1] Chapter 20, Sections 2 and 3.

[2] *Overseas Hindustan Times*, December 26, 1963.

"In rural areas specially there is an acute and widespread feeling that nothing is ever done by the officials with whom they have to deal without bribes having to be paid." (G. L. Nanda, then Union Minister of Labour, Employment, and Planning, in *A.I.C.C. Economic Review*, July 7, 1962.)

[3] Chapter 20, Sections 1 and 2.

erous left-wingers bent on creating speedily a highly industrialized socialist state. But since the beginnings of independence, it has become more and more obviously a political machine, which has had to attach primary importance to keeping its internal dissensions within bounds. Effective political opposition tends to come from within the ruling party rather than from other parties. At the state level, for instance, it is often the organizational wing of the Congress that acts as the opposition in offering itself as an alternative government. In this situation the primary aim of other parties must be to influence groups within the ruling party. That the Congress Party is an entire party system in itself thus gives other parties an influence quite disproportionate to their numerical strength. This, in turn, tends to polarize the ruling party still further. It also means that in its preoccupation with arranging the local bargains and compromises by which divergent interests are reconciled, the Congress Party has become a less effective instrument for realizing national purpose and effort or for exacting public discipline and service. As a political machine, however, the Congress is still very powerful. From the 1962 general elections it again emerged as the dominant party at the center and in most of the states. It lost a few seats in Parliament and rather more in the states, mainly to right-wing parties. For this reason it is possible to regard the election results as indicating a shift to the right in Indian politics. But as our analysis will endeavor to make plain, the ruling party has itself been moving in a more conservative direction, in practice if not in theory, ever since it came to power.

Against this background the political consequences of the border conflicts with China and, later, Pakistan have been anything but healthy. As we observed in Chapter 5, boundary troubles in South Asia tend to arouse national fervor and, in a sense, ease the task of national consolidation. This was, for instance, the effect of the Indian conquest of Goa shortly before the general election in 1962.[1] But the excitement thus generated does not provide a very stable foundation and it has been used for other political ends as well. Thus the large-scale Chinese assault on the Himalayan frontier in October of 1962 at first evoked a spontaneous affirmation of national unity and integrity, much of it in the form of melodramatic gestures and oratory. Even Nehru, in an outburst of Churchillian rhetoric, called for a "Dunkirk spirit." The conflict, he asserted, had made India a nation, and the war effort it now necessitated would accelerate rather than delay the pace of its economic development. But no sooner had the fighting ceased than the mood of national purpose and determination evaporated. The politicians resumed their mutual recriminations and factional feuding;[2] discontent with food shortages, increased tax burdens,

[1] Chapter 4, Section 7.

[2] The following is a fair analysis: "The external threat to the nation's security was expected to awaken Congressmen to the need for unity in the party. But except for an

and rising prices fed the vocal opposition to the government, and the state of emergency declared at the outbreak of hostilities became the subject of cynical comment. Meanwhile, it was apparent that India's prestige and influence in international affairs – resulting from Nehru's policy of non-alignment in the cold war and his independence, particularly, of Western opinion – had evaporated.[1]

As the border dispute developed, Nehru came under sharper attack, especially from conservative groups within and outside the Congress, for showing too much moderation toward Chinese claims. In accusing him of flouting Parliament by not keeping it fully informed of Chinese frontier intrusions,[2] his opponents touched a sensitive spot and thereby ensured that subsequent negotiations were conducted as a noisy type of open diplomacy, mainly directed to public opinion in India and, increasingly, to India's friends abroad. Under mounting pressure, Nehru seemed uncertain whether to claim credit for defending India or for loving peace; he tried to subsume both under the notion of "patriotic non-alignment," which he contrasted with the "super-patriotism," as he described it, of his critics. The vocal Gandhians were utterly confused; some developed into reckless nationalists. The Indian Communists were split between ideological affiliation and national patriotism, and from time to time many of them were arrested.

The conservative attack was directed as much against the government's domestic as its foreign policies. "Doctrinaire" economic policies as well as non-alignment were responsible, they alleged, for the country's unpreparedness. All manner of policies, attitudes, and personalities were called into question. They successfully clamored for the ouster of Krishna Menon, the left-wing Defense Minister, and relentlessly sought to discredit Nehru himself. At bottom their real target was the social and economic revolution he stood for and which they had already done so much to obstruct or emasculate. It was thus the conservatives, not the radicals, who embarked on the propaganda struggle against China with most enthusiasm, for they saw that it offered the Indian public an exciting diversion, though at the expense of sinking them all the more deeply in the very conditions that were responsible for national weakness in the first place.

It must be remembered that these shifting currents of attitude and opinion took place mainly within a small upper-class group, though in

---

all too brief period marred by invidious attempts to undermine the leadership and force changes in policy, there was no such awareness of the new responsibility thrown on the party. Deep-seated ambitions and jealousies were muffled only for a few days and broke to the surface again with renewed force for having been restrained." (*Link*, August 1, 1963.)

[1] Chapter 5, Section 8.

[2] Chapter 5, Section 7.

India, as in all of South Asia, they are referred to as "middle class" and their views as "public opinion." The masses did not participate much in the political process except as mobs to be roused to riot and demonstrations or as voters to be cajoled by appeals that had little to do with national issues.

5 *Further Consideration of the Mechanism of Causation*

The decline of public spirit in Indian politics, the struggle for prestige, power, and private gain, the indifference to national purpose and welfare, the dissensions and factional rivalries at the state level, and the alleged increase of corruption in politics and administration are discussed in India in moral terms that add up to the assertion that there is a deterioration in the character of the politicians and even of the ruling upper strata. This is not, by itself, a necessarily wrong or unrealistic view, since the phenomena it seeks to diagnose are certainly related to attitudes and patterns of behavior that legitimately enough can be judged from a moral standpoint. It is pointed out that the heroic traditions of the independence struggle have been steadily weakening. The cherished national leaders of that time have died or are getting old. Among the younger generation of politicians there are no successors of similar integrity and ability or with any comparable appeal to the articulate Indian opinion. At all political levels under the national leadership, there are said to be far fewer devoted workers for the national good and many more opportunists and self-seekers, catering to and nurtured by essentially parochial interests and demands. After independence, internal divisions could no longer be sublimated in the interests of the national struggle; there was not the same urge to work together for a supreme cause.

All these may be correct observations. But the social scientist is still interested in the how and why, in the mechanism of causation by which the changing character of Indian politics may be explained. To begin with, it must be recognized that the process by which individuals are selected and advanced in politics, the way they are conditioned to feel, think, and act, and the type of appeals they can employ to win support have all become very different from what they were in the national liberation movement and in the first flush of independence. In the liberation movement, there was little to gain from politics, except perhaps personal acclaim, and much to lose by way of personal sacrifice. The over-riding aim of political activity was simple and unifying: to win national political independence. Service to the Congress was identified with service to the nation. The principal tasks were not those of government but of political propaganda and organization. Policy commitments could be broad and radical; they belonged to the uncertain future. The liberation movement naturally appealed to the intellectuals of the so-called "middle class," and it was they who took leadership.[1] After independence, the day-to-day tasks of practical politics appealed much less to this detached intelligentsia. But they did appeal to quite another type in the "middle class," less interested in ideals and still less in a life of self-sacrifice for the national welfare. We have already pointed out that the strained situation immediately following independence and partition put a premium on the capacity for taking practical decisions in contrast to forming broad policies and also that the privileged position of those who stepped into power must have dampened their eagerness to implement radical social and economic reforms. A new type of politician with few ideological inhibitions about working for special interests invaded the arena of politics at the center and still more in the states.[2]

As politics became increasingly concerned with practical issues, so the pressure of vested interests on the politicians grew stronger, and with it, corruption and nepotism became profitable. The Congress high command could lay down high principles for policies and for the selection of candidates for political posts; but the political machines were in the hands of state and local bosses, who were intent on winning elections. Accordingly, communal and caste appeals often decided the selection of candidates.[3] In this situation it is understandable that reform policies ostensibly

[1] "The leadership of the independence movement right from the village level to the national level had been in the hands of the middle class. The historical explanation apart, in every society and more so in a semi-literate society, the educated members tend to take a lead in social and political matters. The involvement of the masses in the direct action is thus rooted in their social relations with the members of the middle class." (Rajni Kothari, "Direct Action: A Pattern of Political Behaviour," *Quest*, January/March, 1960, p. 35.)

[2] In the 1962 general election, for example, the guiding principles of the Congress high command were virtually ignored by the State Congress Committees. The following analysis of the scramble for Congress tickets before the election appeared in the July 23, 1961, issue of *Link*, a left-wing weekly that has always held up Nehru as its hero:

"As the average number of aspirants for every Congress ticket varies from state to state, so does the social strata to which the ticket seekers belong. In Punjab most of them are rich peasants, the traditional leaders of public opinion in the villages of the State. In Madras according to the PCC spokesman, 60 per cent are 'townsmen engaged in business and trade,' including 13 industrialists (of whom six are textile magnates), 10 buss transport operators, three bankers and two newspaper proprietors; others in this category can be classed as 'prosperous city people.' . . . Most of them joined the Congress in recent years. Only five per cent of the Madras applicants have claimed the Congress ticket on the ground of their contribution in the freedom struggle. In Punjab, too, there are quite a few applicants with 'business contacts.'

"In both states most of the aspirants are post-independence Congressmen. But unlike Madras, most of those who have applied for tickets in Punjab have described themselves as 'active workers' even when they have joined the Congress only recently."

[3] There are those who regard the de-idealization of politics and the emergence of organized interest groups on specific policy issues as a force for political stability. "Once ideological questions can be reduced to specific issues, compromise and dis-

intended to alleviate the desperate poverty of the masses turn out to subsidize those who are relatively well off.

The type of appeal that can be made by politicians has also changed greatly since the liberation movement. They can no longer put the blame for poverty and stagnation on colonial masters, but must explain why there is not greater progress now that India is independent. Nor is personal sacrifice a means of inspiring confidence. Very few of the present leaders have made any sacrifices, and any that were made belong to a much earlier period. Politics now is commonly considered an avenue to privileges and patronage; to be a politician is to be regarded as a self-seeker and opportunist. Thus it is to the particularist interests of those who command the votes and to the emotions and superstitions of a deeply fissured society that the politicians address their appeal. It is in this respect that Indian politics has changed most since the beginnings of independence. But what it really reflects is a shift in the basis of political power in Indian society.

Any government action, whether a law or an administrative decision, to be effective must be enforced at the lower levels of the political structure — in the states, districts, and localities. But because of the poverty, ignorance, and apathy of the masses and their habitual dependence on and submissiveness to people of wealth and status, real power at levels below the center is mostly wielded by peasant landlords, merchants, and moneylenders. These small upper strata see to it that policies averse to their interests are not put into effect or are turned to the benefit of themselves or their dependable "clients" alone. To exercise control from above in a country as vast, diversified, and stratified as India is extremely difficult and in most cases virtually impossible. Moreover, since these groups are also the political brokers who command the votes of the poor, unorganized masses, the national leaders dare not affront them. Thus in the 1962 elections far more attention was paid to influencing community leaders and "key men" than to public meetings and mass propaganda. Since the masses are docile and "amenable," they need not be approached directly; it is enough to win over the dominant group that controls them. This kind of political structure is unavoidable when a national party does not have a cadre of dedicated workers in direct contact with the masses. In India this applies to every party, including the Communists, who have not as yet succeeded in mobilizing a mass following, especially in the rural areas, except on a caste basis as in Kerala.

The attitudes of the political bosses, who wield the real political, social,

---

cussion are possible and prospects for a stable political party system will improve." (Weiner, *Party Politics in India*, p. 289.)

But this kind of political stability, as we shall shortly argue, may well be incompatible, in a country like India, with economic growth and a broadening of the basis of active political participation.

and economic power at the local level and, indirectly, at the state and federal levels, are far removed from the lofty modernization ideals of the Congress movement and quite often at variance with the policies actually pressed by the central government. That the character of Indian politics would change in this way after independence now seems inevitable. The Indian sociologist, M. N. Srinivas, has described the inherent conflict of interests as follows:

> The rural elite has emerged as a class keenly conscious of the political and economic opportunities lying before it. It does not have any inhibitions about exploiting these opportunities to its own advantage. . . . A basic contradiction needs to be mentioned here. In implementing programmes for the benefit of rural areas government officials tend to be guided by the rural leaders who are part of the rural elite. But it is forgotten that there is a fundamental conflict between the interests of the rural elite and the rural poor. . . . The rural elite are, as a group, aggressive, acquisitive and not burdened by feelings of guilt towards the people they exploit. Hierarchy and exploitation are so deep-seated in rural India that they are accepted without questioning. Neither the urban politician nor the administrator can do without the rural elite and the latter know it.[1]

Under pressure to show results, the officials administering development programs require the cooperation of the rural elite.[2] No wonder, then, that the evaluation studies invariably conclude that these programs have helped mainly those in the rural population who were already relatively well off. Suffrage has given the rural elite a power that state ministers and legislators must respect. Political decentralization, or panchayat raj, has strengthened their position still further by offering them more opportunities for political office and patronage. *Democracy itself thus plays into the hands of petty plutocracy.*[3] As one Indian journal put it: "One cannot help wondering whether the drive to political maturity is, after all, a good thing in a country which has still not had a proper social revolution. It may well result in premature old age."[4]

Thus a key to the understanding of the power of the political bosses is

[1] M. N. Srinivas, "Changing Attitudes in India Today," *Yojana*, October 1, 1961, p. 26.

[2] Chapter 18, Section 12.

[3] "Adult franchise has placed much power in their [the rural elite's] hands as each rural leader commands the votes of a certain number of caste-fellows and clients." (Srinivas, *loc. cit.*)

[4] "Maturity or Age," *The Economic Weekly*, October 7, 1961.

The article observes that the growing strength of the rural elite is a threat to the power and influence of the urban elite: "Whatever may be said of the narrow social base of this urban elite [who dominated Congress in earlier times], it has been, all through the last four or five decades, a progressive force saturated with the ideals and lessons of the French and the Russian revolutions, and pushing the country in the right direction. . . . But the rural upper class is innocent of all this. It is not inhibited by troublesome ideas of social justice or cramped by the emergence of new forces demanding its place under the sun. After having been denied political power for centuries the rural upper class is now not only conscious of its power but determined to use it to further its own ends."

the inherited social stratification of India and, above all, its caste system. At election times the caste groups function as political vote banks whereby the ballots of their members are joined to the candidate with a party label.[1] For this reason alone the local political bosses have a vested interest in preserving the social and economic *status quo* and exploiting it as a matrix for political action.[2] But the caste system, as we noted earlier, is also connected with regional and linguistic differences and tends in consequence to strengthen the pull of these centrifugal forces. Asoka Mehta, a political theorist as well as a practical politician, long ago called the tendency to regionalism, reinforced by caste, "the biggest danger that Indian democracy faces during the next twenty years, when it will be under the severe strains of economic development."[3] He regards Indian democracy as little more than a clever balancing of the castes against each other. Activating this process are the political bosses, who exploit what is continually condemned in India as "casteism, communalism, provincialism, and linguism."

This exploitation of particularist tendencies is a threat to peaceful, orderly government, especially as Indian politics has preserved from the liberation struggle so much of an inclination to "direct action." It is the political bosses, working on prejudices, grievances, and frustrations, who are often responsible for student unrest at Indian universities,[4] and even

[1] "Indeed, one of the factors providing sustenance to casteism is that castes are reservoirs of political power which political parties are obviously shy to ignore and which, to pamper prove to be to their benefit." ("Notes and Comments on Social Education and Casteism," *Indian Journal of Adult Education,* Vol. XIX, No. 3, October, 1958, p. 1.) See also W. H. Morris-Jones, "Stability and Change in Indian Politics," in Saul Rose, ed., *Politics in Southern Asia,* Macmillan, London, 1963, p. 29.

[2] Srinivas illustrates this point with the following story: "I remember a remark made to me by the Headman of Rampura in 1948. The Headman wanted electricity and the loan of a bulldozer and tractor for the village from the Mysore Government. I told him the village badly needed a good school but he did not agree with me. According to him a school only meant that the sons of his servants and labourers would become uppish and none would be available to till the fields. The Headman was also not in agreement with the attitude of the Government towards Harijans [Gandhi's term for the untouchables]. He did not want them to be admitted into temples, and the grant which the Government gave towards providing Harijan houses with country tiles for roofing, he doled out in such small instalments that the Harijans spent it on toddy. He cited this as decisive proof that nothing could be done to help the Harijans." (Srinivas, "Changing Attitudes in India Today," *Yojana,* p. 26.)

[3] Asoka Mehta, "The Political Mind of India," *Foreign Affairs,* July, 1957, p. 682.

"God knows," Jayaprakash Narayan has remarked, "what there is in this caste system that it has withstood all the shocks received by it throughout history. . . . Now, this caste system is feeding upon this system of parliamentary democracy. Casteism is growing at the cost of parliamentary democracy." (*Towards a New Society,* p. 87.) See also K. William Kapp, *Hindu Culture, Economic Development and Economic Planning in India,* Asia Publishing House, Bombay, 1963, p. 37.

[4] More precisely, the student agitator, allied to the political bosses, exploits the sense of frustration and insecurity Indian students commonly exhibit. In a more general way, political parties since independence have sought to build up student political movements as training grounds for future party leaders or simply as centers of opposition to the government. See Chapter 33, Section 6.

more often for communal riots and friction over language problems and state boundaries. Such conflicts are harmful to national consolidation both directly and also indirectly in that they deflect interest from the larger issues that must be solved if Indian economic development is to outpace population growth. There is another angle to the threat to national consolidation from the new political boss class. Since their power is strong in the districts and the states and weakest at the center, their activities and pressures must tend to strengthen the former against the latter. It is very much in their interest to resist the efforts of the center to control state policies and activities. In the Indian political system, as we noted earlier, the states have responsibility for most matters that directly affect the lives of the people. The political bosses, who have a vested interest in perpetuating existing conditions, therefore foster a "state nationalism"—what in India is usually referred to as "provincialism"—at the expense of a nationalism embracing the whole nation.

It is often argued in India, though mainly in private, that the very conditions which inhibit the masses from effectively organizing to push their own interests, namely, their poverty, ignorance, and isolation, and the hierarchical power structure of Indian society, have made it possible for India to hold general elections, based on universal suffrage, without endangering political stability.[1] Even the fact that economic and social reforms are largely ineffective in practice can, in a sense, be described as "stability." But this kind of stability has only been achieved through the incapacity of the political system to induce the social and economic changes that development calls for. *By leaving real power with the opponents of economic and social change, political stability implies stagnation.*[2]

The upsurge of centrifugal forces and the build-up of resistance to fundamental social and economic change in India since independence thus follow naturally from the attempt to base political power on universal suffrage in a harshly inegalitarian and extremely poor society, without first effecting social and economic revolution. The enlightened members of the Congress leadership anticipated that social change would be brought about gradually by the democratic political process. But what they are now learning by experience, as their recently expressed anxieties

[1] "The upper classes need not resist when the lower classes are not demanding." (*The Economic Weekly,* December 1, 1962.)

[2] "Political stability is not, of course, the only good thing in the world; economic development is probably more important in the long run; indeed, it could be said that the price of India's political stability is her declining growth rate." (*Ibid.,* October 5, 1963, p. 1673.)

This was early seen by Maurice Zinkin, who wrote in the mid-1950's: "But the larger the actively interested electorate, the more conservative it is likely to be. This is a great source of political stability. But it can also be a considerable brake on the sort of change which is needed to improve the standard of living." (Maurice Zinkin, *Development for Free Asia,* Chatto & Windus, London, 1956, p. 72.)

about national integration have shown, is that the Indian polity itself is endangered unless the divisive forces within society can be controlled. To this theme we shall return often in the course of this study.

6 *National Consolidation in the Balance*

The operation of the mechanism of political causation set in motion by the achievement of Indian independence was, of course, plainly visible to those public leaders who personify the great traditions of the Congress movement, above all Nehru, and to many journalists, university people, and intellectuals generally. To complete the picture, therefore, we need to take account of the countervailing pressures they have exerted.[1] To begin with, there is the impact and momentum of the ideology of modernization. This is still the ruling ideology, indeed, something like a state religion, from which no conservative group within the Congress Party, nor any other political party, dare deviate very far. It sets the groundwork within which public debate is conducted.[2] A fairly large group of intellectual leaders continue to proclaim the modernization ideals, and positions of considerable authority are still occupied by those who led the struggle for independence or who firmly adhere to this great legacy from the liberation struggle.

At their head until 1964 stood, of course, the towering figure of Nehru himself. Whatever time Nehru could spare from his multifarious and exacting roles in the government and from the endless details of administration, which in large measure he failed to delegate,[3] he devoted to speaking, on all sorts of occasions and often several times a day, against

[1] This is not done, for instance, in Selig Harrison's otherwise well-documented study, *India: The Most Dangerous Decades.*

[2] In a speech to the Constituent Assembly, B. R. Ambedkar, the Chairman of the Drafting Committee for the Indian Constitution, had commented on the Directive Principles, where this ideology was expressed, and pointed out: "He [the politician] cannot ignore them. He may not have to answer for their breach in a Court of Law. But he will certainly have to answer for them before the electorate at election time. What great value these directive principles possess will be realized better when the forces of right contrive to capture power." (Quoted in Pylee, *India's Constitution,* pp. 25–26.)

[3] As one of his biographers has remarked: "The fact of the matter is that Nehru is an inept administrator. Decisions are concentrated in his hands to an incredible degree, not only because of objective pressures, but also because of his all-consuming interest in the pettiest of details. He lacks both the talent and temperament to coordinate the work of the various ministries. More important, he has never shown a capacity or inclination to delegate authority. The result has been the 'administrative jungle' which he bemoans." (Brecher, *Nehru, A Political Biography,* p. 622.)

This observation agrees with the writer's own personal observations. Nehru even answered many unimportant personal letters himself and any ambitious visitor to India could see him. He was prepared to advise in matters he should not have had time to bother with. He made things more difficult for himself by not insisting on having a like-minded cabinet.

"casteism, communalism, provincialism, and linguism" and for the modernization ideals, economic and social reform, national consolidation, and development. With unflagging energy he hammered away at the need for a social revolution and for a complete change in outlook on the part of the Indian people. It was as if he wanted to use every minute, while he was still on the scene, to drive home the gospel of modernization so that it would be permanently fixed in the national consciousness.[1]

He was not alone in this: similar impulses motivate many other Indian politicians and intellectual leaders. Indian newspapers give so much space to their speeches that they, too, appear to be mainly concerned with enlightening their readers along the lines of the modernization ideals. In the tradition established immediately after independence, legislation is frequently used for the same purpose even when it must be clear that the intentions and spirit of the laws are being nullified in practice. The five year plans have formulated general goals remote from their practical proposals. The annual conferences of the Congress Party, and sometimes the Parliament, have been persuaded to adopt resolutions far in advance of the actual policies pursued. If there was a discernible trend in all this ideological activity, it was in Nehru's time toward more explicit, radical commitments whereas, as we have noted, practical politics moved in a pragmatic and conservative direction.

A persistent gulf between promise and fulfillment cannot be altogether politically healthy. It implies the depreciation of principles and governmental functions, and must breed cynicism.[2] Many politicians who echo Nehru and other high-minded leaders in propounding the modernization ideals cannot be completely sincere, or are not very clear in their thinking. They have helped to enshroud social and economic problems in an atmosphere of unreality and make-believe. This is the more unfortunate because of the tendency of Indians to be less interested in facts than in generalities. They live and talk on several ideological planes, and their beliefs about facts and their valuations are obviously not kept firm and in accord with reality.[3] Even highly educated Indians, in solemn conclave or in

[1] "This is how the mind of Mr. Nehru works sub-consciously if not consciously: his failure or refusal to build anything like an ideologically homogeneous party, group or even cadres is made up for by his almost epic endeavour to transform the whole nation into a land of Nehrus which would act, ultimately, as a powerful national deterrent against any reactionary leader or group reversing the basic engine of our policy." (R. K. Karanjia, *The Mind of Mr. Nehru,* Allen & Unwin Ltd., London, 1961, p. 67.)

[2] "The Congress leadership has generated general apathy by making promises and refusing to carry them out. All the time it has kept on talking of a socialistic pattern of society, of welfare state, of social justice, of equal opportunities for all, and the other catch phrases from the Fabian Bible, with the result that the rich at the top are annoyed by its talk and the poor are dismayed by its performance." (*The Economic Weekly,* November 2, 1963, p. 1808.)

[3] There is, with all differences, something of a similarity in this respect between Indian and American civilization.

contact with foreigners, are found to believe that India is a "welfare state" and is developing toward a "classless society." They point to the constitutional injunction and explain that caste is abolished. There seems, indeed, to be no end to the lack of realism about what has been happening in the field of policy. It would be an interesting and important study to probe this whole complex of "double-think." One indication is, of course, the hiding of their privileged position by including themselves in the "middle class."

Thus in the short run this propaganda effort through speeches, resolutions, plans, and legislation must have the negative effect of confusing and concealing problems. But in the long run it must also have the positive effect of preserving an influence for the modernization ideals. We should not underestimate the importance of getting a political creed firmly outlined and accepted, even if its realization lags well behind. In line with these ideological activities, there has also been, as we observed, a vigorous continuation of the practice, inherited from British rule, of making factual surveys and honest evaluations of the results of policies. Here again the basic value premises are the modernization ideals. The work of most Indian social scientists, much of which is in the nature of "challenges" to policy, is cast in the same mold. Within the framework of ideological activities and studies there is, in addition, the impact of planning as an ongoing process. Since planning is closely integrated into the central government and increasingly into the state governments as well, it exerts an influence for greater coordination of policies at all government levels, and hence for national integration. The fact that this political planning process is kept moving and is centrally directed is important. By bringing local and state politicians to look at problems from the standpoint of national development, and by disseminating factual information from the same standpoint, organized planning activity must encourage changes in attitudes. And planning involves more than the formulation of projects and proposals. In many fields it has brought into being huge operational machinery that, although it must be worked with consideration for local and regional interests, is to a considerable extent under central direction. The Indian constitution itself exhibits, as we saw, a strong bias in favor of centralization. Finally, the fact that the center is much less under the influence of the vested interests of the political bosses than are local and state governments strengthens still further the strategic position and momentum of the modernization ideals.

The central Parliament is another unifying force and a potentially powerful instrument for the political education of its members as well as of articulate opinion outside. No less important, the Congress Party still retains from the liberation struggle a considerable degree of central direction that cannot escape being partly under the influence of the modernization ideals. It is true that in the last resort the national leadership depends on the state and local bosses to back and implement its decisions and to get out the vote. This again undoubtedly enables the political bosses at these levels to obstruct or frustrate policies running counter to their interests. But it must not be forgotten that national political activity, like economic planning, is a two-way process in that the party image is continually being conveyed downwards even when party policies are being thwarted from below.

Another hope inspired and initiated from the center is that a system of locally elected bodies, the panchayat raj, better known under the label "democratic decentralization" or "democratic planning,"[1] will encourage the masses to participate in the management of local affairs and thereby weaken the power of the local political bosses. For this purpose the most important unit of self-government is the village panchayat, or council. Panchayat raj is the favored answer today to most of the disappointments encountered by the community development programs in their efforts to arouse the rural masses from their torpor and stimulate local initiative. As we noted previously, however, the most conspicuous immediate effect of such efforts has been to strengthen the grip of the rural elite, the self-elected boss class, over the masses. Whenever locally elected bodies are given powers worth scrambling for, they are almost invariably run in the interests of the dominant caste in land and wealth.[2] The system of panchayat raj, like the basic democracies in Pakistan,[3] has not, in general, thrown up any new leadership in rural areas. It is difficult to see how any other result could have been expected.[4] But it is equally difficult to see any alternative to the imposition of "democratic decentralization" from above. This problem will be discussed in Chapter 18.

In the long run, however, "democratic planning" should nevertheless tend to reduce the power of the rural elite. In any place as backward as the Indian village, an election must be something of a shock. Sooner or later the electorate may come to realize that they have the right to throw out their representatives and secure some advantages for themselves. Press reports of minor clashes between untouchables and caste Hindus indicate that the former are occasionally asserting their rights. With the

[1] Chapter 18.

[2] To quote Srinivas again: "The conferring of vast powers to panchayats [village councils] places great temptations before the locally dominant caste to use the money and power available to it in favour of its own members and at the expense of the other and dependent castes." (Quoted in A. M. Rosenthal, "Mother India Thirty Years After," *Foreign Affairs*, Vol. 35, No. 4, July, 1957, p. 626.)

[3] Chapter 8, Section 8; Chapter 18, Section 9.

[4] Jayaprakash Narayan was among those who had no delusions on this score: "You take the village as it is and you give it the right of electing the panchayat and carrying on certain functions and duties. What will happen in such a village? Either the dominant castes or a few leading families or the bullies will capture the panchayats, and run them for their own use. Therefore, there is need for a revolution before the foundational units of democracy could be created." (*Towards a New Society*, p. 94.)

spread of education it may become more difficult to keep them and all others among the poor and disadvantaged in their lowly status. Caste rests upon custom and habit not being challenged; consequently, every challenge to the latter, however unsuccessful at first, should weaken its authority.[1] The modernization ideology, in short, may be seeping downwards and in time making it more difficult to deny elementary rights to people hitherto regarded as outcasts. But as things are, and are tending to become, *there is not much time left for gradual changes to evolve,* and in the short run democratic decentralization, like general suffrage at all levels, works mostly for reaction and stagnation.[2]

All of this points up the urgency of raising educational levels. But these efforts are hampered by the population increase. Moreover, they require that teachers be of high quality and, in particular, that they be trained to induce changes in attitudes and not merely to give formal schooling. Adult education is especially needed to effect rapid changes in attitudes. The problems of education will be taken up in Chapters 32 and 33.

7 *The Upshot*

For the reasons indicated in the preceding sections, the progress of India toward national consolidation is uneasily balanced by a host of interacting forces, some negative and some positive. The outcome cannot be gauged with any degree of certainty. Much will depend on the pace of economic development itself, and in this respect the omens are far from favorable. The prospects have been made less encouraging by a rate of population growth that has exceeded all expectations.

The international setting is another influence that has changed for the worse in recent years. On the one hand, the improvement in relations between the Soviet Union and the West has eased the strain of those intensely competitive situations in which India's position of non-alignment gave it international prestige and occasionally considerable influence. On

[1] See, for example, Morris Edward Opler, "Factors of Tradition and Change in a Local Election," in Richard L. Park and Irene Tinker, eds., *Leadership and Political Institutions in India,* Princeton University Press, Princeton, 1959, pp. 137–150.

[2] ". . . Panchayati Raj, visualised as an instrument for development in the countryside, and for the exercise of local initiative, is a major threat to the power and influence of the urban elite. . . . Nothing is more unrealistic than the assumption – which the Congress seems to make – that the masses in the countryside are going to gain power and initiative in the near future through Panchayati Raj. Indeed, it would not be surprising if, even at the next election [to Parliament and State Assemblies], the rural upper class captures the sources of political power in India, and begins to dominate the [Congress] party which has given this opportunity. And, if this happens, it does not require a prophet to predict that the pragmatic approach of the party will rapidly gain strength, and its ideological urges get further diluted, before the time comes for drafting the next election manifesto." (*The Economic Weekly,* October 7, 1961.)

the other hand, India's own international problems have become more difficult. The wars with China and Pakistan, leaving the contested issues unresolved, and India's increasing dependence on foreign grants and loans have given comfort to the forces of conservatism and outright reaction in India. The outbursts of resentment against other countries occasioned by these pressures may momentarily appear to ease the task of national consolidation. But ill-feeling toward other countries is not a safe foundation on which to build national unity.

Nor can much, if any, encouragement be derived from recent trends of domestic politics in India. The ruling party appears to evade its ideological commitments in the day-to-day pragmatic decisions. "It elevates the politics of amorphousness to the level of a political doctrine," one Indian journal caustically remarked.[1] The Congress Party's conservative wing dominates its political machine and slows down the processes of economic and social change. The trappings and emoluments of office appear to be the main concern of most Congress politicians, and party factions fight one another to achieve or retain them. Other parties, it should be added, set no higher example.

> A fundamental will-lessness manifests itself in Government's actions. The Congress organisation, with a dwindling leadership at the top and bloated ranks below, can keel over in a crisis of any magnitude. The other political parties which are insignificant in the larger political context, have reconciled themselves to functioning as mere lobbies. This political uncertainty is the direct parent of divisive tendencies, of centrifugal social factors.[2]

In August, 1963 Nehru attempted to revitalize the Congress and its image by persuading a number of senior officials, mostly of a more conservative leaning, to resign from ministerial posts at the center and in some of the states to undertake organizational work for the party. They were expected to root out corruption and factionalism in the party and to demonstrate the need for spiritual renewal among the people. The whole exercise was ostensibly intended to revive the pre-independence spirit of selfless service. Instead, it seems to have intensified dissidence within the party, particularly at the state level where the purged ministers sought to build up positions of strength that would take them back into power. In any case this sort of exercise will not cure the frustrations and disaffections that spring from the hiatus between the government's declared objectives and its actual achievements. The government and the Congress Party will only regain momentum by translating the national objectives into concrete measures they are prepared to implement. The important question then arises, however, whether this is feasible given the present social base of the ruling party.

[1] *The Economic Weekly*, Special Number, July, 1963, p. 1115.

[2] Editorial in *Overseas Hindustan Times*, August 23, 1962.

Another imponderable that long agitated the minds of Indian and foreign observers alike was what would happen when Nehru left the scene. His stature had been such that for some years he was a factor of instability, as when the mighty pillar supporting an edifice begins to crumble. His health became something of a political obsession, and the impression was sometimes created that Indian parliamentary democracy could not survive his departure. This gloomy view was unwarranted, as, we may hope, is the notion, occasionally expressed, that the Congress Party was showing alarming similarities to the Kuomintang under Chiang Kai-shek after the Second World War.[1]

As a matter of fact, Nehru's hold over the Congress Party had been far from complete. Certainly after the debacle of the border conflict with China his authority became much less unquestioned. Yet even in later years Nehru remained supreme in the eyes of the public; he personified national purpose and identity. His political strength was thus in a sense India's weakness. Nehru himself, however, was deeply convinced that the function of leadership is to make institutions the custodians of social and political power and that the fate of a democratic system should not be made to depend on the availability of exceptional men. Moreover, the impress of his ideas and personality seemed unlikely to vanish quickly after his death.

All the same, it was widely feared that the choice of a leader to succeed Nehru would rend the Congress Party asunder. In the event, the succession was managed smoothly and with a sense of responsibility and dignity that few other countries have matched in similar circumstances. Congress politicians congratulated themselves on the way the parliamentary party rallied to elect Lal Bahadur Shastri unanimously as its new leader.

Shastri had risen to prominence as an effective worker for the Congress Party and owed his election to the stage management of its organizational wing. Indeed, "machine politics" is apt to become more influential, if only because the new generation of Indian politicians have made their beginnings in state politics, unlike the "old guard" whose formative years were spent in the national liberation movement. The central government is now more nearly a cabinet of equals and this puts a premium on disciplined, collective leadership. At the same time, as the mishandling of the food shortages under the Shastri government makes plain, the power of the center is heavily dependent on the will of the state leaders, who in turn depend on the local bosses. And in a number of states, the Congress Party has been reduced to a shambles of personal cabals.

It is against this political background that a rising crescendo of public concern with "emotional integration" has been expressed for several years,

[1] "The Congress is in decline. To many it appears to have alarming similarities to the Kuomintang under Chiang Kai-shek after the second world war." (Brecher, *Nehru, A Political Biography*, p. 496.)

particularly since mid-1961, following serious riots between linguistic groups and religious communities and much student unrest. In a display of concerted effort, committees and conferences of governors, ministers, political parties, and educational leaders were called to discuss the subject and make recommendations. Parliament passed legislation making it a violation of electoral procedures to promote enmity between classes in the name of religion, caste, race, community, or language. In the summer of 1963 it amended the constitution to permit state governors to impose restrictions on all activities aimed at the disintegration of the country and to prohibit political parties from making secession from India an election issue. The Indian penal code was amended to make disturbance of communal harmony a criminal offense. During a "national integration week" people were asked to sign a pledge that they would not resort to physical violence in any dispute. Codes of conduct were drafted for the guidance of political parties, employers, workers, students, and the press.

Judged by the election campaign of 1962, the early effects of this whole debate were not encouraging.[1] It is not realistic, however, to expect mere exhortations from above to bring about rapid changes in Indian political life. The reports of the innumerable committees and conferences concerned with "emotional integration" give the strong impression that the participants must have felt quite helpless. The emphasis in the end is placed on education of the sort that Nehru called "training people's minds" – a rationalistic variation of Gandhi's prescription, "a change of heart." In India an intellectual and moral conversion tends to be advanced as a panacea for all kinds of ills. But to change attitudes without changing social institutions is a rather hopeless quest. This remains the basic dilemma and challenge of Indian politics.

[1] In a broadcast on the eve of Independence Day in 1962, President Radhakrishnan said: "The recent elections showed that the system of caste and feeling for groups – linguistic and communal – had not loosened its hold on the masses of our people. These have impaired the health of our democratic structure. Even in panchayat raj, we should be careful that the spirit of caste panchayat does not vitiate its working." (*Overseas Hindustan Times*, August 23, 1962, p. 12.)

Chapter 8

PAKISTAN

1 *Initial Difficulties and the Lack of National Purpose*

As we pointed out previously in discussing partition,[1] few modern states started their independent existence on such a tenuous basis and under such severe initial difficulties as Pakistan. Not only was the new country split into two wings, separated by over a thousand miles of Indian territory; many vital arteries were severed in the process. Thus the east wing lost its principal port, the pivot of its railway system, and the industrial complex that had processed its jute, while the west wing's frontiers with India cut across the extensive and all-important Punjab irrigation network, leaving several vital headworks in Kashmir and India. The only undivided provinces Pakistan inherited from British India were Sind and the North-West Frontier Province, both relatively small and backward. Pakistan was even less industrialized than India and had few natural resources. It gained no main offices of major firms, very few banks, and virtually no industry. It inherited proportionately fewer administrators, clerks, professional and business people, and skilled workers than India, and received a proportionately larger number of refugees. Lacking an established political and administrative capital and a commercial and financial center, Pakistan had to improvise the entire apparatus of government and business. Born in communal strife and political and economic chaos and bordered by hostile neighbors, the country's mere survival as a political unit was remarkable.

[1] Chapter 6, Sections 1 and 3–5.

Behind the unfavorable circumstances of its origin was a fundamental predicament – the lack of a clear conception of the kind of state that should be created and the aims it should pursue. The struggle for Pakistan was exclusively concerned with freeing Moslems from Hindu domination. As a prominent leader expressed it: "The Muslims of the Sub-Continent wanted to build up their lives in accordance with the teaching and traditions of Islam, because they wanted to demonstrate to the world that Islam provides a panacea to the many diseases which have crept into the life of humanity today."[1] This was the declared *raison d'être* of the new state. That mass appeal to religious faith could be used to incite Moslems against Hindus – and vice versa – was tragically proved by the events preceding and following partition. But its positive value in creating a sense of national identity and purpose was to prove rather illusory.

This outcome could have been foreseen. Islam, like Christianity but unlike Hinduism, is a universal rather than a national religion. Indeed, many religious Moslems, especially some of their most learned men, either held aloof from or actively opposed the struggle for an Islamic state on the Indian subcontinent as heresy or something close to it. On the practical level they could ask what the attitude of a Moslem state that identified religion with national patriotism should be toward the millions of Moslems remaining in India – or toward the many Hindus and other non-Moslem minorities within its own borders. These critics considered the establishment of an Islamic state to be without foundation in the Koran. While popular enthusiasm for Pakistan mounted as events reached a climax and religious fanaticism came to prevail among both the Moslem and Hindu masses, many Moslem intellectual leaders remained detached and critical. Some of these leaders even stayed in India after partition.

In this connection it should be remembered that from the outset the Muslim League was led mostly by a Westernized upper-class group who were usually not very religious but had appealed to the need of the Moslem masses to assert themselves against the Hindus. Some of the leaders were plainly indifferent to religion or were agnostics; others were secularists who tried to adapt the injunctions of the Koran to the conditions and opportunities of modern living.[2] Few, if any, could be classed as devout

[1] Liaquat Ali Khan, *Pakistan: Heart of Asia,* Harvard University Press, Cambridge, 1951, p. 2.

[2] Jinnah himself was certainly in this second category, if not in the first. For obvious reasons the folklore about his worldliness is cultivated with particular relish in India. Louis Fischer, in *This Is Our World* (Jonathan Cape, London, 1956), refers to Jinnah as follows (p. 18): "Somebody called him 'one of the best-dressed men in the British Empire.' He drank liquor, ate pork, seldom went to the mosque, knew no Arabic and little Urdu. In these respects, as well as in surname, origin, and temperament, he was as un-Islamic as anyone could be, and he adopted the program of a separate Moslem state very late in life."

Undoubtedly, the rationalist character of Islam on the "higher" level, and, more

Moslems.[1] Their ideas about the future state of Pakistan had few roots in Islam. As Keith Callard pointed out in reviewing Pakistan's origins and early political history: "The background of the men who organized the campaign was not theology and Islamic law but politics and the common law, not Deoband but Cambridge and the Inns of Court. Mr. Jinnah and his lieutenants such as Liaquat Ali won Pakistan largely in spite of the men of religion. They led a secular campaign to create a state based on a religion."[2] The leaders of the Muslim League occasionally expressed the secular nature of their political strivings;[3] their predicament drew ironical comments from Moslem intellectuals who stayed behind in India.[4] But, as we shall see, partition defined in the religious terms of the two-nation doctrine and the mass appeal of Islamic solidarity came to have political significance. It gave justification to conservative traditionalism, represented by the influence of the mullahs. None of the leaders of the new state dared to openly suggest a complete separation of religion and politics for fear of being branded anti-Islamic.

The Western-educated leaders of the Muslim League thus acclaimed

particularly, the reaction of intellectual Moslems to some elements in Hinduism, such as idolatry and cow worship, encouraged the intellectual elite in Pakistan to retain their ties with Islam. An American writer, F. S. C. Northrop, who in *The Taming of the Nations: A Study of the Cultural Bases of International Policy* (Macmillan, New York, 1952) analyzes Asian problems entirely in literary, ideological, and theological terms, has this to say (p. 149): "To turn from the literature of Hindu-Buddhist-Taoist-Confucian Asia to that of Islam is, to a Westerner, like moving from a low hanging humid, all-embracing haze into an upper region of fresh, clear air. There is a realistic, implicitly expressed definiteness and directness about the Quran and its Islam which permits one of the West to breathe more easily and to see things more clearly, as if one were at home in the clime to which one's physiology is adapted. From the outset also there is an emphasis upon the moral as the determinately lawful. Allah is a God of justice and his creatures are going to be judged."

[1] The Jama'at-i-Islami leader, Maulana Maudoodi, stated unequivocally that "From the League's Quaid-i-Azam [Jinnah] down to the humblest leader, there was no one who could be credited with an Islamic outlook and who looked at the various problems from an Islamic point of view." (Munchi Abdur Rahman Khan, in a 1956 work, quoted in Khalid Bin Sayeed, *Pakistan, The Formative Phase*, Pakistan Publishing House, Karachi, 1960, p. 216.)

[2] Keith Callard, *Pakistan, A Political Study*, Allen & Unwin Ltd., London, 1954, p. 200.

[3] A. K. Brohi, the Pakistan Law Minister from 1953–54, explained: "I have never said that I do not want an Islamic Constitution in this country; all I have said is that having regard to the accepted notion of what constitutional law is, it is not possible to derive from the text of the Quran any clear statement as to the actual content of the constitution of any State." (Quoted in Keith Callard, "The Political Stability of Pakistan," *Pacific Affairs*, Vol. XXIX, March, 1956, p. 29.)

[4] Maulana Maudoodi inquired: "Who will build up the required Islamic atmosphere? Can an irreligious state, with Westernized persons at its helm, do the job? Will the architects who are well-versed only in building bars and cinemas spend their energies in erecting a mosque? If the answer is in the affirmative, it will indeed be a unique experiment of its kind in history; godlessness fostering godliness to dethrone itself." (Quoted in Khalid Bin Sayeed, *Pakistan, The Formative Phase.*)

Islam as the supreme cause, yet were guided by Western political principles and precedents in their efforts to build the new state.[1] This unresolved contradiction concerning the kind of state that was being created accounts in part for the long delay in producing a constitution. When at last Pakistan's first constitution was promulgated in 1956, the Moslem heritage was recognized in the designation of an "Islamic Republic" and in the statement in the preamble that "the principles of democracy, freedom, equality, tolerance and social justice as enunciated by Islam should be fully observed," and that "the Muslims of Pakistan should be enabled individually and collectively to order their lives in accordance with the teachings and requirements of Islam, as set out in the Holy Quran and Sunnah."[2] The Directive Principles of the constitution bound the state to safeguard the rights and interests of non-Moslems, including their religious rights and their due representation in federal and provincial services, though the President of Pakistan had to be a Moslem. Early drafts of the constitution gave the professional orthodox religious leaders a virtual veto over legislation, but after a storm of protest from the secularists this safeguard against the passing of laws repugnant to the Holy Koran and Sunnah was removed and the good faith of the legislators was simply relied on. The state was to endeavor to make compulsory the teaching of the Koran. By such provisions did the new constitution support the cause of the religious traditionalists, but these trappings were of no great practical importance. It was clear that a secular state had, in effect, been created.

The campaign for Pakistan also left confusion about the aims and policies to be pursued by the new state. As was pointed out in Chapter 6 (Section 5), the Muslim League in pre-independence times was so locked in the fight for partition that it never developed a social and economic program as did the Indian Congress. What the new state should do for its citizens — other than free them from Hindu domination — was left vague and uncertain. The political inclinations of most of the leaders of the League were probably similar to those of British conservatives a few generations ago: they wanted the new state to be secular and in some sense modern, not only in its formal political institutions; it should even be progressive, provided their privileged position was not jeopardized. Opposing the Westernized leaders were the mullahs, equally or more conservative but more obscurantist. The two groups shared a hearty dislike of the radical reform program of the Indian National Congress.[3]

[1] "Their minds often operate upon two different levels: a level of fundamental principle on which they sincerely accept the authority of Islam and the level of practical reality on which they are guided by facts and figures and legal precedents. . . . The resulting conflict has been the cause of a great deal of confusion in the attempt to define the meaning of an Islamic state." (Keith Callard, *Pakistan, A Political Study*, pp. 201–202.)

[2] Pakistan, Government of, Ministry of Law, *The Constitution of the Islamic Republic of Pakistan*, Government of Pakistan Press, Karachi, 1956.

[3] Chapter 6, Section 2; Chapter 7, Section 1.

The class background of the leadership that came to power on the achievement of statehood explains much of its political conservatism. They were mainly professional politicians, related to the Moslem hereditary landlords of the northern part of imperial India, with only a sprinkling of the type of industrialists and commercial people who were so important among the supporters of the Indian Congress.[1] Partition had induced or compelled many of those living in the northwestern part of what was going to be India to take refuge in West Pakistan. However, they generally managed to bring much of their wealth with them and quickly found opportunities for its aggrandizement. In Sind, West Punjab, and the border areas to the north and west there was already a class of strongly entrenched absentee landlords. Until the recent land reform about half the area of West Pakistan consisted of holdings of more than 500 acres.[2] In the Punjab nearly 60 percent of the land belonged to big zamindars, while in Sind, that citadel of exploitative feudalism, a few hundred landlords owned practically all the arable land. In East Pakistan by contrast, a large number of the zamindars had been Hindus. With partition they generally fled to India and the tenants took over the land. As we shall see, this difference in land ownership and in the acquisition of land after partition by wealthy refugees, most of whom went to West Pakistan, was to affect crucially relations between the two wings of Pakistan. Higher civil servants and army officers, like the League leaders, were also linked by birth or marriage to the Moslem landowners of northern British India. They, too, combined the conservativism of this class with a Westernized and secular outlook.

The political situation in Pakistan during the first decade of independence was largely shaped by these wealthy refugee groups from the Moslem minority provinces of former British India, which had had more than their share of the membership of the Muslim League Council and its Working Committee in the years immediately preceding partition. These

[1] In 1942 landlords formed the largest single group in the Muslim League Council, accounting for 163 members out of a total of 503. The Punjab, with 51 landlords, contributed the largest share, followed by the United Provinces and Bengal. Of Sind's 25 members in the Council, 15 were landlords. The Secretary of the League at that time, Liaquat Ali Khan, was a big landowner in the United Provinces and so was Ismail Khan, the Chairman of its Committee of Action. The next largest group in the Council were lawyers. Merchants, bankers, and industrialists, though increasing in number, were far less influential. (See Khalid Bin Sayeed, *Pakistan, The Formative Phase,* p. 244; and Mushtaq Ahmad, *Government and Politics in Pakistan,* Pakistan Publishing House, Karachi, 1959, p. 91.)

O. H. K. Spate has stressed the different class background of the Muslim League and the Indian Congress and its consequences for the way the two countries started out. See his classic work, written soon after independence and partition, *India and Pakistan, A General and Regional Geography,* 2nd ed., Methuen, London, 1957, p. 242.

[2] Some 7.5 million acres of cultivated land in holdings of more than 500 acres was owned by 1 percent of the landowners, whereas around 65 percent of the owners held about 7.4 million acres in lots of less than 5 acres each. (Khalid Bin Sayeed, "Martial Law Administration," *Far Eastern Survey,* Vol. XXVIII, No. 5, May, 1959.)

men of wealth and power dominated the politics of Karachi, occupied strategic positions in the central bureaucracy, and carried over the patterns of behavior and thinking to which they had been conditioned.[1] Over the vehement protests of the Bengalis, they imposed Urdu as the official language of the nation though it was used by only a small minority of Pakistanis.[2] Toward the mass of poor refugee peasants, laborers, and artisans the attitude of the wealthy refugees and of the upper strata they became allied with in West Pakistan was ambivalent, if not plain callous.[3] Rejecting considerations of Moslem brotherhood, the landlords opposed any plans for resettling and rehabilitating poor refugees by breaking up the large estates.[4] To make matters worse, much of the property of evacuees to India passed into the hands of local landlords and wealthy refugees, with the connivance of public officials, and so was unavailable for rehabilitation purposes. During the first decade of independence the whole problem had low priority.[5] The negative and conservative leanings the Muslim League had acquired in its opposition to the Indian National Congress thus coincided with the class interests of those who controlled it both before and after partition.

[1] One prominent member of this class ironically remarked to this writer that Pakistan was largely "a conquered country." "We have given them," he went on, "the administration, the industrial leadership, the culture and indeed the language."

[2] In its spoken form Urdu derives largely from Sanskritized Hindi and Persian and is fairly closely allied to Punjabi; it is written in an Arabic script. As Urdu was used during the last phase of the Mogul Court at Delhi, its rehabilitation as an official language signified that Pakistan represented the continuation of a great cultural tradition. Shortly after independence both Jinnah and Liaquat Ali Khan declared flatly that the state language of Pakistan would be Urdu and nothing else. "Pakistan is a Muslim State and it must have as its lingua franca the language of the Muslim nation," said Liaquat Ali Khan in 1948. Yet Jinnah himself spoke little Urdu and at mass meetings of the League before independence his speeches had to be translated from English. (Curiously enough, when Nehru spoke in the vernacular, it was Urdu he knew best.) According to the 1951 Pakistan Census (Vol. I, p. 71), the proportion of the population speaking Urdu was 7.2 percent, Punjabi 28.4 percent, Pushto 7.1 percent, Sindhi 5.0 percent, and Bengali 54.6 percent.

[3] After describing his government's plans to aid them, one prime minister blurted out to the writer: "Here they come, these small black people and destroy our race!" Indeed, it has been reported that at the time of partition, when primitive urges were laid bare on both sides of the new border, the hope was expressed in some government circles that with the onset of cold weather pneumonia would kill off many of the uprooted poor and so lessen the burden. See Penderel Moon, *Divide and Quit*, Chatto & Windus, London, 1961, p. 256.

[4] Of the uncompromising attitude of the big landowners in Sind, for instance, the then Pakistan Finance Minister, Ghulam Mohammed, said in 1948: "The people who had money, the Zamindars, were so much poisoned against the refugees that in some places not only were they turned out but they were attacked. The refugees had no place to live, whereas houses were lying vacant and they were kept for their favourites, for Sindhis and none else." (Quoted in Khalid Bin Sayeed, *Pakistan, The Formative Phase,* p. 289.)

[5] As late as February 20, 1959 the newspaper *Dawn,* reporting on the results of a field survey, stated that 527,535 people in Karachi were classed as "shelterless" and of these, 84 percent were refugees.

Closely related to its lack of a social and economic program was another important characteristic of the Muslim League: its lack of collective leadership and internal discussion. Jinnah ran the League like a general issuing orders to his troops and local commanders. This was the more unfortunate because of his death a year after Pakistan became a state.

Pakistan's initial situation on attaining statehood should also be taken into account when explaining its poor showing in comparison with India during the first decade of independence.[1] In the long period before a constitution was framed, Pakistan had no general elections. No clear-cut and lasting demarcation of smaller political units – in Pakistan called provinces – and no division of power and responsibility between them and the center were worked out. No far-reaching social legislation was instituted. Pakistan's First Five Year Plan was presented first in 1956 and never became operational. For a long time no serious attempts were made to carry out a land reform – except in East Pakistan where the revolutionary activities following partition involved an expropriation of Hindu property. Community development efforts – in Pakistan called village aid – agricultural extension, and rural uplift generally were more spurious and on a smaller scale than in India.

At the end of Section 3 of Chapter 7 we sketched in the abstract terms of a model the essential causal factors of a mechanism that has progressively dragged down national consolidation and economic development in India. Applying the same model to the early history of Pakistan we find:

(1) The Muslim League did not afford Pakistan much of the momentum that the Congress did in India.

(2) The urgent problems arising out of independence and partition were very much graver than in India and certainly did not create favorable conditions for social and economic reforms.

(3) The lack of a successful start rather tended to slacken what momentum there was.

(4) Pakistan, like India, was a "soft state," though the absence of the Gandhian philosophy of non-violent resistance to authority should have made it somewhat easier in Pakistan to overcome the inhibitions and obstacles to enforcing discipline, if other conditions for doing so had been present.

(5) The upper-class status of those who stepped into power was even more pronounced in Pakistan than in India, and was weighted heavily toward the landlord class.

(6) This group had fewer inhibitions about using power in its own interests, particularly as the masses were even less activated to defend theirs.

(7) Economic and social inequalities were generally as great as in

[1] Chapter 7, Section 2.

India, even if not fortified by as rigid a caste system, and whatever Pakistan had of a democratic political process tended to strengthen the conservative forces.

(8) The absence of far-reaching social and economic reforms was even more pronounced in Pakistan than in India and hampered economic development, the lack of which, in turn, strengthened the conservative forces.

2 *The Confrontation with Democracy*

As in the other liberated countries of South Asia, it was commonly agreed that Pakistan should be a democratic state in which fundamental rights and social justice were guaranteed to all and power resided with the governed. To the legally trained politicians of the League this meant the adoption of the British form of parliamentary government. Not only was this the system most familiar to them, but its adoption provided an opportunity to expose the racial insult implied in the long-time denial of their fitness to administer the kind of government regarded as best by their former rulers. As in India, therefore, little thought was given to any alternative structure of government.

A Constituent Assembly consisting of representatives from the provincial legislatures,[1] inherited as in India from colonial times, had to frame a constitution and act as the national legislature until a general election could be held. As a legacy of its overwhelming victory in the provincial elections of 1945–46 in undivided India, the Muslim League initially controlled all the provincial legislatures and therefore dominated the center as well.[2] Indeed, many members of the Constituent Assembly were also members of the legislatures and cabinets of provincial governments. Despite the commanding position occupied by the League at the outset, Pakistan took almost a decade to frame its first constitution, and even then no general elections were held to bring it into force. During the first decade of independence parliamentary government was arbitrarily suspended once at the center and several times for considerable periods in the provinces. Public meetings were frequently banned to preserve law and order, and military rule was twice imposed over large areas to pre-

[1] The seats set aside for the princely states that acceded to Pakistan were filled by the nomination of their rulers. Princely states were of little importance, however; they accounted for only about 5 percent of the total population of the country, a much smaller proportion than in India.

[2] It is relevant to note that the provincial legislatures were not chosen in 1945–46 with a view to their future as electoral colleges for the national legislature, and also that, because the right to vote in those elections was narrowly based on a property and education qualification, "it is unlikely that anywhere more than 15 per cent of the total population was entitled to vote." (Keith Callard, *Pakistan, A Political Study*, p. 77.)

vent rioting and insurrection. On the face of it, these symptoms of political instability and indiscipline appeared to be due to the intrigues of irresponsible politicians and to provincial rivalries and ideological confusions. But in retrospect a deeper mechanism of causation stands out.

An important factor was the reluctance of the ruling upper strata to seek electoral support for their policies. Although they thought of no other form of government, parliamentary democracy generated no enthusiasm as a "moral principle of social relationship."[1] For one thing, in culture and aspiration the country's leaders were, and still are, separated from the masses even more than in India, and there was among them little of that ideological identification with the interests of the masses which in India both Gandhi and the radical intellectuals in the Congress had nurtured. In addition, they were inhibited by the genuine difficulty of trying to explain the secular goals of an Islamic state to the illiterate poor in rural villages and urban slums and even to their more educated countrymen. The fight for partition had given them no experience in doing so since their appeal had then been to religious fanaticism. As we have seen, they had evolved no constructive program; they had promised nothing but freedom from Hindu domination. So long as Pakistan was yet to be achieved, all Moslems were supposed to subordinate their personal interests and differences to this one objective. "We shall have time," Jinnah had declared, "to quarrel ourselves and we shall have time when these differences will have to be settled, when wrongs and injuries will have to be remedied. We shall have time for domestic programme and policies, but first get the Government. This is a nation without any territory or any government."[2] The impression conveyed to the masses by the campaign for Pakistan had been that Islam gave the answers to all political, social, and economic problems. In these circumstances, the Westernized League leaders must have feared that if policy issues were openly debated, the "mullah element" would get the better of the argument.

Moreover, the class interests of those who came to power militated against the establishment of a truly democratic state. They had campaigned for self-government, not to bring about social change, but to escape the consequences of majority rule in an undivided India. They recognized and probably overestimated the threat that a parliamentary system and universal suffrage posed to their natural inclination to retain the privileges of power.[3] The civil servants and officer corps, whose unu-

[1] Keith Callard, *Political Forces in Pakistan 1947–49*, Institute of Pacific Relations, New York, 1959.

[2] Quoted in Khalid Bin Sayeed, *Pakistan, The Formative Phase*, pp. 195–196.

[3] As the *Pakistan Times* wrote on February 26, 1957: "The crux of the matter is that the undue economic privileges bestowed on the landlords has brought in its train a disproportionate share of political power, and now this undeserved near monopoly of political power is being used to maintain the outdated system which guarantees their special economic rights."

sual role will be commented on later, had acquired in their service under the British a sense of superiority to the politicians. They had no serious commitment to democracy or belief in politics as a means of producing social and economic change. The unabashed scramble for the spoils of office immediately after independence only confirmed their view that politicians make a mess of things.

The tradition of the Muslim League had been to keep control in the hands of a small group instead of indulging in the popularism the Indian National Congress movement had sought. Since the League was the founder of the new state, any opposition to it was in the beginning considered tantamount to treason. Its leaders believed that only they had a valid moral claim to political office and preferment. Unfortunately for Pakistan, its leaders did not develop a tradition of discipline based on collective discussion. Jinnah's prestige was immense, his control virtually absolute; as the first Governor General of Pakistan and the president of its Constituent Assembly and the Muslim League, he wielded more power than any British Viceroy had ever commanded. Yet he undoubtedly held his power by popular consent, if not veneration. Had he not died in September, 1948, Pakistan might very early have become a political dictatorship with some democratic trappings. A move in that direction would not have been difficult to justify: the need for strong executive action to cope with the desperate plight of the country; the unpreparedness of the League ideologically and otherwise for democratic procedures; the success with which Jinnah had run the League; the tensions with India. In a sense, the potentialities for the military takeover in 1958 were already present ten years earlier.

Liaquat Ali Khan succeeded Jinnah, and while he enjoyed considerable prestige as the right-hand man of the Quaid-i-Azam during the fight for Pakistan, he was neither as dominating nor as brilliant as his former chief. He found it necessary to rely more on the support of other League leaders and provincial League organizations. But most of those leaders, inexperienced in the exercise of authority and accustomed only to carrying out Jinnah's orders, were not capable of constructive rethinking of Pakistan's problems. With no program on which to unite and no tradition of collective leadership, the League soon disintegrated into warring factions and cliques, each intriguing for preferment and the spoils of office. After the assassination of Ali Khan in October, 1951, the trend toward bossism of a blatantly corrupt and ruthless nature became increasingly pronounced.

Out of these dissensions and rivalries in the League emerged new parties. Their formation was prompted by frustration at the preferment accorded to rivals at the center rather than by principles and programs. Their leaders, like those of the League, did not take a national view of issues and few of them maintained a consistent stand on any issue. The parties were mainly vehicles for personal political advancement. Government at the center became largely a series of caretaker coalitions precariously based on shifting alliances negotiated behind closed doors. The premiership was conferred or denied by powerful interests outside the parliament, and a prime minister could not provide leadership to his cabinet or command the loyalty of his colleagues once this appointing authority had disowned him. The politics pursued in Pakistan during its first decade of independence was thoroughly inimical to social change and national consolidation.

3 *Provincial Rivalries*

Many of the cleavages and tensions within the body politic were closely related to the strains and rivalries among the different regions of Pakistan. It was generally accepted that the country's geography dictated a federal union; but the basis of representation at the center and the distribution of powers between the center and the provinces became the subject of sharp and continuing controversy. This again is largely attributable to the origin and social background of the leadership of the Muslim League.

The Pushtoons of the North-West Province, if not openly rebelling against Karachi, mistrusted and feared the dominating role in the capital of political elements from the larger and wealthier Punjab. So did the Sindhis, who had the additional special grievance of having lost their capital, Karachi, to the federal government. From Baluchistan threats of provincial secession were occasionally heard. The decision of the Governor General of Pakistan in 1955, Ghulam Mohammed, himself a Punjabi, to merge the provincial subdivisions of its west wing into one political unit only confirmed fears that the powerful landlord class of Punjab were bent on consolidating their political hold over the country. It was the virtual eclipse of the Muslim League in the east wing provincial elections the previous year that prompted Ghulam Mohammed to enact the "one unit" reorganization of the west wing. This maneuver provided a more effective counter-balance against the Bengalis since it prevented them from making alliances with provincial subdivisions of the west wing and thereby capturing political power at the center. The most dangerous threat to the consolidation of Pakistan came, in fact, from the mounting tension between its east and west wings.

East Pakistan – or East Bengal, as the people persisted in calling their region until 1956 – accounts for roughly one-seventh of the total area of Pakistan, but for over half its population. Its people have little in common with those in West Pakistan except their religion. But the Moslem elite of northwestern British India, the traditional center of Moslem power, who after partition had concentrated in West Pakistan, trace their faith to Arabic and Persian antecedents and their ancestry in some cases to the

Mogul invaders. They tend to be condescending toward the Bengalis, who are economically more backward, regarding them as poor fighters and as descendants of converts to the faith or, worse still, opportunists who embraced Islam merely to avoid a lowly caste status in Hindu society. Although the common faith sets both wings apart from India, in West Pakistan relations with Hindus are now confined mainly to external issues, while in East Pakistan Hindus, since they are still a significant minority of the population, constitute an important domestic concern. Because of this substantial Hindu minority, West Pakistanis do not regard East Pakistan as embodying the true spirit and cultural heritage of Pakistan. Significantly, the national legislature in 1956 approved separate electorates in West Pakistan for provincial and national elections but, at the insistence of Bengali members, a single roll or joint electorates in East Pakistan.[1]

The intense pride of Bengalis in their cultural tradition and the feeling of superiority to which this gives rise have contributed to the widespread belief in Karachi and Lahore that East Pakistanis regard themselves as Bengalis first and Pakistanis second. Political awareness among somewhat broader strata of the population and a community of language are also more developed in East Pakistan. In West Pakistan, which is less unified culturally and politically, there is, in contrast, the local pride of the Punjabis, Pathans, Sindhis, or Baluchis. Furthermore, whereas the dominant group in West Pakistan and Karachi politics were big landlords, in East Bengal the big landlords were mainly Hindu zamindars who fled to independent India when partition was enacted. East Pakistan thereupon improvised a land reform[2] – a social and economic change that provided a rather more popular basis for politics. In West Pakistan no re-distribution of land accompanied or followed independence.

The celebrated Bengali appetite for politics certainly had many grievances to feed on. Although East Pakistan is poorer and more densely populated than West Pakistan (it was one of the most neglected parts of British India), after partition investments for economic development were much more vigorously pushed in West Pakistan. The East provided about three-fifths of the country's foreign exchange earnings, but vir-

[1] The only hope for political influence for Hindus in Pakistan was to cease being spokesmen for minority interests and participate instead in joint electorates. In pressing for separate electorates throughout the whole country, the Muslim League leaders in West Pakistan were not simply carrying over the mentality they had acquired in their struggles with the Congress movement before partition; they also sought to limit Bengali influence by keeping the Moslem and Hindu communities in East Pakistan from making common cause on national issues and on regional issues between the two wings.

[2] Under the State Acquisition and Tenancy Act of 1950 all rent-receiving interests were to be abolished over a ten-year period. See Chapter 26, Section 13.

tually every index of prosperity favored the West by a large margin.[1] The East had very few industries at the time of partition and West Pakistanis acquired a large stake in those subsequently established. As might have been expected, Bengalis became convinced that they were not getting a fair share of the tax revenues and development expenditures of the central government and that their wealth was being drained away for the benefit of West Pakistan.

The administration of the central government was dominated by West Pakistan officials,[2] who in the early years of independence were not noticeably sympathetic to the development problems and needs of the East. And, since there had been virtually no East Bengali Moslems in the entire Indian Civil Service in British times, after partition the senior administrative positions in East Pakistan had to be staffed by Moslems from other areas, especially Punjab and the former United Provinces. The Pakistan Civil Service, which was more centrally organized than the Indian Civil Service had been under British rule, represented national interests as against the forces of provincialism. But to Bengalis these officials were simply outsiders and agents of the central government who did not serve the true interests of East Pakistan. The non-Bengali officials even expected the Bengalis, who cherished their own language, to learn Urdu or English, and generally sneered at Bengali culture.[3] The senior officers of the armed forces, which absorbed about two-thirds of the central government's revenue, also came predominantly from West Pakistan (in part because the British had been accustomed to recruit the so-called martial races from the northwestern areas of British India); in East Pakistan, especially during the period of governor's rule in 1954, they were looked upon almost as an occupation force.

The idea of Pakistan had gained support in East Bengal from the simple expectation that material well-being and opportunities for advancement would suddenly increase when the wealthier and better educated Hindus were removed from commanding positions in the social structure. But with independence Bengalis found they were underrepresented at all levels of policy-making and were scorned by the West Pakistanis who

[1] For 1957–59 it was calculated that income per head in the East was 30 percent lower than in the West. (*Report of the Panel of Economists on the Second Five Year Plan (1960–65)*, Government of Pakistan Press, Karachi, 1959, p. 14.)

[2] In the mid-1950's West Pakistanis outnumbered East Pakistanis by five to one in the central services. (Khalid Bin Sayeed, *Pakistan, The Formative Phase,* p. 392.) Moreover, because of the operation of seniority rules, few Bengalis reached higher positions at the center during the first decade of independence.

[3] "The non-Bengali administrators, who came to occupy almost every senior post in East Bengal, often conducted themselves with the arrogance of imperial guardians and hardly ever as fellow-countrymen." (Stanley Maron, "The Problem of East Pakistan," *Pacific Affairs*, Vol. XVIII, No. 2, June, 1955.)

were now in command. Jinnah had regarded the Punjab as the heart of Pakistan.[1] Yet East Bengal had given more fervent and solid support to the Muslim League before partition than had any of the territories later included in West Pakistan, and Bengalis did not expect the new state simply to substitute dominance from Karachi for that from Calcutta. Having felt exploited in the past by the British and Hindus, they readily ascribed the lack of improvement in their living standards after independence to the new exploiters from West Pakistan. Disaffection in East Pakistan was tinged with an almost anti-colonial resentment, particularly against "Punjabi imperialism." Provincial autonomy – sometimes virtual secession – became a favorite theme of its politicians. To substantiate their case they recalled the historic Lahore resolution of the Muslim League in 1940, which declared Pakistan to be a state "in which the constituent units shall be autonomous and sovereign." But the nature of the Muslim League leadership and the urgent need for strong administration to cope with a succession of emergencies following partition led to greater centralization of power rather than to provincial autonomy.

The sense of betrayal in East Pakistan reached a climax when the central government decreed Urdu to be the national language of Pakistan. Bengalis saw this as not only a mortal blow to their culture but a threat to perpetuate their underrepresentation and inferior status in the administrative services, especially in relation to Punjabis, by putting them at a disadvantage in all competitive examinations. The decree provoked student riots at Dacca University and doomed the Muslim League to massive defeat in the East Pakistan provincial elections of 1954 at the hands of an electoral alliance or "United Front" of other parties. The virtual annihilation of the League in East Pakistan, by the same token, challenged its right to dominate the center and speak for the nation. It proved to be the signal for a violent outburst of Bengali feelings against non-Bengalis, which in turn provided the pretext for the central government to dismiss the United Front ministry and establish governor's rule and martial law. Actually the United Front had been united only on the one aim of defeating the Muslim League and securing a greater degree of provincial autonomy.[2] Soon after the election it disintegrated through lack of agreement on other issues.

Its election victory nevertheless marked an important landmark in Pak-

[1] In the constructed name of Pakistan there is no letter standing for Bengal; see footnote 3 on p. 232.

[2] One of the principal points in its election manifesto read: "Secure all subjects, including residuary powers, except Defense, Foreign Affairs and Currency for East Bengal, which shall be fully autonomous and sovereign as envisaged in the historic Lahore Resolution, and establish Naval Headquarters and ordnance factory in East Bengal so as to make it militarily self-sufficient." (Keith Callard, "The Political Stability of Pakistan," *Pacific Affairs*, Vol. XXIX, March, 1956, p. 13.) This last demand reflected the desire of East Bengalis to equalize the military power of the two wings.

istan politics. Some intermittent attention was subsequently given to the grievances of East Bengalis. The constitution adopted in 1956 recognized both Bengali and Urdu as national languages and endorsed the principle of parity in recruitment for all spheres of federal administration. More important, the annihilation of the Muslim League in East Pakistan greatly aggravated political instability at the center by making the game of forming and dissolving coalition governments much more difficult to play. Finally, the subsequent suspension of parliamentary government in the East foreshadowed its eventual collapse at the center as well.

4 *The Impotence of Political Action*

From the outset politics in Pakistan was characterized by factional maneuvering, chicanery, coercion, and widespread corruption, all of which were so much part of the mores as hardly to need concealing. Not alone idealism but even public decency was at a discount. From this low level of behavior, economic as well as political chaos quickly followed.

The mass of Pakistanis or even the larger part of the educated class were not really involved in the game of politics except intermittently and haphazardly: as voters to be bribed or intimidated, or as mobs to be swayed. Provincial elections, except possibly those of East Pakistan in 1954, were a farce. Prime ministers and cabinets at the center rose and fell in rapid succession. The Constituent Assembly functioned at the sufferance of the executive instead of as a check upon it. It did not make or break governments, or educate the public on national issues, and it became less and less representative of the country as the years went on. Attendance in the Assembly was poor and debate was superficial. There was little scrutiny of government legislation; economic policy evoked so little parliamentary interest and concern that when the country's First Five Year Plan was produced in 1956 no general debate on it was initiated.[1] A very few people made all the important political decisions at every level of government, a tradition established by Jinnah. Even major decisions on framing a constitution took place outside the Constituent Assembly.

The authority of the politicians at the center did not rest on electoral support since no national election had yet been held. Not that the experience of provincial elections and the nature of the political parties gave

[1] In April, 1958 the then prime minister observed: "I was staggered to learn that until a few days ago the Five-Year Plan had not even been authenticated by the Government for publication. With hardly two more years to go, the Plan continues to be regarded as routine departmental file, meant only for recording of prolific notes and cross-notes. Even a properly coordinated machinery for the implementation of the Plan has not yet been evolved." (Quoted in Mushtaq Ahmad, *Government and Politics in Pakistan*, p. 68.)

any assurance that a general election would solve Pakistan's serious problems. But its constant postponement gave parties no incentive to formulate clearly differentiated, national programs. Even when the protracted debate on the constitution at last ended in 1956, the promised general election necessary to implement it was further postponed. Those at the top plainly feared that such elections would endanger their control and privileges. It could also be argued, however, that without stable, disciplined parties, each with a well-defined program and some support among the people, the adoption by Pakistan of the British system, as provided for in the constitution, would lead to experiences like those of the Fourth Republic of France.[1] In the absence of national cohesion the constitutional division of powers between the center and the provinces was more likely to consolidate and intensify regional loyalties.

The maintenance of a parliamentary façade for a whole decade during which the prospects for a democratic system of government grew dimmer was inevitably demoralizing. National self-confidence was further undermined by Pakistan's lack of success in bringing pressure against India over the Kashmir dispute. Few Pakistanis, therefore, mourned the demise of this sham parliamentary government when it was replaced by military dictatorship and martial law in 1958. The politicians had lost real power long before.

An important factor contributing to the weakness of the politicians in this first decade of independence was the excessive influence accorded to the higher civil servants and zealously guarded by them. Already under Jinnah civil servants had been given authority, if not actual control, over ministries and politicians. Under Liaquat Ali Khan their influence was often decisive in removing ministers from political office. If their British training made it unlikely that they and the armed forces would actively plot to overthrow parliamentary democracy, neither were they likely to uphold it. Although it should be said in fairness that the considerable authority acquired by the civil servants from the outset is the reason Pakistan did not completely disintegrate as a political unit, their very authority released the politicians to "play politics" and obscured the need for radical reforms. As Adlai Stevenson once remarked, power corrupts, but the lack of power corrupts absolutely. Here again the Pakistan situation offers, *mutatis mutandis,* a parallel to France. And the unique position the civil servants occupied in an increasingly corrupt political milieu tended to corrupt their own public morals.[2] The extent to which the civil

[1] It is no accident that the constitution later given to Pakistan by President Ayub Khan's military regime appeared to have been inspired by the one General de Gaulle provided for the Fifth French Republic.

[2] When, for example, import controls were imposed after 1952, the industrialists' need for a permit often matched the officials' need for a higher income. "According to an official survey of the activities of the Special Police Establishment in 1951–52, of the 1,134 persons proceeded against under the Foreign Exchange Regulations Act

service became part of the wealthy classes in Pakistan was a visible measure of the deterioration of its standards.

The arrogance and aloofness of the civil servants were frequently criticized in the press and legislative assemblies, particularly in East Pakistan. They were charged with a colonial mentality, which set law and order above all else. Since much of the credit for restoring order out of the violence and near anarchy that accompanied independence must go to the civil administration, this function naturally seemed paramount to them and their ministers. As a consequence, however, the Pakistan Civil Service was not prepared, either in outlook or in organization, to assume and promote the functions of economic development.[1] After the assassination of Liaquat Ali Khan the administrators and military officers began to invade the sphere of the politicians more openly and even to replace them. Thus Ghulam Mohammed, who succeeded Jinnah as Governor General and increasingly took over the reins of power after the death of Ali Khan, was himself a former civil servant. Following the debacle of the Muslim League in the East Pakistan elections of 1954, he dismissed the central government and Constituent Assembly and replaced them with a "Ministry of Talent," which included General Ayub Khan as Defense Minister[2] and General Iskander Mirza as Minister of the Interior. When Mirza, in turn, succeeded Ghulam Mohammed as Governor General, he chose as his Prime Minister Chaudry Mohamad Ali, yet another civil servant turned politician. Mirza was outspokenly contemptuous of the politicians and advocated some kind of "controlled democracy."

It was under the rule of these men that Pakistan departed from the more independent foreign policy pursued by Ali Khan and concluded military alliances with the United States in 1954. This was done less out of strong sympathy with the West than as a bulwark against India.[3] The

---

and the Hoarding and Blackmarketing Act, 735 were government servants." (Mushtaq Ahmad, *Government and Politics in Pakistan,* p. 83, f.n.)

A few weeks before the imposition of martial law by Ayub Khan, the Chief Minister of West Pakistan admitted that "now from top to bottom, there was hardly a person who was not corrupt." (*Pakistan Times,* August 26, 1958.)

[1] "So far as law and order, administration of justice and collection of revenues . . . are concerned, the system continues to serve the country reasonably well. The efficiency of the system within this essential field invests it with a factitious appearance of adequacy for all purposes, including the new and supremely important task of planned development. This, on the one hand, creates a psychological atmosphere of complacence unfavourable to reform, and, on the other, increases the inertia of the system, its power of resisting change." (Pakistan, Government of, National Planning Board, *The First Five Year Plan, 1955–60,* Karachi, December, 1957, Vol. I, p. 99.)

[2] When he subsequently became Pakistan's military dictator, Ayub Khan revealed that he had been asked several times by Ghulam Mohammed to take over the country but had refused.

[3] Chapter 6, Section 7.

The Mutual Defense Treaty concluded with the United States in 1954 might well have encountered serious opposition in Pakistan, especially in East Bengal, if Indian reactions had not been so shrill and hostile.

effect, somewhat surprisingly, was not to lessen but to increase Pakistan's burden of military expenditures.[1] This, in turn, strengthened the size and position of the officer corps whose ties were with the most conservative sectors of society. Thus the Mirza government, which struck the final blow at the ramshackle façade of parliamentary democracy in Pakistan, openly represented the combined power of the higher civil servants, army officers, big industrialists, and landlords.

5 *Economic Development in the First Decade*

The economic life of Pakistan in its first decade of independence was not much different in essence from its politics, though there were some specific accomplishments. A good beginning was made in developing consumer goods industries. Behind a protective wall a textile industry was built up at a rate that, within seven years of independence, transformed Pakistan from an importer to an exporter of textiles. In agriculture, however, the situation was quite different. From an over-all food surplus as late as 1952, Pakistan moved to a continuous and critical food shortage in almost every subsequent year. Its consequent dependence on large-scale food imports, although they came to be substantially financed by American aid under P.L. 480, nevertheless constituted a drain on the country's foreign exchange reserves. Along with the developing food shortage the collapse of the boom in raw material prices after the Korean War caused a rapid decline in Pakistan's foreign exchange earnings. Drought and floods contributed to the perpetual state of crisis in agriculture.

No great effort was made in these years to increase the very low agricultural productivity. Neither the increase in acreage brought under irrigation nor the improvements in water supply and drainage offset the colossal waste of land inherent in absentee landlordism. Agricultural output stagnated, and hoarding and smuggling of food-grains into India reduced marketable supplies still further.[2] The actual living standards of the masses probably deteriorated during the first decade of independence,[3] particularly in East Pakistan.

[1] "To an economist . . . the inescapable conclusion would seem to be that Pakistan, which was already spending too much of her own resources on military purposes, was encouraged by the U.S. military aid program to spend even more on military purposes." (David Bell, Deputy Director, Pakistan-Iran Advisory Group, Graduate School of Public Administration, Harvard University, in Hearings on the Mutual Security Programs, House of Representatives, 86th Cong., 1st sess., January 22, 1959.)

[2] "It is not nature that has capriciously reduced us to such a position. The fault lies with ourselves: our Central and Provincial Governments have proved to be complacent, negligent or even inefficient, and the bulk of our landlords, *zamindars,* big cultivators and middlemen in the food-grain business have proved thoroughly unpatriotic." (*Dawn,* September 4, 1952, quoted in Tibor Mende, *South-East Asia Between Two Worlds,* Turnstile Press, London, 1955, p. 245.)

[3] The Chief Economist of the Planning Board reported in 1955: "It is . . . probable

The Constituent Assembly readily voted large expenditures for development which benefitted the financial backers of the ruling parties, but it never accepted the kind of tax discipline that planned economic development necessitates. It preferred, instead, to countenance inflation while it retained the high international value of the rupee, which distorted priorities and encouraged less essential types of consumption. Large investments took place in residential construction for the upper classes (and foreign experts, mostly Americans); fortunes were rapidly accumulated by building shoddy hotels, running cinemas, moneylending, and dealing in import or export licenses. The profits from these and from many manufacturing activities as well were extremely high. So was the element of state subsidy they implied. Evasion of taxes became a common practice, unchecked by the government. Smuggling, black-marketeering, and the auction of licenses and permits to replenish party funds were prevalent. Corruption became almost a way of life in business. All this was openly discussed and deplored, though sometimes excused on the ground that Pakistan, unlike India, was a free enterprise society. In the circumstances economic planning did not and could not become an important instrument of government policy or a force for national consolidation.[1]

Toward the end of the first decade of independence there was an all round decline in food production. The rate of growth of industrial production was slowing down, not least because of inadequate supplies of spare parts and raw materials. At about the same time Pakistan experienced its largest balance of payments deficit. These symptoms of creeping economic paralysis, together with disaffection in the east wing, failure to initiate any effective land reform in the west wing, pressure of inflation, distrust of the new industrial class, and rampant corruption, produced a general demoralization in public affairs and an ever deeper mistrust of the professional politicians. It was in these conditions that the army and General Ayub Khan took over in October, 1958 and imposed martial law.

---

that the per capita income after 1954–55 would be less than what it was about seven years ago. Inequalities in income have increased. A smaller national income, relatively to the size of the population, more unequally distributed than before, implies that the living standards of the masses of the people which were already very low, have deteriorated still further." (M. L. Qureshi, Address delivered at the Conference of the Pakistan Economic Association, Peshawar, 1955, p. 11.)

[1] "The first five-year plan was commissioned in 1955, full eight years after independence. It did not receive formal approval of the Government till 1957. During these years there was a total neglect of the primary sector of our economy – agriculture; we squandered the windfall surpluses of the Korean war boom in buying, on open General Licenses, European cosmetics and radiograms. It is not only that we failed to develop basic heavy industries. We did not even make any provisions for their future establishment; not even to the extent of starting to get our men trained in basic technologies. And, lastly, we completely neglected the exploitation of our minerals. Not even a survey was undertaken." (From an address by Professor Abdus Salam, President, *XIII Annual All Pakistan Science Conference*, Dacca, January 11, 1961.)

6 *The Collapse of Parliamentary Democracy*

It was fashionable at first for the defenders of the army coup to put all the blame for the failure of parliamentary democracy on the corrupt professional politicians.[1] But, as Ghulam Mohammed and General Mirza had openly demonstrated, the real levers of power had, in fact, already passed into the hands of those who still hold them under Ayub Khan. In any case it is misleading to talk of the offending politicians as a separate and independent group in society; all of them belonged to or were in the service of the upper class of landlords, civil servants, industrialists, and professional men – and, still in the background, the army officers.

On later reflection Ayub Khan admitted that on one fundamental point the politicians were rather sinned against than sinning: "That is, they were given a system of government totally unsuited to the temper and climate of the country."[2] With its high illiteracy rate, primitive communications, and overwhelmingly rural population barely touched by life outside the villages, Pakistan did not have, in his opinion, the prerequisites for a parliamentary system founded on general suffrage. However, some of the politicians Khan dispossessed thought it misleading to talk of the failure of parliamentary government since the constitution was abrogated before it became fully operative. They felt that the system had not been given a chance to prove itself. Some Pakistani and outside commentators were inclined to ascribe the nation's political troubles to the fact that under colonial rule the actual business of government had been divorced from political aspirations. This dichotomy bred men of action, unused to government by discussion, and political agitators unmindful of the capabilities and limits of state action.[3] The independence movement of the

[1] In a broadcast to the nation on October 8, 1958, President Ayub Khan blamed the existing chaotic conditions on "self-seekers who in the garb of political leaders have ravaged the country or tried to barter it away for personal gains." (Quoted in Mushtaq Ahmad, *Government and Politics in Pakistan*, p. 236.)

[2] Ayub Khan, "Pakistan Perspectives," *Foreign Affairs*, Vol. 38, No. 4, July, 1960, p. 550.

[3] "The inherent weakness of colonial government lies in the alienation between administration and popular aspiration. Administration carried on without a sense of accountability to popular aspirations is deprived of imagination; at best it tends to be sterile; at worst it becomes oppressive. The evocation of general aspirations without regard for actual operating requirements and limits of government results too often in producing giddiness and demagoguery. Political communication is deprived of realism and the result is likely to be the politics of agitation and utopia." (H. S. Suhrawardy, "Political Stability and Democracy in Pakistan," *Foreign Affairs*, Vol. 35, No. 3, April, 1957, pp. 423–424.)

Charles Burton Marshall, an American advisor to the Pakistan prime minister during 1955–57, recalled that a Pakistani once remarked to him: "Pakistan had produced only two types of men in its public life. One type he described as men who believe in action without discussion. The other type is men who are devoted to discussion without action. The colonial experience, he said, encourages and indeed compels this disjunction." (Hearings on the Mutual Security Programs, House of Representatives, 86th Cong., 1st sess., January 21, 1959.)

Muslim League embodied popular sentiments and therefore had a moral claim to obedience: the business of political action was to defy alien British rule and reduce it to impotence. As all anti-government actions were considered legitimate, the idea of a "loyal opposition," so essential to the British parliamentary system, could never take root. After independence this struggle for supremacy continued between the executive (and the higher civil servants), as heirs to the British raj, and the Constituent Assembly as the legatee of the British Parliament. But these reflections on the collapse of parliamentary government in Pakistan do not explain how it was able to function better and survive in India. Pakistanis and Indians shared much the same political experience under colonial rule. Why, then, should the Indians be so comparatively successful in operating the same form of government, particularly in the first decade of independence? No one, least of all Ayub Khan, suggests that Pakistanis are inferior to Indians in education, intelligence, and capabilities.[1]

As we noted earlier, there was a significant difference in the political preparation of the two countries: whereas the Indian National Congress had provided the new government of India with a program of action, the Muslim League concentrated on a single aim, the negative one of freeing Moslems from Hindu domination. Behind these dissimilar objectives was the very different class basis of those who set the tone of the two movements. The Congress drew its strength from the urban classes of northern India; the League largely from the wealthy Moslem landlords, who abhorred the reform program of the Congress. The intellectual vacuity of the League went hand in hand with the cult of the Great Leader. Once the authoritarian leadership of Jinnah and that of Ali Khan came to an end, the League quickly fell prey to squabbling and personal intrigues. The clue to the survival of parliamentary government in India and its failure in Pakistan is thus to be sought in the traditions, character, and leadership of their respective independence movements rather than in the suitability of this political system for a poor and largely illiterate peasant society. To this should be added the very much greater initial difficulties that faced independent Pakistan.

7 *The Military Takeover and After*

Upon seizing power, General Mohammad Ayub Khan abrogated the constitution, dismissed the central and provincial governments, dissolved their legislatures, abolished political parties, exiled President Mirza, and imposed martial law. Freedom of the press and public discussion and the

[1] Regarding Ayub Khan's point about high illiteracy rates in Pakistan constituting an obstacle to the adoption of the British parliamentary system, it may be remarked that the rate of illiteracy in the population 15 years of age and over was not much greater in Pakistan than in India; see Chapter 32, Section 4.

power of the courts to enforce fundamental rights were circumscribed, though repression did not go so far as to prevent the cautious expression of views on relatively inconsequential matters. Apart from unrest in Baluchistan, which had to be forcibly suppressed, the military takeover was accepted quietly. Although it came as something of a shock to the Western world, it was inevitable in the circumstances. The parliamentary regime that the army displaced was truly decrepit; not even the small upper-class groups whom it served believed in it. There had already been much arbitrary interference with its functioning. The "controlled democracy" for which Iskander Mirza had expressed a preference was not far from the type of government Ayub Khan set about creating.

What the general initially established, however, was a co-dictatorship of the higher army officers and civil servants. The first task undertaken by the military regime was to purge civilian administration and public life generally of the worst forms of anti-social behavior and regenerate public morality and discipline.[1] To this end an elaborate screening of public servants was instituted; but surprisingly few higher civil servants actually lost their jobs.[2] Convictions for political patronage or for raising party funds were far more numerous; in fact, it was against the professional politicians rather than the civil servants that the cleansing operations of the military were conspicuously directed. With few exceptions the politicians emerged debauched and humiliated, though most of the worst compromised exercised their option to disappear from public life and went unpunished. As in the case of the civil servants, punitive action was not excessive: normally it amounted to no more than rustication. Similarly, tax dodgers who had made false declarations and those who had fraudulently accumulated foreign exchange were given a chance to declare their illicit wealth without suffering serious punishment or impoverishment. Through price controls, limitation on commercial profit margins, and prohibition of hoarding, the precipitous rise in prices was halted. Finally, to escape the pressures of vested economic interests, the capital was moved to Rawalpindi, the headquarters of the Pakistan army.

In view of the sins of commission and omission of the previous parliamentary regime, it is probable that most of the articulate and informed strata of the population generally approved the initial cleansing impulse

[1] Ayub Khan announced in a broadcast to the nation on October 8, 1958: "Martial law regulations will be produced which will tighten up the existing laws on matters like malingering or inefficiency amongst officials, any form of bribery and corruption, hoarding, smuggling or black marketing, or any type of anti-social or anti-State activity. Such matters will be dealt with ruthlessly and expeditiously." (Quoted in Mushtaq Ahmad, *Government and Politics in Pakistan,* Appendix, p. 238.)

[2] According to a statement of the Home Minister as reported in *Dawn,* November 1, 1960, only four civil servants and two higher police officers were compulsorily retired as a result of this screening. See also K. J. Newman, "The Constitutional Evolution of Pakistan," *International Affairs,* Vol. 38, No. 3, July, 1962, p. 358.

of army rule. The new regime quickly won the confidence of the Western diplomatic corps in Pakistan although it was actually an abnegation of what the "free world" purported to represent. Some even talked of Ayub Khan as another Ataturk.[1] To the United States it was especially gratifying that the new regime initially ignored the advocates of a more independent foreign policy and cast its lot with the West. Occasionally, however, and especially regarding British and American reluctance to bring pressure to bear on India over the Kashmir issue, Pakistan newspapers were allowed, if not encouraged, to pursue a different theme as a sort of warning to the West not to take the country's friendship for granted.[2]

The relative mildness of the repression practiced by the regime was also reassuring to its Western friends. On the whole, the new regime seemed to be returning to principles observed by the British raj.[3] This is not surprising, for the *putsch* was mainly a defensive regrouping of the old ruling class. What Ayub Khan and the higher officer corps wanted was not so much a fundamental re-distribution of power as a return to the decency, probity, and sense of public service the British had exemplified.

In other respects there was little analogy between the military junta's approach to Pakistan's problems and that of the British colonial rulers. For one thing, the new regime publicly endorsed the whole gamut of modernization ideals, including the need for planning, greater equality in the distribution of wealth, the liquidation of feudalism, and the emanci-

[1] As Charles Burton Marshall observed: "In the meager reporting that is supposed to inform us of events in a place like Pakistan, the debacle tends to be presented in terms of accomplishment, as if something fine and constructive had taken place when the political institutions were overturned and thrown aside. The formula of interpretation has been a simple one, a lot of bad old things have been swept out by a good new broom. We have in our minds a lot of mythology about redemption and heroes. It supplies a lot of clichés for reporting and a lot of handy patterns for dictatorial regimes to explain themselves to us in ways calculated to reassure and to please." (Hearings on the Mutual Security Programs, House of Representatives, 86th Cong., 1st sess., January 21, 1959, p. 12.)

[2] The American and British decision to strengthen India's armed forces following the Chinese assault on the northern frontier fostered criticism of the United States and its Western allies even from the government spokesmen. Pakistanis feared that this assistance would also strengthen India's military pressure against Pakistan since the scale of it, they argued, was out of all proportion to the danger facing India from China. They complained also that "neutral" India was getting without strings the same sort of assistance that Pakistan obtained only by concluding a formal alliance with the United States. In fact, of course, United States aid to Pakistan, both military and civilian, has been running at a higher level than its aid to India.

[3] The writer, who was in Pakistan a few days before the military takeover, and later in Delhi, can testify how well the new regime in Pakistan had impressed American visitors in particular. "It is just as in the British time," one American explained, "the country is efficiently run by the civil servants and the military people." To this a Britisher present replied a little wryly: "Yes, it is as in the British time – except that then there were members of Parliament in London who could take up matters that were not satisfactorily handled, there was a free press, in spite of all the infringements, and, finally, in the British time there was a vociferous opposition which worked so effectively that in the end it brought down the British regime."

pation of women. These ideals were frequently proclaimed to be in accord with basic Islamic doctrine purged of later distortions. Be that as it may, the military regime took important steps toward the interdependent goals of more rapid economic development and national consolidation that the parliamentary regime had been too weak to pursue. With administrative reorganization and the effort to improve the quality and efficiency of government administration, committees and other agencies preparing new policies began to work with commendable speed and relative freedom from the pressures of special vested interests. The regime set out to design a legal system that would be more efficient and simpler than that inherited from the British. The educational system was to be similarly overhauled in order, first, "to develop among the people a sense of public duty, patriotism and national solidarity and to inculcate among them the habit of industry, integrity and devotion to service," and secondly, "to provide facilities for the development of talent and to produce men of character and ability required for the development of the country in different fields."[1] The regime courageously espoused birth control.[2] The rehabilitation of refugees also began to be tackled with greater sympathy and vigor than the parliamentary regime had shown.

To inculcate a sense of coordinated national effort toward explicit goals, so conspicuously lacking in the first decade of independence, the military junta gave economic planning a strategic role and strengthened the Planning Commission. It carried out an evaluation of the First Five Year Plan and duly formulated and enacted a second one, to run from 1960 to 1965. The aim of the Second Five Year Plan was to increase Pakistan's national income by over one-fifth by 1966. But with the rate of population growth at much over 2 percent a year, the increase in income per head would have to be much less. Top priority was given to agriculture and education, and as it turned out, Pakistan has in recent years had more success in economic development than India. After the stagnation in the first decade, yields in agriculture picked up, and the target of the Second Plan of a 21 percent increase in production was reported to have been reached one year ahead of schedule. Even though the rate of population growth proved much higher than was estimated in the plan, food requirements were met without price rises – thanks mainly, however, to large-scale imports from the United States under P.L. 480. Prospects for the fulfillment

[1] *Dawn,* December 16, 1958.

[2] Chapter 28, Section 8.

In reference to religious objections against birth control, Ayub Khan commented: "I cannot believe that any religion can object to the population control because no good religion can object to anything aimed at the betterment of human lot, because all religions, after all, come for the good of the human race and human beings do not come into the world for the religions." (*Pakistan Times,* February 25, 1959, quoted in Khalid Bin Sayeed, "Martial Law Administration," *Far Eastern Survey,* Vol. XXVIII, No. 5, May, 1959.)

or overfulfillment of the plan's target of a 24 percent growth in national income were considered to be good. Nevertheless, the Governor of the State Bank in his 1964 annual report referred to the social and political problems implicit in the "widespread feeling that disparities in income and wealth in Pakistan have tended to increase."[1] A Third Five Year Plan, to begin July 1, 1965, even more ambitious than the Second Plan, was prepared. The Rann of Kutch operations and, still more, the full-scale war with India over Kashmir later in the year strained Pakistan's resources, at a time when future financial aid from the West was left pending. As a result, the Third Plan has been curtailed substantially for the first year; generally, the future seems more uncertain.

The problem of land reform in West Pakistan was also taken up promptly, and its general lines were decreed by January, 1959.[2] As later carried out the reform was anything but drastic or radical. One estimate reckons that it probably redistributed not more than 2 percent of all cultivated land.[3] Nor does it appear to have been rigorously enforced. Prior dispositions to relatives were common and even officially sanctioned, and there were many rumors of favoritism in allocations. More important, the high ceilings on holdings left all but a few landowners unaffected. In keeping with the conservatism of the new regime, the reform aimed, in fact, at stabilizing the position of the hereditary landlords: Ayub Khan could hardly afford to alienate the higher officer corps and civil servants, the main props of his regime, who were closely related to the landlord class. But the parliamentary regime had never tackled land reform at all, and, however mild the present government's program, it may serve as a beginning for more effective reform in the future.

In the field of foreign policy Ayub Khan has tried with some success to lessen the neurotic strain in Pakistan's relations with neighboring states. Although Afghanistan's demand for a separate Pathan state[4] has not explicitly been given up, the fact that Ayub Khan is himself a Pathan and that Pathans have played a conspicuous part in his regime has undoubtedly helped to blunt the edge of the agitation. By May, 1963 the two countries became reconciled on other issues. Pakistan has also been cultivating closer relations with Nepal. But perhaps the most substantial gain from the greater confidence Ayub Khan brought to the conduct of its foreign relations was the agreement Pakistan reached with India in September, 1960 for ending their dispute over the distribution of the Indus basin waters. Admittedly this was made possible only because the

[1] *The Times* (London), September 4, 1964; *Pakistan News,* Embassy of Pakistan, Stockholm, October 27, 1964.

[2] Chapter 26, Section 14.

[3] *The Economist,* London, December 2, 1961, p. 935.

[4] Chapter 5, Section 5.

Western powers agreed to finance almost the whole cost of the scheme. All the same, this was a dispute the parliamentary regime had felt unable to settle in the face of the anti-Indian sentiment it did nothing to allay.

The desire to put relations with India on a saner basis partly reflected Ayub Khan's concern for the security of the whole subcontinent following China's military occupation of Tibet and its rejection of the existing Himalayan frontier line.[1] But his suggestion of a common Indo-Pakistan defense strategy only earned him at that time a rebuff from Nehru. Both sides continued to base the training and disposition of their armies on a hypothetical struggle for Kashmir that would be resolved on the plains of the Punjab. In the event, as we have seen, while Pakistan concluded from its point of view a satisfactory border agreement with China, India's costly conflict with its northern neighbor has not yet been settled. In recent years Pakistan has consistently cultivated ever more friendly relations with China, to which India has responded with anxiety and anger.[2]

The Kashmir issue remains the principal stumbling block to better relations with India because for both sides, as noted earlier,[3] it represents a continuation of the political struggle between the Muslim League and the Congress that preceded partition. However, the inability of India to withstand the Chinese assault on its northern frontier while a large part of its army was massed before its western frontier, compelled it, under American and British pressure, to agree to further talks with Pakistan about Kashmir. Both governments at first showed some inclination to settle the dispute by partitioning the state, but they were as far apart as ever on where the line should be drawn. After a series of fruitless talks the issue remained stalemated. On the Pakistan side, anti-Indian agitation on the Kashmir issue has flared up intermittently. On the Indian side, the government and newspapers seized on Pakistan's frontier agreement with China[4] as evidence of its overriding ill will toward India and lack of conciliatory purpose over Kashmir. It is true that Pakistanis badly concealed their delight at the discomfort China had caused India. But from the Pakistan point of view, Ayub Khan may be excused for not rejecting

[1] He expressed this anxiety in 1960 as follows: "As a student of war and strategy, I can see quite clearly the inexorable push of the North in the direction of the warm waters of the Indian Ocean. This push is bound to increase if India and Pakistan go on squabbling with each other. If, on the other hand, we resolve our problems and disengage our armed forces from facing inwards as they do today, and face them outwards, I feel we shall have a good chance of preventing a recurrence of the history of the past, which was that whenever this sub-continent was divided – and often it was divided – someone or other invited the outsider to step in." (Ayub Khan, "Pakistan Perspectives," *Foreign Affairs,* Vol. 38, No. 4, July, 1960.) His reading of the lessons of Indian history is similar to that of nineteenth century British Viceroys, except that for them it was principally Russia, not China, that constituted "the inexorable push of the North"; see Chapter 5, Section 8.

[2] Chapter 5, Section 8; Chapter 6, Section 7.

[3] Chapter 6, Sections 6–8.

[4] Chapter 5, Section 7.

the opportunity of a firm agreement with China for the entirely speculative hope of a settlement over Kashmir, especially since it is from India, as the country mainly in possession, that the really significant concessions required for an acceptable solution must come. To the Western powers it has seemed a fair assumption that India is unlikely to get a more moderate Pakistani leader to negotiate with than Ayub Khan. We noted in Chapter 6 (Section 7) Nehru's attempt in the last months of his life to reach an agreement on the basis of a condominium over Kashmir.

As we mentioned, the military regime started out with substantial good will in the Western countries, especially in the United States. The previous regime, being conservative and non-revolutionary, had already enjoyed much sympathy on the part of most Western observers; the firmer rule of the military regime, its stand against corruption, and its initiatives in regard to planning and social and economic reforms were acclaimed in the West as evidence that conservatives could be progressive. This sympathy also was based on an appreciation of the secular and Westernized philosophy and modes of living of the ruling strata, made possible by the inherent rationalism of Islam in its higher and more sophisticated forms;[1] the military junta brought to power leaders who were even more Westernized in this respect.[2] Later, the rapprochement with China and, still later, the war with India dampened Western sympathy. At the beginning of 1966 the future orientation of Pakistan's foreign policy seems uncertain. When the conflict with India was brewing, it was announced that Pakistan would have a policy of "maintenance of an equipoise in relations with the East and West"[3] (see Chapter 6, Section 6). The fact that Pakistan is entirely dependent on Western aid would seem, however, to necessitate a move back toward its earlier policy, at least to the extent of not having too warm relations with China.

8 *Reconstructing the Framework of Political Action*

None of the initiatives taken by the military junta was more keenly felt by the supporters of the old regime than its sweeping program of political reform. The military coup, Ayub Khan maintained, was not directed

[1] Footnote 2, p. 306 above.

[2] The remarkable effectiveness of Pakistan's public relations with Westerners, especially Americans, has from the beginning and even more since the military takeover undoubtedly been attributable in part to the worldly outlook and modes of living of the Pakistani leaders. They mix with Westerners without any marked inhibitions about dressing, eating, drinking, joking, or philosophizing about life. The average upper-class Hindu in India, however Westernized, appears to the unsophisticated Westerner as more tense, introverted, haughty, and lacking in humor and the simple graces of human togetherness.

[3] *Pakistan News*, Embassy of Pakistan, Stockholm, March 23, 1965.

against democracy as such, but "only against the manner in which its institutions were being worked."[1] The suspension of constitutional government was explained to be a temporary necessity in order "to prepare the country suitably for representative forms of government to come in and flourish."[2] The declared aim of Ayub Khan, in fact, was to restore democracy,[3] but a democracy that "all the people could understand and effectively participate in up to the level of their mental horizon and intellectual calibre." The political process should "put to the voter only such questions as he can answer in the light of his own personal knowledge and understanding without external prompting." It must also be able to produce reasonably strong and stable government. There is no recognition in his argument, it will be noted, of a need to curb the arbitrary exercise of executive power by democratic processes and institutions.

In pursuit of these objectives the military junta in late 1959 first introduced a system of local councils, beginning at the village level with union councils or in urban areas with town committees, in which delegates from one level are represented at the next level and so on up the pyramid to the provincial councils. Direct elections on the basis of full adult franchise, including voting rights for women, are confined, however, to the lowest level, the "basic democracies" as they are called; above that level there is indirect suffrage. Even at the lowest level considerable controlling powers have been given to the government officials who also serve on the councils. As the pyramid rises so the proportion of nominated and official members grows.[4] The basic democracies were to perform local government functions and focus the consciousness of the rural population on economic development needs and activities. It was hoped they would help to build up the capacity for self-government, make the business of government seem close and responsive to the people, and produce a fresh supply of local and national leaders.[5]

[1] Ayub Khan, "Pakistan Perspectives," *Foreign Affairs,* Vol. 38, No. 4, July, 1960.

[2] Ayub Khan, Speech to Karachi High Court Bar Association, January 15, 1959. (Quoted in Mushtaq Ahmad, *Government and Politics in Pakistan,* p. 209.)

[3] "There are two main reasons why we in Pakistan cannot but adhere to a democratic pattern of life and government. In the first place as Muslims, we are brought up on two basic ingredients of democracy, namely, equality and fraternity. Anything to the contrary would be the negation of our spiritual faith and practice. And secondly, we have to fight a long and arduous battle for progress and development in which every man, woman and child of Pakistan must participate to the fullest possible extent. Democracy provides the only healthy and dignified way for arousing the willing cooperation of the people and harnessing it to a sustained national endeavor." (Ayub Khan, "Pakistan Perspectives," *Foreign Affairs.*)

The quotations following in the text are from the same article.

[4] "The experiment in some ways resembles the steps by which, during the evolution of British colonial rule. popular opinion was slowly associated with the official element in the governor's council." (*The Economist,* December 2, 1961.)

[5] Chapter 18, Section 10.

The election of some 800,000 persons to 8,000 basic democracies took place at the end of 1959 and the beginning of 1960.[1] The candidates had to confine themselves largely to extolling their personal qualities, since no criticism of the new political system nor discussion of regional claims, religious beliefs, or foreign policy was permitted. In fact, the elections did not indicate whether the voters favored one set of aims or policies over another. Nor did they seem to yield new leadership. Considering the economic and social hold of the landlord over the peasant and his family, the failure of any alternative leadership to emerge is hardly surprising. On the contrary, the system of basic democracies has actually strengthened the position of the local landlords – first, because it is easier for them to manipulate and intimidate a small electorate than a larger one, and secondly, because the candidates must reside in the locality, thus making it impossible to provide the peasants with alternative leadership of the kind that might arise if constituencies were large enough to include both larger towns and villages. The effect of the new system has thus been to associate the local landowners or their nominees with the official machinery of government, a result that is in keeping, as we have argued, with the character of the so-called revolution Ayub Khan enacted in October, 1958.

Having launched the basic democracies, the military junta next turned to the construction of a framework for national political action. From Ayub Khan's forthright condemnation of the old regime something could be learned of the constitution he would put in its place. While not denouncing his countrymen's belief in Islam as the greatest source of inspiration and enlightenment, Ayub Khan turned a deaf ear to the self-appointed spokesmen for Islam who advocated a withdrawal into a comfortable but unproductive mysticism. Under the new constitution promulgated in 1962 the official designation of the country became simply the Republic of Pakistan.[2] Such concessions as it made to Moslem ideology were, if anything, even less than those contained in the 1956 constitution.[3] Pakistan, in short, remains a secular state. The statement of aims in the new constitution retains a commitment to the full range of modernization ideals – for instance, greater social and economic opportunity for all including the prevention of undue concentration of wealth or capital, equitable adjustments of rights between employers and employees and between landlords and tenants, the advancement of underprivileged classes, and the eradication of illiteracy.

As regards the institutional framework of political decision-making, a

[1] The constituencies of the basic democracies consist of 1,000 voters each, as compared with the 100,000 voters that formed the parliamentary constituencies under the old constitution.

[2] As a result of mounting pressure, however, Ayub Khan agreed early in 1963 to change the name of the state back to the Islamic Republic of Pakistan.

[3] Section 1 above.

return to a parliamentary system of government was not seen to be desirable or even feasible. The Muslim League tradition from pre-independence and early independence times could not be rejuvenated; the later emerging party system, which Ayub Khan regarded as a curse,[1] had been in process of decomposition long before his coup d'état. With one-party dominance there was no chance of inaugurating the Indian type of parliamentary democracy. Power would have to be preserved for a ruling elite, and past experience suggested that to maintain discipline within its ranks a much smaller group of high military officers and civil servants would have to retain substantial initiative and control.

The prescription thought to fit these needs best was a presidential system of government along the lines designed by de Gaulle for the Fifth French Republic. Ayub Khan justified it, however, as being in accordance with Islamic traditions. Under the new constitution the President, who must be a Moslem, is the sole repository of executive power. He appoints and governs through a Council of Ministers at the center and through governors appointed and directed by him in East and West Pakistan. He has unquestioned responsibility for all public expenditure; the National Assembly cannot vote on his budget or vote appropriations or introduce a money bill. He must validate all legislation passed by the National Assembly, which can only over-ride his veto if three-quarters of its membership so agrees. The constitution gives the President the right to dissolve the Assembly and govern by ordinances. He is directly elected by the basic democracies, the electoral colleges, for a term of five years. He can be impeached or removed from office only by a vote of at least three-quarters of the National Assembly, and there are provisions to ensure that such a move is not undertaken lightly. Thus, if less than half the National Assembly vote for his impeachment or removal, the members sponsoring such a resolution, who must in any case constitute not less than one-third of the total membership, shall lose their seats. In general, any matter that is in dispute between the President and the Assembly can, at his choice, be decided by a simple majority vote of the "basic democrats," as the members of the elected local councils are called. Finally, any amendment of the constitution requires the support of at least two-thirds of the National Assembly.

The National Assembly is composed of 75 members each from East and West Pakistan, elected by the electoral colleges or basic democrats. In addition three seats from each of the two wings are reserved for women members, though women may also stand for the general seats. No seats

[1] "I believe that instead of blind-foldedly following the pattern of the West we should try to run our representative institutions based on the concept of consensus of opinion. If we can do that, and I don't see any reason why we shouldn't – because the whole of our past social history and religious tradition is based on that – then we might be able to do away with the curse of the party system." (*Pak Jamhuriat*, October 27, 1960.)

have been reserved for religious minorities. On being appointed a minister a member of the Assembly must resign his seat.[1] Provincial legislatures are as much subordinate to provincial governors as the National Assembly is to the President. Furthermore, provincial government in general is clearly subject to central direction. One significant indication of this is that under the new constitution national economic planning and coordination are reserved exclusively to the center whereas under the constitution of 1956 responsibilities under this heading were divided between the center and the provinces. As a concession to East Bengali feelings the new constitution makes Dacca the principal seat of the National Assembly though retaining Rawalpindi as the principal seat of the central government until the new capital of Islamabad is built. Bengali and Urdu continue to be the two national languages, though English may be used officially until arrangements are made for its replacement.

Ayub Khan had thus framed a constitution well suited to provide strong leadership, stability of administration, and continuity of policy. Despite some democratic features it is in reality autocratic.[2] In the range of discretionary power given to the executive and unchecked by parliamentary processes, it falls short of what a Western liberal democrat could approve. The fundamental rights it purports to guarantee are qualified in ways to prevent judicial processes from thwarting the ends of executive action. Political arrests of opposition leaders have not ceased. All the same, from the Western liberal's standpoint it is a good deal better than martial law, and the government clearly does not exercise pervasive control over the opinions and activities of the articulate strata of the population. Given the failure of the old parliamentary system to even prepare the country for democracy in the Western sense, it is doubtful whether anything but an autocratic regime could now work.

After more than three years of military rule the new constitution came into force in June, 1962 and martial law was ended. Elections to the National Assembly and to the provincial assemblies were held during the previous two months. Ayub Khan, hoping that candidates would be selected on their personal merits, forbade them to campaign on a party basis. Yet by all accounts political issues, including the restoration of full civil liberties, direct elections, and the revival of political parties and parliamentary government, dominated the manifestoes of many candidates. The results were no less portentous. No member of a minority community, nor any woman, won a general seat. More important, while members re-

[1] Under pressure from east-wing members, Ayub Khan issued an order in June, 1962 allowing ministers to retain their seats in the Assembly. But in May, 1963 the Pakistan Supreme Court ruled that this order was unconstitutional.

[2] "The document bears all the hallmarks of a Constitution devised by the Executive, to be imposed through the Executive and for the Executive." (K. J. Newman, "The Constitutional Evolution in Pakistan," *International Affairs,* Vol. 38, No. 3, July, 1962.)

turned from East Pakistan included some trade unionists, journalists, and politicians of moderate means, the new members from West Pakistan were mostly men of property — nawabs, landlords, and industrialists.[1] Indeed, the latter groups outnumbered all others in the National Assembly. In addition most of the successful candidates were former party men, with old Muslim Leaguers forming the largest single group. From the nature of their election campaigns it was apparent that many of them were not going to rest content with the subsidiary role the new constitution accorded them. Despite restrictions on the formation or revival of political parties, the new members of the National Assembly quickly proceeded to organize themselves into like-minded groups. Fortunately for Ayub Khan, a slight majority of them supported him unconditionally.

Two clear tendencies have since dominated Pakistan politics: first, an attempt in the name of democracy to wrest power from the executive and return it to the legislature; and secondly, the insistence of East Pakistan that it should receive an equal share in all the benefits and opportunities of government. Proponents of these views have combined in a sustained attack on Ayub Khan's regime. Above all, they have demanded fundamental constitutional reforms, the revival of political parties, direct elections, justiciable rights, and trial in open court of all political detainees. To forestall a mounting pressure for the removal of all restrictions on organized political activity the government in July, 1962 rushed its own Political Parties Bill through the National Assembly. No restrictions were to be placed on the number of political parties that could be formed or on their assumption of old labels.[2] But to the anger of the opposition about a hundred former leading politicians, including some past premiers and ministers, were debarred from membership and office in any political party; to ensure that they remained politically impotent, Ayub Khan subsequently tightened the definition of political party and political activity. They could, however, appeal to the President for a reduction or remission of their disqualification, a right of pardon Ayub Khan no doubt intended to bargain for their loyalty. This determination to silence disqualified politicians capable of arousing a following is to some extent an admission by Ayub Khan of his inability to win any comparable support among the politically articulate, particularly in East Pakistan. Finally, the bill required a member of the legislature to resign his seat on changing his party after an election, a provision aimed at preventing the shifting, opportunistic allegiances that plagued the old parliamentary regime.

[1] Sardar Buhadar Khan, the President's brother, likened the East Pakistan representation to a "House of Commons" and that from West Pakistan to a "House of Lords." (*Overseas Hindustan Times*, August 2, 1962.)

[2] The Political Parties Bill forbade the formation of parties to propagate opinions or act in ways prejudicial to Islamic ideology or the security of Pakistan, including parties that are foreign-aided. This provision, in effect, banned non-Moslem parties and the Communist Party.

Continuing political arrests tended to isolate the military regime still further from popular support in the articulate strata and opened it to the charge of repressing political opposition more harshly than the British had done. It is in East Pakistan that opposition to the new constitution has been most vocally and actively expressed. And just as the students there were in the forefront of the revolt against the Muslim League, so they have figured prominently in the opposition to Ayub Khan. In January, 1962, when their political hero, Suhrawardy, was arrested for his defiance of restrictions on civil rights, they rioted and Dacca University was closed. Although Ayub Khan has tried in various ways to conciliate the east wing, its sense of colonial subordination to the west wing has not noticeably lessened. The central government claims that, according to the plan, a greater share of its revenue is now being allotted to the east wing, though less was actually spent there. It has admitted, too, that by 1963 out of 790 junior civil servants recruited by the martial law regime, only 120 came from the east wing,[1] and the situation has not changed very radically since then. The educated upper and middle classes in East Pakistan evidently remain very discontented with the pace at which new opportunities for them are being created.

In the face of the opposition to the constitution, Ayub Khan began to waver and make new concessions. By the beginning of 1963 he was prepared to make fundamental rights justiciable, though not those martial law regulations already frozen into the constitution. He conceded in principle that members of the national and provincial assemblies could be directly elected, but insisted that the President himself must continue to be elected indirectly, by the basic democracies. However, subsequent electoral successes of the opposition parties persuaded him later to preserve indirect elections for the legislators as well. The opposition continued to demand a return to full democracy. Opposition leaders resent the subordinate role of the National Assembly because its inability to compel ministerial change makes it a less attractive outlet for political action. They also resent the fact that the constitution makes the President responsible to the electorate and not to the legislators. If Ayub Khan shows litle faith in the legislators, they in turn show little faith in the ability of the basic democrats to choose a President and decide disputed issues by referenda.

As popular sovereignty hardly existed under the old parliamentary regime, as little attempt was then made to educate the public on political issues, as arbitrary political arrests were not unusual, and governments did not hesitate to put the safety of the state above political liberty or to circumvent the protection the courts afforded the citizen, the veneration for true democracy professed by Ayub Khan's opponents can be ques-

[1] *The Times*, London, March 28, 1963.

tioned. The political parties now active in Pakistan are either old groups in the parliamentary regime that have been resurrected or rival claimants for the name and property of old parties, especially the Muslim League. Personal cliques riven by provincial rivalries are becoming the rule now as before 1958. Although the opposition marches under the banner of democracy, the indications are that what is developing is the same old pattern of factional bargaining for regional interests and the spoils of office. There is still no attempt to formulate true party programs that prescribe for the country's immense economic and social problems. Until the middle of 1963 Ayub Khan, like de Gaulle, tried to remain above politics, rather than put himself at the head of a "government party" within the National Assembly. But he was unable to stay outside the political maelstrom[1] and later that year he joined the pro-government faction of the splintered Muslim League. Against his better judgment he has been compelled to "play politics" just as the "strong men" before him did by dividing and dominating the opposition.

If his position seems more solid – in January of 1965 he won a clear victory, even in East Pakistan, over Fatima Jinnah, the sister of Mohammed Ali Jinnah, who had been put up as a candidate of all the opposition parties in the presidential election – this is largely due to the inability of the opposition parties to make common cause on anything but their desire for power, under cover of a campaign for the return to democracy.

9 *A Look Toward the Future*

Any government in Pakistan that tries to engender national consolidation and development must cope with certain basic difficulties. It is a very poor country without a history of political identity or national allegiance. Its population is divided by widespread social and economic inequalities and its solidarity further strained by a geographical division into two roughly equal units whose principal tie is a common religion and a shared animosity to the large neighbor that separates them. Clearly, religion and resentment against a neighboring state are precarious foundations on which to build a modern state.

It should nevertheless be possible to overcome regional strains within Pakistan. One lesson of history is that a national boundary, no matter how artificial from an economic or any other standpoint, can become natural in time. With enlightened and effective government, the split

[1] On June 11, 1962 the *Pakistan Times,* an ardent supporter of Ayub Khan, wrote: "Actually President Ayub needs a party more than anybody else, because he alone is the author of a new political philosophy and it needs to be inculcated, broadcast and projected by a powerful popular organization."

would eventually become self-perpetuating as the disparate parts were made to function as a true unit. A strong government in Pakistan also has a better chance of effecting cooperative arrangements with India aimed at making partition less detrimental economically. The pursuit of vigorous policies to raise living standards, decrease harsh inequalities, reduce the alarmingly high birth rate, and generally enlist the participation and cooperation of the people could undoubtedly create the reality of nationhood for ever larger sections of Pakistan's population.

Against admittedly formidable odds, then, it is possible to envisage a progressive and nationally consolidated state of Pakistan. That it survived in the first place was almost a miracle. And it was remarkable as well that after the passing of the initial leadership, sense of direction, and willingness to sacrifice for the national cause there was not more political disintegration than occurred. In its strivings for national consolidation, Pakistan even has certain advantages in comparison with other South Asian countries. Like India, but unlike Ceylon and the countries of Southeast Asia, it has no ethnic minorities of a distinct foreign culture that are difficult to assimilate. Its Hindu minority is not very dissimilar to the Moslem majority and, like the Moslem minority in India, can undoubtedly be integrated into the new state if given equal opportunity and security. This assumes that the religious character of the state is not emphasized – which is in any case a pre-condition of modernization and development. Pakistan is also fortunate in that its caste system is less ramified, and certainly less solidified by religion, than India's. Neither caste proper nor the much more prevalent and important inequalities of a non-caste or less-than-caste character, which in districts like Sind keep large sections of the rural population almost in servility, have any sanction in the Koran. Islam is egalitarian and in its "higher" manifestations has traits of rationalism that should permit it to be integrated more readily with the modernization ideals than, for instance, Hinduism in India. This, in turn, should facilitate the economic and social reforms required for national consolidation.

Given these circumstances, if Pakistan is to instigate and maintain progress, it must have a regime with a vision of national goals, in contrast to the lack of program that characterized the old Muslim League. The emphasis on economic planning, and the other initiatives taken by Ayub Khan after he seized power, were important steps in that direction. To preserve the momentum, however, the regime must frequently apply policies that, in the short view at least, run counter to the vested interests of the upper strata of landlords, big industrialists, merchants, and professionals to which the men around him belong or are intimately connected. It must be remembered, as was emphasized earlier, that Ayub Khan did not instigate a true revolution, but rather a defensive maneuver of regrouping and disciplining the real wielders of power within the upper strata. Some politicians who were badly tainted and a few civil servants were punished; more generally, politicians who had been active during the old regime were rusticated. In the main the country is ruled by very much the same upper class as before, except that within it the higher military officers, and alongside them the higher civil servants, have taken firmer command. To the extent that this inner controlling group has sufficient integrity and vision to move decisively against the interests of the upper strata whenever these conflict with the development needs of the country, the momentum of reform can be maintained. But an upper-class regime with army backing, even one that remains orderly and incorrupt, can easily be a static and protective framework, especially when its leadership becomes accustomed to power.

The political opposition that exists seems too inept to keep the regime on the alert in regard to national issues of a substantive character. The "middle class" (i.e., those below the very top level represented by the regime) – a motley assortment of former politicians who have not been effectively purged, lawyers and journalists, small traders and merchants, teachers and students – who form the core of the opposition parties, are united only in fighting for an undefined "democracy"; on every other issue the opposition parties are split among and within themselves or are simply disinterested.[1] Indeed, no other issue is important except as a political weapon. In this respect – that they have no economic and social program – these opposition parties are perpetuating the most damaging tradition of the old Muslim League. Fighting for power in the name of democracy in the same way the League fought for separation from India, they exert no pressure on the Ayub Khan government to adhere to, and promote, a program of social and economic reform. Thus there is no opposition to hinder that regime from becoming static and protective, or to offer a progressive alternative.

One may then also ask: Will not the present regime in time deteriorate politically, ideologically, and morally? Protected as it is by constitutional safeguards – and ultimately by armed force – and able if necessary to repress public criticism, can it continue the fight it began against corruption? Can it, indeed, avoid becoming corrupt itself? Not long after the coup d'état the incorruptibility of the military junta came into question. It was not so much that speculation, black-marketeering, tax evasion, and other fraudulent practices had decreased, people were saying, as that the cost of bribery, because of the greater dangers, had increased.[2] Yet

[1] During the election campaign, Ayub Khan likened the five opposition parties that had joined together in support of Fatima Jinnah to "five cats tied by their tails." (*The Economist*, February 13, 1965.)

[2] Mr. Kayani, Chief Justice of the West Pakistan High Court, expressed this skepticism when he said: "These officers are our own sons and nephews and cannot outpace our vices." (*The Guardian*, Manchester, August 29, 1960.)

nothing will more effectively reduce the momentum for reform initiated by the new regime than a sliding back into the old slough of corruption.

The dilemma is obvious. Even the most devoted friend of political democracy cannot see much hope for national consolidation and development in the fight being waged in the name of democracy by the present opposition parties. Were they to win, it is difficult to see how the result could be other than a return to the conditions that existed during the first decade of Pakistan's independence. Thus what hope there is for progress in Pakistan must be attached to the present quasi-dictatorial regime: to its ability, despite its very narrow class basis, to advance national goals of planning, equality, and consolidation and to purge the state of corruption.

Chapter 9

CEYLON AND SOUTHEAST ASIA

I

Ceylon

1 *National Consolidation: The Dimensions of the Problem*

From the standpoint of national consolidation, Ceylon began life as an independent nation with certain clear advantages over the neighboring states of India and Pakistan. In the first place, there are obvious reasons of geography that make it natural for Ceylon to be viewed as a single political entity. Since it is a small compact island territory, it has no problems of spatial definition and no boundary worries. Its geopolitical position, with only poor peaceful India as a near neighbor, has given Ceylon a sense of national security that has enabled it to keep its military expenditures at a much lower level than those of any other country in the region.[1] The conception of Ceylon as a political entity, or rather the notion

[1] Insofar as the Ceylonese ruling elite had any stake – besides a financial one – in the British military bases that were allowed to remain on the island after independence, it was that they provided insurance against possible internal troubles. External threats seemed remote, though concern was occasionally expressed about Communist or irredentist appeals gaining a hold over the Tamils in South India, hereditary enemies of the Singhalese.

of a Singhalese nation, is firmly rooted and goes far back into history, a fact that, in romanticized form, has obvious ideological significance at the present time. The territory was never incorporated in a South Indian kingdom in pre-colonial times. Colonial rule, lasting four hundred years, did not always encompass the whole island, but the island was never split or joined with an outside territory for administrative purposes. The British did not attempt to rule Ceylon, like Burma, as a subordinate province of imperial India.

With a flourishing and efficiently run plantation industry, Ceylon has for some time enjoyed much higher levels of living than India. Malnutrition is far less common and the level of literacy in colonial times was the highest in South Asia, except for the Philippines. Inequalities are generally smaller than in India. In particular, the social stratification in Ceylon is more egalitarian and women are less subjugated.[1] The existing inequalities are less rigidly rooted and unyielding, a major reason being that, although Ceylon has more than a vestige of a caste system, this is not nearly as obtrusive as in India. In particular, employment and political conduct are less blatantly influenced by caste loyalties and antipathies. Ceylon has no Brahman caste, or, strictly speaking, any equivalent of the untouchables, though some of its lowly placed castes suffer similar disabilities. More important, the dominant or highest caste, the Goyigama caste of cultivators, comprises the majority. Ceylon's long exposure to the processes of Westernization, and the economic and professional opportunities this opened up, ensured that such caste distinctions as existed were thoroughly penetrated by class distinction.

The preparation for self-government had proceeded more rapidly and smoothly in Ceylon than anywhere else in the region, except the Philippines.[2] When political independence arrived, the country had a relatively large number of politicians steeped in the lore of parliamentary democracy under conditions of universal suffrage and with experience of executive action as well. It also had a larger and better trained indigenous civil service than that possessed by any other country in the region except India and the Philippines. The transition was managed with a minimum of constitutional change and a minimum of upset. There were no uncertainties about boundaries, no partition, no murderous upheavals, no stream of refugees, and no harsh memories of national struggle and sacrifice, as on the Indian subcontinent.

The liberation effort in Ceylon – it would be misleading to call it a

[1] Women in Ceylon were enfranchised on the same basis as men in 1931, well before the women of any other Asian country. The reason given was that women's services would be of special value in coping with the high infant mortality rate on the island and with the need for better housing and improved child care, midwifery, and pre-natal services.

[2] For an amplification of the content of this and the following paragraph, see Chapter 4, Section 9.

movement — never really reached down, as it did in India, though mostly in the northern part of the subcontinent, to touch the mass of the people. It barely extended beyond the confines of a comparatively small and well-to-do upper-class group, whose economic interests had become closely allied with those of the British and who had a personal and professional interest in playing the game of politics. The members of this group formulated no ambitious program of economic and social reform as did the Indian National Congress. Neither by conviction nor by force of circumstance did they feel the need to do so. Their brand of nationalism, though welfare-directed, was not markedly radical in temper. Their prevailing political outlook might more accurately be described as conservative in the way of fairly modern political conservatism in Britain.

There were important nuances of difference between this upper stratum and its counterpart on the Indian subcontinent. For one thing, the elite in British India adhered more to their traditional culture. The Moslem landowners had acquired their social and economic position in the distant past under dynasties of their own kin and came in a later period to regard British rule as a defense against the Hindus. Many of the newer class of Hindu businessmen felt themselves to be in competition with the British. Even the professional men and higher civil servants were, to a larger extent than in Ceylon, opposed to their colonial rulers, if not actively, at least in their hearts. The nationalist effort in Ceylon thus lacked the élan of the liberation movement on the Indian subcontinent. The implications were not altogether healthy, politically speaking. The manifesto of the Sri Lanka Freedom Party (S.L.F.P.), which was launched in 1951 to represent the interests of those indigenous social forces the ruling elite had neglected, explains why this is so:

> Unlike other countries such as India, Pakistan, Burma, Indonesia, Ireland, etc., which advanced to freedom through the instrumentality of mass movements based on clear-cut principles and policies, our freedom movement was really one proceeding from the top and cut off to a great extent from the masses. The importance of this fact must be clearly understood. It has created a feeling in the minds of some people that our freedom is not something that the people have obtained but one that a few individuals have succeeded in getting, and one therefore that is looked upon to a great extent as the private property of some individuals, the benefits of which should be chiefly enjoyed by them and their posterity.[1]

The political feeling underlying that comment is not the only reason why, despite an apparently favorable initial situation, Ceylon has not made much progress toward national consolidation, including in that concept both effective government and the "emotional integration" of the

[1] *Manifesto and Constitution of the Sri Lanka Freedom Party*, Wellampitiya, 1951, p. 3.

population. Not only is the social structure of the country divided vertically, between a privileged, well-to-do, English-educated upper class and an indigenously educated lower class; it is also divided horizontally, between different ethnic communities.[1] Community, class, language, and religion are by no means perfectly correlated. Language, religion, and social customs generally separate the Singhalese majority from the Ceylon Tamil minority. The division has a geographic dimension as well, insofar as the Singhalese are concentrated in the island's center and southwest, including the Kandyan or hill-country districts that experienced a shorter period of Westernization than the low-country areas, whereas the Tamils chiefly inhabit the northern and eastern districts. But within both communities — and among Burghers and other population groups outside them — a tiny upper stratum of English-educated and often Christian Ceylonese held a bridgehead of privilege against an indigenously educated, largely underprivileged majority. The Indian Tamil laborers on the plantations, from which the Ceylonese Tamils had kept aloof, were another separate lower-class group.

The political development of Ceylon since independence is largely a story of how these fissures in its social structure, which the British and Ceylonese elite had long kept under control, were increasingly exposed and exploited for political ends. Communal peace was shattered by politics. An irresponsible radical nationalism became the order of the day. The record since the early 1950's is replete with riots, strikes, and other symptoms of a distempered political condition. This dizzy descent from order and stability that marked the transfer of sovereign power contrasts strikingly with India's political experience since independence. When India started out on the path to parliamentary democracy under conditions of universal suffrage, the result was to strengthen the forces of conservatism and make for a kind of political stability. Ceylon's higher standard of living and of literacy, its less rigid social structure, and, in particular, the long education of the people in the power of the ballot box go some way toward explaining this difference. But any explanation must identify a number of other cogwheels in a complex social mechanism.

2 *The Emergence of New Social Forces*

Independent Ceylon inherited a constitution modelled on the British pattern, the basic features of which have survived intact to the present day. The British Crown, represented by a Governor General, is Head

[1] Of a population of roughly 11 million in the 1953 census, about 70 percent spoke Singhala and 22 percent spoke Tamil. The latter group consisted of Ceylon Tamils and Indian Tamil estate workers in equal proportion. Moslems and Burghers of mixed European and Singhalese descent accounted for the remainder.

of State, and the British Privy Council is the final court of appeal. The cabinet is responsible to the House of Representatives. The Senate, or upper house, is of little practical importance, save as an outlet for political patronage: its powers are less than those of the British House of Lords. It offers, however, a convenient way of including non-elected members in the legislature, which has been used by all Ceylonese governments. It is worth noting that, unlike that of India, Ceylon's constitution contains no policy directives and, except for stating that the legislature cannot restrict religious freedom or discriminate against any religion or community,[1] it ignores the issue of equality and human rights. It fails, in short, to spell out the modernization ideology.

In the general election of 1947, the newly formed United Nationalist Party (U.N.P.), the party of the Westernized elite, won 42 of the 95 elective seats in the House of Representatives. Six more members were appointed by the Prime Minister to represent important interests otherwise under- or unrepresented, and the U.N.P. could also count on the support of most of the 21 independent members returned. The opposition consisted of the representatives of the Ceylon Tamils and of a few small leftist parties adhering to a "Marxist" doctrine; the latter were led by upper-class Western-educated intellectuals who were at loggerheads with each other on ideological questions. This weak and thoroughly split minority presented no serious parliamentary challenge to the ruling party. In appealing to the electorate the U.N.P. had pledged itself to what it called "practical socialism." In practice this amounted to little more than the initiation or extension of social welfare schemes in a period of easy money. The U.N.P. stood for such politically popular aims as free and universal education, better medical services, the control and improvement of working conditions, and the continuation of wartime food subsidies. Its social conscience was inspired by humanitarianism and charity rather than by the revolutionary ideas of social justice and equality.

The U.N.P. government inherited large sterling balances as a result of British and Commonwealth wartime expenditures on the island, and export prices were good. No major economic troubles disturbed its complacency. It accepted the need for industrial development and sought it through the encouragement of private enterprise and cottage industries. There was no attempt at serious economic planning, much less any intention of interfering with the foreign estates on which the prosperity of the economy was founded. Large-scale agricultural settlements and irrigation schemes were promoted, but not fundamental agrarian reform. The nationalist appeal of the ruling party was non-communal and secular. Its

[1] The force of this proviso hinges on the definition of "community." Thus when the Tamils challenged the Singhala-only language policy of the government on the ground that it discriminated against them, the Attorney General argued that they were not a community. (*The Times* (London), October 30, 1962.)

ranks included Ceylon Tamils as well as Singhalese, Christians as well as non-Christians. It bridged different communities and all religions and sought to bring into being a united Ceylon. In foreign affairs, which excited little interest, the U.N.P. was friendly to the West and did not establish diplomatic relations with Communist countries. For some years the U.N.P. governed easily. In the second general election of 1952 it won a clear majority of 54 seats. That was, however, the high-water mark of its electoral fortunes. In the 1956 election the U.N.P. won only 8 seats. What had brought about this dramatic change in its popular appeal?

The U.N.P. was never a strong and well-constructed political machine. It had no grass roots organization, no tradition of collective leadership, and no firm party discipline. It could be described as a loosely knit grouping of the camp followers of its leading personalities. The inner core of its leadership was so family-centered that it became known as the Uncle and Nephew Party.[1] Family quarrels, extensive political nepotism, and reports of graft and corruption brought it increasingly into disrepute.[2] Also working against it was the fact that the economic climate had become less favorable by the early 1950's. Declining export proceeds made the U.N.P.'s welfare policies more burdensome, and the government reacted in a way that showed it to be out of touch with popular feeling. In 1953 it removed the subsidy on rice, not to devote more funds to national economic development, but merely to end the mounting drain on the budget. The poorer sections of the population suffered – both the rice producers, who were mainly peasants, and the masses of rice consumers – while no sacrifice was asked of the well-to-do. The resulting public disorder and rioting were used against the U.N.P. in the general election three years later. In a longer perspective, it was evident that the rapid growth of population was holding down improvements in living standards and making it more difficult for educated young people to get employment commensurate with their ambitions. Above all, the ruling elite neglected the aspirations of the indigenously educated Singhalese, who felt discriminated against in their homeland. It was this group and its allies that spearheaded a wave of radical nationalism that drove the U.N.P. out of office in 1956.

Beneath the topmost layer was a stratum of small businessmen, landowners, traders, middlemen, and moneylenders. In addition the spread of

[1] The first Prime Minister, Don Stephen Senanayake, was succeeded by his son, Dudley Senanayake, in 1952. In 1953 his nephew, Sir John Kotelawala, took office.

[2] "It is significant . . . that . . . plausible explanations of cabinet divergence under the U.N.P. centered around alleged family and social status differences or competing personal ambitions. That there should be honest disagreement between informed and thoughtful men regarding the merits of policy appeared implausible." (W. Howard Wriggins, *Ceylon: Dilemmas of a New Nation,* Princeton University Press, Princeton, 1960, pp. 109–110.)

vernacular education under British rule had produced a rural intelligentsia of Singhalese school teachers, notaries, and indigenous or *ayurvedic* physicians. Less Westernized than the ruling elite, these groups were overwhelmingly Buddhist, and mainly or solely Singhala-speaking. They shared the common South Asian feeling that an educated person must have a clerical job, preferably in government service, the largest and best paid source of such employment. As their numbers increased they found it more and more difficult to get jobs, both because the white-collar positions in government service were limited and because the English-educated, who were also increasing rapidly, monopolized the best positions available. The frustration and tension thus generated fanned the embers of communal and religious antipathy in ways we shall examine later.

The attitude toward the Indian Tamil laborers on the tea estates had early indicated which way the nationalist winds were blowing. Historically, the foreign-owned plantations in the hill country had encroached on village lands and pushed the Singhalese peasantry down into the valleys where their rapidly growing numbers gradually made for an acute land shortage. At present perhaps more than a third of the rural population is landless. For reasons to be discussed in another chapter,[1] the plantations had recruited their labor supply from South Indian Tamils and often provided better working and living conditions for them than existed in the neighboring Singhalese villages. Not surprisingly, the Singhalese peasantry came to resent both the plantations and the Indian Tamils. Feeling against the Indian Tamils was also nurtured by their isolation in the plantation enclaves, although this was caused as much by Singhalese aloofness as by the Tamils' refusal to be assimilated into the surrounding Singhalese and Buddhist society.[2]

When independence arrived, the majority community was generally opposed to the Indian Tamils' keeping the political rights the British had given them. Only some politicians of the "Marxist" parties stood up for them, which was one reason for the poor showing of these parties at the polls. Under pressure from the hill-country Singhalese, in particular, the U.N.P. government promulgated nationality laws that effectively denied civic status to the overwhelming bulk of the Indian Tamils;[3] further legislation restricted voting rights to Ceylonese citizens, thereby disenfranchising this minority. Ceylon was the only country in South Asia to mark its independence by restricting the franchise enjoyed under colonial rule. Other handicaps were imposed on the Indian Tamils. For instance, they

[1] Chapter 10, Section 7; cf. Chapter 11, Section 6.

[2] Before the Second World War certain hill-country constituencies tended to return Indian Tamil representatives on a communal ticket.

[3] According to the 1953 census nearly one million Indians, mainly Tamil estate workers, were not citizens of Ceylon. An insignificant number of European and Pakistani residents were in the same position.

were not eligible to receive allocations of Crown land for farming and a number of urban occupations were closed to them. Successive governments have felt that the only permanent solution to the problem was to repatriate the Tamils to India, but obviously this would require India's agreement. The U.N.P.'s failure to reach such an agreement contributed to its growing unpopularity.

The Indian Tamils were a hardy perennial of parliamentary debate in Ceylon until the official language of the country became the more vital issue. As the number of those with a vernacular education increased, the use of English became a focal point for Singhalese resentment toward the Westernized upper class. For as long as English remained the language of the government and the medium of communication in the best schools, the indigenously educated were seriously handicapped in competing for the most coveted jobs.[1] In any case, it was an odd sort of democracy when more than 90 percent of the electorate did not speak the language of their government. But replacing English solely with Singhala would hurt not only the upper class, who monopolized these jobs, but also the Ceylonese Tamil community. Many Ceylon Tamils, concentrated in the poorer agricultural areas of the country, had taken advantage of the educational opportunities offered by the Christian missionary schools, with the result that they had acquired more than their share of government jobs and other socially rewarding positions. The up-country Singhalese had fared less well, not least because relatively fewer missionary schools had been established in their districts.

As a minority community the Ceylon Tamils tended to be on the defensive in politics. They had opposed the abolition of communal representation when the British decreed universal suffrage in 1931. After independence some of them wanted a federal state with local autonomy for Tamil-speaking areas, while others favored cooperation with the Singhalese majority. As long as the U.N.P. was in power, it was possible to hope for a compromise that would not endanger their special interests. But once the language issue came to the fore in politics, as it did in the election of 1956, the proponents of federalism gained strength and became the principal spokesmen for the community. The Ceylon Tamils saw in the prospect of Singhala becoming the national language a threat to their culture, their identity, and their economic status. It made them a fighting party. They were forced to demand the recognition of Tamil as a national language too, whereas previously they had been content to have English serve this purpose.

What brought the issue to the fore was the rise of the Sri Lanka Free-

[1] Not more than 6 to 8 percent of the population were proficient in English, though 60 to 70 percent were literate in Singhala; see Chapter 31, Section 8.

dom Party. The S.L.F.P. was founded in 1951 by S. W. R. Bandaranaike, the owner of large and prosperous cocoanut plantations. Bandaranaike was English-educated, aristocratic, an Anglican Christian, and, until 1951, a prominent member of the U.N.P., though its family-centered leadership did not treat him as a complete equal. Politically shrewd and ambitious, he sensed the mounting indignation of the educated Singhalese and set out to capitalize on it as the champion of the underprivileged and the defender of a besieged culture. To this end, he mounted a vigorous campaign to have Singhala made the sole official national language. Buddhist religious associations helped the S.L.F.P. to gain a popular following. The title of the new party was calculated to appeal to these groups. Sri Lanka – the old Singhalese name for Ceylon – has much the same spiritual connotations for Singhalese Buddhists as Israel has for the Jews. The Buddhist priesthood distrusted and disliked the Christian-founded and -controlled schools that had produced the English-educated elite. It assailed the Western way of life and called for a revival of Singhalese values and social practices. Some of its fervor was due to the fact that many Buddhist priests were drawn from the stratum of Singhalese society that felt socially and economically frustrated. Religious identification and protest, though not unimportant, had always been much less pervasive in Ceylon than on the Indian subcontinent. Even aroused, it was essentially a convenient vehicle for the aspirations of the not-so-privileged. Nevertheless, it helped to precipitate and emotionalize the language issue.

In building up a popular following based on the Singhalese aversion to the Ceylonese and Indian Tamils and the Buddhist dislike of Christian influence, the S.L.F.P. under Bandaranaike, in effect, stoked the fires of communal and religious bigotry. In the process the electoral support of the basically non-communal and secular U.N.P. melted away. In the 1956 election it went down to spectacular defeat. On the eve of the election, it had abandoned its stand for parity between Tamil and Singhala and come out in favor of making Singhala the only official language, but the conversion came too late to carry conviction. Resurgent and radical Singhalese nationalism had apparently struck a decisive blow at the political dominance of the Westernized elite. Yet ironically enough, the bulk of all the candidates in that election were drawn from the well-to-do sections of the population, which had received an English education.[1] Political leadership remained in the hands of the upper stratum; the only difference was that those who had taken power were more responsive to the aspirations of the educated Singhalese.

In his successful bid for electoral victory, Bandaranaike had engineered an alliance with tiny groups of "Marxists" and Singhalese communalists,

[1] Cf. I. D. S. Weerawardana, *Ceylon General Election 1956,* M. D. Gunasena Co. Ltd., Colombo, 1960, especially Chapter IV.

so that all the organized political parties except the Tamils were lined up against the U.N.P.; this explains why the U.N.P. lost proportionately more seats than votes. The Bandaranaike coalition, or People's United Front (P.U.F.), as it was called, won 51 seats and had an absolute majority in the national legislature as long as it held together and the opposition remained disunited. It was perhaps less significant that "Marxists" entered the government for the first time than that the Tamil Federal Party made a clean sweep of what could be called Tamil constituencies and gained 10 seats. Bandaranaike had triumphed, but at the cost of undermining the nation's unity.

3 *The Trend Toward Radical Nationalism*

The People's United Front had campaigned on a thoroughly radical platform. Apart from the "Singhala-only" plank, it included the repatriation of Indian estate workers, the expansion of village lands at the expense of the plantations, the elimination of non-Singhalese control over trade and distribution, the guarantee of minimum wages, the nationalization of private schools (these were mainly Christian), foreign-owned plantations, banking, insurance, transport, and key industries, the elimination of British military bases on the island, non-alignment in world affairs, and the inauguration of a republic. The least controversial of these was the pledge to reorient Ceylon's foreign policy, and this was done without delay. Bandaranaike demanded, and was readily conceded, the withdrawal of British military bases. He established diplomatic relations with Communist countries and actively pursued the Indian path of non-alignment. All this was in tune with Singhalese nationalism, but it did not meet with fierce resistance from any section of the population, especially as there was no question of Ceylon leaving the Commonwealth; the British Crown remained the Head of State, and the British Privy Council the last court of appeal.

It is open to question how seriously Bandaranaike and those closest to him took the rest of the P.U.F. platform. It had served him well when he was seeking office, but when he began to govern, it brought him a bitter harvest of political and communal discord. His power rested not on a political machine but on his personal ability to please the new and diverse social forces that had swept him into office. In the event, his improbable coalition of disparate elements failed to hold together. There was an extraordinary lack of collective discipline and responsibility in the cabinet. Vitally opposed on ideological issues, the conservative and "Marxist" factions of the P.U.F. scandalously attacked each other in public until, in 1959, the former pressed the latter out of the government altogether. The Singhalese bourgeoisie was not prepared to tolerate any radical experiments at the expense of its own economic interests. Meanwhile, the political life of the country slid out of control. In 1958 an attempt to implement the Singhala-only policy had led to an ugly outbreak of communal rioting, and a state of emergency had been declared. The initiative for preserving order passed to the Governor General. Having rallied and enlisted the forces of communal and religious extremism in his bid for power, Bandaranaike now found himself their prisoner. His ironical dilemma was tragically terminated when, soon after his coalition government broke up, a fanatical Buddhist priest assassinated him.

A period of utter confusion followed, with the ruling party in disarray, parliamentary government reduced to a shambles, and the air thick with rumors of an impending military coup. No cohesion existed anywhere along the political spectrum. The stage was set for a comeback by the conservative U.N.P. Now without scruples, it conducted a virulently communal campaign and emerged from the general election in March of 1960 as the strongest single party, with about a third of the seats in an enlarged lower house of 151 members. But its triumph was short-lived, for it was defeated on the first parliamentary vote of confidence.

In new elections a few months later, the S.L.F.P. capitalized on the carefully nurtured martyrdom of Bandaranaike and made his widow its leader. It again concluded electoral pacts with "Marxist" groups, and this time the formula proved more successful. The S.L.F.P. won so commanding a parliamentary majority that it could form a government on its own. Freedom from the chronic pressure-group politics that had racked her husband's coalition government gave Mrs. Bandaranaike the chance to lead the country out of the political morass into which it had fallen. That advantage was not taken of this opportunity was due to the S.L.F.P.'s lack of any unity of purpose and its commitment to fulfill the radical nationalist urges of the Singhalese-educated class. When it endeavored to extend the Singhala-only policy to government administration, the Tamils reacted so violently that a state of emergency had to be declared which this time lasted two years. The country had grown accustomed to emergency rule, accompanied on this as on other occasions by parliamentary alarums of an impending military coup. Almost as if to satisfy this fear, Mrs. Bandaranaike's government in January, 1962 unearthed a plot by high-ranking army and police officers to seize the levers of power. That a large proportion of the conspirators were Christian and Western-oriented gave the plot a counter-revolutionary character in the eyes of the S.L.F.P. and the "Marxist" parties.

There is still some mystery about this alleged coup. In any case, there are reasons to believe that it would be exceptionally difficult to establish a military dictatorship in Ceylon. The country has not faced, and does not now face, any actual or potential threats to its territorial integrity, and for this reason the army, even with the police added in, is small. It has no glorious tradition behind it, and is not an essential ingredient of national pride. It is not really regarded as a national army; its officer corps has been so recruited that it seems to consist of men who are strangers to the common people, particularly the educated people who are the spearhead of Singhalese and Buddhist nationalism. Army revolutionaries would have to rely heavily on the civil service. But the higher ranks of the civil service are recruited in the same way. Ceylon has had a long history of parliamentary responsibility, and its small size has made it easier for politicians to take the measure of its problems. The transition to independence was so untroubled that there was no occasion for the civil service to establish its authority as a "steel frame" of government, like its counterpart on the Indian subcontinent. Constant political interference and attack, the latter stemming at times from the refusal of ministers to accept responsibility for their actions, have reduced the effectiveness of the civil service and weakened its morale; allegations of corruption have lowered its standing. Whether this is viewed as fortunate or unfortunate, Ceylon lacks the conditions that would make a dictatorship possible. It has to remain a democracy, even though its functioning as such has not been very successful until now.

The most immediate cause of the communal unrest and violence that wracked the country after 1956 was the resistance of the Ceylon Tamils to the Singhala-only language policy of the S.L.F.P. governments. Bandaranaike had pledged himself to accept a "reasonable use of Tamil" in Tamil-speaking areas, and also the right of Tamils in other areas to correspond with the government in Tamil; Tamil officials already appointed would not be forced to adopt Singhala when carrying out their duties, and Tamil applicants for the public services would have the right to be examined in Tamil. But militant Singhalese and Buddhist extremists forced Bandaranaike to make this concession ever thinner in content. The protests of the Tamil community then escalated into communal rioting. Only after ugly disorders, and attempts to put down the insurgents by dictatorial measures, including the proscription of the Tamil Federal Party (F.P.) and the arrest of its leaders, did the legislature pass the Tamil Language Act; implementation of this law was, however, delayed and only partial. On January 1, 1961 all government administrative agencies switched from English to Singhala, though evidently with insufficient thoroughness, for the change-over subsequently had to be pushed more energetically.[1] The Tamil federalists continued to press for the recognition of Tamil as a regional language and the language of administrative officials in their areas. When the government refused, the Tamils again resorted to direct action, and were answered with another and longer bout

[1] The treasury threatened to withhold the salary increments of any civil servants who did not become proficient in Singhala. (*The Times* (London), October 20, 1962.) Feeling their prospects blighted, many Tamil civil servants left the administration.

of emergency rule. The government made no conciliatory gestures to allay the Tamils' fears that their social and economic position and culture generally were seriously menaced. In the prevailing political atmosphere, Singhalese extremists would have regarded any concessions as a betrayal of their interests.

As for the Indian Tamil laborers on the estates, the government's desire to repatriate them met with continued resistance from India. They were, in fact, Ceylon's only serious international problem. The U.N.P. government and Nehru had agreed that the Tamil laborers could not be compelled to leave Ceylon; India had undertaken to facilitate their registration as Indian citizens, but did nothing to implement this pledge. Neither country applied its citizenship laws liberally. Articulate Indians argued that the long residence of the Tamil laborers in Ceylon and their service to its economy entitled them to Ceylonese citizenship. The S.L.F.P. governments maintained that the country could not afford to keep them;[1] they were not "stateless," as India suggested, but Indian nationals. In the absence of agreement, Mrs. Bandaranaike decided to push ahead with the Ceylonization of employment outside the plantations, a policy that would threaten the jobs of some Tamil laborers and so compel them to apply for Indian citizenship. However, the recent "eviction" of Indians from Burma and India's need to counteract Chinese pressures by cultivating better relations with its smaller neighbors greatly improved Ceylon's bargaining power. Toward the end of 1964 the two countries came to terms. Over the next fifteen to twenty years, it seems, India will repatriate 525,000 Tamils and Ceylon will give civic status to 300,000. The future of the remaining 150,000 was left for further discussion the following year. Whether Singhalese laborers can replace the Tamil laborers without disrupting the plantation economy remains to be seen, but the period envisaged should be long enough for a planned substitution. As for the Tamils scheduled to become citizens, later pronouncements of Mrs. Bandaranaike made it appear doubtful that they would ever be accepted as equals in Ceylon.

Mrs. Bandaranaike also satisfied Singhalese nationalist fervor by organizing the state-aided religious schools under a consolidated national plan, despite opposition from Catholics, the denomination most affected. The government conceded, however, the right of religious minorities to run private schools which did not receive a public grant. The creation of such a state system of education is hardly a startling innovation and

[1] As Mrs. Bandaranaike later put it: "Ours is a small country and unemployment is very high. In a total population of about eleven millions it [the Indian Tamil problem] constitutes a great economic burden for us. We say India should take these people back. . . . With our own population increasing very rapidly, and the foreign exchange problem created by the need to import foods such as rice and sugar, we just cannot absorb these people in our economy." (*The Guardian*, Manchester, July 21, 1964.)

could be regarded as long overdue.[1] But in the context of Ceylon politics it was bound to be interpreted as part of the gathering attack on the privileged Westernized elite and their way of life. The protracted efforts of the government to bring the press under public control may also be attributed to a radical nationalist impulse, especially since the two leading newspaper groups have not supported the official language policy or the resurgence of Buddhism. Curiously enough, the Buddhists, who had been hostile to the press, are strenuously opposed to the government takeover, while the "Marxist" group Mrs. Bandaranaike brought into her cabinet in 1964 supports what it previously condemned. Such is the political confusion created when language and religion are exploited for political ends.

On the economic front things went in many respects from bad to worse. The economy had been plagued with wave after wave of strikes and slowdowns by organized labor. Political parties competed for the allegiance and control of trade unions and used them to intimidate the government. The port workers of Colombo, especially, were used to hold the government up for ransom. Not surprisingly, Colombo became notorious as a slow and congested port. Meanwhile, the terms of trade tended to worsen. Unwilling or unable for political reasons to cut welfare expenditures, including those designed to hold down the price of food – any attempt to cut the subsidized rice ration would invite political disturbances and electoral defeat – the government continued, in effect, to pump money into the economy. The resulting inflation drained away the country's external reserves. Hence the government had to apply increasingly stringent controls over imports. These controls were also used to drive non-Singhalese traders out of business.[2] In these circumstances a population increase of nearly 3 percent a year not only weighed heavily on Ceylon's economic resources; it also necessitated, because of built-in voting pressure, ever larger government expenditures on social welfare. In real terms, income per head probably did not rise much in the 1950's[3] and has been stagnating since then. The problem of finding jobs was becoming more acute. In terms of rice production per acre, Ceylon still ranks low as a food producer. Since domestic rice producers are also subsidized, the more successful the government is in increasing production, the greater will be the financial burden on the budget. There were few effective efforts to spur industrialization, in either the private or the public sector.[4] On the whole, industrial investment was neglected. The tax measures of the govern-

[1] Chapter 33, Section 1.

[2] Chapter 17, Sections 1 and 11; Chapter 19, Section 5.

[3] Chapter 11, Section 2.

[4] Chapter 17, Section 11.

ment, and the anti-foreign bias of its policies generally, discouraged investment from abroad and led to the sale of many foreign-owned estates and business enterprises.

Government policy-makers were mainly concerned with freeing the economy from the control of European and Indian business interests. Bandaranaike's election platform in 1956 had already contained a commitment to nationalize a wide range of activities. This program was now implemented to the extent that subsidized private schools, some types of banking, life insurance, transport, ports, and the import and distribution of oil were all taken under government jurisdiction. Apart from the small amount of industry that exists, the government failed to fulfill its pledge only with regard to the foreign-owned plantations. This was an all-important exception; taking these estates over would have involved nationalization on a scale unprecedented in South Asia. Although blowing hot and cold on the issue, the government was unwilling to risk the serious economic dislocation this might entail and, at the same time, unwilling to withdraw its statement of intent. This was probably the worst of all policies from the point of view of economic development.

Radical nationalism in Ceylon, although imbued with the vague socialism Bandaranaike professed, has been more concerned with jobs than with ideology. As in Burma and Indonesia, it is rooted in resentment against the exceptional economic role of alien minorities; it also reflects a mistrust of the elite who hold the best positions in business and government. Socialism in this context, as we shall later note,[1] provides an opportunistic rationalization for measures to oust these elements, or at least ensure a better distribution of the spoils. Ideological confusion is the inevitable result, the more so because of the absence not only of pomposity but also of seriousness about ideology in Ceylon. Unlike articulate Indians, the Ceylonese intelligentsia think it ridiculous to stress broad goals and ideals. Along with this attitude goes a lack of political responsibility. As the amazingly uninhibited parliamentary debates make plain, politics is pursued as a game — without restrictive rules — where arguments have their main value in winning a point or hurting an adversary. When one is disheartened by the Indian propensity toward double-thinking, a good antidote is to consider where an extreme of political cynicism has led Ceylon.

It is in this context that the absence of serious planning in Ceylon must be viewed. The idea that there should be planning was, of course, generally accepted, but it was mainly used to belabor opponents in the political game. In 1956 Bandaranaike had appointed a planning council that was placed outside of politics. When, in 1959, it presented a Ten Year

[1] Chapter 17, Sections 1 and 11.

Plan, this had high qualities as an intellectual exercise, but nobody took it seriously, least of all the government.[1] Ceylon's experience clearly demonstrated that, to be important for policy formation, planning efforts should be part of the political process and aimed at formulating a political program.[2] Furthermore, effective economic planning requires a strong and unified government, which up to now has been denied Ceylon. Policies have not been considered from a national point of view, but only in terms of how they will affect the interests of a particular group or community. An inability or unwillingness to plan on a national level was the price paid for, or a reflection of, the particularist form of nationalism that has imbued Ceylon's politics and absorbed the interests of its politicians. On the other hand, the lack of planning as an integral part of the process of government left the field free for antagonistic forces and produced shortsighted, haphazard, and expedient policies. The goals of political stability and national unity, which involve regularizing relations between the majority and minority communities within a system of representative government, seemed as far away as ever.

To recapture its lost drive and bolster its dwindling support, the ruling S.L.F.P. in 1964 once more invited a "Marxist" group into the government. Shortly thereafter the government lost a vote of confidence in the Lower House, the defeat being administered by a motley combination of all the parties in opposition, aided by a right-wing insurrectionist group from its own ranks.

4 *A Change in the Trend?*

The new elections in March, 1965, forced by the downfall of Mrs. Bandaranaike's government, brought the U.N.P. again into the position of being the strongest party in the Lower House. Its representation was increased from 30 to 66 members out of a total of 151, while the S.L.F.P. went down from 75 to 41. After effecting a coalition with the main Tamil party – the F.P., with 14 members – and some smaller parties, it formed a government under Dudley Senanayake and could then add 5 nominated members. This assured the government a secure majority as long as unity could be preserved within the leading U.N.P., including the affiliated rebels from the S.L.F.P., and with the F.P.

The new government immediately took some important and wholesome initiatives in non-controversial fields. Thus, for the first time in Ceylon's history, it made planning a serious business and established a new Ministry of Planning and Economic Affairs, to work under the Prime Minister. It

[1] *The Economist* (August 22, 1959, p. 549) observed that it was "cold-shouldered by the public at large, and unfavourably received by the intellectuals."

[2] Appendix 2, Section 15; Chapter 15, Section 7.

endorsed in unequivocal terms a population policy directed toward spreading birth control among the masses. In other respects the government took care not to manifest a break with established policies. In foreign policy it has adhered to non-alignment, though it has made this policy more balanced by moving away from the anti-Western tendency that had been growing under the previous government. No attempts have been made to reverse the steps that had been taken to nationalize foreign interests, but the new government has been somewhat more generous in giving compensation. The threat to nationalize foreign plantations was quietly but definitely shelved. In order to stabilize the economy and provide financing for the planned development expenditures, the government has exerted itself to restore more friendly relations not only with the World Bank and the International Monetary Fund, the United States and Britain, but with the Soviet Union as well. It has made no move, however, to curtail social welfare expenditures; in particular, the rice subsidies have been retained, though a curtailment of these in order to improve Ceylon's balance of payments is reported to have been a Western request, passed on by the Bank and the Fund. The government has made no move to undo its predecessor's policy of placing the private subsidized schools under state control, but has merely hinted at a more "flexible implementation." In regard to the Indian Tamils, the government has stated no other intention than to hold to the agreement with India reached by Mrs. Bandaranaike's government shortly before it fell; the F.P. has not shown any greater interest than before in the fate of the Indian Tamils, and can be counted on not to cause any difficulty by seeking more protection of their interests.

But on the communal language question an understanding between the U.N.P. and the F.P. must be reached in order to hold the two main coalition parties together; as yet, at the beginning of 1966, no definite solution seems to have been reached. In keeping with the government's careful avoidance of major departures from established policies, it has been declared that what is intended is nothing more nor less than the fulfillment of Bandaranaike's pledge in 1958, which he himself and, later, his wife had drifted away from. But there has been no legislative and administrative implementation of this declaration. Contradictory statements by U.N.P. and F.P. spokesmen in the legislature, the disinclination to make public the initial agreement between the two parties when the new government was formed, and rumors in the press of disagreements among the U.N.P. members of the government and also among the leaders of the Ceylonese Tamils inside and outside the government, have added to the confusion and tension. If the Senanayake government should fall, it will be mainly because of the inherited and intractable communal issues that center on the language question but also involve religion and, in particular, jobs. The F.P. would, perhaps, seem to be a powerless hostage in the government coalition, as the Tamil minority cannot possibly count on finding more understanding from the S.L.F.P. But as the Ceylon Tamils are also stirred up and have a tradition of direct action by communal rioting, there are limits to what the F.P.'s representative in the government and his party in the legislature can agree to. In the U.N.P. there are, on the other hand, many who are staunch Singhalese nationalists. The opposition, of course, uses this issue ruthlessly against the government, and there have been demonstrations, strikes, and riots.

Even if the coalition government would seem to have a secure majority in the national legislature and should be able to stay in power without elections until 1970, this assumes a unity within and between the two coalition parties that may not be able to outlast the onslaught from the opposition. The difficult foreign exchange situation and the rising cost of living give the opposition more basis for their propaganda. A new election could go heavily against the U.N.P.; during the last decade, the Ceylonese electorate has proven exceedingly volatile. Under these conditions it is too early to predict that the trend toward radical nationalism has turned in Ceylon.

II

Burma and Indonesia

5 *Southeast Asia Generally*

From the standpoint of national consolidation the countries of Southeast Asia, dealt with in this and the next part of this chapter, exhibit a wide variety of conditions and problems. Nevertheless, they have some features in common that set them apart from their neighbors to the west. First of all, their populations are much smaller than those of India or Pakistan, except for Indonesia, whose population is probably a little larger than Pakistan's. Their territories tend to be fairly compact, like India's, although Indonesia and the Philippines are fragmented into many islands of varying size. The region has not been free from boundary troubles,[1] but they have not as yet been so disruptive an influence in Southeast Asia as in India or Pakistan – aside, of course, from the raging conflict about the cold war frontier now dividing Vietnam.

Most of the countries of Southeast Asia are less poor than Pakistan and India, although the distinction is not marked in Burma's case. Levels of literacy are generally higher, and malnutrition, in the sense of insufficient

[1] Chapter 5, Sections 9–13.

caloric intake, is less common. Natural resources are more plentiful in the Southeast Asian region. People there have more elbow room; Java is crowded, but Indonesia has plenty of open space on its other islands, even though resettlement there of people from Java is expensive and can, at best, only proceed slowly. The population of Southeast Asia is increasing even more rapidly that of India and Pakistan.

In some of the particulars just enumerated the countries of Southeast Asia are more similar to Ceylon. Also, like Ceylon but unlike India and Pakistan, the Southeast Asian countries are ethnically divided. The Indians in Burma and the Chinese there and throughout the rest of this region constituted the principal foreign elements at the time of independence. Aside from the special position of these "Oriental aliens," inequalities in economic and social status are less blatant and unyielding than on the Indian subcontinent. Social structures are more egalitarian if only because, as in Ceylon, the existing inequalities are less firmly embedded in a caste system. It is commonly accepted that in Burma and Thailand there is a tradition of human equality without parallel on the Indian subcontinent, and much the same tradition is shared by the common people of Malaya, Indonesia, and the Philippines.

Unlike not only India and Pakistan but also Ceylon, the whole of Southeast Asia was over-run by the Japanese during the Second World War. The consequences were varied and complex. In general the Japanese occupation destroyed the political *status quo* and released suppressed or quiescent energies, particularly in countries such as Burma, the Netherlands Indies, and French Indo-China, where the participation of the indigenous intellectual elite in the processes of government had been least encouraged by colonial officials.[1] Only in Malaya and the Philippines, where special factors prevailed, did this interlude fail to give a direct and immediate impetus to a liberation movement – Thailand merely returned to its pre-war independent status, once the conquerors departed. In the former group of countries, the Japanese occupation evoked a pattern of anarchism, which gathered force when the Dutch and French attempted to reimpose their political control at the end of the war. Internal rebellions accompanied the arrival of independence in Burma and Indonesia, followed it in the Philippines, and delayed it in Malaya. With the dissolution of colonial rule most of the new states in Southeast Asia became involved in an all-engrossing and sometimes protracted struggle to establish their authority over their territorial inheritance. To a varying extent they also had to cope with the ravages of the war, a problem nonexistent in India, Pakistan, and Ceylon.

The fact that the initial situation of the Southeast Asian countries was quite different from that of India, Pakistan, and even Ceylon, has given a

[1] Chapter 4, Sections 8, 11, and 12.

distinctive framework to their political life since independence. Nevertheless, a useful distinction may be made between Burma and Indonesia, where the political trend has gone in a radical direction, and countries such as Malaya, Thailand, and the Philippines, where government policies have been cast in a more conservative mold. On this basis South Vietnam, under American tutelage, belongs with the latter group, but it is now so engulfed in internal and external strife and confusion as to defy clear analysis of its political development in these terms.

6 *National Consolidation in Burma and Indonesia*

As we saw in Chapter 4 (Sections 8 and 11), the ending of colonial rule in Burma and the Netherlands Indies was far from smooth and orderly. Burma was propelled into independence on the crest of revolutionary fervor; Indonesia won it after a prolonged and bitter struggle against the Dutch. Both countries had been exceptionally ill-prepared for political independence. The legacy of indigenous administrators left by the colonial regime was much poorer than in Ceylon, India, and even Pakistan. Burma and Indonesia were little better off when it came to experienced personnel in other fields. While in Ceylon colonial rule had resulted in the emergence of a substantial indigenous upper class of business and professional people as well as civil servants, in both Burma and Indonesia this upper class was largely composed of aliens. The Western-educated nationalists in both countries who took charge of the struggle for independence were too few in number to constitute a distinct layer of society.

Foreigners almost completely monopolized the modernized sectors of the Burmese economy. Western interests, particularly British, dominated the exploitation of Burma's mineral, oil, and forest resources and controlled the major portion of its foreign trade, internal transport, and banking; internal trade and the non-British segments of foreign trade and banking were largely in the hands of Indians and Chinese. Indian moneylenders had a significant stake in absentee land ownership; Indians staffed the middle and lower ranks of the public services and a few had filtered into the higher ranks. Indian coolies, who were willing to work for less than Burmese laborers, were employed at a variety of low-grade manual tasks. The *laissez-faire* economic policies of the British colonial government and its treatment of Burma as a backward province of India until 1937 largely explain why the territory became as much an Indian as a British colony. Not surprisingly, Burmese nationalism was directed against Indians as well as Britons and other Westerners; the Chinese were less disliked and, in fact, were regarded as somewhat distant "cousins." Nationalist sentiment was also directed against what there was of an elite in Burmese society, as this was largely alien. Much the same situation prevailed in the Netherlands Indies, where the Dutch, to a degree matched only by the French in Indo-China, particularly in Vietnam, dominated not only the modernized sectors of the economy but – together with Eurasians – virtually all save the very lowest posts in the public services. Chinese merchants, moneylenders, and small businessmen were the principal Asian alien element in the colony and dominated the quasi-modernized sectors of the economy.

The liberation movements in Burma and Indonesia lacked the organization, discipline, and collective leadership of that in India. Those involved never developed well thought-out programs for social and economic reform. Non-violence was of no consequence, either as a philosophy or as a tactic. In Burma the nationalists tended to concentrate on direct action; indeed, the frequency with which riots, revolts, and banditry threatened law and order suggests that the country had only been superficially pacified by the British. Dutch repression had driven the Indonesian nationalist struggle into conspiratorial channels, thereby making it especially difficult to form a united movement. Consequently, more than one center of resistance developed. In both countries, the Japanese occupation put a further premium on conspiracy at the same time that it strengthened the determination and ability of the nationalists to resist the return of the European colonial rulers. In both Burma and Indonesia uprisings broke out at various places simultaneously when the colonial powers finally departed. To sum up, the nature of the liberation struggle was such that the main political education of the nationalist leaders in both countries was in agitation, rebellion, and conspiracy rather than in the responsible exercise of power. Also, groups and areas acquired a habit of resisting central authority that has plagued the search for political stability ever since. Considering the record since independence, it is a wonder that both states have not completely disintegrated. To this day, neither state exercises effective control over the whole of its territory.

Much of the difficulty in establishing national unity is traceable to the way these countries had been governed as colonies. Burma had been conquered piecemeal, and in their comparatively short reign the British did not treat it as a unit. The hill peoples in the border regions were generally protected and controlled through their hereditary feudal rulers; many of them were considered "martial races" and their strongholds served as recruiting bases for the army, from which the Burmese were kept out. These more conservative elements, it should be added, had little in common with the young revolutionary Buddhist idealists who spearheaded the independence struggle. Dutch policy in the Netherlands Indies was designed to protect and preserve traditional regional cultures, which often meant, in political terms, that local centers of feudal power opposed to the Western-educated nationalists were undisturbed. In both countries, then, colonial rule militated against the formation of any national outlook. Indonesia's geographical fragmentation has facilitated and encouraged the continuation of separatist and particularist tendencies. Scattered over thousands of islands and over great distances, Indonesians have very little contact with one another. The practical political difficulties this fragmentation created were exemplified after the first and only general election in September, 1955, when it proved physically impossible to assemble the new legislature until the following March. Burma's geographical compactness made it a far more natural political entity.

Neither Burma nor Indonesia began its independent existence with any very strong unifying elements to offset the powerful centrifugal forces at work. Both enjoy a tradition of human equality that should facilitate the attainment of national consolidation. In each country there is one predominant religion – Buddhism in Burma and Islam in Indonesia. The spread of the Islamic faith in Indonesia is historically a rather recent development and among the Moslem majority there are wide regional variations in the strength of the religious attachment. Religion played a part in building up the nationalist movement in both countries, though more in Burma, but since independence its role has been ambiguous. The spread of a common language is probably a more positive unifying influence in both countries. In Burma, the necessity for making Burmese the official language of the state has generally been accepted. Indonesia has adopted a romanized and modernized form of basic Malay, called Bahasa Indonesia, as its official language, although it is still a long way from replacing various regional languages, particularly in the older generation. In neither case has the language question aroused the divisive passions it did in Ceylon or, for that matter, in India and Pakistan.[1]

Both countries preferred a unitary to a federal constitution. The Burmese constitution, which was drafted in 1947 with remarkable speed, gave statehood to the Shan, Kachin, Kaya, and Karen frontier regions and created a special administrative division for the Chin community. However, the governments of these districts were responsible to councils consisting of members of the Union Parliament from those regions and not to separate legislatures. Appearances notwithstanding, Burma created a unitary system. All the separate state governments have, in any case, been dependent on large subventions from the Union government. A federal constitution would appear more appropriate for Indonesia, but the fact that the Dutch, in contradiction to their pre-war policy, had sponsored a federal political framework as part of their campaign to destroy the emerging republic was a sufficient reason for Sukarno to prefer a unitary state. It may be added that a federal constitution would have required many more trained administrators and capable politicians than a unitary state that pooled these scarce talents at the center. Both countries started

[1] Chapter 3, Section 3.

out with a cabinet system of parliamentary government, founded on universal suffrage, and with a president as the ceremonial head of state.

7 *The First "Democratic" Phase*

Burma began its parliamentary experience with a single ruling group, the Anti-Fascist People's Freedom League (A.F.P.F.L.), which was a loose national federation, under the leadership of the Buddhist ex-university students who had negotiated the final transfer of power. A socialist wing provided its official ideology. Owing to widespread disorders, the first general election was postponed until 1951. The A.F.P.F.L. won an overwhelming victory then and retained a very comfortable parliamentary majority in the next election five years later. During the first decade of independence, no serious parliamentary opposition that could provide the nucleus of an alternative government emerged. Thus the party caucus and not the Union Parliament was the real locus of power.

The A.F.P.F.L. was by no means a well-organized and disciplined political machine. For over a decade it did not even attempt to frame a constitution for itself. It never developed any grass roots support. It claimed to be the voice of national unity and treated all opposition as trifling, yet it itself became riddled by personal rivalries and finally split in 1958 into two factions, the "stable" and the "clean." When U Nu, who had been the country's premier for most of the period since independence, decided to accept Communist support for his "clean" faction, the reaction was so violent as to persuade him to abdicate in favor of a caretaker, army-imposed government. The parliamentary regime had been discredited, moreover, by the inefficiency and corruption pervading public life; the prevalence of corruption was a constant theme of U Nu's public utterances.[1] The failure to heal the rifts between the border regions and the center was another black mark against it. The Shans, Karens, Chins, Arakanese, and Mons feared and resented the domination of the Burmese and their "master race" attitude. In addition, these hill peoples, who were politically conservative, opposed the socialist ideology of the ruling class. All this nourished separatist feelings, which in the case of the Karens, gave birth to a prolonged rebellion against the central government. Communist insurrection also plagued the government, but those rebels who called themselves Communists were more radically inclined;

[1] "I have to admit with shame," he declared in 1952, "that I am painfully aware of the prevalence of corruption, like mushrooms, around politicians, government servants and business men. But although we may know these things, we cannot take action when actual proof is lacking. We can but look on with folded hands. . . . Unless the guilty persons overcome their greed, the Union of Burma will go to rack and ruin." (Quoted in Hugh Tinker, *The Union of Burma*, Oxford University Press, London, 1959, p. 86, f.n. 3.)

basically, they were radical nationalists – when they were not simply gangs of bandits – and seem to have had no formal relationship with the Communists in China or the Soviet Union.

Despite the poor showing that had been made by representative democracy in Burma, the army stepped down from power in 1960 and gave parliamentary government another chance. In fresh elections, the U Nu faction of the old A.F.P.F.L., which now called itself the Union League, won a convincing victory. After a short bout of army reform and discipline, the electors evidently favored a return to soft government, however inefficient and corrupt.[1] The experiment, however, was not a success. In 1961, the government of U Nu decided to make Buddhism the official state religion, though without denying other religions the freedom guaranteed by the constitution. Although this merely affirmed a viewpoint established in the pre-independence days of the nationalist movement, the hill peoples, many of whom were Christians or Moslems, feared this policy would lead to discrimination against them in the competition for government jobs; they also saw it as a demonstration of Burmese domination. Consequently, it incited disaffection and worsened the problem of internal security. At the same time the government's promise to create constituent states for the Arakanese and Mons gave a fresh impetus to particularist tendencies in the body politic. Furthermore, the new cabinet was neither united nor loyal; corrupt practices sprouted weed-like into public prominence, and regional disaffection, especially among the Shans, once more threatened the security of the state. Consequently, the army decided in 1962 to stage an outright coup and abolish parliamentary government altogether. We shall examine in the next section the special character and role of the Burmese army.

Parliamentary government also collapsed in Indonesia, but the process and the outcome were different. For reasons indicated earlier, no umbrella-type political organization like the A.F.P.F.L., much less one as unified and efficient as the Congress in India, emerged from the struggle for independence. The Indonesian governments were based on stopgap coalitions of the most important of a multitude of parties. The Masjumi Party was the largest organized Moslem group, and derived its principal support from the more prosperous rural elements in the outlying islands and Western Java. Although modernist to a degree, it became noticeably more conservative as the influence of the main radical groupings rose. The

[1] "At almost every level of society army rule proved that the Burmese people were not prepared to make heavy demands upon themselves in order merely to improve their land and strengthen their country." (Lucian W. Pye, "The Army in Burmese Politics," in John J. Johnson, ed., *The Role of the Military in Underdeveloped Countries*, Princeton University Press, Princeton, 1962, p. 247.)

Nahdatul Ulema Party was an orthodox Moslem party. The Indonesian Nationalist Party was more secularist; it professed a syncretism founded on the Pantja Sila principles of nationalism, humanism, democracy, social justice, and belief in God, which Sukarno first enunciated in 1945, and which were incorporated in the preamble of the provisional constitution drawn up for the newly proclaimed Republic of Indonesia at the end of the Japanese occupation. The prestige and appeal of this party originated from its part in the successful fight against the Dutch and its association with Achmed Sukarno. In time it became closely linked with the bureaucratic governing elite, the large landowners, and the groups that benefitted most by the takeover of foreign-owned enterprises. It had no strong roots outside Java. The third main political grouping and by far the best organized and disciplined was the Indonesian Communist Party. After an abortive revolt against the emerging republic in 1948, it regained its political prominence and public appeal by identifying itself closely with Sukarno's radical nationalism. But for this reason, and because Java was its political stronghold, it competed directly for popular support with the Nationalist Party. Among the smaller parties was a dwindling Socialist Party, which was mainly supported by intellectuals and never achieved a real mass following.

Without collective cabinet responsibility for major policy directives, government proved grossly ineffective and unstable. There were six cabinets between 1945 and 1948, seven between 1949 and 1957. General elections were not held until 1955, a delay that gave the parties little incentive to identify themselves as the proponents of clear-cut programs rather than as instruments of personal power and ambition. The elections did not put an end to unstable and irresolute government through party coalition. The major parties were deeply divided internally and were subject to all manner of extra-parliamentary pressure. Corruption, graft, and fraud on a colossal scale were conspicuous features of public life.

The most serious challenge to Indonesia's existence as a political entity arose, however, from a succession of revolts in the outlying islands against the highly centralized government in Djakarta on Java. Fears of Javanese domination were nourished by a conservative distrust of the radical ideological pressure exerted by the mainly Javanese-based Nationalist and Communist Parties. The inhabitants of the outer islands felt that they were not getting their due share of development projects and funds, though they earned the bulk of the country's foreign exchange. Most foreign exchange earnings were, in fact, spent on Java's imports and the principal beneficiaries were backers of the Nationalist Party and the army. These remote populations also resented the corruption and incompetence of the central government. The failure of parliamentary democracy to avert national disintegration eventually persuaded Sukarno, or gave him a pretext, to attack its substance and then, in 1959, with the all-important backing of the army, to abolish it altogether. Democratically elected government had lasted only four years in Indonesia.

Not surprisingly, the Burmese and Indonesian economies were adversely affected by the turbulent and erratic course of national politics. To the severe war damage they had sustained was added the dislocation caused by the forced departure of the alien administrators and capitalists who had dominated their modernized sectors – a movement that was slower and less systematic in Indonesia than in Burma.[1] In Indonesia, monetary mismanagement and inflation, by widening the gap between the official and the black market rate of exchange, put a premium on illicit direct trading and smuggling between the outer islands and Malaya, Singapore, and the Philippines and worsened the country's foreign exchange position. The rebellions that broke out in Sumatra, Kalimantan (Borneo), and Sulawesi (Celebes) during the 1950's aggravated the economic difficulties of the central government in Java. The Burmese economy was also plagued by mismanagement and insurrections.

Planning was taken seriously in Burma from the outset and, indeed, was prescribed in the constitution. The U Nu government commissioned American consultants to formulate a comprehensive plan of rehabilitation and development. The result was published in 1953. This was not a particularly well-constructed plan, and it depended heavily on optimistic assumptions about rice export earnings, which were not fulfilled. Insufficient allowance was made for the lack of stable and effective government and the shortage of indigenous managers and technicians. The government showed little willingness or ability to implement a plan. Most of the few new industrial development projects that were actually undertaken were concentrated around Rangoon because of the lack of security upcountry, the high costs of inland transport, and the biases of Burmese politicians. Shortly before the beginning of the first period of army rule in 1958, U Nu admitted that the country was floundering in a morass of uncoordinated and ill-conceived schemes. Soon afterwards all attempts at serious economic planning were virtually abandoned. Output stubbornly remained below pre-war levels. No major changes – of either an institutional or a technical nature – had been induced in agriculture. There was no determined and sustained attempt at planning in Indonesia during this first phase, although the West, particularly the United States, urged that this be done and offered its assistance.[2] It should be added that from the

[1] See Section 9 for an elaboration of this point.

[2] A somewhat closer view of the development of economic policy in Burma and Indonesia will be given in Chapter 17, Sections 12 and 13.

beginning Indonesia has been more ardent and successful than other South Asian countries in promoting educational reform.[1]

8 *The Second "Dictatorial" Phase*

The Burmese and Indonesian armies played a crucial role in the collapse of parliamentary government, and they continued thereafter to exert a major influence on the conduct of public affairs. Their antecedents and character thus deserve attention. In neither case was the army an inherited professional corps as in Pakistan and India. Nor was it fashioned by a monolithic independence movement. It was molded, instead, out of the armed bands that emerged in the struggle for independence. Nevertheless, Burma succeeded in evolving an efficient, disciplined, and remarkably professional officer corps. The role that it came to play in the nation's affairs is without parallel in South Asia. The social and educational background of the senior Burmese officers was very similar to that of many of the leading politicians. Nonetheless, they succeeded in isolating themselves from politics by concentrating on their military tasks; for a long time they accepted a non-political role under civilian direction. They were, it is true, a privileged group and they enjoyed conspicuously higher living standards than any other group dependent on incomes from public funds. Yet, when they eventually seized power, they tried to formulate a policy in the national interests of Burma without regard to the interests of the upper class of landlords, businessmen, and officials to which they belonged or were closely related. Whatever faults they have demonstrated in policy formation, they are not those of exploiting power for selfish purposes.

By contrast, the Indonesian army has always been deeply involved in partisan politics. Unlike the Burmese army, it was never placed under firm central military command, much less civilian direction. Many army commanders regarded their units as instruments of personal power. They tended to live off the land and to enrich themselves by participating in illicit export and import deals and other foreign exchange manipulations. The espousal of regional rebellions by some of them was a form of "warlordism." It was largely because regional disaffection had the support of local army commanders that centers of independent political power frequently arose to defy the central government. Dissension in the officer corps prohibited the army from seizing control of the state, as in Burma, even when the politicians made patent their inability to govern effectively. At the same time, the army was the only instrument for enforcing national

[1] Chapter 32, particularly Sections 3 and 4; and Chapter 33.

policy in the outer islands and its support was obviously necessary to Sukarno when he resolved to impose "guided democracy" on the nation. Although it became an integral part of the government structure, many of its officers proved to be as corrupt and inefficient as the civilian administrators. The officer corps, no less than other elite groups, sought the spoils of power and acquired a relatively high living standard. The army certainly offered no hope for a more development-minded government in Indonesia. If it was opposed to a Communist takeover, this was as much because the Communists were a threat to the privileged position of the officer corps as because of any ideological antipathy. In short, it is difficult to disagree with the following judgment:

> Being involved in, rather than detached from, current politics, the military acquired the habit of settling for small gains, individual rewards or, at best, tactical objectives. Thus they have failed . . . to close ranks and use their collective strength to create a strong and efficient government. Under these circumstances, moral deterioration and material corruption have set in.[1]

The Burmese army first took over the government in 1958, ostensibly at the behest of the ruling premier, U Nu, and with the overwhelming approval of Parliament. Without giving much thought to a formal development plan, it saw the establishment of orderly government as its first duty. It demonstrated during this first period a regard for honest dealing and an ability to get things done. Among other accomplishments, the military government brought about greater internal security, cleaned up Rangoon, curbed the activities of hoarders and black-marketeers, stabilized the cost of living, increased exports and foreign exchange reserves, and successfully negotiated a border agreement with China.[2] Having thus given the country its most efficient government since independence, the army confounded the experts by abdicating in favor of a parliamentary regime; this is said to have been army commander Ne Win's personal decision, taken against the will of many of the younger officers who had actually been running the various branches of the government. Only when the politicians again demonstrated their incapacity to avert national disintegration did the army stage an outright coup, in March, 1962. Ministers were arrested, Parliament was abolished, and all political parties and trade unions were banned. All the old-guard politicians who had taken over the reins of power at independence were removed from the national scene; many of them, including U Nu, are still imprisoned or confined to country residences. In place of the old parties the army founded a national front, a single Burma Socialist Program Party, to express the united will of the nation. The army has interpreted this to mean

[1] Guy J. Pauker, "The Role of the Military in Indonesia," in Johnson, ed., *The Role of the Military*, p. 201.

[2] Chapter 5, Section 9.

an uncompromising extension of radical nationalism – a point to which we shall return in the next section.

The vast authority Sukarno assumed after 1959, when he abolished democracy as it is commonly understood, was rationalized under the slogan of "guided democracy." According to Sukarno the latter revives the best traditions of Indonesian village rule, which through its emphasis on mutual assistance, discussion, and general agreement is held to have exemplified the people's natural genius for harmonious cooperation. In practice "guided democracy" on the national level meant replacing a democratically elected parliament with an appointed assembly to advise the President. This assembly consisted of representatives of organized functional groups, such as workers, peasants, businessmen, women, veterans, youth, the armed forces, and religious devotees, together with "acceptable" political parties. The cabinet was replaced by a National Advisory Council and ministers were appointed by and responsible to the President alone. The whole scheme really amounted to an attempt to govern through a national front, which was sometimes called NASAKOM (nationalist, religious, and Communist).[1] Sukarno argued that his "guided democracy" offered the only hope of eliminating the debilitating and destructive consequences of a Western-type party system. To this end, the press and educational and religious institutions have increasingly been "guided," if not coerced, by official directives on the true nature of the "Indonesian revolution." The Masjumi and Socialist Parties, which had stood up for the supremacy of the elected parliament during the "democratic" phase, were banned altogether since some of their leaders had been implicated in the rebellion that led to the organization of a rival provisional government in central Sumatra in 1958.

"Guided democracy" failed to give more direction to economic policy in Indonesia. The output of all the traditional plantation crops stayed below pre-war levels. Mismanagement continued to impair the productive capacity of processing plants, transport facilities, and public utilities. Persistent monetary inflation, smuggling, and rebellions drained the country's central exchange reserves. The currency was devalued from time to time, but the black market price of foreign currency continued to rise. The efforts at planning were not impressive. In 1960 the Indonesian

[1] Sukarno's concept has been officially and more grandiloquently expressed as follows: "'Guided-Democracy' is the democracy of the family system, without the anarchy of liberalism, without the autocracy of dictatorship. It is the concept of life, the ideals of the 1945 Revolution, which animates our activities, and to this we must direct and subordinate all layers of our national life. Guided Democracy emphasises that every individual has the obligation to serve the public interest, to serve society, to serve the nation, to serve the state and also that every individual has the right to a proper living within that society, nation and state." (*Manipol-Usdek in Question and Answer,* Department of Information, Republic of Indonesia, Special Release 84, Jakarta, January, 1961, p. 39.)

National Development Council, set up the previous year, produced a bulky and diffuse Eight Year Plan. Although the revenues available to the government were grossly overestimated, the plan did not set up goals that would imply real economic growth. At best the plan amounted to a shopping list of uncoordinated projects; that these would be completed in an orderly and effective way seemed improbable from the outset, particularly as there was no improvement in the administration. As General Nasution, Minister of Defense and Security, admitted, corruption in the management of state enterprises reached "fantastic proportions."[1] A not very far-reaching land reform act was passed in 1960, but delays and evasions, in which officials connived, made it largely ineffective.

In preparation for the campaign to acquire West Irian, military expenditures were allowed to skyrocket. Even though much of the hardware had been provided on easy credit terms by the Soviet Union – and some had been sent as "aid" by the United States – the call to arms put an extraordinary financial burden on the country and left little room for development efforts. The later "confrontation" with the Federation of Malaysia suggested that a major portion of Indonesia's economic resources would be devoted to military purposes for some time to come.[2] The banning of trade with the federation hurt Indonesia's two chief exports, rubber and oil,[3] even though Indonesian leaders hailed it as a blessing in disguise. Urban living standards almost certainly deteriorated for all but a few privileged groups. Over large areas of central and east Java, people were reportedly badly fed, though at nothing like the near-starvation level familiar in many areas on the Indian subcontinent. Outside of Java the peasants continued to be largely unaffected by the economic and financial mismanagement at the center.

In Burma the military dictatorship did not lead to a decisive upturn in economic activity. The Ne Win government concentrated on suppressing the rebellions, overhauling the administration, and pursuing a policy of nationalizing what was left of alien influence over the economy. So far, the negotiations with rebellious groups have not led to their complete surrender, and still less to their integration in the national front. Driving out the foreigners will not, by itself, raise the level of economic activity; judging by the budget for 1964–65 the gross national product decreased as a result of the nationalization drive. Now that the anti-foreign drive is coming to its logical end, it remains to be seen whether the Ne Win regime will stay united and incorrupt, and whether, in the intellectual vacuum

[1] *The Times* (London), March 17, 1964.

[2] Chapter 5, Section 12.

[3] Traditionally, about 80 percent of the rubber from Indonesian smallholders, or about two-thirds of Indonesia's total rubber exports, went to Singapore for processing. Malaya and Singapore bought nearly two-thirds of Indonesia's refined petroleum products.

it has created, it can frame and implement a program for economic development and national consolidation. As there is very little discussion in Burma – politicians, trade unionists, independent journalists, student leaders, and other articulate persons have been silenced – and as the government is not very forthcoming, it is not possible to foresee what the future may hold. At the beginning of 1966 it would seem, however, that from a political point of view and without looking too far ahead, Burma has one of the most stable regimes in South Asia. Indonesia, in contrast, has been in violent upheaval for several months (Section 10).

9 *The Drift Toward Nationalistic Radicalism*

Both Burma and Indonesia had started out with a commitment to socialism,[1] but a socialism that was expressed in very vague and confused terms. This was due in part to the relative scarcity of intellectuals capable of articulating and developing the socialist ideology, and in part to efforts made to incorporate religious beliefs. But it also reflected the fact that socialism was given such a strongly nationalist accent that the broader issue of the organization of the economy escaped close attention. The nationalist direction of the aspirations in both countries was explainable, and to an extent justifiable, not only by the political subjugation they had endured – both countries entered the era of independence in a mood strongly antipathetic to everything associated with colonial rule – but also by the fact that almost all of their productive capacity outside of peasant agriculture had long been controlled by aliens. The small but growing indigenous elite resented being excluded from the most rewarding positions in their own countries; they also tended to blame foreign interests for the fact that the living standards of the masses deteriorated in colonial days and failed to rise once independence had been achieved. On a more practical level, it is difficult to see how Burma, especially, could have framed any plans for its future economic development without first bringing the large foreign-owned enterprises in the country under government direction.[2]

Immediately upon the advent of independence, Burma dismissed all non-Burmese officials. It also started out with the avowed objective of taking over all the large and powerful foreign-owned enterprises within its territory. A basic difficulty in making an economic success of this nationalization policy, and in pushing ahead with the industrialization projects outlined in its plans, was the extreme scarcity not only of civil servants but also of managerial and technical personnel. The government was

[1] Much of the content of this section will be developed further in Chapter 17, Sections 12 and 13.

[2] Chapter 17, Section 12.

forced to experiment with "joint ventures," but their results were not impressive. Faced with the general failure of planning and with widespread corruption and mismanagement in state enterprises and the administrative services of the government, U Nu in the late 1950's was forced to retreat from his initially radical program and come out in favor of private enterprise. Even land reform measures and other attempts to improve the indigenous sectors of the economy were stripped of their effectiveness.

The first period of army rule in 1960–61 did not bring any fundamental change in policy, but only an attempt to make the administration more effective. When in 1962 the army took over the reins more definitely, it marked time for a year or so and then – reportedly after some internal struggle – issued a radical policy statement that inaugurated a sweeping extension of state enterprise.[1] Entitled "The Burmese Way to Socialism," it employs Communist terminology and is quite devoid of the religious and spiritual overtones of the various definitions of Burmese socialism during U Nu's regime. It is clear that the policy of nationalizing such productive assets as the rice mills, the oil industry, the banks, all trade in principal commodities, including rice, and gradually all retail trade, is aimed at the foreigners in Burma and at the Indians in particular. In this respect the military regime is following and sharpening policy lines that evolved in the first years of the earlier regime. First excluded from the public services and then dispossessed of their landholdings, the Indians who remained in commerce were now driven out of their businesses and back to India by the action of the Ne Win regime.[2] There has been no sign of a similarly radical will to reorganize and improve agriculture and crafts, from which by far the larger part of the indigenous population derive their livelihood. With the nationalization measures went an increasingly hostile attitude toward all foreign contacts, even those which brought with them offers of assistance. In international affairs, Burma may be said to have withdrawn into its own peculiar type of isolationism.

The socialism of the Indonesian articulate elite – vague and confused to start with – did not gain in clarity in the second phase of "guided democracy." While the army regime in Burma cloaked its aims in "Marxist" terminology, the Indonesian leaders, especially Sukarno, increasingly associated their socialism with national traditions and, less emphatically,

[1] This manifesto is quoted in Chapter 17, Section 12.

[2] "The expropriation of small traders, predominantly Indian, fits into a long tradition of anti-Indian feeling. Only the most humanitarian of middle-class Burmese feel regret at the pitiful exodus of poor Indians now jamming the harbour and airport at Rangoon. The emigrants, almost literally robbed at source by punitive regulations, are often further fleeced by customs officials. So far, the government of India has restricted itself to restrained protests." (*The Economist*, September 5, 1964.)

with the Islamic religion.[1] The result, which is supposed to denote the true nature and aims of the "Indonesian Revolution," is merely a hodgepodge of borrowed slogans that can be invoked to justify all manner of opportunistic policies. Like U Nu in an earlier epoch of Burmese history,[2] Sukarno appeared to be convinced he could blend all philosophies, from Mohammedanism through Jeffersonian democracy to Marxism. He has described the Indonesian revolution as "greater than the American or Russian revolutions, which were only political."[3] He has also confessed to being a romantic revolutionary.[4] By stoking the fires of an emotional nationalism he attempted to hold together a badly integrated nation; he claimed to personify Indonesia's unity, which in a sense he did. But nationalistic declamations cannot of themselves create a well-reasoned and feasible program for economic development, and neither did they prove to be an effective means for making a reality of Indonesian nationhood.

Even more than the Burmese, the Indonesians felt that the revolution that won political independence would not be complete until they had made a "national economy" out of their "colonial economy." The place of political parties along the political spectrum was partly determined by their views on the speed and manner in which the process should be car-

[1] The rival political parties that existed during the parliamentary phase of the country's political development were far from agreed on the extent to which the new state should be guided by Islamic principles and, indeed, on what those principles were. Sukarno has been reluctant to base the Indonesian state too firmly on religion lest this provoke the non-Moslem communities into secession.

[2] See Chapter 17, Section 1, particularly p. 800, footnote 1.

[3] *The Observer*, London, September 22, 1963.

In a speech on the fifteenth anniversary of the day when the Republic of Indonesia was proclaimed, Sukarno declared:

"The Declaration of Independence does not contain social justice and socialism. The Communist Manifesto needs an element of the sublime from Belief in God the Almighty. Both of those documents are very progressive for their period. Now we are in the second half of the 20th Century. It is the reality that with those two alone, the world of man has been split into two blocs.

"That is why the Indonesian people are proud to have Pantja Sila, and recommend it to all nations. It is a universal basis, that can be used by all nations, and a basis that can guarantee the welfare, peace and brotherhood of the world." (*Indonesian News and Economic Bulletin,* Indonesian Embassy Information Department, Stockholm, October 28, 1960.)

[4] "I tell you frankly, I belong to that group of people who are bound in spiritual longing by the romanticism of revolution. I am inspired by it. I am fascinated by it. I am completely absorbed by it. I am crazed, I am obsessed by the romanticism of revolution. . . . That is why I, who have been given the topmost leadership in the struggle of the Indonesian nation, never tire of appealing and exhorting: solve our national problems in a revolutionary way, make the revolutionary spirit surge on, see to it that the fire of our revolution does not die, or grow dim, not even for a single moment. Come then, keep fanning the flames of the leaping fire of revolution! Brothers and sisters, let us become logs to feed the flames of revolution!" (Quoted in Benjamin and Jean Higgins, *Indonesia, the Crisis of the Millstones,* Van Nostrand, Princeton, 1963, p. 115.)

ried out. Yet the ouster of Dutch officials and the wholesale nationalization of Dutch property was an expression of political pique over Holland's refusal to give up West Irian; it was not a calculated move toward a well-defined objective. Similarly, British and then American properties were seized as a mark of Indonesia's dislike of British and American support for the Federation of Malaysia and American policy in Vietnam. The measures directed against the Chinese community, on the other hand, were less fortuitously determined. The Chinese had suffered ill treatment from both sides in the nationalists' war against the Dutch. Their loyalty to the new state was felt to be in doubt, especially since only about a third of them had accepted Indonesian citizenship by the mid-1950's. To the dislike that stemmed from their reputation as rapacious traders and moneylenders was added antipathy arising from their traditional social exclusiveness. Nor did it assuage nationalist feelings that many Chinese looked to China to safeguard their basic interests. China did, in fact, protest when, in 1960, the Sukarno regime banned Chinese merchants and moneylenders from Indonesia's rural areas. Its intercession in their behalf put the Indonesian Communist Party in the politically embarrassing position of having to espouse an unpopular cause. At various other times the Indonesian government also closed down Chinese schools, imposed discriminatory taxes on the Chinese, and took over their business enterprises.

The governing elite sought to redistribute wealth and income at the expense of foreigners. This policy was strongly associated with the feeling that an end of the colonial drain on the country's wealth would usher in a period of unprecedented prosperity. However, the expropriation of foreign income transfers is a once and for all process, and the mismanagement of the enterprises taken over suggests that Indonesia has to some extent been living off accumulated capital. Too often, the attempt to open up opportunities hitherto monopolized by foreigners merely bred a new class of parasitic businessmen or swelled the ranks of incompetent and corrupt bureaucrats. The officer class benefitted, as did the landlord class, but it is not evident that the masses in Indonesia derived any profit from the nationalizations.

10 *Turmoil in Indonesia*

Indonesia's foreign trade and exchange balances have been deteriorating further in recent years, and in 1965 the outlook was worse than ever, partly because the foreign exchange claims for servicing Indonesia's foreign debts were increasing, while foreign "aid" failed to increase.[1] Inflation was be-

[1] See *Bulletin of Indonesian Economic Studies,* Department of Economics, Research School of Pacific Studies, Australian National University, Canberra, No. 1, June, 1965, pp. 2–4, and No. 2, September 1965, pp. 1–5.

coming rampant. The official cost of living index rose by 50 percent from January to August, 1965. Most of this rise occurred in the last two months, July and August, and was especially apparent in the price of the staple food, rice; in September the trend gathered momentum. This stupendous rise in prices implied hardship for the masses of people but opened easy roads to riches for a top layer of officials and private businessmen.

As the title of his 1965 Proclamation Day (August 17) speech, Sukarno chose "Reach to the Stars – A Year of Self-Reliance,"[1] and he used the occasion to issue warnings, not only to foreign imperialists, but also to internal enemies:

> We possess all the requirements needed to solve the 'food and clothing' problem. Those who interfere with the solution of this problem should be brought before the Court of Justice of the People and of History. We have rich national resources, our People are industrious, but so far, the fruits of their labour have been devoured by the landlords, the brokers, money-lenders, the 'idjon' brokers, and the other 'village devils.' I have given enough opportunity to those who doubt the Revolution to adjust themselves; I have been very patient, I have displayed the patience of a father, but there is a limit to my patience, still more, to the patience of the people! I have given sufficient opportunity to implement land reform; I even postponed the time limit, and if necessary I am willing to extend it yet another year; I have been very patient, I have displayed the patience of a father, but, I repeat, there is a limit to my patience, still more to the patience of the People!

This was a rather serious indictment of the results to date of his "Indonesian Revolution," the harshness of which was hardly mitigated by Sukarno's defense and praise of such "prestige projects" as the National Monument, whose eternal flame had been lighted the night before.

At the political level, Sukarno had, in the phase of "guided democracy," been performing a balancing act between the opposing pressures of the army and the large and well-organized Communist Party (P.K.I.). The latter had closely identified itself with his branch of radical nationalism, but not without some loss of ideological identity. For if the "class struggle" is subordinated to nationalist policies, what, then, is the distinctive ideological character of the Communists in Indonesia? To reap political advantage from the deteriorating living levels of the masses, the party would have to propose far more radical solutions to national economic problems than Sukarno has offered.[2] And it could be assumed that the army – or the larger part of it – would resist them.

In the years immediately preceding the events that were to rapidly

[1] *Ibid.*, September, 1965, pp. 1 and 64–67. Sukarno announced the year's slogan to be "standing on one's own feet"; the preceding year it was "a year of living dangerously."

[2] In central Java, where the P.K.I. is particularly powerful, the party had, in fact, already in 1964 organized "unilateral actions" by peasants to implement the land reform legislation in defiance of the local authorities.

transform the P.K.I. from a major government party into a hunted opposition, the party had continually strengthened its power positions, apparently with Sukarno's support. It gained increasing representation in the cabinet, in the several appointed advisory bodies, and even in the bureaucracy. It used pressures to gain dominance over other parties and to immobilize persons and parties that resisted. By the same tactics it increased its influence over the press and over civic, professional, and trade organizations; even some of the younger officers in the army seemed to be won for the party, or at least for a "leftist" outlook. This advance of the P.K.I.'s power positions in the Indonesian body politic was undoubtedly related to the increasingly anti-Western policy line of the government and its orientation toward closer cooperation with China. In the spring and summer of 1965, the P.K.I. had been pressing ever harder to "arm the people" by organizing civilian militias and distributing weapons to them. Sukarno had announced that he was considering the matter.

On September 30 a junior army officer, Lieutenant-Colonel Untung, launched a coup; six high-ranking, conservative army officers were killed, but General Nasution, the most prestigious man in the army and Sukarno's defense minister, escaped. Much still remains in doubt about the objectives of the coup, who planned it, and who took part in the conspiracy. In particular, it is still an unsettled question whether the P.K.I., or a faction of that party, were the instigators; it has even been suggested that Sukarno had been informed about it. What truth there is to the allegation of a "generals' plot," aimed at taking over the power in Indonesia, also remains to be established. All three allegations might be true or less than true. In any case, the coup was rapidly beaten down by loyal army units, and this outcome set off a violent storm, directed at the liquidation of the P.K.I. and, indeed, the Communists; another target for persecution was the Chinese minority. The victims have been reckoned in the hundreds of thousands.[1] Apart from the war in Vietnam, this has been the cruelest and most massive butchery since the partition of imperial India. The cool reporting of it in the Western press as a welcome major setback for the Communists, and for China, illustrates the lowering of moral standards that has followed in the wake of the two World Wars and the cold war – and, naturally, also the lower degree of compassion felt when the sufferers are others than white Western people.[2]

[1] "Estimates of the number of killings since October range from 87,000 – officially admitted by the president – to gossip of 350,000. . . . Army sources estimate the deaths at between 185,000 and 250,000. In the East Java district of Malan a welfare organisation has already registered 400,000 children orphaned since October." ("The Army Waits Through a Cruel Winter," *The Economist,* January 29, 1966, p. 398.) There have been even higher estimates of the number killed.

[2] In character, this reaction in the West is not different from the equanimity of most Germans under Nazism, when Hitler set out to liquidate all potential sources of

The killings were carried out, organized, or indulged in by the army; also active in the persecutions were mobs of Moslems. Only in a few areas, mostly in central and eastern Java, could the Communists put up armed resistance. A total reorganization of the power structure in Indonesia was taking place. The Moslem parties and organizations to the right, which had been banned, and the rightist leaders in the other parties, who had been immobilized, reappeared and drove out those Communist sympathizers who did not now find it opportune, or were not given a chance, to follow along in the general drift. The press, the mass media, and the professional and trade organizations were reorganized and redirected, through army regulation and continued pressure from the army and the Moslem "Action Body." Under this onslaught, the whole laboriously constructed Communist power structure crumbled like a house of cards. The P.K.I.'s large mass following proved valueless, as they had few weapons. Sukarno continued in his position as President, but could not stand up against the army and the course of events.

Meanwhile, the Indonesian economy, already near bankruptcy, was utterly destroyed. Food became very scarce in the urban areas; prices skyrocketed, industries were at a standstill, and unemployment mounted; much of the agricultural land was deserted. In mid-December the rupiah was devalued to one-thousandth of its previous value, and rice was placed under price controls. But these and other policy measures were symptoms, not remedies, of the grave economic crisis. When speculating on why the army left Sukarno in office and did not take over the formal trappings of military dictatorship, Western experts have not only referred to his continued, though waning, popularity among the masses, but have also wondered whether it is not in the army's interest to avoid as long as possible shouldering responsibility for doing something about the desperate economic situation and the sufferings caused by it. So far as can be judged from outside, no reports exist of constructive ideas as to how to deal with the aggravated economic crisis, which has worsened from week to week. The new forces emerging in Indonesia are all marching under the banner of the "Indonesian Revolution," and have even adhered to Sukarno's latest slogan of "standing on one's own feet." It is also difficult to see from what source foreign assistance could come in substantial amounts, as long as the political situation in Indonesia is so fluid and the economy is drifting toward ever greater calamity.

Much remains unknown about recent happenings in Indonesia, and the story we have pieced together from the reports in newspapers and period-

opposition – and the Jews. From the point of view of our moral tenets it is no excuse that a different outcome of the coup might have unleashed a similar beastly orgy (to which, however, people in the West would have reacted differently).

icals is only intended to give the very broadest account. To form a judgment about what the future holds is still more difficult – indeed, impossible. One thing which seems certain, however, is that any future government in Indonesia that wants to come to grips with its grave problems will have to be a dictatorship. The country has experienced a long period of virtual lawlessness, and even to restore a minimum of order will require firm measures. To stabilize and gradually develop the economy will necessitate taking many policy measures that will hurt various interest groups and, considering how the situation has been allowed to develop, often add to the sufferings of the masses. As guidance, such a government would need competent planning of a type Indonesia has had very little of, as yet.

Only the army could conceivably carry out this type of relentless but benevolent and enlightened dictatorship. It would have to take firm control over its recent allies, the rightist Moslem groups, as it has already suppressed the Communists and their collaborators. This could mean starting out with the great majority of the people against the government, which is a serious thing for any dictatorship. Moreover, the army would have to initiate serious planning, for which until now it, like other important groups in Indonesia, has shown little inclination or ability. Finally, and as a pre-condition for meeting the other two requisites, the army would have to subordinate private interests to the national cause, and itself become united, firmly disciplined, and incorrupt. In view of the history and character of the army, discussed in Section 8, it is most unlikely that these requisites will be met. Consequently, Indonesia's desperately serious problems, aggravated by recent events, are not likely to be solved in the near future.

To speculate on Indonesia's foreign policy orientation seems still less rewarding. However, Indonesia's friendly relations with China, until the September coup, will probably be severed more permanently. Since there is no love lost between Chinese businessmen in Indonesia and their indigenous Indonesian competitors, and since the Chinese merchants can easily be blamed for the scarcities and the rising prices, anti-Chinese demonstrations and persecutions could still readily be organized. This, and the slaughter of Chinese and Indonesian Communists, together with the barring of the P.K.I., will continue to create hostility in China against the new regime in Indonesia. Without the backing of China, Indonesia's self-assertion in foreign affairs, including its "confrontation" with the Federation of Malaysia, becomes a hopeless undertaking, and may gradually be relinquished with some face-saving round-about movements. To break its isolation Indonesia might rejoin the United Nations. As Indonesia will be desperately short of foreign exchange and in need of aid, and can hardly hope to get much from the Communist countries any longer, it will have every reason to begin courting the United States and even Britain, though here again it would have to save face. How far and how fast

Indonesia will travel in order to join the "free world" will depend in part on the response of the Western powers.

It is unlikely that such a reorientation of Indonesia's foreign policy would bring about the radical reforms in its internal situation and policies required to set the country on the road to economic progress and national consolidation. If serious sufferings among the masses, on the one hand, and incompetence, corruption, and bickering for power and spoils among the upper strata, on the other, continue to be the rule, violent outbreaks cannot be excluded, even if foreign aid should be granted.

III

The Rest of Southeast Asia

We turn now to a brief survey of Malaysia, the Philippines, Thailand, and the states that emerged from the dissolution of French Indo-China and did not come under Communist rule. This rather motley collection is difficult to treat as a unit since the political life and problems of these countries have been shaped by strikingly different historical experiences. Thailand had preserved, throughout the era of imperialism, its formal political independence as a buffer zone between the British and French empires. As we have shown in Chapter 4, the other countries had been subjected to sharply contrasting systems of colonial rule and had won their independence in different ways. One thing all these states have in common is a rather conservative orientation. The ruler of Cambodia, Norodom Sihanouk, professes what he calls Khmer socialism, but this seems to amount to little more than a vague rationalization of certain traditional features of Cambodian society; it is not comparable to the radical nationalism of Ceylon, Burma, or Indonesia, nor to the program of a "socialist pattern of society" upheld in India. The conservative leanings shared by these states emanate, however, from widely differing social structures and internal and external forces. For this reason we shall deal with each of them in turn, beginning with Malaysia.

11 *Malaysia*

Indonesia's "confrontation" policy, Britain's determination to protect the new and enlarged state against this threat, evidenced by the deployment there of large British military forces (together with some from Australia and New Zealand), and the undefined but real connection between this conflict and the war in Vietnam form an international setting that is bound to restrict the Federation of Malaysia's opportunity to develop solely according to its own ambition and capacity. Sukarno's belligerence probably, on balance, helped to maintain political stability within the federation, particularly in Malaya. Perhaps the sweeping electoral victory of the Alliance in 1964 reflected a sense of concern about national survival in the face of this threat. There have certainly been plenty of patriotic gestures in Kuala Lumpur and clarion calls for national unity. However, the low rate of recruitment into the armed forces and the modest national defense budget suggest that no great effort is being made to mobilize the strength of the new nation. A greater Malaysian defense effort would entail larger sacrifices from the wealthier classes of the population – a prospect they would not greet with enthusiasm; this is the more important since these classes have a monopoly on political power everywhere, except in Singapore. Most of these wealthier people are Chinese; the fact that they are discriminated against politically cannot increase their enthusiasm to carry heavier defense burdens. Meanwhile, whatever exigencies justify Malaysia's dependence on British and Commonwealth forces, their presence on a large scale is bound to foster doubts about its credentials among potential Afro-Asian friends and weaken its will to defend itself. Not least from the point of view of international relations, the Federation of Malaysia seems a fragile structure, more fragile indeed than the earlier, less encompassing Federation of Malaya.

Focussing our attention first on internal political developments in Malaya, the only part of Malaysia that has as yet any history as an independent state to review, its main political problem has been the promotion of harmonious relations and a sense of national solidarity within a system of parliamentary democracy among ethnic communities sharply differentiated by economic condition, religion, customs, and language. Malaya is unique in South Asia in that indigenous Malays constitute a minority; there are nearly as many people of Chinese origin, while the rest of the population is mainly Indian. In average terms Malaya stands out as by far the richest country in South Asia – Singapore is richer still and the two territories on Borneo, though less advanced, should not hinder economic development in the federation. There are, however, great economic inequalities between the several ethnic groups and, especially, between the different classes within them. There is a tiny but socially and politically fortified upper stratum of Malays surrounding the Sultans and consisting mostly of landlords and administrators, but most Malays eke out an existence as very poor farmers. The urban and mining populations are predominantly Chinese, and the Chinese also dominate retail distribution and moneylending in rural districts. There are conspicuously few Chinese in rice farming and fishing – and in the administration, which is mainly a Malay preserve. Chinese-owned rubber plantations and mines invariably employ Chinese labor, while those owned by Europeans employ Indian labor. A minority of Indians is also found in trading, moneylending, and the professions. The Chinese earn and receive a disproportionately large part of the national income – there are millionaires among them – but the great majority of Chinese are poor.

As we pointed out in Chapter 4 (Section 10), Malaya engaged in no real struggle for independence and was only galvanized into purposeful political activity after the Second World War by the fact that the British clearly intended to withdraw as quickly as possible. Even then political consciousness developed along communal lines, with the Malays and the Chinese forming their own political organizations and the Indian community following suit. An association of the wealthy leaders of the three main communal parties, called the Alliance, negotiated the final transfer of power with the British. In the negotiations leading up to independence, the Federation of Malaya was constructed so as to grant and preserve political advantages and privileges to the Malays, while allowing the Chinese to enjoy the fruits of their more commanding position in the economy. Its citizenship laws were drawn so as to ensure an electoral majority of Malays. Because all those born in Malaya after independence are automatically citizens and because the Chinese are multiplying faster than the Malays, this electoral advantage will tend to diminish. However, the Electoral Commission was empowered to adjust the ratio of seats to voters and has, in fact, done so in such a way as to favor rural areas where the Chinese are less numerous. In the new and larger federation this prerogative can also be used in Sabah and Sarawak to strengthen the political power of indigenous peoples, mainly Malays and kindred ethnic groups.

The Malay aristocratic class has been conspicuous in the leadership of the Alliance and Malays account for the greater proportion of the candidates the Alliance sponsors in elections. A main objective of the Malay-dominated government has been to preserve the privileges this group enjoys in areas such as administration, land ownership, and education, and also to promote and advance the economic and social ambitions of the Malays more broadly, without upsetting communal relations. The greater part of its civil expenditures, for instance, has been directed toward rural development. As wealthy and privileged individuals, the leaders of the three communal organizations have an obvious vested interest in political stability; consequently they have adopted a cautious approach to economic and social change. Their conservatism is inherent in the political compromises necessary to hold the Alliance together. They have not been tempted to indulge in the sterile economic nationalism of neighboring Indonesia. Neither have they been inclined to engage in comprehensive economic planning, as this would endanger communal relations or their particular economic interests. State planning would almost inevitably involve taking land away from the Malay aristocracy or interfering with the industrial enterprises of the Chinese business classes. As the country is rich, by South Asian standards, its foreign exchange situation favorable, and as the Chinese provide a steady flow of business initiative, planning and state intervention do not, for the time being, seem necessary to the same degree as in India and Pakistan, for instance.

The fact that the leaders of all three communal parties making up the Alliance are upper-class and English-speaking affords a basis for their cooperation. But the masses of their followers undoubtedly find it much more difficult to cross communal barriers and probably do not always understand and trust the bargains struck in their behalf. The existing inequalities between and within the major communities pose a constant threat to internal political cohesion, and they are likely to increase as the population expands. Recent developments in Ceylon – a country that, like Malaya, won its independence without much of a liberation movement and for almost a decade was ruled by a conservative government bent on communal peace – provide a stern warning of possible future difficulties. Until now, however, the Alliance has successfully weathered two sorts of political challenge. The first has come from left-wing inter-racial parties in predominantly non-Malay areas, which have tended to demand more economic reforms and to favor the removal of discriminations against the Chinese. These parties have not been united and have made little headway in elections. The second challenge has come from Islamic-based parties in predominantly Malay areas, especially on the east coast, which have expressed an extreme Malay nationalism. Since in a vague way they favor a "Greater Indonesia" that would bring all Malay-speaking Moslem peoples together, the government regards them as potentially subversive, particularly in view of the deterioration of relations with Indonesia. If communal relations become inflamed, they could well gain more electoral support, a development that would force the Chinese in Malaya to take more aggressive action to defend their rights.

The recent merger of Singapore, Sabah, and Sarawak with Malaya was, as we saw,[1] primarily prompted by concern for the international political security of the area. Aside from this problem, it cannot be said that the formation of the Federation of Malaysia eased the task of national consolidation or made the rule of the Alliance more secure. The radical inclinations of the overwhelmingly Chinese population of Singapore presented a special challenge. The relatively moderate socialist People's Action Party (P.A.P.) of Lee Kuan Yew, which rules Singapore, must appeal to the masses of the poorer Chinese and cannot very well accept the claim of the wealthy leadership of the Malayan Chinese Association, a partner in the Alliance, to represent the interests of all the Chinese. The P.A.P. believes, and probably rightly as far as Singapore is concerned, that a left-wing multi-racial party offers the only hope of preventing the

[1] Chapter 5, Section 11.

Chinese masses from supporting the Communists. It feels that the Alliance, and Tunku Abdul Rahman, the federal Prime Minister, in particular, do not understand the problems of the urban Chinese population. The increasing urbanization of other parts of Malaysia could increase this party's chances of gaining in appeal throughout the federation. That could end the reign of the Alliance and steer the Malays into more extreme political agitation.

Singapore has its own potentially explosive problems. Its population is growing extremely rapidly, contains a large proportion of very young people, and threatens a mounting unemployment burden. The socialism of the P.A.P. is directed toward welfare schemes rather than toward a program for reordering the entrepôt's economic affairs. At the same time, the Malay minority in Singapore demanded much the same preferential treatment, including reserved quotas for government jobs, as that which the federal government offers. The P.A.P. government rejected this demand but is plainly worried about the economic and social frustrations that lie behind the ugly racial riots that broke out in Singapore in 1964.

Sabah and Sarawak, at much lower levels of constitutional and political development than Malaya and Singapore, are not free from the type of communal problems that threaten the cohesion of Malaya. Their indigenous peoples fear the economic and educational superiority of the Chinese in their midst, who are multiplying at a faster rate than they themselves. They also distrust the Malays on the mainland and apparently feel that federal government development expenditure may bring a form of Malayan hegemony. It is instructive to note that, apart from a Minister for Sabah Affairs, not a single minister in the federal government originates from any constituent state outside Malaya. It would not be surprising, then, if anti-Malayan sentiment developed in these territories. As elsewhere in the federation, the Chinese in Sabah and Sarawak resent the special privileges and safeguards granted to the indigenous peoples.

The whole structure and stability of the federation thus rested on a contrived balance of interests among contrasting ethnic communities at varying levels of social, economic, and political development and internally split by great economic inequalities. The external dangers might, at least for a time, serve as a cohesive force, but they might also introduce subversion or at least cause economic difficulties. Thus the future course of political development in Malaysia could hardly be forecast with any certainty.

This was how things appeared at the beginning of 1965 when the above text was written. In August, Singapore was expelled from the federation. Relations between the two major units of Greater Malaysia had been deteriorating since Lee Kuan Yew brought his P.A.P. into the political struggle in Malaya in 1964. The party presented a program of equality between the ethnic groups, fought for a "Malaysian Malaysia," and sought cooperation with the various opposition parties to the left of the Alliance. This aroused suspicion and anger in the dominating Malay organization in the Alliance, and finally Tunku Abdul Rahman decided to inform Lee Kuan Yew that Singapore had to leave. The British government, which had been seeking preservation of the federation, only learned of this move at the last moment, whereupon it tried to have it postponed, but to no avail.

Singapore now became independent in its own right. Its government declared a foreign policy of non-alignment; while not demanding withdrawal of the British military base on the island – which is an important source of employment and income – it declared such limitations on its use as to weaken the British desire to hold it for the long-term future. At the beginning of 1966, economic relations between Singapore and Malaysia are not fully settled. Without a common market, industry is bound to suffer in Malaya, while Singapore's interest in having Malaya as an import and export market is probably even stronger.

The repercussions in Sabah and Sarawak were serious. The decision in Kuala Lumpur to expel Singapore from the federation had been taken without consulting their officials, not even the Sabah representative in the union government, who immediately resigned. Tunku Abdul Rahman and his government had generally been heavyhanded in their relations with the faraway, smaller states in the federation. The British, Australian, and New Zealand governments are reported to have come to the rescue of what remains of the federation by making it plain that their defense commitments to the two states on Borneo apply only as long as they remain in the federation. As for the future, much will depend on developments and policies in Indonesia.

12 *The Philippines*

In moving next to the Philippines we approach a country that, except for its geographical position, seems hardly to belong to the Asian region at all. Several centuries of Spanish rule sufficed to give it a distinctly Latin American complexion, and a further half century of American tutelage completed the mutation by superimposing a political system patterned on that of the United States. The result was to reinforce and legitimize in a modern democratic framework the hierarchical power structure created under the aegis of Spain.

The Philippines is unique among Southeast Asian countries in that the date of its independence had been determined long in advance.[1] So, for

[1] Chapter 4, Section 6.

that matter, had its political constitution. Furthermore, it boasted a civil service that had become almost entirely indigenous. As in the case of Ceylon, the arrival of full independence heralded no sharp break with the past. No deep-seated frustrations awaited release and there was no inclination to repudiate and reject the colonial heritage. If anything, the Filipinos – or rather their articulate upper strata – became even more emotionally attached to all things American. They had no ambivalent attitudes toward modernization and blithely talked of pursuing it along American lines. Indeed, the Filipinos, like the Americans, generally accept that the free enterprise system is the foundation and safeguard of their democratic way of life. There is no ideological support for the extension of government enterprise, especially since the existing examples are often riddled with graft and corruption. In theory, government corporations are tolerated only because private enterprise is unwilling or unable to perform their function; in practice, the politicians have a vested interest in creating and maintaining them as a source of patronage and graft. More generally, it should be added, the lack of any ideological attachment to "socialism" of the type that is so common in South Asia accords perfectly with the interests of the wealthy ruling elite. In foreign relations the Philippines has faithfully aligned itself behind the United States in complete opposition to all Communist regimes and influences, a policy that has done little to reduce its comparative isolation from the rest of the region.

Maintaining the exceptionally close relationship that had existed with the United States in pre-independence times was, and is now, virtually a necessity for the economic viability of the Philippines. In fact, if not in form, this relationship has been regulated by package deals; originally they specified that special consideration be given to various United States interests, but they have gradually been modified in favor of the Philippines. Several issues – for instance the amounts to be paid for wartime damage or the "priority rights" guaranteed American citizens as part of the price paid for commercial advantages and substantial American assistance toward post-war reconstruction – have given rise to irritation with the United States. The younger generation of Filipinos, particularly the students, have expressed strong disapproval of another type of American privilege, namely the extraterritorial rights of American military personnel based in the Philippines.[1] But even if there is an occasional flare-up of anti-American sentiment, not only the reality of Philippine dependence on United States markets and United States military forces but also the close links between American business interests and the Filipino ruling elite should be a powerful deterrent to the adoption of radically nationalist policies. A movement aimed at breaking the established close ties with the United States could only develop as part of a general realignment of

[1] In August, 1965, the United States agreed to give Philippine courts wider jurisdiction over offenses by Americans both on and off the bases.

Philippine politics, implying the rise of political awareness on the part of the low-income groups, and such a development would not necessarily be given an anti-American slant.

The Philippines constitutes a well-defined geographical area, has a relatively homogeneous ethnic structure, and an overwhelmingly Catholic population. Communal and religious divisions thus play little or no part in its political life. The Chinese minority that forms the principal alien element is only a tiny fraction of the total population. But as elsewhere in the region, its conspicuous role in commerce has attracted national resentment. A "Filipino First" sentiment, which demands primacy for Filipinos over foreigners in all fields of activity, has been mainly directed against the overseas Chinese;[1] otherwise it has not been much of a political force. The population has trebled over the past half century and is now increasing by more than 3 percent annually. This has caused little anxiety and there is hardly more than the start of a birth control movement, a fact that, of course, reflects the dominant position of the Catholic Church. The Philippines has an average level of income above the poorest but below the richest countries in the region. But this conceals an extremely unequal distribution of wealth and income, and the masses of the people are very poor. Living levels among the lower-income groups have not improved as compared with pre-war years.

There is an unusually high rate of unemployment in the urban areas and, at the same time, an extraordinary display of wealth and luxury on the part of a few. The economic inequalities in agriculture, where two-thirds of the labor force is situated, are equally glaring and they have a long history. Probably over one-half of those engaged in agriculture are landless and, through the medium of population increase and a mounting burden of indebtedness to landlords and moneylenders, their number continues to rise. It is thus easy to understand why the history of the Philippines has been punctuated by frequent peasant revolts, such as that which broke out after the Second World War. Born out of armed resistance to the Japanese, the Huk movement, as it was called, early came under Communist leadership and militantly demanded, among other things, far-reaching agrarian reform. It took nearly a decade and American assistance to suppress this rebellion. A successful policy of land resettlement played an important role in putting down the Huks, but all moves, including those backed by the United States, looking toward more general agrarian reform have been blocked or blunted by a Congress dominated by powerful landed interests. The latter control the rural vote, especially in remote

[1] Chapter 17, Section 14. The Retail Trade Nationalization Law of 1964 was designed to squeeze the Chinese out of their dominating position as middlemen but its form was such that it threatened some large American corporations as well. While the Chinese look for convenient loopholes and opportunities for political payoffs, the United States will probably succeed in having the law modified insofar as American interests are at stake.

areas, and often the police and the courts as well. The vote is in any event restricted by a literacy qualification to not much more than half the adult population. The Catholic Church is a considerable power on the side of the landlords. Acceptance by the Catholic hierarchy can be an important avenue to office and non-acceptance the death knell of political ambition. Even the small beginnings of trade unions and peasant organizations are very much under the control of wealthy landowners and churchmen.

Against this background it is not surprising to find national policies shaped by personalities and landlord-controlled lobbies more than by issues and principles. Since the urban business class is still weak, the strongest political lobbies are the producers' associations built around commercial agricultural products like rice, tobacco, cocoanuts, abaca, and sugar cane. Although public opinion is not entirely ineffective, shifting coalitions of these interest groups tend to set the limits of government action. The two major parties, the Nationalists and the Liberals, the second an offshoot of the first, are ideologically indistinguishable, have a fluid membership, no permanent organization, and rely on local and provincial bosses to deliver the vote. Elections are held mainly to choose leaders and they have at times been marred by intimidation, violence, and outright gangsterism. Political allegiance in the articulate upper strata is largely determined by private and family interests and may be bought for jobs, public works contracts, foreign exchange, and other favors dispensed by the prevailing spoils system. Much of Philippine politics centers, in fact, on patronage. A not surprising consequence is that graft and corruption permeate all levels of public life. Perhaps in no other country in South Asia is political dishonesty so widely recognized, accepted, and talked about as part of the political game. For politics is a national pastime, indulged in with gusto. Given the hierarchical power structure of Philippine society, it may be inferred that such freedom of expression is only tolerated because it does not threaten the position and interests of the privileged upper class. That is perhaps a measure of the country's political stability.

In sum, it is the almost baronial power wielded by the landed interests that largely explains why, despite its comparative prosperity, the Philippines has experienced so little industrial progress, agrarian reform, and democratization of its society in depth. What the future holds in store is most uncertain. One possible line of development would be the continuation of present policies. In view of the very rapid population increase, this would mean that the masses could expect little but continued poverty and, probably within not too long a time, an increase in their misery.

Another possible line of development would be a change in the direction of social and economic reform. The Philippine literacy rate is among the highest in South Asia and is still rising; a very large proportion of the literates have more than a smattering of English. Representative government has a long history in the Philippines and would seem to be firmly established; the country has had the experience, rare in the region, of two changes in national leadership via the ballot. Under these circumstances it would seem possible that politics could gain a broader democratic base by more organized participation on the part of the low-income groups. This could well lead to the break-up of the present political power structure and the initiation of large-scale reforms, primarily those of an agrarian nature. As already suggested, such a political development need not affect the alignment of the Philippines with the United States. From the time of the Bell Mission the American government – though not always American business – has pressed such reforms, and this policy should have more backing than ever in an America that has declared "unconditional war on poverty" at home and defined its national goal in terms of The Great Society.

A third possibility is the spread of Communism. It is commonly said that the Catholic allegiance of the population is a protection against such a development, as is the fear of China and the mistrust of what in neighboring countries is seen as Communist influence. If one recalls the Huk movement, which for years was on the verge of winning control over the Philippines, the strength of these protective forces should not be overestimated. If present policies are not changed radically, it is conceivable that the Philippines will be more ripe for a Communist movement in a later stage of development. The rise of unemployment among the educated could then be a potent catalyst. Nevertheless, with American military bases spread over the archipelago, and with the close relationship that exists between the American and Filipino officer corps, a Communist takeover seems improbable. Instead, the outcome of a rise of Communist influence could easily be a military dictatorship, which would put an end to the present well-established system of representative government.

The actual course of events will, of course, also depend on what happens in the rest of Southeast Asia. In pointing out these various possibilities we are merely stressing the uncertainty of the future.

13 *Thailand*

In dealing with the new states we have frequently emphasized the way their problems and political development have been shaped by colonial rule and the manner of its passing. Thailand provides an illuminating example of a state that escaped the shock of colonial domination, with profound consequences for the present character of its political system.

First of all, the absence of colonial government meant that no Western language was pressed upon Thailand. An ambitious Thai was not obliged to acquire a Western education in order to take advantage of the opportunities opened up by alien rule and no sizeable Western-educated class emerged. The country needed to take and apply only such foreign ideas as its rulers felt would help it to preserve its national identity and precarious independence. So the impact of Western culture on Thailand's political institutions was relatively weak. The authoritarian traditions of the country were not seriously modified, and changes in the character of the state and the administrative machinery proceeded slowly and under strong central control; there was no sharp break with the past. Naturally enough, Thailand never experienced the tensions and frustrations that characterized independence or resistance movements elsewhere in South Asia, and there were no appeals to the people to resist established authority.

The escape from colonial domination fortified the view of the Thai ruling elite that a strong centralized government was necessary if their country was to avoid a disunity that invited foreign intervention. Along with this attitude went a certain expedient bowing before the prevailing political winds. Having made a number of concessions to foreign interests before the First World War,[1] the rulers shrewdly took advantage of the respite the outbreak of hostilities afforded them, and entered the conflict on the winning side. Shortly before the Second World War, the Thai government veered toward the Japanese camp. It collaborated wholeheartedly with the Japanese during the war and actually declared war on Britain and the United States. In return, the Japanese allowed it to indulge some pan-Thai pretensions at the territorial expense of Cambodia, Laos, and Malaya. Thailand also suffered much less war damage than any other country in Southeast Asia. An external political situation dominated by the West after the war brought about a new opportunistic adjustment inside Thailand. The discredited wartime government made way for a seemingly more liberal regime. However, once the country had firmly aligned itself behind the West, the ruling elite correctly observed that it mattered little to its allies what sort of regime ruled so long as it was stable and staunchly anti-Communist. An interesting question, therefore, is what sort of adjustment could be expected if the Thais should come to believe, as the neighboring Cambodians apparently do, that China will ultimately be the major external power influence on Southeast Asia.

Concern with the need for internal stability and a strong central government in the face of foreign pressure has been a force making for conservatism in the political life of Thailand. It has conditioned the ruling elite to believe that the masses should be sheltered from the impact of disruptive changes occurring elsewhere in the region. It has also provided a convenient justification for the methods by which a ruling oligarchy has maintained an unchallenged hold on the spoils of power. The task of main-

[1] Chapter 5, Section 2.

taining a conservative political front has been made easier by the fact that this ruling oligarchy is extremely small. It consists primarily of the top echelons of the officer corps and civilian bureaucracy; since the former have their roots in the latter the two groups overlap. There is no indigenous elite in business as in Ceylon. A close observer of the country's affairs has depicted its ruling class as a three-tiered pyramid:

> The top level includes perhaps ten to fifteen persons who do or could dominate the ruling class and the country as a whole by a manipulation of the various political forces. This group includes senior military commanders, a few men of great reputation gained in the revolution of 1932 or in the interplay of politics since, and perhaps two or three men around the throne. At any given time there have never been more than six or eight such men in power. The second level of the pyramid is made up of perhaps a thousand persons including military officers of the rank of colonel or general, special-grade civil servants, prominent members of parliament, some princes, and perhaps some particularly powerful businessmen. Although the top group dominates, it is only through their manipulation and control of the second group that they gain, hold and use power. The base of the ruling-class structure is what may be called the political public. It is made up of educated and articulate citizens in Bangkok and the provincial towns who interest themselves in the details of political activity. For the most part high school and university graduates, they are largely in the bureaucracy but also include professional people, journalists and other writers, and Thai members of the commercial white-collar group. It may be estimated that the ruling class as described is between 1 and 2 percent of the total adult population of the country.[1]

The political horizons of the ruling class are narrow and often purely personal. They have no doctrine to implant, no program to implement. Their political concerns consist largely of maneuvers for status and the rewards and privileges that go with it. The military coup has become the recognized way of changing the government because military power is the only secure source of political authority. Since the coup that brought absolute monarchy to an end in 1932 there have been very few years when the army, including the para-military police force, has not ruled the country. For a short time after the Second World War, when the West dominated the external political situation once more and civilian leaders came to the fore in Thai politics, an attempt was made to give the country constitutional government, with a fully elected assembly and wide freedom of political activity. The experiment was tarnished, however, by wholesale corruption, financial scandals and mismanagement, and by strikes and riots between Thais and Chinese. A predominantly army coup was therefore staged in 1947 to "save" the nation from weak and dishonest government. Rival cliques within, or related to, the military and police establishments then contended for the fruits of power and from their struggles there

[1] David A. Wilson, "Thailand," in George McTurnan Kahin, ed., *Governments and Politics in Southeast Asia*, Cornell University Press, Ithaca, 1959, pp. 36–37.

emerged in 1958 a total dictatorship under General Sarit Thanarat, who was an admirer of the direct methods of government of leaders like de Gaulle. Sarit declared martial law and dropped all pretense of governing on even a quasi-constitutional basis. All political and judicial power was concentrated in the executive. Sarit himself became Prime Minister, Supreme Commander of the armed forces, Director General of police, and Minister for Economic Development. Political parties were banned, the radio was controlled, and the press muzzled. No criticism of the regime was tolerated. All rights and freedoms became subordinate to his own conception of the national interest. Yet curiously enough Sarit acknowledged that "anyone can launch a revolution, but the snag about it is that once a revolution is staged, how to win public approval."[1] To a limited extent his regime undertook to improve public welfare but otherwise it sought no popular support.

Another army general succeeded Sarit in 1963. There has been some parcelling out of the many official responsibilities the latter had assumed; at least for a time the exploitation of positions of political power may have been curtailed; there might even be another experiment with constitutional government. But there is little prospect of changing the basic features of the regime.

Coups of the traditional kind have been attempted, but they have been suppressed. As in the past, the game of changing the guard in Bangkok is played well above the heads of the masses, who live out their peaceful, unpolitical lives in the villages and the poorer quarters of the cities. We can only suppose that they accept whatever government comes along as their destiny. A large majority of the people are farmers with their own land. There is no estate problem in Thailand and average levels of living are comparatively good by Asian standards. Certainly there is little sign of the abysmal poverty to be found on the Indian subcontinent. Chinese residents generally dominate all the trades and professions except for government services and rice farming. They control, for instance, the overwhelming bulk of the retail shops, most of the timber mills, the skilled labor force, and the rice trade. On the other hand, they are much better integrated in Thailand than elsewhere in the region. Cultural affinity has long facilitated their intermarriage with the Thais, and complete assimilation usually follows by about the third generation. This makes it difficult to assess the number of Chinese in the population.[2] One observer estimates that they form roughly 20 percent of the total population;[3] the proportion is, in any case, much larger than in any other Southeast Asian country

[1] Quoted in *Link*, May 26, 1961, p. 23.

[2] The Chinese are legally defined as Chinese citizens holding alien registration certificates. Every child born to a Thai woman is counted as Thai unless it is formally registered at a foreign consulate.

[3] Alice Tay Erh Soon, "The Chinese in South East Asia," *Race*, Vol. IV, No. 1, November, 1962, p. 34.

except Malaysia. The policy of successive Thai governments toward the Chinese has tended to waver between outright repression and measures designed to force their assimilation. The Chinese fared badly under the pro-Japanese government that came to power shortly before the Second World War. Their schools, newspapers, and choice of occupation were severely curtailed, and Thais were discouraged from marrying them. Since the war they have been less openly harassed and more encouraged to assimilate through naturalization and marriage.

The southern provinces contain a Malay Moslem majority whose aspirations for union with Malaya had to be forcibly suppressed after the war. If only because it needs the cooperation of Thailand in ferreting out Communist guerrilla remnants in the jungles bordering this frontier, Malaya is unlikely to encourage separatist movements in this area. Thailand's northeastern provinces, where about one-third of the population live, present a rather more serious problem to the central government. Here the majority of the population are Lao-speaking and have close cultural affinities with the trans-Mekong Laotians. Indeed, the Mekong River is not so much a frontier as a traffic artery between Laos and Thailand. With its dry, barren scrubland, which is hard to irrigate, this northeastern region has long been the poorest and most neglected part of Thailand. Fearing that Communists would foment separatist feelings in the region, the Sarit regime, with substantial American assistance, initiated a program to raise the living levels of its inhabitants. Concern for political security in that region also induced the regime to take an active interest in the political affairs of war-torn Laos.

There has been little real planning in Thailand and almost no ideological debate on economic and social goals. A tradition of imaginative and constructive statesmanship scarcely exists. The government owns many enterprises but also encourages private initiative and foreign investment. In both spheres the military and civilian rulers — and their wives — have been favored with shares and directorships. A policy of Thaifying the economy is ostensibly directed against the Chinese; in practice it is often used to blackmail the Chinese into giving the Thai rulers a share of the fruits of their industry. From the standpoint of government officials the whole economy is one vast spoils system. It is the impulse to exploit political position for personal gain, and not any ideological principle, that accounts for the existence of a large public or quasi-public economic sector in Thailand.[1] After Sarit's death, in 1963, it was revealed that, in the span of barely more than a decade, he had acquired a huge fortune in lands, houses, cars, companies, and bank deposits.[2]

[1] Chapter 17, Section 14.

[2] The cornerstone of his wealth was a state lottery, which never announced any winners. After his death a new Director of the State Lottery revealed that £4.3 million of its funds had been misappropriated. (*The Observer*, March 29, 1964.) Family

A particularly dynamic factor in the political life of Thailand would seem to be the rapid increase of a Western-educated class of intellectuals, who have contact with the rest of the world through the universities and through international organizations. Since the West has no political interest in changing the way of life in Thailand as long as that country is staunchly anti-Communist, and since the members of the rising intellectual elite have plenty of opportunity for good living, this Western influence may not cause much trouble for a long time to come. Moreover, there is a tradition in Thailand of permitting sophisticated members of the upper strata considerable freedom of expression; as individuals they can voice radical views, provided they stay out of politics. The masses of people in the villages and cities are even more passive than those in other South Asian countries, for reasons already alluded to: Thailand has never had a liberation movement that tried to incite the people against the rulers; there is less exploitation of the masses by landlords and moneylenders; and levels of living are, on the whole, both relatively high and improving. Nevertheless, future political developments in Thailand are unpredictable. What happens will depend, in the first place, on how the conflict raging in the former Indo-China area affects the surrounding countries. Given the absence of ideological commitment and the tradition of opportunism in Thailand, it provides the extreme justification for John Foster Dulles' domino theory – much more than do the successor states to French Indo-China themselves.

14 *Cambodia*

Cambodia and Laos achieved their political independence without great exertion, for it came about by the Geneva settlement in 1954 (see below), as a virtual by-product of what was largely a Vietnamese struggle against the French colonizers. But when Vietnam became a vital stake in the cold war, it was inevitable that Cambodia and Laos should be viewed in the same light and subjected to much the same external pressures. Of the states that emerged from the break-up of French Indo-China, only Cambodia managed to avoid being engulfed in civil war. The Vietnamese war against the French continued in South Vietnam as armed rebellion against an American-sponsored regime. A similar movement in Laos became closely linked with the Vietnamese struggle and likewise led to a *de*

---

squabbles over Sarit's estate, provoked by his numerous "minor wives," most of whom were beauty queens and actresses, led to further revelations. In November, 1964 a government investigating commission found that he had misused the equivalent of £10.4 million of state funds; the estimated total of his estate was £46 million. (*The Guardian*, December 19, 1964.) These revelations of plunder on a gigantic scale by a man who had meted out arbitrary punishment for minor peccadillos hardly rippled the calm surface of Thai public life.

facto partition of the country that persisted after the French departed. Once these movements came under Communist leadership, a development for which French intransigence was largely responsible,[1] the whole area became a battleground of cold war strategies, with the United States assuming the role of protector of all anti-Communist regimes. Unlike the other successor states, Cambodia achieved its independence without violence or any loss of territory to Communist-led resistance movements.

French rule had had less of an effect on Cambodia's traditional social and political structure than on Vietnam's. No Cambodian class emerged with interests closely linked to those of the colonial rulers. The French traded mostly with the Chinese and relied on immigrant Vietnamese to fill those administrative posts they did not reserve for themselves; of these two foreign minorities, the Vietnamese were probably the more resented. Foreign-owned plantations did not substantially encroach on land resources and, since the population was relatively sparse, the Cambodians were not cramped for living space. Broadly speaking, the easy-going ways of a stagnant rural society were not seriously disturbed.

At the end of the war, there were only a handful of French-educated Cambodians capable of challenging the existing monarchical political order and initiating parliamentary government. Personal rivalries, intrigues, and a failure to unite on a clear ideology or program discredited their efforts and enabled the king, Norodom Sihanouk, to suspend parliamentary procedures and take credit for negotiating complete independence from the French. Sihanouk then descended into the political arena to organize the popular following, or national rally – the Popular Socialist Community – through which he has ruled the country ever since. Like the nationalist political groups he outflanked, his national rally has no collective leadership or discipline and no clear program and ideology. Its "socialism" is thoroughly imbued with Buddhist religious doctrines and ethics and apparently aims to preserve the tradition of human equality and cooperation that is held to be a natural feature of Cambodian village life. The linchpin of the political system is Sihanouk's personal power, combined with a mandarinate of civil servants.

Unlike neighboring Thailand and South Vietnam, Cambodia established relations with Communist countries, including China, and declared itself to be unaligned in world affairs. This choice was dictated partly by principle and partly by the realization that pro-Western leanings would play into the hands of the Communists. Sihanouk is not pro-Communist, and many Cambodian army officers fought with the French against the Viet Minh. Nevertheless, his foreign policy envenomed relations with Thailand and South Vietnam. Since the Vietnamese and Thais are the traditional foes of Cambodia, this development has enabled Sihanouk to

[1] Chapter 4, Sections 3 and 12; Chapter 5, Section 13.

discredit his political opponents by branding them as foreign agents or the enemies of a monarchy and a religion that are deeply revered. The policy also paid off economically, for many of the public economic projects launched by Sihanouk have been provided by foreign aid, awarded by both sides in the cold war. Despite these projects, there have been no fundamental efforts to modernize Cambodia or to arouse its people out of their accustomed torpor.

In 1963 Sihanouk renounced United States aid, ostensibly out of pique at that country's failure to curb what he regarded as the aggressive designs of Thailand and South Vietnam. The following year Cambodia nationalized foreign trade and banking, both until then dominated by foreigners, but not the few foreign-owned rubber estates. What prompted the step is unclear but it may well have stemmed from Sihanouk's quite natural obsession with national survival. At any rate, his latest maneuverings, including a break in diplomatic relations with the United States in 1965, seem to reflect his belief that China, and not the United States, will ultimately succeed to France's role as the guarantor and protector of Cambodian independence.

15 *Laos*

Laos was drawn into the cold war struggle when the Pathet Lao, a militant resistance movement related to the Viet Minh, occupied the northern part of the country, and stayed there after the Geneva settlement in 1954. In fact, warring factions adorned with cold war labels have made the Laotian state a fiction. The factional leaders are either members of old princely and aristocratic families or ambitious army officers. Their baronial feuding has acquired international importance only because of the outside political and military backing they have received. Thus the "left-wing" Pathet Lao has been supported by North Vietnam and China, and a "right-wing" faction by Thailand and the United States. A "neutralist" faction between these two extremes has become generally accepted in international discussions as providing the only possible basis for a solution that would remove all forms of outside intervention. Left-wing, right-wing, and neutralist labels in this context are merely crude indications of where the rival factions stand in relation to the cold war. Of their attitude toward the future aims and character of a Laotian state next to nothing is heard. For instance, Prince Souphanouvong, the leader of the Pathet Lao, is reportedly a "Marxist" who supports the monarchy and Buddhism.

Laos has a long history of dynastic strife that survived foreign interference and sometimes invited or provoked it. The present division of the country between the Pathet Lao and the factions that oppose it is, for instance, a rough parallel to the rival Siamese and Annamese spheres of influence in the nineteenth century. The unity created by French domination was rather superficial. It never curbed the authority of the princely families over their former fiefs, nor did it end the ancient animosity between the northern hill tribes, who now incidentally support the Pathet Lao, and the Laotians in the Mekong valley. In other respects, too, the country failed to make any substantial progress under the French. Only a handful of Laotians gained a Western education, and most of these came from princely or aristocratic families. There was no political evolution to speak of and at the lowest level of society a lethargic peasantry passed a largely self-sufficient existence. The superimposing of cold war political values on this feudal system has greatly impeded the pacification and unification of the country. The situation has been the subject of numerous international parleys and a singularly futile international control commission. But all attempts to effect a reconciliation between the warring factions have foundered on the fear that an agreement would enable one side to gain a decisive political or military advantage over the other.

Laos must now have the largest proportion of soldiers to total population of any country in South Asia. Soldiering has become in effect a relatively well-paid civil service career, though the Laotians appear to have little zest for fighting. The United States undertook to finance completely the formation and maintenance of a Royal Laotian Army, but substantial American assistance also bred inflation and colossal and unabashed corruption. Luxury imports, cars and houses, and profits from black-market currency dealings or trading in import licenses are among the more obvious perquisites of political influence. Struggles for power and wealth within the officer corps are not the least of the reasons for the military ineffectiveness of the opposition to the Pathet Lao.[1] No reliable reports exist of the extent to which the Pathet Lao is dependent on outside aid.

It is patently clear that there can be no hope of peace and stability in Laos unless there is a settlement of the more bloody struggle in Vietnam such as to bring about a slackening of cold war tensions throughout the whole area of what was formerly French Indo-China.

16 *South Vietnam as a Separate State*[2]

The Geneva Declaration of July 21, 1954, issued in connection with the agreement on the cessation of hostilities in what had been French Indo-

[1] When General Phoumi Nosavan, a so-called "strong man" and onetime protégé of the United States, fled the country in February, 1965 after an abortive coup, it was reported that the sources of wealth he controlled "included a monopoly of imports of gold, wines and spirits as well as ownership of the biggest opium parlour in Vientiane." His access to riches evidently aroused the bitter enmity of some fellow officers. (*The Observer*, February 7, 1965.)

[2] The background and beginning of the war in Vietnam were described in Chapter 4, Sections 12 and 13, and Chapter 5, Section 13.

China, stressed that the military demarcation line at the 17th parallel was "provisional and should not in any way be interpreted as constituting a political or territorial boundary." Country-wide elections were to be held after two years; negotiations between "authorities" in the two military zones on methods of organizing the elections were to begin within one year. Meanwhile, "the sovereignty, the independence, the unity and the territorial integrity" of Cambodia, Laos, and Vietnam should be respected and "interference in their internal affairs" refrained from. The Geneva Agreement and Declaration contained a number of other clauses, the most important of which prohibited the introduction of any further troops, military personnel, arms, and ammunition into the two zones, the establishment of foreign military bases there, the Vietnamese involvement in military alliances. Bao Dai, whom the French had installed as Emperor early in the struggle, and who a few days earlier had appointed Ngo Dinh Diem as Prime Minister of his government, dissociated himself from this settlement; the United States made a "unilateral declaration" supporting it with some provisos, the main and substantive one being that the elections in Vietnam should be supervised by the United Nations.

Emperor Bao Dai, who had long resided in France, concluded from the situation created by the conference and the settlement that his authority was now limited to the part of Vietnam that was south of the 17th parallel, and he dispatched Ngo Dinh Diem to Saigon. By means of a spuriously democratic referendum, Diem soon ousted the Emperor, declared South Vietnam an independent country – the Republic of Vietnam – and had himself elected President. Diem made it clear from the beginning that he had no intention of permitting the unifying elections in all of Vietnam that had been stipulated in the Declaration. Despite some perfunctory proddings from France and Britain, he consistently declined to enter upon the prescribed negotiations. The United States, having given Diem its full backing from the beginning, and very soon thereafter also economic and military support on a large scale, strongly encouraged him in his stand. The reason for this changed position on the part of the United States was openly declared to be the conviction that such elections would be won by the Communists.[1] However, this judgment could equally well have been made before the Geneva settlement, and by implying that in the name of democracy the Vietnamese should be prevented from following their own will,[2] it put United States action in the Vietnam conflict in an awkward light.

[1] Cf. Dwight D. Eisenhower, *White House Years: Mandate for Change, 1953–1956*, Doubleday, New York, 1963, p. 372.

[2] "If 80 percent of the people supported Ho, as Eisenhower was to state later in his memoirs, the threat to the Diem government would presumably come from the people themselves, and free world support of the Diem government would mean frustrating the popular will. But, as the U. S. view had it, the people chose Ho because they had not yet been offered a better way. The U. S.-supported Diem government would become the alternative." (Robert Scheer, *How the United States Got Involved in*

Through the gunsmoke of almost a decade of bitter war against the French, and the mechanism of an international settlement, the Vietnamese attained independence. But a military demarcation line, which was meant to be provisional, came to divide their relatively homogeneous country into two political entities, between which – contrary to the terms of the Geneva settlement – even trade and other normal exchanges were prohibited. North Vietnam, of course, refused to recognize South Vietnam as a permanently separate state, while Diem and other spokesmen for the government in South Vietnam refused to give up their ambition to "liberate" North Vietnam. As the situation developed, each government began to assemble evidence showing that the other – and the great powers backing it in the wider political conflict – had broken the Geneva settlement. That settlement has been rendered invalid by the course of events since 1954, but in the propaganda war it is still frequently invoked by both sides without much concern for its actual contents.[1] The government in Hanoi continued to press for the elections prescribed in the Geneva Declaration, and at least until 1959 did not give up hope that they would ultimately come about. The government therefore had an interest in holding to the Declaration, but Diem had denounced it from the beginning. The result was that the International Supervisory Commission, set up as a consequence of the Geneva settlement, soon had to report that it was not able to supervise the implementation of the agreement in South Vietnam. And in its Sixth Interim Report, in 1956, it stated unanimously: ". . . the degree of co-operation given to the Commission by the two parties has not been the same. While the Commission has experienced difficulties in North Vietnam, the major part of its difficulties has arisen in South Vietnam."[2]

The situation in that part of Vietnam south of the 17th parallel was desperate from the beginning, and the prospect of creating a secure and stable political order there seemed hopeless. Monarchists, politico-religious sects, warlords, and nationalists with a variety of political affiliations – among them those loyal to the Viet Minh who had fought the French – all possessing their own armies or guerrilla bands, were at one another's throats, while organized gangsterism controlled Saigon and more than 800,000 refugees poured in from the north.[3] The economy had been rav-

Vietnam, Report to the Center for the Study of Democratic Institutions, South Santa Barbara, California, 1965, p. 19.)

[1] Walter Lippmann expressed astonishment over the United States' assertion that "we seek no more than a return to the essentials of the agreements of 1954." (*New York Herald Tribune,* Paris Edition, April 2, 1965.)

[2] *Sixth Interim Report of the International Commission for Supervision and Control in Vietnam,* September, 1956, quoted from *Vietnam,* No. 1 (1957), Her Majesty's Stationery Office, London, 1957, p. 30.

[3] One provision of the Geneva accord was that civilians should be permitted and helped to go to the zone where they wanted to live. The bulk of the refugees going

aged by war and rampant inflation and was further damaged by the fact of partition and the withdrawal of not only the French armed forces but also a great deal of French capital and enterprise. Much land had lain fallow during the war and agricultural production was at a low ebb. To deal with all of these problems the Diem government had only a large but disjointed army and a weak and jumbled administration inherited from the French era. As we pointed out in Chapter 4 (Section 12), the French authorities had not encouraged the creation of an indigenous civil service nor, for that matter, the development of a large indigenous Western-educated intelligentsia or business class. In addition, as Hanoi was the traditional capital, all the central administrative offices were located there, together with the head offices of most businesses and, incidentally, the university. It is no exaggeration to say that the Diem government had to create an army, a police force, and a civil administration almost from scratch and put them to immediate use restoring order, at the same time that it was getting the economy going.

Considering all the adverse circumstances, the first few years of Diem's government must be considered an era of remarkable achievement. In a bid to establish his power, Diem won the loyalty of crucial cadres of officers and had the army reorganized under American guidance and equipped with efficient, modern arms provided by the United States. Meanwhile, he cunningly outmaneuvered and then smashed the politico-religious sects and the organized banditry. Diem's reorganized army and police forces also held their own against the remnants of the Viet Minh guerrillas. The refugees were resettled, and in this connection a land reform was initiated, under American guidance, that in terms of ultimate goals and some of the early accomplishments compared favorably with any attempt in that direction made elsewhere in South Asia – a standard that is not very high. The population was fed and production gradually resumed. None of these policies would have had any chance of success without the massive American military and civilian aid that was forthcoming from the very beginning, or the advice and direction associated with it – which, at this stage, Diem was usually willing to accept. But neither would America's involvement in South Vietnam have had these positive results without Diem's ruthless singlemindedness and resourcefulness. For a time the combination of Diem's forceful and shrewd political leadership at home and America's all-out and diversified assistance seemed about to accomplish the miracle of building up anarchic and destitute South Vietnam to the point where it would become a politically stable and economically viable, separate state.

---

south fell into two groups: members of the French colonial army and Catholics who had enjoyed a protected status under the French regime and raised militia fighting on the French side. Only some 150,000 refugees went north; others were discouraged by the Viet Minh, which in the expectation of the elections did not want to decrease its sympathizers in the South.

Diem was a remarkable man. Because of his upbringing as a Catholic and a mandarin, he had refused to participate in either the rebel government of Ho Chi Minh, the Communist leader of the national liberation movement that finally won the war against the French, or Bao Dai's puppet government. Diem had spent most of the early 1950's in the United States, where he had acquired the confidence of many in powerful circles. He accepted the Emperor's call to head his government only when the Geneva settlement was imminent, ruled for a few months without taking any direction from him, and disposed of him in 1955. French colonial policy had either compromised so many potential leaders or driven them over to the nationalist groups under Ho Chi Minh's leadership, that Diem had a unique position in a South Vietnam that defined itself as anti-Communist and, at the same time, was bent on freeing itself from French tutelage. For his lack of political and administrative experience he substituted natural shrewdness and courage, though, as we shall see, he devised a type of personal rule that later would stir up rebellion all around him. In his first few years in office, his political strength derived very much from the wholehearted backing given him by the United States and the fear that American protection and aid, needed for feeding the population, would be withdrawn if he was overthrown. Given its chosen role in the cold war to build an anti-Communist bastion in the southern part of Vietnam, the United States had good reasons for its confidence in Diem, judging from his early accomplishments.

In colonial times the economy of the southern provinces of Vietnam had depended heavily on the export of rice to the northern provinces and the sale of some rubber on the world market. While French capital had dominated the rubber trade, a Chinese minority had controlled the rice trade. The Chinese were also prominent in other non-agricultural economic activities, including retail distribution. In other words, the Vietnamese had had little share in the modern or quasi-modern sectors of their economy. After the establishment of South Vietnam as a separate state, all Chinese-born residents there were required to assume citizenship in the new country, adopt Vietnamese names, pay taxes, and register for military service. Those who did not comply were automatically regarded as foreigners and as such debarred from a number of their normal business activities. Unfortunately, most Vietnamese were in no position to assume the economic functions of the Chinese. This became clear when the Chinese later reacted to political intimidation with an economic boycott that seriously disrupted the rice trade.

Even though an indigenous urban upper and middle class emerged after the French exodus – profiting not least from the buying and selling of imported consumer goods financed by American aid – along with a large urban proletariat, the majority of the people in South Vietnam continued to derive their income from agriculture. Most of them were very poor peasants and tenants. There was, however, in addition to some French landowners who had held on to their property, an upper stratum of Vietnamese landowners. The latter had closely identified themselves with French interests; they now stood in the way of the American-directed land reform policy – which, had it been vigorously pursued, might have given the Diem government a foundation of popular support. Many in this landlord class, and in the top echelons of the army and the bureaucracy, were Catholic converts; indeed, it was by virtue of their superior education under the French that the Vietnamese Catholics, although constituting only about 10 percent of the population, came to hold a disproportionate share of the wealth and higher social positions in the country. Their number was increased by upper-class Catholic refugees from North Vietnam, many of whom were appointed to important government posts. This development tended to inflame old suspicions and animosities between the South and North Vietnamese, and, more particularly, between Catholics and Buddhists. Underlying these feelings, however, were social and economic inequalities and conflicts of interest.

Increasingly, once relative order and stability had been restored, the people of South Vietnam came to regard the Diem regime as in essence a family-centered junta deriving its main support from the Catholic elite and the United States. Diem had no belief in the value of democratic processes but, in deference to his American protectors, he promulgated in 1956 a seemingly liberal constitution patterned on that of the United States. This provided for an executive president, a sovereign legislative assembly, universal suffrage, an independent judiciary, and a bill of rights.[1] Nevertheless, government in South Vietnam continued to be anything but democratic. No independent and legally organized political opposition was permitted, elections were rigged, the radio was controlled, the press muzzled, and public discussion stifled. The National Assembly and the judiciary became tools of the executive; government policy was generally established by presidential decree. Diem tried to manufacture a semblance of government by consent by coercing and cajoling people, including civil servants, into joining his Movement of National Revolution. Arbitrary arrests, a political spy network, and even concentration camps were among the methods used to enforce docility and obedience. As a result, there came to be no middle ground between total acceptance of the Diem

[1] In outlining his constitutional recommendations to the National Assembly in 1956, Diem declared: "We affirm that the sole legitimate end and object of the State is to protect the fundamental rights of the human person to existence and to free development of his intellectual, moral and spiritual life. We affirm that democracy is neither material happiness nor the supremacy of numbers. Democracy is essentially a permanent effort to find the right political means for assuring to all citizens the right of free development and of maximum initiative, responsibility, and spiritual life." (Wells C. Klein and Marjorie Weiner, "Vietnam," in Kahin, ed., *Governments and Politics of Southeast Asia*, pp. 362–363.)

regime and the clandestine opposition of the National Liberation Front, or Viet Cong as it was usually called in Saigon and the United States, a rebellious guerrilla movement that stemmed partly from the Viet Minh resistance to the French.

Only American insistence explains why, in the first place, the Diem regime agreed to operate behind a Western-type democratic façade instead of rationalizing its authoritarian rule under some heading such as "guided democracy."[1] In 1961, when the National Liberation Front was intensifying its efforts, all pretense of constitutional government was abandoned and a state of emergency was declared; at the same time the United States was forced to relax its pressure for reforms. From this point on, the only ideology in regard to government that Diem professed was the ambiguous doctrine of personalism, which affirms the absolute value of the human person but stresses that this value is realized only in the context of civic duty and discipline. It was a measure of the rootlessness of his regime and its isolation from the masses that he could propound such a doctrine as an alternative to the radical nationalism of the National Liberation Front. In fact, of course, the regime did not check the rebellion. On the contrary, the number of rebels and the size of the territory they controlled began to expand manyfold. It is a matter for argument to what extent the unfolding opposition to the Diem regime was due to genuine Vietnamese nationalism. The presence of Americans wherever there were decisions to be taken and the steadily growing number of American military "advisors" and regular soldiers were bound to provoke an emotional reaction. So, too, was the refusal of the Diem regime to enter into negotiations with North Vietnam preparatory to holding the elections stipulated in the Geneva settlement. Certainly the rebel movement made the most of these nationalist sentiments in its propaganda. The specifically "Communist" element in its ideological armoury was a demand for radical land reform and a better deal for the common people generally. There seems little

[1] A reporter from the *U. S. News and World Report,* who asked Diem for his reaction to the criticism that his government was "semi-authoritarian, permitting no opposition," received the following reply:

"I do not answer criticism. Rather, I try to solve that historical problem which consists of achieving democracy in a state of underdevelopment, a problem which not only Vietnam but all the countries of the 'third world' face. As you know, all the underdeveloped countries are under authoritarian or dictatorial regimes, which is a historical and general phenomenon having nothing to do with individuals or governments and which corresponds to a historical need for centralization of power to wipe out the age-old poverty and humiliation of the people. The problem is how to get out of that situation.

"You also know that the governments which have tried to establish Western-style democracy from the top down in an underdeveloped country have all been liquidated by military coup d'état." (Quoted from *News from Viet-Nam,* No. 230, March 4, 1963, Vietnamese Embassy, London.) The inaccuracy of the last observation needs no underlining.

doubt, however, that the rebellion gained far less from the positive program of the rebels than from the glaring shortcomings of the Diem regime; it was because of these shortcomings that the nationalist propaganda appealed to so many Vietnamese minds.

It was widely known and cynically accepted that graft and corruption permeated all facets of public life. At the village level rapacious officials extorted labor and tribute from the peasantry with the result that the peasants were disinclined to support the war against the rebels.[1] The manner in which Diem surrounded himself with sycophants undermined morale in the public services and sheltered him from unpleasant facts and critical attitudes. American efforts to induce more liberal and effective government were increasingly ignored as misplaced idealism or denounced as interference in the internal affairs of a sovereign state. In addition, Diem's constant, whimsical meddling with the military chain of command – designed apparently to prevent any officer from becoming sufficiently powerful to challenge his supremacy – reduced the effectiveness of the military campaign against the rebels.

As early as the spring of 1960, eighteen Vietnamese nobles, including a number of former ministers, had petitioned Diem to liberalize his regime and stamp out inefficiency and corruption. In the autumn of that year the paratroopers rose in revolt, but were crushed after 400 had been killed. Buddhist agitation finally provided the rallying point for all the discontent rife in Saigon and those other areas of South Vietnam that were controlled by the Diem government. While the Buddhists could and did represent themselves as a truly indigenous spiritual force opposing an alien religion, their mounting agitation against the government was more political, social, and economic than religious. The Diem family reacted with a blind intolerance that was to prove its undoing. When in 1963, after martial law had been imposed, government forces began shooting Buddhists, sacking their temples, and arresting their leaders, the United States commenced to withdraw its support, and reports of the unpopularity of the Diem regime finally began to prevail in Washington. Other reasons for the United States wanting to get rid of Diem were rumors that the President's powerful brother, Ngo Dinh Nhu, and his wife might be prepared to change sides; Diem himself indulged in frequent diatribes against the United States. Denied American protection, the government was overthrown with contemptuous ease by an army junta. Diem and his brother were murdered and other prominent members of the family were arrested or exiled.

[1] A provincial leader has been quoted as saying: "When you have an official who will deal sternly with the Viet Minh, it is of secondary importance whether he is honest or otherwise capable. It is better to have a district chief who steals than a district full of Communists." (Roy Juniper, "Mandarin Bureaucracy and Politics in South Vietnam," *Pacific Affairs*, Vol. 30, 1957, p. 52.)

The new rulers suspended the constitution and dissolved the National Assembly, but promised a swift return to constitutional government and a liberal political framework. This proved easier said than done. For one thing, the army junta did not speak with one voice; it had been united only in its detestation of the Diem regime, and offered little competent political leadership. Furthermore, the state apparatus Diem had constructed was not easily dismantled. To remove the thousands of officials who had a vested interest in its corrupt and repressive practices would have severely crippled all administrative services. On the other hand, the continued presence of these officials, particularly the Catholics, was a standing provocation to the Buddhists and other opponents.

As government in South Vietnam gave way to a whirligig of riots, demonstrations, and coups, the United States found itself in an increasingly difficult position. From a holding operation that would enable an independent and democratically ruled South Vietnam to lay the foundations of political, economic, and social reform, its involvement developed into a military commitment to protect, almost regardless of cost, any regime that could be mounted and was prepared to fight on in the civil war against the National Liberation Front. As the American public were told by their professional reporters in the press, corruption and maladministration reached even higher levels than under Diem. But United States prestige had now been even more definitely stacked, and the fear that all the countries of Southeast Asia would topple like so many dominoes if South Vietnam should fall to Communism had become a sacred tenet of American policy. This might be true, but the civil war in Vietnam, as it is now being fought, might in the long run give an even greater impetus to the spread of Communism in the area. In any case, a commitment to help a Saigon government win the civil war becomes untenable if the people in South Vietnam are unwilling to fight on the American side. A considerable number of the rebels may be Communists in some sense — and more are probably becoming Communists — but they are also, and more fundamentally, Vietnamese. In the Saigon camp the American presence was becoming ever more visible, as, in its time, was the presence of the French. Although Westerners, as well as the upper strata in South Asia generally, prefer to ignore it, the racial issue is increasingly evident. To the people in the villages and the paddy fields, the Americans coming in their helicopters and jet planes to spread fire and death are more than powerful and dangerous strangers; they are "white devils" — a concept with a long tradition in this part of the world. Even above that level of intuitive reaction, the contention that the Saigon government, however much it changes in the sequence of coups, is merely a puppet government, set up and defended by foreigners for their own purpose, and that it offers nothing but death and arbitrary, corrupt rule, must look embarrassingly plausible to simple-minded people.

The deployment of American military personnel was gradually increased from less than 800 men in 1960, when President Eisenhower's term expired, to 21,000 toward the end of 1964. "Escalation" on a grand scale came in 1965; a target in August for the end of 1965 of 125,000 men was later raised to 200,000. At the beginning of 1966 more than 180,000 American soldiers are in South Vietnam, and the trend is toward ever higher figures. Although there has been no declaration of war, the role of the American forces has gradually changed. Instead of mere "military advisors," they have become regular combat troops, participating in war operations.

Certain common traits are apparent in this continual intensification of United States participation in the Vietnam war. For one thing, almost every step-up has been motivated – even if this was not announced at the time to the American public – by an acute danger that the rebels were on the verge of a decisive victory; this was the case also when the decision on large-scale escalation was made in February, 1965. With equal regularity, each increase in the war effort has left the situation as bad as it was in the beginning, if not worse. This has assured a constant pressure driving the escalation of American war efforts ever higher without coming nearer the goal. A third trait has been that after each new step-up of United States military engagement, U. S. government officials expressed high hopes that the tide was turning and the end of the war was in sight. Their optimism diminished after mid-1965, and toward the end of the year the announcements became more sober. The American public was then, for the first time, given to understand that winning the war might take many years and necessitate the involvement of even more troops.

Under these circumstances it is only natural that President Johnson has accompanied the most recent phase of accelerated military escalation with peace offers, which by now have risen to the pitch of a diplomatic peace offensive. These peace offers have been needed for internal reasons in the United States; it is, indeed, questionable whether, without them, the nation would accept the ever-growing commitment of American soldiers in a war now seen to be of indeterminate length. Expressing honestly held convictions, the President affirms that the United States does not seek any territory in Vietnam, and that it is prepared to withdraw its troops as soon as South Vietnam is in a position to determine its own future freely, without interference from North Vietnam. To the outside world – and we mean not only North Vietnam and other Communist countries – there are, however, some flaws in these declarations, which make it understandable that the response from Hanoi has not been positive. These flaws are all a consequence of United States relations with the government in Saigon.

The latter government is, to be sure, dependent for its very existence and for all its policies on the United States, but as things have developed the United States is, at the same time, equally dependent on having a government of that type in Saigon. A change of leaders, while preserving the main policy line of carrying on the war, is less tempting to the United States after all the coups since the liquidation of Diem, and could make little difference anyhow. The very weakness of the Saigon government increases United States dependence on it. Thus the usual disadvantage of having satellites and puppet governments – that the powerful, supporting government easily becomes the hostage of its client and dependent on his precarious circumstances – is one more factor in the automatic, accelerating escalation of the war in Vietnam.

The Saigon government stands in danger of losing whatever security it has if the United States were to take account of the reality of civil war in South Vietnam and in unequivocal terms declare itself ready to negotiate with the party it is fighting against, the National Liberation Front. Likewise, the Saigon government cannot possibly accept an unequivocal declaration by the United States that it would be prepared to acquiesce in the choice by the South Vietnamese people of a Communist regime and union with North Vietnam, if that were the popular will, and thereafter withdraw its troops. The United States has to detour around the possibility of such an outcome and maintain that its moral duty is to assist the brave, freedom-loving South Vietnamese nation, fighting valiantly in order not to succumb to military aggression by another nation. Nor is it certain that the President, if he wanted to, could get the American people and the Congress, at this stage, to accept a clarification on these two points; it is certain, however, that the South Vietnam government would not be prepared to risk it. The United States has, indeed, pushed that government to the practical limit of possible concessions in that it no longer announces as its goal the "liberation" of North Vietnam, as was done not only by Diem but also, as late as the summer of 1964, by the head of one of the several later governments, General Khanh.

While accelerating its military operations and at the same time engaging in peace offensives, the United States has intensified its efforts to secure improvements in social conditions in South Vietnam, and has set aside huge sums and a large group of personnel for this purpose. Recognizing that, in the final instance, the main thing is to win the people, United States officials now speak of the need for a "social revolution" in South Vietnam. But the Saigon government and the United States troops probably have stable and effective control over less than 30 percent of the territory of South Vietnam, compared with about 80 percent at the beginning of 1962. Not only does this fact make it even more difficult than in the past to lead the ruling group in Saigon to the active pursuit of a policy of large-scale social and economic reform and of stamping out corruption and inefficiency; it gives military action an even higher priority than before. Unless a large increase of the securely "pacified" area can rapidly be achieved, the "social revolution" is in danger of being a card played too late.

How this vast human tragedy, the war in Vietnam, evolves in the months and years to come will depend not only on the decisions of those governments that are directly and indirectly involved in the conflict, but also on the actions and reactions of other governments – and of the Vietnamese people. In contemplating this grave uncertainty, it is worth bearing in mind a fundamental point that is commonly overlooked. Vietnam has been lumped together with the rest of Southeast Asia by many commentators, including ourselves in this book, when by virtue of the political traditions, language, administrative system, and religious and philosophical outlook of its articulate strata, it belongs to East Asia. The Vietnamese have much the same culture, much the same ideals and ideas, and much the same attitudes and abilities as the Chinese. Yet for many centuries Vietnam defended itself against Chinese encroachment and sought a distinct identity. There is no reason to suppose that this tradition would not be kept alive under a Communist regime – unless, of course, people felt that they were the object of a relentless attack from the West. To the Vietnamese people a Communist state, intent on preserving a maximum of independence from China, could hardly be a worse alternative than a prolongation of the misery they have suffered these past twenty years. In view of the mounting material, political, and moral costs of present U. S. policies, it is difficult to understand how the situation can look different to the United States.

In general, the development problems of the successor states to French Indo-China have been given only cursory attention in this study. We have dealt with the political problems in Vietnam a little more fully because what happens in this corner of the region is bound to have serious repercussions in all the South Asian countries.

Part Three

ECONOMIC REALITIES

In this part of the book we shall deal with the economic facts of the South Asian countries. We shall sketch, in broad outline, the main features of the national economies: levels of total output, structure of production, position in world trade, the impact of alien elements on the economy, levels of living, and the extent and consequences of income inequality.

We are still in the introductory, descriptive stages of our study of the economic problems in South Asia. However, the attempt to make valid generalizations and inferences from the facts implies some preliminary efforts to understand why and how things have come to be as they are and what the alternatives and prospects are for further economic development. We cannot, therefore, avoid reference to the historical background and the major issues of planning that are discussed more fully elsewhere.

The attempt to sketch economic reality, to find out what the present situation is and discern dominant trends, is severely restricted by the lack of precise and reliable statistics and other information. Even more fundamentally, we are restricted by inconsistent, unrealistic, and even misleading concepts in attempting to grasp and interpret the facts. Much of Part Three, particularly Chapters 11 and 12, will therefore be given to a critical appraisal of conventional economic concepts as applied to South Asia. "Reality" in South Asia will be found to be a rather elusive notion when viewed through glasses shaped by Western experience.

Chapter 10

POPULATION AND THE DEVELOPMENT OF RESOURCES

1 *The Paramount Importance of Land and Its Utilization*

The aim of the present chapter is to set out the basic features of economic geography in South Asia and to explain in broad terms how these facts of nature – together with the impact of Western domination, including the opportunity created for population increase – have shaped the economic structure of the countries in the region and influenced the distribution of population. We have tried to draw a highly simplified picture in order to outline the main historical trends and indicate the broad similarities and differences among these countries today.[1]

Throughout South Asia, agriculture continues to be the dominant branch of production. Productivity in agriculture, in contrast to those parts of the world where agriculture embraces a smaller share of population and production, is the main determinant of national levels of income and living. Moreover, there are narrow limits to the extent to which imports can be relied on to feed an increasing population; and since any increase in income

[1] The tables and graphs accompanying this chapter were compiled at an early stage of the study; as more recent developments are discussed in other chapters of this book, we have not attempted to update them.

per head from the present low levels also will considerably increase the demand for food, the man/land ratio, together with the utilization of the land and of the labor available to work it, is of crucial importance for the prospects of development and the problems of planning for development.

2 *Population Density*

Let us first consider how population size is related to land resources. South Asia is often thought of as a very densely populated region. It certainly has more people per unit of land than other tropical regions in Africa and Latin America. If, however, South Asia is compared with the non-tropical parts of the world, it cannot unqualifiedly be called a densely populated region, as will be seen later. Here we need only note that the average population density of the whole region of South Asia is roughly the same as that of Europe, without the U.S.S.R., and about four times that of the United States.

Figures for population density arrived at by dividing the total number of people in a region by the total area of the region are, of course, highly inadequate as indicators of the relative scarcity or abundance of land resources in different regions, even supposing that the figures are statistically sound. First, regions differ in degree of industrialization, and so in the proportion of population that gains its livelihood from agriculture. Secondly, the agricultural population is never spread evenly over an entire region, so that aggregates and averages have limited meaning even when they are confined to the agricultural population. Thirdly, there are great differences between regions in the proportion of land that is cultivated or can be cultivated. Fourthly, there are differences in quality of land, both cultivated and cultivable. Finally, there are differences in crop patterns and in agricultural techniques employed.

These differences are apt to make all general and simple comparisons of population density misleading. The refinement sought by relating the population, or the agricultural population, to cultivated land rather than total land area removes some of the difficulties, but it does not necessarily give a more correct measurement of population pressure. Population density so measured does not take into account either the scope for expansion in the cultivated area or the quality of the cultivated, and the cultivable, land. The observation that in a given country the cultivated area per head of population, or of agricultural population, is small may mean that land resources are nearing exhaustion so that a unit of arable land has to carry the burden of an abnormally high number of people. But it may also mean that agricultural techniques are so primitive, capital so scarce, and the political, institutional, and attitudinal barriers so high, that only a part of the cultivable land is in use. There is also the question of the intensity with which land is cultivated, related to crop patterns and agricultural techniques. Ideally one would want to know to what extent – and under what conditions, not only in regard to costs – the land resources could be increased, either extensively, by bringing more land under cultivation, or intensively, by applying irrigation, fertilizers, or otherwise increasing the yield from presently cultivated land.

In Chapter 26, Section 6, we shall discuss the potential land resources of the several countries in South Asia; in this broad survey we shall content ourselves with the less refined traditional yardsticks. In Table 10–1, total population and agricultural population in the region as a whole, and in a few other regions and countries, have been related to agricultural area and output. It is hardly necessary to say that the figures have a wide margin of error, especially those in columns 3 to 6.[1] The orders of magnitude should be sufficiently reliable, nevertheless, to bring out the main similarities and contrasts.

The first thing to note is that, contrary to what is often assumed, the man/land ratio in South Asia is not strikingly high in comparison with that in other parts of the world. The number of inhabitants per unit of cultivated land is comparable to the European average; it is half that of China; and, of course, much lower than in Japan, about one-sixth of the Japanese average according to the table. What really distinguishes South Asia is the very low output per unit of agricultural land (column 4) and per unit of labor (column 6). Per hectare, South Asia as a whole produces probably only about half as much as China[2] or Europe and only about one-fifth as much as Japan. Indeed, per hectare output in South Asia is of the same order of magnitude, roughly speaking, as in the United States and the U.S.S.R. – even though these countries, with more than three times as much agricultural land per head of total population, can afford very extensive cultivation and, at their levels of industrialization, use a much smaller proportion of their total labor force for agricultural production (about one-half the South Asian figure in the case of the Soviet Union, and about one-tenth in the case of the United States). The basic fact to account for the low degree of economic development in South Asia is that its agricultural output, whether measured per hectare or per man engaged, is lower than that of most major regions. Those countries whose output per hectare is equally low have the advantages of a greater area of land per inhabitant and an even greater area per unit of labor devoted to agriculture. In the light of these figures, South Asia appears to have the worst of both worlds.

[1] Of the basic estimates, those of population and of cultivated area are fairly reliable, except for China and, to a lesser extent, South Asia; those of volume of output and, even more, of men in agriculture are crude in every case. As a result the figures in column 6 in particular have a very wide margin of error.

[2] This refers to Chinese levels of output before the recent sharp changes, upwards and downwards. This way of making the comparison is, perhaps, the more appropriate one, as the South Asian countries have not had much in the way of land reforms and have experienced few large-scale attempts to change agricultural techniques, let alone the type of revolutionary changes introduced in China by the Communist regime. See Chapter 26.

Table 10–1

AGRICULTURAL POPULATION AND OUTPUT IN MAJOR PARTS OF THE WORLD

	Total population (Mid–1955 estimate. Millions) (1)	*Number of Inhabitants per hundred hectares of cultivated land*[a] *(Around 1955)* (2)	*Percent of "economically active" males engaged in agriculture*[b] *(Around 1955)* (3)	*Volume of agricultural output*[c] *(Average 1952–56. Index: Average for South Asia = 100)*		
				Per hectare of cultivated land (4)	*Per inhabitant* (5)	*Per "economically active" male in agriculture* (6)
South Asia	646	275	70	100	100	100
China	608	560	70–75	180	90	90–100
Japan	89	1,620	35	510	85	175
Europe	409	275	30	(250)	(250)	(580)
U.S.S.R.	200	90	40–45	(70)	(215)	(350)
United States	166	90	15	(125)	(380)	(1,780)

Sources: See note on Sources following Table 10–2.

[a] Arable land plus land under tree crops. Land under permanent grass is excluded.

[b] "Economically active" has been placed in quotation marks for reasons discussed in Chapter 21, Part III.

[c] The figures for South Asia, China, and Japan were arrived at by applying Indian farm prices, averaged for 1952–56, to the average quantities of output in every country during that five-year period. Only plant production was considered. The figures for Europe, the U.S.S.R., and the United States are broad guesses. They are supposed to include animal production. The figures in parentheses are subject to especially wide margins of error. All figures except those in column 1 have been rounded to the nearest 5. Column 6 is based on the other columns and on estimates of the percentage of active males in the total population.

Broadly speaking, farming as practiced today is of two distinct types. Sparsely populated lands like North America, Australia, or the Soviet Union utilize the soil extensively; they have a very low output per unit of land. The second type, intensive land utilization with high yields per hectare, is practiced in regions with a high man/land ratio as, in varying degree, in Europe, China, and Japan. South Asia fits into neither of these main groups. It forms a third and very unfortunate category, namely, that of extensive land use combined with a high man/land ratio. Naturally, this constellation results in disastrously low levels of nutrition and real income. For not only is agricultural output per head of population low, but almost three-fourths of the total labor force is tied up in the production of a meager diet in which cereals usually account for more than two-thirds of total calorie intake.[1] Thus in South Asia only about one out of every four male workers is available for activities other than the direct production of food, while in the United States nine out of ten and in Europe two out of three males can devote themselves to non-agricultural occupations.

Over-all comparisons such as these indicate the dimensions of the basic economic problems of the region. More particularly, they suggest that higher agricultural output per unit of land is an essential condition for raising levels of living and for supporting industrialization. As we shall demonstrate in later chapters, much of the discussion about draining off an alleged surplus of manpower from agriculture as a pre-condition for economic expansion is beside the point. Even on the most optimistic assumptions, productive work opportunities outside the agricultural sector will not be capable of absorbing more than a small fraction of the natural increment in the population of working age in the decades immediately ahead. The so-called surplus manpower must in fact remain in agriculture, and the foundation for economic advance must be laid by intensifying agricultural production. The achievement of this result will require a much heavier labor input both from the present agricultural population and from the increment in the agricultural work force made available by rapid population increase. In Part Five we shall take up the systematic analysis of these questions.

3 *Population Density and Types of Agriculture*

There are sharp contrasts in density of settlement within South Asia, as Figure 10–1 shows. Huge populations are concentrated in a few pockets where the number of people per unit of territory is often comparable to that of highly industrialized areas in Western Europe. East Pakistan, with one-seventh of the area of Pakistan, has almost four-sevenths of the popu-

[1] Some smaller countries in the region, where plantations play a major role – as Malaya and Ceylon – or where agriculture, even without plantations, is export oriented – as Burma and Thailand – do not fit into this generalization; see below.

Figure 10–1

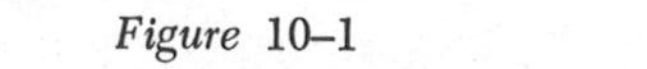

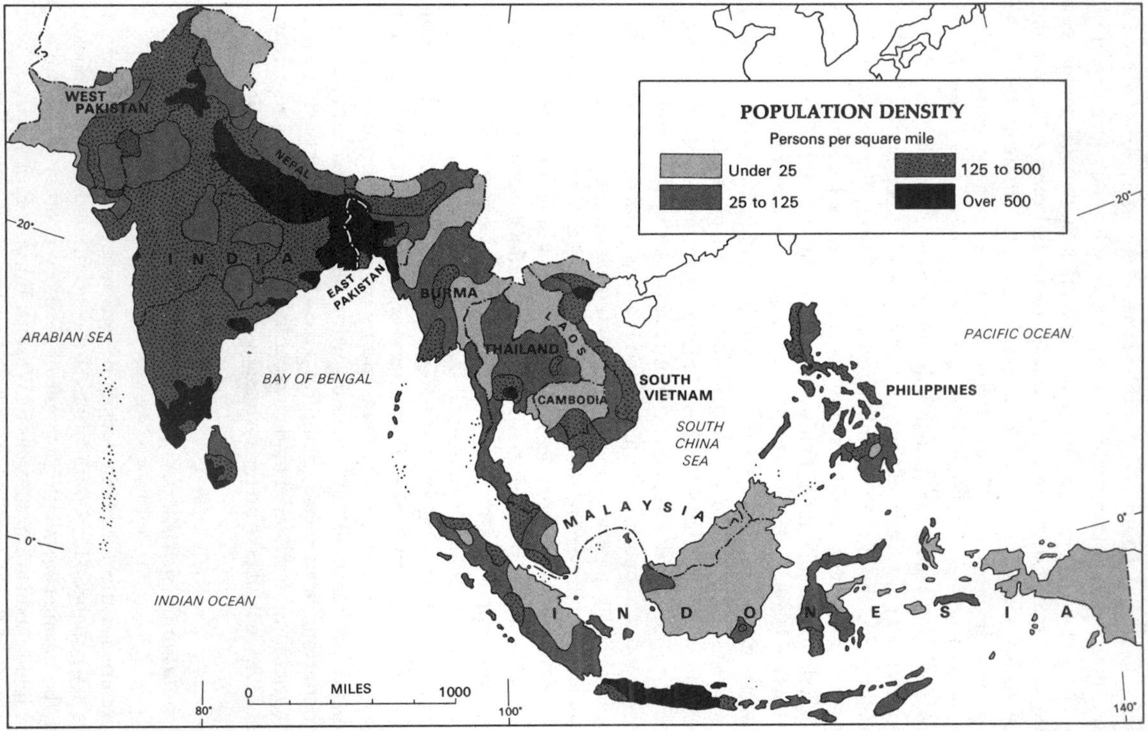

Sources: India: *Census of India 1951, Paper No. 1,* New Delhi, 1957. Pakistan: *Census of Pakistan 1951,* Vol. 1, p. 36. For other countries the chart is based mainly on E. H. G. Dobby, *Southeast Asia,* University of London Press, London, 1950, p. 388 *et passim,* supplemented by information from the *Demographic Yearbook* of the United Nations.

lation; the concentration is even greater in the central part of East Pakistan. Half the population of India lives on less than a quarter of the total available land, and one-third is concentrated on less than 6 percent of the land. At the other extreme, vast areas continue to be almost uninhabited. It is in the logic of things that the most densely populated countries are the "big" countries when bigness is counted in numbers of people and that, in all countries, the most densely populated areas weigh heaviest in any population comparison. This is to say that people live in denser concentrations than a simple comparison between population and total or cultivated area would suggest, either for the region as a whole or for the several countries.

These contrasts in population density are closely connected with differences in cropping pattern and in character of agriculture. Broadly speaking, the pattern of settlement can be explained in terms of four types of land utilization: (1) wet paddy cultivation; (2) cultivation of plantation crops; (3) sedentary dry farming; and (4) shifting cultivation. The first two are associated with high population density, the others with more scattered settlement. Obviously the distribution of population as shown in the map also reflects differences in degree of urbanization in the various areas.[1] But these differences are of limited importance in the present context, partly because the share of urban population in total population is small throughout South Asia and partly because the location of the urban centers, notwithstanding some conspicuous exceptions such as Bombay, Delhi, and Singapore, is in turn determined largely by the agricultural conditions of the hinterland. The non-agricultural rural population in the villages is, of course, still more dependent on the agricultural population, and thus indirectly on agricultural production.

The highest concentrations of population are invariably found in those areas where conditions are favorable for the growing of wet paddy. These are, first of all, the fertile river valleys and coastal plains in Southeast Asia, where the population has been concentrated for centuries or millennia. The silt deposited by the rivers when they overflow during the monsoon rejuvenates the soil, enabling cultivation to continue for centuries without danger of soil exhaustion. The main areas of wet paddy cultivation of the highest type are the Irrawaddy Delta in Burma, the lower range of the Me Nam in Central Thailand, the Red River in North Vietnam and – more recently and less densely populated – the Mekong Delta in South Vietnam. Good conditions for the growing of wet paddy contributed to the early growth of population in Java and on the island of Luzon in the Philippines. River valleys, deltas, and coastal plains of the wet paddy type exist also on the Indian subcontinent. But there they account for a much smaller share of the cultivated land than in Southeast Asia. Paddy is produced, most often in monoculture, on less than a fourth of all cultivated land in India as

[1] See below, Section 11.

against one-third in Indonesia and from half to three-fourths in continental Southeast Asia. Most of the paddy cultivation on the Indian subcontinent is concentrated in East and South India and in East Pakistan where conditions for agriculture are somewhat similar to those of Southeast Asia.

Part of the wet paddy cultivation in the main producing districts of Southeast Asia has been aided by man-made irrigation, the works in some cases dating from centuries before European rule. The extent to which irrigation canals have supplemented the natural sources of water – rainfall and the unregulated discharge of rivers – has generally varied with the density of population. In crowded Java, at one extreme, irrigation works for paddy cultivation have been intensively developed while in Lower Burma, which is less densely settled, cultivators have not taken much interest in irrigation works but have found the rainfall and annual flooding reliable enough for their needs.

Although the regions of wet paddy are mostly those of very ancient civilization, the cultivation of plantation crops, the other type of land utilization associated with dense settlement, is of quite recent origin. The greatest concentrations of plantation crops are found in Ceylon, along the western coast of the Malayan Peninsula, on Java and Sumatra, and in the Philippines. On the Indian subcontinent, again, plantation crops play a far smaller role. The deep impact of the plantations on the recent economic history of South Asia will be briefly described later in this chapter.

There are vast areas of land where the predominant form of agriculture is of the third type – sedentary dry farming – and where the population density is considerably lower than in wet paddy or plantation areas. In Southeast Asia, the only major regions where such cultivation prevails are the dry zones in central Burma and northeastern Thailand. In these places an annual dry period, even if relatively short, makes it possible to have permanent cultivation without the soil being destroyed by continuous leaching.[1] In India and West Pakistan, on the other hand, sedentary dry farming is practiced over large areas. The predominance of this relatively poor form of agriculture reflects the climatic handicap of much of India and West Pakistan as compared with the other countries of South Asia. The summer monsoon is weak and unreliable, and the winter monsoon wholly or nearly absent, in West Pakistan and North and Central India. Although wetter than the desert parts of West and Central Asia, these areas are not as wet as monsoon Asia proper.[2] Here the original form of primitive agriculture, burning patches of forest land (see below), seriously depleted the land and left a dry and poor sedentary agriculture as the only alternative.

[1] When rainfall is concentrated in a few prolonged storms, as in the truly monsoon climate, the soluble elements in the soil needed for plant growth are dissolved and either buried deep or washed away. This "leaching" of the soil can be beneficial to the extent that it washes away salts and other harmful elements, but usually the process must then be carefully controlled to ensure that desirable elements are not also removed. See Appendix 10, Sections 2 and 4.

[2] Appendix 10.

Where irrigation facilities have been provided they have often failed to produce impressive changes in yields or in agricultural practice, for the cultivators have tended to regard irrigation more as an insurance against drought than as a resource to be exploited in order to improve performance.[1]

In the physical conditions governing agriculture, the Indian subcontinent is thus seen to be intermediate between Southeast Asia and West and Central Asia. Geographically and agriculturally, the region of South Asia can be divided into two main parts, a Western and an Eastern one, with the borderline running through India from north to south, bending to the west so as to include South India in the eastern part. The "Western region," consisting of West and Central India together with West Pakistan, is characterized by dry farming and, in limited areas, by wet farming under artificial irrigation; in other words, the agricultural pattern is fairly similar to that of West and Central Asia. The "Eastern region" embraces East and South India, East Pakistan, Ceylon, and the whole of Southeast Asia. Wet paddy cultivation and the production of plantation crops are here the principal forms of agriculture.

The fourth type of agriculture, and the one associated with the lowest man/land ratio, is that of shifting cultivation. It is practiced by clearing a field in the forest, by burning down the existing vegetation, and sowing food crops, mostly rice or millets, then moving on after a few years, when the fertility provided by the ashes has been used up or when the field has become overgrown by weeds. While a new clearing is opened and cultivated in another place, the wild forest reconquers the soil. This type of cultivation requires less heavy work than does permanent tilling of the soil and it can be done without the help of draft power. But it can of course support only a scattered population and requires the existence of vast stretches of forest land. It continues to be a typical form of subsistence farming in Indonesia outside of Java and throughout the mountain districts of continental Southeast Asia. Even in some parts of otherwise densely populated Ceylon, shifting cultivation still provides many farmers with a considerable share of their subsistence. It is less widespread in India because of the scarcity of large forest districts; but where forests do exist – mainly in East and Central India – shifting cultivation is still prevalent. In other hilly districts, and in the Himalayas, sedentary farmers practice shifting cultivation as a subsidiary occupation, in much the same way as in Ceylon. In what was just called the "Western region" of South Asia, land not under continuous cultivation consists largely of deserts or denuded rocks; in the sparse forests where shifting cultivation occurs it is likely to be more damaging than in the "Eastern region" because the dry climate enhances the danger of uncontrolled fires.

These broad relationships between physical conditions, type of agricul-

[1] Chapter 26, Section 9.

Figure 10–2

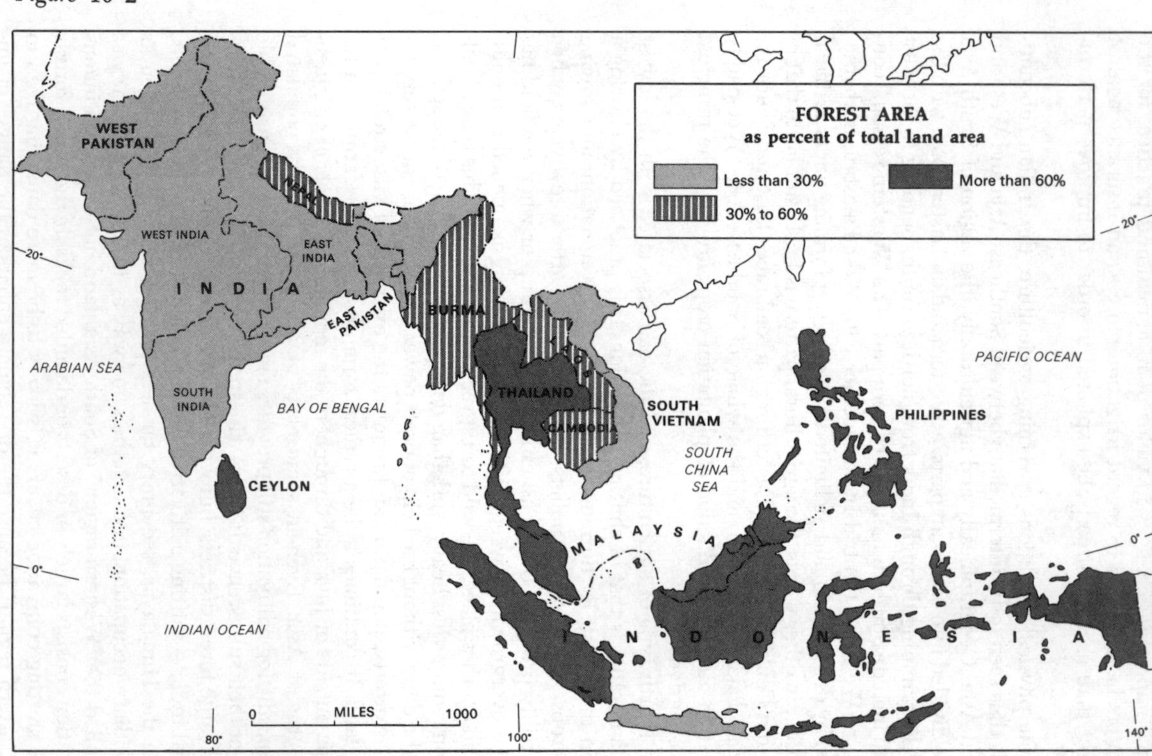

Source: World Geography of Forest Resources, American Geographical Society Special Publication No. 33, Ronald Press, New York, 1956.

Figure 10–3

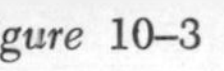

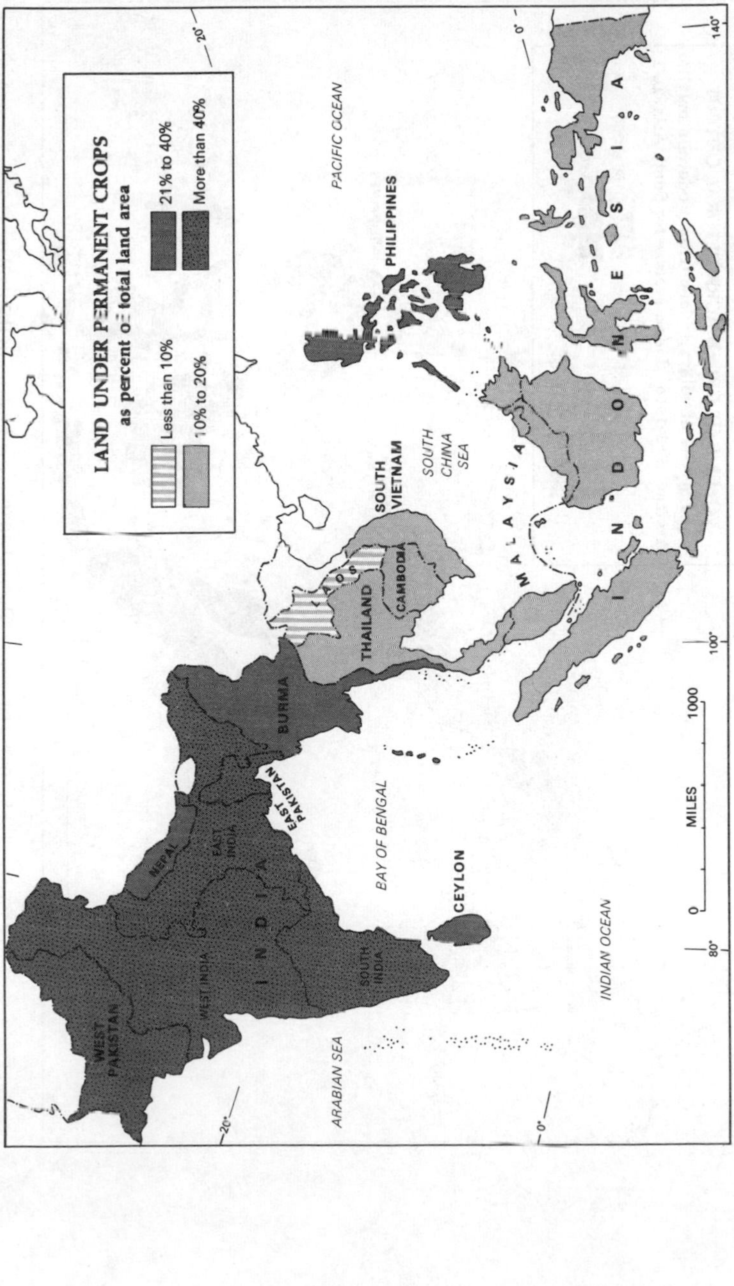

Source and Notes: Data from United Nations, Food and Agriculture Organization, *Production Yearbook 1964,* Table 1, pp. 2–8. There may be wide variations among reporting countries; many countries supplied data only for areas under major crops. Data are for the early 1960's except for Indonesia (1954) and Pakistan (1958). For India, Pakistan, Nepal, Indonesia, and the Philippines the base is a reporting area smaller than the total area.

Figure 10–4

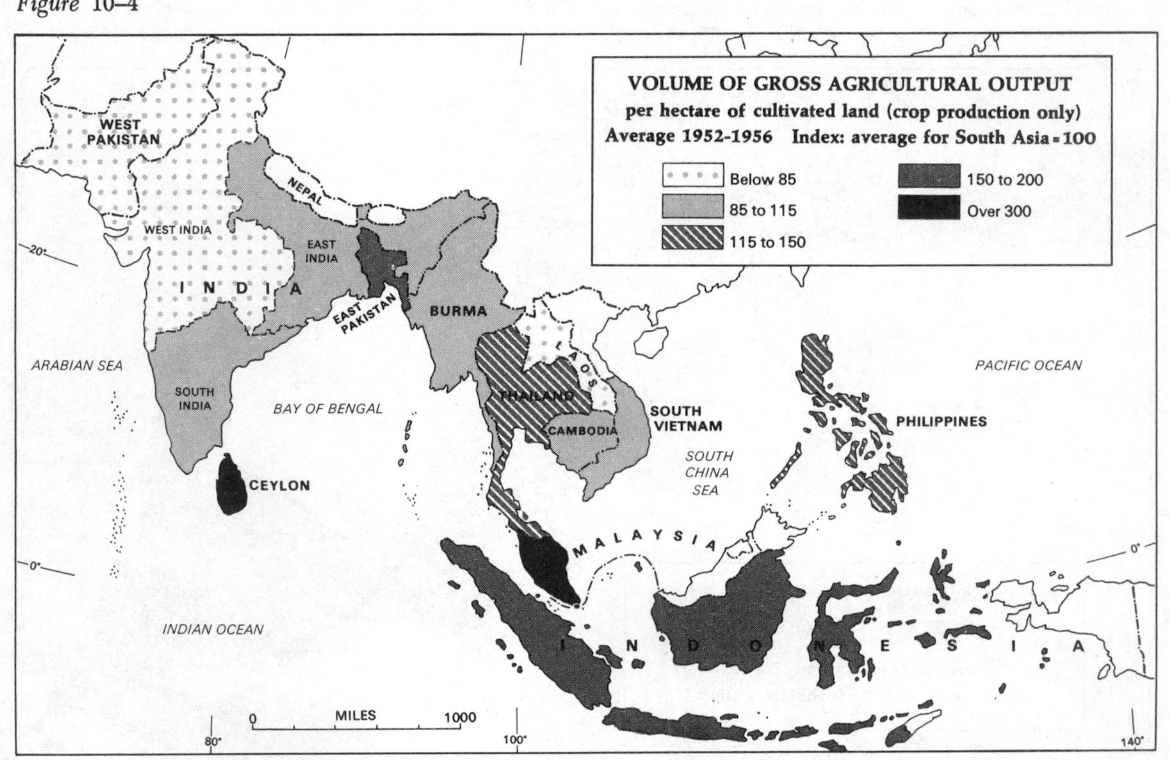

Source: Table 10–2. Data are for the mid-1950's; see the notes to that table.

ture, and density of population are illustrated in three charts. As can be seen in Figure 10–2, the share of forests in the total area exceeds 60 percent in most of Southeast Asia. At the other end of the scale, forests account for less than 30 percent of the area throughout the Indian subcontinent. As would be expected, the proportion of land that is cultivated is low where forests predominate and vice versa (Figure 10–3).

Finally, the differences in forms of agriculture are reflected in Figure 10–4, which shows variations in crop production per hectare of cultivated land. Of the four main types of agriculture, plantations yield by far the highest returns per unit of land, followed by wet paddy, sedentary dry farming, and shifting cultivation, in that order. Correspondingly, the highest per hectare output is found in Ceylon and Malaya where plantations are particularly important, and the next highest in Java and Sumatra, and East Pakistan. Output rates are lowest in West India, West Pakistan, and Laos.

4 *Population Density and Agricultural Productivity*

In Table 10–2 an attempt has been made, despite seriously deficient statistical data, to give somewhat more precise quantitative expression to these relationships between population density and agricultural productivity in each of the countries in the region and in major parts of some of them. The first three columns of this table show the population density according to three different measures: (1) the crude territorial density; (2) the over-all density per unit of cultivated land; and (3) the "agrarian density," i.e., the number of men[1] engaged in agriculture per unit of cultivated land. The three following columns show the volume of crop production in relation to cultivated land, to agricultural manpower, and to total population, expressed in each case as a percentage of the weighted average for South Asia as a whole. As with the preceding table, the figures have a wide margin of error. Although detailed computations were made for each crop in each country, and annual fluctuations were eliminated by taking the average of five consecutive years, the figures arrived at can be no more than crude approximations.

A few main features of the table may be pointed out. First, a comparison can be made between the Indian subcontinent and the region of Southeast Asia (rows 19 and 21). On a purely territorial basis (column 1), the Indian subcontinent is seen to be more than twice as densely populated as Southeast Asia. But if the population, or the portion that is dependent on agriculture for its livelihood, is related to the cultivated area (columns 2 and

[1] Owing to wide discrepancies in methods of statistical reporting, an attempt to include female employment in agriculture would impair the inter-country comparability even further.

Table 10–2

POPULATION DENSITY, AGRARIAN DENSITY, AND AGRICULTURAL PRODUCTIVITY, BY COUNTRY AND REGION

Country or region	No.[a] of Inhabitants		No.[a] of active males in agriculture per 100 ha. of cultivated land (3)	Volume of gross agricultural output (crop production only, average 1952–56. Index: Average for South Asia = 100)		
	Per 100 ha. of total territory (1)	Per 100 ha. of cultivated land (2)		Per hectare of cultivated land (4)	Per active male in agriculture (5)	Per inhabitant (6)
1. West India	70	155	35	55	92	96
2. East India	170	345	75	109	81	86
3. South India	160	280	50	90	99	88
4. Total India	115	240	50	79	89	90
5. West Pakistan	45	230	45	73	90	86
6. East Pakistan	325	510	120	173	80	93
7. Total Pakistan	85	325	75	109	84	90
8. Ceylon	130	570	85	312	206	150
9. Federation of Malaya[b]	45	275	50	354	399	357
10. Burma	30	225	(40)	88	(129)	107

11. Thailand	50	260	55	129	126	136
12. Cambodia	25	220	(50)	(92)	(103)	(117)
13. Laos	5	140	(30)	(52)	(100)	(104)
14. South Vietnam	70	365	65–75	115	85–96	87
15. Java and Madura	410	585	(115)	207	(98)	97
16. Outer islands of Indonesia	20	345	(65)	198	(167)	156
17. Total Indonesia	55	470	(95)	206	(122)	119
18. Philippines	75	370	55	145	149	109
Averages:						
19. India and Pakistan	110	255	50	83	88	90
20. Ceylon and Fed. of Malaya	75	395	65	338	295	236
21. Southeast Asia (excl. Fed. of Malaya)	45	350	65	148	122	115
22. Total South Asia	80	275	55	100	100	100
23. China	60	560	(100)	178	(97)	87
24. Japan	240	1,620	160	508	174	86

[a] Number rounded to nearest multiple of five.

[b] For all of Malaya (i.e., the Federation and Singapore) the figures in columns 1, 2, and 6 would be 55, 325, and 295 respectively.

Note: Many figures in this table had to be estimated by crude methods on the basis of insufficient statistical data. Figures in brackets are particularly uncertain and may be misleading even as indicators of broad orders of magnitude. For details on sources and methods of estimation, see the appended note.

Sources and Methods for Tables 10–1 and 10–2

1. *Geographical area and cultivated area.* Data are from *FAO Yearbook of Production,* various issues, and national sources as follows: India: *Agricultural Situation in India,* February, 1958. Pakistan: *Pakistan Statistical Yearbook 1955; Report of the Economic Appraisal Committee,* Karachi, 1953, p. 59. Indonesia: *Statistical Pocketbook of Indonesia 1957; Ekonomi dan Keuangan Indonesia,* Djakarta, September, 1955. South Vietnam: *Statistical Yearbook of Viet-Nam, 1956.* The cultivated area in South Vietnam was estimated on the basis of information on the area under paddy (United States Operation Mission to Viet-Nam, *Annual Statistical Bulletin,* data through 1957) and on the share of paddy in total cultivated area (Gene Gregory, *A Glimpse of Viet-Nam,* Saigon, 1957, p. 49).

2. *Total population.* Estimates for mid–1955 taken mainly from United Nations, *Demographic Yearbook, 1956,* but corrected for latest census returns. For China, the 1955 population was taken from U. N., *Economic Survey of Asia and the Far East 1961,* Bangkok, 1962, p. 168. The regional figures for India and Pakistan were estimated on the assumption that the rate of growth since 1951 was the same for each of the regions considered.

3. *Active males in agriculture.* In most cases the figures were based on census results as given in *United Nations Demographic Yearbook* and *FAO Yearbook of Production.* The figures include people engaged in fishing and forestry. The census figures, relating in most cases to years between 1945 and 1951, were raised to an estimated 1955 level on the arbitrary assumption that the male work force in agriculture had been growing at the same rate as total population. Country details are as follows:

India: The figures were based on the *Reports of the 1951 Census* (Parts II B and II C), and some adjustments were made to take account of the subsequent changes in State boundaries, and to include persons engaged in plantations, stock raising, forestry and fishing. Finally, the agricultural work force in South India was semi-arbitrarily raised from 15 to 17 million in order to offset what appears to be a gross under-estimation in the census figure.

Pakistan: The source of the data is *Pakistan Statistical Yearbook 1955.* A rough estimate for the North-West Frontier Region was added.

Burma, Indonesia, Cambodia and Laos: In the absence of reasonably recent and complete census data very rough guesses were made, based on scattered estimates of total population around 1955 and the share of rural population in total population. The ratio between active males in agriculture and total rural population was freely estimated on the basis of available information from other countries in the region with broadly similar economic structure. The unreliability of the resulting figures cannot be sufficiently stressed.

Ceylon: The census figures for men engaged in agriculture include the personnel of tea factories. A deduction was made, based on information on factory employment in Indian tea plantations as given by the National Sample Survey.

China: It was assumed that active males in agriculture account for 25 percent of the population attached to agriculture.

4. *Volume of gross agricultural output.* For each country, the quantity produced of each single crop (average 1952–56, for China 1952–55) was multiplied by the aver-

Sources and Methods for Tables 10–1 and 10–2 continued

age price paid to Indian farmers (or, in some cases, Indian wholesale prices) during the same period. No attempt was made to include the output from animal husbandry.

The sources of information were *FAO Yearbook of Production* and national harvest statistics. For China, *Report of the Indian Delegation to China on Agricultural Planning and Techniques, 1956.* For Indonesia, information received directly from the Bureau of Statistics, Djakarta. Indian farm prices were taken from *Agricultural Prices in India* and other official publications.

Some crops, notably soy beans, sugar beet, palm kernel, and abaca, are not grown in India but are important in other countries of the region. In the absence of an Indian price for these products, a somewhat artificial procedure had to be adopted: For each of these "non-Indian" crops a "hypothetical Indian price" was computed on the basis of the ratio in some other country between the price of that crop and another crop closely related with respect to end-use. The "hypothetical Indian prices" thereby arrived at were as follows (for equal units of weight):

Soy beans	76	percent of the Indian price of	groundnuts
Sugar beet	38	–do–	potatoes
Palm kernel	80	"	copra
Abaca and hard fibres	154	"	jute
Flax	175	"	hemp
Ramie	300	"	cotton

In the case of rubber and tea, Indian prices were available only for the products at plantation factory (rubber sheets and dried and packed tea). In order to avoid an over-estimation of the relative level of agricultural output in the countries where plantation products predominate, a rubber price reduced by 15 percent was applied. Similarly, the price quotation for tea was reduced by 35 percent so as to arrive at a hypothetical price of green tea.

Since Indian farm prices are available for rice (rather than paddy) and gur (rather than sugar cane), the harvest figures, in terms of paddy and cane, had to be converted to a rice and gur basis. The conversion ratios applied were 3:2 and 10:1, respectively.

A final and serious shortcoming of these computations must be mentioned. The official harvest figures are naturally subject to a wide margin of error, even as an indication of the output from the area that is supposed to be covered by the statistics. Moreover, the statistics usually fail to include some minor crops, and the incompleteness in this respect varies from country to country. One particular aspect of this problem is that the statistical data usually include only field production proper, and not what is produced on the villager's small "compound" within the village itself. The relative size of the production that thus escapes the statistics may vary from negligible, for instance in Northwest and Central India, to a substantial proportion in some parts of Southeast Asia. There was no means of making systematic corrections for this factor. It was felt, however, that the omission of production from the "compound" involved a particularly serious under-estimation of the level of output in Java relative to that of other parts of South Asia. In order to correct for this factor, even if in the crudest way, the output figure for Java was raised by the arbitrarily chosen percentage of 15.

3), the picture is reversed, and on this reckoning Southeast Asia would appear to have the higher density and might be expected, *prima facie,* to be saddled with a more serious problem of population pressure. Since, however, plantation crops and fertile areas of wet paddy are more predominant in Southeast Asia than on the Indian subcontinent, agricultural output per hectare of cultivated land (column 4) is far higher in Southeast Asia. And this difference in productivity outweighs that in density, so that even if reckoned per head of agricultural or total population (columns 5 and 6), the volume of agricultural output in Southeast Asia is higher by more than one-fourth than that in the Indian subcontinent.[1] As we would expect from the foregoing, East India and East Pakistan conform more to the Southeast Asian pattern.

Among the individual countries and regions listed in the table, East Pakistan and Java stand out with particularly high over-all densities, even higher than that of Japan. Ceylon, where much of the land is still under jungle, joins this group if density is measured on the basis of cultivated land rather than of total territory – though by this measure its density is less than a third of Japan's. But here again differences in cropping pattern are controlling. The plantations, with extremely high output per hectare, and also per man employed, bring Ceylon's agricultural output per inhabitant (column 6) to a level almost 60 percent higher than India's. East Pakistan and Java also have an intensive cropping pattern owing to the predominance of wet paddy, and some plantations; but this is sufficient only to secure an output per head that, despite the much higher population density, is close to the average for the region as a whole. Similarly, the volume of agricultural output per head of population comes out at fairly equal figures for East and West Pakistan, the huge difference in population density being more than offset by the far higher output per hectare in East Pakistan.

In a general way, the table suggests that agricultural output per head of population does not differ from country to country as much as might be expected. In other words, the densely populated countries and regions are also those where land resources have been more intensively utilized. The conspicuous exceptions to this generalization are of course Ceylon and Malaya. In these two countries, agricultural output per head of population is between two and a half and three and a half times that of either the Indian subcontinent or the rest of Southeast Asia. Highly productive plantations in those two countries are, of course, mainly responsible for their high rating. If we compared output per head of the paddy growers, the difference would be greatly reduced.

Crude territorial densities per unit of cultivated land are, then, unreliable indicators of population pressure. In forest areas where shifting culti-

[1] For the purpose of these comparisons, Malaya was left out from the group of Southeast Asian countries, since its economic levels and structure are highly untypical.

vation is practiced, or in the areas of dry farming, the actual pressure of population against available resources may be as high as or higher than in the densely settled paddy deltas. It will often be true, on the other hand, that the regions of dry farming offer more long-term scope for increasing the productivity, and thus the carrying capacity, of land through irrigation than do the paddy lands or the plantation areas. And regions with forests or with irrigable desert land have more unused, though cultivable, land.

In many cases such improvement will require organized migrations and settlement of the migrants, together with the organization of large-scale investments in land clearance and irrigation, which are beyond the economic power of the individual farm or the small village community or are precluded by present land tenure regulations. This certainly is true if a large-scale and rapid change is wanted. The radical intensification of agriculture in the regions where it is now extensive and, particularly, the bringing under the plow of empty land are therefore dependent on public intervention in the form of settlement schemes. The experience and future possibilities of such policies will be discussed in later chapters.[1] With the pattern of population density adjusted, by and large, to the present agricultural facilities and techniques in each area, there appears to be rather limited opportunity for an equalization of levels of living through a spontaneous, unorganized flow of people from high-pressure to low-pressure areas.

This, it must again be stressed, is not to say that the agricultural resources of the region are very fully utilized. They are, of course, in limited areas, notably Java and the Tonkin Delta in North Vietnam. But the outer islands of Indonesia have hardly begun to be opened up, and in Burma, Thailand, and Malaya, not to mention Laos, there are vast stretches of cultivable but uncultivated land. It is true that the reserves of usable land in India and Pakistan are rather small by Asian standards, but in view of the low output per hectare at present, a considerable intensification of agriculture should be possible. As we shall point out, this would assume, however, crucial reforms of institutions and attitudes.[2]

5 *Agrarian "Overpopulation" and "Underemployment"*

The problems of population and labor utilization in South Asia are commonly discussed in terms of "overpopulation," "unemployment," and "underemployment." A huge disparity is supposed to exist between agricultural resources and the manpower stocked up in agriculture. It is said that because the land is overcrowded, much of the available labor supply

[1] Chapter 26, Section 6; Chapter 27, Section 14; and Appendix 11.

[2] Chapter 26, Parts II and III.

is unemployed or is employed at very low levels of productivity, often assumed to be zero at the margin and, indeed, far inside the margin. The corollary is that the main requirement for achieving higher over-all productivity, which is the aim of economic development, must be to reduce the agrarian density by "skimming off" the redundant manpower in the villages. The problems of labor utilization and population are central to our analysis of the development problems of South Asia. They will be taken up for intensive analysis in Part Five. There we shall challenge the concepts commonly used and the theories implied in these concepts. It is already apparent, however, that certain facts brought forward in the three preceding sections dictate caution in accepting without important qualifications this common view that South Asia is severely "overpopulated" and that the density of population, resulting in "unemployment" and "underemployment," is the main cause of poverty in the region.

To begin with, we have seen that in South Asia as a whole the density of population in relation to cultivated land (Table 10–1) is about the same as in Europe, if the Soviet Union is excluded. The agrarian density, i.e., the number of persons engaged in agriculture per unit of cultivated land, shown in Table 10–2, is, of course, considerably higher than in Europe. Typically, there are not much more than two hectares per agricultural family in South Asia as against some five hectares in Europe. To bring this comparison into the right perspective, allowance must, however, be made for the huge difference in agricultural techniques. In South Asia, human labor and bullocks are still, in the main, the sole sources of power. Countries like India and Pakistan are at an intermediate stage – that of the bullock – in regard to agricultural techniques. Looking far ahead, the desired policy is eventually to substitute the oil pump, the truck, the tractor for the bullock. But the same tasks – pumping, transporting, digging, levelling, and even plowing – can be done by human muscle power, as they largely are in China and Vietnam. In fact, if individual countries are compared, an agrarian density as high as that of China is found only in Java and East Pakistan and in parts of Ceylon, West Bengal, and Kerala, and even there the ratios are far below that in Japan. In the larger part of India, West Pakistan, and continental Southeast Asia, the agrarian density is intermediate between the European average and the Chinese one.

In comparison with Europe, the crop pattern in South Asia also implies a more labor-intensive agricultural production. Paddy and most plantation crops require far more labor per unit of land than do wheat and maize, even with comparable techniques. When taking into account both the more labor-intensive techniques applied and the choice of crops requiring more labor input, the agrarian density in South Asia is perhaps not surprisingly high, even if we should be aware of the opposite causal relation, that the labor-intensive patterns are partly a function of the high man/land ratio.

Moreover, if agrarian overcrowding itself were the main explanation of low productivity in South Asia, one would expect to find a fairly close inverse correlation between output per man engaged in agriculture and the man/land ratio. We have seen that this is not the case (Section 4). There is, instead, a certain equalization of yield per head of the agricultural population, with a tendency toward a positive correlation, if any. This tendency becomes accentuated, of course, for the areas in Malaya and Ceylon where plantation crops are responsible for especially high yields not only per hectare but also per head. Again, Japan has almost three times as high an agrarian population density as South Asia in terms of active males per hectare, but has over five times higher output per hectare and roughly double the output per active male.

More generally, the very low average agricultural yield per hectare in the larger parts of South Asia (Table 10–2) contradicts the impression that, throughout the region, rural pauperization is mainly the result of too much labor being devoted to too little land. If the over all view is taken, the agriculture in the region, in spite of the labor intensity in regard to production methods and crop patterns, has rather to be characterized as an "extensive" one, as was pointed out above. The implication of this conclusion is that, *even without radical changes in technology, it should be possible to extract very much larger yields from the available land by raising the input and efficiency of the labor force* (Chapter 26).

In some parts of South Asia, particularly the Indian peninsula, which is the poorest part, the climate may be partly responsible for the low yields per hectare and the low over-all labor productivity. As we shall stress in Chapter 14 (Section 2), climate has received too little attention in discussions of underdevelopment in South Asia. It has adverse effects on the soil, on the crops and animals, and on the willingness and ability of the labor force to work, and to work diligently and hard. But again the effects of the climate are not a function of high population density; they would not be less severe if the man/land ratio were lower.

Leaving aside for the moment the question of the change in that ratio over time, there are other factors that, by keeping down the labor productivity in most sections of South Asian agriculture, together are responsible for low average incomes and low standards of life: poor nutrition and housing, poor schooling and training, poor sanitary and other health facilities. Very low living levels decrease the amount of labor input and also the intensity and efficiency of the work actually performed on the land by the labor force. Low incomes are only the other side of low labor productivity; a vicious circle makes poverty and low levels of living, or low labor productivity, self-generating. Behind this unfortunate causal mechanism there is, besides the parameter of climate, a social system of institutions and power relations, particularly in regard to the ownership and utilization of land resources, that is severely inimical to productivity, at the same time as low productivity establishes itself as the norm. And within this social system, both shaped by it and upholding it, are the ingrained attitudes of people in all classes. Among the non-physical factors that keep down labor productivity are also the primitive techniques employed in agriculture, likewise both a function of the existing social system, which deprives the tillers of both capital and incentives to greater effort, and a prop to that system (Chapters 22 and 26).

Considering these broad political, social, psychological, and technological causal interrelations,[1] it becomes impossible to see the poverty among the peoples in the region as merely, or even mainly, an effect of population density. At least the causation is not a direct and simple one. But indirectly – and over many intermediate stages, in the course of which conditions altered in some areas – the long upward climb of population has undoubtedly strengthened these other factors that keep down labor productivity. This has been an effect, not of population density as such, but of population growth.

Table 10–3 indicates the broad features of population growth in South Asia since the beginning of the nineteenth century.[2] Very little is known about earlier population trends, but there was probably a modest but sustained natural growth as a normal thing, periodically interrupted and reversed by the ravages of wars, famines, or epidemics. The first impact of colonial domination was to put an end to warfare and internal strife, and, later, to facilitate relief to famine-stricken areas. Everywhere, it led to a secular trend of more or less uninterrupted population increase, which was reinforced by the introduction of elementary sanitary measures, such as smallpox vaccination. In Java, the Philippines, and Ceylon, this trend was quite steady from the beginning of the nineteenth century. In the countries of continental Southeast Asia, which were brought under colonial rule much later, the steady trend started correspondingly later; in Thailand – which preserved a precarious independence throughout the colonial era – it did not really begin until around the turn of the last century. In India, there was an acceleration in population growth until the last quarter of the nineteenth century, when a deceleration set in due to recurrent severe famines and epidemics, lasting for about half a century. Following a steady pace of natural increase in the inter-war period, all the countries of the region entered, after the Second World War, a phase of virtually explosive population growth, which is likely to continue in the foreseeable future. Since fertility has always been very high in South Asia, the mortality rate has been the determining factor in the trends described.[3] Only in the colonial history of Malaya and, to a lesser degree, Ceylon did migration play any significant role.

[1] Appendix 2, Part II.

[2] The history of population growth in South Asia will be given in more detail in Chapter 27, Section 3.

[3] Chapter 27, Sections 2 and 3; Chapter 30, Sections 2, 3, and 4.

Table 10–3

BROAD ESTIMATES OF POPULATION GROWTH FROM 1800 TO 1960, AND OF SIZE OF POPULATION IN 1800 AND 1960, BY COUNTRY

Country	Annual growth of population (percent) 1800–1850	1850–1900	1900–1950	1950–1960	Size of population (millions) 1800	1960
Undivided India	1.1[a]	0.4[b]	0.9	1.8	125.0	524.3
Ceylon	0.6	1.2	1.3	2.4	1.6	9.9
Burma	0.6	1.1	1.2	1.4	(4.5)	21.5
Malaya and Singapore	1.0	2.9	2.2	3.2	(0.3)	8.5
Thailand	0.0	0.6	1.8	3.1	(6.0)	26.3
Vietnam, Cambodia, Laos[c]	0.3	1.4	1.3	1.9	(7.0)	36.0
Philippines	1.4	1.4	2.1	3.1	(1.7)	27.8
Java and Madura	1.8	2.1	1.1	2.0	4.0	93.5
Rest of Indonesia	0.6	1.0	1.9		4.5	
South Asia	1.0	0.7	1.0	2.0	155	748

Source: See Table 27–2, Chapter 27.

[a] 1800–1871. [b] 1871–1901.

[c] The figures refer to the whole territory of the former French Indo-China including North Vietnam.

The effects of population growth on the social system have been important. Within the villages, it has undoubtedly had a tendency not only to cause fragmentation of holdings but thereby also to fortify the class structure, to make it more rigid and less egalitarian by increasing the relative number of the landless and poor,[1] and thus ever more inimical to the success of efforts to raise productivity in agriculture. Nevertheless, the upward trend in population has meant that more food has been needed to maintain even the traditionally low levels of nutrition. More labor has had to be put in by a labor force that has been growing at about the same rate as the population. Speaking very broadly, the interplay between the increased needs for food, the bigger labor force, and the slow improvement in productive techniques that has counteracted the tendency to decreasing returns and even to deterioration of the soil,[1] has resulted in an increase in the input of work that has been about what was needed, with labor productivity about constant, to preserve traditional levels of living for the agricultural population. A process of gradual adjustment has constantly given work, or some work, to all, or almost all, in the growing agricultural labor force – except to those who for social reasons have preferred, ac-

[1] See Chapter 22, Sections 4–6.

[1] See below, Section 6.

cording to their custom, to remain idle or work but little; they have been able to indulge in that luxury at little cost since labor has remained very cheap. The whole social situation has thus been subtly arranged to absorb the continual increase in the agricultural labor force.

In part this adjustment has consisted in extending the area under cultivation, or raising its productivity by irrigation, or changing over to other types of cultivation and other crop patterns rendering higher yields per hectare; this will be discussed in later sections of this chapter. But the impulses for change in indigenous agriculture have been weak. In particular, the abundant supply of labor has inhibited whatever impulses there may have been for changes in production methods and crop patterns that would increase the work input of those engaged in agriculture and the efficiency of their labor. The labor force has been utilized, but not as intensively or effectively as it might have been. Consequently, average indexes of yield, whether per unit of cultivated land or per worker in agriculture, have remained low. That considerably higher yields could be obtained through increased intensity and efficiency of work is proved by the example of Japan, and many areas in South Asia itself.

The large scope for a greater input of work on the part of the present and now rapidly increasing labor force in agriculture gives a more favorable cast to prospects that otherwise would appear desperate, not only in India, Pakistan, and Java but also in some other parts of the region. As we shall show in Part Five, even assuming a much more rapid industrialization than is actually taking place, or could be expected, in any of the South Asian countries, by far the larger part of the very rapid increase in the labor force in the next decades will have to stay in agriculture.[1] Naturally, in the countries and areas most densely populated the possibility of utilizing an increasing labor force in agriculture while at the same time raising average labor input and labor efficiency depends on vigorous government policies and offers only a respite, particularly with the sharply rising trends of population increase. But a respite is what is needed from a planning point of view. At a later stage of industrialization work opportunities in non-agricultural pursuits would begin to increase more substantially.

These are broad generalizations that need to be amplified and specified, and the larger part of this volume, especially the chapters in Part Five, will be devoted to that task.

6 *Adjustments Within Indigenous Agriculture*

Despite the major population expansion over the course of a century or more, most people in South Asia – especially on the Indian subcontinent and in Indonesia – have continued to live and work within the confines of

[1] Chapter 24, Section 5; Chapter 26, Section 1 *et passim*.

a traditional agrarian structure in which the production of basic subsistence requirements is the paramount objective of economic activity. The economic history of these countries in this long period has been dominated largely by people's struggle to match the population increase by a corresponding expansion of the production of basic foods in the villages where they were born. Particularly on the Indian subcontinent, this is reflected in a remarkable lack of internal mobility of the population, in spite of the trend toward urbanization and a pattern of marrying outside the local community.[1] Exceptions to this rule in some parts of Southeast Asia will be noted below.

The struggle for higher food output has been conducted in various ways, some of which have involved serious danger of destruction of natural resources. Four main lines of attack may be distinguished:

(1) In the already intensively cultivated and densely populated regions of wet paddy production, such as Bengal and the Tonkin Delta, the natural increase in population, despite some emigration, led to a gradual decline in the amount of land available per family. A precarious nutritional balance was maintained by applying still more labor per unit of land.

(2) Extension of irrigation along the rivers was an important means of intensification in both India and Indonesia. During the fifty years or so before the end of the colonial era, the land under irrigation in Java expanded from one half to three and a half million hectares and the irrigated area in India rose from 13 to 17 million hectares. This implied government initiative and investment. The largest irrigation schemes in India were those in the northwestern wheat districts, where the great rivers of the Punjab are virtually dried up by the use of water in a vast system of irrigation canals. The opening of these lands for more intensive cultivation was accompanied by a considerable influx of families, contrary to the general rule of population immobility. The effects of the investment in irrigation were thus strengthened by the fresh initiative provided by groups of new settlers,

[1] Referring to "the traditional immobility of the Indian population and the slender volume of internal migration," S. Chandrasekhar presents some census figures: "The comparative stay-at-homeness of the Indian population is a regular feature of many an Indian census report. In all the censuses (except the last one of 1951, which period witnessed the Indo-Pakistan population transfers on an unprecedented scale) nearly 90 percent of the people have been enumerated in the districts in which they were born. Another 5 percent have been enumerated in adjoining districts which were more industrialised or urbanised than the districts in which they were born. In 1901, only 9.27 percent of the total population was enumerated outside the districts of their birth. In 1911 this percentage fell to 8.7 and in 1931 this ratio was repeated. Though figures for 1931–41 are not available there is no reason to expect any radical change, for during that decade there was no significant inter-provincial migration, as was witnessed in the last decade consequent on the partition of India." (Sripati Chandrasekhar, "Possibilities of Migration," in *Population and Planned Parenthood in India*, Allen & Unwin Ltd., London, 1955, p. 30.)

There is no reason to believe that the situation was radically different in the period before censuses were taken. Probably mobility was even less before the coming of the railways.

and the Punjab became one of the most prosperous agricultural regions of India.

(3) In areas where no irrigation facilities were made available, the pressure led often to an extension of cultivation to hillsides and other areas in the neighborhood that were previously under forest or used for grazing.

(4) Finally, in the regions of shifting cultivation the length of fallowing periods tended to be reduced.

As a result of the changes under (3) and (4), the area under cultivation increased considerably, but neither in India nor in Indonesia did this increase match the increase in population; at any rate, it fell far short of doing so in the decades after the First World War. And the extension of the cultivated area was by no means an unmixed blessing, for in many places it caused serious and lasting damage to the soil. The pressure for expansion of subsistence production was particularly destructive in areas under shifting cultivation. As long as such cultivation has to support only a scattered population, and groups of families are small, only small fields will be cleared, and after a few years the cultivator will move to another site, allowing the forest sufficient time to reconquer the land. With the increase in population, plots tend to become larger, the periods of cultivation are lengthened, and the intervals of rest tend to be shortened. There is less time for the forest to re-cover a soil already damaged by exposure to the tropical sun, and eventually the forest may be destroyed. In some areas, this kind of destruction was the joint effect of population growth and the encroachment of plantations on forest land formerly available for shifting cultivation. In Ceylon, for instance, the customary rest interval is reported to have been shortened from 15–20 years to 8–10 years, whereas a period of 20–30 years is held by some experts to be the minimum interval between forest clearings, if damage to the soil is to be avoided. The most serious effect was in hilly forest land, where the monsoon rains wash the soil from the denuded hillsides and also damage the lower-lying lands.

This vicious circle of population growth leading to deforestation and deforestation to greater demographic pressure was most dangerous on the Indian subcontinent where the destruction of forests in ancient times had already brought the total forested area below the minimum held to be necessary for soil and moisture preservation. Legal measures to protect the forest cover date back a century in India and Ceylon, but under the pressure of increasing needs for cultivated land and firewood these regulations have largely remained a dead letter. More recently, complaints about damage to forests have been heard in Southeast Asian countries as well. Shifting cultivation causes concern in areas as sparsely populated as Burma and the eastern islands of Indonesia, where the bulk of the territory is under dense forest.

A further problem arising from population pressure on limited land resources is overgrazing. The number of animals has increased in recent decades, partly because the expansion of the area under cultivation and under irrigation raised the demand for draft power, and to a lesser extent because the increase in population raised the demand for animal food; taboos against cow slaughter in India and some of the other countries worked in the same direction.[1] At the same time, the quantity and quality of grazing land tended to decline with the extension of cultivation and the destruction of forests. Overgrazing has become particularly acute in India and Ceylon. The typical Indian village has more animals on its grazing land than it can satisfactorily support. When grasslands are subjected to such treatment, only the plants that animals refuse to eat can flourish. In consequence, the quality of the animal population is kept low while the productivity of the land deteriorates. All over South Asia, and particularly in India, a large part of the land supposed to be under grass is covered by useless growths. Some of these half-deserts now cover what once were centers of great civilizations, such as the dry area in central Burma around the site of the old capital of Pagan.

The two other chief methods for accommodating domestic food output to population growth – the extension of irrigation and more intensive cultivation in the areas of wet paddy – rarely had such destructive effects. There are cases, however, in which irrigation facilities were either constructed or used in such a way that the soil became saline or water-logged, leading to serious declines in yields or to the withdrawal of land from cultivation. These results have been most marked in Punjab and Sind. An American expert in Pakistan expressed the fear that "If this state of affairs is allowed to continue at its present rate, the Valley of the Indus, within less than half a century, will become a desert!"[2] In many parts of South Asia, excessive use of irrigation water and inadequate drainage are causing similar damage, though on a smaller scale.

Given the foregoing, it remains to be explained how food output per head could have been maintained as well as it was, particularly in British India, despite an enormous increase in population. Extension of the cultivated acreage and intensification of production through irrigation could alleviate part of the pressure on food supplies, but these adjustments do not always appear to have been sufficient. Some slow improvement in agricultural techniques may also have occurred, but there is no strong evidence to suggest that its effect was important.

Another factor may also have been at work, though we can only speculate about its significance. Throughout this period, peasant proprietorship was steadily giving way to tenancy and sharecropping. As we shall demonstrate in later chapters, these land tenure arrangements are inimical to

[1] Chapter 3, Section 4; Chapter 26, Section 7.

[2] John O. Bell, in a public address on "American Aid and the Agricultural Crisis in Pakistan," quoted in Edward C. Jandy, "A Decade of Socio-Economic Progress in Pakistan," *United Asia,* Vol. 10, No. 1, 1958, p. 25.

agricultural progress and impose an artificially low ceiling on productivity.[1] Nevertheless, when in the process of being introduced, they may tend to raise the floor beneath which output per head is not permitted to fall. Small holders – whose production, in the first instance, is too low to provide a substantial surplus above the consumption requirements of their families – when turned into sharecroppers who must divide their gross output with landlords, may find themselves obliged to produce more in order to meet the minimum subsistence requirements of their families. Any increase in aggregate food output attributable to this institutional pressure cannot, however, have been sizeable. Although the statistical documentation on trends in food production during this period is notoriously defective, it does suggest, at least for India, that food output per head – which was never conspicuously high – probably declined in the course of the half century preceding independence;[2] so far as the subsistence sector is concerned the trend in the other South Asian countries has probably been the same.

In addition to the rise in population, but not always independent of it, another dynamic factor – the spread of commercialization – has influenced the long-term adjustments that have occurred in indigenous agriculture. The aggregative impact of monetized production on the indigenous agricultural sector has been felt much more forcefully in Southeast Asia than on the Indian subcontinent. The most dramatic changes occurred in the rice-growing deltas of the Irrawaddy River in Burma, the Me Nam in Thailand, and the Mekong in Cochin China. Rice production for export began on a big scale in Burma after 1870; in Thailand and Cochin China it began somewhat later and less spectacularly. An important immediate cause was the opening of the Suez Canal, which made it profitable to export rice to Europe. Another factor was the interruption of rice exports from Carolina during and after the American Civil War. At the same time, the rapid increase of population in the plantation areas developing in Ceylon and Malaya created an export market for rice within Asia.

While the expansion of commercial rice production in the deltas was thus causally connected with the rise of Western plantation enterprises, the South Asian peasant himself took the initiative in seizing these new

[1] Chapter 22, Section 6; and Chapter 26, Section 5 and Part III.

[2] We must again emphasize that the statistical basis for this conclusion is far from satisfactory. A cautious analysis of Indian official sources covering the span from 1893–94 to 1945–46 reaches the conclusion that "gross production of food crops in India during the entire period remained nearly constant. It is remarkable that even the slight change, especially since World War I, has been in a downward direction. This tendency in particular applies to the rice crop, which constitutes roughly half of total food crop production. Changes in the production of other crops have failed to alter this trend, despite considerable expansion of the wheat crop." (Daniel and Alice Thorner, "Long-term Trends in Output," in *Land and Labour in India,* Asia Publishing House, Bombay, 1962, p. 103.) Cf. Chapter 26, Section 2.

opportunities. Neither the resettlement in the Irrawaddy Delta[1] nor the steady expansion of cultivation on the lower Me Nam was organized or supported by government or by Western enterprise.[2] In the Mekong Delta, however, cultivation probably could not have expanded as it did without the large-scale investment in flood control undertaken by the French around the turn of the century.

This response to the new opportunities for commercial farming opened up, particularly in Southeast Asia, in the latter part of the nineteenth century is worth stressing, as it demonstrates that South Asian peasants under favorable circumstances can display as much alertness and market consciousness as peasants anywhere else. Peasants from Upper Burma streamed to the almost uninhabited Irrawaddy Delta, while Vietnamese peasants went south to take up market production of rice in the Mekong Delta.[3] But willingness to migrate is only one expression of market-mindedness demonstrated by some South Asian peasants. Once the merits of assimilating unfamiliar non-food cash crops into their productive pattern have been demonstrated, an impressive number of South Asian producers have readily taken to growing them and indeed have been reluctant to de-emphasize them in favor of the less rewarding food crops. In Java, for example, campaigns to expand food output launched by colonial authorities – and later by the Japanese – encountered difficulties because the peasants were not easily persuaded to substitute food crops for sugar and other profitable commercial crops; and in Malaya, public measures to increase rice production failed partly because the peasants preferred to concentrate on growing rubber for export. In Upper Burma, the peasants have been quick to turn from subsistence crops to groundnuts and cotton when price relations made it attractive to do so. In India, where "grow-more-food" campaigns have been recurrent for decades, the output of non-food crops has risen faster than that of foodstuffs. In part this is because the utilization of newly created irrigation facilities has usually been associated with increased specialization on higher value non-food crops.[4]

[1] In earlier times, much of the Irrawaddy Delta had been under cultivation. The whole area was laid waste in the wars between the Burmese and the Mons in the eighteenth century and had become dense jungle.

[2] For Thailand, see James C. Ingram, *Economic Change in Thailand Since 1850*, Stanford University Press, Stanford, California, 1955, p. 54. For Burma, see J. S. Furnivall, *Colonial Policy and Practice (A Comparative Study of Burma and Netherlands India)*, Cambridge University Press, London, 1957, p. 279 *et passim*. For Indo-China, see Charles Robequain, *The Economic Development of French Indo-China*, Oxford University Press, London, 1944, *passim*.

[3] In the Central Plain in Thailand, on the other hand, the natural increase in population supplied the labor needed for expansion of commercial rice production. Migratory movements could hardly have been expected since there was still plenty of easily cultivable land in the other parts of Thailand. (See Ingram, *Economic Change in Thailand*, p. 55.)

[4] Chapter 26, Section 8.

This alertness on the part of the peasants in exploiting the opportunities to produce more profitable crops has had, on the whole, no counterpart in a willingness or ability to improve production techniques. As H. Myint explains:

. . . peasant export production expanded without the introduction of radical improvements in the agricultural techniques used in subsistence production, and . . . when the peasants took to 'specializing' in export crops it merely meant that they were devoting the whole of their resources to export production. In doing this they took full advantage of the *market opportunities* available to them; but this does not mean that they took full advantage of the *technical opportunities* to improve their productivity . . . . the same combination of land, labour and capital [has] been used throughout half a century of rapid expansion in rice exports from South-East Asia.[1]

In the main, the dramatic responses to opportunities for commercial farming have been confined to those situations in which peasant proprietorship has been a dominant form of agrarian organization. Where sharecropping and leasing arrangements have prevailed, the assimilation of innovations has been much slower, if it occurred at all. One of the ironies in the subsequent evolution of the agrarian structure, however, is that successful entry into commercialized production has tended to undercut the very conditions that originally made it possible. The process has been an involved one and a thorough analysis of it belongs to another context.[2] Stated in most summary form, it has often meant that indigenous agriculturalists who have prospered through participation in monetized exchange have thereby become most exposed to excessive indebtedness and thus to loss of their land. The result, in many cases, has been an erosion of peasant proprietorship and its replacement by some form of sharecropping or tenancy that has later stifled incentives for progress.

7 *The Coming of the Plantations*

The great expansion of plantations in South Asia occurred in the second half of the nineteenth century. In earlier periods, some of the products that were later to be grown in big plantations were cultivated by peasants, while others were not grown in the region at all. In some places, notably Indonesia under the so-called "culture system" (1830–70), the peasants had been forced to cultivate these products directly by the foreign rulers or by their village or feudal chiefs acting as intermediaries for the foreign companies. But although the specific crops were not entirely new to the region, their

[1] H. Myint, *The Economics of the Developing Countries,* Hutchinson, London, 1964, p. 51.

[2] Chapter 22, Part I.

large-scale cultivation in a plantation system was a new and potent force that had substantial economic and demographic impact.

Broadly speaking, plantation crops include rubber, tea, cocoanuts, tobacco, coffee, sugar cane, and spices. These may conveniently be regarded as "wood plants," as distinct from grasses or root crops. As one writer observes:

> . . . today plantation denotes not only a system of agriculture but a system which chiefly grows plants from wood as opposed to plants from grass: tea, coffee, rubber, cocoa, coco-nut, cinchona. No doubt the capital investment required in raising wood plants has been instrumental in bringing these products under the plantation system, though it has not made it impossible for native growers, *e.g.* in rubber, to produce for themselves. . . . In method of exploitation . . . the plantation of to-day is closer to certain forms of forestry than it is to grain crops or roots. One may think of it with advantage as intensive forestry conducted in regions of hitherto sparse population.[1]

Thus plantation crops differ from the more traditional crops grown in South Asia (rice, wheat, jute, and roots) in such a way that production on a large-scale, rationalized basis is required for maximum efficiency.

From the outset, then, the exploitation of plantation crops was fundamentally different from traditional indigenous agriculture. For one thing, little of the output could be consumed on the spot; in fact, with the constricted South Asian markets of the latter half of the nineteenth century, plantations were necessarily export-oriented. Furthermore, the higher plantation output per hectare required more capital than other types of South Asian agriculture – investments to cover the cost of clearing, planting, and foregoing of returns until the plants began to produce (sometimes a period of up to ten years), and the construction of factories for pressing, drying, and similar crude on-the-spot processing. Indeed, given the heavy capital investment required for efficient production, native enterprise was unable to provide adequate financing, even assuming an incentive to do so. The impulse toward establishment of plantations therefore emanated from the West, in response to Western demands.

The labor requirements per unit of land were also considerably higher than in traditional agriculture. This fact had important demographic implications, for it meant that the introduction of plantation crops raised the maximum population that a given territory could support. The higher incomes generated could be used to import food or induce more local food production to support an increased population. To this extent the region where plantation culture developed entered the realm of international or inter-regional trade in response to comparative advantage. Why this failed

[1] C. R. Fay, "Plantation Economy," *Economic Journal*, XLVI, December, 1936, pp. 622–623. Sugar cane is a special case. It is a grass, but is grown under the plantation system.

to trigger an all-round economic growth as somewhat similar developments did in Western Europe will be examined in Section 8.

Despite the usual assumption of a vast surplus population, it should not be surprising that the rapid rise of plantations, especially in the period from about 1880 to the First World War, created problems of labor supply.[1] In Ceylon and Malaya the local peasant population, aside from being insufficient to the need, showed little inclination to take up wage labor on the plantations. Cheap labor was therefore drawn from the densely populated paddy regions in East and South India and in South China. This, of course, alleviated somewhat the population problem of these areas, but it created much of the present-day ethnic difficulties surrounding the Indian Tamils in Ceylon and the Chinese in Malaya. The tea plantations in Sumatra had to draw their manpower from Java (with no equally serious ethnic problem in this instance), while the tea plantations in Assam in northeastern India were mostly manned by importing labor from tribal areas. Only in Java, where the population pressure was already high and the local population had been mobilized for wage labor since before the middle of the nineteenth century, could local manpower for the plantations be recruited.

The fact that the tropical plantations at this time came to be located so largely in South Asia, rather than in other tropical lands in Africa or America, is thus to be explained in part by the relative ease with which labor could be secured within the region, with the aid of some migration, and by the proximity of districts capable of producing rice to feed the workers. Soil and climate were less important factors. The particular locations within South Asia were even more determined by the convenience of transport to Europe. All the major plantation areas are situated along the trade routes between Europe, South Asia, and the Far East, which pass southern India, Ceylon, the Bay of Bengal, and the Malacca Straits. The concentration of plantations is particularly heavy in Ceylon, on both sides of the Malacca Straits – in Malaya and Sumatra – and in Java.

With the opening of the Suez Canal in 1869, the cost of transport from these areas to Europe declined sharply, and increasing needs for industrial materials in Europe and America, together with increasing demands for tea, coffee, and other tropical consumer goods, provided the basis for a secular boom – which was to be interrupted frequently by sharp cyclical setbacks. The expansion was particularly marked in the first decade of the twentieth century, when huge areas were planted with rubber in Ceylon, Malaya, Indonesia, and Indo-China. Another big push followed in the 1920's when the rise of the automobile industry stimulated rubber production and when Java had its sugar boom. The price collapse during the Great

[1] Chapter 21, Sections 2–4.

Depression, and destruction during the Second World War and its aftermath, particularly in Indonesia but also in Malaya, dealt a severe blow to the plantations. Many failed to survive, while others enjoyed a new boom in the post-war inflationary period.

The foregoing discussion suggests that *the development of plantations was, in effect, a process of industrialization.* Plantations themselves are large-scale, capital-intensive, highly specialized commercial enterprises employing wage labor. Although a plantation uses land and is concerned with products grown on land, in its scale and methods of operation it is more analogous to a modern factory than to an owned or rented family farm worked by unpaid family labor or occasional hired help.[1] The spread of plantation culture must be viewed as a spread of industrialized agriculture.

Yet most discussions of "industrialization" neglect this important aspect and give exclusive attention to the creation or rapid growth of a sector of *manufacturing*, frequently thought of as large-scale industry using modern techniques. This concept of industrialization is, naturally enough, drawn largely from the developmental process experienced in Western Europe and the United States, where industrialization meant the growth of manufacturing industry and where the symbols of advancing affluence have been the large integrated steel complex, the chemical, capital goods, and automotive industries. But this growth pattern is not especially relevant to the present situation in South Asia and is atypical of whatever degree of economic development has taken place there since the middle of the nineteenth century. Indeed, as we shall later argue, the difference in initial situations renders growth in South Asia along the lines of the West highly improbable (Chapter 14).

Perhaps the most serious consequence of this vision of the growth process is that it diminishes emphasis on agriculture. Despite the concern shown for agriculture and the attempts to raise agricultural productivity, it is clear that agriculture is viewed as a sector destined to shrink significantly in both output and employment relative to an "industrial sector." Agriculture, when looked at from a sort of "bullock" view, becomes a symptom of underdevelopment that must rapidly make way for an efficient, modern factory sector. This notion, too, stems from Western experience, where the industrial revolution followed upon the rationalization of agriculture – the "agricultural revolution." Since the dynamic element in the West *was* man-

[1] A Ceylon planter notes that "tea estates are highly organised pieces of machinery which cannot function without efficient management and a permanent labour force." On his own estate of 1,400 acres, a permanent "army" of 1,500 men, women and children are employed. He adds that "the estates are so organized that crop is taken six days out of every seven all through the year." (Harry Williams, *Ceylon, Pearl of the East*, 5th ed., Robert Hale Ltd., London, 1956, pp. 191, 206.)

ufacturing, though it rested on earlier fundamental changes in agriculture, it is natural enough to tie the desire for economic growth in South Asia almost exclusively to that type of industrialization.[1]

But Western Europe never possessed the kind of agricultural potential so important to many of the South Asian countries, namely plantations. Indeed, as we shall discuss more fully later, the key to the relatively advanced position today of Malaya and Ceylon is the predominance of plantation culture in their economic structures. It is this factor that explains the higher output per head of Malaya and Ceylon.[2] The measure of economic growth that has occurred in some other countries of South Asia over the past century also has been closely related to the development of plantation crops. Thus an *increase* in the share of agriculture in the economy undoubtedly accompanied whatever growth took place prior to the Second World War. From the beginning the large capitalist plantations were surrounded by smaller, usually less efficient plantations and also by farms growing plantation crops but employing no, or few, workers outside the family. But the momentum was provided by the big plantations, which also accounted for the larger part of the output. In principle, these less capitalized enterprises are not different from the small-scale manufacturing industry and crafts that always – even in Western countries – coexist with large-scale industry and often get their impetus from it.[3]

The introduction of plantations and the growth of plantation crops outside the plantations proper explain many of the present demographic differences among the South Asian countries. The migratory movements not only led to a more rapid population increase but also led to or aggravated ethnic difficulties of current concern, especially in Ceylon and, in another setting, Malaya. Demographic effects of exploitation of the fertile deltas, stimulated by the rise of plantations, were not limited to internal migrations. During the scramble for land in the Irrawaddy Delta, the migrants coming down from Upper Burma were insufficient in numbers to meet the

[1] Chapter 24, Section 1.

[2] See Chapter 11, Section 1.

"But whilst the output of these [plantation] crops accounts for between 35 and 40 percent of Ceylon's national income, their corresponding contribution in India is very much smaller. It is only in a few countries of the region, Malaya being a prominent example, that plantation agriculture plays a comparable role as in Ceylon; and it is not without significance that in Malaya, where plantation output provides a substantial part of national income, income per head is even higher than in Ceylon. Indeed if both the output of plantation crops and the population dependent on it are excluded, Ceylon's per capita income would fall. In fact the importance of the plantation sector is much greater than suggested by such a calculation since no account would be taken of the innumerable activities which have grown out of and are dependent on the plantations." (Ceylon, Government of, National Planning Council, *The Ten-Year Plan,* Colombo, Ceylon, 1959, p. 6.)

[3] The gradations of plantation size, ownership, and efficiency are examined more fully in Chapter 11, Section 6.

demand for labor, and the cultivators, under conditions of commercial farming, tended to lay their hands on more land than they could cultivate with their own family. From the middle of the 1870's, cheap labor from the poorest districts of India – in Bengal and South India – began to stream into Burma, encouraged by the colonial government. The flow continued well into the twentieth century.

Two kinds of migratory movement across boundaries were thus called forth by the new forms of economic activity in the colonial era: the flow of Indian labor to the plantation areas and the flow of Indian agricultural workers to commercial rice farms in Burma. There was also a third kind of migration, namely, a continuous, though more diffuse, movement of Chinese and Indians to countries all over Southeast Asia. Even before the Europeans arrived, traders and moneylenders of Chinese and Indian origin had been present in most commercial centers. With the expansion of Western enterprise – and under continuing population pressure in India and China – this flow tended to increase. Most of the immigrants found a living as coolies, doing the hardest and most despised work in agriculture; but as time went on a number of them managed to find more profitable activities by joining the traders, middlemen, and moneylenders. The Indians of this class, who gradually came to own a large share of the land in Lower Burma, were largely driven back to India during and after the Second World War.[1] But elsewhere in Southeast Asia, urban trade and moneylending – in some areas also rural moneylending – continue to be dominated by Chinese and Indians. In Burma and Malaya there are still, as well, many low-paid Indian and Chinese laborers. The significance of these migratory movements for present social and political relations in South Asia will be discussed in Section 10 of this chapter.

8 *The Weak Spread Effects from the Development Spurts in Agriculture*

As we have just seen, the new developments in agriculture dating from the middle of the nineteenth century signified an era of dynamism and expansion in all the South Asian countries, especially when considered against the background of economic stagnation in preceding centuries. Exports from the region grew rapidly; and the tempo of intra-regional trade likewise increased, the plantations of Ceylon and Malaya serving as mar-

[1] Chapter 9, Section 9. More recently under the second Ne Win government a new wave of expulsion of Indians has taken place; see Chapter 17, Section 12. The Chinese in Burma are less unpopular; they are reckoned as "second cousins." That the Chinese have been permitted to remain, and even to continue to immigrate, is probably to be explained in part by the fact that the Burmese deem it advisable to be more considerate in their dealings with their powerful neighbor to the north.

kets for rice produced in Burma and Thailand. At the same time, these developments in agriculture helped make room for the population increase, referred to in Section 5 above, primarily associated with the relative peace imposed on the region by Western conquest and the introduction of some elementary sanitary reforms.

When we recognize that the growth of plantations was, in fact, a form of industrialization spurred by an increasing demand for exports, this process appears not unlike the beginning phases of industrialization in Western Europe. The fact that most real incomes did not rise, or rise very much, does not constitute a difference; in Western Europe, too, real wages did not increase significantly in the early stages of industrialization. In England they did not do so until the middle of the nineteenth century or later.[1] But in Western Europe, the profits served as sources of capital accumulation, and the early industrialization spurts also had spread effects. Later, real incomes and levels of living also started to rise. The subsequent tendencies then became cumulative and self-reinforcing.

In South Asia, the processes of capital accumulation and spread were frustrated. The plantations, like the mines, remained enclaves in largely stagnant economies while the initial impulses failed to trigger cumulative and self-perpetuating growth. The promising beginning in agriculture did not spill over into other sectors; a generally dynamic response failed to materialize. In short, the subsequent development in South Asia continued to be what Boeke has aptly referred to as "static expansion."[2] The problem of the present section is to explain why the development spurts in agriculture, which occurred to a varying extent in the several countries of South Asia from the middle of the last century, did not give rise to a cumulative process of economic growth or did so only in a very limited way.

The expansion of peasant growing of cash crops undoubtedly meant an increase in monetization. But in India, much of the money went to pay the new taxes imposed by the British authorities.[3] Furthermore, the rise of peasant cash crop production in India was apparently at the expense of food output. Daniel and Alice Thorner have argued that the output of food crops declined between 1893–94 and 1935–36 while commercial crop production increased; the resulting increase in total crop production was hardly sufficient to keep pace with population growth.[4] In the Netherlands East Indies, government policy in the middle of the last century sought to restrict peasant growing of such cash crops as sugar and rubber by forbid-

[1] Chapter 30, Section 3.

[2] J. H. Boeke, *Economics and Economic Policy in Dual Societies* (*as Exemplified by Indonesia*), H. D. Tjeenk Willink & Zoon N.V., Haarlem, 1953, p. 174. George Rosen speaks of "aborted growth" ("A Case of Aborted Growth: India 1860–1900," *The Economic Weekly*, August 11, 1962, pp. 1299ff.).

[3] Daniel and Alice Thorner, *Land and Labour in India*, pp. 53–54.

[4] *Ibid.*, pp. 104–105. See in Section 6 above, particularly footnote 2, p. 440.

ding the sugar refineries to buy cane from native growers and imposing a discriminatory tax on rubber produced by small holders. Although not always successful and later changed, such policies helped discourage native expansion into the dynamic areas and confined the activities of small holders mainly to traditional lines.

Spread effects were also vitiated inasmuch as expansion of output of cash crops by native growers did not in general imply the use of new technology (Section 6). In the main, traditional techniques were employed, so that there was no significant rise in demand for capital equipment, even in Burma and Thailand where the expansion of rice production for sale was greatest. The increase in production meant mainly higher incomes or, more usually, incomes for a greater number of people; these incomes were ordinarily turned into a rising demand for food by the growing indigenous population. The profits from the export trade went almost entirely to foreign commercial firms and were regularly remitted abroad. Even when such profits and fresh investment capital were used to build up ports, roads, and other transport facilities, the necessary capital equipment was imported. The net effect was to arrest the cumulative process short of the point at which new demand in the non-agricultural sector, and in particular demand for home-produced manufactured goods, would have been generated. The rising demands for different kinds of capital equipment and implements of all sorts were satisfied principally from foreign sources, leaving traditional things to be produced in traditional ways by the rural community.

When we turn to plantations, a similar but more involved pattern emerges. The development of plantations was initiated and controlled by foreigners. Managerial functions and ultimate control were in the hands of aliens. Dividends and a large part of the salaries were remitted abroad or used to purchase foreign goods rather than to stimulate demand on the local market. The reinvested profits were used mainly to purchase capital equipment from abroad to the extent they were not spent on the labor needed to establish new plantations or enlarge and improve the old ones. Although expansion gave rise to a demand for local labor, it was for the most part a demand for unskilled labor; more highly skilled workers were brought in from outside.

This is what is usually meant when it is said that the plantations spurred the industrialization of the Western countries but not of South Asia. The plantations were, in effect, extensions of the metropolitan countries: ". . . much of the management, finance, distribution, transport and processing was a part of London and Amsterdam rather than Singapore and Djakarta."[1] The plantations were therefore more closely connected to the West-

[1] Benjamin Higgins, "Western Enterprise and the Economic Development of Southeast Asia: A Review Article," *Pacific Affairs,* Institute of Pacific Relations, New York, March, 1958, p. 75.

ern economy than to the country of their location – their investments stimulated demand in the Western economies much more than in South Asia. The more investment of this type increased imports from abroad, the less were the stimulating effects in South Asia.[1]

Not only did the higher salaries go to alien managers and foremen; much of the wages of unskilled labor also went to workers imported from other South Asian countries – especially in the plantations of Ceylon and Malaya – so that even part of the incomes accruing to low-paid workers on the estates was sent back to their families at home rather than translated into demands for locally produced commodities. It is true that plantation wages, though low, were usually higher than earnings in self-sufficiency farming. And of course aggregate incomes and local spending did rise; remittances abroad merely blunted the total impact. But the countries with the greatest concentration of plantations early became dependent on food imports, the purchase of which took most of the increased earnings. In this way the plantations helped stimulate commercial rice growing in the region, as was explained in Section 6.

A further aspect of the plantation system that strongly bolstered the enclave structure but that has not been given adequate recognition in the literature was the fact of segregation and discrimination. Had the European owners, managers, or skilled workers of the large estates come in close contact with the natives, a diffusion of skills would almost surely have taken place and a much larger group of indigenous personnel would have acquired the requisite abilities. More and more of the demands for higher skills could then have been satisfied locally. But the fact of European ownership and control in primitive regions meant a wide separation between the European upper caste and the masses of unskilled workers that the plantations came to utilize. This was less a matter of "race" or even racial prejudice, at least at the start, than a very real difference in modes and levels of living and, more generally, cultural characteristics. Given the lack of rapport and limited direct contact, even on the job, the raising of native "industrial" capabilities faced a major social obstacle.

[1] "A pipeline across a desert cannot be expected to generate secondary effects. It would not make much difference to the desert economy if all the Sheiks cut down on their concubines and Cadillacs and used the capital thus saved in complementary activities to the pipeline. The only complementary activity is maintenance work on the pipe." (J. J. Puthucheary, *Ownership and Control in the Malayan Economy,* Donald Moore for Eastern Universities Press Ltd., Singapore, 1960, p. 148.)

Much of plantation investment had this "pipeline" character. H. W. Singer even goes so far as to suggest that "the import of capital into underdeveloped countries for the purpose of making them into providers of food and raw materials for the industrialized countries may have been not only rather ineffective in giving them the normal benefits of investment and trade but may have been positively harmful." (H. W. Singer, "Distribution of Gains Between Investing and Borrowing Countries," *American Economic Review, Papers and Proceedings,* May, 1950, p. 476.)

The gulf between the two groups was widened by the use of middlemen, who were very often "Oriental aliens," and by the system of "managing agencies." These institutions tended to shield the Europeans from the consequences of their own activities for the indigenous groups. At the same time, they served as channels of communication designed to inculcate behavior patterns required for the new forms of economic development. The "sieve effect" of these intermediary institutions has been described as follows:

> Even after many years of life in India the gulf between the Europeans and the workers is so wide that the foreigners know very little about the workers and find it almost impossible to understand, much less appreciate their ways, habits and difficulties. The jobber thus becomes an indispensable link in the chain of officials. He interprets the workers' requirements to the manager and conveys, in turn, the latter's directions and instructions to the rank and file. If there is trouble of any kind, the jobber's cooperation is essential for the restoration of normal conditions. The somewhat antagonistic relations between the manager and the jobber are reflected in the manager's usual epithet, "clever rascal," for the jobber. The manager may receive anonymous petitions from the workers, written in quaint English, which acquaint him with their grievances against the jobber. Though he may know the grievances are based on a solid substratum of truth, the manager is usually too dependent upon the jobber to take action.[1]

This gulf between the disparate social groups was, and is, particularly wide in the countries on the Indian subcontinent, where it fit into an inherited social stratification, characterized by inequality, exploitation, and rigidity.

In this social framework what Myint has called a "cheap labor policy" was adopted by the European managements of plantations and extractive industries.[2] This policy, he says, "induced them to use labour extravagantly, merely as an undifferentiated mass of 'cheap' or 'expendable' brawnpower. So through the vicious circle of low wages and low productivity, the productivity of the indigenous labour even in the sparsely populated countries was fossilized at its very low initial level." It was then "not surprising that Adam Smith's vision of the growth of the exchange economy and the division of labour 'improving the skill and dexterity of the people' should remain largely unfulfilled."[3]

The plantations, by their direct and indirect effects, did raise the average levels of income in the countries where they became a relatively large part of the economy — though not everyone shared in this increase. In particular they did permit accommodation of more people. The investments in

[1] B. Shiva Rao, *The Industrial Worker in India,* Allen & Unwin Ltd., London, 1939, p. 91. Cf. Chapter 23, Section 3.

[2] *The Economics of the Developing Countries,* pp. 54ff. Cf. Chapter 21, Section 4.

[3] *Ibid.,* pp. 56, 57, 64. The problems raised by the "cheap labor policy" will be discussed further in Chapter 21, Sections 3–4.

buildings and ancillary facilities such as roads, ports, and railways, even if mainly appendages to facilitate their enclave structure, could be used for other activities. Likewise the modern financial and commercial institutions, though geared to the foreign-dominated export-import sector, became part of the local scene and could be used for wider purposes. Despite these positive aspects, however, the other features already outlined explain the abortive developments in secondary and tertiary industries. The South Asian "agricultural revolution" therefore merely bubbled on the surface of continued general economic stagnation and filtered through to an insignificant extent, leaving the social pattern by and large unchanged. "The productivity of peasant agriculture is not markedly different in Ceylon from other Asian countries," observe the authors of the Ceylon Ten Year Plan,[1] and the same is largely true of Malaya. Indeed, it was part of colonial policy not to "disturb the natives," but to preserve a tranquil environment for a burgeoning economic activity of primary benefit to the industrialized West.

We have characterized the growth of the plantation sector as a South Asian variant of industrialization. A similar development took place in the non-agricultural extractive industries. Mine and forestry output had begun to increase substantially in the latter part of the nineteenth century, under the impetus almost everywhere of foreign, predominantly Western, enterprise. Although Chinese enterprise had early initiated tin mining in the Netherlands East Indies, Thailand, Malaya, and Indo-China, it was Western enterprise, capital, and skills that gave these activities a real push, first in the East Indies and Malaya from around 1865 and after the turn of the century in Thailand and Indo-China. Beginning about 1870, coal and iron ore in India and teak in Burma and Thailand were exploited by Western interests. However, the development of an oil industry in the East Indies and Burma and the mining of other minerals such as bauxite, nickel, and zinc in the East Indies, Malaya, and Indo-China came mainly after the second decade of the present century.[2]

Western exploitation of these natural resources had substantially the same causes and effects as the rise of plantations. The enterprises were, and many still are, financed and controlled by Western interests. The managers, technical personnel, and often the skilled workmen were Europeans. The less rationalized enterprises, as in the plantation system, had the features of small-scale industry; they were ordinarily run by "Asian foreigners," mostly Chinese. The products were not processed beyond the raw material stage and were destined for the export market to provision the expanding manufacturing industries of the West. The enclave structure of the plantation system carried over into the non-agricultural extractive in-

[1] Ceylon, Government of, *The Ten-Year Plan*, p. 6.

[2] Recent trends are discussed in Chapter 11, Section 7.

dustries. As a result there was little capital accumulation and new demands, except for food. Thus what was said about the plantations applies almost equally to these forms of activity.

9 *The Decline of Crafts and Hesitant Beginnings of Manufacturing Industry*

A main reason why plantations and the non-agricultural extractive industrial enterprises remained foreign enclaves and failed to trigger a continual, cumulative industrialization process in South Asia was that manufacturing industries did not develop. Although modern manufacturing even now continues to be a very small sector in the South Asian economies, in terms of both workers employed and value added to the national product, a brief account of what happened in this sector is appropriate at this stage of our analysis in order to understand why the development spurts proved so inconsequential.

Here it is worthwhile taking a longer look backward, for there is general agreement in the literature that in the pre-colonial era, many sections of South Asia were not inferior to the countries of Western Europe in manufacturing of a pre-industrial character. In quality and variety of products as well as production techniques, large parts of the region may even have been somewhat in advance of the West. Higgins points out that "there is little evidence that the level of technology [in Asia] was markedly below that of Europe in the sixteenth century. Countries like Indonesia had gunpowder, and their navigation techniques, modes of land and water transport and techniques of manufacture and agriculture were not markedly inferior to those of Europe."[1] Nehru was able to quote a statement by V. Anstey that even "up to the eighteenth century, 'Indian methods of production and of industrial and commercial organization could stand comparison with those in vogue in any other part of the world.'" As described, with perhaps some understandable exaggeration, by Nehru:

> India was a highly developed manufacturing country exporting her manufactured products to Europe and other countries. Her banking system was efficient and well organised throughout the country, and the hundis or bills of exchange issued by the great business or financial houses were honoured everywhere in India, as well as in Iran, and Kabul and Herat and Tashkent and other places in central Asia. Merchant capital had emerged and there was an elaborate network of agents, jobbers, brokers, and middlemen. The shipbuilding industry was flourishing and one of the flagships of an English admiral during the Napoleonic wars had been built by an Indian firm in India. India was, in fact, as advanced

[1] Higgins, "Western Enterprise and the Economic Development of South Asia," *Pacific Affairs*, p. 76.

industrially, commercially, and financially as any country prior to the industrial revolution.[1]

Not only were many parts of South Asia not significantly behind Western Europe economically, possibly as late as the eighteenth century, but at first contact the West was at a distinct disadvantage. In the sixteenth and seventeenth centuries, Europe had few goods to offer that could not be more easily produced in India and China, and European demand for goods from Asia was high and increasing.[2] Even after improved techniques were introduced in England, India continued to enjoy, for a time, a wide market in a variety of manufactured products. But about this time, the fortunes of South Asia and Western Europe began to diverge. Western Europe had its industrial revolution while the South Asian economies stagnated.

Many factors account for this difference in development. Among them must be included the rigid social stratification in South Asia and the absence of the rationalism that in Europe paved the way for an industrial revolution. The divergent social and political developments must stand as a major explanation of subsequent economic change or failure to change. As Kuznets puts it:

> When the presently developed countries within the European orbit reached their pre-industrialization phase they already possessed a variety of social, political and economic institutions, and particularly a prevailing set of views and scale of values which were extremely useful in that they permitted these societies to make the further adjustments which industrialization brought in its wake or which were essential concomitants.[3]

But no such set of institutions and attitudes evolved in South Asia. That is why it may be doubted whether there would have been an industrial development in the South Asian countries had there been no colonial domination. This is a highly speculative question, but the more pertinent question is what colonial domination implied with respect to industrial development.

To begin with, the colonial governments were careful not to attempt to radically change institutions and attitudes among the people under their rule. They created an educated class but directed its interests to administration and the professions, not to business management and modern technology.[4] Their commercial and financial policies were formulated to the

[1] Jawaharlal Nehru, *The Discovery of India*, 4th ed., Meridian Books Ltd., London, 1956, p. 282.

[2] B. H. M. Vlekke, "The Meeting of East and West: The Western View," *Eastern and Western World*, W. van Hoeve Ltd., The Hague, 1953, p. 31.

[3] Simon Kuznets, *Underdeveloped Countries – Present Characteristics in the Light of Past Growth Patterns*, Paper presented at the University of Texas Conference, April 21, 1958, mimeographed, pp. 10–11.

[4] Chapter 31, Section 3 *et passim*.

advantage of the metropolitan countries. As expressed by one writer: "The colonial relationship subordinated India to British political and economic interests; it stimulated Indian economic development in some ways and inhibited it in others."[1] What is true of British policy toward colonial India holds to at least the same extent for Dutch and French colonialism elsewhere in South Asia.

In general, the colonial regimes in South Asia were inimical to the development of manufacturing industry in the colonies. This was even more true when they gradually gave up, after the 1850's or 1870's, the crudely exploitative policies of early colonialism and began to encourage investment and production. It was predominantly or exclusively the production of raw materials for export that was encouraged. The following judgment on British policy in India can be generalized for the whole region:

> The coming of unrestricted British enterprise to India precipitated the development of the Indian economy on colonial lines. In stepping up the supply of raw materials, the British stimulated Indian economic development. In pressing for the conversion of India into a market for British manufactured goods, the British inhibited India's own manufacturing industries and gradually converted India into an agricultural hinterland of Great Britain.[2]

There are several facets to this side of colonial policy. On the one hand, it sought to protect and stimulate the home country's markets for manufactured goods. This led not only to tariff restrictions against competitive products from the colonies but also to measures designed to force colonial consumption of cheap, machine-made goods from the metropolitan country. On the other hand, as the factories in the home country required abundant and cheap raw materials from the colonies, manufacturing industry in the colonies was inhibited. The result was a lopsided economy precisely suited to the stimulation of manufacturing in the metropolitan country.

The story of the early destruction of the Indian textile crafts has often been told. The same thing happened in Java, where cottage industries gave way to imports of cotton prints first from England and later from Holland. Partly this was the natural outcome of the unequal struggle between an old and a new technology. But the process was helped and hastened by protection in England against Indian products combined with free entry into India of English products manufactured with the aid of power-driven machines. An adaptation of modern technology in India was initially hampered by the legal prohibition of certain machinery exports to India and of the migration there of skilled workmen and technicians. Thus the spread effects were swamped by the backwash effects partly because of policy

[1] Helen B. Lamb, "The 'State' and Economic Development in India," in Simon Kuznets, Wilbert E. Moore, and Joseph J. Spengler, eds., *Economic Growth: Brazil, India, Japan,* Duke University Press, Durham, N.C., 1955, p. 465.

[2] *Ibid.,* p. 467.

measures specifically designed to inhibit the former while facilitating the latter set of forces.

Even later when the *laissez-faire* view was in the ascendant and some of the discriminatory policies were relaxed – the duty on machinery imports into India was removed as early as 1860 – other features of colonial policy continued to hamper industrialization. And by then, while the South Asian countries had been stagnating, the advanced Western countries no longer needed the extra protection in the colonies. Britain could increasingly afford the luxury of greater *laissez faire* in colonial matters. Between economies on such different levels there is a natural mechanism tending toward greater inequality. But this mechanism was continually supported by policy measures. Fiscal policy, instead of allowing tax revenues to be used to bolster the colonial economy, tended to siphon off a large part to pay for expenditures that were in the interest primarily of the metropolitan country. "Much of India's public debt was in essence an accounting device for placing on India – despite the protests of many British officials in India – British military and imperial expenses unrelated to Indian needs."[1] The procurement policies of the government of India (under British control) were largely directed toward England and hence failed to provide a stimulus to native industrialists. In general, it must be concluded that the fiscal as well as the commercial policies pursued by the colonial powers placed strong constraints on the development of local manufacturing industries needed to replace the destroyed crafts. There is therefore truth in the statement by Frederick Clairemonte that "Up to the outbreak of World War I, *laissez-faire* economic policy was hardly distinguishable in its end-effects from mercantilism."[2]

Even the development of the Indian railways, aside from the fact that they were wastefully and expensively built, was oriented toward the foreign-dominated export industries, a situation that was accepted as natural. Freight rates tended to discriminate in favor of raw produce moving toward the ports and thus "helped the port industries and foreign industries in their competition with the industries of the interior."[3] It is scarcely surprising that the railways "neglected the question of the development of local industries along their lines,"[4] or that they "did not give rise to a flood of satellite innovations and . . . destroyed more occupational opportunities than . . . [they] opened up."[5] Being constructed primarily from the point

[1] *Ibid*, p. 490.

[2] *Economic Liberalism and Underdevelopment*, Asia Publishing House, Bombay, 1960, p. 126. See also Chapter 21, Section 3.

[3] D. R. Gadgil, *The Industrial Evolution of India*, 4th ed., Oxford University Press, London, 1942, p. 126.

[4] *Ibid.*, p. 127.

[5] Leland H. Jenks, "British Experience with Foreign Investments," *Journal of Economic History*, IV, Supplement, December, 1944, p. 75.

of view of the British economy, with the aim first of facilitating military security and secondly of getting the raw produce out cheaply and British goods in, as well as providing famine relief, the railways, instead of exerting enormous spread effects[1] as in Western Europe and, later, North America, served to strengthen the complementary colonial relationship and further subordinate the Indian to the British economy. Nor did the introduction of such modern institutions as commercial banks, company law, and labor legislation stimulate modernization, largely because they were brought into the colonies without particular regard to their economic needs or to the peculiarities of the economic, social, and cultural milieu. Thus, "India had the outer form of many British institutions but not the inner core, the shadow but not the substance."[2]

Colonial policy was thus an intricate combination of overt and indirect suppression of indigenous manufacturing industry. Even potential supports, such as construction of social overhead capital and the introduction of modern commercial institutions, failed to stimulate industrialization because of the failure to recognize the specific needs of the South Asian economies. Often the effect was further to subordinate the colonies and keep them longer in the stage of "hewers of wood and drawers of water," as mere appendages to the metropolitan economy. In sum, in the colonial context *laissez-faire* policies failed to trigger much indigenous industrialization. The doctrine of *laissez faire* implied the absence of government aid and protection to manufacturing and to economic development generally, outside of the plantations and the extractive industries producing raw materials. Given this lack of positive industrial promotion and of serious efforts to reform the social system, the emergence of an expanding "free economy" where private initiative would provide the dynamic impulse was rendered almost impossible. In conjunction with active support for the European enterprises in plantations, mining, forestry, and other extractive fields, *laissez-faire* passivity virtually guaranteed an absence of spontaneous industrialization. That some did occur is more to be wondered at than its relative dearth.

One should, moreover, qualify the common characterization of colonial economic policies, especially before the First World War, as *laissez faire*. True, little or nothing was done to encourage industrialization, outside of the plantations and the extractive industries; but the influence of government was used to weight the scales with discriminatory measures that hindered industrialization and enhanced dependence on the production of raw materials for export. The puzzlement expressed by so many writers as to why India did not become industrialized after so many starts is there-

[1] As Marx had expected; see Chapter 5, Section 4, and Chapter 14, Section 4.

[2] Helen Lamb, in Kuznets, Moore, and Spengler, *Economic Growth,* p. 486.

fore misplaced.[1] The Dutch in Indonesia and, somewhat later, the French in Indo-China followed policies similar to those pursued by the British in India, with comparable effects. Although specific details differ greatly, colonial policy generally throughout South Asia up to the First World War impeded native industrialization, either deliberately or otherwise, while it built up an export sector concentrating on raw materials and a native market for Western manufactured goods. When deliberate restrictions were progressively abandoned after the First World War, the change came too late to engender vigorous responses. The serious damage to native skills and industry had already been done. Later, when encouragement to industrialization took a more positive form, the Great Depression intervened to delay even further a real industrial beginning. Right down to the Second World War and independence, therefore, the extent of industrialization in all the countries of the region was negligible.

Of course, the *laissez-faire* policy, despite its mercantilist features, was not without an opportune rationalization. Underlying the grand strategy of free international trade, especially in the latter half of the nineteenth century and into the 1920's as well, was the static theory of comparative advantage. Instead of being viewed as exploitation of poor and underdeveloped colonies in the interest of rich countries – which it was in part, though only in part – colonial policy of the *laissez-faire* variety was rationalized on the ground of mutual advantage. If the South Asian resource endowment made the region peculiarly suitable for plantations and extractive industries, while Europe's resources made it the "natural" center for manufacturing, what could be more mutually advantageous than an exchange of raw materials or agricultural products for manufactured commodities? Specialization along these lines would seem to make economic sense. Yet it was convenient to ignore the fact that the export sectors of the South Asian economies were not run or controlled by or for the local inhabitants and that much of the benefits that should in theory accrue to South Asia went to Europeans. Thus Western Europe received most of the benefits that in other circumstances would have been more widely diffused. Moreover, there was nothing "natural" about the relative degrees of economic development achieved by South Asia and Western Europe. Nevertheless, the static theory of comparative advantage gave intellectual support to the policies pursued even though the abstractions on which it was based inval-

[1] "The Indian case is particularly intriguing, for modern industry came to India more than a century ago. India has long been an important exporter of jute and cotton textiles; an efficient integrated iron and steel industry was established over fifty years back; India developed indigenous entrepreneurship and financial institutions; major industrial nuclei were created over the country, with a wide range of related industrial and service activities; the railways crossed the subcontinent almost one hundred years ago. Yet India was not an appreciably more industrialised nation in 1951 than in the first decade of the century, at least in terms of the relative importance of modern industrial output and employment." (Wilfred Malenbaum, *Prospects for Indian Development*, Free Press of Glencoe, Inc., Division of Crowell Collier Publishing Co., Great Britain, 1962, p. 31.)

idated its relevance to the particular set of colonial relationships in South Asia.[1]

Despite the general impact of colonial policy, some manufacturing did develop. Mainly this occurred in India and in a limited number of fields, cotton textiles and jute first and later steel. Textiles even developed prior to the policy of "discriminating protection" of the 1920's, when Britain began to show some concern for the lack of Indian industrialization. From its beginning, in 1853, the cotton textile industry has been financed, managed, and controlled mostly by Indians. Attesting to its vitality is its survival and growth despite virtually free import of textiles from England, the various world crises, and increasing foreign competition. By 1914, India had become the fourth greatest cotton manufacturing country in the world. Temporary difficulties after the First World War failed to halt the growth of the industry, and it increased its output even during the Great Depression, largely because newly introduced tariff protection enabled it to capture most of the domestic market. The growth of a steel industry in India is another tribute to indigenous entrepreneurship. The Tata Iron and Steel Company, founded in 1907, likewise survived numerous exigencies and expanded its production during the 1930's. Steel benefitted far more than textiles from British support of colonial industrialization after the First World War. The government made large commitments to purchase Tata steel for the State railways and, under the later policy of "discriminating protection," steel was the first industry to be considered; it received protective duties against foreign imports in 1924. By 1934, Tata supplied almost three-quarters of the domestic demand for steel. The Second World War further stimulated the textile and steel industries, as we shall examine later. The development of these two industries indicates that, given some encouragement, there might have been a far greater degree of industrialization much earlier.

Other industries established in India during the colonial period were mostly initiated by Western enterprise and remained for many years under foreign control. The manufacture of jute grew rapidly after 1864, especially in Bengal, in response to rising foreign demand, until 1930 when, like all export industries, it experienced serious difficulties. A number of industries on a rather small scale also grew up, but mostly after 1914 and especially after the policy change in the 1920's.[2] Today, foreign control generally has been replaced by Indian.

[1] See Gunnar Myrdal, *Economic Theory and Underdeveloped Regions,* Duckworth, London, 1957, Chapters 3–5.

[2] "Industrial progress in India has been on a significant scale during the last thirty years. With the exception of textile industries which took root towards the end of the 19th century, many of the important industries developed during this period. The policy of 'discriminating protection' adopted in 1922 and the circumstances created by the second world war and its aftermath contributed to this development. Between 1922–23

In other countries there was even less industrialization than in India. This was due in part to a less industrially oriented resource endowment, but mainly to more restrictive colonial policies. Indeed, Robequain argues that Indo-China was eminently suited for industrialization but that "The free development of industry has never been allowed in any colony; even the possibility of such development was long considered paradoxical, almost inconceivable, by the mother country."[1] Even the Dutch "ethical policy" after 1900 did little to stimulate industry in the Netherlands East Indies[2] until the disastrous effects of the collapse of export markets were brought home in 1931, at which time some encouragement was given to local industry in Java, mainly the manufacture of cheap consumer goods. Up to, and in most cases beyond, the Great Depression, Western capital and enterprise there remained heavily concentrated in plantations and extractive industries, with transport and communication investments mainly geared to provide greater efficiency in these fields. The meager extent of industrialization in all countries of the region shown in Chapter 11, Table 11–5 for 1954–56 indicates strikingly the effects of colonial policy.

Whatever industry, using modern techniques, did develop was partly a substitute for the more primitive crafts. These were first undercut by foreign imports and then by indigenous industry as this began to develop. It is therefore not surprising that on balance the increment in manufacturing was negligible, particularly when measured in terms of workers employed. To this must, of course, be added the destruction during the Second World War, in many countries, of what little industrial capital existed. Wartime damage was particularly heavy in Malaya and Burma;

and 1949–50, the production of coal went up from 19 million tons to 32 million tons and that of steel ingots from 0.2 million tons to 1.4 million tons; industries like sugar, cement, soap and matches quickly attained a level of production adequate to meet domestic demand; and the number of persons employed in industry increased from 1.5 millions to 2.4 millions." (India, Government of, Planning Commission, *The First Five Year Plan, A Draft Outline*, New Delhi, 1951, p. 146.)

[1] *Economic Development of French Indo-China*, p. 269.

[2] "Although, in their original plans, the founders of the 'ethical policy' had paid some attention to the encouragement of industry, during the entire period of 'ethical policy,' right up to the days of crisis in 1930, the government never made any serious beginning with industrialisation. Such industry as existed at the end of the previous century was directed mainly at meeting the requirements of the plantations and railways (assembly shops, for instance, making machines for use in the sugar factories). Shortly after the turn of the century and during World War I – owing to the disappearance of imports from Europe – attempts were made to establish industries, but they never met with lasting success. There was enough room for investment in the well-known fields of agriculture and mining and there were no strong incentives for making a break with this tradition. As soon as better times set in again after the end of the war, the government dissolved the Commission on Industrialisation. The powerful estate companies felt little sympathy for industrialisation, fearing that it might cause labour costs to rise and export possibilities to fall off, as a result of diminished imports of manufactured goods." (W. F. Wertheim, *Indonesian Society in Transition*, W. van Hoeve Ltd., The Hague, 1956, p. 102.)

Indonesia and parts of Indo-China also suffered serious damage to communications, plant, and equipment.

One further aspect of colonial policy deserves mention here, namely, its effect on the proportion of the population in agriculture. In India the decline of traditional indigenous manufacturing, under the competition of foreign industry and, later, of some domestic large-scale industry, compelled large numbers of artisans and craftsmen to turn to the land. As a result it is frequently alleged that from the 1850's until the Second World War "India became progressively ruralized."[1] Evidence to support this rather widespread view[2] is extremely weak, however. Daniel and Alice Thorner, after a careful examination of the census figures, more cautiously conclude that, starting with 1881 (the first All-India census), the

> . . . Indian economy was already overwhelmingly agricultural. The scope for any subsequent de-industrialization was decidedly limited. At best, a plausible inference from our figures is that whatever new employment was created by the introduction of textile mills, rice dehusking plants, and other modern industrial establishments may have been roughly offset by an equivalent falling off in handicrafts. The conclusion forced upon us by the census occupational data is that the industrial distribution of the Indian working force from 1881 to 1931 stood still.[3]

It is scarcely credible that in 1850 little more than half the population was dependent on agriculture as Nehru, among others, has alleged,[4] while by 1881 the proportion was almost three-quarters as it is at present. It is possible that from the beginning of the nineteenth century a gradual "ruralization" of the Indian population occurred, but no adequate evidence is available to support so great a shift in the occupational distribution of the population. In all probability, dependence on agriculture in India was always very widespread. This would fit the pattern of all pre-industrial economies.

But the significant fact is that as agricultural rationalization occurred in Western Europe, it was closely followed by rapid growth of manufacturing industry, with the result that the proportion of the population dependent on agriculture everywhere declined sharply and steadily. Such was not the case in India. The stagnation of the Indian economy is nowhere better ob-

[1] Nehru, *The Discovery of India*, p. 298.

[2] "A century ago only about half the people [of India] were devoted primarily to agriculture; by 1950 this proportion had risen to 70 percent." (Ansley J. Coale and Edgar M. Hoover, *Population Growth and Economic Development in Low Income Countries*, Princeton University Press, Princeton, N. J., 1958, p. 86.)

[3] Daniel and Alice Thorner, *Land and Labour in India*, p. 77. The distribution has stayed put, even between the two last censuses, 1951 and 1961; see Chapter 24, Section 10, particularly p. 1200, footnote 3.

[4] Nehru, *The Discovery of India*, p. 298.

served than in the relative constancy of the occupational distribution of the labor force during the period for which any reasonably reliable figures are available. Whatever degree of agricultural rationalization occurred in India, it is clear that concomitant opportunities did not open up elsewhere; thus the slight extent of industrialization was, as already indicated, more in the nature of a substitute for traditional non-agricultural occupations than a net increase. Even if India did not become progressively ruralized, this does not deny the fact of economic stagnation or, at best, "static expansion."

10 *The Resulting Pattern in Agriculture*

The South Asian countries thus remained rural and predominantly agricultural although the plantations introduced by Europeans represented modern capital enterprise and technology. We have shown in Sections 8 and 9 that the spread effects from the plantation economy toward manufacturing industry were very weak. Within the agricultural sector the smaller plantation crops represented spread effects, mainly of the imitative type, though processing plants, transportation, and a market also had first to exist. But then the spread effects stopped. The plantations had hardly any influence at all on self-sufficiency farming and little impact even on peasant growing of commercial crops of the non-plantation type.

The plantations plus all commercial farming can be regarded as one type of agriculture, and self-sufficiency or near self-sufficiency farming as another. The agriculture of most of India and Pakistan is mainly of the second type. The former type of agriculture, dominated by production for export, is exemplified most clearly by Ceylon, Malaya, and, in Indonesia, parts of Sumatra, where plantation crops became important – though these countries also have large districts where the farms are not of this type – and by the three deltas in Burma, Thailand, and South Vietnam, where commercial paddy production is dominant. In Indonesia, Java is a more mixed case.

The changes in the colonial period that brought about the rise in commercial farming created a pattern of trade among the South Asian countries, which has continued to the present day, based on the distinction between rice-importing and rice-exporting countries. The rice importers are the countries with the largest concentration of plantations, chiefly Malaya and Ceylon, and the rice exporters are the three thinly populated countries on the Southeast Asian mainland where commercial rice production was developed, especially in Burma and Thailand.

Finally, the economic changes in the utilization of land that were described in Sections 6 and 7 gave rise to important migratory movements across territorial boundaries. The poverty in the regions of subsistence

Figure 10–5

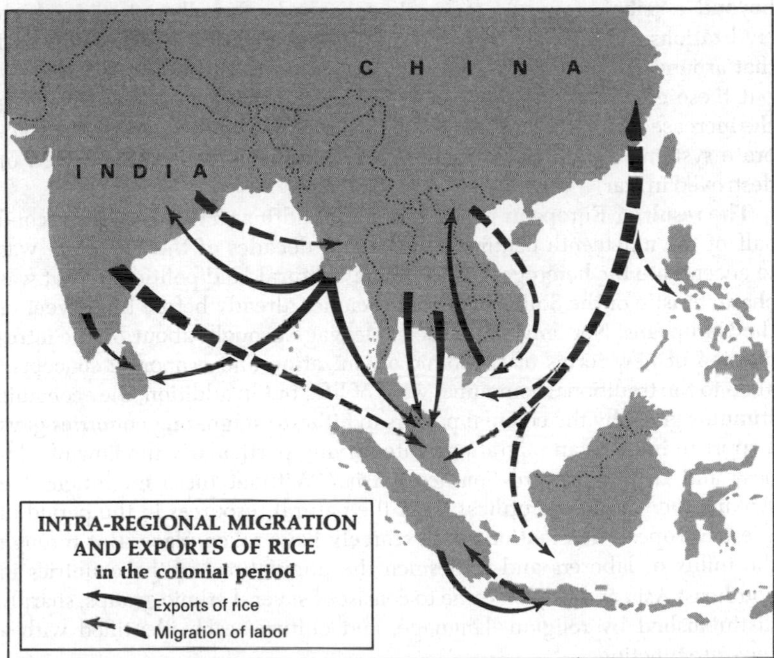

farming in India and South China provided the push, and the pull came from the growth of plantations and, in Burma, from the development of commercial food production. This pattern of intra-regional movements of food and men is shown schematically in Figure 10–5.

These migratory movements are a key factor in explaining the present politico-demographic pattern in Southeast Asia and Ceylon. This is not to say that the ethnic and cultural heterogeneity so characteristic of present-day Southeast Asia was a wholly new feature, arising from colonial domination. Since ancient times, the distinction between shifting and sedentary agriculture had been almost identical with that between the original population and the invaders from the north who occupied the fertile lowlands and pushed the aboriginal tribes to the remote regions. As was mentioned above, the alluvial plains lend themselves to intensive paddy cultivation without risk of soil exhaustion in the long run. They were therefore the regions where stable civilizations could develop. But being dependent on narrowly localized natural resources, these civilizations could not spread to the interior, and there was thus no way of bridging the sharp cleavage in levels of civilization between the fertile, densely populated pockets and the areas of shifting cultivation, where social organization could not advance beyond a tribal stage. In some places outside the alluvial plains high civilizations did arise – the ancient Khmer civilization in Cambodia and that around Pagan in Burma and Anuradhapura in Ceylon are examples – but these could not endure because more intensive cultivation, following the increase in population, led to exhaustion of the soil, or because the elaborate systems of artificial irrigation – as in Ceylon – were neglected or destroyed in war.

The result of European penetration in breadth and depth in the second half of the nineteenth century and the first decades of the twentieth was to accentuate the heterogeneity – ethnic, cultural, and political – that was characteristic of the Southeast Asian societies already before the advent of the Europeans. Not only was a social cleavage brought about by the introduction of new forms of economic organization and economic concepts,[1] alien to the traditional communal ways of life; but in addition, the economic stimulus given by the colonial powers to hitherto stagnating countries gave a spurt to intra-Asian migrations, intensifying particularly the flow of Chinese and Indians toward Southeast Asia.[2] Without these migrations the striking increase in the utilization of the natural resources in the period of West European domination could scarcely have taken place. But through the influx of laborers and tradesmen the populations of the countries in Southeast Asia and Ceylon came to consist of several ethnic groups, sharply distinguished by religion, language, and culture, each identified with a separate function.

Meanwhile, in the traditional non-commercial farming districts on the Indian subcontinent, Java, Ceylon, and even parts of continental Southeast Asia, the size of farms was reduced, through fragmentation of landholdings, when population increased faster than the cultivated area expanded. The poorer classes of sharecroppers and landless laborers tended then to enlarge faster than other classes. With this came the gradual decline of village crafts under competition both from imported consumer goods and from the beginnings of domestic factory production, especially in India.

Under the influence of these forces – and many other concomitant social changes to be described in Part Five – social relations in the agricultural population underwent a transformation that is commonly referred to as a "disruption" of village life.[3] The particular form of the process and its

[1] Such as the Western concept of land ownership; see Chapter 22, Section 2.

[2] Before the coming of the Europeans, Chinese and Indians had established themselves in most of the Southeast Asian societies. It is arguable, says Charles A. Fisher, that until the middle of the nineteenth century, and with the exception of Java and the Philippines, the indigenous way of life was more extensively undermined by foreigners of Asian origin than by the Europeans. (Charles A. Fisher, "Southeast Asia," in W. Gordon East and O. H. K. Spate, eds., *The Changing Map of Asia*, 2nd ed., revised, Methuen, London, 1953, pp. 189–193.)

[3] See also Chapter 18, Section 5.

speed and completeness varied much from country to country. The dissolution of old patterns went perhaps furthest in Burma and least far in Indonesia. The Indian village was less touched by outside influences as the opportunities for production of commercial crops were smaller. The Indian village was also a more closely knit social organization, where the caste system presented a high degree of social rigidity toward external stimuli. The economic effects were hardly less frustrating in India, though, than in Burma.

In the Netherlands East Indies, the more paternalistic colonial policy of the Dutch, especially in matters of land ownership, did give some protection to the villages from encroachment of plantations on their lands. In Ceylon, on the other hand, where the plantations came to occupy a far larger share of the total area, a sharp conflict arose between village and foreign plantation. The planters laid their hands on uncultivated land in the hilly districts around the villages, in the very period when an extension of the land under food crops was becoming urgent as population was increasing. The pressure of the two sectors against each other, especially in the more recent decades, is illustrated in Table 10–4. Until the time around the First World War, the land in the peasant sector could still be increased *pari passu* with the increase in population, despite the expansion of the plantation area. From 1921 to 1946, the plantation area increased further by one-third but the area in the peasant sector remained what it had been, and the land available per man fell by one-third.

To sum up, one can distinguish three main kinds of split in South Asian societies. First, there is the sharp difference in level and character of civili-

Table 10–4

AREA AND EMPLOYMENT IN AGRICULTURE IN CEYLON, 1871, 1921 AND 1946

	1871	*1921*	*1946*
	Area in thousand hectares		
Plantations	80	440	600
Peasant sector	480	690	680
Total agriculture	560	1,130	1,280
	Hectares per worker		
Plantations	0.7	1.0	0.8
Peasant sector	1.7	1.6	1.1
Total agriculture	1.5	1.3	0.9

Source: N. K. Sarkar, *The Demography of Ceylon*, Colombo, 1957, Chapter 10.

zation between the dominant ethnic groups and the tribal peoples in hills and mountains and other remote and sparsely populated places. This dichotomy, which is of ancient origin and unrelated to the episode of European domination, poses problems especially in India, Burma, South Vietnam, and, to a lesser extent, in the Philippines and in the outer islands of Indonesia. Secondly, there is the contrast between modern, market-oriented, and profit-seeking forms of economic enterprise and the traditional subsistence economy. This is most apparent where modern plantation estates exist side by side with a village economy still largely dominated by subsistence farming. This cleavage of the economy into a modern and a traditional sector, with few intermediate forms of enterprise, reflects an economic development that remained partial, localized, and lopsided. The third kind of cleavage, often closely connected with the one just mentioned, is that on purely ethnic lines, resulting from the migratory movements. The most important example is of course that of the Chinese minorities in the countries of Southeast Asia and the Indian Tamils in Ceylon. Sharply defined ethnic, linguistic, and cultural group differences are here associated with almost as sharply defined differences in economic role. In the Federation of Malaya, where the two main ethnic groups – the Malays and the Chinese – are of nearly equal numerical strength, the cleavage on ethnic lines has resulted in a peculiar constellation of power: the Chinese group wields economic power, while political power is with the Malays.

The Southeast Asian societies have thus come to be rather extreme examples of "plural" societies,[1] where the various groups "mix but do not combine."[2] The political, social, economic, and cultural problems thereby created are in some ways similar to those connected with the caste system in India. Naturally, the achievement of national independence has exacerbated the problem of "pluralism." The creation of national states inevitably brought to the fore a number of minority problems – some territorially defined, others not – and has thus thrown into relief what has aptly been called the "demographic immaturity" of these countries where "no lasting adjustment has yet been reached between land and state."[3] These and related problems are discussed in other parts of this book.

[1] The "pluralism" of Southeast Asian societies was first pointed out and explained by J. S. Furnivall in his pathbreaking article "The Organisation of Consumption" in *Economic Journal,* Vol. XX, 1910, pp. 23–30. Despite some close similarities, the concept of "pluralism" should not be confused with that of a "dual economy" as propounded at about the same time by J. H. Boeke, the founder of the Leyden School of "tropical economists." Boeke focussed attention – perhaps too much attention – on the dichotomy between a modern European sector dominated by the motive of profit and an indigenous subsistence sector in which economic incentives are ineffective or less effective. See, for instance, J. H. Boeke, *Economics and Economic Policy in Dual Societies*. For a critical evaluation of Boeke's main thesis, see B. Higgins, "The 'dualistic theory' of underdeveloped areas" in *Ekonomi dan Keuangan Indonesia,* Djakarta, February, 1955.

[2] Furnivall, *Colonial Policy and Practice,* p. 304.

[3] C. A. Fisher, in East and Spate, *The Changing Map of Asia,* p. 236.

11 *Urbanization*

If, in one sense, "demographic immaturity" typifies parts of South Asia, there is another sense in which the region is perhaps demographically "premature." This is in its urbanization. Not only has South Asia experienced in recent decades a rapid rate of urban growth (see Table 10–5) without sig-

Table 10–5

LEVELS OF URBANIZATION

Country or region	Date	Census or estimate	Percent of total population in towns of: 20,000 or more	100,000 or more
World	1950	C, E	21	13
N.W. Europe	1950	C	46	30
U.S.S.R.	1950	E	31	18
Africa	1950	E	9	5
S.W. Asia	1950	E	22	10
Pakistan	1951	C	7.8	5.1
	1961	C	...	7.3
India	1951	C	12.0	6.6
	1961	C	...	8.4
Indonesia	1950	E	9.1	7.0
	1957	E	...	7.0
Burma	1953	C, E	9.2	5.2
Vietnam	1950	E	8.0	6.5
Philippines	1950	E	12.7	5.1
Thailand	1950	E	7.6	6.7
Ceylon	1950	E	11.4	5.4
Fed. of Malaya	1948	C	17.1	7.4
	1957	E	...	10.8
Singapore	1950	E	72.5	72.5

Sources: 1950 estimates from ECAFE *Bulletin*, Vol. X, no. 1, June, 1959, p. 18, which uses totals for censuses nearest to 1950, and (for Belgium, Denmark, Finland, France, Germany (West), Liechtenstein, Luxembourg, Netherlands, Norway, Saar, Sweden, Switzerland, and United Kingdom) U. N., *Demographic Yearbook 1955*, Table 8. The latter source is also used for the earlier Malayan and Indian figures. India: *1961 Census Provisional Population Totals*, Office of the

nificant industrialization,[1] but this growth has been accompanied by relative stagnation of agricultural productivity as already shown. South Asian urbanization has not, therefore, been a response to rapidly rising productivity in either agriculture or industry.

This is contrary to Western experience, where one of the traditional accompaniments of industrialization has been a rise in the relative importance of urban centers not only with regard to population but in terms of output as well. The causal mechanism historically has involved an increase in employment opportunities in urban agglomerations due to the clustering of manufacturing establishments in response to external economies. This process went hand in hand with a rise in agricultural productivity sufficient to create an excess labor supply in rural areas; sooner or later, the excess became absorbed in the expanding industrial centers. In a very general way this process typified the early period of rapid industrialization in Northwestern Europe during the late eighteenth and early nineteenth centuries. In South Asia, the rise in urbanization has not been induced by vigorous economic expansion. It seems to be generally true that:

> The present level of urbanization is high in relation to the degree of economic development [of the region as a whole]. . . . When the major industralized countries of Europe and North America were at a comparable level of urbanization they were far more developed, as is shown by the fact that approximately 55 percent of their labour force was engaged in non-agricultural occupations, as against the present figure [for South Asia] . . . of 30 percent.[2]

[1] It appears to be generally true that "urban growth in under-developed areas is not a function of the expansion of the industrial base but an expression of the severity of the agrarian crises. This fact is borne out by ample data showing that urbanization has grown considerably faster than industrial employment in under-developed countries." (United Nations, ECAFE, *Economic Bulletin for Asia and the Far East,* December, 1959, p. 21, f.n. 65. See also United Nations, *Report on the World Social Situation* [prepared by Bureau of Social Affairs, U. N. Secretariat, in Co-operation with ILO, FAO, UNESCO, WHO], New York, 1957, pp. 111–143.)

[2] U. N., ECAFE, *Economic Bulletin,* Vol. X, No. 1, June, 1959, p. 19. The advanced state of urbanization relative to economic development has also been observed for an earlier period. See Gadgil, *Industrial Evolution of India,* p. 134.

Sources to Table 10–5 continued

Registrar General, New Delhi, 1961, pp. xiii, xxxv–xxxix; Kerala is excluded; population of Delhi State from p. 80, assumed to be in "over-100,000" area, except for rural council regions. Pakistan: over-20,000 from ECAFE, *loc. cit.;* over-100,000 from Census of Pakistan, 1961, Bulletin no. 1, Preliminary Release, 28 February 1961, p. 13. Burma: *First Stage Census 1953,* vol. I, Government of Union of Burma, Rangoon, 1957, pp. 2–3, with our population estimate for the whole country. Indonesia: 1957 estimate from *Statistical Pocketbook of Indonesia,* Biro Pusat Statistik, Djakarta, 1960, p. 11. Malaya: 1957 estimate from United Nations, Department of Economic and Social Affairs, *The Population of South-East Asia (Including Ceylon and China: Taiwan), 1950–1980,* Future Population Estimates by Sex and Age, Report III, Population Studies No. 30, New York, 1958, p. 46.

Table 10–6

NATIONAL AND URBAN RATES OF POPULATION GROWTH

Area	Period	Yearly compound percentage rate of growth of population in: Whole of area	Urban areas	Cities of over 100,000
Pakistan	1951–61	2.1	. . .	6.1
British India (excl. Burma)	1921–41	1.2	2.1	3.6
	1931–41	1.4	2.9	5.5
Indian Union area	1941–51	1.3	3.6	4.8
	1951–61	2.0	. . .	3.8
Indonesia	1930–56	1.2	. . .	5.1
	1952–56	1.5	. . .	3.9
Burma	1931–41	1.4	. . .	2.4
	1931–53	1.2	3.0	2.9
Philippines	1931–48	1.9	2.2	. . .
	1948–60	3.2	. . .	3.7
Ceylon	1931–46	1.6	2.4	1.7
	1946–53	2.8	2.7	2.4
Fed. of Malaya	1931–47	1.6	3.0	2.2
	1947–57	2.5	. . .	6.2

Sources: U. N., *Demographic Yearbook 1951,* Table 2; *1952,* Tables 3, 5, 6; *1955,* Tables 6, 7, 8; V. Nath, in *Proceedings of the 1954 World Population Conference,* U. N., New York, 1955, Vol. 2, p. 843; O. H. K. Spate, *India and Pakistan,* 2nd ed., Methuen & Co., London, 1957, p. 115; Kingsley Davis, *The Population of India and Pakistan,* Princeton University Press, Princeton, N.J., 1951, p. 127; India, *1961 Census Provisional Population Totals, op. cit.* (see last table for details of this source and the method); 1961 Census of Pakistan, Bulletin no. 1, *op. cit.* (see last table for details of this source); Union of Burma, *First Stage Census 1953, op cit.* (see last table); *Statistical Pocketbook of Indonesia 1959,* Biro Pusat Statistik, Djakarta, p. 11; *Journal of Philippine Statistics,* Vol. XIII, nos. 7–9, July–Sept., 1960, Bureau of the Census and Statistics, pp. 2–3.

In all countries of the region, most cities are growing at a faster rate than the entire population (Table 10–6). In the 1940's the Indian urban population grew by about 45 percent,[1] several times the rate of growth of total population. Several (though not all) of the cities with over a million inhabitants in 1961 had grown at rates well above the Indian average in the pre-

[1] U. N., ECAFE, *Studies on Population Growth and Economic Development* [Preliminary Report], February, 1958, mimeographed, p. 66.

ceding ten years.[1] And between 1921 and 1951 the "urban population living in localities with 20,000 or more inhabitants increased by 2.8 times."[2] The growth rates of Djakarta and Bandung between 1930 and 1958 were four to five times that of Indonesia as a whole. In Burma, the growth rates of Mandalay and Rangoon in the mid-1950's were some four times the national average. The rate of growth of Karachi was over 80 percent between 1951 and 1961, several times the increase of about 24 percent for all Pakistan.[3] The urban growth rates in Ceylon, the Philippines, and Malaya were somewhat less but still in excess of the national averages.[4]

Despite the roughness of the data and the varying conceptions of "urban" and "rural" among the countries, the evidence supports a relatively rapid increase in urbanization in South Asia. Yet the sex composition and mortality differences between urban and rural areas yield lower rates of natural population growth in urban centers than elsewhere.[5] It is clear, then, that net migration from rural to urban areas is the main reason for the more rapid growth of the latter.[6] But the movement cityward is largely unrelated to any vigorous expansion of urban employment opportunities, for, as will be discussed later, the cities are beset by serious unemployment and "underemployment" problems[7] of their own. And in view of the squalor, overcrowding, inadequate housing and sanitation in urban centers, the movement toward the cities cannot in general be motivated by any increase in their "net attractiveness"; recent studies indicate the reverse.[8]

[1] India, Government of, Ministry of Home Affairs, Office of the Registrar General, *1961 Census Provisional Population Totals,* New Delhi, 1961, Table 18.

[2] U. N., ECAFE, *Studies on Population Growth,* p. 63.

[3] Pakistan, Government of, Population Census Commission, Ministry of Home Affairs, *Census of Pakistan, 1961 Provisional Tables of Population,* Karachi, February 28, 1961, Tables 1 and 6.

[4] The somewhat slower rise in Malaya and Ceylon doubtless reflects in part the different form of "industrialization" in these countries, which creates less agricultural stagnation.

[5] P. M. Hauser, ed., *Urbanization in Asia and the Far East,* UNESCO, Calcutta, 1957, pp. 107–127.

[6] Vishwambhar Nath, "Urbanization in India with Special Reference to Growth of Cities," in *Proceedings of the World Population Conference, 1954* (Rome, 31 August–September 1954), Papers: Vol. II, United Nations, New York, 1955, and Kingsley Davis, "Internal Migration and Urbanization in Relation to Economic Development," in *ibid.,* pp. 763–800.

[7] See also Chapter 11, Section 4.

[8] Studies of urbanization in Bangkok, Bombay, Dacca, Delhi, and Djakarta show that "economic hardship, in varying degrees, was the real reason for practically all migration." (UNESCO, *The Social Implications of Industrialization and Urbanization, Five Studies in Asia,* Calcutta, 1956, p. ix. See also B. Hoselitz, "The City, the Factory and Economic Growth," *American Economic Review,* May, 1955, Papers and Proceedings Supp., pp. 177 ff.)

V. Nath argues, though unconvincingly, that "The principal cause of urbanization in India, as in other countries, is the growth of modern type industry, commerce and service occupations." (V. Nath, *Proceedings of World Population Conference, 1954,* p. 846.)

If this is so, then the principal cause of South Asian urbanization must be an increase, relative to urban areas, in rural poverty and insecurity, at least in certain strata of the rural population, which creates a "push" toward the cities.[1] The dynamic element would therefore appear to be the very rapid growth of population in the region; this, in the first instance, presses on the lower strata in the rural sector and then spills over, as it were, into the towns and cities. Urbanization is thus more a reaction *against* the lack of vigorous economic growth than a response to rising levels of income per head. Indeed, much of it is due to factors inhibiting economic development, such as civil wars, instability,[2] and crop failures, as well as to excessive rates of population growth. Instead of standing as a symptom of growth, as it was in the West, urbanization in South Asia is an aspect of continued poverty.

[1] Consistent with this conclusion is the fact that the migrants cling to their relation with the village. S. Chandrasekhar explains: "However, during lean years a migration from villages to towns does take place. It is not a voluntary and willing migration. Only economic pressure of the worst kind forces the agriculturist into the city in search of a job – any job – to earn a livelihood. He hopes that it is only temporary and longs to return to the village. Hence he leaves behind his wife and children and goes to the cities. . . ." (Sripati Chandrasekhar, *India's Population, Fact and Policy*, 2nd ed., Indian Institute for Population Studies, Chidambaram, 1950, p. 56.)

There are also "push back" factors operating in the urban areas. As Ashish Bose points out, "migration analysis based on push and pull factors tends to be an oversimplification." ("Internal Migration in India, Pakistan and Ceylon," United Nations World Population Conference, Belgrade, August 30–September 10, 1965, A.3/I/E/132.)

[2] Partition of India and Pakistan led to a rapid rise in urban areas. Some two million Pakistanis moved to Indian urban centers alone following partition. (V. Nath in *Proceedings of World Population Conference, 1954*, p. 844.)

Of the 3.2 million Pakistan refugees into the Indian Punjab, almost half settled in urban areas. The urban share of the Indian Punjab population increased from 18.6 percent in 1941 to 25.0 percent in 1951. See I. N. Chawla, "The Urbanization of the Punjab Plains," *Indian Geographer*, December, 1958, pp. 30–38.

Chapter 11

NATIONAL OUTPUT AND STRUCTURE OF ECONOMY

The preceding chapter gave a broad overview of the economic structure of the several countries in South Asia in its geographic, demographic, and historical setting. As the overwhelming majority of the populations in these countries get their livelihood from agriculture, our interest was focussed mainly on the man/land ratio and on the utilization of the agricultural resources. With considerable justification,[1] all these countries now see their long-range opportunity for development in industrialization. In this chapter, the closer analysis of the present economic structure and recent trends takes this aspiration into account and gives greater attention to the degree and character of industrialization in the several countries of the region. To provide a background for this analysis, we shall first consider levels and trends of national income – or output – per head of population.

Much of this chapter will be devoted to demonstrating the extreme frailty of the statistical material available; we deem this an important scientific task, since in the analysis of the development problems of these countries unreliable figures are often used with a naive credulity that greatly impairs the value of the conclusions drawn.

[1] See Chapter 24, Section 2.

1 *National Output and Income Per Head*

National output or income per head plays a central role in the discussion of underdevelopment and development of the South Asian countries. The level of this magnitude – these magnitudes, rather, since output and income may differ, as will be shown below – is usually taken as an indication of a country's relative state of underdevelopment; and the rate of change in this index – when it is rising – as an indication of the speed of development. The plans regularly fix as a target a specified rate of increase during the plan period.[1] In Appendix 2 (Section 7) we give the reasons why, rationally, output or income per head and its rate of change can never give anything more than a rough indication of, respectively, underdevelopment and the speed of development. Both underdevelopment and development are composite concepts; they cannot be defined merely in terms of a single aggregate or average. If this point is recognized, figures for national output or income and of its changes over time are nevertheless considered to be sufficiently indicative of underdevelopment and development to merit serious attention.

Table 11–1 purports to give, for the years 1954 through 1956, average national income per head figures for the countries in the region and a few countries outside it. It is with great hesitancy that we publish this table, or any other tables that give, or imply, national income figures. That these figures have any precise meaning at all is doubtful; we see no possibility of estimating even roughly the margins of error. Although we use the available data, it cannot be emphasized too much that they are extremely tenuous. To begin with, not only is national income per head a very crude indicator of the degree of development or underdevelopment, as already suggested, but there are certain logical difficulties involved in the way such an aggregate is defined and the data are compiled. The appropriate definition depends, of course, on the purpose one has in mind or the use one proposes to make of the national accounts. For example, an aggregative measure of total output during a particular time period may refer to production within a geographical or national boundary. Such a measure is termed "net geographical product," or sometimes "net domestic product." On the other hand, a measure of the incomes accruing to normal residents as a result of current productive activity, referred to as "net national income," is also useful for some purposes.

For the industrialized countries of the West, the discrepancy between these two aggregative measures is relatively small. But for any economy with a large enclave-type, alien-dominated sector involved in substantial remission of interest, profits, salaries, and even wages, as well as factor payments to foreigners or non-residents, a serious discrepancy exists be-

[1] Appendix 4, Section 1.

tween "net geographical product" and the income actually received by normal residents, "net national income." Especially for Ceylon, Malaya and, before the large-scale nationalization of foreign property, Indonesia, where the export sector accounts for a significant share of total output and where it is also largely owned, controlled, and managed by aliens, this divergence may be rather substantial. It is only somewhat less so in the other countries of South Asia. In other words, although in a purely accounting sense, the value of output necessarily equals the value of input (i.e., income), a difference can and usually does exist, especially if the extent of alien economic control is fairly large, when one concept is construed on the basis of "normal residence" or citizenship and the other is viewed in geographical terms. So long, therefore, as the plantations, mines, and other segments of the South Asian economies remained largely under foreign domination, the incomes received by the indigenous populations were less, by varying amounts, than the value of the net geographical output.

Jonathan Levin has expressed this as follows: "The existence of foreign factors, remitting their income abroad, casts serious doubt upon the validity of several widely accepted fundamental assumptions, the most important of these being the identity between production and income within a geographic area."[1] In the pure logic of the case this is not quite correct. An identity, in an accounting sense, as indicated above, necessarily holds, but there is no identity when output is viewed geographically while income is viewed in terms of "normal residence" or citizenship. It is only in this sense that the basic assumption of an identity is erroneous. This assumption is, of course, a product of social accounting concepts developed in the West, where the discrepancy was never very important, at least at the time when social accounting was initiated. But the assumed identity for some of the economies of South Asia can be misleading. Furthermore, since the concept of "normal residence" is an elusive one the distinction between geographical product and national income is somewhat arbitrary.

The national accounts data presented in this chapter refer basically to what we have termed "net geographical product." Although most of the data are defined as "national income," they are usually deduced from a prior measure of what is in reality "net geographical product" (or "net domestic product"), by subtracting a figure specified as "net factor payments abroad." We believe that this deduction is substantially underestimated and fails to give adequate consideration to unilateral transfers or remittances. As a result, the figures regularly published show a closer correspondence than we believe exists between incomes actually received and retained within the national boundaries by normal residents (not counting amounts spent on imports) and the value of geographical out-

[1] Jonathan V. Levin, *The Export Economies,* Harvard University Press, Cambridge, Mass., 1960, p. 173.

put.[1] Depending on the country involved, net geographical product may or may not coincide closely with income received by normal residents. In the present chapter, the estimates used pretend to be net income, but they might better be regarded as output produced within the national boundaries.

In South Asia, the discrepancy between output and income has progressively narrowed. Since independence there have been curbs on remission of dividends and interest, nationalization in some countries, and increased taxation of alien-dominated enterprises, and, everywhere, greater participation by normal residents in the higher posts of public administration and in what were formerly European economic preserves. These tendencies reduce whatever degree of distortion is involved in assuming output to be identical with income; but for that reason they make the data less comparable over time. Any attempt to make inter-temporal comparisons must face up to this difficulty as well as to the problem of deflating for price changes.

While, therefore, the figures presented in Table 11–1 may overstate the position of Ceylon and Malaya, in particular, if viewed as "incomes received by normal residents," we have not made any arbitrary deductions from these figures, which already suffer from large statistical deficiencies (as we shall discuss later) because of the lack of adequate and comparable data, for all of the countries, on the extent of income remission and foreign factor payments. It may, in consequence, be useful to look on these figures as measures of output or of "potential income" for the average resident of the various South Asian countries. In the latter regard they should become more realistic as native personnel increasingly take over the ownership and control of assets within their national boundaries.[2] It should be clear that this income-output discrepancy and its magnitude, which was much greater in the nineteenth century, accounts in part for the weakness of the spread effects of the coming of Western enterprise. To the extent that incomes generated within a territory gave rise to no concomitant demands for the output of that territory, the stimulus was that much weakened. Unilateral remission of incomes and payment of non-resident foreign

[1] In India, which in general has national accounts estimates superior to those of the other South Asian countries, it has been pointed out that "Information regarding items like donations and remittances is incomplete, . . . [and] no clear indication is available regarding the net outflow of factor incomes from the country . . ." (India, Government of, Department of Economic Affairs, Ministry of Finance, *Final Report of the National Income Committee February 1954,* Government of India Press, New Delhi, 1954, p. 104.)

[2] This assumes that in the process of such takeover, productivity of the plantations, mines, and some heavy industry will not be adversely affected. This assumption, as Indonesia's experience indicates, is far from universally valid. Again, if compensation for the assets is made, say in the form of bonds, there will be an increase in interest payments to aliens, who may or may not be residents, that will partly offset the above-mentioned tendencies.

Table 11–1

AVERAGE YEARLY INCOME PER HEAD, 1954–56
(*Indian rupees*)

Country	*Income per head at official exchange rates* (*1*)	*Estimated income per head* (2)
Pakistan	207	220
India	263	260
Indonesia	585	300
Burma	211	300
South Vietnam	592	350
Philippines	771	380
Thailand	350	400
Ceylon	558	460
Malaya	995	780
Italy	1,700	–
U. K.	4,067	–
Sweden	5,293	–
U. S.	9,258	–

Sources: Column 1 from Table 4 of Appendix 13. Column 2 from Table 6 of that appendix.

factors represent, therefore, a separable part of the leakage from domestic aggregate demand over and above the demand for imports, as already discussed in Chapter 10 (Section 8).

There is yet another difficulty with respect to national accounting in South Asia beyond its weak statistical basis, namely, the valuation of output. Large sections of the economy are non-monetized and without much of a link with any markets. To value the non-marketed or bartered output at prices of the same or similar commodities in existing markets, even if in close proximity, implies both that tastes and preferences in the monetized and non-monetized sectors are identical and that the market prices would not be very different if the non-marketed output were offered for sale.[1] Either implication is subject to considerable doubt. In South Asia, moreover, it is the rule rather than the exception for goods that do enter markets to be sold under conditions of substantial market imperfection. But some markets are more nearly perfect, and some goods are even priced in markets related to highly competitive international markets. The relative valuations of commodities established in such divergent ways cannot be expected to reflect preferences and scarcities in any con-

[1] See William J. Barber, *The Economy of British Central Africa,* Oxford University Press, London, 1961, p. 98.

sistent fashion. This raises serious doubts about the aggregation of these data into a single figure purporting to represent "output." Such an aggregate has more meaning in Western economies, where most goods and services are sold in relatively competitive markets, though even there caution is needed.[1] But in South Asia the aggregate cannot have any clear and unambiguous meaning.

Aside from these major logical and conceptual problems, the statistical basis for the figures of Table 11–1 is extremely weak, though more so for some countries than for others. Nearly all efforts to calculate national income for countries in the region date back only a few years.[2] Only in some of them has national accounting become a regular practice as yet. In all South Asian countries that, either fairly regularly or sporadically, have carried out calculations of national income, these calculations have had to be founded to a very large extent – much larger than in developed countries – on crude estimates. The reasons for this may be briefly listed: (1) The "organized" or "large-scale" sector, for which comprehensive statistics are available, accounts for a very small share of total income generated. (2) Accurate quantitative information about the much larger "unorganized" or "small-scale" sector is only very seldom and partly available. (3) The non-monetized part of the economy is very large, since it includes a very large share – in many countries by far the largest share – not only of food production but also of the production and consumption of other consumer goods and services, and also a considerable part of total investment, especially in agriculture and house construction. (4) Particularly in the case of foodstuffs, the supply appearing on the market has to a large, though varying, extent been mobilized not by a market process but by a "squeezing" process determined by tradition and power, with landlords and moneylenders as the active agents. (5) The statisticians available to piece together the scattered and heterogeneous information obtainable for the purpose of national accounting are insufficiently trained and too few, particularly in top-level positions.[3]

[1] ". . . statistics giving international comparisons of national incomes are among the most uncertain and unreliable statistics with which the public is being confronted. . . . This is a field where politics reigns supreme. . . ." (Oskar Morgenstern, *On the Accuracy of Economic Observations,* 2nd ed., Princeton University Press, Princeton, N. J., 1963, p. 282.)

[2] Only for India and Indonesia were national income estimates made before the Second World War. These were unofficial estimates worked out by individual scholars; see V. K. R. V. Rao, *An Essay on India's National Income, 1925–1929,* Macmillan & Co. Ltd., London, 1939, and *The National Income of British India, 1931–1932,* Macmillan & Co. Ltd., London, 1940; J. J. Polak, "The National Income of the Netherlands Indies, 1921–1939," unpublished paper (no date). For detailed comments on the various estimates made of India's national income prior to 1951 see Daniel and Alice Thorner, *Land and Labour in India,* Asia Publishing House, Bombay, 1962, Chapter VII.

[3] For a discussion of procedures, see Harry J. Oshriva, "National Income Statistics

The examination of national accounts statistics that we have made permits a rough evaluation of their comparative quality among the several countries. Our judgment is that the data for India and the Philippines are the best in the region and those of Indonesia and South Vietnam the poorest,[1] while the other countries fall somewhere in between. Yet even the material for India leaves much to be desired, and has recently come in for some rather trenchant criticism.[2] The Philippine data have received less criticism than the Indian, but doubtless because they have not been examined with the same care.[3] For the other countries the national income

---

of Underdeveloped Countries," *Journal of the American Statistical Association*, June, 1957, pp. 162–175.

[1] National accounts figures for Indonesia are "rough estimations and extrapolations based on the national income estimates for the years 1951–1952 prepared by Dr. D. S. Neumark." (United Nations, Statistical Office of the United Nations, Department of Economic and Social Affairs, *Yearbook of National Accounts Statistics 1960,* New York, 1961, p. 114.) South Vietnam last produced national accounts in 1956.

A recent study flatly states that "Indonesia lacks any reliable estimates of national income and its composition, whether considered from the point of view of investment, saving and consumption, or the industries in which income originates." (U. S. Economic Survey Team to Indonesia, *Indonesia: Perspective and Proposals for United States Economic Aid,* A Report to the President of the United States, Yale University Southeast Asia Studies, New Haven, 1963, p. 39.)

[2] Thorner has pointed out a serious inconsistency in two official series purporting to show physical agricultural output in India, one of which is used by the National Income Unit of the Central Statistical Organisation to estimate agricultural income. (Daniel Thorner, "India's Elusive Agricultural Output Figures," *Economic Weekly,* January, 1960, pp. 199–200.) Since income originating in agriculture constitutes almost half of total national income, any basic weakness in this component casts serious doubts on the total.

Another writer recently complained that "whatever national accounts there are in India provide the same sorry picture as the national income estimates: a few islands of sound and solid ground in a treacherous marsh of Derived and Baseless Statistics." (A. Rudra, "National Income Estimates, Why Not Discontinue Them?," *Economic Weekly,* February 4, 1961, p. 211.) His classification of statistics into two groups, "Informative" and "Derived and Baseless Statistics," reveals a very substantial share of the national income data by sectors as falling in the latter category (*ibid.*, p. 213), and he uses this finding to support his plea for discontinuance of national income estimates as presently prepared. Little has complained that in India, "National income figures exist, but are very unreliable." (I. M. D. Little, "The Strategy of Indian Development," *National Institute Economic Review,* No. 9, May 1960, p. 20, f.n. 3.) Aside from these adverse comments on the Indian estimates there are numerous considerations that raise questions about their accuracy; for example, the failure until recently to provide figures on depreciation and estimates of aggregate consumption, investment, and other such categories on the expenditure side. In the light of these considerations we think it is overly optimistic to conclude that the maximum error in the aggregate figure is only 10 per cent (India, Government of, Department of Economic Affairs, Ministry of Finance, *Final Report of the National Income Committee February, 1954,* Government of India Press, New Delhi, 1954, p. 105) or that the national income figures available since 1948–49 are "firm estimates" (G. S. Gouri, "National Income Estimates in India 1931–1949," *Indian Economic Journal,* July, 1954, pp. 58–59). However, the *Final Report* also stated (p. 105) that the "margin of error may possibly be somewhat higher."

[3] It may be worth noting that the national income estimates given in the Philippine plan differ substantially from those reported by the Economic Commission for Asia

estimates are far more tenuous. Thailand under-reports agricultural income.[1] The Indonesian data were revised upwards by over 20 percent in a single year, 1955.[2] More recent estimates of national income in Indonesia have been subjected to severe criticism.[3] In Pakistan, the estimates of income originating in "minor agricultural crops," "livestock," "fisheries," and "forestry," accounting for over one-third of total agricultural income, remained unchanged in every year from 1953–54 through 1957–58[4] and were only revised in the Second Five Year Plan.[5] The data for a rather substantial proportion of the important agricultural sector, in short, remained "provisional" for about six years and still are unreliable. Official Pakistan estimates of food production may be in error by as much as 20 percent according to one analyst.[6] The Ceylonese figures for gross domestic product originating in agriculture were reduced in the 1960 *Yearbook of National Accounts Statistics* compared with the 1959 edition for every year between 1953 and 1958 by about 4 or 5 percent although total gross domestic product remained the same.[7] This adjustment was unaccompanied by explanatory comment. The data for South Vietnam suffer from obvious frailties, as pointed out in Section 3 below. In Malaya basic information on such an important magnitude as rice yield per acre has been estimated to range as much as "40 percent over and 90 percent under actual measured yields" in various districts. Since crop statistics are deemed to be "among the most accurate recorded in Malaya,"[8] whatever national

---

and the Far East. Compare Philippines, Government of the, National Economic Council, *The Five-Year Economic and Social Development Program for FY 1957–1961*, Manila, January, 1957, mimeo. Generally, however, the relatively high caliber of the Philippine data is confirmed by other observers. For example, Golay has stated that "Philippine statistics are plentiful and relatively good." (F. H. Golay, *The Philippines: Public Policy and National Economic Development*, Cornell University Press, Ithaca, New York, 1961, p. 100.) Similarly, Higgins has commented on "the relatively large number of trained people, plus an unexplained Filipino passion for statistics." (Benjamin Higgins, *Economic Development*, W. W. Norton Co., New York, 1959, p. 742.)

[1] U. N., *Yearbook of National Accounts Statistics 1958*, New York, 1959, p. 217.

[2] Compare figure in United Nations, ECAFE, *Economic Survey of Asia and the Far East, 1959*, Bangkok, 1960, p. 112, Table 5 with the same survey for 1960, p. 126, Table 5.

[3] J. M. van der Kroef, "Indonesia's New Development Plan," *Eastern World*, February, 1961, p. 28.

[4] Pakistan, Government of, Central Statistical Office, *Statistical Bulletin*, February, 1959, p. 139.

[5] Pakistan, Government of, Planning Commission, *The Second Five Year Plan (1960–65)*, Karachi, June, 1960, p. 45.

[6] Christopher Beringer, *The Use of Agricultural Surplus Commodities for Economic Development in Pakistan*, The Institute of Development Economics, Monograph No. 12, January, 1964, Karachi, p. 36.

[7] Compare U. N., *Yearbook of National Accounts Statistics 1959*, p. 45, Table 2, with the same source for 1960, p. 43, Table 2.

[8] L. A. Peter Gosling, "The Location of 'Problem' Areas in Rural Malaya," in Norton Ginsburg, ed., *Essays on Geography and Economic Development*, University of

accounts data exist are therefore subject to serious reservations. These random selections of conflicting evidence (many others could be given) provide important caveats concerning the caliber of the data in the region.

It is extremely important to stress these things, for to the extent that planning in South Asia relies on the data available it is apt to be misguided, in some cases very seriously. Whether as a tool for planning or as an indicator of results, the statistics are unreliable and inadequate. As I. M. D. Little suggests in regard to India, "It is extraordinary what little fuss the Planning Commission makes about the poverty of Indian statistics."[1] A similar comment is even more relevant to the other countries of the region.

In Table 11–1 are included figures for a few countries outside the region. This has been done mainly to give us the occasion to state that, even apart from the logical difficulties and the extremely shaky statistical basis of the figures for the South Asian countries, we see no real meaning in a comparison of national incomes per head among countries so different in levels of development, economic organization, composition of foreign trade, structure of prices, and, more pertinently, modes and levels of living, levels of "saving" and composition of "consumption."[2] When column 1 of this table shows, for instance, that the United States has a national income per head about 35 times higher than India's, this seems to be nothing else than giving an entirely unwarranted and false precision to the obvious fact that the United States is a very much richer country than India. A study by Everett Hagen concludes that comparisons of income per head that are based on official exchange rates seriously overstate the differences between countries on different levels of development since, "Typically, goods and services produced and used within a low-income country are cheaper, relative to the same goods and services in say the United States, than those that enter into foreign trade, so that conversion of the country's national income to dollars by use of the foreign exchange rate understates the true income."[3] A recomputation suggests that the disparity between the United States and India is more nearly of the order of 12 to 1 rather than the ratio of 35 to 1 obtained from a straight com-

---

Chicago Press, Chicago, 1960, pp. 127–128. See also E. H. G. Dobby and others, "Padi Landscapes of Malaya," *Malayan Journal of Tropical Geography*, October, 1955, p. 7.

[1] "The Strategy of Indian Development," *National Institute Economic Review*, p. 20, f.n. 3.

[2] The terms "saving" and "consumption" are placed in quotation marks for reasons given in Chapter 12, Section 2, and Appendix 2, Section 21.

[3] Everett E. Hagen, "Some Facts About Income Levels and Economic Growth," *Review of Economics and Statistics*, February, 1960, p. 63.

parison of incomes per head at official exchange rates.[1] However, though perhaps a better and in some sense a more "realistic" comparison, any such figure represents a rather spurious attempt at simplifying what is in essence complex. How much "better off" the average American is than the average Indian cannot by any method be so succinctly or empirically shown on the basis of presently available data; least of all can it be pressed into a simple and precise quantitative relation. A deeper analysis of the entire economic and social situation would be required to understand fully the relative levels of well-being in countries so vastly different. And even if all the facts were in our possession, there are logical reasons why it would not be possible to express the results in an index number.

Comparisons between South Asian countries[2] are also hazardous, but a little less so since conditions are more similar. We have deflated the figures by a simplified method, described in Appendix 13, and presented them in column 2 of Table 11–1. Although the deflated figures seem to agree better with what is generally known about differences in economic level between the South Asian countries, the reader is warned to take this comparison with more than a small grain of salt,[3] not only because our method of deflation is very crude, but also because the basic data, including some of the population estimates, are extremely frail.

Given the foregoing logical, conceptual, and statistical problems that cast doubt both on the relative magnitudes involved and on what they would mean if they were statistically accurate, the question arises whether the figures deserve to be published at all. Later in this chapter, when we

[1] Hagen's readjustments involve multiplying the per head incomes below $100 by 3, those between $101 and $300 by 2½, those between $301 and $600 by 2, and those between $601 and $1,200 by 1½. Using these very rough adjustments and a value of the Indian rupee equal to about one-fifth of a U. S. dollar, less substantial average income differences than those implied in Table 11–1, column 1 between the less and more developed economies are obtained.

Another study argues that the gap between incomes per head is regularly and systematically overstated primarily because of the treatment of transport costs in national accounting procedures. Revised data for Thailand using U. K. prices suggest that Thai income would be five times higher than when estimates are used based on the conversion of bahts to pounds at official exchange rates. (Dan Usher, "The Transport Bias in Comparisons of National Income," *Economica,* Vol. XXX, No. 118, May, 1963, pp. 140–158.)

[2] The figure for Thailand may be unduly low. The deflation procedure, described in the note to Table 11–2, is crude and it involved use of the cost-of-living index for Bangkok, which may not be especially representative of price changes throughout the rest of the country.

[3] Owing to the tremendous difference between the items and their relative weights in any budgets that could be used for ascertaining differences in price levels between the developed countries and the underdeveloped countries in South Asia, the calculation of deflated figures for the former countries would have meant taking a further step in illusory precision; hence column 2 has been left blank for the developed countries.

examine the component parts of the aggregate data, further difficulties and inconsistencies will become apparent. If the figures are so frail and have little real meaning, the merits of presenting them are highly questionable. We have hazarded their publication for several reasons.

In the first place, figures on national income play an important role in economic planning in the region. Indeed, changes in national income are frequently viewed as the main indicator of success or failure of the efforts involved in carrying out development plans. Furthermore, the bulk of contemporary scientific discussion concerning economic growth in underdeveloped countries is couched in terms of this magnitude and its component parts. But if the national income figure, which has some meaning and a degree of accuracy in market economies, has so little meaning and is subject to an exceptionally large range of statistical error in South Asia, it is clear that much of the emphasis on national income is both excessive and misleading as far as South Asia is concerned. The publication, therefore, of the estimates in Table 11–1 was partly designed to give us the occasion to comment on their fundamental weaknesses. Other tables in this chapter provide further illustrations of inadequacies and inconsistencies.

Secondly, such comments as we have already made lay bare the overwhelming importance of clarifying the concepts and perhaps changing the entire focus of the discussion of development and planning for development in South Asia. The uncritical application of Western concepts to a completely alien environment cannot, except by accident, materially assist in resolving the pressing problems of South Asia.

Finally, there is, of course, a possibility that the evidence presented in this chapter may have some rough relationship to reality and in a very crude way have some meaning, although until a deeper analysis of the concepts and statistics is made, we cannot be certain that this is the case. Thus it may not be too unreasonable to present these figures on the hypothesis that it is better to paint with a wide brush, of unknown thickness, than to leave the canvas blank. Alternatively, the reader may wish to view the empirical comparisons simply as a mathematical exercise, designed not so much to capture South Asian reality as to stress the serious inadequacies of the material and to suggest the magnitude of the research job remaining to be done.

We wish, however, to reiterate that the publication of the data does not mean that we attach much significance or even relevance to them. When we later analyze and deduce certain other magnitudes by crude techniques from the already inadequate figures, we are acutely aware that this may represent mere algebraic manipulation. When we seek to account for apparent differences in the magnitudes among the countries in the region, it is entirely possible that the recorded differences may be largely spurious. Our excuses for so doing have been presented above and while they may not fully justify publishing and using the data, it is often the case that even error is heuristic. With this *apologia* we turn now to an examination of Table 11–1.

Broadly speaking, this comparison of national incomes per head indicates a wide disparity between the poorest country in the region – Pakistan, with an estimated income per head of only 220 rupees per year – and the most opulent – Malaya, with an average income of 780 rupees per year, or more than three and a half times as much. If we omit Malaya, which stands out as exceptional for the region, the spread narrows considerably. Although not much confidence can be placed in the absolute differences shown, the ranking may not be an unreasonable version of relative well-being in South Asia. Pakistan and India emerge as the poorest countries; the Philippines, Thailand, Ceylon, and Malaya – in ascending order – appear relatively much better off; and Indonesia, Burma, and South Vietnam lie somewhere between.

Despite the crude techniques employed in making these estimates, the ranking of the countries in terms of relative poverty for the years 1954–56 shown in Table 11–1 may be sufficiently realistic to warrant attempts to account for it. This is the task of later sections. It should be mentioned that in all tables in this book, the listing of the countries follows the order indicated by the estimates of average income per head presented in Table 11–1.

2 *The Trends of Change in National Income Per Head*

Comparisons of the rates of change over a period of time either in individual countries or between countries should be more meaningful.[1] The assumption is that the period is so short that alterations in organizational factors, including the relative size of the non-monetized sector, in market and price structure, in composition of production and consumption, and so on, are so relatively minor that they can be disregarded; even comparisons with more developed countries should under the same assumptions make more sense. In addition, however, such comparisons of rates of change assume both that no major revisions in the methods of estimating and computing national income have occurred and that no changes have occurred in the ascertaining of the primary data, two assumptions that can-

[1] However, Oskar Morgenstern has argued (for the developed countries, where the concepts are clearer and the statistical data vastly more reliable) that "There is no possibility of making concessions as far as the scientific use of growth rates is concerned. As available today, they are worthless in view of the exacting uses to which they are being put. The data are limited and untrustworthy, and the method of computation is at best based on the tremendous oversimplification that there are no errors in gross national product." (*On the Accuracy of Economic Observations*, p. 300.)

not generally be made in those underdeveloped countries attempting to improve their statistics. Comparisons over time involve, furthermore, reflating the rates of change to a constant value basis. To effectuate such a reflation is a most difficult problem in countries where price statistics are so fragmentary and uncertain.

Notwithstanding these difficulties, in Table 11–2 we have attempted to derive or bring together estimates showing the trends in what may be construed as aggregate real output or income per head from 1950 through 1960 for all those countries of South Asia where data for this period are available. We have limited the period under review to 1950–60 because of empirical problems associated with the evidence since 1960, much of which is either not yet available (e.g., Indonesia) or is still in provisional form. Where evidence is available indicating the more recent experience, we have commented on this in the text.[1] Table 11–2 also includes evidence for several countries outside the region, which is obviously somewhat more meaningful in this context than in one of static contrasts, despite several problems already mentioned and others to be mentioned later. However, the concept of aggregate real output used differs from country to country, as indicated in the notes to the table. For the data to be comparable, this implies that the relationships between gross national product, gross domestic product, national income, and similar aggregates, at either market prices or factor cost of some particular year, are stable for each country. This may or may not be the case, since the sketchiness of the available data for most countries does not permit a close check of this point. Nonetheless, it does not seem unreasonable to assume a relatively high degree of stability of these relationships over time; at least, there should not be so much instability as to render the comparisons meaningless.

An examination of the data suggests that among the South Asian countries, Burma has exhibited by far the fastest rate of growth. Other estimates also suggest that its rate has been impressive.[2] Several comments are in order regarding the apparent record of Burma. In the first place, Burma's population growth has been variously estimated as anywhere between 1.1 and 2.5 percent per year. It is generally believed, however, that

[1] Cf. United Nations, ECAFE, *Economic Survey of Asia and the Far East, 1965*, Bangkok, 1966, Table V–3, p. 157.

[2] For example, depending on which of two available sets of population estimates is used, Burma's real output per head rose by either 2.9 percent or 3.3 percent annually between 1948–49 and 1959–60. See Arthur A. Wichmann, "Economic Development and Capital Formation in Burma," *Review of Economics and Statistics*, August, 1962, p. 326. Data cited by Louis Walinsky suggest a growth rate of over 4 percent compounded annually between 1948–49 and 1959–60 and even higher if 1949–50 is used as a base. (See Louis J. Walinsky, *Economic Development in Burma 1951–1960*, Twentieth Century Fund, New York, 1962, pp. 660–661.) See also United Nations, ECAFE, *Economic Survey of Asia and the Far East, 1961*, Bangkok, 1962, p. 11, where a growth rate of 3.9 percent between 1951 and 1959 is recorded.

Table 11–2

GROWTH OF REAL OUTPUT PER HEAD
(*Index: 1952 = 100*)

Country	*1950*	*1951*	*1952*	*1953*	*1954*	*1955*	*1956*	*1957*	*1958*	*1959*	*1960*
Pakistan	103.9	100.9	100	103.0	103.5	100.0	105.2	104.3	102.2	103.0	105.6
India	96.9	97.7	100	103.9	104.7	104.7	107.8	104.3	109.4	109.0	114.5
Indonesia	–	98.5	100	104.9	111.5	113.4	114.1	120.2	113.3	111.6	. . .
Burma	86.8	95.8	100	105.5	107.6	112.1	114.1	123.9	117.1	122.6	128.4
Philippines	93.6	94.8	100	104.6	106.7	111.6	113.5	115.0	115.9	119.3	119.0
Thailand	116.0	110.7	100	98.3	94.1	105.5	101.3	96.1	89.4	98.8	102.1
Ceylon	89.7	95.5	100	96.4	96.6	100.2	92.5	95.9	92.3	100.9	104.7
Italy	92.9	98.1	100	107.7	114.0	120.5	125.0	131.2	137.7	147.3	157.1
U. K.	98.9	100.9	100	104.0	108.1	110.2	113.2	114.1	112.8	114.8	118.3
Sweden	98.3	97.9	100	101.9	107.6	110.6	113.3	116.6	117.2	122.2	126.7
U. S.	94.7	99.2	100	101.9	97.9	104.1	105.1	104.2	100.4	105.8	106.3

Sources: Pakistan: Central Statistical Office, "Estimation of National Income in Pakistan," *The Pakistan Development Review,* Vol. 1, No. 3, Winter, 1961, p. 88.

India: Press Note included in Central Statistical Organisation, *Estimates of National Income 1948–49 to 1959–60,* March, 1961. Figure for 1960 is a preliminary estimate from *A.I.C.C. Economic Review,* March 22, 1962, p. 37. Real output data refer to net national output per head.

Indonesia: U. N., *Economic Survey of Asia and the Far East, 1961,* Bangkok, 1962, Table 3–23, p. 109. Real output data refer to gross product per head in prices of 1955.

Burma: U. N., *Yearbook of National Accounts Statistics,* various years. Data on real output refer to gross domestic product in prices of 1948. The population estimates have been made on the assumption that the percentage change from 1950–51 was 1.5 and that the growth rate rose by one-tenth of a point per year reaching 2.4 percent between 1959 and 1960. In view of the usual acknowledgment that Burma's population growth is seriously understated, we have adopted the above procedure as preferable to the use of existing estimates.

Philippines: U. N., *Economic Survey of Asia and the Far East, 1961*, Bangkok, 1962, Table 3–7, p. 74. Real output data refer to gross national product per head.

Thailand: National income in current prices from U. N., *Economic Survey of Asia and the Far East, 1961*, Bangkok, 1962, Table 5, p. 170: deflated by cost-of-living index in *ibid.* and earlier issues of *Economic Survey*. Population estimates made on the basis of data in Table 3 of Appendix 13 and assumed growth rates of 3.1 percent from 1956 to 1960 and 2.5 percent from 1950 to 1954. This is consistent with the latest census estimate of 26.3 million for 1960.

Ceylon: U. N., *Yearbook of National Accounts Statistics*, various years. Data on real output refer to gross domestic product in 1948 prices. According to the 1957 and 1959 Yearbooks, the figures for 1950–54 refer to gross *national* product at 1948 prices. However, the gross national product and gross domestic product estimates for 1953 and 1954 are identical in the 1959 and 1960 Yearbooks. We have therefore assumed that the series is continuous in terms of gross domestic product from 1950 to the present. Population data from U. N., *Monthly Bulletin of Statistics*, November, 1962, Table 1, and U. N., *Demographic Yearbook, 1961*, Table 4.

Italy: U. N., *Yearbook of National Accounts Statistics*, various years. Data on real output refer to gross national income at prices of 1954. Population data from same source as Ceylon.

Sweden: Sources same as for Italy. Real output refers to gross national product at prices of 1954.

United Kingdom: Output data refer to net national product at factor cost of 1954 and are taken from Central Statistical Office, *National Income and Expenditure 1961*, Table 13, p. 9.

United States: Output data refer to national income deflated by gross national product deflator, taken from Department of Commerce, *Survey of Current Business*, July, 1962, Table 1, p. 6 and Table 6, p. 8.

population growth is seriously understated in most publications, and in Table 11–2 we have tried to compensate for this shortcoming. Also, there is doubt regarding the reliability of the real aggregate product estimates. As has been said, "Burma's growth rates of aggregate and *per capita* product seem to have been over-estimated; growth of its aggregate product cannot be reconciled with that of agricultural production, and growth of *per capita* product is further exaggerated by the use of an unusually low deflator for population growth."[1] Even accepting the data as reliable, all estimates suggest that as late as 1960, the level of living was still about 15 percent below that prevailing in 1939.[2] The apparently high growth rate, even if overstated, may reflect reconstruction following the Second World War and the insurrection, so that "early and rather substantial increases in aggregate output were relatively easily attainable."[3] All of these considerations suggest that it was probably premature at the end of the 1950's to class Burma as an economy well on the way toward economic success. Indeed, a United Nations calculation suggests that income per head in Burma declined rather sharply between 1960 and 1964.[4] This is consistent with a recent observer's view that "General Ne Win's authoritative regime is still trying to create unity and economic stability in the face of declining per capita income."[5] The most one can say regarding over-all economic growth in Burma is that, while the evidence is mixed, there is a strong probability that stagnation or even a decline has occurred in recent years.

Although Indonesian growth appears rapid, through 1957, it will be recalled that the Indonesian national accounts are very unreliable. A rough alternative computation, using a cost-of-living index analogous to the method used for Thailand, suggests a much slower growth rate between 1951 and 1957 than Table 11–2 indicates. Another estimate places the growth rate at 1.6 percent between 1951 and 1959.[6] Furthermore, it has been suggested that Indonesian "national income per head in the middle of the fifties was below the 1939 level, . . . probably below the 1929 level and may even be below the level of 1919,"[7] and the evidence shows a

[1] U. N., *Economic Survey of Asia and the Far East, 1961,* p. 11.

[2] Walinsky, *Economic Development in Burma,* pp. 660–661. One writer suggests that in 1962 Burma's gross domestic product per head was about 24 percent *below* the 1938 level. See J. H. Badgley, "Which Road for Burma?," *Challenge,* June, 1963, p. 27.

[3] Wichmann, "Economic Development and Capital Formation in Burma," *Review of Economics and Statistics,* p. 326.

[4] Data for these years taken from U. N., *Economic Survey of Asia and the Far East, 1964,* Table 5, p. 231.

[5] Badgley, "Which Road for Burma?," *Challenge,* p. 26. Cf. Chapter 9, Section 8.

[6] U. N., *Yearbook of National Accounts Statistics 1960,* p. 267.

[7] Benjamin Higgins, "Indonesia's Development Plans and Problems," *Pacific Affairs,* Vol. XXIX, No. 2, June, 1956, p. 110.

sharp decline since 1957. As things look at the beginning of 1966,[1] there seems to be little prospect of rapid economic growth in Indonesia.

The general picture for South Asian countries whose data seem somewhat more reliable appears to be roughly as follows: Pakistan, Thailand,[2] and Ceylon have been relatively stagnant in terms of output per head. However, there are indications that in recent years Pakistan has emerged from the stagnation of the previous decade. The latest available data suggest an over-all rate of growth of 2.0 percent in income per head and an over-all rate of growth of 4.8 percent in gross national product between 1959–60 and 1964–65 (as projected). These figures contrast sharply with an average rate of growth in income per head in the 1949–50 to 1959–60 decade of barely 0.1 percent. Whether this is a valid and sustainable acceleration of the growth rate cannot be said at this time; the period is far too short and the terminal figures for 1964–65 are "extrapolated trends,"[3] doubtless taken from recent experience. Aside from statistical problems, it is still premature to suggest that anything approaching this degree of dynamism can be maintained over time. The evidence clearly reveals a decided improvement in Pakistan's rate of achievement, but it should be assessed with all the previously mentioned caveats clearly in mind. Thailand seems to have had a much more rapid rise of national income per head since about 1958 – a rise of perhaps 5 percent, which is a higher rate than has been experienced anywhere else in the regime.[4] For Ceylon, it has been argued that "'real output' per capita is probably not so very much greater [in the mid-1950's] than in 1926 or 1938."[5] Income per head seems to have remained fairly static, with perhaps a slight upward trend.[6] The Federation of Malaya, not included in Table 11–2 since consistent estimates back to 1952 are not available,[7] recorded a slight gain of less than

[1] Chapter 9, Part II, particularly Section 10.

[2] For Thailand we have used a high population deflator, though one consistent with the latest census results. However, the 1960 *Yearbook of National Accounts Statistics,* p. 268, shows a growth rate of only 3 percent between 1952 and 1959. A more recent study estimates that during the 1951–61 period "real output *per capita* has increased by almost 2.5 percent a year." (Puey Ungphakorn, "Thailand," *Asian Economic Development,* Cranley Onslow, ed., Weidenfeld & Nicolson, London, 1965, p. 160.)

[3] Pakistan, Government of, Planning Commission, *Outline of the Third Five-Year Plan (1965–70)*, Karachi, August, 1964, Table 1, p. 1.

[4] U. N., *Economic Survey of Asia and the Far East, 1965,* Table V–3, p. 157.

[5] Henry M. Oliver, Jr., *Economic Opinion and Policy in Ceylon,* Duke University Commonwealth-Studies Center, Duke University Press, Durham, N. C., 1957, pp. 112–113.

[6] Gamani Corea estimates that gross national product per head in real terms increased at an average rate of approximately 0.7 percent per year between 1948 and 1962. ("Ceylon," in *Asian Economic Development,* p. 29.)

[7] According to one estimate, Malaya's gross national product per head in real terms increased by 1.8 percent per year in the period 1947–60. (Lim Chong Yah, "Malaya," in *ibid.,* p. 112.)

7 percent in real gross domestic product per head in the seven years between 1955 and 1962[1] but a higher rate in more recent years. Even this gain has been jeopardized by the problems associated with the Indonesian "confrontation" and the increase in internal tensions as a result of Malaya's incorporation in Greater Malaysia.[2] The Philippines showed a steady and fairly rapid growth of income per head during the 1950's, but in later years this index has shown a tendency to decline.[3]

In India it is believed that by 1948–49, income per head was almost 16 percent below the 1931–32 level.[4] Patel estimated that income per head in India fell slightly between 1916–25 and 1946–55 and that the planned level for 1960, which was not attained, would merely have brought it back to the level prevailing around the turn of the century.[5] Patel had not taken into account the higher than estimated population increase during the 1950's, which would have accentuated his conclusion considerably. There seems, however, to have been during the 1950's a slow but fairly steady rise, as shown in Table 11–2. While the growth rate was scarcely impressive[6] – a little over 1 percent per year over the decade – it appeared to be a reversal of the historic trend. The published statistics for the first two years of the 1960's suggest virtual stagnation in net national output per head; then, after two years of fairly rapid advance, the last year of the Third Plan period, 1965–66, when a bad crop coincided with the war with Pakistan,[7] brought the estimated national income per head down to the level it had reached in the first year of the plan period.[8]

[1] The estimates, in Straits dollars of 1959, are as follows:

Year	*GDP per head*
1955	722
1956	724
1957	721
1958	704
1959	710
1960	751
1961	765
1962	770

These figures are from *Interim Review of Development in Malaya Under the Second Five-Year Plan*, Kuala Lumpur, December, 1963, Table 3, p. 10.

[2] Chapter 5, Section 12.

[3] *Economic Survey of Asia and the Far East, 1965*, Table V–3, p. 157.

[4] U. N., ECAFE, *Economic Survey of Asia and the Far East, 1950*, New York, 1951, p. 113.

[5] Surendra J. Patel, "Long-term Changes in Output and Income in India: 1896–1960," *Indian Economic Journal*, January, 1958, Table III.

[6] This growth rate in income per head was confirmed in the *Press Note* attached to India, Government of, Central Statistical Organization, Cabinet Secretariat, *Estimates of National Income 1948–49 to 1959–60*, New Delhi, March, 1961, table on p. 2, column 7. As it is not large enough to fall outside the range of possible error in the national income figures, even this low growth rate may be in part a statistical illusion.

[7] Chapter 7, Section 4.

[8] India, Government of, *Estimates of National Income 1964–65*, New Delhi, 1966,

Except for the Philippines and Burma, the countries of the region thus had a very slow and erratic rise in the output per head indicator during the 1950's; and during the first half of the 1960's this indicator has declined or become negative except in Thailand, Malaya, and, to an extent, Pakistan. Furthermore, recent levels of income per head may mostly be below whatever peak they reached in pre-war times. The data are, of course, very tenuous as we have emphasized and should be taken with a large dose of skepticism. But, granting this, the only objective indicators we possess belie any notion of vigorous economic growth and development as a general trend in the region despite the efforts of the past decade. Since the more highly developed economies have continued to grow in the post-war era, and have far surpassed pre-war income levels,[1] it is abundantly clear that the discrepancy between the economic well-being of the haves and the have-nots, so far as South Asia is concerned, is rapidly widening.[2]

Indeed, the figures showing changes in output per head over time may understate the actual discrepancies between growth rates in the Western economies and the underdeveloped economies. That is, the figures for the underdeveloped countries may contain an upward bias as these countries are eager to show progress and are less restrained from adjusting the data upward because of their weak and often highly conjectural statistical basis. Often, too, as the statistics improve over time, the increase in the monetary sector will reveal an earlier underestimate. On the other hand, the tendency to keep some items in the national income accounts constant over

---

p. 1, Table 1; and *Fourth Five Year Plan: A Draft Outline,* New Delhi, 1966, p. 3. The latter source gives the following figures for national income per head in rupees at 1960–61 prices:

1960–61	*1961–62*	*1962–63*	*1963–64*	*1964–65*	*1965–66*
326	326	323	331	348	325

[1] It will be noted that the growth rate of the United States was singularly sluggish from 1955 until 1961 and subject to considerable fluctuations. But in the most opulent developed economy failure to grow rapidly has substantially less welfare impact than it does in the poor countries in South Asia. The U. S. economy, moreover, has far surpassed the pre-war levels and since 1961 has resumed a higher growth rate than typified the late 1950's. Concerning the relative stagnation of the United States and its causes, see Gunnar Myrdal, *Challenge to Affluence,* Pantheon, New York, 1963. The other developed countries, except Canada, grew more rapidly than the United States during the decade 1950–60.

[2] We should have liked to include in Table 11–2 comparisons with the Soviet Union and the other Communist countries. But there are serious conceptual problems involved in making such comparisons meaningful and, in fact, there is much controversy concerning actual growth rates in these economies independently of attempts to compare the concepts of "output" with those of the West. Our failure to include at least the Soviet Union and China in this table should not be taken to mean that such a comparison would not be extremely valuable. On the contrary, we deem it to be of the utmost importance, but the lack of firm evidence and data comparable to those used in the table, and a lack of expert knowledge of conditions outside the Western world and South Asia, have forced us reluctantly to limit the comparison to certain Western economies.

relatively long periods – as previously indicated in the case of Pakistan – may serve to understate the rate of growth in some of the underdeveloped economies, although this is very uncertain. For the developed countries, there appears to be a downward bias because of failure to account fully for improvements in quality of the national output[1] and the increase in leisure. Although these observations do not necessarily hold in every instance and are not valid to the same degree for each country, they appear sufficiently plausible to warrant the suggestion that, on balance, the available evidence may understate the apparently increasing discrepancies between the economic growth of the more developed economies and the underdeveloped countries of South Asia, especially when compared with pre-war levels of output.

3 *The Share of Agriculture*

When trying to get a broad picture of the structure of the economy in the South Asian countries, the natural course would be to break up the aggregate figure for national income into its component parts and relate the income originating in each main sector to the number of persons employed in, or having their livelihood from, that sector. Unfortunately, the statistics on occupational distribution are especially unreliable. Indonesia and Burma have had no complete census for several decades and the census data on occupational distribution for India,[2] Pakistan, Ceylon, and the Philippines are known to be particularly weak. Nor can the figures for the other countries of the region be considered superior since many of them are listed as "estimates," "provisional," and so on.[3] In addition, there are various sample surveys and other studies; they regularly yield results in apparent contradiction to the census figures. For a variety of reasons, such

[1] Quality changes are generally absent from the price indexes as now computed because of the difficulties involved in measurement. Some estimates for particular products have been made. One estimate indicates that a "quality" correction for automobile prices of the "low-priced three" manufacturers in the United States would show that "the corrected average price of an automobile fell by 18 percent from 1950 to 1959." (Price Statistics Review Committee, *Price Statistics of the Federal Government*, National Bureau of Economic Research, 1961, p. 36.) On the other hand, the U. S. consumer price index reports an increase of 31 percent, and even this ignored changes in dealers' concessions. (For details see *ibid.*, pp. 35–37 and p. 53, and George Jaszi, "The Measurement of Aggregate Economic Growth: A Review of Key Conceptual and Statistical Issues as Suggested by United States Experience," *Review of Economics and Statistics*, XLIII, No. 4, November, 1961, pp. 325–328.)

[2] Some of the problems of interpreting as well as measuring occupational classifications in India are explored by Daniel Thorner, "De-Industrialisation in India, 1881–1931" in *First International Conference of Economic History*, Contribution and Communications (Stockholm, August, 1960), Mouton & Co., Paris, 1960; and Daniel and Alice Thorner, *The Working Force in India 1881–1951*, Indian Statistical Institute, Bombay, 1960.

[3] I.L.O., *Year Book of Labour Statistics, 1960*, Geneva, 1960, Table 4, and notes thereto.

as incomplete enumeration, inadequate sampling, and vague and shifting demarcation of vocational lines, the available statistics on occupational distribution are extremely weak.

Thus we shall stress only the simple distinction between the agricultural and non-agricultural sectors, although we also wish to distinguish as far as possible the "manufacturing" component within the broad and heterogeneous non-agricultural category. Even this simple two or three sector split up of the national income aggregates leads to rather anomalous results; this illustrates further the weakness of the figures discussed in Sections 1 and 2. This impression is fortified by an analysis of the more detailed national income split-up, which we have undertaken but refrained from publishing.

With considerable hesitation, therefore, we present in Table 11–3 figures on the proportion of income and population in agriculture and on agricultural productivity. The data on proportion of income originating in agriculture (column 1) reveal rather wide variations, but they are spurious. The figure for South Vietnam is clearly too low and appears at odds with the very high estimates of population and work force in agriculture.[1] It is scarcely credible that although over 80 percent of the work force is deemed to be in agriculture, this sector accounts for only about one-third of the total output. This would imply an extremely low level of agricultural productivity, which seems inconsistent with the estimated level of income per head for South Vietnam. The relatively low figure for share of income originating in agriculture in Burma may be partly due to the low domestic price paid to rice producers under the State Agricultural Marketing Board[2] despite generally rising prices elsewhere in the economy. Even the figure for Thailand seems out of line if we note the extremely high proportion of the population in agriculture. This may be explained in part by the fact that much of subsistence agriculture is not included in the Thai national income estimates.[3]

[1] An alternative estimate of the income originating in agriculture puts the figure even lower — around 25 percent. The data, as this source points out, "are based on estimates of the production of agricultural crops for the agricultural component only provided by the Department of Agriculture from *judgment* estimates by local officials." Why this should lead to a gross underestimate is not clear. The same source, however, states that the "commerce" component of gross domestic product is computed as a residual. Since this sector accounts for the largest proportion of total output it seems that the residual method of estimation leads to serious overstatement, especially when it is admitted that "It is impossible to give a numerical measure to the margin of error existing in the aggregate figures." This may account in part for the apparent underestimation of agriculture. (See United States Operations Mission to Viet-Nam, *Annual Statistical Bulletin,* No. 3, Data through 1959, June, 1960, p. 14.)

[2] For details on this see Levin, *Export Economies,* pp. 224–261.

[3] U. N., *Yearbook of National Accounts Statistics 1958,* p. 217. Later statistics on agriculture's share in the national product do not make more sense; see "National Development Perspectives of Agriculture in the ECAFE Region," *Economic Bulletin for Asia and the Far East,* Vol. XVI, No. 1, June, 1965, p. 4, Table 3. The figures are presented as "for 1961 or the nearest available year"; Vietnam's percentage figure is 30, Burma's 43, Thailand's 39.

Table 11–3

PRODUCTIVITY IN AGRICULTURE, MID-1950's

Country	*Percent of income originating in agric., 1954–56* (1)	*Percent of active population in agric.* (2)	*Economically active persons as percent of total population* *Male* (3)	*Female* (4)	*Total* (5)	*Income, in Indian rupees of 1954–56, rounded to nearest 10* *Per person in agric.* (6)	*Per active male in agric.* (7)	*Volume of gross agric. output per hectare (Index: So. Asia = 100)* (8)
Pakistan	57	71	29	2	31	170	600	109
India	47	71	28	11	39	170	740	79
Indonesia	56	60	27	10	37	280	1,040	206
Burma	42	70	27	18	45	18C	670	88
S. Vietnam	34	82	24	14	38	150	610	115
Philippines	41	62	24	15	39	250	1,030	145
Thailand	50	86	27	24	51	230	860	129
Ceylon	55	53	28	9	37	470	1,680	312
Fed. of Malaya	54	57	26	8	34	740	2,830	354

Sources: Col. 1 from Appendix 13, Table 5, col. 3. Cols. 2–5 from I. L. O., *Year Book of Labour Statistics, 1960,* Tables 1 and 4. Estimates are for various recent years. The population totals are the I. L. O.'s for those years. For Pakistan, the Philippines, and Thailand, the census and subsequent *Sample Survey* ratios are averaged. Indonesia: Human Relations Area Files, *Indonesia* (New Haven, 1957), Vol. VI, p. 870, applying the 1930 census work force's sex ratio to the estimated 1953 work force. Burma: H. R. A. F., *Burma* (New Haven, 1956), Vol. III, pp. 1457–61, applying the 1930 census work force's sex ratio to the estimated 1955 work force. South Vietnam: Col. 2 from the U. S. Operations Mission, *Annual Statistical Bulletin,* No. 3 (June, 1960), pp. 8–9; col. 5 for South Vietnam is the average of the latter's figure and I. L. O.'s. Col. 8 from Table 10–2, Ch. 10. Cols. 6 and 7: Unrounded estimates of national income per head were obtained from Appendix 13 and multiplied by col. 1 above. (i) To obtain col. 6 above, the results were then divided by col. 2 above. (ii) For col. 7 above, the results of *i* were divided by the percentage of active males in agriculture to the population (obtained from the same sources as cols. 2 to 5 above). The Indian figure in cols. 3 to 5 includes earning dependents; the figure from which col. 7 was calculated excludes them, and is the I. L. O.'s figure as adjusted by them for comparability.

Looking at column 2 of Table 11–3, the proportion of active population in agriculture, there are similar difficulties beyond those already mentioned. Various countries treat "unpaid family workers" in different ways. For example, Ceylon excludes this group entirely while the Philippines and Thailand appear to include them.[1] The evidence for Pakistan appears utterly conflicting. The 1951 census reported a rise in the share of agriculture in the labor force between 1931 and 1951 from 78.8 to 84.1 percent in East Pakistan and from 60.0 to 66.2 percent in West Pakistan. It was stated that "practically the whole of the increase in the Labour Force has gone into agriculture."[2] This is difficult to reconcile with the steady rise in the proportion of urban dwellers from 6.5 percent in 1931 to 10.4 percent in 1951.[3] Even more surprising is the apparent sudden reversal of the rising share of agriculture. That is, an "official estimate" for 1954–56 in Pakistan puts the share of agricultural labor at only 64.7 percent,[4] compared with 76.5 percent stated in the 1951 census. A decline of this magnitude in a period of four or five years is especially suspect in view of the apparent trend since 1931; the 1961 census records the percentage of the labor force in agriculture to be 75.0.[5] Aside from such instances of dubious statistics, in most countries the absence of independent estimates of the number of people deriving their livelihood from agriculture[6] requires us to assume that the proportion of total population in agriculture is the same as the proportion in the work force.

These few examples illustrate the frailty of much of the data pertaining to the South Asian economies and suggest that the wide divergences among the countries indicated in columns 1 and 2 of Table 11–3 may be largely a statistical illusion. But acknowledging all these weaknesses it appears generally to be the case that over half of the national income originates in the

[1] Details on the varying census definitions and practices are given in United Nations, Economic Commission for Asia and the Far East, *Studies on Population Growth and Economic Development,* Preliminary Report, February, 1958, mimeographed, pp. 52–57; and Hilde Wander, *Trends and Characteristics of Population Growth in Indonesia,* Interim Report for United Nations Technical Assistance Organisation, Djakarta, July, 1959, pp. 33–34. See also United Nations, *The Asian Population Conference 1963,* New York, 1964, pp. 194ff.

[2] Pakistan, Government of, *Census of Pakistan 1951,* Vol. I, Karachi, 1956, pp. 107–108.

[3] *Ibid.,* p. 80.

[4] I.L.O., *Year Book of Labour Statistics, 1960,* Table 4.

[5] See United Nations, *Economic Survey of Asia and the Far East, 1964,* Bangkok, 1965, p. 8, Table 1–1. The figures in that table showing changes in the percentage of the labor force in agriculture in several of the South Asian countries do not invite confidence.

[6] The Pakistan census commented on this point as follows: "In the early planning stages of the census consideration was given to the possibility of obtaining information from which Dependents might be analysed according to the industry or activity of the person on whom they were dependent. It was found, however, that this information had proved unreliable in the past and was likely not to be reported with sufficient accuracy or completeness." (Pakistan, Government of, Office of the Census Commissioner, *Census of Pakistan, 1951,* Census Bulletin No. 4, Karachi, March, 1953, p. ii.)

agricultural sector and about two-thirds or three-fourths of the people obtain their livelihood from this source.

Further data on the economically active population are shown in columns 3, 4, and 5. The figures indicate the numbers of "active" males and females as percentages of total population. Since in each country there are nearly equal numbers of men and women, the figures in columns 3 and 4 if multiplied by two also afford a rough idea of the degree of economic participation for each sex. These figures, which do not possess any greater accuracy than those already presented, reveal a rather wide variation in female economic participation among the countries of the region. In Thailand, women seem to be economically active to the same degree as men, but in Pakistan, Malaya, and Ceylon, a large majority of women confine their activities to the household. The extent of variation in female participation is undoubtedly overstated, for in countries where religious or social prejudices require that women refrain from work outside the household there is a natural tendency to under-report such activities. If the evidence is overstated it nevertheless appears broadly correct since it shows large differences between Moslem countries such as Pakistan and countries like Thailand and the Philippines where there are few prejudices against women engaging in productive work. For men, participation rates vary much less – from 24 percent of total population in the Philippines (according to the 1948 census) to 29 percent according to an "official estimate" in Pakistan. It is therefore safe to infer that most of the variation among countries in the proportion of population (male as well as female) in the economically active category shown in column 5 reflects varying degrees of female participation. Generally those countries with the highest proportion of economically active people also have the largest extent of female participation, and vice versa.[1]

If then we wish to compare agricultural productivity among the countries it is necessary to adjust for the varying rates of female participation. This is the more essential in view of the lower rates of remuneration for women than men in the region and the relatively shorter hours worked per day and per month by women. Accordingly, to reduce the distortion from these sources we have computed only income per head of the total population in agriculture and income per active male. These figures are shown in columns 6 and 7 respectively. Of course, since they are derived from the inadequate data already described, there can be no claim that they possess any high degree of accuracy. Nevertheless, in a very rough way, if they may be assumed to be broadly representative of reality, then in terms of income both per head and per active male in agriculture, Malaya and Ceylon stand far above the other South Asian countries. (Indonesia appears to be an exception to this statement, but the data for

[1] For further discussion of the problem of participation ratios in agriculture, see Chapter 22, Section 7 *et passim.*

this country, along with those for Burma and South Vietnam, are among the weakest in the region and may be provisionally ignored.) Indeed, Malaya and Ceylon have a level of agricultural productivity per active male about three to five times that of India and Pakistan respectively.

This is also borne out by the relative output per hectare indicated in column 8. As argued in Chapter 10 and spelled out later in the present chapter, this wide disparity in agricultural productivity is directly related to the predominance of plantations and plantation crops in the economic structures of Malaya and Ceylon. It is also noteworthy that the figures on output per head in agriculture (excluding South Vietnam and Indonesia) provide a ranking that coincides with the levels of national income per head previously obtained, except that Thailand is placed below the Philippines whereas it had approximately the same income per head. Recalling that the income originating in agriculture is understated in Thailand, we can reasonably assume a complete coincidence of rank between the estimates of national income per head and those of agricultural income per active male. If this is not entirely a spurious relationship, as it might be since agricultural output is only about half of the total, it suggests that the role of plantation culture is even more pervasive and significant than indicated above. This is discussed more fully below.

More significant for the future than the static picture of economic structure and productivity as it pertains to agriculture are the apparent trends. In this context one would naturally like to know what changes have taken place in recent years in the share of agriculture and in agricultural output per head and per active male. But the available data lead to anomalous results. National accounts statistics for Thailand indicate a decline in the share of agriculture in total output from 57 percent in 1950 to 47 percent in 1953, and only 36 percent in 1962,[1] which seems inconsistent with the reported increase in the proportion of the work force in agriculture from 85 to 88 percent between 1948 to 1954.[2] The decline in the proportion of output originating in agriculture shown for Ceylon – from 58 to 48 percent between 1950 and 1959 – likewise seems excessive in view of Ceylon's relative stagnation in terms of income per head; and the figures for the Philippines indicate a drop from 43 percent in 1953 to 35 percent in 1959,[3] a level inconsistent with the degree of economic development apparently achieved in that country. The data therefore appear to be highly suspect. For the other countries in the region, the share of agriculture has remained relatively stable over the past decade. For example, about 51

[1] See U. N., *Economic Survey of Asia and the Far East, 1963,* Table 6, pp. 187–188.

[2] I.L.O., *Year Book of Labour Statistics, 1960,* Table 4.

[3] U. N., *Yearbook of National Accounts Statistics 1960,* Table 3, pp. 270–276. Estimates for 1962 put the share of agriculture for Ceylon and the Philippines at 46 and 33 percent respectively. (*Economic Survey of Asia and the Far East, 1963,* Table 6, pp. 187–188. See also *ibid., 1964,* Tables 1–6, p. 12.)

percent of India's national income originated in agriculture in 1950 while in 1958 the share remained relatively high at about 50 percent. Substantial fluctuations in this share have occurred (e.g., it fell to almost 45 percent in 1954) and while there is some evidence of a decline, it is occurring, at most, at the pace of a glacial drift.[1]

The data on trends in occupational distribution are not only extremely weak, as already shown, but are not sufficiently plentiful to permit a realistic assessment of major trends since 1950. Thus it is difficult to derive any unambiguous conclusion with respect to the importance of the agricultural sector over recent years. This precludes any meaningful analysis of trends in productivity in the agricultural sector. However, data are available that purport to show the behavior of food production per head. These indicate relative stagnation or an actual decline for India, Indonesia, Pakistan, the Philippines, and Burma between the average for the years 1952–53 to 1956–57 and the figure for 1963–64. On the other hand, the data for Ceylon show a modest rise in food output per head, while those for the Malayan Federation and Thailand show a sharp increase over the four-year base period.[2] It is difficult to reconcile the relative stagnation of food output per head indicated for the Philippines with the trend in average national income. Perhaps this inconsistency can be explained in part by the sharp and steady rise in manufacturing production and the fairly steady increase in mining and construction coupled with the decline in the relative importance of agriculture over the period.[3]

In general the data are so unreliable that not much importance can be attached to them. Broadly, however, it would appear that agricultural output per head remained relatively stagnant in the region as a whole during the 1950's and early 1960's, and this must account in large measure for the failure of national income per head to show signs of vigorous expansion. It seems likewise reasonable to infer that whatever trends are occurring in agricultural structure, as well as productivity, are far from dramatic if we can dismiss the remarkable evidence of declining agricultural shares in national income, especially in Thailand and Ceylon where there are no signs of rapid economic growth. Perhaps the only safe conclusion to be derived from the empirical material is that far more needs to be done in the way of efficient data collection to ascertain what is in fact happening in the vital agricultural sector of the South Asian economies.

[1] Data from U. N., *Yearbook of National Accounts Statistics 1960,* Table 3, pp. 270–276, in terms of current prices. Preliminary estimates for 1962–63 put the share of agriculture at 45.3 percent. (India, Government of, *Estimates of National Income 1948–49 to 1962–63,* New Delhi, February, 1964, Table 2.1, p. 3.)

[2] Data given in U. N., *Economic Survey of Asia and the Far East, 1960,* Table 9, and the 1964 issue of the same publication, again Table 9.

[3] *Economic Survey of Asia and the Far East, 1960,* pp. 133, 137; and *ibid., 1964,* p. 12.

4 *Share of Non-agricultural Occupations*

In Table 11–4 we have attempted to summarize the relevant data pertaining to the non-agricultural sector. The aforementioned strictures on the caliber of the empirical material apply with equal force to columns 1 and 2 of this table since these are simply the mirror images of the same columns in Table 11–3. Nor do the data in columns 3 and 4, showing non-agricultural output per head and per active male outside of agriculture, possess a higher degree of accuracy than those purporting to represent agricultural productivity. The extremely high levels of productivity indicated for South Vietnam and Thailand will be noticed. The overestimation of agricultural population relative to output, previously commented on, gives these countries a non-agricultural efficiency almost five times that of the poorer countries in Table 11–4. The extreme variations in relative efficiency within the agricultural and the non-agricultural sectors shown in column 5 are thus especially suspect for Thailand and South Vietnam.

The other ratios shown in column 5 indicate much less variability among countries and between the two broad sectors. These figures, too, are doubtless spurious. In addition to the apparent overestimation of the agricultural population in some countries, there is the problem of incomplete reporting of agricultural output since much of it is directly consumed by the producer. Even where estimates of direct consumption are made, they are subject to wide margins of error. On top of this is the problem of valuation. Generally, there seems to be a relative underestimation of agricultural incomes, especially in view of the protection of industrial products destined for home consumption by the imposition of tariffs and import restrictions. Agricultural products of export economies, on the other hand, are valued at or below world market prices and sold in a more competitive environment. Partially offsetting this is the fact that the processing performed on plantations is included as agricultural income when in reality it is manufacturing activity. As the available data do not permit segregation of the value added by such processing, there is an inevitable overstatement of agricultural income and productivity.[1] For most of the countries of the region, where the share of the plantation sector is relatively

[1] For example, it is acknowledged that "The extent of industrialisation in Ceylon is somewhat understated . . . since employment and production in tea and rubber factories are included in the category of agriculture." (Ceylon, Government of, National Planning Council, *The Ten Year Plan*, Colombo, 1959, p. 28.) The same is true in Indonesia. A government study found that "it was not possible to separate the activities of estate processing factories from estate agricultural activities." (Indonesia, Government of, *The Contribution to the National Income of Indonesia, 1957 and 1958 by the Agricultural Sector*, Preliminary Report of the Working Group of the National Income Committee, Djakarta, February, 1960, p. 3.) On the other hand, a study of Malayan national accounts explicitly makes this separation. (Department of Statistics, *National Accounts of the States of Malaya 1955–1961*, Kuala Lumpur, no date, pp. 11–12.)

Table 11–4

PRODUCTIVITY OUTSIDE AGRICULTURE, MID–1950's

Country	*Percent of income originating outside agriculture* (1)	*Percent of population outside agriculture* (2)	*Income, in Indian rupees of 1954–56, rounded to nearest 10* — *Per person outside agriculture* (3)	*Per active male outside agriculture* (4)	*Ratio of non-agric. to agric. productivity* (5)
Pakistan	43	29	320	1,100	1.8
India	53	29	480	2,040	2.8
Indonesia	44	40	330	1,230	1.2
Burma	58	30	590	2,180	3.2
S. Vietnam	66	18	1,290	5,350	8.8
Philippines	59	38	590	2,440	2.3
Thailand	50	14	1,420	5,260	6.1
Ceylon	45	47	440	1,560	0.9
Malaya	46	43	830	3,200	1.1

Sources: Same as Table 11–3. Col. 1 is 100 – col. 1 of Table 11–3. Col. 2 is 100 – col. 2 of Table 11–3. Col. 3 is obtained as col. 6 in Table 11–3, and col. 4 as col. 7.

small, the overstatement involved is of little consequence. Only in Malaya and Ceylon is it likely to make much difference. Indeed, in the Federation of Malaya it was estimated that over 40 percent of the gross domestic product originating in manufacturing came from rubber processing on the estates in 1960.[1]

On balance, it is safe to say that the productivity differential between the agricultural and non-agricultural sectors is to a large but varying extent overstated in the figures of Table 11–4.[2] These spurious ratios serve as a warning against the entire national income calculus. Nevertheless, a real differential between agricultural and non-agricultural productivity favoring the latter does appear to exist for all countries except Ceylon, and this differential provides part of the incentive toward "industrialization" or channelling resources away from agriculture. The evidence also points up the extreme poverty in agriculture except in Malaya and Ceylon, where the prevalence of plantation culture not only provides high average agricultural productivity but also reduces substantially the gap between agricultural and non-agricultural output per active male, as the ratios in

[1] *Ibid.*, Table 11, p. 23. No earlier estimates for Malaya are available. Thus the above comments and those that follow regarding Tables 11–3 and 11–4 pertain to Malaya as well.

[2] This problem is discussed further in Chapter 24, Section 2.

column 5 show. Even in these countries, however, productivity and income levels are very low in ordinary farming.

The "non-agricultural occupations" category is, of course, a mixed bag. It comprises such occupational groups as services, construction, manufacturing, mining, and commerce. The boundaries of these classifications are highly flexible and different countries exclude and include different items in each. There are also differences in the reliability of the figures themselves. Thus the data are even more difficult to compare than those previously examined. We have therefore refrained from publishing an occupational breakdown, except for manufacturing, which is examined later. We shall simply comment on the non-agricultural occupations in general terms before attempting a more detailed analysis of "industrialization."

Putting aside for the moment manufacturing industry and crafts, the general impression is that retail trade, domestic service, and governmental administration all tend to occupy an excessively large proportion of the population, particularly in view of the low productivity attached to such activities. The proliferation of retail outlets and petty traders, and the large and growing number of middlemen of all kinds, are frequently observed phenomena. There are many references to the "long chain of dealers and middlemen."[1] A report by the Indian Central Cotton Committee lists the following steps in cotton marketing: the grower sells to the village dealer, who then sells on the market through a broker; the cotton next goes through "one or more" middlemen (ginning is done at this stage), then passes through "one or more" commission agents, and is finally sold to an exporter or merchant.[2] It is common to have "as many as six intermediaries intervene between the producer and the consumer."[3]

Perhaps the most striking picture of the excess of retail outlets and traders is afforded in the towns and cities where

> . . . much of the retail trade is conducted in small family shops, commonly located in bamboo structures which also serve as living quarters. In Rangoon, for example, there are thousands of such individual shops, grouped near the large bazaars, which specialize in one or two varieties of goods. There are also many thousands of itinerant street peddlers selling all kinds of goods.[4]

[1] Manilal B. Nanavati and J. J. Anjara, *The Indian Rural Problem,* Indian Society of Agricultural Economics, Bombay, 1944, p. 46.

[2] B. B. Ghosh, *Indian Economics and Pakistani Economics,* A. Mukherjee and Co., Calcutta, 1949, p. 137.

[3] K. R. Kulkarni, *Agricultural Marketing in India,* Vol. I, 2nd ed., V. V. Bhapat, Bombay, 1956, p. 350.

[4] Human Relations Area Files, *Burma,* Vol. III, New Haven, 1956, p. 1397. See also Wendell Blanchard *et al., Thailand,* "Country Survey Series," Human Relations Area Files Press, New Haven, 1957, p. 326, and Human Relations Area Files, *Indonesia,* Vol. III, New Haven, 1956, p. 1120.

Free-lance traders abound throughout the region, engaging in a sort of *ad hoc* trading. In 1947 more than half of the persons active in "commerce" in Malaya were hawkers, peddlers, and vendors on their own account.[1] The large numbers engaged in such trading activities do not perform a very efficient or sophisticated function, nor is the turnover of retail trade very high. Indeed, much of this activity is essentially underutilization of labor,[2] facilitated by both the underutilization of labor in agriculture and the ease of entry into such trading pursuits. In short, the plethora of petty traders and peddlers is not so much a response to a rising demand for their services as a reaction against the prevailing low productivity and cheapness of labor. This reaction, when coupled with a disinclination to work for an employer, induces a "push" into "own account" employment, channelled along these lines by the meager capital and minimal skills required.

A similar situation exists in traditional crafts where markets have been dwindling because of imports and, in more recent times, expanding domestic industrialization. The main difference between these backwash effects and the spread of petty trading and hawking is that the persons affected tend to remain in the area of the traditional crafts while performing less work, whereas the growth of petty trading represents a more dynamic response to a trend toward urbanization that is not closely related to, nor caused by, rising employment opportunities in the industrial sectors. Both reactions perpetuate the low levels of labor input and labor efficiency.[3]

Conditions are not fundamentally different in the realm of public administration.[4] Not only have public expenditures for government activity risen, both in absolute terms and as a proportion of national income,[5] in response to the increase of real needs arising from the developmental efforts and newly won independence, but the number of people employed in the civil service has risen even more significantly. In Burma, employment in the civil service in the late 1950's was "over three times greater than before independence" and much of it involved "the recruitment of many 'political' civil servants."[6] In Indonesia, government employment rose by a greater percentage (more than 250 percent) than that of any other occupation between 1930 and 1953,[7] while the number of civil servants

[1] J. J. Puthucheary, *Ownership and Control in the Malayan Economy*, Donald Moore for Eastern Universities Press Ltd., Singapore, 1960, p. 3.

[2] This problem is discussed further in Chapter 23, Sections 4 and 9.

[3] We shall return to this subject in Chapter 23, Sections 2, 4, *et passim;* government policies to support and strengthen crafts and "small-scale industry" will be discussed in Chapter 25.

[4] Chapter 23, Section 9.

[5] U. N., *Economic Survey of Asia and the Far East, 1960*, Table 17, p. 56.

[6] Hugh Tinker, *The Union of Burma*, 2nd ed., Oxford University Press, London, 1959, p. 156.

[7] Human Relations Area Files, *Indonesia*, p. 260.

in the employ of the Ceylonese government was three times as high in 1958 as in 1938.[1] The pattern is similar in the other South Asian countries. Of course, not all of this rise in public employment can be deemed excessive. Some of it is called for by an extension of essential governmental activities, and it cannot be denied that key personnel of high quality are too few in numbers and probably overworked as well.[2] But much of the rise in employment occurs at the lower levels of the civil service hierarchy. Thus Hugh Tinker observes that "The passages of the Secretariat are taken up by slovenly youths, lounging and smoking, . . . The casual, amateurish atmosphere in the government offices may largely be attributed to the appointment of large numbers of political nominees."[3] The lower ranks of most civil service organizations in the region are even differentiated along "craft" lines. Often there is one person whose sole function is to usher in visitors to the office while another carries files; neither is fully occupied. Similar inefficient use of manpower is not unknown in the West, but it appears to be far more extensive in South Asia. Duplication of functions, splitting of departments into new ones with parallel tasks, noting and passing of files through many hands, all tend to expand employment in the public sector at the expense of efficiency. While it may be true that efficient use of manpower is less essential when the labor force is large and when labor is generally underutilized, nonetheless such a growth in bureaucracy causes delays in important developmental projects and is inherently inflationary since incomes are paid for no concomitant increase in output. Furthermore, since the aim of the various developmental plans is to raise output per head, any type of boondoggling, either in the public or the private sector, is detrimental.

An explanation of the apparent increasing waste in the public sector lies in the pressure exerted by the so-called "educated" unemployed living in towns.[4] They seek clerical positions, and a high prestige is attached to civil service posts. The inability of the "soft state"[5] to resist such pressures doubtless accounts for a rise in the number of lower civil servants out of proportion to real needs. There is a general awareness of this problem in the region. Thus the Pakistani Finance Minister called for "a thorough examination of the nonproductive field of Government expenditures."[6] Yet the political difficulties that stand in the way of reductions in government expenditures, strong as they are, loom even greater when personnel cut-

[1] Anders Östlind, *Ceylon's Plantation Economy*, typed manuscript, Colombo, 1960, p. 4.

[2] *Indian Journal of Public Administration*, July-September, 1956, p. 276.

[3] *Union of Burma*, p. 134. See also Walinsky, *Economic Development in Burma*, Chapter 24.

[4] Chapter 23, Section 6.

[5] Chapter 18, Sections 13–14 *et passim*.

[6] Pakistan, Government of, *The Budget of the Government of Pakistan for the Financial Year Ending March 31, 1958*, Speech of the Finance Minister, Karachi, 1957, p. 29.

backs are proposed. As a consequence, little is accomplished along these lines despite the general awareness of the problem. For example, the Indonesian budget for 1953 was regarded as "heroic" because it envisaged the dismissal of 150,000 governmental employees including civil servants, soldiers, and policemen. But there was a revenue carry-over from the previous budget and little contraction in personnel occurred.[1] Given widespread unemployment among the educated, there are strong social as well as political pressures to increase the ranks in government service and still more to resist large-scale dismissals. The entire system therefore becomes self-reinforcing. Governments hesitate to aggravate the substantial unemployment among the "educated" through reductions in employment in the public sector even though many civil servants are underutilized.[2] The chain of circular causation stretches even farther: many of the "educated" go to universities in the first place because they are unemployed.[3]

It is worth noting that recent estimates available for Malaya, Ceylon, Pakistan, and the Philippines all indicate a rise in the proportion of the labor force in the categories of "services and commerce" as the above discussion suggests.[4] The number of people in the category of "services" alone exceeded that in "manufacturing" for all of these countries and also for Thailand and India.[5] This indicates the comparatively minor role that industry presently plays in the economies of the region.

The data are statistically unreliable, but they confirm in a vague way what is generally known. They suggest that the widely held view that the

[1] Benjamin Higgins, *Indonesia's Economic Stabilization and Development*, Institute of Pacific Relations, New York, 1957, p. 10, f.n. 3.

[2] The office set up in New Delhi for this study employed for some time an ambitious and skilled male secretary, who for this purpose got leave of absence from his low-paid job in the railway administration. He informed us that he was virtually without anything to do and that a great many of his comrades were in the same situation. Actually he feared he would lose his skill in typing. When it was suggested that the staff should be decreased he showed no understanding. His permanent civil service employment represented his security; according to him none in the higher ranks would contemplate shrinking the number employed.

A particularly able minister told the writer that of the employees in his ministry below the level of under secretary, the larger number were of no use whatsoever; it would be easier to do the job without them. Even if they had been recruited as "educated," they hardly maintained their ability to write, for lack of exercise. A suggestion that the ranks should be decreased met with a shudder: it was politically impossible. Also, all the administrative routines were adjusted to a situation of wide-scale underutilization of labor and they could not easily be changed.

[3] Chapter 32, Section 6 *et passim*.

[4] I.L.O., *Year Book of Labour Statistics, 1960,* Table 4 and notes thereto.

[5] It is curious to note that the number of economically active people in the service category in Pakistan apparently more than doubled between the 1951 census and the official estimates for 1954–56, but there was less than a 100 percent increase in manufacturing employment despite an increase in the index of manufacturing production of over 250 percent. See *ibid.*, Tables 4 and 5.

Table 11–5

RELATIVE SIZE OF MANUFACTURING INDUSTRY

Country	*Percent of national income originating in manufacturing, 1954–56*	*Percent of active population in manufacturing*	*Percent of active males in manufacturing*
Pakistan	11	6 (1951)	6
		11 (1954–55)	N/A
India	17	9 (1951)	8
Indonesia	10[a]	11[d] (1930)	7
Burma	11	11[e]	N/A
S. Vietnam	14[b]	2[c] (1957)	2
Philippines	13	6 (1948)	3
		11 (1959)	4
Thailand	13	2 (1947)	1
		2 (1954)	2
Ceylon	5	10 (1953)	7
Malaya	N/A	6 (1957)	5

Sources: U. N., *Yearbook of National Accounts Statistics 1959,* New York, 1960, country pages for output from manufacturing. Work force data from I.L.O., *Year Book of Labour Statistics 1960,* Geneva, 1960, Table 4.

[a] U. N., *Yearbook of National Accounts Statistics 1960,* p. 114, average of 1954–56.
[b] United States Operations Mission to Viet-Nam, *Annual Statistical Bulletin 1959,* June, 1960, p. 15.
[c] *Ibid.,* p. 9.
[d] Human Relations Area Files, *Indonesia,* New Haven, 1955, p. 870.
[e] Consists of 1.3 percent in "factories" plus 9.4 percent in "handicrafts." Human Relations Area Files, *Burma,* New Haven, 1956, p. 1458.

number of people in tertiary occupations increases as a country becomes richer is *not* applicable to the underdeveloped countries in South Asia. Even though few countries in the region appear to have made much economic progress, especially compared with the pre-war situation, most of them have a very high percentage of their non-agricultural population in tertiary employment, and this percentage is increasing. This should not be particularly surprising, given the rapid growth of the labor force in the face of relative stagnation in agriculture and an inability of the as yet tiny industrial sector to absorb much of the increase. We have already pointed out that these facts induce a "push" into employment or self-employment in areas where the difficulties of entry are not formidable. Typically such areas are to be found in petty trading, services, and the like. This provides yet another example of a particular trend that accompanies economic growth in the West but that in South Asia is more symptomatic of failure to achieve rapid growth. The emergence of processes in South Asia analogous to those experienced in the West may thus result from quite contradictory forces, as we saw also with respect to urbanization.[1] The applicability of Western developmental processes to South Asia should therefore, as we have stressed, be regarded as questionable.

Some figures on the extent of manufacturing industry are given in Table 11–5. The quality of the empirical evidence concerning "manufacturing" leaves much to be desired. Most handicraft activity is included under that term, while processing on plantations is excluded altogether, as indicated in Section 3. Thus, to the extent that "industry" is assumed to imply the use of modern equipment and a strictly non-agricultural orientation, the data are apt to be misleading. Generally speaking, the available evidence reveals the relatively minor role of manufacturing, even where it includes crafts. In no country of the region did the share of the labor force in industry in this wide sense exceed 12 percent and nowhere did the value of industrial output exceed 20 percent of national income during the middle or late 1950's. Further details on manufacturing are given in Sections 8 and 9.

5 *Partial Industrialization of Agriculture*

The statistical information relating to industry excludes the important industrialized sector that has for a long time existed in agriculture. As stressed in Chapter 10 (Section 7), the cultivation of plantation crops must be viewed as a form of industrialization, despite its agricultural orientation. The traditional notion of "industry" as relevant only outside of agriculture is too confining where plantation crops are feasible. Thus the fact that there have been opportunities, in varying degrees, for this type of cultivation in the South Asian countries is a distinguishing mark that makes the Western view of industrialization inappropriate, at least when we look to the past.

As previously noted, plantations are highly specialized productive units employing wage labor on a regular basis. Moreover, capital investment is much greater in plantations than in other forms of agriculture, if only because of the longer period of gestation of the crops. When the industrialization and heavy investment become overt in the form of processing plants whose added value frequently exceeds that of several manufacturing plants, and when it is further recognized that the larger estates also contain hospitals, dispensaries, schools, and cooperative stores,[2] the distinction between traditional farming and plantation culture becomes even

[1] Chapter 10, Section 11; and Chapter 23, Sections 4 and 5.

[2] In 1951, the 6,075 estates in Ceylon were reported to contain 130 hospitals, 758 dispensaries, 801 schools, 973 crèches, and 254 cooperative stores. Some 1,533 estates

more obvious. If we ignore the processing and other activities, the designation of plantations or estates as industrial enterprises still holds. Indeed, the plantations themselves – on which the greater part, though not all, of the typical plantation crops are grown – are generally far more efficient than other branches of agriculture and even have a higher productivity than most segments of non-agricultural activity. For example, the value of output per active worker in the Ceylonese plantation sector (defined as tea and rubber estates and cocoanut plantations, and so presumably excluding most of the small holdings) was several times that in "all other agriculture" and greater than that in industry in the 1950's.[1] A study of plantation industry in India places the rate of gross profits on total capital employed for the years 1955–58 at 10.1 percent for 167 tea plantations and over 15 percent for 43 rubber and coffee plantations. These rates of return compare favorably with the average rate of 8.8 percent for 1,001 companies in many other industries. Plantations other than tea had the second highest profits of all industries listed, including iron and steel, cement, paper, and chemicals.[2] These profit rates are suspiciously low, but the contrasts among them might be indicative; the higher rates for plantations are not the result of a monopoly situation, as most plantation crops are sold in competitive international markets whereas domestic industry in the region operates, to a very large extent, within highly protected internal markets.[3]

In view of these facts it is questionable whether plantation output and employment are properly designated as part of agriculture instead of industry. The figures purporting to indicate the extent of "industrialization" are thus somewhat understated, especially for Ceylon and Malaya and to a lesser extent for Indonesia and the Philippines, where plantation culture has for many decades represented a continuous process of industrialization, though without the spread effects that typified the commercialization of agriculture in Western Europe during the nineteenth century. Since plantations play so large a role in the economic life of the South Asian countries, particularly the smaller ones, it is important to examine them in more detail.

6 *The Structure of Plantation Industry*

Within the plantation sectors of the countries of the region there is substantial variation. Yet they all have one thing in common – a very high

had their own power and electricity facilities. (Ceylon, Government of, Department of Census and Statistics, *Census of Agriculture 1952, Part IV – Agriculture,* Colombo, 1956, p. 108.)

[1] Ceylon, National Planning Council, *The Ten Year Plan,* p. 93.

[2] "The Plantation Industry," *Eastern Economist Blue Supplement,* New Delhi, February 24, 1961. All figures about profits are, however, unreliable.

[3] Chapter 19, Section 7; Appendix 8, Part I, *et passim.*

export orientation. For example, over 90 percent of the rubber output of Ceylon, Indonesia, Thailand, South Vietnam, and Malaya is regularly exported, as is about three-fourths of tea output in Ceylon and Indonesia and the Philippine sugar production. This compares with the export of well below one-third of the rice produced in Burma and Thailand, the largest rice surplus countries in the region.[1]

There are systematic differences in methods of cultivation – in size of holding, type of ownership, and degree of efficiency. Holdings range from very large estates of over several thousand acres to only a few bushes, trees, or plants on plots of small householders, but ownership is closely related to size. Europeans are dominant in the larger estates, "Oriental aliens" in the medium to small size estates, and natives in the small-scale segment of the industry. Thus Europeans owned less than 24 percent of the rubber estates in Malaya in 1957 but these accounted for over 63 percent of the acreage.[2] A similar situation holds for the rubber and tea plantations in Ceylon.[3] Middle-sized estates tend to be in the hands of non-indigenous but non-European people. In Thailand, for example, over 40 percent of all the rubber holdings in 1954 were owned by Chinese nationals.[4] Alien control has greater weight in total production, for efficiency is closely linked to both size and type of ownership. The larger estates tend not only to be more efficient in themselves but to have, or have access to, superior financial resources, which permits "generous treatment with fertilizer and improved agricultural practices."[5] The larger rubber estates have generally a greater proportion of acreage planted in younger and more productive trees and make a better provision for the future by replanting than do the smaller holdings.[6] In short, the more efficient production of plantation crops takes place on the larger estates, mostly controlled by Europeans, whereas the least efficient production is found on small-scale native holdings. Whatever industrialization or rationalization of agriculture has taken place is basically confined to the larger, foreign-dominated holdings. For the small holdings under native control there is much less industrialization and a closer analogy to non-plantation crops.

[1] Rice exports from both Burma and Thailand were about half of total production before the war.

[2] Federation of Malaya, Department of Statistics, *Malaya Rubber Statistics Handbook, 1958,* Kuala Lumpur, 1959, p. 10.

[3] Ceylon, *Census of Agriculture 1952,* p. 10.

[4] G. William Skinner, *Chinese Society in Thailand: An Analytical History,* Cornell University Press, Ithaca, New York, 1957, p. 350.

[5] The direct correlation between size and efficiency in terms of output per acre is clearly shown for Ceylon, and applies to tea, rubber, and cocoanuts. See Ceylon, *Census of Agriculture 1952,* pp. 18 and 19.

[6] See, for example, Report of a Mission Organized by the International Bank for Reconstruction and Development, *The Economic Development of Malaya,* Johns Hopkins Press, Baltimore, 1955, pp. 245–252 and pp. 48–58; see also Ceylon, *Census of Agriculture 1952.*

In terms of the dynamics of the situation it is the progress of the large plantations that has greatest significance and stands out in contrast to agricultural developments in Northwestern Europe before and during the industrial revolution.

Of course, this three-fold relationship among size, ownership, and productivity does not hold in every case. Nor does it apply with equal force to each plantation crop; it is more generally valid for tea and rubber than for cocoanuts, sugar, cocoa, and spices. In Ceylon, for example, we find that the percentage of acreage under small holdings is only about 20 percent for tea and 50 percent for rubber but as high as 70 percent for cocoanuts; for paddy, a non-plantation crop, the proportion of acreage in small holdings is almost 97 percent.[1] A similar progression is found in the use of fertilizers.[2] The proportion of alien control also differs rather systematically among the various crops. Indeed, the significant structural feature of the plantation economy is that a similar pattern is discernible for each plantation crop.

The generally high productivity of plantations suggests a direct relationship between the share of plantation crops in a country's total agricultural output and the level of productivity in its agricultural sector. And the latter is found to be directly related to the level of income per head. Thus differences between countries in income per head are largely attributable to the relative significance of the plantation sector. The emphasis on plantation culture, with its superior productivity, in turn implies not only that a high proportion of exports typically consist of agricultural products but that exports themselves constitute a significant percentage of national income. We should not be surprised, therefore, to find that the ratio of exports to national income is highest for Ceylon and Malaya and lowest for Pakistan and India.[3] The rationalization of present levels of income per head boils down to this: predominance of an agricultural sector organized along plantation lines with a heavy export orientation.

This suggests two main avenues of growth open to the poorer countries in the region: to rationalize agricultural techniques, and to reduce the relative significance of traditional agriculture. Both imply some sort of "industrialization," which all countries are emphasizing. However, the concentration on one or a few export crops, although it appears to account for present high levels of income per head, creates a precarious situation. Not only does it subject the entire economy to substantial instability due to demand fluctuations in particular markets, but the future prospects of such concentration do not appear conducive to rapid or sustainable economic growth. Putting all the eggs in one basket is a dangerous way to

[1] Ceylon, *Census of Agriculture 1952*, p. 18.
[2] *Ibid.*, p. 25.
[3] For details and analysis see Chapter 13, Section 2 *et passim*.

live and an improbable basis for steady development.[1] Apart from questions of stability and the adequacy of world demand, Malaya and Indonesia have the space to extend their plantation acreage, particularly for rubber. Ceylon has less scope for extending the area but, here as in the other plantation economies, much can be done to raise the yields of existing acreage through replanting and more intensive use of fertilizers.[2] For the other countries the prime focus must be on ordinary agriculture, and here the analogy to past Western experience is much closer except for two ominous facts: first, that a significant rise in agricultural productivity has not taken place prior to industrialization; and, secondly, that whatever induced "agricultural revolution" is to occur must be achieved despite a long history of rapid population growth and present growth rates that are two or three times those experienced by the Western economies in their early periods of development. The population explosion casts a shadow, because, even at best, industrial employment can grow only very slowly.[3]

7 *Industrial Resource Base*

Since the South Asian countries look to industrialization outside of the agricultural sector, it is important to outline the present structure and trends in manufacturing. One factor conditioning both present and future attempts to industrialize is, of course, the amount and variety of natural resources available for industry. Parallel to the discussion of the man/land ratio in the preceding chapter, we shall first examine the industrial resource base in these countries. As we shall find, it is in general not very satisfactory.

Lack of resources required by modern industry may be an important constraint on both the level and the direction of industrial activity in an underdeveloped country. Any nation desiring to industrialize without adequate resources will be faced with the necessity of importing substantial amounts of raw materials. The relative burden of such imports depends largely on the level of wages and labor productivity. If output per unit of available labor is relatively high – which implies a high degree of discipline and efficiency of the labor force actually used and a high capital intensity – the importation of raw materials or other needed industrial supplies will obviously be less of a hindrance to economic growth. Not only can an economy with an efficient, hard-working, and skilled work force and a high capital intensity more easily afford more imports than one at lower levels of

[1] These notions are discussed more fully in Chapter 13.

[2] Ceylon, *The Ten Year Plan*, pp. 167 ff.

[3] Chapter 24, Sections 5–6.

productivity, as the costs for the imports are a smaller share of total production costs, but these imports will be more effectively used.

The ability to offset the initial disadvantages of resource scarcity, therefore, is directly related to efficiency levels. The examples of Denmark, Switzerland, and Japan immediately come to mind. Denmark has little in the way of natural resources except the sites to put the factories on. Switzerland has, in addition, only hydropower, while "Japan's natural resource position is definitely inferior to that of China, India, Indonesia, or Burma, and was recognized as such throughout her period of development. Her only resources were skilled manpower, waterpower, and (in the 20th century) electricity."[1] Yet for these countries the necessity to import large quantities of parts and materials was not an insuperable barrier to progress and this seems largely attributable to their high degree of labor discipline and efficiency.

Furthermore, once labor becomes relatively scarce and/or skilled, wages per unit of labor input rise; it then becomes more natural as well as more economic to achieve progress through the substitution of capital for labor, and this further enhances labor productivity, and reduces even more the burden of importing large amounts of raw materials. But where capital is scarce and labor is plentiful and cheap it is difficult to raise productivity simply by capital substitution. Thus a combination of resource scarcity, scarcity of capital, low levels of labor skills, work discipline and efficiency, all resulting in low productivity and wages in the underdeveloped economies of South Asia, tends to make the relative burden of raw material imports more severe, at the same time as such imports place a heavy burden on their already precarious balance of payments situation. In this light, the adequacy of resources takes on added significance despite the fact that the relationship between economic growth and the natural resource base is highly tenuous and complex. It is the combination of adverse features that makes the South Asian resource endowment more significant than it would otherwise be.

In general, nature has not been particularly generous to South Asia. Of the countries of the region only India possesses iron ore, coal, or power resources in quantities adequate for a high degree of industrialization. As a consequence, the production of basic raw materials is largely concentrated in India. It is evident from Table 11–6 that India produces a wide variety of basic raw materials, with the notable exceptions of petroleum and tin. Estimated coal reserves and known iron ore reserves per head are shown in Table 11–7, which bears out India's superior resource endowments. All the other countries of the region have smaller absolute reserves

[1] M. Bronfenbrenner, "Some Lessons of Japanese Economic Development, 1853–1938," August, 1960, mimeographed draft, pp. 6–7.

Table 11–6

OUTPUT OF BASIC RAW MATERIALS, 1957 AND 1959

(*Thousand tons unless otherwise stated*)

Country and year	*Pakistan*		*India*		*Indonesia*		*Burma*	
	1957	*1959*	*1957*	*1959*	*1957*	*1959*	*1957*	*1959*
Coal	694	744	43,500	47,830	717	637	...	1
Petroleum (crude)	294	312	...	464	15,468	18,218	397	528
Natural gas (1,000,000 cu.m.)	414	640	...	...	...	2,232	...	...
Iron ore[a]	23	2	5,071	7,930	...	...	4	4
Tungsten ore (tons)[a]	...	...	15	...	...	...	397	237
Chrome ore (tons)[a]	18,150	16,019	78,542	85,200	...	...	...	...
Manganese ore[a]	...	...	1,602	1,190	30	45	1	1
Copper ore[a]	...	...	{ (404) 8[m]	(411) 8[m] }	...	...	...	...
Lead ore[a]	...	...	5	7	...	...	27	19
Zinc ore[a]	...	...	8	10	...	...	16	21
Tin ore[a]	...	...	...	...	28	22	1	1
Bauxite	4	2	96	124	241	381	...	...
Gypsum[a]	69	86	920	857	...	...	...	2
Asbestos[a]	...	...	2	1	...	...	...	...
Cement	1,078	1,008	5,688	6,948	...	...	36	36
Salt	460	284[c]	3,670	3,178	347	314[c]	116	110

	South Vietnam		Philippines		Thailand		Ceylon		Fed. of Malaya	
	1957	1959	1957	1959	1957	1959	1957	1959	1957	1959
Coal	...	20	191	140	100[l]	109[l]	...	...	155	77
Petroleum (crude)	...	...	...	...	...	...	...	...	...	...
Natural gas (1,000,000 cu.m.)	...	...	...	...	...	...	...	...	...	...
Iron ore[a]	...	...	1,346	1,230	9	6	...	...	3,020	3,821
Tungsten ore (tons)[a]	...	...	...	...	907	463	...	...	51	20
Chrome ore (tons)[a]	...	...	725,516	653,487	...	...	...	...	...	...
Manganese ore[a]	...	...	30	35	...	...	...	...	...	...
Copper ore[a]	40[m]	50[m]	...	...	...	...	...	...	...	2
Lead ore[a]	...	...	814[m]	355[m]	7[b] (lead and zinc)	3	...	...	...	...
Zinc ore[a]	...	...	302[m]	5[m]		...	...	...	...	...
Tin ore[a]	...	...	...	...	14	10	...	...	60	38
Bauxite	...	...	...	...	...	...	...	...	331	388
Gypsum[a]	...	...	...	2	2	4	...	...	...	...
Asbestos[a]	...	...	...	...	...	...	...	...	...	...
Cement	...	...	393	740	402	481	49	95[c]	126	192
Salt	80	61[c]	105	175	263	460[c]	82	...	...	...

Sources: U. N., ECAFE, *Mining Developments in Asia and the Far East, 1957,* Bangkok, 1959; and *Mining Developments in Asia and the Far East, 1959,* Bangkok, 1961.

[a] Concentrates. [b] Mixed lead and zinc concentrates. [c] ECAFE, 1960, Table 12. [l] Lignite.
[m] Metal content in concentrates.

Table 11–7

INDUSTRIAL RESOURCES PER HEAD OF POPULATION

	Coal reserves (estimated) (tons)	*Iron ore reserves (tons)*	*Potential water power (kilowatts)*
Pakistan	2	0.7	0.12
India	175	54.2	0.09
Indonesia	30	0.1	0.03
Burma	13	0.1	1.01
Philippines	2	1.3	0.07
Thailand	–	–	0.05
Ceylon	6	0.4	0.06
Malaya	10	–	–
Japan	233	0.7	0.25
United States	10,245	41.0	0.65
United Kingdom	3,396	73.4	0.02

Source: United Nations, "Economic Development and Planning in Asia and the Far East, Industrialization," *Economic Bulletin for Asia and the Far East,* December, 1958, p. 40, Table 13.

Note: A dash (–) indicates the amount is nil or negligible. Population data refer to the year 1956 and prior to revised figures. Estimates of resources are from earlier studies. For details see notes to original table.

of most raw materials and substantially less diversity. Thus the mineral wealth of Pakistan

> . . . is practically confined to oil, salt, chromite, and a very little inferior coal and iron ore; further she has little hydro-electric potential actually within her borders. . . . However, the discovery in 1951 of a very large natural gasfield greatly changed her power position—present estimates indicate that these reserves are the thermal equivalent of three times her coal reserves.[1]

Most countries in the region are specifically endowed with only one or a few major metals or minerals. Burma possesses copper, lead, and zinc deposits at Bawdin and tin and tungsten deposits at Mawchi. Ceylon is the world's largest graphite producer. Malaya, Indonesia, and Thailand accounted for some 35.9, 18.2, and 9.0 percent respectively of the world's mine production of tin during 1956–58. Indonesia leads the region in petroleum output by a substantial margin although its production contributed only 2.2 percent of world output in 1958 and its proven reserves represented only 1.6 percent of the world total.[2]

[1] W. Gordon East and O. H. K. Spate, eds., *The Changing Map of Asia – A Political Geography,* Methuen, London, 1958, p. 148.

[2] United Nations, Department of Economic Affairs, *Development of Mineral Resources in Asia and the Far East,* Report and Documents of the ECAFE Regional Con-

Despite the relative paucity of industrial resources, exports of some of these materials provide an important source of foreign exchange earnings. For example, exports of tin and iron ore accounted for 14.2 and 2.8 percent respectively of Malaya's export earnings during 1956–58. By 1963 these percentages had risen to 23.6 and 6.5. In 1956–58 tin and petroleum exports provided 5.7 and 30.5 percent of Indonesia's total export income; in 1963 these percentages were 2.8 and 38.5. The Philippines regularly derives roughly 7 to 10 percent of its export earnings from metal and mineral exports, while Thailand has earned around 6 to 7 percent of its foreign exchange from tin exports in recent years.[1] Other materials that may be mentioned are sulphur and bauxite. Although sulphur has only been found in Indonesia, its major product, sulphuric acid, may be obtained from other deposits found in India, Malaya, and the Philippines. The importance of sulphuric acid for the region lies in the manufacture of fertilizers. Bauxite, used in the production of aluminum, has been found in India, Indonesia, and Malaya.[2]

Besides the above-mentioned resources, forestry products provide some export earnings and serve important domestic uses, especially in Burma, the Philippines, and Thailand. Forests of varying quality cover more than three-quarters of the land area of Malaya and Thailand and over half in Burma, Ceylon, and the Philippines. Only in India and Pakistan is the forest area exceptionally small. Burmese forests contain about three-quarters of the world's teak stands although exports of teak by value accounted for only 6 percent of total Burmese exports in 1959, a decline from the pre-war average of 7 percent. The physical reduction in annual average teak exports was steep – from over 227,000 tons during 1936–40 to less than 75,000 tons during 1956–60.[3] Log production in the Philippines has steadily increased since the Second World War and exports of "logs, lumber and timber" accounted for over 15 percent of total Philippine exports in 1959 and 20 percent in 1963. Teak exports from Thailand, however, account regularly for less than 3 percent of total exports by value. Forest reserves constitute an as yet only partially exploited natural resource in most of the countries in the region although they have long served as sources of fuel and housing for the inhabitants and support rather extensive saw-milling activities in Malaya, Thailand, Burma, and the Philippines.

ference on Mineral Resources Development, Tokyo, April 20–30, 1953, Bangkok, 1953, p. 55.

[1] Data from U. N., *Economic Survey of Asia and the Far East,* various years.

[2] U. N., *Development of Mineral Resources in Asia and the Far East,* p. 281. See also United Nations, *Mining Developments in Asia and the Far East,* Mineral Resources Development Series No. 24, New York, 1965.

[3] Burma, Government of, Ministry of National Planning, *Second Four-Year Plan for the Union of Burma 1961–62 to 1964–65,* A Draft Outline, Rangoon, 1961, p. 108.

It is clear from the general picture of resource endowment that only India possesses enough of the required resources to concentrate on heavy industry to a large extent in its development plans. For the most part, the industrial resources of the other countries do not appear adequate to support large-scale, indigenous manufacturing activity. This conclusion needs to be tempered because geological mapping is not complete;[1] the possibility of major new resource discoveries cannot be neglected. Nevertheless, present information suggests that South Asia has not been very generously endowed with industrial resources. Nor do any of the countries, except India, have an appropriate combination of resources for industrial development. Each country has one or several types of natural resource, but a favorable combination of them is conspicuous by its absence.

Few of the countries have really been pushing against the limitations of natural resources. Where resources are being exploited this is often only for export of the raw materials rather than to supply an expanding domestic industry. In part this reflects the lack of a favorable combination of resources, but it must be stressed that the very meager extent of industrialization in the region is less a product of resource scarcity than of the other limitations and inhibitions discussed in the last chapter and many following ones.

8 *The Structure of Manufacturing Industry: Product Breakdown*

This section and the next examine respectively the product composition of manufacturing output and the types of establishments. The statistical data available on manufacturing include crafts or cottage industry and other small-scale enterprises as well as the larger, more highly organized firms. Within this very mixed group the quality of the statistics varies considerably. As would be expected, figures for the organized factory sector are fairly firm.[2] Comprehensive information about small-scale manufacturing industry is more difficult to come by because of the larger number of units and their greater geographic dispersion; and if accounts are kept at all they are usually less reliable and comprehensive than in the larger firms. Statistics on crafts and cottage industry are still more elusive.[3] Hence, the validity of information about manufacturing varies

[1] United Nations, ECAFE, *Coal and Iron Ore Resources of Asia and the Far East*, Bangkok, July, 1952, pp. 11–14.

[2] See, for example, Little, "The Strategy of Indian Development," *National Institute Economic Review*, p. 20.

[3] An impression of the range of ignorance about the number of workers engaged in all forms of manufacturing, and particularly in cottage enterprises, can be obtained from such observations as the following concerning Pakistan: "In the census of 1951, only 1,400,000 workers reported themselves employed in industry, large and small

Table 11–8

PERCENTAGE SHARES OF DIFFERENT INDUSTRIES IN TOTAL VALUE ADDED BY MANUFACTURING

	Pakistan (*1954*)	*India* (*1954*)	*Philippines* (*1956*)
Consumer goods industries:			
Food processing, beverages and tobacco	15.0	10.9	44.9
Textiles	46.7	50.7	4.5
Wearing apparel, footwear including leather products	4.8	0.4	5.6
Wood and cork products including furniture and fixtures	0.1	0.3	5.7
Paper and paper products	1.4	2.1	1.9
Printed and published materials	3.0	—	3.1
Rubber products	0.8	—	1.0
Total	71.8	64.4	66.7
Producer goods industries:			
Chemicals and chemical products	} 8.4	8.4	9.6
Products of petroleum and coal		—	[a]
Basic metals	1.7	11.4	0.9
Metal products	2.5	1.8	3.6
Machinery, including electrical machinery	1.4	9.2	1.9
Transport equipment	1.2	0.6	2.0
Non-metallic minerals	3.4	4.2	5.0
Total	18.6	35.6	23.0
Miscellaneous	9.6	—	10.3

Source: U. N., *Economic Survey of Asia and the Far East, 1958,* Bangkok, 1959, Table 25, p. 89.

[a] Included in "Miscellaneous."

directly with the predominance of larger scale firms using modern techniques. On the whole, the information presented in this and the following section is probably more dependable than much of the data hitherto

scale alike. This was probably a substantial underestimate. Even if it were correct, and if allowance were made for those employed in large-scale industry, it would indicate that about 1,100,000 were employed in cottage and small-scale industry. The figure commonly stated for employment in cottage and small-scale industry is three to four million, and figures as high as seven million have been mentioned." (Pakistan, Government of, National Planning Board, *The First Five Year Plan, 1955–60,* Karachi, 1958, p. 595.) For India, a scrutiny of various sources, including the national sample surveys, reveals similar inconsistencies in regard to cottage industry. Statistics for the other South Asian countries are even less reliable, except perhaps in the case of the Philippines. These observations concern employment in cottage industry; estimates of production are equally inadequate.

examined. This is especially true of output data in those fields where firms tend to be fairly large. Employment figures are less reliable since smaller firms and, in particular, craft enterprises, account for by far the largest part of the "industrial" work force.

One outstanding feature of the composition of manufacturing output shown in Table 11–8 for India, Pakistan, and the Philippines is the large proportion of such output devoted to consumer goods. Approximately two-thirds of the value added by manufacturing came from production of consumer goods, whereas in the United States in 1954 the share of national income originating in consumer goods industries within manufacturing, including automobile production, was slightly in excess of 42 percent. Despite problems of classification that make direct comparisons difficult, it is apparent that manufacturing in India, Pakistan, and the Philippines has a substantially greater consumer orientation than in the United States and the Western world generally.[1] Since 1954 the emphasis on heavy industry in planning in India and, to a much lesser extent, Pakistan has undoubtedly led to a reduction in the ratio of consumer goods output to total manufacturing. In India three new steel plants raised steel ingot capacity to a total of 6 million tons by 1960–61 and there has been a sharp increase in mechanical industries. Partly because heavy industry does not operate as close to capacity as consumer industry, but mainly because, even in India, producer industries still constitute a very small economic sector (the high percentage increases reflect the small initial base), the industrial structure has not changed very much in India despite an earlier start.[2]

The other outstanding feature is the overwhelming predominance of textiles in India and Pakistan and of food processing in the Philippines, which of course reflects the lack of diversity of output generally found in underdeveloped economies. In India, for example, five major industries – basic iron and steel, cement, paper, cotton textiles, and sugar – accounted for 60 percent of the employment of all twenty-nine industries included in the 1951 Census of Manufactures, and generated about 60 percent of

[1] The ratio of consumer to producer goods output in manufacturing is sometimes considered indicative of the degree of industrialization, with the "highest stage" that in which the ratio approaches unity. By this criterion Pakistan is clearly the least industrialized of the three, and India and the Philippines are approximately equal. The ratio for Japan in 1955 was less than unity; the United States had a ratio less than one in 1954. (See United Nations, ECAFE, *Economic Development and Planning in Asia and the Far East, Industrialization*, Vol. IX, No. 3, December, 1958, pp. 10–11.)

[2] Cf. National Council of Applied Economic Research, *Indian Economy, 1961–63*, New Delhi, 1963, pp. 33ff.

". . . the bulk of [India's] industrial income, nearly 60 percent, is from traditional industries like cotton and jute textiles, wheat flour, sugar, oil-crushing, leather, etc., all of which can be classed as agricultural-processing industries, and a few others from such industries as cement, glass, etc., based on non-metallic mineral resources." (*Ibid.*, p. 35.)

Table 11–9

COMPOSITION OF INDUSTRIAL OUTPUT IN CEYLON, 1952

Industry	*Net output (Rs millions)*	*Percent of total net output*
Coir fibre and coir goods	22	10
Printing, bookbinding and kindred industries	20	9
Cocoanut and oil milling	51	23
Engineering	48	21
Electricity	13	6
Total	154	69

Source: Ceylon, Department of Census and Statistics, *Statistical Abstract of Ceylon, 1960,* Colombo, 1960, Table 157, p. 180.

total value added.[1] Cotton textiles alone accounted for one-third or more of the totals reported in that census for the following items: capital employed, number of workers, gross value of output, value added, and payment to workers during the period 1949–53.[2]

For the other economies in the region less detail is available, but the following remarks indicate the general pattern of industrial output. For Ceylon, statistics refer only to the "factory" sector of industry, defined as "every industrial establishment which – (a) has not less than five paid employees; (b) has a working capital of not less than three thousand rupees; and (c) uses mechanical power in any of its production processes."[3] The value of the net output of the 692 establishments in 1952 was some 225 million rupees, or about 5 percent of the national income. Of this amount, five industries contributed almost 70 percent, as shown in Table 11–9. Again the high concentration of output in a few industries is apparent. It is interesting to note that the number of workers in the "factory" sector as defined above was only 54,000 in 1952[4] whereas in all manufacturing in 1953 there were an estimated 300,000 workers.[5] This implies, according to the same source, that about five-sixths of the workers in manufacturing were "self-employed or working in small shops with virtually no capital to raise their productivity or . . . [were] engaged in handicraft and artisan activities at a moderate level of skill."

[1] George Rosen, *Industrial Change in India,* Free Press, Glencoe, Illinois, 1958, p. 20.

[2] *Ibid.,* p. 36.

[3] Ceylon, Government of, Department of Census and Statistics, *Census of Industry, 1952,* Colombo, 1954, p. 175.

[4] Ceylon, Government of, Department of Census and Statistics, *Statistical Abstract of Ceylon 1960,* Government Press, Colombo, 1960, p. 180, Table 157.

[5] W. Howard Wriggins, *Ceylon: Dilemmas of a New Nation,* Princeton University Press, Princeton, N. J., 1960, p. 64.

In the Federation of Malaya, industry has been similarly oriented toward handicrafts and processing of raw materials. These activities accounted for some 57 percent of employment in 1947. The other segments of industry tend to be of a localized nature where high transport costs provide natural protection. The food, drink, and tobacco categories absorbed about 13 percent of those employed in industry while engineering and "other manufacturing" employed 16 and 14 percent respectively. The last category includes enterprises producing bricks, soap, metal containers, newspapers, and so on, all generally small-scale and localized. Indeed, it has been suggested that "No private manufacturing firm in Malaya employs more than a few hundred workers; the average firm has perhaps 20, the majority less than 10. In the Federation nearly 40% . . . of the 'industrial' labor force consists, not of wage-earners, but of own-account workers and unpaid family helpers."[1]

Burma, recovering from wartime destruction[2] and civil war, had failed to achieve by 1958–59 a level of real gross domestic product equivalent to that of 1938–39, and, indeed, real output per head is about 15 percent below that of 1938–39. The small industrial and mining sector that existed before the war has shown an even more sluggish rate of revival. In physical terms none of the minerals produced in 1939 had achieved by 1957–58 even 50 percent of its 1939 output level. Though physical output of specific industries such as cigarettes, sugar, brine salt, cotton yarn, and bricks had generally increased between 1953–54 and 1958–59, these contributed a minute proportion of value of gross domestic product.[3] The total share of manufacturing amounted to only 12 percent of output, and almost half of the manufacturing component consisted of the output of cottage industry. Of the remaining 6 percent, more than half originated from rice milling.[4]

The story in Indonesia is much the same as in Burma except that somewhat greater progress seems to have been made in increasing mining and industrial output.[5] In Thailand, industry is almost entirely confined to processing raw materials, fabricating a few consumer products (playing cards, jewelry, toys, furniture, etc.), and manufacturing building materials (cement, timber, bricks). Apart from a small steel mill, there is no important heavy industry.[6] A survey conducted in 1958 indicated that almost 60

[1] International Bank for Reconstruction and Development, *Economic Development of Malaya,* p. 422.

[2] As a consequence of the Second World War, "at least half of Burma's capital of modern communications and industry was destroyed." (Tinker, *Union of Burma,* p. 285.)

[3] Burma, Government of, *Economic Survey of Burma 1959,* Rangoon, 1959.

[4] Human Relations Area Files, *Burma,* p. 1339.

[5] See *Report of the Governor of the Bank of Indonesia for the Financial Year 1958–1959,* G. Kolff & Co., Indonesia, pp. 208–220.

[6] Blanchard *et al., Thailand,* p. 326.

percent of employment was concentrated in two types of establishments, saw milling (which accounted for 41 percent alone) and rice milling. Employment in printing, sugar milling, weaving, ceramics, ice factories, flour milling, engine repair, foundry and machine shops made up most of the balance.[1]

From the foregoing it is evident that two main activities characterize the industrial structure in South Asia: handicrafts of all types and processing of domestically available raw materials, mostly foods (such as rice, sugar, and cocoanuts) and so requiring little elaborate capital equipment. Heavy industry, producing consumer durable or producer goods, is conspicuously absent, except in India. There are, of course, oil refineries, steel mills, and other heavy industrial plants, but these tend to stand as isolated symbols of future aspirations rather than to be closely integrated with existing facilities. Again India, with a superior base of industrial resources, is exceptional, having a long-established and not unsubstantial steel and textile industry.

But of greater importance for future industrialization than specific product types is the nature of the so-called "industrial" establishments within particular branches of manufacturing.

9 *The Structure of Industry: Types of Establishment*[2]

Three main types of establishment may be distinguished: cottage industry, small-scale industry, and large-scale industry. Precise definition of each is difficult and contentious, but for present purposes an outline of the key distinguishing features will suffice.

Cottage industry, as the name implies, is small in scale and frequently confined to a single dwelling unit. It is characterized by production of traditional commodities using traditional (i.e., non-power-driven) equipment and techniques. Employment usually involves members of the household rather than hired labor. Production has a strong rural orientation; raw materials are procured locally and marketing seldom extends beyond the village confines. For many workers and their families cottage industry provides part-time employment and a welcome, though uncertain, addition to family incomes.

Small-scale industry, on the other hand, is increasingly characterized by production of non-traditional, or less traditional, commodities, some-

[1] International Bank for Reconstruction and Development, *A Public Development Program for Thailand,* Johns Hopkins Press, Baltimore, 1959, Table 5, p. 90.

[2] This section relies heavily on P. N. Dhar and H. F. Lydall, *The Role of Small Enterprises in Indian Economic Development,* Asia Publishing House, Bombay, 1961. See also Chapters 23, 24, and 25, where problems of industrial structure are discussed from an institutional and a planning and policy point of view.

times using modern techniques. In India and to a lesser extent the other countries, such products as radio sets, electric motors, bicycle parts, sewing machines, machine tools, and spectacle frames emanate from small-scale industry, if produced at all. Some of these industries (textiles for example) are direct competitors of cottage industry, frequently to the disadvantage of the latter; that is, they sometimes employ more modern techniques to produce traditional products. There are also small-scale industries using more traditional techniques to produce more or less modern products. For example, Western-style shoes, furniture, soap, matches, and brushes can be made by labor-intensive, capital-saving techniques in small-scale industry (as well as sometimes in cottage industry). Small-scale industries are generally located in towns or cities, rather than villages, since they require a wider immediate market than the village economy provides, to say nothing of the other external economies of urban agglomeration. Their raw materials are obtained from widely scattered sources and marketing occasionally extends to the international sphere. They employ hired labor at established or bargained wage rates. Thus our use of the term "small-scale industry" is rather broad and applies to any enterprise using primarily hired labor, though not in very large numbers.

Large-scale industry may then be defined as predominantly capital-intensive enterprise using substantial amounts of raw materials. Its location is determined in large part by the extent of weight loss of the important resources used during manufacturing. Thus the steel industry locates near iron ore or coal reserves, aluminum near power supply, and so on. Barring any strong locational pull by virtue of weight-losing raw materials, large-scale industry tends to have a distinct urban orientation. Hired labor is used exclusively and in relatively large numbers, frequently with union representation. Sales have a much wider geographical scope than in either cottage or small-scale enterprises. All of "heavy" industry clearly falls into this category. Most enterprises are organized as corporations even when families retain control.

We shall attempt to assess the relative significance of these three broad classifications and to sketch their distribution along product lines. The most extensive data are for India, but the picture they provide may be fairly typical of the region, except that India has relatively more large-scale industry, particularly heavy industry.

The breakdown of employment between rural and urban in India, given in Table 11–10, generally confirms the substantial rural orientation of cottage industry. If the urban employment of enterprises in the largest size class seems less than that implied in the above conception of "large-scale," this may be largely a statistical illusion; for the table shows employment in terms of workers' residence and some of the workers surveyed may work in urban areas but reside in rural. The noteworthy feature is the

Table 11–10

NUMBER OF EMPLOYEES BY SCALE OF ENTERPRISE AND URBAN OR RURAL RESIDENCE OF WORKERS, INDIA, 1955
(*Thousands*)

Type of Enterprise	*Rural*	*Urban*	*Total*
1. Employing less than 10 with power, or 20 without, using mainly household labor (cottage industry)	8,068	2,821	10,889
2. Employing less than 10 with power, or 20 without, using mainly hired labor	833	897	1,730
3. Employing 10–49 with power, or 20–99 without	197	298	495
4. Employing 50 or more with power, or 100 or more without	1,438	1,650	3,088
Total	10,536	5,666	16,202

Source: Special tabulation made for the Perspective Planning Division of the Planning Commission from employment data collected in the Ninth Round of the *National Sample Survey,* May–November, 1955. All data taken from P. N. Dhar and H. F. Lydall, "The Role of Small Enterprises in Indian Economic Development," mimeographed copy prepared for the Center for International Studies, Massachusetts Institute of Technology, July, 1960, p. 7.

overwhelming preponderance of cottage industry. Almost 70 percent of the workers surveyed reported employment in cottage industry whereas relatively few reported employment in the intermediate sizes of enterprise (rows 2 and 3).

Of more interest is the breakdown by industry for establishments of various types, shown in Table 11–11. Although the classification of industries as "mainly traditional," "mixed," and "mainly modern" is admittedly rough, it does indicate the general preponderance of cottage industry in the traditional sector. However, the study from which this table is derived reveals important size and technical differentials within specific industries. Taking textiles (wool and silk) for example, there are a relatively large number of establishments in the largest size class compared to the second largest. In terms of value added per worker, there tends to be a positive correlation with size and technique of enterprise. Indeed, as of 1943, the ratio of value added per worker in large-scale plants using power machinery to value added per worker in handloom, cottage industry was over 14 to 1.[1]

In short, if industrial productivity measured by value added is corre-

[1] For textiles, see U. N., *Economic Development and Planning in Asia and the Far East, Industrialization,* p. 55, where productivity differences among types of industrial establishment are given.

Table 11–11

NUMBER OF EMPLOYEES, BY INDUSTRY AND SCALE OF ENTERPRISE, INDIA, 1955
(*Thousands*)

Industry	*Household enterprises*	*Non-household below 10–20*	*10–49 with power, 20–99 without*	*50 or more with power, 100 or more without*	*All enterprises*
Mainly traditional:					
Foodstuffs	2,209	284	61	271	2,825
Tobacco products	240	160	66	97	563
Wool textiles	109	13	2	23	147
Silk textiles	149	76	31	32	288
Miscellaneous textiles	813	202	49	44	1,108
Wood and wood products	1,516	119	21	52	1,708
Leather and leather products	535	56	27	24	642
Miscellaneous	608	73	6	40	727
Total	6,179	983	263	583	8,008
Mixed:					
Cotton textiles	2,725	316	41	843	3,925
Pottery, bricks, glass, etc.	813	160	59	204	1,236
Metals and products (excl. machinery)	732	83	28	328	1,171
Total	4,270	559	128	1,375	6,332

Mainly modern:					
Beverages	177	27	14	439	657
Jute products	57	4	7	215	283
Paper and paper products	15	—	4	38	57
Printing and publishing	25	46	23	48	142
Chemicals	60	30	34	278	432
Machinery, electrical and transport equipment	106	41	22	112	291
Total	440	158	104	1,130	1,862
Grand Total	10,889	1,730	495	3,088	16,202

Source: Dhar and Lydall (cited at Table 11–10), p. 9.

Table 11–12

ESTIMATED DISTRIBUTION OF MANUFACTURING ESTABLISHMENTS BY NUMBERS OF EMPLOYEES, INDIA, 1956

Number of persons per establishment[a]	*Number of establishments*	*Total number of persons employed (thousands)*
Under 5	5,000,000	10,200
5–9	130,000	910
10–19	43,000	600
20–49	18,000	560
50–99	4,660	340
100–249	2,550	380
250–499	840	270
500–999	470	330
1,000 and over	580	1,410
Total	5,200,000	15,000

Source: For establishments employing 50 or more: *Occupational Pattern in Manufacturing Industries, 1956,* Planning Commission, Government of India, 1959, pp. 45–46. For those below 50, see text. Data from Dhar and Lydall, *op. cit.*, p. 11.

[a] Includes working proprietors and unpaid family workers.

lated with size and technique, as seems generally true, the numbers and/or employment of establishments of different types will be a significant determinant of over-all industrial output per man-hour. In this regard Table 11–12 is especially revealing. Over two-thirds of manufacturing employment occurs in enterprises employing less than five persons. It may be assumed that most of these establishments lack mechanical power in view of the rural incidence of cottage enterprises and the lack of rural electrification in large parts of India. It seems clear, then, that achievement of significant gains in productivity will require a considerable adjustment in the role of cottage industries relative to small and large-scale enterprises in India.

Scattered evidence reported in the previous section generally bears out the ubiquity of the Indian pattern. For Pakistan, the United Nations study already referred to reported that "employment in 1953 in cottage industries amounted to 1,176,000 workers (of whom 779,000 were in food and textiles) as compared to 200,000 in establishments operated by power."[1] Typically, then, industry in South Asia is dominated, in terms of employment, numbers of enterprises, and techniques, by rural enterprises employing little capital and few workers with very low output per worker.

[1] *Ibid.*, p. 9, f.n. 12.

The consequences of this are not difficult to assess. Not only does it keep down the over-all level of industrial productivity, but it tends to perpetuate the low living levels of rural areas. The familiar pattern of cumulative causation appears once more: output per man in cottage industry is limited by the constricted village market, which in turn is limited by low agricultural and, to a lesser extent, industrial productivity. Thus both the ability and incentive of cottage enterprises to increase efficiency are blunted by existing circumstances. Again we arrive at the question of how to break out of the trap of low-level productivity on the village level.

Were it not for the enormous numbers of people involved in cottage industry an obvious solution would be to stake everything on accelerating the growth of factories. But large-scale, and even small-scale, enterprises of this sort are generally labor saving and capital intensive, neither of which feature is particularly attuned to economies characterized by underutilization of the labor force and capital scarcity. A rapid destruction of cottage industry would not only eliminate a source of supplementary rural income, but would also accentuate the push toward urbanization and further aggravate congestion in urban areas, where in-migrants cluster in the low productivity sectors referred to in Section 4.

A discussion of industrial policy against the background of development trends and with a view toward the future will be postponed until Chapters 24 and 25. There we shall note that, while trying to industrialize, the South Asian countries have more than sentimental reasons for protecting rural cottage industry, particularly in the field of consumer goods. Such a policy can perhaps be only a holding operation during a period of transition, but that period may have to be long.

Chapter 12

LEVELS OF LIVING AND INEQUALITY

1 *Introduction*

In this chapter, our attention will be focussed on levels of living, by which we mean the amount of goods and services regularly consumed by the average person in the various countries of South Asia. At the same time, since average figures of consumption hide the high degree of inequality that exists, we shall attempt an assessment of this aspect of South Asian reality as well. Basically our aim is to ascertain, as far as the available evidence permits, the consumption levels of the vast majority of the people.

Levels of living are of course important in themselves. Indeed, it is a major goal of planning for development in the region to raise the abysmally low levels of living for the mass of the people. A rise in these levels has thus an independent value in setting the goals for planning,[1] and provides an important test of plan achievement. But in addition, a rise in levels of living has an instrumental value. By the circular causation attending changes in social conditions, a rise in levels of living is likely to improve almost all other conditions, in particular labor input and efficiency and thus productivity, but also attitudes and institutions.[2]

[1] Chapter 2, Section 4; Chapter 15, Section 1; Appendix 2, Sections 7, 12, and 13. Closely associated with this goal is a reduction in the extent of inequality; see Chapter 2, Section 4; Chapter 15, Section 1; and Chapter 16, Part I.

[2] Appendix 2, Part II and Section 21; Chapter 21, Section 15 *et passim*.

It is an important fact that a rise in levels of living has a much greater instrumental value in South Asia than in the advanced countries. In the latter, levels of living are already so high that on the margin the productivity effect of a change is nil or slight. Therefore the income of an individual, a group, or a whole nation can be divided, with reasonable accuracy, into two parts, one used for consumption and the other for savings, which is to say investment.[1] Normally, then, the level of living, when measured as consumption by "final" purchasers, is obtained by subtracting "savings" from income. These "savings" correspond to the tangible assets accumulated through the non-consumption of some part of current output. But in the underdeveloped countries of South Asia, levels of living are so low as seriously to impair health, vigor, and attitudes toward work. Consequently, increases in most types of consumption represent *at the same time* "investment," as they have an immediate and direct effect on productivity. In this situation the identity between investment and the stock of physical assets, changes in which correspond *ex post* to the magnitude of current savings, is not satisfactory. Savings and the "investment" logically associated therewith should be more broadly defined to include all those expenditures having a positive impact on productivity; and some of them, as we mentioned, are at the same time consumption. This is one reason for doubting the usefulness for South Asia of Western-type economic models, which stress the relationships among output, employment, savings, and investment. These issues are taken up more fully in Appendix 2 (Sections 20 and 21). In the present chapter, this methodological difficulty will not seriously inconvenience us, since our interest is to establish what can generally be known about levels of living without, at this stage, inquiring how changes in these levels affect productivity and output.

In the next section we shall attempt to give some indication of average consumption levels. Thereafter we shall examine the apparent consumption of the more important goods and services. The subject of income inequalities will be discussed in Sections 7 and 8, and also in Appendix 14.

Throughout this chapter we must keep in mind the gross inadequacies, both logical and statistical, of national income figures in South Asia (Chapter 11, Section 1).

2 *Average Levels of Consumption and "Savings"*

A natural starting point in measuring consumption by "final" purchasers would be to obtain data on aggregate consumption from the national ac-

[1] There are, of course, even in the developed economies, logical and definitional problems associated with this distinction, such as how to classify expenditures on education or health, and the usual difficulties attendant on short-run vis-à-vis long-run effects. But for items such as food, clothing, and shelter, and even elementary education and health facilities generally, present levels of consumption in the advanced countries are so high that marginal changes cannot have much impact on individual labor input and efficiency either in an attitudinal or physical sense.

counts. However, none of the countries attempt to supply a breakdown of national output by expenditure category to show what part of it is consumed. India, Pakistan, Indonesia, and Malaya develop some breakdowns of national income by industrial origin, but they do not regularly publish estimates of the amount devoted to expenditures on consumption. Where estimates of aggregate consumption are available, as in the cases of India and Malaya, they are extremely unreliable.[1] In the Philippines "private consumption expenditures" are calculated as residuals.[2]

We have therefore attempted to calculate average consumption levels by deducting from the data on income per head in Chapter 11 some crude estimates of what are taken to be "savings" in the sense of that portion of income which goes into "investment" and hence is unavailable for consumption.[3] This procedure also gives us an opportunity to comment on the gross inadequacies of the measurement of "savings." It will be apparent how little justified is the great concern with which small changes in the alleged rate of "savings" are frequently attended in the literature on the development problems of the South Asian countries.

Difficulties of a conceptual nature emerge when one attempts to deduce

[1] See United Nations, ECAFE, *Economic Survey of Asia and the Far East, 1961*, Bangkok, 1962, p. 172, and subsequent issues.

[2] United Nations, Statistical Office of the United Nations, Department of Economic and Social Affairs, *Yearbook of National Accounts Statistics 1960*, New York, 1961, p. 178.

[3] The concept of "saving" used here is the usual one referring to that portion of income generated by current production deemed not to have been spent on "final" consumer goods and services during the same period in which productive activity is measured. By the same token, investment means that portion of current production which has not been "used up" (i.e., consumed) during the period: it is essentially "product left over" as a result of production and consumption. Since production and income are formally identical in money terms, then logically, savings and investment, *ex post*, are likewise identical. From this point of view, an export of part of a nation's production becomes investment because it represents an increase in claims against the rest of the world that can be used at some future date to purchase foreign goods and services – it has not been used up currently by the exporting nation. Comparable treatment requires that imports be regarded as "disinvestment." Hence the balance of trade (exports minus imports of goods and services) is referred to as "net foreign investment."

A nation's total investment arising from current economic activity consists therefore of two parts: (1) that part of current production not consumed domestically which represents an increase (or decrease) in the stock of durable assets and inventories, referred to as "domestic investment"; and (2) the increase (or decrease) in claims against the rest of the world, or net foreign investment. In accounting, national saving (net or gross) equals domestic investment (net or gross) plus net foreign investment.

We may then measure national saving in two ways: (1) deduct from national income those figures purporting to be consumption and/or (2) add domestic investment to exports less imports. (Details on these alternative computations are given in the notes to Table 12–1.) Sometimes, however, investment is construed as the increase in the stock of physical assets within a nation, whether this results from retaining some part of current output or comes from foreign sources. From this point of view an import of, say, machinery would be deemed to represent "investment" while an export of any tangible good would represent a reduction in physical stocks within the nation. This is precisely opposite to the treatment of the trade balance in contemporary

levels of consumption by the approach just indicated. One of these is the discrepancy between net geographical output and net national income due to income remission and payments to non-residents, which we discussed in Chapter 11 (Section 1). We do not see any feasible way of accurately estimating such income transfers abroad. The average income of "normal residents" may, as we noted, be somewhat overstated for this reason, especially in the cases of Ceylon and Malaya.

Secondly, there is a serious conceptual problem with respect to government "consumption," since there is little possibility of distinguishing clearly between consumption and investment expenditures in the budget of the public sector. As we point out in Appendix 4 (Section 3), the "development" or "investment" budget contains very large sums that are not strictly investment because they do not represent an increase in the stock of physical capital. Furthermore, increased outlays on military equipment may augment the stock of assets but do not, strictly speaking, represent capital formation. Consequently, when public and private "investments" are aggregated to obtain total investment, which is logically equivalent to "savings," the aggregate is a hodgepodge of entirely disparate expenditures. Private investment is defined as physical stock accretions, while government investment is usually construed more broadly. Since estimates of savings are frequently derived from calculations of private and government "investment," it is clear that the resulting figure may consist of a variety of elements that need to be differentiated.

Finally, the calculations of national income are made after deducting the value of imports from the value of exports. Yet, to ascertain amounts actually consumed, we should logically add consumer goods imports, rather than subtract them, and subtract, rather than add, exports of consumer goods. Unfortunately, serious data limitations for all the countries preclude the isolation of a strictly "consumer goods" category from either exports or imports. Rather than attempt to make crude adjustments of this nature in already tenuous estimates, we have followed the simpler proce-

---

national accounting. It nevertheless has intuitive appeal. The underdeveloped countries are trying to increase the quantity of real capital at their disposal regardless of source. Furthermore, if some of the capital imports are financed by gifts or grants requiring no subsequent repayment, this is the usual treatment.

It is useful to keep in mind this alternative way of viewing investment. However, to relate a magnitude defined as domestic investment plus imports minus exports (and minus net factor incomes from abroad) to a national accounting aggregate that treats exports and imports the other way around seems to be misleading and yields a ratio whose meaning is very unclear since the numerator and denominator treat the same items, exports and imports, in a contradictory fashion. To construe exports as, in some sense, "disinvestment" seems particularly distorting. A recent study has, however, defined a concept of "gross savings" (domestic plus foreign) in just this way. (U. N., *Economic Survey of Asia and the Far East, 1961*, Chapter 2, Tables 2–1, 2–3, and pp. 43, 46.)

Although useful for some purposes, this approach to capital formation should not be confused with the more usual definition of savings and investment adopted here and used in constructing Table 12–1.

dure of deducting savings estimates from the income per head data presented in Chapter 11.

When these further problems are considered alongside those indicated in the previous section, the reader scarcely needs to be warned again to view the estimates of savings and consumption levels offered in this section as highly speculative.

Only in two countries, India and Ceylon, have serious attempts been made to estimate savings directly. For all the other countries savings either are estimated from a prior calculation of private and public investment or are computed as a residual after deducting an amount deemed to represent "consumption," both private and public, where such figures are available, from a national income figure to which is added back "indirect taxes net of subsidies." The former technique runs up against the difficulty already mentioned, that the "investment" calculation is a composite of rather disparate items. The latter (residual) approach, even setting aside the problem of separating government consumption from investment, is fraught with possibility of grave error since small errors in either the national income or consumption estimates lead to greatly exaggerated errors in the savings figures. Moreover, since no figure of national income can be considered accurate within 10 percent, and even this is excessively optimistic, it is clear that enormous scope is opened up for overestimation or underestimation of savings.

Special difficulties, both conceptual and empirical, surround the attempts to measure savings directly. Savings estimates of the household sector are particularly weak. In both India and Ceylon, the direct estimates exclude inventories of durable consumer goods. Data on rural housing and other asset changes, especially in cottage and small-scale industry, are impossible to obtain with any degree of accuracy. Thus, even where direct estimates of savings are available, they are acknowledged to rest on very shaky foundations. As was remarked in a study on savings carried out by the Reserve Bank of India, "the factual basis for making any firm estimates is extremely inadequate. Under the circumstances, no fair degree of accuracy or precision is claimed for the year to year estimates presented in this study . . ."[1] Again, a study of savings in Ceylon points out that "Lack

[1] "Estimates of Saving in the Indian Economy," *Reserve Bank of India Bulletin*, March, 1960, p. 1.

Similar caveats are stressed in National Council of Applied Economic Research, *Saving in India – A Monograph*, New Delhi, 1961.

The attempt to measure savings directly in Malaya suffers from such extreme data limitations that we have not used the estimates in this section. See "Saving of the Federation of Malaya, 1954–58: A Preliminary Estimate," *Economic Bulletin for Asia and the Far East*, Vol. XIII, No. 1, June, 1962, pp. 17–33. This study suggests that gross savings constitute 11–13 percent of gross domestic product. More recent estimates, derived by deducting public and private consumption expenditures from gross domestic product, suggest a range of 13–25 percent. See U. N., Report No. TAO/MAL/10, *Report on the National Accounts of the Federation of Malaya 1955–1960*, prepared

of data in most sectors has made accurate estimates impossible."[1]

In view of all these warnings, the savings figures in Table 12–1, even for India and Ceylon, should be regarded with the greatest skepticism. They cannot be said to provide a picture even broadly representative of reality. The derived figures of savings would suggest that Burma's savings ratio is higher than Ceylon's, though Burma is much the poorer country, and that it is double India's ratio and over three times Pakistan's.[2] The estimate for India comes out as higher than that for the relatively well-off Philippines. The derived figures on consumption per head shown in column 3 of the table have somewhat more validity than the estimates of savings, but only because they constitute a much larger magnitude. Savings estimates could be 100 percent overstated without causing a much higher range of error in consumption. By the same token, however, the calculated figures on consumption must be less reliable than the national income estimates, even if savings ratios were completely accurate, and we have already shown the weaknesses of the national income data (Chapter 11, Section 1).

For whatever the evidence is worth, column 3 indicates exceedingly low average consumption levels, generally below 400 rupees annually per head (which is only $80 U. S. at official exchange rates). For Pakistan and India, the figures confirm the prevalence of extreme poverty, with consumption averaging only about 200 to 250 rupees per head per year (a mere $40–$50 U. S. at official exchange rates).[3] When we later consider the uneven distribution of income, these low figures will appear very much on the high side for the bulk of the population.

These findings are a meager harvest considering the effort involved in obtaining them. Furthermore, since nobody assumes, and, except for Burma and Malaya, few of the estimates suggest, that net saving (i.e., non-

---

by Dorothy Walters, February 15, 1963. Although there are conceptual and other differences between the two studies, this variation highlights the ambiguity surrounding the whole notion of "savings."

[1] W. Rasaputram, "Savings of the Ceylon Economy, 1950–59" (a study made partly in connection with the ECAFE project on "Sources of Savings and Methods of Raising the Rate of Saving in Countries of the ECAFE Region"), *Bulletin,* Central Bank of Ceylon, January, 1961, p. 1.

[2] One source does suggest that the Burmese figure should be lowered substantially, since it is possible that "Burma's national product is understated by 50 percent." (U. N., *Economic Survey of Asia and the Far East, 1961,* p. 44.)

[3] Consumption per head for India has been directly computed by the National Sample Survey (11th round, August 1956–February 1957) as 17 and 25 rupees per month for rural and urban areas respectively. Since about 80 percent of the population lives in rural areas, this would put the national average at about 223 rupees per person per year, a figure not inconsistent with the 1954–56 figure of 246 for India in Table 12–1, which also includes "governmental" consumption. (Data from India, Government of, Department of Statistics, Central Statistical Organization, "Member Secretary's Draft Report, Committee on Income Distribution," New Delhi, June, 1962, Tables (3) and (4), pp. II–(19) and II–(10).)

Table 12–1

GENERAL CONSUMPTION LEVELS, 1954–56

Country	*Income per head* (*Indian rupees*) (*1*)	*Ratio of net savings to national income* (*percent*) (*2*)	*Estimated government and private consumption expenditures per head* (*Indian rupees*) (*3*)
Pakistan	220	5[a]	209
India	270	9[b]	246
Indonesia	320	5[c]	304
Burma	310	18[d]	254
South Vietnam	370	−12[e]	414
Philippines	390	7[f]	363
Thailand	390	9[g]	355
Ceylon	450	12[h]	396
Malaya	810	17[i]	672

Sources: Col. 1 from Appendix 13. For col. 2 see notes below. Col. 3 is computed from columns 1 and 2.

Note: To derive net savings we have added to national income "indirect taxes less subsidies" and subtracted from the resulting figure the sum of what are defined as private and government "consumption." The net investment figure is computed by subtracting from gross domestic investment the estimated figure for "depreciation," adding to this "exports less imports of goods and services," and subtracting, if negative, or adding, if positive, data on "net factor income payments abroad." In several cases, the results did not yield an equality between net saving and net investment because no adjustment had been made for "residual error" or because the data for the various components were very rough. The estimates of the savings ratio were obtained in this fashion for South Vietnam, Burma, Thailand, and Malaya from data in ECAFE, *Economic Survey of Asia and the Far East, 1961,* Table 7, p. 172 or as indicated below. For Thailand the figures for net savings differed substantially from those for net investment while the discrepancies were very small or non-existent for Burma, South Vietnam, and Malaya. The savings estimates for the other countries are as cited below.

[a] Pakistan: Ratio of *gross* savings to gross national product is given as 6 percent in Government of Pakistan, Planning Commission, *The Second Five Year Plan* (1960–65), June, 1960, pp. 28–29. Ratio of net savings to national income at market prices is assumed to be about 5 percent in ECAFE, *Economic Survey of Asia and the Far East, 1956,* Bangkok, 1957, p. 54, Table 14 for the year before the First Five-Year Plan. It is probably not unreasonable to assume a 5 percent net savings ratio over the period 1954–56. See also Government of Pakistan, *Outline of the Third Five-Year Plan* (*1965–1970*), August, 1964, p. 7.

[b] India: The 9 percent figure is obtained by averaging the results of the revised estimates of the Reserve Bank of India and the "direct" and "indirect" estimates of the National Council of Applied Economic Research (N.C.A.E.R.) for the years 1954–55, 1955–56, and 1956–57. (See "Estimates of Saving and Investment in the Indian Economy: 1950–51 to 1958–59," *Reserve Bank of India Bulletin,* August, 1961, and

consumption) is much more than a few percentage points of national income, one wonders whether the national income figures themselves, unreliable as they are, do not provide an equally serviceable measure of consumption — the more so since it is apparent from the foregoing comments that there is little chance to refine the measurement by using the available, frail statistics on "savings." The main point of this exercise has been to highlight the difficulties surrounding certain magnitudes that are all too frequently used in an uncritical and undiscriminating fashion.

As would be expected, there is no reliable evidence that could be used to impute trends in average consumption from changes in savings ratios and trends in income per head. The revised direct estimates of savings in the Indian economy made by the Reserve Bank of India indicate a rather static rate from 1950–51 through 1958–59. During 1950–51 the ratio of savings to national income was 6.7 percent but by 1958–59 it had only risen to 7.7 percent. However, an average for the years 1950–51 through 1952–53 compared with 1956–57 through 1958–59 indicates a rise from 5.9 to 7.9 percent.[1] A generally rising trend of saving is also reported by the National Council of Applied Economic Research (N.C.A.E.R.), whose estimates

[1] "Estimates of Savings and Investment in the Indian Economy: 1950–51 to 1958–59," *Reserve Bank of India Bulletin,* August, 1961, p. 5, Table II. This second study of savings by the Reserve Bank provided data for an additional year and modified the results of the earlier study already cited.

Notes to Table 12–1 (continued)

N.C.A.E.R., *Saving in India,* New Delhi, 1961, Table 2.2.1, p. 70.) The estimates (in current prices) of the Reserve Bank, N.C.A.E.R. direct, and N.C.A.E.R. indirect were, respectively: 7.1, 7.6, and 8.8 for 1954–55; 9.1, 10.3, and 11.4 for 1955–56; 8.8, 8.2, and 9.3 for 1956–57.

[c] Indonesia: ECAFE, *Economic Survey, 1956,* p. 54, Table 14.

[d] Burma: ECAFE, *Economic Survey, 1959* for 1954 and 1955 and ECAFE, *1960* for 1956.

[e] South Vietnam: ECAFE, *Economic Survey, 1960,* p. 128; refers to years 1955 and 1956.

[f] Philippines: National Economic Council, *The Five-Year Economic and Social Development Program for FY–1957–1961,* January, 1957, p. 53 states that the "level of savings is low, from 92 to 94 percent of output going to consumption." Data relating consumption expenditures to net national product at market prices indicate a rate of consumption of over 98 per cent. ECAFE, *1959* for 1954 and 1955 and ECAFE, *1960* for 1956. We have used the former estimate to obtain the savings ratio of 7 percent.

[g] Thailand: ECAFE, *Economic Survey, 1960;* refers only to 1956. If computed on the residual basis the ratio is about 17 percent for 1956.

[h] Ceylon: *Savings of the Ceylon Economy, 1950–1959,* no date, Table I, p. 18. Average for the years 1954–56.

[i] Malaya: ECAFE, *Economic Survey, 1961;* refers to 1955 and 1956 average.

imply that the "national average saving-income ratio in India increased from 6 percent in 1948–49 to 1950–51 before the First Plan to about 9 to 10 percent in 1956–57 and 1957–58, the first two years of the Second Plan."[1] The discrepancy between the N.C.A.E.R. and the Reserve Bank estimates is due not only to the limited data available but also to somewhat different coverage. As the Reserve Bank acknowledges, "On the basis of such fragmentary information . . . and taking a qualitative view, it appears that the aggregate saving-income ratio may be about *two* percentage points higher than that estimated in this study."[2] This would make the two sets of estimates agree very closely for the later years in absolute amounts as well as in terms of the rising trend. On the other hand, the Ceylonese direct estimates indicate wide fluctuations and a definite downward trend from 1950 through 1959. The ratio of savings to national income was 13.0 percent in 1950 and only 6.0 percent in 1959. The average for 1950 through 1952 was 9.1 percent and that for 1957 through 1959 was 6.0 percent.[3]

Little reliance can be placed even on these figures, computed by the direct method, although they may be of some limited value as trend indicators. For the other countries the weaknesses of the estimation procedures and the empirical evidence preclude any meaningful trend imputation.

The sharp increase in military expenditures requires special note since these are contained in the estimates of public consumption. India's border conflict with China, the tension between India and Pakistan that in the autumn of 1965 exploded in open warfare, Indonesia's "confrontation" of Malaysia, and the war in Vietnam have created an acute sense of insecurity throughout South Asia and a consequent rise in defense outlays. Given a relatively static level of national output, the accelerated defense activities reduce the amounts left over for food, clothing, shelter, and other household needs. Moreover, defense spending diverts attention from pressing developmental needs and obviously distorts development planning. Among other effects it absorbs young people with higher training, for example doctors, and cuts down the manpower available for productive activities. Indian defense outlays rose sharply in 1962–63 and were expected to rise again in 1963–64, by more than 70 percent above the record high reported in the previous year. Indonesia's expenditures on defense appear to have almost quadrupled between 1959 and 1964. In the other countries of the region except Ceylon, defense spending has also increased in recent years, though less dramatically.[4] But the inclusion of what are deemed to

[1] National Council, *Saving in India,* p. 11.

[2] "Estimates of Savings and Investment," *Reserve Bank of India Bulletin,* p. 1. As to coverage, see the same page and cf. National Council, *Saving in India,* Part I.

[3] Rasaputram, "Savings of the Ceylon Economy, 1950–59," p. 18, Table I.

[4] Estimates derived from United Nations, ECAFE, *Economic Survey of Asia and the Far East, 1963,* Bangkok, 1964, Table 36, pp. 236–237.

be defense outlays in public consumption means that consumption estimates for recent years somewhat overstate actual levels of living. Whatever trends are observed in consumption per head must therefore be tempered by the increasing allocation of resources to the military sector.

In general, however, the empirical and conceptual problems involved in the use of national accounting aggregates force us to discuss trends in levels of living primarily in terms of estimates of physical production or availability of key consumer commodities. Indeed, even for a particular year, physical indicators of consumption per head provide a truer picture of levels of living than the extremely weak monetary measures of Table 12–1. To these indicators we now turn.

3 *Physical Indicators of Levels of Living*

Human welfare depends on many different goods and services even in primitive society. As only a few of these can be taken into account in the most comprehensive set of indicators of levels of living, the selection of the most central and relevant items is always difficult.[1] It is especially so in the South Asian context where many factors militate against obtaining representative, accurate, and comparable data. We are at this stage of our study concerned only with existing levels, and shall reserve for later chapters the analysis of causes and effects.

Nevertheless, we have ventured to choose for somewhat detailed statistical analysis those items that seem to cover the most pertinent aspects of levels of living in South Asia. These are:

(1) food and nutrition;
(2) clothing;
(3) housing, including sanitation;
(4) health facilities;
(5) educational facilities;
(6) information media;
(7) energy consumption;
(8) transportation.

For each of these eight components of consumption – except housing, for which no meaningful indicator is available owing to the great diversity of dwelling arrangements – some available, in every way imperfect, summary statistical evidence is presented in Table 12–2. The figures relate mostly to the late 1950's and 1960–61, and include comparative data for three advanced Western countries.

[1] For an apt discussion of this problem, see United Nations, *Report on International Definition and Measurement of Standards and Levels of Living*, Report of a Committee of Experts convened by the Secretary-General of the United Nations jointly with the International Labor Office and the United Nations Educational, Scientific and Cultural Organization, New York, 1954.

It must be emphasized that most of these indicators refer to facilities for consumption rather than to its actual level, which may not and often does not reach the full potential of the existing facilities. This method of trying to show how people are actually living, consuming, and working is beset by several other difficulties. In the first place, the relative importance of these items in total consumption varies substantially, particularly between the South Asian and the advanced countries. For example, the share of necessities, especially food, in total consumption is very high in South Asia, whereas it may be well below one-half in the Western countries. Thus the quantities shown in Table 12–2 tend to understate the real differences in the consumption levels of the underdeveloped and the advanced countries. Secondly, the figures shown in the table fail to convey the vast differences in quality, especially as compared with the West. South Asian foodstuffs frequently have a low nutritional value, those sold in the market are often adulterated, and they are, at least for the bulk of the population, available in far less variety than in the West. A "commercial vehicle" in South Asia may easily be a broken-down, fully depreciated automobile or truck incapable of very efficient use. Radio receivers are seldom of the modern type and are often out of order. The quality of educational facilities is not comparable to that in the West; nor is the quality of "physicians," many of whom have received but a rudimentary training. Certainly there is not the same ubiquity of highly skilled specialists as in the developed economies. Generally, the quantitative differences understate by a substantial amount the actual discrepancy between South Asian and Western countries, owing to the great gap in quality. Thirdly, and perhaps more important, averages, because they are averages, fail to reveal the enormous inequality in the consumption of these items by different income, social, or ethnic groups, by urban as opposed to rural areas, and by different regions. Fourthly, and related to this bias, many of the items for which data can be obtained to make inter-country comparisons are in large part available to or consumed by a tiny upper-class minority in South Asia, usually concentrated in urban centers. Only the more affluent persons — frequently Europeans — can afford the luxury of, say, an automobile; it is still "an article of fashion, the privilege of the upper middle class and the plaything of the rich."[1] Generally, not only the greater number but also the highest quality of radio receivers and telephones are in the possession of the upper income groups, mainly city dwellers. Whole villages count themselves fortunate to have a single radio; and in the absence of widespread rural electrification, telephones, adequate lighting, and so on are not possible. Thus inequalities of income and of physical facilities imply a heavy concentration of the very low average quantities shown in the table within urban areas and the upper class. It is true that

[1] E. S. Rao, *Surveys of Indian Industries*, Vol. I, Oxford University Press, Oxford, 1957, p. 78.

Table 12–2

PRINCIPAL INDICATORS OF LEVELS OF LIVING FOR SOUTH ASIA AND THREE ADVANCED COUNTRIES

Economic indicators	Year	Pakistan	India	Indonesia	Burma	South Vietnam	Philippines	Thailand	Ceylon	Fed. of Malaya	Sweden	United Kingdom	United States
1. *Food*													
1.1. Calories per head per day	1958	2,030	2,050	2,125	2,150	. . .	2,145	2,185	2,060	2,290	3,020[a]	3,290	3,100
1.2. Proteins per head per day (grams)	1958	54	57	48	51	. . .	56	45	46	51	87[a]	86	91
2. *Clothing*													
2.1. Annual textile consumption (kilograms per head)	1956–58	2.2	2.4	1.2	1.7	1.7	2.1	2.0	2.0	3.5[b]	10.2[c]	11.7	15.5
2.2. Of which cotton (percent)	1956–58	96	92	73	93	66	84[d]	89	65[e]	95[b]	58[c]	49	67
3. *Physicians* – number per 100,000 population	1960	9.1	17.6	2.1[f]	9.1	3.4	18.6[f]	13.3	22.2	15.6	90	104	125
4. *Literacy and education*													
4.1. Literacy, by sex (population aged 15 years and over)													
Males	around 1960[g]	29	41	57	80	23	74	79	83	66	. . .	. . .	. . .
Females	around 1960[g]	8	13	30	40	10	70	56	62	22	. . .	. . .	. . .
4.2. Percent of age cohort completing primary school; both sexes	around 1960[g]	15	(30)	(40)	(20)	(30)	35	35	85	(70)	. . .	. . .	. . .
5. *Newsprint, radios & telephones*													
5.1. Annual newsprint consumption (kilograms per head)	1960	0.1	0.2	0.2	0.5	0.4	1.3	0.7	1.5	0.8	23.6	24.9	36.6
5.2. Radio receiver licenses per 10,000 population	1960	30	50	70	60	90	220	70	360	360	3,670	2,890	9,410[h]
5.3. Telephones per 10,000 population	1960	8	10	13	6	11	41	16	37	110	3,525	1,562	4,285
6. *Energy* – annual consumption of coal equivalent (kg. per head)	1961	68	150	140	49	60	154	67	105	259	3,523	4,925	8,042
7. *Transportation*													
7.1. Motor vehicles per 10,000 population[i]	1957	6	11	15	18	35	62	30	96	166	1,316	1,070	3,922

7.2. Ton-kilometers of road and rail freight per head	1957	84	199	31	50	35	75	86	104	187	1,555	1,399	7,691
7.3. Percent of rail, road, and inland waterway freight traffic accounted for by rail	1957	55	88	17	26	5	9	45	31	30	. . .	43	56
7.4. Passenger-kilometers per head	1957	240	304	180	380	338	1,282	595	895	615	(4,395)	4,208	6,450
7.5. Percent of total rail and motor passenger traffic accounted for by rail	1957	56	59	31	12	11	2	16	19	13	17	17	4
7.6. Length of railroad in kilometers per 10,000 population	1957	1.34	1.29	0.78	1.46	1.03	0.41	1.65	1.58	3.33	19.8	5.93	20.59

Sources: Rows 1.1 and 1.2: U. S. Department of Agriculture, Foreign Agricultural Service, *The World Food Deficit, A First Approximation,* Washington, D. C., March, 1961, p. 22 for the South Asian countries; and United Nations, *Statistical Yearbook 1960,* New York, 1960, Table 127, pp. 315–316 for Sweden, U. K. and U. S.

Rows 2.1 and 2.2: Food and Agriculture Organization of the United Nations, *Per Caput Fibre Consumption Levels 1948/1958,* Commodity Bulletin No. 31, Rome, 1960.

Row 3: From Table 30–2.

Rows 4.1 and 4.2: From Tables 31–3 and 31–4.

Rows 5.1 and 5.2: U. N., *Compendium of Social Statistics: 1963,* Table 65, pp. 345–347.

Row 5.3: United Nations, *Statistical Yearbook 1962,* New York, 1963, Table 150, pp. 416–418.

Row 6: U. N., *Statistical Yearbook 1962,* Table 122, pp. 290–292.

Row 7.1 through 7.6: *Economic Survey of Asia and the Far East,* Bangkok, Vol. XI, No. 3, December, 1960; and Wilfred Owen, "The Transport Revolution," in J. Frederic Dewhurst and associates, *Europe's Needs and Resources,* Twentieth Century Fund, New York, 1961, esp. pp. 285–295.

[a] 1954–56. [b] Includes Singapore. [c] 1955–57.

[d] Unusually low; the remainder was almost entirely rayon tissue imports.

[e] 33 percent of all textile consumption constituted of imported artificial fibers, as against 3 percent in 1943–50, showing that the low cotton ratio is largely the consequence of the relatively unrestricted import policy pursued by Ceylon until recently.

[f] Government service only. For the Philippines 1961.

[g] For Malaya 1957; the Philippines and Thailand 1960; Pakistan, India, and Indonesia 1961; Burma and South Vietnam 1962; Ceylon 1963.

[h] The number of radio receivers in all U. S. possessions, not licenses.

[i] Excluding government vehicles in Thailand and U. K. The figure for Indonesia includes three-wheeled vehicles, military vehicles, ambulances, and hearses, all of which are excluded from the other countries.

differentials between income groups, social classes, and rural and urban areas exist also in developed countries, but the degree of inequality is far less than in South Asia. Few regions of the United States, for example, do not have electricity; most rural homes have radios, television sets, telephones, and all the mechanical conveniences associated with rural electrification and a high level of income per head.

Considering the quality differences and the uneven distribution, it is clear that the figures drawn together in Table 12–2, even if completely reliable, could not adequately convey how most of the people really fare with regard to these few items of consumption. Some of the series are particularly weak. Especially in the case of health and educational facilities, varying definitions among the countries and serious problems of enumeration render the data tenuous for any close inter-country comparisons. For the other items listed, the data should be better, since these, with the exception of non-rail transport, are mostly produced in large-scale, organized sectors, where the empirical evidence is generally more accurate. But the figures on energy consumption overstate the case, since most energy goes for production and is not available for household use.

As we proceed to examine in some detail these indicators of how people are living and what their consumption is it must be remembered that the information assembled in Table 12–2 is set forth primarily to point up the research task still to be done. In regard to health and educational facilities in particular, a more intensive analysis is provided in Part Seven, which examines problems of population quality.

4 *Consumption of Food*

About two-thirds or more of total private consumption expenditures in South Asia are devoted to food whereas in the developed economies the proportion is normally well below two-fifths.[1] Thus a very pertinent indi-

[1] For India, it has been estimated that almost 77 percent of the consumption expenditures of agricultural workers were for food in 1956–57. (International Labor Office, *Year Book of Labour Statistics, 1959,* Geneva, 1959, p. 437.) In Thailand the comparable figure for farm households in 1953 was 71 percent. (Food and Agriculture Organization, *State of Food and Agriculture 1959,* Rome, 1959, p. 187.)

If we include non-agricultural households the ratio drops somewhat, as would be expected in the light of the rural-urban income differential. For example, urban workers in Rangoon devoted approximately 66 percent of their consumption expenditures to food in 1958 (I.L.O., *Year Book of Labour Statistics, 1959,* p. 437), and the figure for the average spending unit in Ceylon for 1953 was 60 percent (Central Bank of Ceylon, Department of Economic Research, *Survey of Ceylon's Consumer Finances,* Colombo, 1954, Table 24); for wage earners in Djakarta, almost 60 percent in 1957; and for wage earners in Saigon in 1955, 63 percent (I.L.O., *Year Book of Labour Statistics, 1959,* p. 437).

The developed economies show much smaller ratios. In Sweden, all households devoted only some 32.6 percent of consumption expenditures to food in 1958 (Sweden, Official Statistics of, *The Consumption of Households in 1958,* Stockholm, 1961, pp.

cator of levels of living is provided by food consumption levels. Food consumption, in turn, is measured most appropriately by the average daily calorie intake per person. Table 12–2, row 1.1, gives such estimates for the South Asian countries in 1958. Ranging from 2,030 calories per head per day in Pakistan to 2,290 calories in the Federation of Malaya, the ranking of the national averages roughly corresponds to that of the incomes per head derived in Chapter 11 (Section 1). There are three important deviations, however: the nutritional position of rice-exporting Burma and Thailand appears to be better than their general economic situation would imply, while the opposite is true for Ceylon, which relies heavily on imported foodstuffs.

The accuracy of these estimates is hard to judge, but in all likelihood they lend an optimistic rather than a pessimistic bias to the prevailing food situation. This may be presumed, for example, from the underrating of population size in the calculations. And in fact, other available evidence points to somewhat lower nutritional levels. Thus the calorie supply estimates of the F.A.O. for 1957–59, given in Table 12–3, column 1, are lower than the U. S. Department of Agriculture estimates shown in Table 12–2, row 1.1, and considerably lower for two countries – for the Philippines by 275 calories and for India by 150 calories. Since the basic statistics are shaky in all the countries of the region, the estimates are frequently conflicting. The apparent small discrepancies in food supply among the various countries may therefore not be real at all. They may be much wider and the order of rank of the countries may differ substantially.

Food balance sheets, available for four of the countries – Pakistan, India, the Philippines, and Ceylon – are reproduced in Table 12–3.[1] Tenta-

18–20). In Canada, where food is comparatively cheap, the figure for urban wage earners in 1955 was only 28 percent (I.L.O., *Year Book of Labour Statistics, 1959,* p. 437).

[1] Aside from data inaccuracies, the estimates of calorie intake per person per day are broad averages and are based on a population that includes children and retired people, as well as working adults. Calorie requirements differ among these groups, and indeed vary in accordance with the kind of work performed. Furthermore, the figures on intake refer to daily averages over the course of a year. Yet during the busy seasons in agricultural regions, peasants and farm workers generally eat better than at other times. As Harry T. Oshima explains: "The employer traditionally supplies a mid-morning or mid-afternoon meal or both to the workers during the long hours of the peak seasons. In addition, because of the scarcity of workers, wage rates tend to rise in such periods." ("Underemployment in Backward Economies, An Empirical Comment," *Journal of Political Economy,* June, 1958, p. 262.) Thus nutritional levels tend to vary directly with the physical effort expended at different times of the year, a fact hidden by these averages. A rough recalculation by Oshima reduces significantly the gap between the required and actual intake of calories. As we note below, however, some of the factors mentioned are taken account of in the estimates given (i.e., the reference is to adults at body weights and at temperatures relevant to the region), and the extreme inequality of consumption would offset the effect of such upward recalculations as suggested by Oshima in the case of large numbers of people. But the general weaknesses of a daily average as an indicator should be acknowledged.

Table 12–3

CALORIE AND PROTEIN CONTENT OF POST-WAR FOOD SUPPLIES
(*Per head per day*)

	Calories				
			Percent accounted for by:		
Country and year	*Total* (*1*)	*Deficit of requirements* (*percent*) (*2*)	*Cereals* (*3*)	*Animal products* (*4*)	*Proteins* (*grams*) (*5*)
Pakistan					
1949–50	2,010	– 8.9	78	9	48
1951–53	2,000	–11.2	75	9	46
1954–56	1,990	–11.6	74	9	47
1957–59	1,980	–12.0	76	8	46
1960/61[a]	1,970	–12.4	78	8	45
India					
1949–50	1,630	–29.1	70	7	44
1951–53	1,700	–26.1	70	7	46
1954–56	1,840	–20.0	67	7	49
1957–59	1,900	–17.4	67	6	51
1960/61[a]	1,990	–13.5	68	6	53
Philippines					
1952/53[a]	1,790	–18.3	68	7	46
1957–59[a]	1,870	–15.0	67	10	47
1960[a]	1,950	–11.4	65	9	51
Ceylon					
1952–53	1,990	–13.1	58	4	43
1954–56	2,070	– 9.6	59	4	44
1957–59	2,030	–11.4	61	5	45
1961[a]	2,060	–10.0	60	4	44

Sources: U. N., *Statistical Yearbook 1962*, Table 128, pp. 330–332; U. N., *Compendium of Social Statistics: 1963*, Table 18, p. 163; and Food and Agriculture Organization, *Production Yearbook*, Vol. 16, 1962, Rome, Table 96B, pp. 251–252.

[a] Tentative data.

tive at best, they give some evidence that the average person in South Asia does not receive adequate nutrition. Estimated minimum calorie requirements are 2,200 to 2,300 and protein requirements about 65 grams per day per adult person at body weights and temperatures relevant to the region.[1] Tables 12–2 and 12–3 indicate calorie and protein intake below these figures for each of the countries. Thus, while calorie intake in the advanced countries significantly exceeds the requirements, in South Asia it falls short of minimum needs by at least 10 percent and probably by much more, with the possible exception of Malaya. The protein intake is even farther below needs. Moreover, because of the serious inequalities of consumption in the region, a substantial proportion of the population receives even less than these low averages. One writer has estimated, for example, that the family of a typical attached farm laborer in Uttar Pradesh in the mid-1940's ate only between 60 and 70 percent of the minimum required to maintain health.[2] He adds that "the proportion of those who have enough to eat is insignificant." Even in the urban areas, according to another report from Pakistan, "There is hardly 10 percent of the population which gets adequate food required for maintenance of good health. A large number of the remaining 90 percent are either semi-starved or ill-nourished."[3] Some 50 percent of Pakistani students examined medically were found to suffer from malnutrition or from deficiency diseases.[4] A 1950 survey found that among Bombay factory workers, who are probably better off than most Indians, the incidence of anemia, largely an iron-deficiency disease, was over 50 percent and animal protein intake was much too low.[5]

Although calorie and protein intake appears to be insufficient throughout South Asia, some improvement during the 1950's in India and the Philippines is indicated by the figures in the first column of Table 12–3.

[1] See, for example, U. S. Department of Agriculture, Foreign Agricultural Service, *The World Food Deficit, A First Approximation,* March, 1951, pp. 4–5, and U. N., *Economic Bulletin for Asia and the Far East,* Vol. VII, No. 1, May, 1956, p. 1.

A detailed discussion of the effects of age, weight, and outside temperature on calorie requirements is contained in F.A.O., *Calorie Requirements,* Report of the Committee on Calorie Requirements, Washington, June, 1950, p. 35, f.n. 1. Accordingly, the daily calorie requirements per head have recently been put at 2,250 in Pakistan, 2,300 in India, 2,200 in the Philippines, and 2,290 in Ceylon. These requirements are lower than in the advanced countries; for the European countries the estimated needs vary generally from 2,600 to 2,800 calories per head per day. (U. N., *Compendium of Social Statistics: 1963,* Table 18, pp. 163–164.)

[2] Mohinder Singh, *The Depressed Classes,* Hind Kitabs Ltd., Bombay, 1947, pp. 109–110.

[3] Pakistan, Government of, Ministry of Food and Agriculture, *Report of the Government of Pakistan to the Food and Agriculture Organization, 1955–57,* Karachi, May, 1959, p. 60.

[4] *Ibid.,* p. 62.

[5] Mello, Modi *et al.,* "Bombay Nutritional Survey," *Indian Journal of Medical Science,* Vol. 4, 1950, pp. 357–360.

Some of the Hindu depressed classes are reported to subsist largely on *gobraha,* grain picked from cowdung. See Singh, *Depressed Classes,* pp. 116–117, and Kusum Nair, *Blossoms in the Dust,* Duckworth & Co. Ltd., London, 1961, p. 82, f.n. 1.

Table 12–4

APPARENT CONSUMPTION OF CEREALS, 1934–38 AND 1955–57

Country	Period	*Production* (1)	*Gross exports* (2)	*Gross imports* (3)	*Apparent consumption* (4)	*Population (millions)* (5)	*Apparent consumption per head (kilograms)* (6)	*Domestic production as percent of consumption* (7)
			(million tons)					
Pakistan	1934–38	12.0	0.4	–	11.6	66.0	176	103
	1955–57	13.3	0.1	1.0	14.2	84.4	168	94
India	1934–38	48.0	0.6	2.2	49.6	304.3	163	97
	1955–57	57.9	0.1	2.0	59.8	392.4	152	97
Burma	1934–38	5.0	3.1	–	1.9	15.6	125	260
	1955–57	4.3	1.7	–	2.6	20.1	129	165
Indonesia	1934–38	6.2	0.1	0.4	6.5	67.4	96	95
	1955–57	9.9	–	0.7	10.6	85.1	125	93
Philippines	1934–38	2.0	–	0.1	2.1	15.4	136	95
	1955–57	3.2	–	0.4	3.6	22.7	159	89
Thailand	1934–38	3.1	1.4	–	1.7	14.5	116	180
	1955–57	5.1	1.4	–	3.7	21.1	175	138
Ceylon	1934–38	0.2	–	0.6	0.8	5.7	139	25
	1955–57	0.5	–	0.7	1.2	9.2	134	42
Malaya and	1934–38	0.4	0.2	0.8	1.0	4.9	198	40
Singapore	1955–57	0.5	0.1	0.8	1.2	7.7	163	42

Source: ECAFE, Economic Survey, 1959, p. 78, Table 30.

Pakistan and Ceylon showed little change over this period. In view of the weakness of the basic data, however, the evidence cannot be accepted as conclusive, though some stabilization may actually have taken place. Comparisons with pre-war times, equally inconclusive, suggest that by 1958 the calorie supply slightly surpassed the 1934–38 level in the Philippines and the Indian subcontinent but was about the same or a little lower elsewhere.[1] In the light of this evidence it is rather surprising to note from Table 12–4 that consumption of cereals per head apparently declined between 1934–38 and 1955–57 in India, Pakistan, Ceylon, and especially Malaya (including Singapore), but increased in the other countries. It cannot be assumed that the Indians and the Pakistanis turned increasingly to other types of foods: the high proportion of cereals in the diet, indicated in Table 12–3, column 3, does not support such an interpretation. Alternative estimates show a fairly substantial increase in cereal supplies (defined as production plus imports minus exports of cereals) per head of population between 1951/52–1953/54 and 1960/61–1962/63 for India and Indonesia; in the case of the other countries they show either relative stagnation or a slight decline.[2] There is little general consistency between these apparent trends and changes in the average daily calorie intake between the early 1950's and 1960 or 1961 as shown in Table 12–3. Indeed, the estimates purporting to show apparent consumption of cereals per head in kilograms in Table 12–4 differ widely from the figures derived by a similar method in the publication cited in the preceding footnote. It is difficult to determine which of these conflicting sets of evidence errs less. This means, of course, that for individual countries the trends in average cereal consumption are ambiguous, although the over-all impression of relative stagnation on an insufficient level appears to be grounded in fact.

Table 12–3 (columns 3 to 5) points up clearly at least one facet of the food situation in South Asia: the monotony of the diet. Cereals constitute more than 70 percent of the Pakistani calorie intake and about two-thirds of the Indian and Philippine, compared with less than one-quarter in the United States. Rice alone accounts for half of the calories consumed in Pakistan.[3] It has been estimated that in the Far East as a whole "staple

[1] If the calorie intake figures given in Food and Agriculture Organization, *Second World Food Survey* (Rome, 1952, p. 13) are taken as indicative of the pre-war (1934–38) food situation, the figures in Table 12–2 for 1958 imply the following changes in the interval, measured in calories:

Pakistan	+ 60	Philippines	+225
India	+ 80	Thailand	0
Indonesia	− 85	Ceylon	− 80
Burma	−200	Malaya	− 50

[2] See U. N., *Economic Survey for Asia and the Far East 1964*, Table II–5, p. 43.

[3] F.A.O., *Food Supply Time Series*, Rome, 1960.

cereals and starch roots comprise about 73 percent of the average diet."[1] This heavy reliance on one or a few crops not only fails to provide the needed balance of protective elements against disease[2] but leaves the consumer precariously vulnerable to crop failure due to adverse weather conditions or plant disease.

Concentration on cereals has gone so far that, despite the calorie deficit, the total production of cereals in India in 1957 was estimated to exceed the "balanced-diet" requirements of this particular type of foodstuff by about 6 percent.[3] Available supplies of pulses, fruits, milk, sugar, fish, meat, and eggs were reported to be substantially below requirements. Even if adults are assumed to require only 10 ounces of milk per day (as against the ideal 20 ounces), the actual availability of milk fell short of the needs by 55 percent according to the same report. Nevertheless, the milk consumption in India is rather high by South Asian standards, though this advantage is offset by reduced consumption of other animal foodstuffs.[4] Generally, calories of animal origin comprise but a very small proportion of the low total energy intake, ranging from 4–5 percent in Ceylon and 6–7 percent in India to 8–10 percent in Pakistan and the Philippines (Table 12–3). In the advanced countries the proportion varies from 35 to 50 percent of a considerably larger total calorie supply. Studies of the intake of minerals and vitamins in South Asia are few. However, the composition of the diets and the nutritional condition of school children and hospital patients indicate widespread inadequacies. The low consumption of meat products throughout South Asia leads to anemia due to iron deficiency. The shortage of calcium and phosphorus is also widespread, and in certain areas goiter is endemic owing to the lack of iodine. Deficiencies in all essential vitamins are, in varying degree, evident throughout the region. The diet is markedly lacking in vitamins A, the B complex, C, and D.[5]

[1] U. N., *Economic Survey of Asia and the Far East, 1960,* p. 12. The percentages for the United Kingdom and North America given in that report are 31 and 25 respectively, and they are still declining rapidly.

[2] *Ibid.;* and Douglas H. K. Lee, *Climate and Economic Development in the Tropics,* Harper, New York, 1957, p. 107.

[3] India, Government of, Ministry of Health, *Report of the Health Survey and Planning Committee,* Vol. I, New Delhi, 1961, p. 188.

[4] According to the estimates of pre-war consumption by F.A.O., milk products supplied an Indian with 156 calories a day, whereas they provided a Filipino with 68 calories per day and other South Asians with even less. However, because of the negligible consumption of meat, the Indian intake of animal proteins is below the South Asian average. In pre-war years, the net supplies of animal proteins were in Indonesia 4 grams a day, in undivided India 9 grams, in Ceylon 11 grams, while they were in Burma 32 grams and in the Philippines 25 grams. The total protein intake is more uniform; the range was from 43 grams a day (Indonesia) to 73 grams (Burma). (F.A.O., *World Food Survey,* p. 38.)

[5] Food and Agriculture Organization, *Report of the Nutrition Committee for South and East Asia, Third Mtg.,* Bandung, Indonesia, June 23–30, 1953, Rome, 1953, p. 19; and J. S. Simmons, T. F. Whayne, G. W. Anderson, H. M. Horack *et al., Global Epidemiology, A Geography of Disease and Sanitation,* Vol. I, J. B. Lippincott Co., Philadelphia, 1944, *passim.*

The monotony of the diet, which largely explains the above-mentioned deficiencies, is not caused by poverty alone, although poverty is the main reason why people take to one staple food – rice or, in the central and western parts of the Indian peninsula, some other cereal. Ignorance of the nutritional value of various foods and tastes that disregard nutritional considerations, together with poor methods of food preparation, also play a part. Thus the deficiency of vitamin A, which may affect vision and for which the paucity of green leafy vegetables in the diet is chiefly responsible, is not always most common in the lowest income group.[1] Deficiency of vitamin B, and consequent susceptibility to beriberi, has been on the increase since the Second World War, because people have turned more and more to the consumption of polished rice, which tastes better than home-husked rice, is easier to store, and saves them laborious pounding.[2] This malpractice is probably most serious in Burma and Thailand, where rice constitutes the main part of the diet; but the problem is by no means unknown elsewhere in the region.[3] Although Burma is a large food exporter, "Malnutrition and undernourishment do not spare the well-to-do – they are found among the children, women, urban laborers, peasants, clerical workers and other such groups at various economic levels."[4] This is hardly surprising when it is considered that – as one study suggests – 29 percent of the proteins, 64 percent of the iron, and 84 percent of the calcium and phosphorus are lost in milling.[5] Choice as well as availability also accounts for the low consumption of milk. As one study group observed: "Milk, unfortunately, is not relished, and even children get little

[1] F.A.O., *World Food Survey*, p. 19.

[2] It was noticed in Malaya during the depression of the early 1930's that the food situation was then better than in prosperous times, as the people, being less busy on the rubber plantations, cultivated more food plants and husked their rice at home. (Pierre Gourou, *The Tropical World*, Longmans, Green, London, 1954, p. 73.)

[3] There are many reports on the prevalence of the consumption of polished rice and its consequences. For example: "Highly polished rice, eaten with a curry sauce, is the mainstay of the Burmese daily fare. In the rice milling process most of the vitamin and mineral content is discarded with the bran. . . . Highly polished rice stores easily without danger of spoiling, . . . Most Burmese dislike the less polished and more nutritious product." (Human Relations Area Files, *Burma*, Vol. I, New Haven, 1950, p. 523.)

In Thailand, "Following the introduction of small rice mills and the inadequate intake of other protective foods . . . the incidence of beri-beri is increasing." (Thailand, Ministry of Agriculture, *Report of the Government of Thailand to FAO*, 1955–57, Bangkok, 1957, pp. 63–65.)

In the Philippines beriberi is said to be common in "the major rice-producing provinces where there is a monotonous intake of highly polished rice and a marked deficiency in vegetables and proteins." (Human Relations Area Files, *The Philippines*, Vol. III, New Haven, 1955, p. 1226.)

Likewise, in Malaya, "the bulk of the rice eaten . . . is 'polished' rice." (B. W. Hodder, *Man in Malaya*, University of London Press Ltd., London, 1959, p. 125.)

[4] Human Relations Area Files, *Burma*, p. 459, citing a Nutrition Survey by Dr. V. Maung.

[5] Hodder, *Man in Malaya*, p. 125. This study refers to husked rice imported into Malaya from Thailand, but its results probably apply elsewhere as well.

of it."[1] Religious taboos and traditions, too, play some part in the faulty diet, though their influence varies from country to country. Thus in Ceylon "meat is eaten only by the more affluent and those who have no dietary scruples against beef or pork or any once-living creature (strict Hindus and Buddhists cannot even eat eggs, which may be fertile)."[2] On top of all this, the nutritional value of food consumed is reduced, or the amount required is increased, by the presence of intestinal worms, which afflict a large proportion of the South Asian population.[3]

Another factor that tends to aggravate the food situation is the inadequacy of storage and transportation facilities. Although no statistical data are available, it is known that large quantities of cereals and other foodstuffs go to waste because they are spoiled by heat and humidity or are eaten by birds, rodents, or insects before they can be transported to community centers. What such losses imply for the consumption figures quoted is uncertain. Some seasonal concentration of consumption occurs of necessity – perishables such as meat and milk products have to be consumed immediately – but concentration of consumption is due as well to ceremonial feasts and to lack of foresight. The months before harvest are usually the leanest, and undernourished workers cannot perform their harvesting tasks with optimal efficiency. Here again is evidence of the vicious circle of poverty: lack of an adequate diet reduces worker productivity both through excessive absenteeism, due to illness, and reduced energy when on the job; but the low productivity is in turn a key "cause" of poverty and thus of malnutrition.

By force of circumstance or custom, certain population groups – infants and growing children, expectant and nursing mothers – seem to be particularly vulnerable to malnutrition in South Asia. Although women are generally provided somewhat better food during pregnancy,[4] their diet is far from satisfactory, and custom sometimes demands that they abstain from foods considered "hot" – for example, meat, certain pulses and fruits, and spices.[5] It is not surprising, therefore, that anemia is one of the most

[1] *Report of the FAO Mission for Siam,* p. 9.

[2] John Tressider, *Ceylon, An Introduction to the "Resplendent Land,"* Asia Library, D. Van Nostrand Co., Princeton, 1960, p. 55.

[3] W. Burridge, *Climate and Labour,* Kitabistan, Allahabad, 1944, p. 54.

[4] This is sometimes contradicted, however. The United Nations' *Economic Survey of Asia and the Far East, 1965* (Bangkok, 1966, p. 73) points out that "the prevalence of the patriarchal system gives to the adult male – even in the consumption of food – a place of priority," and also that in several South Asian countries "expectant mothers [starve] themselves because they fear that an abundant growth of the fetus (contributed to by a rich diet) may result in a difficult birth." Cf. Jacques M. May, *The Ecology of Mal-nutrition in the Far and Near East,* Harper, New York, 1961, *passim.*

[5] Oscar Lewis, *Village Life in Northern India,* University of Illinois Press, Urbana, 1958, p. 47; N. D. Wijesekera, *The People of Ceylon,* M. D. Gunasena & Co. Ltd., Colombo, 1949, p. 69; UNESCO, *Cultural Patterns and Technical Change,* Margaret Mead, ed., Paris, 1953, p. 58.

important causes of maternal mortality in South Asia.[1] The inadequate nutrition of the mother also affects the development of the fetus; hence, babies are small and weak at birth and have poor chance of survival. However, malnutrition seems to have the most adverse effect on children in the weaning and post-weaning ages (from 9 to 36 months); they are generally fed on rice gruel and are not given foods containing sufficient protein for proper nutrition.[2]

In summary, it is probably safe to say that the average person in South Asia simply does not get enough to eat. Even where food intake is above the starvation level, it is generally inadequate in nutritional content to provide minimal safeguards to health. Above all, there has been no substantial general improvement in diets since the late 1930's. When the inequalities in the region are taken into account, the situation appears even worse than the broad averages would lead one to suppose. The health aspect of nutritional deficiencies will be taken up in Chapter 30 (Section 11 *et passim*).

5 *Textile Consumption, Housing and Sanitation*

It is impossible to obtain satisfactory empirical data on the adequacy of clothing that would permit reasonable comparisons between countries in South Asia or between them and other parts of the world. Figures on textile consumption per head are frequently cited, but they cannot portray the quality of clothing, its comfort and durability, especially where different climates and customs are concerned. Such figures are very unreliable in any case because of the notorious deficiency of statistics relating to that large part of clothing and textile production which in underdeveloped countries takes place outside of large-scale factories.

Estimates of textile consumption per head are given in Table 12–2, row 2.1, and the share of cotton textiles in row 2.2. The relatively high figures for India and Pakistan reflect, of course, the large domestic textile industries in these countries and the cheapness of cotton goods. The comparisons with more highly developed economies indicate the general poverty of South Asia in terms of textiles – and probably understate it as there is no adjustment for quality. Some of this discrepancy is due to climatic differences, but the greater part is symptomatic of the low levels of productivity in South Asia. Even Italy and Portugal have substantially greater textile consumption and less concentration in cotton goods. The monotony observed in the South Asian diet carries over into clothing.

[1] P. K. Wattal, *Population Problem in India*, Minerva Book Shop, New Delhi, 1958, p. 81.

[2] F.A.O., *Report of the Nutrition Committee for South and East Asia, Third Mtg.*, p. 9.

Moreover, the poorer classes do not consume anywhere near the national average. Large numbers of South Asians have only one set of clothing, which is seldom washed, except in bathing. Typically the same clothes are worn day and night since pyjamas and even underwear are luxuries a great many people can ill afford. The hygienic consequences are easy to imagine. Few people, especially in the poorer classes, have shoes or even sandals. Children up to the age of seven or so often wear practically nothing when at home; beyond this age many wear only a piece of cloth covering the hips and thighs. Women generally have more and better clothing than men, except for the very poorest women who often have to be content with one *lungi,* covering the body from the waist to the knees.

While clothing is in general probably better suited to the climatic conditions and needs than is food, there are many millions in South Asia whose raiment is well below minimum standards of health. Nor should it be forgotten that large sections in northern India and Pakistan have cold seasons with quite low night temperatures, as do some regions at higher altitudes in other South Asian countries. Those people fortunate enough to possess blankets must often use them to protect their cattle against the cold. Figures of textile consumption per head tell nothing about everyday realities such as these.

When we turn to housing and sanitation we are obliged to rely even more on illustrative and impressionistic information than was the case for food and clothing. There are virtually no comprehensive statistics in this field. It is possible, however, to make three broad generalizations with respect to shelter in South Asia. First, the majority of the people live in poorly built, overcrowded, unsanitary, and scantily furnished homes lacking nearly all amenities. Indeed, next to food, poor housing is the most obvious component of the low levels of living. Secondly, there are important geographical variations in the adequacy of housing. The housing situation is least desperate in those rural areas where lumber is available, mainly in Southeast Asia and to some extent in the hilly regions in India and Ceylon. It is most wretched in the urban slums. Finally, average housing conditions tend to be correlated with national economic levels, being somewhat better in the less poor countries.

The typical house in most rural areas of Southeast Asia is made of wood or bamboo, has a thatched roof, and is often built on piles, 4 to 6 feet high.[1] Thus the living space, most often from one to three small rooms, is safe from the dampness of the ground and from animals and reptiles, and fresh air circulates freely from beneath. But when dirty water spills down

[1] Hodder, *Man in Malaya,* p. 60; Robert A. Polson and Agaton P. Pal, *The Status of Rural Life in the Dumaguete City Trade Area, Philippines 1952,* Cornell University, Ithaca, June, 1956, mimeographed, p. 27; United Nations Social Services Mission to Burma, *Social Services in Burma,* New York, October 1, 1950, p. 22.

through the flooring the ground becomes slushy, a breeding place for mosquitoes. As animals are often tethered under the house, animal dung and urine create a further nuisance. The unsanitary atmosphere is mitigated only by the smoke fires lit to keep mosquitoes away and by a strong sun. Aside from the space underneath, which may be used also for storage or for a workshop, most of these houses lack a separate room for washing or for the preparation of food.

In central India and West Pakistan,[1] where the climate is arid, over two-thirds of the dwellings are of mud, which is easily eroded and far from waterproof. The earth roof, though quite cool when it can be erected over timber battens and joists, is flat, and often lets through the water that collects on it. There is often only a single room,[2] perhaps with a front veranda and a curtained-off kitchen and stove.

Where the climate is too humid to allow mud to remain dry for long, as it is in East Pakistan and parts of southern and northern India, dwellings are often built of bamboo. In Assam, in northeastern India, for example, some two-thirds of the dwellings are largely or wholly of bamboo. Bamboo is frequently used for roofing, alternately or in combination with grass, reeds, leaves, bark or cocoanut shells. These materials, though cooler and cleaner than mud, usually last only three years unless specially treated. Moreover, bamboo is attractive to ants and borer beetles, subject to fire risk, and receptive to fungus infestation. There are some timber dwellings in East Pakistan and Assam, but not often for poor people. About 14 percent of Burma's homes are of timber, and many more combine timber with bamboo. Ceylon, faced with overcrowding, is turning increasingly to its natural timber resources, for the development of which there seems to be considerable scope in the country.

If housing in rural areas must be judged inadequate in varying degrees, there is little such variation in the extent of squalor in the slum areas of large cities. The situation has worsened in the last decade of rapid urban growth.[3] Today the bulk of the urban population lives in dwellings far more crowded and inadequately ventilated, and usually with poorer sanitation facilities, than those in rural areas. It has been conservatively estimated that from one-quarter to one-half of all city dwellers live in slums or makeshift arrangements.[4] The "houses" themselves are often little

[1] United Nations, ECAFE, *Survey of Housing and Building Materials in Asia and the Far East, 1956,* Bangkok, 1956, pp. 31, 89.

[2] "The houses [in Madhya Pradesh] were generally built of mud. . . . The floor and the walls were smeared with cowdung. The house of an agricultural labour family generally had one room, one verandah and a shed for cattle." (India, Government of, Ministry of Labour, *Agricultural Labour Enquiry,* Vol. VI (Central India), Delhi, 1955, p. 27.)

[3] Chapter 10, Section 11.

[4] United Nations, Department of Economic and Social Affairs, *1963 Report on the World Social Situation,* New York, 1963, p. 171.

more than shacks or hovels, thrown together from cast-off materials. Large numbers of people do not possess even these miserable shelters and regularly spend the night under monuments and bridges or in the open on the streets.[1] Smoke from cowdung fuel fills the air, as there are generally no chimneys from the primitive stoves used in preparing food. Eyes are constantly sore and smarting, throats irritated, and lungs affected. Potters, soap-makers, smiths, bakers, tanners carry out their menial trades in and about their homes.[2] Although such conditions are not conducive to anyone's health, the risks seem to be greatest for infants.[3]

Even industrial workers suffer from unhealthy housing conditions.[4] In the hovels set up for migrant laborers, who are obliged to leave their families behind in their village homes and for whom housing conditions are the very worst, there may be forty to fifty men living, with one or two women, in a room licensed for less than a quarter of that number, as a Royal Commission found in Rangoon in 1931.[5] The tenement *chawls* of Bombay offer a similarly miserable existence:

> There are rooms so dark that even during the day inmates cannot see each other in passages, or in the single living rooms, without the help of a light or fire. Fresh air is completely lacking. Very often there is no passage of air from room to room, many of which are built back to back. . . . The single room serves as a living room, bed-room, sick-room, kitchen, dining room, etc., and to add to this the number of persons living in a single room ranges from 4 to 10.[6]

In India, not less than 95 percent of the houses occupied by industrial laborers are estimated to be unsatisfactory for healthful habitation.[7] In Malaya, which has the highest national income per head in the region, "Over 50% of the urban population . . . live in shophouses, the rooms of which are commonly divided into one-family cubicles, leading to very high floor-space densities and producing units of accommodation in

[1] UNESCO, *The Social Implications of Industrialization and Urbanization, Five Studies in Asia,* Calcutta, 1956, pp. 62 and 186; and United Nations, *Report on the World Social Situation* (prepared by Bureau of Social Affairs, UN Secretariat, in co-operation with ILO, FAO, UNESCO, WHO), New York, 1957, p. 132.

[2] Bharat Sevak Samaj, *Slums of Old Delhi,* Atma Ram & Sons, Delhi, 1958, p. 32.

[3] For example, in Bombay City in 1925, infant mortality per 1,000 births was 503 for babies born to families living in single-room tenements. For two-room tenements the figure was 242, and for tenements of four or more rooms, 157. (Vera Anstey, *The Economic Development of India,* 4th ed., Longmans, Green, London, 1957, p. 582.)

[4] Chapter 23, Section 3.

[5] J. S. Furnivall, *Colonial Policy and Practice, A Comparative Study of Burma and Netherlands India,* Cambridge University Press, London, 1957, p. 149.

[6] V. B. Singh, "Housing for Industrial Workers," in V. B. Singh and A. K. Saran, eds., *Industrial Labour in India,* Asia Publishing House, London, 1960, p. 320.

[7] J. S. Simmons *et al., Global Epidemiology,* p. 115. Although the statement refers to pre-war times, the situation has not changed for the better despite some efforts to clear slums. For a more recent assessment see UNESCO, *Social Implications of Industrialization,* p. iv.

which there is often no direct access to light or fresh air."[1] There are, of course, examples of good housing in South Asia. But the decent homes of some industrial workers in Kerala[2] and the mansions of the wealthy stand out as isolated phenomena, only accentuating the mass poverty. Especially in the cities, the vast gulf separating the few rich from the innumerable poor is nowhere more apparent than in the utterly different housing accommodations for each, often in close proximity.

The effects of overcrowded dwellings are aggravated by the congestion typical of human settlement in South Asia. Even villages of less than 500 inhabitants, which comprise about 68 percent of all villages in India,[3] are mostly compact clusters, while the cities with their shanty towns are teeming mazes that have grown without plan and without provision for open spaces, adequate traffic routes, water pipes or other sanitary facilities.[4] A recent ECAFE survey concludes:

> Under the thrust of rapid population growth, the housing situation in most Asian countries is assuming the proportions of a first-rate crisis. The overcrowding of city slums and the mushroom growth of shanty towns on urban fringes is proceeding virtually unchecked, and the construction of new housing and urban facilities is insufficient to have any appreciable improving effect. Although less obvious to the casual observer, housing conditions in the villages and rural areas are still worse, if only because they affect the greatest numbers of people and do not provide even the minimal amenities of city life. Whether urban or rural, such conditions tend to undermine both public health and public morale, which in turn are powerful determinants of economic development.[5]

Some attempts have been made to alleviate slum conditions in both urban and rural areas, but as with so much else in South Asia the rate of achievement has fallen steadily behind the rising needs, leading the survey to state that "the general housing situation seems bound to become even worse than it is at present." Investment in residential construction generally amounts to between 15 and 25 per cent of gross investment, but it "mainly represents private buildings in the cities, often of a luxury nature."[6]

Related to the housing problem is the problem of sanitation. Again the deficiencies are tremendous and improvement slow. This is particularly obvious in the case of water and sewerage facilities. In rural areas, the

[1] Hodder, *Man in Malaya,* p. 123.

[2] Nair, *Blossoms in the Dust,* Chapter II.

[3] India, Government of, Ministry of Health, *Report of the Health Survey and Planning Committee* (August 1959–October 1961), New Delhi, p. 144.

[4] Samaj, *Slums of Old Delhi,* p. 7.

[5] U. N., ECAFE, "Review of the Social Situation in the ECAFE Region," *Economic Bulletin for Asia and the Far East,* Vol. XVI, No. 1, June 1965, p. 37.

[6] *Ibid.,* p. 38.

shallow wells are usually open and may be merely holes dug in the ground. They may run dry in the dry season, but at other times are surrounded and polluted by puddles of stagnant water.[1] Very little is done to clean them and other water sources, or to use disinfectants.[2] On the contrary, each villager as he draws water in his bucket helps spread disease from house to house. Drinking water is seldom boiled, though drawn from the same wells and tanks used for watering animals and for washing clothes and bodies. Rivers, streams, and canals serve these household purposes while serving also for transport and carrying away wastes. As most villages and even many urban areas lack sewerage, refuse is thrown into lanes and backyards, where flies breed unhampered, and is washed into water sources by the rains.[3]

The greatest problem of all is perhaps the disposal of human waste. In rural districts throughout South Asia, it is common practice to defecate in fields, bushes, or jungle areas near human habitation. In consequence people walking barefoot are daily exposed to hookworm; the wind-blown fecal dust makes eyes sore; and when it rains the parasites that thrive in human waste are washed into streams, wells, and tanks. Where there are latrines, they are usually poorly constructed and unclean.[4] In many cities, especially in the slums, sanitary provisions are hardly better and may be worse. For example, a government-sponsored survey depicts the conditions in Old Delhi as follows:

> On the basis of the number of families using them [the latrines] we arrive at an estimated average of 4 families per one latrine. This, however, is to grossly understate the lack of this facility because those particularly of the dry variety are latrines only in name. In most cases there is no proper shelter over them and they hardly provide any privacy. This situation is the most keenly felt among the slum dwellers. It places their women-folk in an impossible position; they cannot think of easing themselves during the day . . . what makes the situation much worse is the lack of urinals which can be used by them during the day. . . . It may be added that the high proportion of the dry variety among the existing latrines is accounted for by absence of proper sewer connection.[5]

Where latrines are dry, scavenging has to be done manually. The scavengers, who are of the lowest caste, tend to perform their job indifferently

[1] M. S. Randhawa, "Health and Sanitation Problems," in M. S. Randhawa, ed., *Developing Village India,* Orient Longmans Ltd., Bombay, 1951, p. 237.

[2] D. N. Majumdar, *Caste and Communication in an Indian Village,* Asia Publishing House, Bombay, 1958, p. 322.

[3] N. D. Wijesekera, *The People of Ceylon,* M. D. Gunasena & Co. Ltd., Colombo, 1949, p. 54.

[4] Fraser Brockington, *World Health,* Penguin Books Ltd., Harmondsworth, Middlesex, 1958, p. 74; Randhawa, "Health and Sanitation Problems," in *Developing Village India,* p. 238; Simmons *et al., Global Epidemiology,* pp. 3, 108–109 *et passim.*

[5] Samaj, *Slums of Old Delhi,* p. 30.

and their carelessness accentuates health hazards. Such sewers as exist are often clogged with trash. Most are only open drains, which both spread germs and give off obnoxious odors.[1] Efforts to improve sanitation have not often been successful; constructed latrines, for instance, are not used. And because of public indifference, improvements are not maintained. In some areas there has been a one-sided expansion of water supply, with deleterious effects on drainage, as sewerage schemes have seemed to the local governing bodies less remunerative.[2]

According to a recent estimate, roughly 6 percent of the total population of India has a protected water supply while only 3 percent has a sewerage system.[3] About one-tenth of the Indian municipalities are estimated to have adequately protected water supplies and about one-fourth inadequate supplies, whereas two-thirds of urban areas have no protected water supply at all. In the rural areas the situation is worse.[4] In Ceylon, there seems to be a better supply of protected water, but even there only one in three houses has a sanitary latrine accommodation.[5] In the Philippines, protected water supply systems serve a third of the population, whereas in Burma only a few of the major towns have adequate piped water. Provisions in Indonesia, Pakistan, Thailand, and South Vietnam appear to be equally unsatisfactory. In the absence of a safe water supply and proper sewage disposal, it is no wonder that South Asia abounds in diseases spread by inadequate sanitation.

Health problems related to deficiencies in the consumption of food, textiles, housing, and sanitation will be discussed further in Chapter 30 (Section 11).

6 *Other Important Components of Consumption*

While levels of consumption of the items we have so far dealt with have been generally stable or declining, levels of consumption of the items enumerated in rows 4 to 7 in Table 12–2 have generally been rising. However, we must again remind the reader of the great inadequacy of such data for the South Asian countries, particularly where inter-country comparisons are concerned.

Health facilities will be discussed in Chapter 30 (Sections 4–10); in Table 12–2, row 3, they are represented by the number of physicians

[1] "How Clean Are Our Cities?", *Link,* July 9, 1961.

[2] India, *Report of the Health Survey and Planning Committee,* pp. 153, 155, 160.

[3] *Ibid.,* p. 152.

[4] *Ibid.,* p. 154.

[5] World Health Organization, *First Report on the World Health Situation 1954–1956* (Official Records of the World Health Organization, No. 94), Geneva, May, 1959, p. 220.

around 1960. In the fuller treatment in Chapter 30 we shall note the evolution of health facilities from the colonial era till more recent years, as well as the plans and prospects for future development. In the present context only a few general observations are in order. Not only are physicians and health facilities typically scarcer in the South Asian countries than in the developed countries, but the quality of the services available is substantially lower. In all the South Asian countries, though to differing degrees, doctors, auxiliary health personnel, and hospitals are concentrated in the cities and serve mainly the more wealthy inhabitants. There has been an increase in public health centers and clinics of various types to meet the needs of the masses, but, aside from the successful campaigns against malaria and a few other contagious diseases, most people, particularly in rural areas, receive little protection against, or treatment of, preventable or curable diseases. Differences among countries in the availability of health facilities are rather closely correlated with differences in economic levels. Ceylon, though not the richest country, ranks highest in health facilities, but is closely followed by Malaya and the Philippines.

Educational facilities will be analyzed in Chapters 32 and 33. In Table 12–2 consumption of this important component of living levels is shown primarily by literacy rates and secondarily by percentages of children receiving elementary schooling. Weaknesses of the statistics on literacy are discussed in Chapter 32 (Section 4). For now, suffice it to say that the literacy rates, by sex, presented in row 4.1 should be regarded with skepticism; in particular, the figures for India and Burma are probably too high. A more general observation concerns the different meaning of literacy in South Asia and in the Western countries. In the West, the ability to read is ordinarily acquired at an early age and is strengthened by subsequent schooling and utilization, so that it is functional; but in South Asia literacy for most people is to a large extent marginal. The figures in row 4.1 indicate that complete illiteracy is much more common in South Asia than in the West. Within the South Asian region the literacy rate is generally correlated with economic conditions; however, the Buddhist countries have a higher rate of literacy than their economic circumstances would suggest. As our analysis in Chapter 32 will show, literacy is invariably higher in urban than in rural areas. It is considerably lower among women than men, particularly in the poorer countries and in rural areas.

Discussions of the advance in schooling usually rest on statistics relating enrollment to the total population. As will be shown in Chapter 33 (Section 2), these statistics are grossly misleading because many enrolled children do not attend school, and still more do not finish primary school, which is a necessary condition for attaining any degree of literacy. Also, the age distribution of the population is markedly different in South Asia than in the West. In row 4.2, therefore, we present our estimates of the number of children in the relevant cohort of children, who actually finish primary school; these estimates are exceedingly uncertain, but they are superior to the enrollment figures usually quoted. As is shown in Chapter 33 (Sections 3 and 7), the quality of elementary education is much lower in South Asia than in the West. Within the region there is a rough correlation between the percentage of children completing primary school and the economic levels of the several countries, while within the individual countries that percentage is higher in urban than in rural areas and higher for boys than for girls. The quality of schooling as well as attendance rates for rural areas and for girls tend to be lower in the poorer countries. Generally speaking, the school system is a less effective instrument for equalization in the poorer countries. (Chapter 33, Section 7).

Formal schooling is, of course, not the only means of acquiring and retaining functional literacy, and in Chapter 32 (Section 4) we shall discuss adult education and the utilization of information media. Adult education is generally neglected in South Asia, though less so in Indonesia and the Philippines than elsewhere in the region. Here, where we are interested in indicators of levels of living, we restrict ourselves to presenting the available statistics on newsprint consumption, radio receivers, and telephones. We have already commented on the quality and regional differentials that make aggregation in such instances a dubious process (Section 3), but taking the averages as they stand, Table 12–2 shows that newsprint consumption per head (row 5.1) is extremely low compared with the West. The higher levels of education and literacy in the Philippines, Thailand, and Ceylon are manifest in newsprint consumption, per head of population, between four and ten times that in India, Pakistan, and Indonesia. The very small number of radios and telephones per head (rows 5.2 and 5.3) compared with the West is to be expected in view of the frequent absence of rural electrification. The incidence of such amenities is closely related to income levels; within the region, the wealthier countries, Malaya, Ceylon, and the Philippines, rank substantially above the poorer countries, especially Pakistan, India, and Burma. The number of radios and telephones per unit of population has risen fairly sharply since about 1955, but less under the stimulus of economic growth than of urban concentration. The failure of newsprint consumption to rise much in relation to population may be attributed in part to the slow growth of literacy and education, even in cities. Too much should not be read into the trends in these items, however, for they have as yet little importance in the South Asian economies.

The statistics on energy consumption are particularly defective for our present purpose. Aside from the difficulties of obtaining adequate basic data on production of energy-producing materials there are serious problems in making comparisons among the materials. Sources of energy are usually compared on the basis of "the heat energy which can be obtained from them under ideal conditions."[1] Although various conversion factors are used, details on varying qualities or types of, say, coal currently produced are generally not available in South Asia, so that the conversion factors themselves fail to mirror divergences in quality of the energy-producing materials.

Furthermore, the figures on energy refer to primary energy (coal, coke, waterpower, mineral oils, etc.) and say nothing about secondary energy, the power and heat derived from animal and vegetable waste. The latter is the kind of energy typically consumed by the great majority of South Asians. In India, for example, the contribution of cowdung to total energy consumption has been variously estimated as between 32 and 77 percent.[2] Generally, the relative contribution of farm wastes has remained remarkably high and stable in the underdeveloped countries whereas in the industrialized economies the proportion of secondary energy is now negligible. Thus the figures in row 6 of our table omit the more relevant aspects of energy consumption. In addition, a very small proportion of the energy produced from primary sources is consumed by households. An estimate for India lists "domestic" use as less than 10 percent for every year between 1950 and 1954, and use by agriculture as below 3 percent.[3] Total consumption of primary energy rose for every South Asian country between 1955 and 1959. The India study just cited indicated a slight percentage rise in household use from 1950 through 1954 (from 8.76 to 9.80 percent), but the data are so rough that no upward trend should be imputed from so small a change. As with the other indicators shown in Table 12–2, the averages hide great inequality. There is, as we noted, little rural electrification in South Asia; indeed, by far the greater proportion of electricity is available only within the larger urban centers. It has been estimated that toward the middle of the 1950's Bombay and Calcutta alone consumed about 40 percent of the total power produced in India;[4] insofar as they used this for consumption it can be assumed that much, perhaps most, went to the top strata, partly for the luxury consumption of refrigeration. In countries where 80 percent of the population lives in rural areas a distribution such as this means extreme inequality of power consumption. As a result, those in the countryside are forced to rely mainly on secondary

[1] United Nations, Statistical Office of the United Nations, *World Energy Supplies 1955–1958,* Statistical Papers, Series J, No. 3, New York, 1960, p. vi.

[2] National Council of Applied Economic Research, *Utilization of Primary Energy in India,* Occasional Papers No. 3, Asia Publishing House, New Delhi, 1958, p. 67.

[3] *Ibid.,* Table 22, p. 58.

[4] A. B. Das and M. N. Chatterji, *An Introduction to Indian Economics,* Bookland Ltd., Calcutta, 1955, p. 15.

fuel and power sources. Except for a few weak oil lamps, most of the villages are completely dark after sunset. Even if the literacy rate were far higher and newspapers or books were available in rural communities, the inadequate lighting would preclude much reading, and this fact, of course, stands in the way of raising standards of literacy and expanding the availability of printed matter. The familiar mechanism of cumulative causation is once again apparent.

Two crude and partial measures of transport availability are included in Table 12–2: number of motor vehicles per 10,000 population (row 7.1) and length of railways on the same basis (row 7.6). Not only are the figures of questionable relevance, because of the varying quality of rail lines and the wide range of what may be termed a "motor vehicle," but they provide a very incomplete picture of transport availability since they neglect roads, canals, port facilities, and units of equipment such as boxcars, locomotives, ships, and bicycles. Except for railway statistics, basic data are not available for most forms of transport. For inland and coastal shipping and transportation by bicycle, draft animal, and small boat, accurate information is almost completely lacking. Yet these are very important forms of transport in South Asia. Indeed, in India, where roads are very poor, bullock carts may still be carrying more freight than railways.[1]

[1] India has "barely 9.7 miles of all-weather roads for every hundred square miles. The condition of the roads, with minor exceptions, is execrable." (E. S. Rao, *Surveys of Indian Industries*, p. 103.)

As recently as 1955 it was estimated that India possessed "about 9 million bullock carts . . . carrying over a hundred million tons of goods and a large number of passengers." (Das and Chatterji, *An Introduction to Indian Economics*, p. 300.) Official estimates of freight originating on the Indian railways give 95 million tons in 1951–52 and 109 million tons in 1955–56. (India, Government of, *India Pocket Book of Economic Information*, New Delhi, 1961, Table 10.2, p. 66.)

Some details of bullock cart operations in five areas are given in a 1963 publication (India, Government of, Programme Evaluation Organisation, Planning Commission, *Case Studies of the Role of Bullock Carts and Trucks in Rural Transport*, 1963). Unfortunately, the information covers a tiny fraction of the territory of India. So far as it goes, it indicates a trend toward substitution of truck transport for bullock carts, but at a very uneven rate from case to case, as the road network was expanded in the decade of the 1950's. The study concludes that "the cart continues to occupy an indispensable place in the rural economy. . . . A major shift in the use of [motor] trucks can only come after . . . changes in the unit of farming and marketing take place" (p. 142). It is therefore anticipated that the bullock cart will continue to play an important role in Indian villages for a long time to come.

There is furthermore a certain nostalgia regarding the bullock cart. Thus one writer says:

"I cannot imagine an India without bullocks and carts. Through centuries of conquest, opulence, famine and strife it was the unobtrusive bullock that made agriculture, transport and life possible. Even today no countryside landscape would be complete without the bullock cart, and it is still what moves our rural economy.

"Few people know how many thousand miles of cartway are listed in official statistics, but it is safe to double this mileage without exaggeration, for like the jeep the

The few comparisons with Western countries presented in Table 12–2 show much greater disparity between number of motor vehicles than between length of rail lines per head. This, of course, reflects the high cost of motor roads compared with other forms of right of way. Roads are poor in all the South Asian countries, though generally not as bad as in India. The Philippines are unusual in relying more on road than on rail transport. Indonesia and South Vietnam have very low rail line averages, but principally because of their superior endowment with waterways. Thus, while their proportionate use of railroads in terms of ton-kilometers is very low, their reliance on water transport is substantial – over 57 percent for Indonesia and 74 percent for South Vietnam. In general, passenger and ton-kilometers of traffic are more informative than data on the facilities available, even though they ignore differences in quality of service and have other serious weaknesses.[1] Here the high ton-kilometer figure for India and the large proportion generated by railroads reflects the preoccupation with heavy industry, so noteworthy in India's developmental program, and the large pre-war railway investments. At least since 1948, traffic has increased in all countries at a much faster rate than national income. Annual rates of increase in road and rail ton-kilometers have ranged from a low of 6 percent in Pakistan to a high of almost 20 percent in Thailand. In every country, the share of motorized road ton-kilometers in the total traffic volume has risen relative to rail transport, a pattern familiar in the West. By 1957 the share of road transport had assumed large proportions in South Vietnam and in the Philippines and Ceylon (over 70 percent), but remained very small in India and Pakistan (under 6 percent of the total for rail, road, and water).[2] The percentage increases in total traffic and in motor transport, where high, are mainly due to the low levels for the base years, and they cannot be presumed to have had, as yet, a significant impact on the bulk of the population in agriculture. Yet the continued rise in goods and passenger transport and the rapid in-

---

bullock cart is independent of roads. Many of the paths it takes are just a pair of parallel, hardly visible wheel tracks in the scrub, and often it leaves the earth-blazed trail altogether and goes cross-country, especially in sandy places." (M. Krishnan, *Jungle and Backyard*, India, Government of, Publications Division, Ministry of Information and Broadcasting, Delhi–6, Job Press Private Limited, Kanpur, June, 1961, pp. 93–94.)

Just as the small units of production and marketing retard the use of motor trucks, the inadequacy of roads forces reliance upon what would otherwise be a most inefficient transport technique. See V. V. Ramanadham, *Economy of Andhra Pradesh*, Asia Publishing House, Bombay, 1959, pp. 172–182, for details of the extent of the road system in one state and the economic consequences of its serious inadequacy. Some 88 percent of the roads in Andhra Pradesh are designated by this writer as "bad" (p. 180).

[1] See, for example, George W. Wilson, *Essays on Some Unsettled Questions in the Economics of Transportation*, Bureau of Business Research, Indiana University, Bloomington, 1962, Chaps. 2 and 3.

[2] United Nations, ECAFE, *Economic Bulletin for Asia and the Far East*, December, 1960, Tables 1 and 2.

creases in capacity are indispensable conditions for economic progress, not only by widening the market but by breaking down regional isolation as well. One difficulty, of course, is the heavy concentration of transport facilities in urbanized areas. Until the vast rural areas are brought within the network of improved transportation, regional inequalities will widen and backwash effects will help perpetuate rural poverty. Industry will then continue to be of an enclave character even though under control of indigenous personnel.[1]

7 *Over-all Income Distribution*

Because the notion of an average consumption level in any of the South Asian countries hides tremendous inequalities, we must attempt to obtain some estimation of the extent of these inequalities besides the impressionistic evidence already indicated with reference to particular items of consumption. In the present section we shall examine the over-all income distribution in order to place in better perspective the figures on national income per head presented in Chapter 11 and to obtain further insights into levels of living. In Section 8 we shall look at examples of specific income inequalities.

In Section 2 we assembled some estimates of savings ratios in the South Asian countries. Ideally, of course, savings should be subtracted from income in order to measure consumption. However, even when conceptual and logical problems are set aside, the data on savings were found to be so weak and, in many cases, inconsistent that we suggested consumption be construed simply in terms of income per head – provided it is remembered that the level of consumption is then overstated by the amount of income "saved." On the average, savings in South Asia are relatively small. When we now take up the question of inequality in levels of consumption, the failure to consider savings, indeed the inability to do so, makes more difference, since the savings ratio tends to be positively related to levels of income – at least under the definition of consumption we have used, which includes productive consumption, and at least beyond the lowest income brackets where savings scarcely exist.[2] This means that income is somewhat less evenly distributed than consumption expenditures are.

[1] Chapter 24, Section 3 *et passim*.

Further details on the development of transport within South Asia can be found in U. N., *Economic Bulletin for Asia and the Far East,* December, 1960. This entire issue is devoted to analysis of transportation. See also U. N., *Economic Survey of Asia and the Far East, 1961,* pp. 138–143. For a broad discussion of transport and underdevelopment see Wilfred Owen, *Strategy for Mobility,* Brookings Institution, Washington, D. C., 1964.

[2] See Rasaputram, "Savings of the Ceylon Economy, 1950–59," pp. 14–16; and Gustav Ranis, *Urban Consumer Expenditure and the Consumption Function,* Institute of Development Economics, Karachi, August, 1961, Table 1, p. 22.

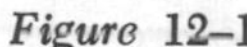

Figure 12–1

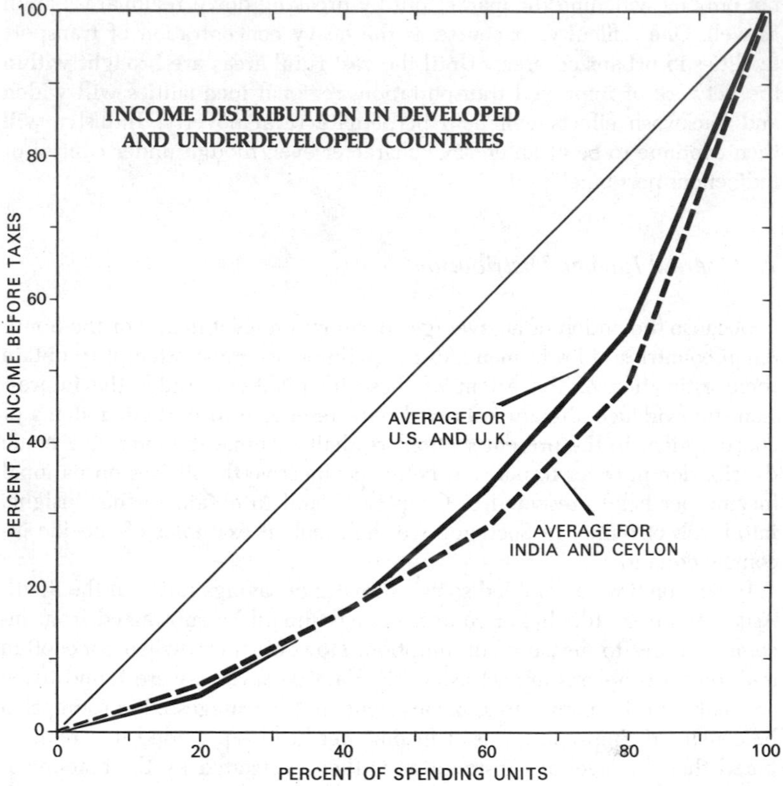

Source: Appendix 14, Table 1.

In general, because of the unreliability of savings estimates and the dearth of studies relating savings to income levels, we are forced to analyze inequality of consumption expenditures in terms of inequality of incomes. Even then we run into serious problems. When attempting to piece together information on over-all income inequality, the inadequacy, incompleteness, and subjectivity of the data are major stumbling blocks. It has therefore not been possible to provide any detailed assessment of over-all inequality for more than a few countries of the region. Even for these the evidence is shaky.

It is generally believed that inequality of income distribution tends to be greater in the underdeveloped economies than in the developed countries.[1] A rough indicator of the degree of over-all income inequality is the so-called "Lorenz curve," which shows the share of total income received by any given percentage of the population, or of spending units or income recipients. A pair of such curves is presented in Figure 12–1; details of the computations and sources are set forth in Appendix 14. Despite the weaknesses of the data, especially for India, the pattern of the curves supports the general impression of greater inequality in the underdeveloped regions. That is, the Lorenz curve for the United States and the United Kingdom generally lies closer to the line of perfect equality than does that for India and Ceylon.[2] This means that in India, for example, not only is the average income extremely low, but the dispersion around this average is also relatively wide. A survey for 1955–56 indicated that half of India's population was living on 14.6 rupees or less per month (about 10 cents in U. S. currency per day), or 175.2 rupees or less per year. Writing in 1958, P. C. Mahalanobis concluded that "only about 10 or 11 percent of the population of India can spend more than one rupee a day."[3] In short, the very low average income does not begin to plumb the depths of misery in India, or even relatively better-off Ceylon. It seems reasonable to suppose that the distribution of income in the other countries of the region is not markedly different, though no usable evidence is available.

The plight of the masses of people in the underdeveloped economies of South Asia would be serious enough if income were evenly distributed. Each inhabitant or each income recipient in each country would then receive an amount equal to the extremely low national average. The high degree of inequality means that the vast majority in each nation are forced to eke out an existence on annual incomes well below the al-

[1] See, for example, Irving B. Kravis, "International Differences in the Distribution of Income," *Review of Economics and Statistics,* XLII, No. 4, November, 1960; T. Morgan, "Distribution of Income in Ceylon, Puerto Rico, the United States and the United Kingdom," *Economic Journal,* December, 1953; Simon Kuznets, "Economic Growth and Income Inequality," *American Economic Review,* XLV, No. 1, March, 1955. H. T. Oshima has criticized Morgan's discussion; however, Morgan's reply and subsequent information on Ceylon support the view of greater inequality in underdeveloped regions. See H. T. Oshima, "A Note on Income Distribution in Developed and Underdeveloped Economies," and "A Rejoinder," by T. Morgan in *Economic Journal,* March, 1956, pp. 156–164.

For additional information on inequality in Ceylon, see Central Bank of Ceylon, *Survey of Ceylon's Consumer Finances,* 1954, Table 10.

[2] This is consistent with the findings of Kravis, "International Differences," *Review of Economics and Statistics,* with respect to the relative degree of inequality. He finds that the United States, the United Kingdom, and Japan have roughly comparable concentration ratios whereas the ratio for Ceylon is somewhat greater.

[3] P. C. Mahalanobis, "Science and National Planning," *Sankhya: The Indian Journal of Statistics,* September, 1958, Vol. 20, Parts 1 & 2, pp. 74, 75. See also Indian Statistical Institute, *The National Sample Survey,* 10th round, December, 1955–May, 1956, and Appendix 14, Table 4, where independent evidence supporting this statement is given.

ready quite inadequate national average. Regardless of the crudity of the empirical evidence, even if it is flagrantly biased downwards (and there is no evidence of persistent bias either way), it cannot and in fact does not conceal the reality of massive poverty.

Several other features of Figure 12–1 are worthy of note. The proportion of income accruing to the very lowest and very highest income groupings – for example, the lowest and highest deciles – is larger in the underdeveloped countries than in the developed. This reflects the common view that "there is a sharp contrast between the preponderant proportion of population whose average income is well below the generally low countrywide average, and a small top group with a very large relative income excess."[1] Furthermore, in countries with very low average incomes, it is clear that the proportion of income accruing to the lowest decile could not be as low as that possible for more developed countries – "otherwise, the groups could not survive."[2] It is only because of the high average income in the United States and the United Kingdom that the lowest decile there can subsist while receiving barely 1 or 2 percent of total income. Thus the lowest quintile in India and Ceylon receives about 5–7 percent of the total income, compared with 4 percent in the United States.[3] This imparts an apparent higher degree of equality at the lowest levels for the underdeveloped economies compared with developed economies than would otherwise be the case. At the top levels, the reverse is true.

It should also be noted that Figure 12–1 refers to pre-tax income and ignores the important redistributional effects of progressive taxation and social security benefits of various types. Direct progressive taxes are imposed on a much larger sector of the population in the developed countries than in South Asia, and, what is particularly important, taxes are far more efficiently assessed and collected. Indeed, tax assessment and collection is notoriously lax in South Asia and more weight is placed on indirect taxation, which tends to be regressive in nature.[4] When these facts are considered along with the far greater volume of social services provided by the developed countries to low income groups and the tendency of social policy measures in South Asia to benefit the not-so-poor income strata,[5] one would naturally expect that the differences in income inequality would widen very considerably as between the developed economies and South Asia when viewed after taxes and redistribution effects.

[1] Simon Kuznets, "Economic Growth and Income Inequality," *American Economic Review,* XLV, No. 1, March, 1955, p. 22.

[2] *Ibid.*

[3] It is possible, however, that part of this difference is attributable to the fact that the figures for India and Ceylon refer to households, whereas the British and American figures refer to spending units, which are often smaller.

[4] Appendix 8, Sections 8–9.

[5] Chapter 16, Section 7, *et passim.*

In other words, when income after taxes and redistributional policy measures is analyzed, the degree of inequality in developed countries decreases fairly sharply whereas no comparable change would be expected for the South Asian economies. Some evidence to support this is afforded by a comparison of after-tax income distribution between India and the United Kingdom.[1] Thus, the available evidence, weak as it is, confirms the view that income inequality is greater in the underdeveloped countries of South Asia than in the developed economies for both pre-tax and, more particularly, post-tax incomes, and would be still greater if account could be taken of various social services which in rich countries tend much more to favor poor people.

But even if the degree of over-all inequality were comparable to that in the Western economies (and the crudity of the data do not preclude the possibility),[2] it would have much more adverse consequences in the countries of South Asia since a given degree of inequality wreaks considerably more hardship on the less developed economy. For example, assume that the starvation level of income in two nations is 100. The difference of 100 percent between income levels of, say, 100 and 200 in the poorer country implies more hardship than the difference of 100 percent between income levels of 1,000 and 2,000 in the richer country, even though the Lorenz curves for the two countries coincide. Thus the indication given above that over-all inequality is greater in the poorer countries is much more serious than it appears on the surface.

Furthermore, a representation of over-all income distribution for the South Asian economies does not have quite the same connotation as in the Western nations, independent of the difference in the average level about which incomes are distributed. In the Western countries, social stratification is less rigid and occupational and spatial mobility much greater than in South Asia. In South Asia, a person's social and economic position tends to be static; the limitations on upward movement are severe. Thus the income inequality manifest at a particular point of time portrays more of a permanent situation for South Asia while, in a Western setting, not only does the average level of income tend to rise more rapidly, but individuals have more opportunity to improve their relative income position. If we could take age into consideration, a more considerable rise in income over the years for more persons would probably appear.

[1] See H. F. Lydall, "The Inequality of Indian Incomes," *Economic Weekly*, Special Number, June, 1960, p. 874.

[2] Indeed, it has recently been argued that "the pattern of income distribution in India is more or less similar to the patterns in some of the developed countries." (P. D. Ojha and V. V. Bhatt, "Income Distribution: A Case Study of India," *American Economic Review*, September, 1964, p. 719.) However, this conclusion is based on a set of estimates that differ widely from other calculations of Indian income distribution. Details of this and other studies appear in Appendix 14.

Generally, opportunities in the West for the individual to advance, to move out of his particular location, occupation, or social status, are much freer. Consequently, even if the Lorenz curve were to remain rigidly fixed over time, considerable changes among individuals at various income levels could be continually taking place. In South Asia, on the other hand, identical Lorenz curves at different points of time would reflect a more static social situation.

The relative fullness of opportunity is therefore not adequately represented in Lorenz curve comparisons between countries at such different levels of economic well-being. Underneath an unchanging distribution of income there may be either substantial movement, change, and social dynamism or, as in South Asia, immobility and stagnation. The portrayal of income inequality as in Figure 12–1 sheds no light on opportunities for personal advancement. The opportunities for advance afforded to individuals in the lowest income group in the West are far greater than in the corresponding group in South Asia, even if both obtain the same share of total income. A high turnover or circulation of individuals in different income classes typifies the West, but not South Asia.

In addition, it is possible that income inequality within each particular sector in one country may be greater than within each corresponding sector in another country, while at the same time the over-all curve of income distribution for the two countries is identical or at least not very different. In South Asia the extent of inequality within occupations or sectors appears to be much greater than in the developed countries. Problems of finding comparable occupational classifications and other statistical deficiencies preclude much valid empirical documentation of this assertion. On *a priori* grounds, however, a higher degree of occupational and regional inequality is to be expected where mobility is restricted. Large wage and salary differentials of a non-equalizing kind can obviously persist longer when possibilities for economic and social movement are few. Since economic and social rigidity is far greater in South Asia than in the Western countries, it follows that inequalities within particular segments of the South Asian economies are more substantial and persistent than in the West. These particular differences may coexist with over-all income distributions for South Asia and the West that are not very different.

What this implies is that as we pierce through the veil of the over-all income distribution,[1] we find greater inequalities in particular segments of the economy than are revealed by the aggregate measure. In other words, as we come closer to "reality," to the actual conditions of the individual

[1] A recent commentator on income inequality in the United States, where inadequacy of data is less troublesome certainly than in South Asia, has pointed out that "it is far more revealing to look at the subgroups in society with particularly low or high incomes than to work with a measure [i.e., the Lorenz curve] which hides almost everything interesting." (James Morgan, "The Anatomy of Income Distribution," *Review of Economics and Statistics,* August, 1962, p. 281.)

who, after all, lives in a particular village, has a particular occupation at a particular level of skill, works in a particular environment, and has particular social contacts – which, in a country with low mobility, are much more real and vital to him than the broader national society – we find more inequality of various kinds.

To these considerations must be added another aspect of South Asian reality. Low average income, income inequality, and social stratification are causally interrelated. But social stratification is itself an aspect of inequality, one that need not uniquely correlate with income distribution. The degree of income inequality among the poorer classes in South Asia cannot be very great, since their average income is so close to the bare subsistence level. Thus it may well be the case that the upper strata in a poor village in India do not have a significantly higher income than sharecropping tenants or landless peasants. Yet there is an important difference between these groups: the former often receive incomes without working while the latter do not. A distribution of income by social strata would therefore indicate a high degree of equality when in fact the social structure is harshly inegalitarian. Hence, far more pronounced inequalities would appear if distribution statistics could be made to reflect the broader facts of social stratification. Particularly in the South Asian rural setting, inequality is in fact mainly a question of land ownership – with which are associated leisure, enjoyment of status, and authority. Income differences are considered less significant.

But a close connection exists among these economic and social factors. The inequality in social status creates major incentives to withdraw from productive activity, especially if its pecuniary rewards are minimal. The status accorded to leisure is naturally high relative to that of income where economic opportunities are felt to be limited. By the same token, economic prospects are curtailed by status restrictions. The fact, therefore, that everyone in a village may be almost equally poor does not imply that everyone is equal; on the contrary, they are all so poor because they are so unequal. Inequality of social status is not only made more rigid and permanent by low levels of income, especially if income is equally distributed, but itself tends to perpetuate its major cause.[1] Even in those cases, then, where income inequality is less in South Asia than in the West – mainly among the poorer classes – the fact of far greater social inequality not only offsets this but ensures the perpetuation of rigidity and lack of opportunity.

It is not possible to provide adequate evidence of the trends in over-all income inequality. The general impression, however, seems to be that the extent of such inequality has either remained constant over the past decade (or longer) or has increased, with the possible exception of Ceylon.

[1] The social structure of the village economy is analyzed in Chapter 22, Section 7.

For India, K. Santhanam, Chairman of the (Parliamentary) Committee on Policy, Resources and Allocations, is reported to have said that "the general impression of the members was that inequalities of wealth and income had increased rather than diminished" during the 1950's.[1] It has also been stated that:

> All available evidence points to the conclusion that . . . [the real income of the vast majority of rural and urban classes] has either been stagnant or actually decreased in the last ten years. The two Plans did not provide for any planned redistribution of national income and no information is available as to how the additional income generated in the last decade has been shared amongst different sections of the community. . . . The presumption, however, is that owing to the continuous and growing inflationary pressure and the balance of forces in the country, the industrialists, big merchants and other privileged classes have mainly benefited from the increase of production and national income.[2]

Somewhat more concretely, the so-called Mahalanobis Committee reports on a study suggesting that between 1952–53 and 1956–57 – "the period during which the tempo of development quickened" – the proportion of income accruing to the top 5 and 10 percent had increased substantially and the share of the bottom 20 percent of the population had also increased, though slightly.[3] The report refers to several other studies, among them one by the Reserve Bank of India that reached the conclusion that "the degree of inequality in overall income distribution does not seem to have changed significantly."[4] The report itself does not find it possible to reach any definite conclusion, on the basis of presently available data, about the trend in regard to income distribution in India.[5] The general recognition that development in India in the post-war era has resulted in inequality was referred to in Chapter 7 (Sections 3–5) and will be discussed further in Chapter 16 (Section 6); cf. Chapter 19 (Section 7).

[1] Reported in *Link*, January 1, 1961, p. 26.

The discussion of inequality in the Indian Second and Third Plans implies that no important change had occurred. See India, Government of, Planning Commission, *Second Five Year Plan*, New Delhi, 1956, pp. 32–37, and *Third Five Year Plan, A Draft Outline*, New Delhi, June, 1960, pp. 12–14.

[2] Gyan Chand, "Social Purpose in Planning," in India, Government of, Ministry of Information and Broadcasting, *Problems in the Third Plan, A Critical Miscellany*, Delhi, January, 1961, p. 82.

[3] India, Government of, Planning Commission, *Report of the Committee on Distribution of Income and Levels of Living*, Part I, New Delhi, 1964, p. 12 and Table 3.4, p. 66. Over the same period the percentage of the Indian population living on less than Rs. 200 per year was found by one writer to have risen from 50 to 65. However, the data are very tenuous and the writer himself states that "it will not be advisable to draw any definite conclusions from them." (Sreelekha Basu, "A Note on the Distribution of Income by Size Classes of Personal Income," *A.I.C.C. Economic Review*, October 7, 1960, p. 15.)

[4] *Report of the Committee on Distribution of Income and Levels of Living*, Part I, p. 13.

[5] *Ibid.*, p. 22.

Benjamin Higgins has argued that despite the apparent growth of income per head in the Philippines, "the standard of living of the masses of the . . . people has improved but little over prewar levels" because "Postwar increases in income, even more than wealth, have been concentrated in the hands of the upper-income groups."[1] Similar views are generally expressed about the other South Asian countries, though exception is sometimes made for Ceylon, which, as we shall find in various contexts, is ahead of the other countries of the region in realizing the beginning of the welfare state.[2] Although most of these are merely impressionistic statements, they nevertheless support the view that income inequality is as high now as in the recent past, and probably higher.[3] Clearly one would have to have more up-to-date and comprehensive surveys in order to make a firm imputation of trend.

It is generally believed that in the early stages of industrialization in Western Europe the income distribution became more unequal and that only later, with the diffusion of spread effects and rising production, and later as an effect of social legislation, this tendency was reversed. From this point of view, increasing inequality may be thought to be symptomatic of economic growth and dynamism. But we have already noted the lack of vigorous development in South Asia, except perhaps to some extent for the Philippines and lately for Thailand (Chapter 11, Section 2). Thus if inequality is in fact increasing in most of the South Asian economies, this provides another example of the irrelevance of past developments in the West for the present situation in South Asia. As with urbanization and the relative growth of tertiary industries, the apparent increase in inequality has not accompanied rapid growth. Indeed, as with urbanization, it may be

[1] Benjamin Higgins, *Economic Development,* W. W. Norton Co., New York, 1959, p. 65. This view is supported by F. H. Golay, *The Philippines: Public Policy and National Economic Development,* Cornell University Press, Ithaca, 1961, pp. 422–423.

[2] Gamani Corea speaks of "the likelihood that income distribution in Ceylon might have changed in favour of the lower income groups" and explains: "There are no precise statistics to provide an accurate picture of income distribution or its change in Ceylon. But the changing patterns of Government finance, with the growing emphasis on welfare outlays and transfer expenditure of one kind or another coupled with steep increases in taxation whose incidence on the upper income groups was particularly marked, does suggest that changes in income distribution are likely in Ceylon, more perhaps than in other developing countries, to have favoured the lower income groups. All this points to the possibility that the average standard of living, or at least the standard of living of the mass of the population, may well have increased at a somewhat faster rate, though not at a markedly faster rate, than the average annual increment of 0.7 percent in real *per capita* product." ("Ceylon," *Asian Economic Development,* Cranley Onslow, ed., Weidenfeld & Nicolson, London, 1965, p. 30.)

[3] In an article "Socialism and Private Business" in *Indonesian Economic Studies,* No. 1, June, 1965, pp. 13ff. (Research School of Pacific Studies, Australian National University, Canberra), the conclusion is reached that "In spite of official reiteration of the goal of a just and prosperous society, the impression of many observers has been that along with a decline in per capita income, the contrast between rich and poor has actually sharpened. Real wages have fallen heavily. Yet the scale of conspicuous consumption in Djakarta seems to have grown."

the result of failure to develop rapidly. It should also be noted that, in contrast to the Western countries especially in their early stages of development, the South Asian countries are attempting to spur and direct development by planning, and they have generally emphasized equality as a main goal of planning. In Chapter 16 we shall return to this subject and explain why in South Asia greater equality would spur rather than hamper economic growth (Section 3).

8 *Specific Income Inequalities*

The over-all pattern of income distribution, while more revealing than the national average income, is nonetheless an aggregative concept that also submerges many of the more pertinent aspects of inequality. The present section will therefore examine particular manifestations of income inequality. Even this more particularistic approach involves broad averages that conceal important inequalities, as already shown with respect to specific items of consumption.

One of the obvious areas of inequality is that among districts within a country. Although income data pertaining to subdivisions of any country are even less reliable than figures relating to the nation as a whole, some rough estimates are available for Pakistan and India that suggest the magnitude of geographical differentials. For example, income per head in West Pakistan in 1957–58 is estimated to have been about 30 percent above that calculated for East Pakistan.[1] Estimates for 1949–50 and 1959–60 put the differential at 29 and 34 percent respectively, thus suggesting some widening of the gap during that period, though more recent estimates suggest a change in that trend.[2] The heavy concentration of development expenditures in West Pakistan during the First Plan period (1955–60) lends support to this finding. The strategy since then has been to try to redress that imbalance. By the end of the Second Plan, in 1965, East Pakistan's share in total government expenditure was expected to exceed 50 percent, against 26 percent in 1949–50.[3] Between 1959–60 and 1963–64, income per head in East Pakistan is reported to have risen at an annual compound rate of 2.2 percent, compared with a rise of 2.0 percent in West Pakistan. But even though the relative gap may appear to be closing, the absolute differential is large and has grown.

[1] *Report of the Panel of Economists on the Second Five Year Plan (1960–65)*, Government of Pakistan Press, Karachi, 1959, p. 14.

[2] Pakistan, Government of, *Outline of the Third Five-Year Plan (1965–1970)*, August, 1964, Table 12, p. 11. Income per head, expressed in rupees of 1959–60 value, is given as:

	1949–50	*1959–60*	*1963–64*
East Pakistan	252	250	273
West Pakistan	326	336	363

[3] *Ibid.*, p. 12.

Table 12–5

(NET NATIONAL) INCOME PER HEAD IN INDIAN STATES, 1955–56 AND 1957–58

State and zone	*Rupees, at 1955–56 prices*		*Percentage change*
	1955–56	*1957–58*	
Andra (S)	221.0	208	−6.1
Assam (E)	256	253	−1.3
Bihar (E)	158	149	−5.5
Bombay (W)	302	316	+4.6
Kerala (S)	257	265	+3.0
Madhya Pradesh (C)	231	219	−5.2
Madras (S)	242	248	+2.3
Mysore (W)	190	184	−3.1
Orissa (E)	171	166	−3.3
Punjab (N)	297	332	+11.6
Rajusthan (N)	223	223	–
Uttar Pradesh (C)	212	214	+1.0
W. Bengal (E)	357	379	+6.2
Delhi (N)	804	892	+11.0
Himachal Pradesh (N)	168	169	+0.6
Manipur (E)	102	104	+2.0
Tripura (E)	214	217	+1.3
All India	241	245	+1.4

Source: "The Character of Regional Changes in Income: 1955–56 to 1960–61," *Quarterly Report of the Indian Institute of Public Opinion*, No. 21, July, 1959.

Zones: N: Northern; C: Central; E: East; W: West; S: South.

For India substantial regional differences in income per head exist, as shown in Table 12–5. Moreover, although the data are extremely weak, it appears that, in the period covered by the table, incomes were growing at a somewhat faster rate in the states already above the national average than in those below it. The disparity among states in average annual earnings of industrial workers seems, however, to be narrowing.[1] The two sets of figures, if correct, imply a regional difference in industrialization and/or a growing regional inequality in the non-manufacturing sectors.[2] Wide variations between states in consumer expenditures per head were recorded in a National Sample Survey for September, 1957–May, 1958. The

[1] India, Government of, Cabinet Secretariat, Central Statistical Organization, *Statistical Abstract, India 1956–57*, New Series, No. 7, New Delhi, 1958, Table 181, p. 611.

[2] Other evidence exists of increasing regional inequality. See, for example, P. K. Chaudhuri, "Balanced Regional Growth," *Economic Weekly*, October 8, 1960, pp. 1501–1504.

state of Orissa had consumer expenditures per head only 70 percent of the all-India average of 20.2 rupees per person per month, whereas Assam and Punjab were 129 and 133 percent of the average and Union Territories were 180 percent.[1] Striking income differences have also been found within states. Within the state of Maharashtra the following incomes per head were reported for 1955–56: Greater Bombay, 474 rupees; Nagpur, 426 rupees; Panch Mahals, 186 rupees; Ratnagiri, 190 rupees. In Gujarat, Ahmedabad had 470 rupees per head and Kaira only 186.[2] If these states are at all representative, it is clear that the structure of inequality is substantially more significant than interstate comparisons reveal it to be.

Clear-cut data on regional inequality are less accessible for the other countries in South Asia. However, the available evidence suggests that regional inequality is substantial.[3] It may also be inferred that such inequality is increasing insofar as it is closely tied to widening urban-rural differentials, indicated by the faster increase in industrial production, with its urban orientation, than in agricultural output in the post-war period. As the U. N. Economic Commission for Asia and the Far East has pointed out:

> The progress of industrialization in the ECAFE countries seems to have been accompanied by increased inequality of incomes. The incomes of industrial workers and employers, and purveyors and traders have risen much more than those of other groups. Wartime and postwar inflations have further accentuated the inequality of income in favour of industrial producers and traders of goods, at the expense of fixed income groups and peasant producers. The latter have been unable to make headway owing to their weak bargaining position.[4]

This suggests that the more urbanized or industrial areas within countries have been increasing their incomes at a faster rate than the national average, thereby accentuating regional inequality. It is indeed noteworthy that annual income per head for agricultural laborers in India was reported to be not only very low in 1956–57 (only Rs. 99.4) but lower than in 1950–51 (Rs. 104.0).[5] This is confirmed by a study made in Uttar Pra-

[1] India, Government of, *Committee on Income Distribution*, Table 7, p. II–(14).

[2] "The Regional Incomes of Maharashtra and Gujarat," *Quarterly Economic Report*, Indian Institute of Public Opinion, January, 1960, pp. 38–40. Details on regional inequalities within Andhra Pradesh are contained in Ramanadham, *The Economy of Andhra Pradesh.*

[3] See, for example, Wendell Blanchard *et al.*, *Thailand*, "Country Survey Series," Human Relations Area Files Press, New Haven, 1957, Chapter 14; J. Russell Andrus, *Burmese Economic Life*, Stanford University Press, Stanford, 1948, Chapter XXI; Ma and Seng, "Economic Characteristics of the Population," *Malayan Economic Review*, October, 1960, p. 32.

[4] *Economic Survey of Asia and the Far East, 1959*, Bangkok, 1960, pp. 74–75.

[5] India, Government of, Ministry of Labour and Employment, Labour Bureau, *Agricultural Labour in India, Report on the Second Agricultural Labour Enquiry 1956–57*, Vol. I. *All-India*, 1960, p. 165.

desh: in terms of 1948–49 prices the rural income was Rs. 198 in 1949–50 and no more than Rs. 193 in 1958–59.[1]

There are strong *a priori* reasons for expecting a high and growing degree of regional inequality within the countries of South Asia. The frequently observed negative correlation between degrees of economic development and inequality[2] is explicable largely by the process of cumulative causation and the general weakness of spread effects relative to backwash effects in underdeveloped countries.[3] Furthermore, these factors are instrumental in aggravating inequalities where market forces are allowed free play.[4] In short, the available evidence, frail as it is, bears out general economic reasoning as it pertains to development and inequality, when planning is not effectual.

Closely connected with these phenomena, as both cause and consequence, are specific rural-urban inequalities. Thus one important factor in the disparity between East and West Pakistan is the fact that East Pakistan has a much smaller proportion of its population in urban centers than West Pakistan.[5] And within East Pakistan urban-rural differences are pronounced, as in Dacca, for example, where industrial wages are reported to be generally double wages in agriculture.[6] In India, Punjab, which ranks among the wealthier states, has also had a high level of urbanization and rate of urban growth.[7] In general, the more urbanized states in India report incomes per head well above the Indian average. Monthly consumption expenditures per person in India have been estimated as about one-third higher in towns than in villages, and in cities more than twice those in rural areas.[8] The remuneration of industrial laborers in towns is about twice that of agricultural labor. Indeed, "In Bombay City . . . the average family monthly income is more than four times that of an agricultural labour family in the countryside."[9] Urban-

[1] Reported in Baljit Singh, *Next Step in Village India,* Asia Publishing House, New York, 1961, p. 38.

[2] United Nations, Economic Commission for Europe, *Economic Survey of Europe in 1954,* Geneva, 1955, Chap. 6.

[3] These phenomena have been discussed with special reference to regional inequality in Gunnar Myrdal, *Economic Theory and Under-developed Regions,* Duckworth, London, 1957, Chapter 3. (American edition, *Rich Lands and Poor,* Harper, New York, 1957.)

[4] *Ibid.,* pp. 51ff.

[5] W. Nelson Peach, Mohammad Uzair, and George W. Rucker, *Basic Data of the Economy of Pakistan,* Oxford University Press, Karachi, 1959, p. 13.

[6] UNESCO, *Dacca: Human and Social Impact of Technological Change in East Pakistan,* 1956, p. 115.

[7] I. N. Chawla, "The Urbanization of the Punjab Plains," *Indian Geographer,* December, 1958, pp. 34–35.

[8] Indian Statistical Institute, *National Sample Survey, No. 13, Consumer Expenditure,* p. 7. This study "imputed values in cases of supplies obtained in kind" (p. 6).

[9] P. M. Hauser, ed., *Urbanization in Asia and the Far East,* UNESCO, Calcutta, 1957, p. 147.

rural differences appear to be less pronounced in Ceylon,[1] but in Thailand a Bangkok survey indicated that the urban diet was far superior to the rural.[2] A substantial degree of rural-urban inequality seems, therefore, to exist throughout the region, and to account for much of the apparent inequality between countries and between districts within countries.[3]

But while the average income per head is higher in urban than in rural areas, the variation within urban centers is enormous. The cities contain some of the workers with the very lowest incomes, but also, at the other extreme, most of the professionals, businessmen, and absentee landowners. It has been pointed out that "the most typical feature in city life, particularly in Asian countries, is the glaring difference between the rich and the poor . . . Where in Western countries the ratio of income of a professional and an industrial worker may be 3 or 4 to 1, it is 15 or 20 to 1 in Asia, or even higher."[4] In India, income in urban areas appears to be much more highly concentrated than in rural areas. Two recent studies suggest that the top 10 percent of households in all urban centers receive 9–12 percent more of the total urban income than the top 10 percent in the rural sector.[5] The concentration ratio worked out for the Reserve Bank of India data shows urban concentration of .40 and rural concentration of .31.[6] Considering the accelerated urban growth rates discussed in Chapter 10 (Section 11), the already high level of inequality in urban centers appears to be on the increase.[7]

Interrelated with these factors are the agricultural–non-agricultural inequalities. As indicated in Chapter 11, Table 11–4, non-agricultural pro-

[1] *Ibid.*, pp. 147–148.

[2] Thailand, Ministry of Agriculture, *Report of the Government of Thailand to FAO*, Bangkok, 1950, pp. 24–26.

[3] On rural poverty – and inequality – see India, Government of, *Report of the Study Group on the Welfare of the Weaker Sections of the Village Community*, Vol. I, New Delhi, 1961.

[4] UNESCO, *Social Implications of Industrialization and Urbanization, Five Studies in Asia*, p. iv.

[5] See Appendix 14, Table 4.

[6] The concentration ratio is the ratio of the area between the Lorenz curve and the diagonal to the area under the diagonal. A concentration ratio of zero implies perfect equality and a ratio of unity implies complete inequality. The figures cited are from Ojha and Bhatt, "Income Distribution," *American Economic Review*, Table I, p. 714.

[7] Ojha and Bhatt conclude that, even with their estimates showing far greater equality of urban income distribution than the N.C.A.E.R. estimates (both of which are shown in Table 4 of Appendix 14), the "distribution pattern in the urban sector seems to be more uneven in India than in some of the developed countries, and the trend seems to be towards an increase in the degree of inequality." (*Ibid.*, p. 719.)

That in India income inequality in urban areas (and even among the non-farm population in rural areas) is greater, and that it is increasing, is recognized in the *Report of the Committee on Distribution of Income and Levels of Living* (pp. 12ff. and tables).

Table 12–6

INCOME BY RACE, ALL-CEYLON, 1953
(*Rupees per month*)

	Arithmetic mean	*Median*
Kandyan Singhalese	90.7	67.2
Low Country Singhalese	115.9	73.5
Ceylon Tamils	124.7	83.0
Indian Tamils	61.1	48.2
Moors and Malays	110.2[a]	87.5
Others	400.8	218.3
All races	107.4	66.3

Source: Central Bank of Ceylon, *Survey of Ceylon's Consumer Finances,* Colombo, 1954, Table 15.

[a] Adjusted according to statement in the source, p. 20.

ductivity, in terms of income per head or per active male, is generally well above productivity in the agricultural sector. An Indian survey indicated that the ratio of the wage rate for casual male workers in agriculture to wages of unskilled workers in the cotton textile industry was only around 25 percent in eight centers, although in West Bengal the agricultural wage was about 60 percent of the industrial.[1] The relative rates of remuneration in the agricultural and non-agricultural occupations exhibit a similar pattern for the other South Asian countries, as would be expected in view of the generally low level of agricultural efficiency outside of the plantations.

The final particular aspect of inequality to which we wish to draw attention is that along ethnic lines. The available evidence from a few of the countries suggests substantial ethnic inequality, when average incomes are compared. Ceylonese data shown in Table 12–6 indicate that the average (mean) income of the lowest income group, the Indian Tamils, is less than half that of the highest paid single group, the Ceylon Tamils. The discrepancy narrows somewhat when median incomes are compared but it remains substantial, and the Indian Tamils still emerge as the low income class. The fact that the Indian Tamils have the highest ratio of persons with no schooling[2] suggests a degree of educational exclusiveness as well. This inequality, of course, actually reflects differences in occupational distribution and urbanization. The Ceylon Tamils include a large number of traders with high incomes, which brings up the average

[1] India, Government of, *Agricultural Labour in India*, pp. 127–128.

[2] Central Bank of Ceylon, *Survey of Ceylon's Consumer Finances,* Tables 6 and 7.

figure. If they were excluded, the difference in average income would decrease or even disappear. For Malaya in 1947, over 47 percent of the Malays occupied in producing the three main products, rice, tin, and rubber, were low-paid paddy growers but only 6 percent of the Chinese so occupied were in this low-paid group.[1] Generally in Malaya "Indians and to a greater extent Chinese specialise in estate work, Malays in smallholder cultivation."[2] Since estate workers' wages are higher than the earnings of men employed on small holdings,[3] there is an inevitable income inequality between the two racial groups. Differences between these groups are reflected in urbanization. According to the 1957 census, of the total urban population in Malaya (2.7 million), 63.9 percent were Chinese, 10.7 percent Indians, 22.6 percent Malays, and 2.8 percent others, whereas the distribution of ethnic groups in Malaya as a whole was 37.2 percent Chinese, 11.3 percent Indians, 49.8 percent Malays, and 1.8 percent others.[4] This relative concentration of Chinese in urban centers, where incomes are somewhat higher, reinforces the degree of inequality. However, this picture of the Chinese in Malaya being "on the average" somewhat better off needs to be modified since rather extreme inequality is found within the Chinese group. A survey conducted in Singapore revealed that a larger percentage of Chinese than Malays are in the poorest, as well as the wealthiest, class.[5] In general a high degree of inequality within ethnic groups exists. This must be kept in mind when making comparisons. In Thailand, the Chinese constituted about half the population of Bangkok in 1947[6] but only some 13 percent of the total population. Generally the Chinese in Thailand are dominant in the higher paying trades and professions and in the skilled portion of the industrial labor force.[7] As in Malaya, however, there is substantial inequality within the Chinese group.

The story is similar in other countries of the region, although in India and Pakistan caste and religious distinctions are more important than distinctions along purely racial lines. If statistics were available according to caste, Brahmans would probably be found to have a higher average income because they are still overrepresented among officials, professionals, and the educated class generally although the major part of the Brahman

[1] Hodder, *Man in Malaya,* p. 49.

[2] *Ibid.,* p. 47.

[3] Indian Council of World Affairs, *Labour in South-East Asia,* P. P. Pillai, ed., New Delhi, 1947, p. 148.

[4] H. Fell, *1957 Population Census of the Federation of Malaya,* Report No. 14, Department of Statistics, Kuala Lumpur, 1960, pp. 3, 9.

[5] See Keng Swee Goh, *Urban Incomes and Housing,* Department of Social Welfare, Singapore, 1956, cited in J. J. Puthucheary, *Ownership and Control in the Malayan Economy,* Eastern Universities Press, Singapore, 1960, p. 177.

[6] Blanchard *et al., Thailand,* "Country Survey Series," p. 66.

[7] *Ibid.,* p. 279.

caste may not be very much better off than some other castes. In addition, of course, there are the extreme instances of inequality found in all the former European colonies owing to the concentration of Westerners in the higher paying posts, especially in business. Restrictions against alien groups, including "Oriental aliens," have become prominent in the development programs of several of the ex-colonial countries,[1] with the object not only of limiting "foreign domination" but also of opening up some of the preferred positions to the native-born.

The foregoing specific manifestations of inequality are all closely interrelated. The disparity between agricultural and non-agricultural average income is obviously tied to the urban-rural differential, as cause and as consequence, and both are linked intimately with regional inequalities and with the ethnic composition of town and country. The latter, of course, are products of the social stratification that excludes certain ethnic or caste groups from the more highly paid, urban positions in industry, commerce, and administration, and that restricts certain low status groups, in the countryside as well as in the towns, to menial work. Intermingled with this, again as cause and effect, is the skill disparity, which reflects educational opportunity and the access of various segments of the population to it.

The entire structure of inequality is bolstered by the caste system, the color line, ethnic discrimination, nepotism, and the general set of social and religious taboos. The vicious circle of cumulative interrelation and causation is thus perpetuated, and even accentuated, by existing institutions confronted with divergent sectoral growth rates, notably between the agricultural and industrial sectors, and serious inflation in several of the countries. Present institutional arrangements, therefore, impede the rise of social, regional, and occupational mobility and encourage the persistence of multi-dimensional segmentation of social and economic life, which is a major obstacle to economic growth. How social and economic inequality acts as an impediment to economic development will be discussed in Chapter 16 (Section 3), Chapter 26, and in many other contexts.

[1] See Chapter 9, *passim;* Chapter 17, Sections 1 and 11–14.

Chapter 13

FOREIGN TRADE AND CAPITAL FLOWS

1 *Outline of the Argument*

As we pointed out in Chapter 10, the economic structures of the South Asian countries, as they exist and function today, are, to a large extent, the product of international economic and political relationships developed over the past century. Expansion in external demand was mainly responsible for whatever degree of economic development occurred in the region. In particular, the appearance and subsequent growth of plantation industry in many of the South Asian countries and the enlargement of rice cultivation in Burma and Thailand were responses to the opening up of new or increased export possibilities in colonial times. So was the growth of mining activities in Malaya, Burma, Indonesia, and Thailand. The manufacturing starts in India, by contrast, took place in spite of a colonial policy that actively worked against such development. That foreign trade and colonial policies had both positive and negative effects was also shown in Chapter 10 (Sections 7–9). Although rising European demand for raw materials stimulated key sectors of the economies, increased competition from cheaper European goods helped destroy some local industries, especially handicrafts and other traditional industries. By stressing exports of raw materials and discouraging industrialization while leaving non-commercial agriculture in a state of "static expansion," colonial policy throughout the nineteenth century facilitated a lopsided development.

As earlier in the Western countries, the increase in exports paved the way for further capital imports to perpetuate and stimulate the developmental process. In South Asia, direct investment in plantations and mines and later re-investment of profits in similar enterprises, together with capital made available to the colonial governments and quasi-public corporations for building ports, railways, and so on, bolstered this trend and accelerated the expansion of commercial activities. The countries where these commercial activities accounted for a relatively large part of output and employment naturally fared better and shared more in the dynamism induced by the growth in exports. That is why, today, income levels in Ceylon and Malaya exceed those in India and Pakistan.

In Western Europe, North America, and Australasia, economic growth also took place initially within the context of a buoyant and expanding volume of international trade, but there the external stimuli generated expansion on a broad front. In South Asia, the response to rising external demand was made primarily by foreigners from Western Europe, who regularly remitted dividends and salaries to the home country, purchased foreign goods for personal and business use, and seldom assimilated with the local population. Economic growth in the colonies was subordinated to the needs of the metropolitan countries. The enclave structure of plantation and mining ventures and the tenor of colonial policy reduced considerably the effects of expansion in these fields on other economic sectors. Instead of having spread effects, economic development was largely confined to the foreign-dominated sectors; it left the great majority of the people and the major part of the economies hardly touched.

Thus, while export opportunities expanded rapidly and more or less steadily right up to the First World War, they failed to trigger rapid over-all growth in the South Asian economies. Since independence, efforts have been made to ensure that the activities even of foreign-dominated plantations confer a greater benefit on the indigenous economies. Spread effects should therefore tend to be larger than in the past. However, the international situation has changed. There is no longer any significant stimulus to be derived from export markets.[1] In fact, demand for most of South Asia's traditional exports is expected to rise hardly at all. There would, of course, be substantial demand for many types of manufactured goods if the South Asian countries could produce them, and could readily sell them to the industrial countries. But there are serious internal impediments to the production of non-traditional commodities for export. Such internal impediments — to be examined later — are precisely those which hinder economic growth in general. While export expansion and diversifi-

[1] With the possible exceptions of rubber in Malaya and rubber and oil in Indonesia. Export prospects are discussed below.

cation are made difficult enough by all of the internal barriers implicit in the very notion of underdevelopment, the problems are aggravated by the restrictive import policies of the industrial countries. The developed countries of the West all too frequently impose tariffs, quotas, and other restrictions upon the products of allegedly "cheap" foreign labor. Nor have the Communist countries yet adopted trade policies that would assure substantial outlets for manufactured products from South Asia.

If development is to occur in the South Asian countries, it will not come as a response to foreign demand for the products in which the region has traditionally had a comparative advantage. Not only does this fact mean that economic growth is a more difficult task than it was when the developed countries confronted it, but it implies that there will be much more autarky and much less "automatic" response to external forces in the growth process itself. Development must be internally based and deliberately prodded and nurtured, since the spontaneous growth-inducing stimulus of a relatively free and expanding international trade is no longer present. This is the main thesis of the present chapter. Of course, the South Asian countries differ considerably in their export prospects and import needs, and consequently in their ability to pick and choose among policy alternatives. This will become clear as we proceed with our analysis.

At the outset it should be pointed out that the factual material pertaining to foreign trade is generally far superior to that pertaining to almost any other segment of economic activity in this region. The concepts are clear-cut. Data on exports and imports have been collected for a much longer time than national accounts material. Furthermore, since imports and exports pass political boundaries, registration by both the importing and exporting countries is normally required, and this provides a double check on accuracy. The foreign trade balance is also watched more carefully than many other empirical quantities, which indicates greater concern for accuracy in this sphere. Not the least important stimulus to careful accounting is the generally high dependence of South Asian governments on foreign trade taxes. Of course, foreign trade statistics are not completely accurate. Goods are smuggled into and out of the region, a process which is relatively easy because most of the countries concerned have long coastlines. Also, exporters tend to under-declare their merchandise, in order to acquire foreign exchange outside the national controls, and importers do likewise, in order to bypass the import restrictions; ordinarily this involves bribery and collusion.[1] But in general the statistical material in this field is more reliable than it is in most others.

[1] Indonesia's foreign trade, in particular, is not adequately reflected in the statistics; see, for example, United Nations, ECAFE, *Economic Survey of Asia and the Far East, 1957*, Bangkok, 1958, p. 151; and *Report of the Governor of the Bank of Indonesia for the Financial Year 1958–1959*, G. Kolff & Co., Djakarta, p. 131. The *Economic Survey*

2 *The Relative Importance of Foreign Trade*

The significance of foreign trade to the South Asian countries is indicated by the figures in Table 13–1, which show exports and imports by total value and in relation to both population and national income during the period 1957–59. The substantial variation from country to country is immediately apparent.

This variation is due in part to differences in geographical size. Generally it is true that the larger a country, the greater the amount of trade that is conducted locally, and vice versa. Thus, when Pakistan was separated from India, trade between the two units became international rather than internal. On the other hand, trade between East and West Pakistan is not regarded as "foreign." It is only natural, therefore, that the larger countries – and India especially – tend to have a low ratio of exports and imports to national income. Related to geographical size in determining the relative importance of a country's foreign trade is another purely mechanical factor, namely, the absolute size of its national income. Thus, although India has the largest absolute value of exports and imports of all the South Asian countries, it has a very low ratio of exports and imports to national income, and ranks near the bottom of the list in exports and imports per head of population. Yet a country's geographical extent and the size of its income are less significant than its economic structure. If two countries, each having a high export orientation, were to become one political unit, the sum total of "foreign trade" would not necessarily be reduced very much unless they previously sold substantial amounts to each other. In South Asia, as we shall note, trade among the countries is small.

It is noteworthy that, consistent with the discussion summarized in Section 1 and the analysis in Chapter 11, and omitting Japan, the countries with the highest levels of income per head (Ceylon and Malaya) also have the most foreign trade relative to income or population, while the poorest countries (India and Pakistan) show the lowest foreign trade ratios. Al-

---

of Asia and the Far East, 1964 (Bangkok, 1965, p. 220) reports that Indonesia's estimates of its exports to other ECAFE countries in 1962 "are only 42 percent of the corresponding total reported by partner countries, partly because of undervaluation . . . and partly because of unregistered exports from Indonesia."

In India the value of "smuggled imports of gold" in 1957–58 was estimated to exceed Rs. 271 million, over five times the value of gold production in India in that year. See "Estimates of Saving in the Indian Economy," *Reserve Bank of India Bulletin,* March, 1960, p. 13, Table VII. D. K. Rangnekar provides further evidence of "a considerable volume of concealed transactions," in his study, *Poverty and Capital Development in India,* Oxford University Press, London, 1958, pp. 219–221. And I. M. D. Little reports that, for India, although "The balance of payments estimates are good . . . trade figures are very unreliable for imports." (I. M. D. Little, "The Strategy of Indian Development," *National Institute Economic Review,* No. 9, May, 1960, p. 20, f.n. 3.)

Table 13–1

VALUE OF EXPORTS AND IMPORTS, ANNUAL AVERAGE, 1957–59
(Merchandise exports f.o.b.; imports c.i.f.)

	Total value (Million Indian rupees)		*Value per head (Rupees)*		*Percent of national income*	
Country	*Exports*	*Imports*	*Exports*	*Imports*	*Exports*	*Imports*
Pakistan	1,515	1,888	17	22	7	8
India	6,203	9,445	15	23	5	8
Indonesia	4,120	2,818	47	32	(20)[a]	(14)[a]
Burma	1,025	1,149	46	52	23	25
South Vietnam	335	1,183	26	90	(5)[b]	(25)[b]
Philippines[c]	2,306	2,681	90	105	11	12
Thailand	1,638	1,919	69	80	18	21
Ceylon	1,715	1,842	176	189	33	36
Malaya (Fed.)	6,106	6,545	757	811	53	43
Japan	14,399	17,102	157	186	12	15

Sources: Trade figures from International Monetary Fund, *Monthly Financial Statistics,* January, 1961, country pages. Population figures from latest censuses. National income from United Nations, Department of Economic and Social Affairs, *Yearbook of National Accounts Statistics 1960,* New York, 1961, except India (Central Statistical Organisation, *Estimates of National Income 1948–49 to 1959–60,* New Delhi, March, 1961, p. 1) and Pakistan (Planning Commission, *The Second Five Year Plan (1960–65),* Karachi, June, 1960, p. 28 *less* depreciation estimates calculated as outlined in "Guide to the Plan Tables"). National income data for South Vietnam and the Federation of Malaya from U. N., *Economic Survey of Asia and the Far East,* 1961, p. 170.

[a] The complicated exchange rate structure makes these figures especially tenuous. We arrived at them by applying the average of the principal export and import rates of exchange for each year to the I.M.F. estimates of international trade in U. S. dollars and dividing the results by the very weak national income estimates.

[b] 1954 and 1955.

[c] Imports valued f.o.b. were converted to Indian rupees at official exchange rates.

though the relationship between income per head and foreign trade ratios is less systematic for the other South Asian countries, it is broadly true that economic structure, especially the importance of industrialized agriculture with its superior productivity, correlates closely with the importance of foreign trade. Thus in the accompanying table exports and imports as a proportion of national income are less than 10 percent for India and Pakistan and over 30 percent for Ceylon and Malaya. Pakistan, with a population of over 90 million in the period covered by this table, exports far less than Malaya, with a population of less than 7 million; and India, with about 440 million inhabitants, exports less than half as much as Japan, which has about one-quarter that number of people. In relation to population, the exports of Japan, Ceylon, and Malaya are between ten and fifty times those of India and Pakistan. (The general pattern has not changed since 1957–59.) Such vast discrepancies are more the result of differences in economic structure than of the purely mechanical influences mentioned above.

3 *Composition of Exports and Imports*

Indicative as the general foreign trade ratios may be, the significant aspect of the foreign sector is the composition of exports and imports. The pertinent data on exports are presented in Table 13–2. Of the nine countries listed, five are one-commodity exporters; that is, more than 50 percent of the value of their exports is accounted for by one commodity. These five are Burma (rice), Pakistan (jute), South Vietnam (rubber), Malaya (rubber), and Ceylon (tea). In all these countries but Pakistan, exports constitute a relatively large share of national income as well. Three countries may be classed as two-commodity exporters – the Philippines, Indonesia, and Thailand. Over 50 percent of their export receipts come from two commodities: cocoanuts and sugar in the Philippines, rubber and petroleum in Indonesia, rice and rubber in Thailand. Only India is diversified to the extent that more than four items account for half its export earnings, if we exclude the broad category "other manufactured goods."[1] In addition, only India has significant exports of manufactured goods.

Most countries listed in the table are thus dependent on a few commodities. Moreover, with the exception of rice and, in India and Pakistan, textiles, there is very little internal demand for these commodities: Malaya and

Table 13–2

COMPOSITION OF EXPORTS, BY VALUE, 1956–58

Country	*Commodity*	*Earnings as percent of total earnings*
Pakistan	Jute	53.7
	Cotton	20.2
	Wool	5.0
	Tea	2.3
	Hides and skins	2.6

(*table continued*)

[1] The degree of concentration depends, of course, on how broadly the commodities are classified. For the countries listed in Table 13–2, however, the classifications are comparable. Comparisons with countries outside the region would require similar classification.

Table 13–2 (*continued*)

COMPOSITION OF EXPORTS, BY VALUE, 1956–58

Country	*Commodity*	*Earnings as percent of total earnings*
India[a]	Tea	22.9
	Jute yarn and fabrics	12.6
	Cotton yarn and fabrics	10.0
	Raw cotton	3.5
	Leather and leathergoods	3.4
	Vegetable oils	2.2
	Spices	1.4
	Hides and skins	1.1
	Chemicals	.8
	Other manufactured goods	15.1
Indonesia	Natural rubber	36.8
	Petroleum	30.5
	Tin	5.7
	Copra	4.1
	Tea	3.2
Burma	Rice and rice products	73.7
South Vietnam	Rubber	68.4
	Rice[b]	19.7
Philippines	Cocoanut and products	38.3
	Sugar and products	22.6
	Logs, timber	11.7
	Minerals and metals	10.4
	Fibres and manufacture	8.3
Thailand	Rice	45.2
	Rubber	20.4
	Tin	6.2
	Teak	3.8
Ceylon	Tea	62.4
	Rubber	16.7
	Cocoanuts	10.6
Fed. of Malaya	Rubber	61.3
	Tin	14.2
	Vegetables	4.4
	Iron ore	2.8

Source: U. N., *Economic Survey of Asia and the Far East, 1959.*

[a] Figures for 1956 (reclassified by ECAFE) may not conform exactly with those for 1957 and 1958.
[b] 1956 was an unusually bad year for rice.

Ceylon export over 90 percent of their output of major products, Indonesia also over 90 percent, South Vietnam and Thailand over 95 percent, and similarly for the other countries. Only in the rice surplus countries, Burma and Thailand, is there a large demand for a primary commodity that is a major export product. For the most part, then, the South Asian countries are uniquely dependent on external markets – markets that are largely beyond their sphere of influence, at least on the demand side. At the same time, the absence of internal markets makes their economies more sensitive to changes in external demand for their major product or products, since there is nothing to cushion the shock of a decline in foreign buying.[1]

For those commodities with a high short-run elasticity of supply, output is therefore inevitably volatile. But for commodities whose growth period extends over several years (e.g., rubber, tea) the short-run inelasticity of supply leads instead to wide price fluctuations in response to shifts in demand. We would, in consequence, expect substantial instability in price and output for the major export commodities in the region. We would also expect that changes in export prices and sales volume would often coincide as to direction, intensifying the effects on export returns. For one-or two-commodity countries, where total exports constitute a large share of national income, these fluctuations seriously affect the total volume of economic activity. In short, the typical trade situation in South Asia makes the countries highly sensitive to conditions over which they can exert little control. Even if the foreign trade sector is relatively small, as it is in India, Pakistan, and the Philippines, the instability of export returns creates recurrent balance of payments crises that not only divert attention from other facets of development, but also impede the importation of strategic developmental products.

Regardless of the magnitude of foreign trade, the instability of receipts from major exports must be viewed as a serious weakness as well as an impediment to growth.[2] Indeed, the vulnerability of the South Asian economies to decreases in export proceeds or increases in import prices is largely independent of the relative size of their foreign trade. In this context, the composition of imports is crucial. This is shown in Table 13–3. The term "essential" imports is used in this table to denote those imports deemed necessary for developmental purposes and that portion of food imports which could not be further reduced without adverse effects on nutritional levels.[3]

[1] To illustrate, if 100 percent of domestic production of a given commodity is exported, a 10 percent decline in foreign sales reduces domestic output by 10 percent as well (assuming that change in inventory is zero); but if only 50 percent of domestic production is exported, a 10 percent reduction in foreign sales reduces domestic output by only 5 percent.

[2] For a brief discussion of the problem of instability, see Appendix 15.

[3] Needless to say, the distinction is imprecise and arbitrary. Besides assuming that the items "capital goods" and "material chiefly for capital goods" are essential develop-

Table 13–3

COMPOSITION OF IMPORTS, BY MAJOR CATEGORY, 1957–59
(*Percent of value*)

Country	*Capital goods and material chiefly for capital goods* (1)	*Ratio (percent) of essential food imports to total food imports* (2)	*Essential food imports* (3)	*Total "essential" imports* (4)
Pakistan	53	85[a]	33	86
India	55	75	15	70
Indonesia	39	86	17	56
Burma	47	39	4	51
South Vietnam	37	31	3	40
Philippines	44	56	10	54
Thailand	46	21[b]	2	48
Ceylon	29	68	27	56
Malaya and Singapore	27	48	11	38

Sources: Column 1: U. N., *Economic Survey of Asia and the Far East, 1960,* pp. 146–148.

Column 2: "Essential" food imports are defined as the ratio of "fish and preparations," "cereals and preparations," "potatoes," "pulses," "coffee, tea and cocoa" to total food imports for each country averaged over the three years (data from U. N., *Yearbook of International Trade Statistics 1959,* Volume 1, country pages). Where these details were not recorded, the most similar items were selected to obtain the ratios.

Column 3: Ratios in column 2 applied to the food component percentage listed in *Economic Survey of Asia and the Far East, 1960,* pp. 146–148.

[a] Refers to years 1957 and 1958. Ratio of wheat and rice imports only to total food imports.

[b] 1957 and 1958 only.

Rough as the data and the methods employed to deduce "essential" imports may be, the results indicate that India and Pakistan concentrate more heavily on essential imports than do the other South Asian countries. The ratio of essential food imports to total food imports is also very high

mental imports, we have attempted to isolate the "essential" portion of food imports by a very rough procedure. This procedure is outlined in the explanation of the derivation of column 2 in the table. The percentages of total imports classified as essential are probably somewhat understated since it was not possible to isolate the essential portion of non-food consumer goods. This understatement may be partly offset by the inclusion of all capital goods and "material chiefly for capital goods" in the "essential" category.

in the case of these two countries and Indonesia as well, in sharp contrast to the situation existing in the rice surplus countries, Burma and Thailand. Clearly, little scope exists for reducing food imports in India, Pakistan, and Indonesia as a means of increasing capital imports, which in India and Pakistan already account for a large share of total imports. The latter countries are thus particularly vulnerable to either a rise in import prices or a decline in export earnings. If either occurs, imports must be curtailed, and most of these appear to be in the essential category. Since neither country has substantial foreign exchange reserves, the only alternative is to seek loans or foreign grants. If such unfavorable shifts are deemed to be longer-run or chronic phenomena, a reduction in "essential" imports may be necessary, despite the adverse implications for growth rates. The crucial question then becomes one of longer-run prospects in the export markets. These are discussed below.

The imports of the other countries in the region are not so concentrated in the essential, or developmental, category. Hence, any need to curtail imports will have a much less pronounced effect on development as long as the import reduction is confined to non-essentials. This must not be taken to imply that to have a large proportion of imports in the non-essential category is necessarily desirable. It may be regarded as a sign of general affluence in a developed economy, but not in an underdeveloped one. The opportunity cost of non-essential imports might well be slower over-all economic growth. The point is, however, that if a nation is poor and has geared its developmental planning in such a way that essential imports constitute a very large proportion of total imports, as is the case with India and Pakistan, any substantial cutback in imports will seriously disrupt planned development. Therefore, although India and Pakistan have the lowest ratios of imports and exports to national income in the region, the composition of their imports gives the foreign sector a strategic significance out of proportion to its size.

Broadly speaking, the composition of imports also reflects the past development patterns discussed in Section 1 and the preceding three chapters. Countries like Malaya and Ceylon have large enough exports that they can afford to buy abroad not only large quantities of manufactured consumer goods but also much of their food. Nevertheless, Ceylon has begun to have difficulties; in January of 1961 it instituted stringent import controls to offset a deteriorating balance of payments position.[1] India and Pakistan are considerably less well situated, while the other countries are in an intermediate position.

[1] This move apparently arrested the growing export deficits, at least for a time. A decline of one-seventh in import payments during the first three quarters of 1961 more than offset a small decline in export proceeds. (See U. N., *Economic Survey of Asia and the Far East, 1961,* Bangkok, 1962, p. 152.) In 1962 and 1963 a balance of trade surplus was recorded. The Ceylonese approach to foreign exchange budgeting is described in United Nations, ECAFE, *Economic Bulletin for Asia and the Far East,* December, 1963, pp. 47–51.

More recently each country's import list has been affected by the relative intensity of its developmental efforts. The efforts put forth by the poorest countries have forced them to drastically reduce their non-essential imports, especially of consumer goods; rising defense expenditures have also affected the importation of consumer goods. India and Pakistan have gone farthest in this direction, and little scope appears to be left for significant changes in their import picture. Pakistan's Second Five Year Plan neatly summed up the problems faced by development-minded nations:

> Foreign exchange expenditure fell short of the [First] Plan projections by about Rs. 2,165 million. Food imports were higher than anticipated and other imports had to be cut correspondingly more. Imports of consumer goods were drastically reduced and imports of raw materials and spares were held well below requirements. But these measures did not prevent a disastrous cut in development imports.[1]

The projections for the plan noted an expected increase in demand for essential consumer goods imports but the plan itself held that "no provision can be made for any expansion in imports."[2]

As a result of these factors India and Pakistan have been forced into policies of import substitution,[3] and their scope for policy in general has been severely restricted.[4] The other countries of the region, having higher levels of exports and substantially smaller ratios of essential to total imports, possess greater flexibility and scope for policy. This is especially true of Malaya and Ceylon, although, as indicated above, Ceylon has tended to develop the same problems as Pakistan and India. Malaya, for its part, faces sharply rising defense outlays. The relative seriousness of these factors as far as development is concerned depends to a large extent on export prospects, and these are analyzed in Sections 12–15 below.

4 *Direction of Trade*

Another striking aspect of South Asian foreign trade is its orientation toward far distant countries. Between 50 and 60 percent of the exports from India, Pakistan, and Ceylon are sent to Western Europe and North America (see Table 13–4). More than two-thirds of South Vietnam's exports and over 70 percent of those of the Philippines go to these areas. This pattern of marketing is not wholly attributable to former colonial connections. With the West Irian dispute, Indonesia's trade with the Netherlands fell to a very low level, yet its exports to Western Europe

[1] Pakistan, Government of, Planning Commission, *The Second Five Year Plan (1960–65)*, June, 1960, p. 82.

[2] *Ibid.*, p. 89.

[3] *Ibid.*, p. 96.

[4] See Section 17.

Table 13–4

DIRECTION OF EXPORTS AND ROLE OF FORMER COLONIAL POWER

Country	Year or period	Total value of exports per year to all countries (million dollars)	Percent of total period's exports destined for: South Asia (ECAFE less Japan)	Japan	Western Europe including U. K.	Eastern Europe	North America	Latin America and Oceania	All other areas	Percentage share of former colonial power[a] in: Exports	Imports
Pakistan	1948[b]	618.4	63.8	0.6	21.6	4.0	8.0	1.8	0.2	8.7	20.1
	1950–52	597.3	31.8	11.7	39.5	5.4	5.6	1.5	4.5	13.0	21.3
	1956–58	324.8	18.0	11.9	47.8	3.2	10.9	1.9	6.3	17.1	16.9
	1959	320.0	16.7	8.3	43.1	3.8	10.4	4.6	13.1	18.5	17.7
	1962	393.2	17.7	6.3	40.9	4.0	11.4	4.1	15.6	17.4	17.8
India	1948[b]	1,371.2	26.8	1.0	31.6	1.9	17.8	12.3	9.6	21.6	22.8
	1950–52	1,372.4	19.7	2.6	33.2	0.8	21.2	10.8	11.7	22.8	19.0
	1956–58	1,272.4	11.9	4.5	37.8	3.9	20.7	7.9	13.3	27.7	22.7
	1959	1,308.0	12.6	5.5	38.5	6.9	18.5	6.4	11.6	27.6	19.5
	1962	1,414.8	10.3	5.0	34.7	11.8	21.3	5.8	11.1	23.7	16.6
Indonesia	1948	394.8	22.9	2.4	44.2	0.4	18.0	1.3	10.8	33.0	19.6
	1950–52	1,008.5	35.6	2.5	33.8	0.4	19.4	3.1	5.2	21.0[d]	17.4[d]
	1956–58	868.9	37.5	5.4	31.6	1.2	16.4	2.0	5.9	14.0	9.4
	1959	872.4	38.1	3.8	33.0	2.3	16.7	4.0	2.3	1.1	3.7
	1961	783.6	38.1	7.1	17.4	5.5	23.4	6.1	2.4	0.3	0.9
Burma	1948[c]	228.8	87.2	0.2	10.1	–	1.0	0.3	1.2	8.9	43.8
	1950–52	209.3	67.9	13.1	10.4	–	1.1	–	7.5	6.9	23.3
	1956–58	212.4	63.3	11.2	10.6	8.0	1.1	–	5.8	7.0	20.4
	1959	218.8	66.2	3.8	16.5	4.4	0.9	–	8.2	9.1	19.2
	1962	257.6	59.8	4.7	19.6	7.0	0.3	–	8.6	9.8	15.0

South Vietnam	1955–56	57.0	22.8	1.8	47.7	—	21.4	—	6.3	59.0	38.2
	1957–59	70.0	19.6	3.2	55.4	—	10.9	0.2	11.7	51.7[e]	27.2[e]
	1962	64.0	16.4	5.2	69.3	—	3.6	—	5.5	36.4	13.2
Philippines	1948	317.6	4.2	4.9	16.6	2.5	67.8	1.9	2.1	66.0	82.0
	1950–52	366.3	1.6	8.2	16.8	—	71.0	2.4	—	69.9	72.8
	1956–58	458.7	2.5	18.5	20.0	—	54.0	3.1	1.9	54.0	58.0
	1959	574.8	2.9	22.9	16.8	—	55.1	1.9	0.4	55.1	48.9
	1962	554.4	4.3	23.7	17.7	—	50.9	1.6	1.8	51.6	43.9
Thailand	1948	205.6	65.0	—	7.0	—	25.5	0.4	2.1	...	...
	1950–52	402.0	52.4	13.2	6.6	—	26.2	0.2	1.4	...	...
	1956–58	336.0	53.9	8.0	12.9	—	21.3	0.3	2.2	...	...
	1959	359.2	43.5	11.7	9.4	—	24.7	0.6	10.1	...	...
	1962	454.4	48.2	14.4	20.5	1.5	8.8	0.7	5.9	—	—
Ceylon	1948	305.6	5.9	0.1	40.2	0.7	20.9	12.4	19.8	30.0	17.6
	1950–52	347.7	8.7	0.3	44.1	0.5	19.2	9.9	17.3	27.6	21.7
	1956–58	354.8	12.6	1.6	39.8	0.3	13.9	9.1	22.7	30.1	22.0
	1959	355.2	8.7	2.5	41.0	1.9	15.3	9.1	21.5	28.4	24.7
	1962	370.8	13.4	0.2	40.0	4.5	13.4	7.3	21.2	30.0	20.6
Malaya and	1948	812.8	23.4	1.1	28.8	7.1	29.5	7.7	2.4	13.9	19.2
Singapore[f]	1950–52	1,525.7	22.6	3.0	35.8	3.5	23.4	7.4	4.3	18.4	18.3
	1956–58	1,381.7	24.0	8.7	32.5	4.2	14.5	7.6	8.5	14.2	17.6
	1959	1,434.4	20.6	11.3	31.0	10.7	15.4	7.3	3.7	12.2	14.2
	1962	1,496.8	22.3	8.5	29.3	9.7	16.5	5.7	8.0	8.4	14.7

Sources: United Nations data from various issues of *Economic Survey of Asia and the Far East; Yearbook of International Trade Statistics;* and *Direction of International Trade.*

[a] U. K. for India, Pakistan, Burma, Ceylon, Malaya and Singapore; Netherlands for Indonesia; France for South Vietnam; U.S.A. for Philippines. The shares in 1935–36 for exports and imports, respectively, were: India (including Pakistan and Burma), 32.2 percent, 15.1 percent; Philippines, 80.1 percent, 62.1 percent; Malaya, 12.3 percent, 15.5 percent (League of Nations, *International Trade Statistics 1937*, Geneva, 1938, country pages).
[b] Year begins 1st April. [c] Year ending September 30. [d] 1951–52. [e] 1957–58.
[f] Until 1952, figures for British Malaya are given. Subsequent ECAFE figures separate the Federation of Malaya from Singapore, but exclude trade between Malaya and Singapore. Our figures therefore represent the trade of the two territories, regarded as a unit, with the rest of the world.

as a whole remained substantial. The import situation is quite as striking. Between 1955 and 1957, Malaya and Singapore received over 30 percent of their imports from North America and Western Europe, while Ceylon and Thailand received just over 45 percent. No other country received less than half its imports from these sources. The Philippines received three-quarters of its total imports from these distant countries; India, Burma, Pakistan, and Indonesia each over 60 percent.[1]

Only the big rice exporters, Burma and Thailand, and to a lesser extent Indonesia, send significant shares of their exports to other South Asian countries. The Philippines sends less than 5 percent of its total exports to other South Asian countries and Ceylon under 15 percent, even though, as small countries, they should control a relatively large South Asian market. For India, the comparable figure is well below 15 percent; for Pakistan and South Vietnam it is under one-fifth, and for Malaya with Singapore, just over one-fifth. On the import side, as of 1963, Pakistan, India, Thailand, and the Philippines took less than 15 percent of their imports from other South Asian countries, and the trend since 1957 has been downward for each of these countries. Ceylon, Indonesia, and Burma received between 28 and 34 percent of their total imports from the region in 1963; Malaya, about 40 percent.[2] Indonesia increased the proportion of its total imports coming from the region to almost 30 percent during the early 1960's. Although Ceylon receives close to one-third of its imports from the other South Asian countries, this represents a decline from the figure of over 40 percent recorded in 1957.

Japan is a major importer from South Asia, accounting for over 20 percent of Philippine exports and around 10 percent of exports from Pakistan, Thailand, and Malaya. Aside from those already discussed, no single region is very important, but Australasia occupies a respectable, though declining, position as a buyer from Ceylon and Malaya.

The position of the former colonial powers, though not a sufficient explanation of the very large role of distant regions in both export and import trade of South Asia, is of considerable importance. Over half of the exports of the Philippines go to the United States, and almost half its imports are from that country. About a quarter of India's and Ceylon's trade is with Britain, as is around one-fifth of Pakistan's and one-seventh of Burma's and Malaya's. Only Indonesia does very little business with the former colonial power. Continued reliance on the former metropolitan countries reflects the "enforced bilateralism" of the colonial period. "Behind this massive protection an institutional structure of business was built up, controlled from the metropolitan country, which . . . functioned

[1] U. N., *Economic Survey of Asia and the Far East, 1959*, Bangkok, 1960, p. 80.

[2] *Ibid.*, p. 80; and *Economic Bulletin for Asia and the Far East*, June, 1964, Table 7, pp. 78–81.

to keep out intruders from other trading countries."[1] After independence the institutional structure tended to persist, except in Indonesia where it was forcibly destroyed. Thus India and Pakistan have exceedingly large trading organizations attached to their High Commissions in London and even conduct most of their trade with other West European countries from that city.

5 *Changes in Trading Position in Recent Decades*

Now that colonialism is ended in South Asia, those in charge of the economic destiny of the region view the present economic structure, not as something static, but as a point of departure. Regardless of the diligence with which they pursue the goal of development, however, their efforts may be thwarted by factors over which they have no control. All the countries in the region are excessively dependent on external conditions, and the trends in foreign trade over the past several decades and the prospects inherent in these trends are such as to have a seriously adverse influence on the growth prospects of every country, though in varying degree. As these developments have been recounted in great detail in publications of the United Nations,[2] we are able to treat them with a brevity altogether out of proportion to their importance and concentrate on the broader picture. We would, however, urge the reader to examine the provocative analyses in the works just cited.

Three global trends are directly related to trade developments in the South Asian economies. For one thing, world production has tended to increase more rapidly than world trade since at least the late 1920's,[3] a reversal of the situation in the nineteenth century. And although recent years have seen something of a shift in this pattern, South Asia has not participated in the renewed export dynamism. Secondly, world trade as a whole has increased more than world trade in primary commodities.[4] Because the countries of South Asia rely heavily on exports of such commodities, the world tendency adversely affects their relative position. Finally, it is significant and ominous that the increase in international trade in primary commodities since the late 1920's for the world as a whole has

[1] Gunnar Myrdal, *An International Economy*, Harper, New York, 1956, p. 286.

[2] Department of Economic and Social Affairs, *World Economic Survey 1956*, New York, 1957, Chapters 1 and 3; Economic Commission for Europe, *Economic Survey of Europe in 1957*, Geneva, 1958, Chapters 4 and 5; *Economic Survey of Asia and the Far East, 1959*, Part II; and *Economic Bulletin for Asia and the Far East*, December, 1963.

[3] See, for example, U. N., *World Economic Survey 1958*, New York, 1959, p. 17.

[4] U. N., *World Economic Survey 1958*, p. 17; and U. N., *Economic Bulletin for Asia and the Far East*, June, 1964, pp. 2–3.

exceeded that for the ECAFE region, which encompassses the nations of major concern to this study.[1] These tendencies in international trade over more than a third of a century have all militated against primary producing countries in general and the South Asian nations in particular. Indeed, if we exclude petroleum, which is not at present a major item for the economies of the South Asian countries, the volume of exports from South Asia toward the end of the 1950's appears to have "remained about the same as in 1927–29," and if rubber is excluded, to have declined by about 25 percent.[2] In view of the rapid economic growth in North America, Western Europe, and other areas to which South Asia typically sells, this stagnation of export volume is rather surprising. Certain key factors appear to account for it.

In the first place, demand for food tends, as a general rule, to lag behind increases in income per head. This is true especially of basic foodstuffs such as cereals, but at higher income levels the demand per head for sugar also levels off. A similar situation obtains in textile fabrics. As a result, the demand for four of South Asia's major exportable items – rice, sugar, cotton, and jute – has lagged well behind economic growth in the West. Only for beverages (including tea) and copra has demand expanded at a substantially faster pace than demand for foods in general, but in neither case is there evidence that dynamic growth is in store. In addition to a certain natural sluggishness in the demand for all these items, the region has been adversely affected by the increase in substitutes for textile fibres.[3] The use of synthetic fibres, the substitution of sack paper for jute, and technological advances that reduce the primary fibre content of finished products have combined to bring about a decline in textile fibre consumption per head in both the United States and Western Europe since the 1920's.[4] South Asia has also been affected by the rise of competing exporters, notably Japan, and by protectionist policies in the

[1] U. N., *Economic Survey of Asia and the Far East, 1959*, p. 55; see also U. N., *Economic Bulletin for Asia and the Far East*, June, 1964, pp. 2–3.

The ECAFE statistics relate to eight of the nine countries discussed in our study (South Vietnam is excluded) plus British Borneo and Iran.

[2] U. N., *Economic Survey of Asia and the Far East, 1959*, p. 58. The data refer to the underdeveloped countries in the ECAFE region. The exclusion of petroleum reduces whatever distortion Iran may have imparted to the evidence, and the exports of British Borneo are not such as seriously to distort the general picture.

[3] Production of rayon and non-cellulosics (i.e., man-made fibres) increased from 1.7 million metric tons in 1952 to more than 3.9 million in 1962. Their share in the combined production of man-made fibres, cotton, and wool increased from less than 15 percent in 1952 to over 24 percent in 1962. See United Nations Conference on Trade and Development, *Synthetics and Their Effects on Agricultural Trade*, E/Conf. 46/59, March 6, 1964, Table III.1, p. 51. For further details see *ibid.*, pp. 47–75.

[4] The 1955–57 level for the United States was about three-fourths that of 1927–29; for Western Europe it was some four-fifths. (U. N., *Economic Survey of Asia and the Far East, 1959*, p. 57.)

West designed to support a faltering domestic textile industry. Exports from South Asia of textiles and other important commodities have thus been faced with increasing competition at a time when substitutes, rising efficiency, protectionism and surpluses, especially in the United States and Canada, have operated to reduce the rate of increase of total consumption in the major markets. Indeed, a study projecting exports from countries in South Asia to 1980 suggests that the "outlook is positively gloomy for such commodities as tea, sugar, cotton and jute."[1]

The situation is similar with respect to industrial raw materials. The demand for tin – the most important metal export of the region – although buoyant in recent years, will be increasingly eroded by the growth of substitutes and by technological advances that reduce the quantity of raw material per unit of output, especially at the high prices now prevailing.[2] Although total demand for rubber has increased rapidly with the rise of the automotive industry in North America and Europe, natural rubber has encountered serious competition from synthetic rubber.[3] Both the tin and rubber markets have been subject to governmental intervention in the West, with the United States government, for example, originally sponsoring synthetic rubber research and alternately stockpiling and releasing tin. Synthetic rubber plants have also been established in Western Europe and Japan.

From the point of view of demand, then, it is apparent that the South Asian economies depend heavily on exports of consumer goods whose income elasticities are low. Therefore, economic growth in the major markets of the West has not generated a concomitant increase in sales of these items. This was to be expected and would have occurred regardless of restrictive policies, substitutes, or new suppliers; the effect of the latter has been mainly to accentuate an inevitable sluggishness. A similar, though less pronounced, deterrent to rapid growth in exports of industrial raw materials has been the accelerating pace of technological advance, which has made possible increasing economy in the use of raw materials. Short-

[1] U. N., *Economic Bulletin for Asia and the Far East,* December, 1963, p. 15. See below in Sections 12–13.

[2] See Appendix 15 for recent experience in the tin market.

[3] For example, consumption of natural rubber in the industrialized countries of North America, Western Europe (the United Kingdom and the E.E.C.), and in Japan increased by only 15 percent between 1950–52 and 1955–57, whereas synthetic rubber consumption increased by 44 percent. In each of these countries, the ratio of synthetic to total rubber consumption rose sharply over the same period. ("The Demand for Industrial Materials, 1950–57," *National Institute Economic Review,* No. 5, September, 1959, Tables 12 and 23, pp. 25, 34. Further details on the inroads made by synthetic rubber are given in Charles F. Phillips, Jr., "The Competitive Potential of Synthetic Rubber," *Land Economics,* November, 1960, pp. 322–332.) Between 1952 and 1962 the share of natural rubber consumption in total rubber consumption in the world fell from 62 to 50 percent after having reached 71 percent in 1954. (U. N. Conference, *Synthetics and Their Effects on Agricultural Trade,* Table II.4, p. 25.)

ages during the Second World War and the concern manifested by conservationists over depletion of resources provided an additional stimulus to those kinds of technological change which yield rising output per unit of resource input. In consequence, economic growth in many industries constituting South Asia's raw material markets was not translated into equivalent growth of demand. As in the case of demand for consumer goods, this is a fact independent of, though in this case related to, development of substitute products, new sources of supply, and, on occasion, import restrictions and tariffs designed to support domestic conservation policies that have the effect of raising domestic resource prices relative to those elsewhere, thereby seeming to justify even higher tariffs.

Part of the explanation of the over-all stagnation of exports from South Asia resides, however, on the side of supply. Wartime destruction was especially heavy in Burma and Indonesia and this, in conjunction with post-war political disturbances, which prevented full recovery, reduced total exports. The population increase in the region has tended to diminish exportable surpluses in some lines. For example, exports of rice by the rice surplus countries have been reduced, and the effects of population growth on demand in the rice-importing countries have been partly offset by their attempts at self-sufficiency. In the case of Malayan and Ceylonese rubber there has been concern that new plantings of high-yielding trees are proceeding too slowly.[1] In recent years, however, considerable replanting has taken place in Malaya. Between 1955 and 1963, of the 1.4 million acres planted to rubber, some 73 percent represented replanting.[2] For most of the other commodities, scarcity of an exportable surplus has not been a significant factor. In some instances, of which jute is one, supply has been excessive; in Indian textile manufacturing excess capacity has become very great.[3] Thus far, domestic consumption in India and Pakistan has taken up much of the increased supply of jute and cotton.

Aggregate export stagnation, serious enough in itself, has been accompanied by trends in export composition that cannot be regarded as favorable. As Table 13–5 shows, several countries – notably Burma, Indonesia, and Ceylon – have grown more dependent on a constant or shrinking number of commodities, and such diversification as has taken place has not been significant except for Pakistan and India. Elsewhere the region is becoming more rather than less dependent on developments in particular markets. This tendency has obvious adverse implications for growth when viewed along with the natural sluggishness of demand mentioned earlier.

Moreover, there has been no decrease in dependence on traditional

[1] International Bank for Reconstruction and Development, *The Economic Development of Malaya,* Johns Hopkins Press, Baltimore, 1955, p. 49.

[2] U. N. Conference, *Synthetics and Their Effects on Agricultural Trade,* p. 14, f.n. 1.

[3] See Donald MacDougall, "India's Balance of Payments," *Economic Weekly,* April 22 and 29, 1961, Table 1.

Table 13–5

TRENDS IN COMPOSITION OF EXPORTS, BY VALUE, 1937, 1957–59, AND 1960–62

		Percent of total		
Country	*Product*	*1937*	*Average 1957–59*	*Average 1960–62*
Pakistan	Jute	39[a]	50	43
	Cotton	43[a]	15	8
India	Tea	19[a]	21	19
	Jute and Bagging	21[a]	16	13
Indonesia	Rubber	30	40	42
	Petroleum	17	31	30
	Tin	8	5	5
	Cocoanut products	7	4	4
Burma	Rice	42	74 (Rice and Teak)	66
	Teak	7		9
	Cotton	2	2	3
	(Petroleum)	25	–	–
South Vietnam	Rubber	–	62	62
	Rice	–	27	23
Philippines	Cocoanut products	28	37	28
	Sugar	38	21	24
	Abaca	14	7	–
	Wood	–	13	18
Thailand	Rice	46	43	34
	Rubber	14	23	25
	Tin	23	6	7
Ceylon	Tea	52	62	63
	Rubber	23	17	17
	Cocoanut products	12	11	11
Malaya	Rubber	64[b]	61	56
	Tin	15[b]	13	21

Source: International Monetary Fund, *International Financial Statistics*, Vol. X, No. 9, Sept., 1957, pp. 28–29 (1937 data), Vol. XIV, No. 6, June, 1961, country pages (1957–59 data), and later issues.

[a] 1953. [b] 1950.

products. On the contrary, primary commodities are mostly as important in the export inventory now as in the past, or even more so. But these are precisely the commodities that have exhibited sluggish growth rates and the prospects for which seem least favorable. Not only, then, has the trend in aggregate exports been sluggish, but the composition of the aggregate has either not altered significantly or has changed in such a way as to increase the area's dependence on a few commodities whose prospects do not seem bright.

In contrast to the stagnant over-all export trend, import needs, and actual imports as well, have risen sharply. The increase in imports between 1928 and 1955–57 in the ECAFE region was almost three times the rise in exports.[1] From 1950 to 1960, commodity imports into the ECAFE region grew at a compound annual rate of 4.3 percent, while commodity exports grew at a rate of only 1.9 percent.[2] Import needs, even more than actual imports, have increased substantially for two main reasons: population growth and developmental efforts since the Second World War.

Since the Second World War population has increased at an ever faster pace, a development analyzed in Chapter 27. The rise in food production has been slow, with the result that the exporting countries have had less food available for export, while the importing countries have had to increase their purchases. South Asia, which until the war had been a net exporter, turned into a net importer with an ever bigger deficit. Cereal exports of the ECAFE region as a whole (excluding China) declined from 4.4 million tons in 1927–29 to 3.1 million in 1955–57, while cereal imports rose from 2.3 to 5.4 million tons over this period.[3] Estimates available for 1964–65 suggest that as far as wheat and rice are concerned, the net deficit of the South Asian countries has risen to about 5½ million tons.[4] Despite the rise in total food consumption, nutritional standards have not improved; instead they have mostly tended to decline and are now well below pre-war levels.[5] It is estimated that "unless the past rate of increase of food production can be increased, net import of cereals in 1970, if domestic demand is to be fully met, may have to be increased to as much as 18 million tons,"[6] or about three times the current figure. Of course, some countries have been more successful than others in raising cereal production in relation to population.[7] Thailand, in particular, has done fairly well, as have Malaya and Ceylon, while Indonesia, Burma, and, until recently, Pakistan have made relatively little progress.[8] India's difficulties,

[1] U. N., *Economic Survey of Asia and the Far East, 1959,* p. 55.

[2] U. N., *Economic Bulletin for Asia and the Far East,* June, 1964, Table 1, p. 1.

[3] U. N., *Economic Survey of Asia and the Far East, 1959,* p. 77.

[4] Food and Agriculture Organization, *Monthly Bulletin of Agricultural Economics and Statistics,* March, 1966, Table A, p. 20.

[5] Chapter 12, Section 4.

[6] U. N., *Economic Survey of Asia and the Far East, 1964,* p. 1.

[7] Chapter 26, Section 2.

[8] Food and Agriculture Organization, *The State of Food and Agriculture 1965,* Review of the Second Postwar Decade, Rome, 1965, Annex Table 2B, p. 217.

which raised her estimated annual deficit to 16 million tons at the end of 1965,[1] were discussed in Chapter 7 (Section 4); see also Chapter 26.

Developmental efforts in the South Asian countries have caused demand for capital equipment, industrial raw materials, and spare parts to soar. It will be seen from Table 13–6 that imports of machinery and transport equipment from Western Europe, the United States, and Japan accounted for 40 percent of Indian and Pakistani imports in 1955–57, against 15 percent in 1928. In absolute terms, this represents a three-fold increase in these important requisites for industrial growth. The difference brought out in this table between India and Pakistan on the one hand and ten other countries of the region on the other is very marked. The data for India provide striking evidence of a progressive substitution of essential food, capital, and industrial raw material imports for less essential or non-essential items. Sugar, liquors, manufactured tobacco, and cotton fabrics have almost completely disappeared from India's import list. A major reason is import substitution, especially in the textiles category, where not only India but also Pakistan are net exporters today. But direct import controls have been more thoroughgoing in these countries and have frozen out imports even when domestic substitutes were not available.

In short, with the aggregate volume of imports held down by relatively low and stagnant export levels and by dwindling foreign exchange reserves, it is necessary to regulate the composition of the import total. Unless specific imports are curbed, non-essential imports, especially of consumer goods, will tend to crowd out essential imports.[2] For example, Ceylon, where stringent import restrictions were lacking until the beginning of the 1960's and import substitution has been insignificant, reveals a "pattern of change strikingly different from that in India."[3] Non-essential consumer goods showed the largest increase of any category of Ceylon's imports from 1928 to 1954–56, whereas investment goods increased only moderately. However, Ceylon's Ten Year Plan proposed that the share of consumer goods in total imports be reduced from almost 58 percent in 1957 to 40 percent in 1968.[4] Even though the plan has not been followed in regard to investment for development, the import controls imposed have had the effect of shrinking imports of non-essential consumer goods.

Pressures for increased imports also arise for other reasons. In some countries, welfare measures, such as the rice subsidy in Ceylon, augment supernumerary income, part of which may be spent on foreign goods though it is mainly needed to maintain or raise standards of nutrition. Since independence, maintenance of domestic military establishments has

[1] *Indian and Foreign Review*, December 15, 1965, p. 8.
[2] Appendix 8, Section 1.
[3] U. N. *Economic Survey of Asia and the Far East, 1959*, p. 83.
[4] Ceylon, Government of, National Planning Council, *The Ten-Year Plan*, Colombo, 1959, pp. 83–85.

Table 13–6

COMPOSITION OF IMPORTS FROM WESTERN EUROPE, THE UNITED STATES, AND JAPAN, BY VALUE, 1928 AND 1955–57

Commodity	*Percent of total imports*	
	Ten countries in South Asia[a]	*India and Pakistan*
Food, drink, and tobacco		
1928	6	4
1955–57	7	2
Metals and manufactures		
1928	6	7
1955–57	6	7
Steel		
1928	7	8
1955–57	9	17
Machinery and transport equipment		
1928	19	15
1955–57	28	40
Chemicals		
1928	4	4
1955–57	8	9
Textiles		
1928	29	44
1955–57	17	5
All other goods		
1928	29	18
1955–57	24	20
Total value[b]		
1928	$ 994	$1,142
1955–57	$1,833	$1,376
1955–57 index (1928 = 100)	184	120

Source: U. N., *Economic Survey of Asia and the Far East, 1959*, p. 81.

[a] Burma, Ceylon, Cambodia, Laos, Vietnam, Federation of Malaya and Singapore, Indonesia, Philippines, and Thailand.

[b] Value in millions of dollars at constant 1950 prices.

necessitated imports of armaments, which have grown rapidly of late, particularly in Pakistan, India, Indonesia, and Malaya. The increasing income inequality evident in most of the countries also stimulates demand for imports that may be deemed non-essential. All of these factors, coupled with population growth and developmental plans, augment demand for imports of various types. If export proceeds were large and growing, total imports in all categories would doubtless rise. But the limitation imposed by the relatively sluggish growth of export markets means that a choice must be made among classes of imports. The problem of selection is difficult, especially where the import inventory is already heavily weighted with essentials as it is in India and Pakistan.

In summary, for the region as a whole, the past three or four decades have witnessed a steady acceleration of import needs in the face of export potentialities that exhibit no comparable dynamism. Indeed, the sharp fluctuations in actual export earnings about a secular trend, which itself falls short of the chronically rising import requirements, are apt to involve almost all the South Asian countries in a series of acute and worsening balance of payments crises.[1] Further widening of the gap between needs and prospects is probable, as we shall indicate later in this chapter.

6 *Trends in Direction of Trade*

It is apparent from Table 13–4 that South Asia's dependence on Western Europe as a market for its exports was generally higher in 1961–62 than in 1948. Data available from other sources confirm that in every case the importance of the former colonial power is now somewhat less than in pre-war times.[2] But a larger proportion of South Asian trade is concentrated in Western Europe and North America, taken together, than in 1937. Thus the trading patterns established in the colonial period linger on in the form of export dependence on the developed countries of the West.

Exports to Communist countries are now somewhat larger than before the war, though not in real terms. Estimates suggest that the total imports of these countries from selected Asian countries (Burma, Cambodia, Ceylon, Federation of Malaya, Singapore, India, Indonesia, Laos, Pakistan, South Vietnam, and Hong Kong) were valued, in current terms, at roughly $440 million in 1938 but at about $480 million in 1961.[3] These figures hide dramatic shifts away from China and toward East European Communist countries (including the U.S.S.R.). According to the same series of estimates, China accounted for virtually all (95.5 percent) of the $440 million

[1] See Sections 12–17 below. On fluctuations in export earnings and their impact see Appendix 15. On the necessity of import controls independent of exchange rates, see Appendix 8, Sections 1–2.

[2] League of Nations, *International Trade Statistics 1937*, Geneva, 1938, p. 207; and U. N., *Economic Bulletin for Asia and the Far East*, September, 1960, Tables 4 and 7.

[3] The 1938 estimate is from U. N., *Economic Survey of Asia and the Far East, 1959*, Table 41, p. 98, and the 1961 estimate is from United Nations Conference on Trade and Development, *Trade Between Developing ECAFE Countries and Centrally Planned Economies*, E/Conf. 46/39, January 27, 1964, Table 8, p. 19.

Table 13–7

TRADE WITH COMMUNIST COUNTRIES, 1955 AND 1961

(*Percent of total value of imports and exports*)

Country		1955		1961	
		Imports	Exports	Imports	Exports
Pakistan	A	0.2	1.7	1.3	5.1
	B	0.1	7.9	0.5	2.5
India	A	1.2	0.7	6.2	8.4
	B	0.4	1.1	0.2	–
Indonesia	A	4.5	2.8	4.9	5.5
	B	1.6	0.7	5.0	4.6
Burma	A	1.0	9.9	4.8	3.1
	B	1.3	7.7	9.7	17.2
Thailand	A	–	–	1.0	1.5
	B	–	–	–	–
Ceylon	A	0.5	0.1	2.8	4.7
	B	5.5	6.3	2.0	4.9
Fed. of Malaya and Singapore	A	0.3	1.1	0.7	8.9
	B	3.0	0.3	3.8	0.3

Source: United Nations Conference on Trade and Development, *Trade Between Developing ECAFE Countries and Centrally Planned Economies,* E/Conf. 46/39, January 27, 1964, p. 15.

A = Trade with European Communist countries (including the U.S.S.R.).
B = Trade with Asian Communist countries (China and North Vietnam).

of imports in 1938, whereas the East European countries absorbed around 75 percent of the $480 million in 1961. Although the over-all growth of this trade was not spectacular, it accelerated toward the end of the period. Burma, Ceylon, and, especially, Malaya and Singapore, India, and Indonesia all sent a larger proportion of their exports to European Communist countries in 1961 than they did in 1955. As Table 13–7 shows, as of 1961 most of these countries sent about 10 percent of their exports to the Communist countries, and received about 5–7 percent of their imports from them. Burma's trade was heavily oriented to China, while Ceylon's and Indonesia's trade was about equally divided between the Asian and European Communist nations. The other countries listed in Table 13–7 traded, as of 1961, primarily with Eastern Europe. Because the post-war trade with the Communist countries has shown sharp fluctuations, related to both political and economic circumstances, it is difficult to establish any long-term trend. However, the evidence appears to suggest that over-all trade with the East European Communist countries has generally been rising at a considerable pace, whereas trade with China has been falling off. There are, of course, individual variations: Burma and Indonesia[1] have been trading more extensively with China, while India's trade with China has all but ceased since the border war. But in general it appears that Eastern Europe may provide increasing outlets for South Asian products.[2] The future place of China in South Asian trade will depend on China's ability to stabilize and accelerate its rate of economic growth. If China is successful in this endeavor, it could become a very significant export market, especially for the Southeast Asian countries. As yet, however, there has been no definite indication of growth, and the present level of trade appears to be well below that prevailing in the late 1930's.

Japan is important for South Asia, buying large amounts of cereals from Burma and Thailand and sugar and raw materials from Indonesia and the Philippines while providing manufactured goods to all countries of the region. In 1959, Japanese purchases constituted about 10 percent of total

[1] The Indonesian situation in early 1966 suggests that trade relations with China will deteriorate sharply.

[2] The comments in the text are based on U. N., *Economic Survey of Asia and the Far East, 1959,* Tables 41 and 44, pp. 98 and 99; and *Trade Between ECAFE Countries and Centrally Planned Economies.* Official data from the Soviet Union (Ministerstvo Vneshnei Torgovli, Planovoekonomicheskoe upravlenie, *Vneshniaia torgovlia Soiuza S S R,* for various years since 1955) showing imports from and exports to the South Asian economies yield rather different results. The data from this source are presented in Table 13–8. In almost every case, there is evidence of a fairly sharp rise in trade with the Soviet Union over the 1955–64 period. But perhaps equally important are the big year-to-year changes.

Of some interest is the discrepancy between these figures and those in U. N., *Economic Survey of Asia and the Far East, 1959,* p. 99. The following table shows the differences for one year, based on a conversion factor of 4 rubles equals 1 U. S. dollar:

	Exports to the Soviet Union in 1957, in millions of U. S. dollars	
Exporting country	*ECAFE estimate*	*Soviet estimate*
Burma	9	9
India	37	42
Indonesia	7	20
Malaya*	13	49
Pakistan	4	5
Ceylon	–	–
Total for these 6 countries	70	125

* The gap between the estimates is all the more surprising as the ECAFE estimates include Singapore while those of the Soviet Union relate to the Federation of Malaya.

These differences warn once again against taking the data too literally. However, even accepting the higher Soviet figures, the ratio of exports to the U.S.S.R. to total exports for the six countries listed above was less than 3 percent, whereas using ECAFE data it was less than 2 percent. Total trade with the U.S.S.R. remains very small, even though it has been rising as noted in the text and in Table 13–8.

Table 13–8

TRADE WITH THE SOVIET UNION, 1955–64
(*Millions of dollars;*[a] *exports f.o.b. Soviet ports, imports f.o.b. foreign ports*)

	1955		*1956*		*1957*		*1958*		*1959*	
Country	*Exp.*	*Imp.*	*Exp.*	*Imp.*	*Exp.*	*Imp.*	*Exp.*	*Imp.*	*Exp.*	*Imp.*
Pakistan	0.33	0	0.11	0.66	1.65	5.06	1.98	7.37	.99	3.63
India	7.26	4.40	40.04	18.15	83.82	41.58	128.70	50.38	67.32	59.95
Indonesia	0.11	3.63	0.22	12.76	5.61	19.58	26.95	11.44	15.62	10.89
Burma	0.22	16.61	4.29	12.10	6.38	9.02	2.53	0	1.54	3.96
Thailand	–	–	–	–	–	–	0.33	0	0.88	2.86
Ceylon	–	–	0	–	0	0.22	0.55	4.29	0.55	4.62
Malaya (Fed.)	–	21.56	0.33	83.16	0.66	48.29	0	116.82	0.88	125.4
Total	7.92	46.20	44.99	126.83	98.12	123.75	161.04	190.30	87.78	211.31

Source: Ministerstvo Vneshnei Torgovli, Planovoekonomicheskoe upravlenie, *Vneshniaia torgovlia Soiuza S S R,* for various years.

[a] The ruble was devalued on January 1, 1961; the figures in this table relate to the "new" ruble valued at 90 kopeks per dollar.

exports from South Asia, excluding Singapore. As Table 13–4 shows, Japan has become increasingly important as an export market for the Philippines and Thailand.

Concomitant with the growing importance of the Western countries in South Asia's foreign trade, which until now has been the most important trend discernible, has been the decline in trade within the region. India's and Pakistan's exports to other South Asian countries have fallen off sharply, both in value and in relation to total exports. In the case of India such exports declined from $367 million in 1948 to $140 million in 1962 in current values and much more in real terms. In the rice-exporting countries – Burma, Thailand, and South Vietnam – the share of exports destined for other South Asian countries has also declined sharply and steadily. Only in Indonesia has the proportion of exports going to South Asian countries shown an upward trend since 1948. The rise has been chiefly in rubber, copra, pepper, and petroleum products to Singapore (mostly for re-export outside the region)[1] and, to a far lesser extent, crude petroleum and petroleum products to the Philippines. The import position is similar. In 1949–51 about 20 percent of total South Asian imports were received

[1] This trade declined sharply with "confrontation"; see Chapter 5, Section 12. Indeed, the ending of trade relations with the Federation of Malaysia is estimated to have caused unemployment in Singapore to rise by almost 12 percent of the work force. (See E. L. Wheelwright, *Industrialization in Malaysia,* Melbourne University Press, London, 1965, pp. 141–143.)

Table 13–8 (continued)

	1960		*1961*		*1962*		*1963*		*1964*	
Country	*Exp.*	*Imp.*	*Exp.*	*Imp.*	*Exp.*	*Imp.*	*Exp.*	*Imp.*	*Exp.*	*Imp.*
Pakistan	2.42	4.40	2.97	4.29	5.06	3.85	6.16	9.57	10.89	2.64
India	46.64	67.76	94.49	66.22	123.20	70.95	219.67	93.83	229.46	154.33
Indonesia	16.06	31.13	31.02	33.55	57.97	38.28	49.39	29.48	46.20	25.52
Burma	1.76	4.95	3.85	2.42	5.83	12.21	6.60	13.64	6.49	20.13
Thailand	1.43	3.43	1.65	9.68	0.99	9.24	1.54	3.52	1.76	0
Ceylon	0.99	8.47	1.76	8.91	10.01	6.05	19.03	7.26	24.42	22.06
Malaya (Fed.)	2.09	110.44	1.98	167.86	2.20	159.39	4.29	132.44	3.30	70.18
Total	71.39	230.58	37.72	292.93	205.26	299.97	306.68	289.74	322.52	295.46

from other South Asian countries; by 1955–57 the proportion was approximately 15 percent.[1] An alternative estimate suggests that the share of intra-regional trade in total imports declined from 36 percent in 1950–52 to 23 percent in 1959–61.[2] Regardless of the size of relative shares, the trend has been sharply downward.

There has been increasing awareness that, given the generally unfavorable export climate, a continuation of this trend will deter economic growth. This fact should give added importance to attempts to stimulate intra-regional trade and reverse the present tendencies. Before we can assess the feasibility of such attempts, we must analyze the reasons for the declining importance of trade among the South Asian countries.

Broadly speaking, the basic cause is itself the general lack of economic growth in these countries. This phenomenon acts to depress intra-regional trade in several ways. In the first place, it naturally induces autarkic efforts to prevent continued stagnation, which take the form, in the realm of international trade, of restrictive import policies: each nation tries to pare down its imports to goods required for development purposes, such as capital equipment and heavy machinery. The effect, naturally, is discrimination against other South Asian countries where this type of equipment is also in short supply. The desire to curtail over-all imports because of weak export markets likewise encourages import substitution and self-sufficiency. Since it is easiest for an underdeveloped economy to achieve independence in those lines that require little in the way of scarce capital, the effect is to stimulate the development of industries that are competitive with those of the other underdeveloped South Asian countries. One

[1] U. N., *Economic Survey of Asia and the Far East, 1959*, p. 80.
[2] U. N., *Economic Bulletin for Asia and the Far East,* June, 1964, p. 4.

United Nations study even concludes that the "declining trends in intra-regional trade can be explained mainly by the deliberate import substitution policy."[1] This has become especially apparent in the sharp decline in the trade of cotton piecegoods and rice within the region.

But a more fundamental explanation is provided by the colonial heritage. The trading relations that developed over the past hundred years linked the various parts of South Asia closely to the colonial powers but did not link areas within South Asia itself. Thus transport and communication networks were not set up to foster intra-regional trade. On the contrary, their location and improvement focussed trade patterns on regions far removed, mainly Western Europe. The entire bias was anti-regional, not only as to physical inter-connections but also as to the whole network of commercial and financial transactions. The reasons why these patterns have persisted since independence are not hard to discern. The alteration of long-established trade patterns is an expensive and risky undertaking; none of the countries could very well afford it in the face of more immediately pressing needs, and few dared to try it on any large scale.

Several factors reinforced this natural reluctance. In the first place, the shortage of foreign exchange reserves accentuated the hazards of such experimental changes. Secondly, the entire approach to planning for development leads essentially to introversion. It is India's economic growth that concerns the Indian Planning Commission, not the growth of India's neighbors. In the competitive struggle to move ahead there may even be an unspoken belief that a neighboring country's gain is one's own loss – a Mercantilist form of rivalry that may lurk not very far below the surface especially where inter-country political or religious tensions exist and as no country is registering significant progress. Planning is introverted also because a nation has far more control over its internal affairs than over its international relations. Thirdly, not the least important barrier to changes in patterns of trade has been the fact that the necessary external financing must come primarily from the developed countries, often the former colonial powers. Finally, present trading patterns, especially with the former colonial powers, are maintained partly by preferential treatment, which the favored countries are naturally reluctant to give up. Obviously, all these factors have been made more inhibiting by the lack of vigorous expansion. With substantial economic growth, the ability to change patterns of trade advantageously would have increased, though at the same time the importance of so doing would have declined. A rapid rate of expansion would have eased the pressure on the balance of payments, reduced the amount of external financing needed, and weakened the incentives toward import restriction and import substitution. But it did not occur, and its absence has been of over-riding importance in impeding the growth of intra-regional trade.

[1] *Ibid.*, December, 1961, p. 61.

Beyond the lack of economic dynamism, and to some extent exacerbated by it, are the political problems that were discussed in Part Two. Two related sets of such problems have interfered with the development of intra-regional trade: the particular constellation of tensions between countries within the region; and the policies pursued by countries outside the region, especially the cold war. A simple enumeration of some of the major tensions between countries will indicate the serious emotional obstacles to that minimal degree of trust required for deliberate and sustained trade cooperation. Foremost is the dispute between India and Pakistan over Kashmir. Like many other issues, it is beclouded by religious antagonism. Indians, who are generally disliked by the Burmese, have now largely been driven out of Burma. Relations between India and Ceylon were strained when laws were passed adversely affecting the Indian Tamils on the plantations and the Ceylonese Tamils in the North. Bitterness between Thailand and Cambodia led to a wrangle over the disposition of a Buddhist temple. The smaller countries of the region are inherently suspicious of the bigger ones. Petty jealousies bolstered by ethnic and religious distinctions pervade the whole of South Asia. All of these tensions have deep historical roots, and they are not diminishing. On the contrary, within the framework of economic stagnation, rising nationalist sentiment, and persistent if not mounting tensions among Russia, China, and the United States, with whom the South Asian nations are bound in various ways, there appears to be increasing dissension. Only at the operational and technical levels, where there is less opportunity for political or religious bickering, is there occasionally tangible, if unspectacular, progress.[1]

The policies pursued by outside countries have obviously heightened these tensions, as the region has inevitably been caught up in the cold war. Moreover, the ideological struggle over the appropriate path toward economic growth – symbolized in the emotion-laden words "socialist," "capitalist," and "communist" – creates tensions between factions within the countries, and these tensions inevitably spill over into relations with neighboring states to heighten existing squabbles.

7 *Trends and Fluctuations in Terms of Trade*

The picture with respect to terms of trade – defined as the unit value of exports divided by the unit value of imports – is rather mixed. Although it is reported that between 1927–29 and 1955–57 prices of primary prod-

[1] Instances of cooperation among some of the South Asian countries, such as the Mekong project and the Asian Highway scheme, illustrate what can be accomplished, despite deep-seated antagonisms, when specific problems are approached by expert groups.

Cf. David Wightman, *Toward Economic Cooperation in Asia: The United Nations Economic Commission for Asia and the Far East*, Yale University Press, New Haven, 1963.

ucts rose somewhat faster than those of manufactured items, thereby indicating an improvement in terms of trade of primary commodities generally, the countries of South Asia shared in this improvement less than primary producers as a whole.[1] This is largely because of the particular commodity composition of exports from the region. In addition, the rise in terms of trade of primary products does not necessarily constitute a net gain to countries exporting primary products, since these countries are themselves significant importers of primary products. There is therefore no clear evidence of a long-term trend toward improvement in terms of trade for the countries of South Asia in recent decades.

Given the sluggish demand for exports from the region and the accelerating imports, especially of capital equipment and other commodities needed for developmental purposes, one would expect the terms of trade to have deteriorated drastically. They have not. This may be attributed, in part at least, to the increased domestic demand for some exportable items and to the failure of some industries to achieve pre-war levels of output, or much significant advance over-all. These factors have reduced exportable surpluses and thus tended to maintain higher export prices than would otherwise have prevailed. At the same time, the export difficulties have reduced the demand for imports below the level that might have been attained with more buoyant export proceeds, so that prices of imports have been lower than might otherwise have been the case.

Although individual countries have fared differently, in general there appears to have been an improvement in the terms of trade through the Korean boom. This was followed by a sharp decline, partial recovery to 1956, a fall in 1956 and 1957, recovery through 1960, and a slow decline in the first half of the 1960's.[2] The causes are difficult to unravel without a detailed analysis of the major commodities involved in the export and import trade of each country. Broadly, an explanation may be found in the divergent influences on price as between primary product exports of the region and major import items. In the short run, prices of most primary products are relatively sensitive to demand changes due to low elasticity of supply. Thus these prices tend to vary with the phase of the business cycle in North America and Western Europe, where most of South Asia's primary exports are sold. The prices of developmental imports, particularly capital equipment from the West, are less sensitive to demand fluctuation; indeed, they are largely cost-determined. Given the downward inflexibility of the cost structure in the Western countries, prices of these commodities tend to rise slightly during business expansion, but to stabilize during

[1] U. N., *Economic Survey of Asia and the Far East, 1959,* p. 62.

[2] *Ibid., 1961,* p. 199, Table 24; U. N., *Economic Bulletin for Asia and the Far East,* June, 1964, Table 2, p. 2; and United Nations, *World Economic Survey, 1965,* Part II, roneod E/4221, New York, June, 1966, Table 25, p. 81.

business contraction.[1] During periods of rising demand in the West, prices of both primary products and manufactured goods tend to rise; but when aggregate demand slackens, the former fall while the latter do not, at least not to the same extent. It is not entirely clear whether the prices of developmental imports will rise less sharply than the prices of the primary exports of South Asia during an expansion of economic activity in the West, but it is apparent that the latter will fall more sharply during a contraction. Although much of the volatility in the terms of trade may be explained by these factors, a more detailed analysis of the entire problem is clearly required. The foregoing and the trends in general trading positions as analyzed in Section 5 suggest that the terms of trade for South Asia will tend to deteriorate, assuming that this area persists in relying on primary commodity exports.

The superior adaptability of the more developed countries enables them to respond more effectively and rapidly to changes in relative prices. Thus the advanced countries take a larger share of the poorer countries' output when prices are favorable, but leave them to "bear the brunt of years of low prices."[2] These factors may, however, be more than offset by technological advance in the developed countries, which serves to reduce the cost of important imports necessary for South Asian economic growth.[3] Reinforcing this last is the rise of capital exports to South Asia by the Communist countries. The increasing competitive pressure on certain items by the Communist countries may serve to reduce the cost of needed imports.

Turning now to past trends in export instability, it will be recalled that the heavy concentration by most of the South Asian countries on one or a few commodities for export makes them vulnerable to fluctuations in the volume or value of these commodities. Despite some evidence that the instability of the volume and value of primary exports decreased between 1920–38 and 1948–57,[4] rubber and rice remained about as unstable as in the inter-war period, while tea became somewhat more unstable. Only tin became appreciably more stable in terms of both unit value and volume. The available evidence therefore supports the view that:

> Altogether, the improvement that has taken place in the postwar period as compared with the interwar period has been less in the ECAFE region [and less still in the countries we have been mainly interested in] which continues to be more

[1] See, for example, C. L. Schultze, *Recent Inflation in the United States,* Study Paper No. 1 for Joint Economic Committee, 86th Cong., 1st sess., Washington, D. C., 1959.

[2] Paul Streeten, *Economic Integration, Aspects and Problems,* A. W. Sythoff, Leyden, 1961, p. 146.

[3] At the same time, however, technological advance in the developed countries in lines competitive with traditional Asian exports, such as synthetic rubber and apparel fibres, works to the disadvantage of South Asia's export potential. Cf. Chapter 14, Section 8.

[4] U. N., *Economic Survey of Asia and the Far East, 1959,* p. 70.

affected by the problems of instability than other primary exporting areas of the world.[1]

Since 1958, there appears to have been a decrease in the instability of the unit value of exports of the commodities of major importance to the region, except for jute and copra.[2] In addition, the instability of the index of the unit value of exports seems to have continued to decline through 1963 for each country in the region except Pakistan.[3] Nevertheless, the problem of instability remains serious, especially in view of the South Asian countries' generally depleted foreign exchange reserves.[4]

8 *Trends in Capital Movements Before the Second World War*

Because their export earnings have failed to keep pace with their import needs, the South Asian countries have been confronted with an increasingly serious shortage of foreign exchange. Therefore the success of their developmental efforts will depend to an important degree on their ability to attract adequate amounts of foreign capital on reasonable terms.[5] India and Pakistan are already in urgent need of capital inflows to prevent deterioration of their low levels of living and to at least sustain the inadequate nutritional levels now prevailing. It is important, then, to examine the more significant changes in capital movements in recent times with a historian's perspective and assess their implications.

The empirical evidence on capital movements is extremely tenuous. Although statistics on international movements of goods and services are generally superior to most other data for reasons already given, the same cannot be said of statistics on capital flows. As a United Nations publication has pointed out, "ordinarily the record of these capital movements is incomplete and likely to be less exact than that of 'current' items and gold."[6] Many inconsistent series exist[7] and the several bases of estimation

[1] *Ibid.*, Table 27, p. 70.

[2] See United Nations, *United Nations Conference on Trade and Development*, Vol. III, New York, 1965, Table 2–8, p. 109.

[3] See U. N., *Economic Survey of Asia and the Far East, 1964*, Appendix, Table 26, p. 226.

[4] The instability of export earnings is discussed further in Appendix 15.

[5] This refers to grants, loans, and investments (direct or portfolio) made by private citizens, governments of foreign countries, or international agencies. "Reasonable terms" refers not only to the interest rate and pay-back period for loans, but to the restrictions often attached to grants and loans especially from foreign governments.

[6] United Nations, Department of Economic Affairs, *International Capital Movements During the Inter-war Period*, New York, 1949, p. 6.

[7] See the divergent estimates of net capital movements between 1923 and 1938 as reported in the United Nations report just cited, pp. 10–13; see also W. S. Woytinsky and E. S. Woytinsky, *World Commerce and Governments*, Twentieth Century Fund, New York, 1955, pp. 202–203. Another series showing U. S. capital transactions yields

available yield different results. For example, estimates may be made by using balance of payments data or by direct surveys. The variability in answers obtained is frequently striking. In India, Conan reports, "it was found by direct inquiry that the net increase in foreign business investments between 1948 and 1953 was approximately Rs. 1300 million (£100 million) while the balance of payments estimates . . . showed that during this period there was a net disinvestment of foreign capital."[1] This discrepancy arises in part because balance of payments estimates include only actual payments and take no account of reinvested profits of foreign firms and revaluations of assets. Moreover, Conan notes that "In most cases the [balance of payments] estimates will include not only the known payment of capital but also a residual item which may comprise both long-term and short-term funds as well as the cumulative result of errors and omissions elsewhere." Other writers have pointed out that "generally only a fraction of the private capital transactions come to light in detail sufficient to be recorded."[2] But if the aggregate measures leave something to be desired, measures of various types of foreign investment – private direct investment, portfolio investment, and so on – are even less satisfactory. Present measures of capital flows are in fact so weak that a true assessment probably requires new statistical techniques.[3] We have attempted to check the accuracy of the figures wherever possible, but the evidence can convey nothing more than broad tendencies.

Prior to the First World War, Great Britain was the leading exporter of capital. Of the estimated $44,000 million of long-term foreign investments made between 1874 and 1914, Britain accounted for about two-

---

a third set of estimates, most of which differ by substantial amounts; see United States, Department of Commerce, *The United States in the World Economy*, Economic Series No. 23, Government Printing Office, Washington, D. C., 1943, Table III.

For the United States there is little discrepancy among the three series as to the direction of capital flows, although for 1923 the Woytinsky study has a net annual capital inflow to the United States and the other two studies record an outflow. But for India and the Netherlands Indies there is a large difference between the U. N. and the Woytinsky findings. For example, in regard to India, the two disagree as to the direction of net capital flows for each of the years 1924, 1925, 1926, 1931, 1932, and 1937. Thus, it is clear that many ambiguities exist in the empirical evidence pertaining to capital transactions. Any specific figures cited in this section must therefore be viewed with the utmost caution. As the U. N. study points out (p. 7, f.n.): "When different series exist . . . concerning the capital issues for foreign account – as in the case of the United Kingdom during the inter-war period – they frequently differ considerably."

[1] A. R. Conan, *Capital Imports into Sterling Countries*, Macmillan & Co. Ltd., London, 1960, p. 65.

[2] Mervyn L. Weiner and Romeo Dalla-Chiesa, "International Movements of Public Long-Term Capital and Grants, 1946–50," *International Monetary Fund Staff Papers*, September, 1954, Vol. IV, No. 1, p. 113.

[3] Conan, *Capital Imports into Sterling Countries*, p. 66.

fifths and France for about one-fifth; one-fourth was almost equally divided between Germany, on the one hand, and the Netherlands, Belgium, and Switzerland on the other.[1] The United States was not yet a major capital exporter. Despite the rapid rise of long-term capital exports from the leading developed countries in the several decades prior to 1914 (an increase of over 500 percent), the underdeveloped countries did not receive much help. Only an estimated 10 percent of the total went to Asia (excluding China), whereas North America and Europe accounted for over half. In short, most foreign investment took place among the richer nations and those regions mainly inhabited by Europeans, while the underdeveloped areas of the world "remained largely outside the international economy."[2]

However, British colonial investment in South Asia, especially India, was not inconsequential in amount. By 1914, British investments in India were estimated to be $1,842 million,[3] or approximately 10 percent of all British capital invested abroad.[4] This investment was largely of the portfolio type, floated through the London money market. In the nineteenth century some three-fourths of British foreign investment went as loans to governments (30 percent), railway companies (40 percent), and other public utilities (5 percent).[5] Thus it is "far from correct to assume . . . that the 'colonial' form of enterprise [i.e., direct investment] . . . was the typical pattern."[6] Conan suggests that "in 1914 more than nine-tenths of the United Kingdom's overseas investments" were in portfolio form.[7] Furthermore, while it may *generally* have been true that "the British preferred to invest money in definite projects," so that by 1914 "not more than one-fourth of the British investments abroad consisted of government securities,"[8] the pattern in South Asia seems to have been different, as almost half of British investment in India and Ceylon apparently took the form

[1] U. N., *International Capital Movements During the Inter-war Period*, p. 2.

[2] *Ibid.*, p. 4.

[3] See Raymond F. Mikesell, ed., *U. S. Private and Government Investment Abroad*, University of Oregon Books, Eugene, Ore., 1962, Table II–1, p. 19. The figure of £379 million was converted to dollars by multiplying by 4.86, the exchange rate at that time. A roughly comparable figure is obtained by Jan Tinbergen in *Shaping the World Economy*, Twentieth Century Fund, New York, 1962, Appendix V.

[4] Estimated at $19,389 million in 1913 by A. H. Imlah, *Economic Elements in the Pax Britannica: Studies in British Foreign Trade in the Nineteenth Century*, Harvard University Press, Cambridge, Mass., 1958, pp. 70–75.

[5] Ragnar Nurkse, "International Investment To-day in the Light of Nineteenth Century Experience," *Economic Journal*, December, 1954, p. 747.

[6] *Ibid.*, p. 747. Data for 1909–10 show that over 86 percent of total British investment in India and Ceylon was in the form of government and railway securities, while only 8 percent was ascribed to plantations and mines. See George Paish, "Great Britain's Capital Investments in Individual Colonial and Foreign Countries," *Journal of the Royal Statistical Society*, Vol. 74, 1910–1911, pp. 167–187.

[7] Conan, *Capital Imports into Sterling Countries*, p. 49.

[8] Woytinsky and Woytinsky, *World Commerce and Governments*, p. 194.

of government securities in 1909–10.[1] Even the Indian railway securities had to carry a state guarantee of 5 percent interest, otherwise "capital would not have moved in that direction."[2]

It is probable that reinvested profits in mines and plantations are not fully accounted for in the preceding estimates.[3] Yet the vision of colonial investment as mainly directed toward extractive industries and plantations in private hands, may be particularly lacking in substance with respect to the Indian subcontinent. Colonial investment in India prior to 1914 seems to have been predominantly in portfolio form. In addition, it tended to go largely into railways and other enterprises of a public utility type, or directly to governments, rather than into purely extractive industries. It thereby helped to build up an infrastructure of social capital. Investment in social capital usually has a greater impact on economic activity than foreign investment in purely extractive industries of an enclave kind, particularly in countries at low levels of economic well-being. That in India it did not have more substantial spread effects and failed to trigger much economic development is attributable mainly to basic features of the colonial system and the environment in general.[4]

The pattern in Thailand and French Indo-China in the pre-war period was similar to that in India, but the amounts invested were substantially smaller. As Table 13–9 indicates, direct investments in Thailand constituted less than 40 percent of the total foreign investment in 1914. The balance was made up largely of loans to the government, mainly for railroad construction and other public works.[5] In French Indo-China direct business investments accounted for barely half the total of foreign investments in 1914 (Table 13–9). As Callis points out, "before the first world war a series of loans was extended to Indo-China by financial groups in France for various public works, for flood protection and irrigation, city

[1] Paish, *Journal of the Royal Statistical Society,* Vol. 74, pp. 167–187.

[2] H. J. Habbakuk, "Free Trade and Commercial Expansion, 1853–1870," in *The Cambridge History of the British Empire,* Vol. II, Cambridge, 1929, p. 797. For details of the railway guarantee see Daniel Thorner, *Investment in Empire,* Philadelphia, 1950, Chapters 6 and 7.

[3] As has been pointed out, "it is impossible to measure British investment in India because of the difficulty of calculating the amount of reinvestment of profits made in India. Estimates for the end of the twenties and the beginning of the thirties range anywhere from 354 million pounds to one billion pounds depending on the methods used and the bias of the estimators." (Helen B. Lamb, "The 'State' and Economic Development in India," in Simon Kuznets, Wilbert E. Moore, and Joseph J. Spengler, eds., *Economic Growth: Brazil, India, Japan,* Duke University Press, Durham, N. C., 1955, p. 475, f.n. 17.) See also "Post-war Foreign Investment in India," in U. N., *Economic Bulletin for Asia and the Far East,* June, 1962, p. 1, where private investment in India is cited as £530 million in 1930–31.

[4] Chapter 10, Sections 8 and 9.

[5] Helmut G. Callis, *Foreign Capital in Southeast Asia,* Institute of Pacific Relations, New York, 1942, p. 59. The major loans were floated through the London money market in 1905, 1907, and 1909.

Table 13–9

FOREIGN INVESTMENTS IN SOUTHEAST ASIAN COUNTRIES, 1914, 1930, AND 1937
(*Millions of U. S. dollars*)

Country	*Type* (*1*)	*1914* (*2*)	*1930* (*3*)	*1937* (*4*)
Netherlands Indies:	Entrepreneur	675	1,600	1,411
	Rentier	68	397	853
	Total	743	1,997	2,264
Burma:	Entrepreneur	80	210	225[a]
	Rentier		10	8[a]
	Total	80	220	233[a]
French Indo-China:	Entrepreneur	75	255	302[b]
	Rentier	73	25	82[b]
	Total	148	280	384[b]
Philippines:	Entrepreneur	100	300	315[c]
	Rentier	12	85	61[c]
	Total	112	385	376[c]
Thailand:	Entrepreneur	25	75	90[b]
	Rentier	40	57	34[b]
	Total	65	132	124[b]
British Malaya:	Entrepreneur	150	447	372
	Rentier	44	113	83
	Total	194	560	455

Source: Helmut G. Callis, *Foreign Capital in Southeast Asia,* Institute of Pacific Relations, New York, 1942. Columns 3 and 4 from p. 108. Column 2 from country chapters.

Note: "Entrepreneur" and "rentier" investments are roughly synonymous with the more common "direct" and "portfolio" investments. Usually, Callis employs the term "rentier" to refer to bonds, which are mainly government-issued. As he explains in the preface to his book: "The study has involved a critical review of terminology and has resulted in our giving preference to the term 'entrepreneur' over the term 'direct.' The term entrepreneur for this sort of investment seems to us to put the emphasis in the right place, for they are usually investments by the businessman acting as a businessman. The appropriateness of the contrasting term, rentier, is obvious once the term entrepreneur is accepted. Rentier investments, it may be said without too much danger of ambiguity, are investor's investments; they are usually made by the investor acting as an investor."

[a] 1939. [b] 1938. [c] 1935.

sanitation and electric power, but particularly for railroad development."[1] Thus, in both Thailand and French Indo-China, foreign investment was not directed primarily to extractive industries; rather, as in India, a substantial portion went toward building up an infrastructure. Indeed, Callis refers to the refusal of "French private capital to take the risks involved in the initial development of the colony."[2]

The composition of pre-1914 foreign investment in the Netherlands Indies, British Malaya, the Philippines, and probably Burma was very different. As the estimates in Table 13–9 indicate, foreign investments of the direct variety were 80 percent or more of the total in 1914 in each of these countries. Some of the money directly invested went into what may be termed public utilities, but the great bulk went into extractive industries (mining and oil) or plantations. In the case of the Netherlands Indies, however, the imbalance manifest in 1914 was not indicative of the level of development of public utilities or of prior government investment, since much of the infrastructure had been developed and fully paid for by 1914.[3]

In a very general sense we may thus distinguish two rather different foreign investment patterns in South Asia prior to the First World War. Foreign investment in the Indian subcontinent,[4] Thailand, and French Indo-China was primarily portfolio investment in social overhead capital, whereas foreign capital flowed mainly into extractive industries and plantations in British Malaya, Burma, the Philippines, and, though this is less certain, the Netherlands Indies. Of course, the data are tenuous for this early period and the distinction between these broad investment categories is far from sharp. Boeke has stated that "the amount of capital invested in the Netherlands Indies can hardly be determined. Every estimate that has been made is too arbitrary in character."[5] Nonetheless, in a

[1] *Ibid.*, p. 71.

[2] *Ibid.*, p. 72.

[3] It was only in the late nineteenth century "after the Agrarian and Sugar Laws of 1870 and the opening of the Suez Canal that private enterprise came wholly to overbalance state production." (J. S. Furnivall, *Netherlands India,* Cambridge University Press, 1939, p. 169, cited in Callis, *Foreign Capital in Southeast Asia,* p. 37.)

[4] This probably does not apply to Ceylon where direct investments in plantations predominated. Separate data on Ceylon are not available.

[5] J. H. Boeke, *The Evolution of the Netherlands Indies Economy,* Institute of Pacific Relations, New York, 1946, p. 26. In another work Boeke amplified this by pointing out that "investments consisted chiefly of profits made in colonial enterprise. This means that exports yielded returns which were, in part, converted into fresh capital. . . .

"This investing of profits was not as a rule done by the shareholders of their own free will, but was rather a policy carried out by the directors with a view to rapid writing-off and generous plowing-back of returns. Some entrepreneurs even state that during the years of expansion these re-invested returns were larger than the returns paid out in dividends . . .

"It is on account of this policy that no one can determine the amount of capital invested in Indonesia." (J. H. Boeke, *Economics and Economic Policy in Dual Societies as Exemplified by Indonesia,* H. D. Tjeenk Willink & Zoon N.V., Haarlem, 1953, p. 200.)

very broad sense, the evidence may be sufficiently exact to warrant the above generalization.

Another feature of pre-1914 foreign investment was the relatively favorable terms available to borrowing countries. In the first decade of the twentieth century, for example, "Indian Government Loans were issued at a rate which yielded only 3.2 percent, Indian Railways 3.87 percent, and Colonial and provincial loans 3.7 percent. Dominion and Colonial governments could indeed borrow more cheaply in London, just before the first war, than those home borrowers whose bonds were not trustee securities."[1] The French loans to Indo-China for railroads and other public works between 1896 and 1914 bore interest rates varying from 2½ to 3 percent.[2] The loans were not tied.

After the First World War the United States emerged as the leading exporter of capital. Rough estimates suggest that, from the mid-1920's through 1933, U. S. net capital outflow exceeded that of Great Britain in every year except perhaps 1929.[3] The total volume of capital movements increased somewhat after the First World War. But the rise in the importance of the United States was not an auspicious event for South Asia since U. S. investments – to an even greater extent than European – were channelled largely to other regions.[4] Investment capital during the 1920's, as in earlier decades, flowed largely to the developed or semi-developed economies, especially Germany and some Latin American countries. The underdeveloped countries

> . . . received less capital, absolutely and in relation to the size of their population, than those which had already made substantial progress. . . . India and China for instance, which together represent about 40 per cent of the world's population, each account for a capital influx similar to, or less than, that of Argentina and Australia with only 1 per cent of the world's population.[5]

Although U. S. direct investments in South Asia rose sharply after 1921–22 – the period when the first significant borrowing by Asian countries in the

[1] Arthur Salter, *Foreign Investment*, Essays in International Finance, No. 12, Princeton University Press, Princeton, N. J., February, 1951, p. 5.

[2] Callis, *Foreign Capital in Southeast Asia*, p. 92.

[3] Woytinsky and Woytinsky, *World Commerce and Governments*, Table 78, p. 202. The data in this table are exceptionally tenuous but outline the broad picture. According to a U. N. study (*International Capital Movements During the Inter-war Period*, pp. 10–13), the volume of U. S. net capital outflow exceeded that of the United Kingdom for every year from 1924 through 1933.

[4] Some of the reasons are given in Nurul Islam, *Foreign Capital and Economic Development: Japan, India and Canada*, Charles E. Tuttle Co., Rutland, Vermont, 1960, pp. 90–91.

[5] U. N., *International Capital Movements During the Inter-war Period*, p. 17.

United States took place[1] – they rose from a tiny base, and the amount remained relatively small. It was less than 3 percent of total outstanding U. S. direct investments in book value at the end of 1929,[2] and in terms of capital inflows per head of population in South Asia it was pitifully meager. As for portfolio investment, it is reported that "No capital issues for the account of either China or India were floated in the United States during the period."[3] The supply of foreign capital to South Asia continued to emanate from the colonial powers, Great Britain in particular. But by 1929 British direct and portfolio investments in the aggregate remained at approximately the dollar value of investments in 1914; the real value was much lower than in 1914.[4] Although loans to India and Ceylon floated on the London money market are reported to have risen from an annual average of £2.4 million between 1924 and 1927 to £7.7 million in 1928, and to an average of £20.4 million per year in 1929–31,[5] the total was probably below 10 percent of Britain's aggregate portfolio investment. British direct investments outstanding in India and Ceylon at the end of 1929 are similarly estimated at less than 10 percent of the total.[6] Thus, while the practice of foreign investment revived after the First World War, and the United States became known as a capital exporter, South Asia received an even smaller share of the investment total than in the pre-war period.

Perhaps as significant was the change in the nature of capital flows. If most of British foreign investment was of the portfolio type prior to 1914, during the 1920's direct investment rose sharply. By the end of 1929, British portfolio investments (par value) were estimated at $8,900 million and direct investments at some $7,900 million. Since "figures with respect to

[1] In 1921–22 a large issue of the Netherland Indies was of particular importance. Between 1920–24 and 1925–29 there was almost a doubling of U.S. direct investments in Asia. (U. S., *The United States in the World Economy*, p. 94 and p. 30.)

[2] U. N., *International Capital Movements During the Inter-war Period*, p. 31.

[3] *Ibid.*, p. 28.

[4] Woytinsky and Woytinsky, *World Commerce and Governments*, pp. 204–205; and U. N., *International Capital Movements During the Inter-war Period*, p. 29.

[5] U. N., *International Capital Movements During the Inter-war Period*, p. 38.

The following is revealing of the cyclical behavior of British capital flows to India during the 1920's: "The average dividend paid by the leading cotton mills in Bombay in 1920 was 120% and in some cases as high as 200 and 250%. Dividends of leading jute mills, with a total capital of £6.1 million, showed profits of £22.9 million in the four-year period 1918–21, in addition to £19 million added to reserves. British capital was naturally eager to share in these colossal profits, and the annual export of British capital to India increased from an estimated £14.7 million or 9% of the total in the period 1908–10, to £29 million in 1921 and £36 million in 1922, or more than one-fourth of British capital exports." (K. L. Mitchell, *Industrialization of the Western Pacific*, Institute of Pacific Relations, New York, 1942, p. 284.)

The crisis following the 1920–21 boom led to a drop in annual British capital flow to India to "£2.6 million in 1924, to £2.4 million in 1925, to £2 million in 1926, and to less than £1 million in 1927." (*Ibid.*, pp. 284–85.)

[6] *Ibid.*, p. 32.

outstanding investments are . . . subject to reservations as serious as those regarding capital movements,"[1] and since direct investments may not fully record plowed-back earnings, it does not seem unreasonable to conclude that, for South Asia as a whole, direct investment became more important than portfolio investment. As Table 13–9 shows, Thailand and French Indo-China did not have a preponderance of direct ("entrepreneur") investments in 1914, but the pattern had changed sharply by 1930; the other countries exhibited a continued heavy concentration of direct investment. This would suggest that much of the capital flow of the 1920's went into extractive or plantation industries, which implies a relative shift away from the public utility type of investment that characterized capital movements before 1914.

As indicated in Chapter 10, the enclave character of most direct investments, the dearth of production for the local market, and the policies pursued by the colonial powers, significantly reduced the stimulating effects of this form of capital inflow. Although neither form of foreign investment proved very stimulating to the South Asian economies, the shift to direct investment in extractive industries producing for the external market, and away from investment in social overhead capital, probably reduced the developmental impact of the total capital inflow into South Asia. Not only did the region derive little benefit from the short-lived resurgence of international capital movements in the 1920's, but the funds they received may have had less economic impact than those of the past. Both quantitatively and qualitatively, capital investment in South Asia left much to be desired.

With the onslaught of the Great Depression in 1929 a dramatic change occurred. The United States became a net capital importer in 1934, following a sharp reduction in its capital outflows from a peak of about $1,250 million in 1928 to less than $300 million in 1932 and 1933.[2] Great Britain also became a net capital importer during the 1930's, beginning as early as 1931.[3] Correspondingly, capital flows out of India, necessitated by past investments, exceeded fresh capital inflows from the leading creditor countries. The United Nations' estimates, computed indirectly as the reverse balance on account of goods, services, and gold, indicate net capital outflows from India in the years 1931 through 1934. The Netherlands Indies recorded net capital outflows from 1934 through 1938.[4]

[1] *Ibid.*, p. 7.

[2] U. N., *International Capital Movements During the Inter-war Period,* pp. 10–13. Estimates by the U. S. Department of Commerce indicate a similar pattern and record a peak of $1,195 million in 1928 and about $340 million in 1933 (for both long- and short-term movements), though most estimates for individual years are substantially different from those given by the U. N. (*The United States in the World Economy,* Table III.)

[3] U. N., *International Capital Movements During the Inter-war Period,* pp. 10–13.

[4] *Ibid.*, pp. 10–13. Table 13–9 indicates a higher value of foreign investments in 1937 than in 1930, but this probably reflects revaluation of existing assets and reinvested

By the end of the 1930's total U. S. private investments abroad had decreased sharply while those of Great Britain showed a slight rise.[1] The depression, which had undermined the international capital market, caused a sharp reduction in new portfolio investment. The ratio of portfolio to total long-term investment for the United States fell from about 44 percent in 1931 to less than 35 percent by 1939.[2] The depression thereby accelerated the shift from portfolio to direct investment already under way in the 1920's and, of course, diminished considerably the aggregate volume of new capital investments, though by the end of the 1930's South Asia had more than regained its position with respect to foreign investments.[3]

9 *Private Investment After the Second World War*

In the Western world at large there has been a gradual resumption of large-scale private foreign investment, particularly of the direct type. The United States as the dominating creditor nation has continued, however, to concentrate its private investment in countries outside South Asia. In 1957 the outflow of private U. S. long-term capital to *"all other"* low-income countries except those in Latin America was only $200 million, or less than 8 percent of the total outflow of this sort of capital.[4] Nor is the relative bypassing of South Asia characteristic of the private capital flow from the United States alone. In the same year the *total* net private long-term investment in the low-income countries in Asia (Burma, Ceylon, India, Indonesia, Iraq, Pakistan, the Philippines, Taiwan, Thailand, and South Vietnam) was estimated at less than $100 million, whereas that in

earnings that more than made up for the net capital outflows; a similar situation occurred in India between 1948 and 1949.

[1] The increase in British investments abroad from an estimated $18.2 billion in 1929 to $18.8 billion in 1937 (see Woytinsky and Woytinsky, *World Commerce and Governments,* Table 81, p. 207) is not necessarily inconsistent with net British capital imports during the 1930's, since the latter include gold and "errors and omissions" while the former estimates do not.

[2] *Ibid.,* Table 80, p. 206.

[3] For Southeast Asia as a whole foreign investment was apparently higher in 1937–39 than in 1930; see Table 13–9. Similarly in India, foreign private investment rose from an estimated £530 million in 1930–31 to between £650 and £700 million in 1939. (See U. N., *Economic Bulletin for Asia and the Far East,* June, 1962, p. 1.)

The data for Burma in Table 13–9 may be substantially understated. Alternative estimates suggest that prior to the Second World War foreign investment may have been between $800 and $900 million rather than the $233 million shown in the table. Details of the higher estimates for Burma may be found in J. Russell Andrus, *Burmese Economic Life,* Stanford University Press, Stanford, Calif., 1948, p. 184; G. E. Harvey, *British Rule in Burma 1824–1942,* Faber & Faber, London, 1946, p. 68; and Louis J. Walinsky, *Economic Development in Burma, 1951–1960,* Twentieth Century Fund, New York, 1962, pp. 53–54.

[4] United Nations, *The International Flow of Private Capital, 1956–1958,* New York, 1959, Table 3, p. 20.

Table 13–10

NET INFLOW OF PRIVATE CAPITAL, 1951–62
(*Millions of U. S. dollars*)

Country	*1951–55 (annual average)*	*1956–59 (annual average)*	*1959*	*1960*	*1961*	*1962*
Pakistan	5	4	8	25	28	23
India	–9	–20	–17	59	–10	–
Indonesia	2	–4	1	20	–11	12
Burma	–1	2	3	–10	–2	–
S. Vietnam	. . .	. . .	1	3	1	12
Philippines	38	39	63	74	10	–20
Thailand	5	4	20	18	32	72
Ceylon	–6	–6	–2	–	–2	–
Malaya	. . .	. . .	18	44	54	66

Source: U. N., *International Flow of Long-Term Capital and Official Donations* for the years 1951–59, 1959–61, and 1960–62.

Latin America was $1,500 million.[1] Furthermore, the trend in Latin America has been sharply upwards, while the erratic changes in South Asia have, at least until recently, shown little sign of a drift to higher levels (Table 13–10).

There are differences, however, within the region. The Philippines, Malaya, Thailand, and, in recent years, Pakistan have attracted some private investment.[2] The Indian situation is shown in Table 13–11. Although foreign private investment in India is reported to have increased about two and a half times (from 2,646 million to 6,810 million rupees[3]) between 1948, when it was very low,[4] and 1961, asset revaluation, especially in the plantation sector, and retained earnings accounted for over 80 percent of the total net increase. Over the period, the inflow of fresh private capital from abroad is reported to have exceeded the repatriation of capital by only negligible amounts, and was largely inflow in kind. The course of events has been similar in Ceylon and one commentator observes that "relatively little private capital has gone to India and Ceylon, which at one time were

[1] *Ibid.*

[2] U. N., *Economic Survey of Asia and the Far East, 1959*, p. 86.

[3] Reserve Bank of India, *India's Foreign Liabilities and Assets 1961*, Bombay, 1964, p. 75.

[4] During the war and the immediate post-war years foreign private investment in India had declined sharply. Indeed, estimates indicate it was as low in 1948 as it was at its lowest point during the thirty years preceding independence. (U. N., *Economic Bulletin for Asia and the Far East*, June, 1962, p. 1.)

Table 13–11

FLOW OF PRIVATE FOREIGN BUSINESS CAPITAL INTO INDIA, 1948–61
(*Million rupees*)

	1948–53 (*1*)	*1954–55* (*2*)	*1956* (*3*)	*1957* (*4*)	*1958* (*5*)	*1959* (*6*)	*1960* (*7*)	*1961* (*8*)
Revaluation of assets	150	320	—	—	—	—	—	—
Retained earnings	700	460	192	95	91	146	141	158
Cash inflow	350	30	31	58	48	33	62	40
Inflow in kind	660	130	85	114	142	78	430	170
Total	1,860	940	308	267	281	257	633	368
Outflow	500	320	70	60	255	155	115	75
Net increase	1,360	620	238	207	26	102	518	293

Sources: United Nations, ECAFE, *Economic Bulletin for Asia and the Far East,* June, 1962, Table 6, p. 6 for columns 1 and 2. Data for 1956–61 from Reserve Bank of India, *India's Foreign Liabilities and Assets 1961,* Bombay, 1964, p. 92.

Note: Separate estimates of asset revaluation for each year 1956 through 1961 are not available. The data shown for these years are net of asset revaluation. "The estimates are based on data furnished in the Reserve Bank of India Report on the 1953 Survey of foreign liabilities and assets (pp. 81–84) and in 'Foreign Investments in India: 1959 and 1960 (Preliminary Trends),' *Reserve Bank of India Bulletin,* May, 1961, Table 2. For the period 1954–55, the Reserve Bank of India estimates of retained profits are *net* of transfers abroad of accumulated profits, which were estimated at Rs. 220 million (see Reserve Bank of India Report on the 1955 Survey, p. 18); this amount has been added here to the estimate of retained profits and also, as an offsetting capital outflow, under 'repatriation of business investments by non-residents.' From 1956 onwards, remittances of accumulated profits have been treated by the Reserve Bank also as an item of capital outflow."

able to attract and utilize this type of finance."[1] An expert group working for GATT suggests that "India seems to have ceased attracting long-term private funds on balance."[2] The situation has been no different in the other South Asian countries, except that the three aforementioned small countries and Pakistan have experienced an increase in foreign investments in recent years.

This virtual drying up of the flow of private capital to the main South Asian countries and to India in particular has occurred in spite of a vigorous campaign in the United States, supported by the World Bank and

[1] Conan, *Capital Imports into Sterling Countries,* p. 48; cf. Henry M. Oliver, Jr., *Economic Opinion and Policy in Ceylon,* Duke University Press, Durham, N. C., 1957, p. 87.

[2] GATT, *Trends in International Trade,* Geneva, 1958, p. 32.

influential circles in other Western countries to promote private investment in the region. Interested parties assert that private enterprise is the engine of economic development in underdeveloped countries and urge that private enterprises in the West help to spur that development. The provision of public grants and loans and technical assistance has often been motivated by a desire to create more favorable conditions for private business to come in and make its contribution; various steps have been taken in the field of tax policy and in other fields to make investment in underdeveloped countries more attractive financially. Except for periods in Burma and Indonesia, foreign private investors have, on the whole, been made welcome by the South Asian governments. Often they have been awarded favored treatment; and more regularly they have been assured of their freedom to take home their profits and even their capital, if they should choose to do so.

Nevertheless, with the modest exceptions noted, very little private capital has responded.[1] Political instability has been a deterrent in the case of many South Asian countries, though hardly in the case of India, which has been regarded, at least until recently, as a stable and viable state of the Western type. The cumbersome controls applied to all business[2] have also helped to discourage foreign enterprise from ventures in these countries, as has perhaps, in some instances, the sense of a political climate not congenial to foreign investors. However, the lack of vigorous economic development has probably been a much more important factor, particularly as there has been rapid progress in the rich countries themselves. The somewhat more rapid increase of private foreign investment in Pakistan than in India in recent years[3] may reflect the fact that while India failed to move ahead in the first half of the 1960's, Pakistan under the new authoritarian government made a remarkable recovery from the extreme depression of the 1950's; also, Pakistan has gone further than India in declaring its intention to liquidate controls and has probably given foreign investors greater advantages.

Foreign investments in South Asia have become ever more restricted to direct investments. Since the 1920's, private investors have been reluctant to lend money on a long-term basis, even to governments, and this trend has been particularly evident where the South Asian countries are concerned.

[1] "I noticed with my American friends that they really do believe, very honestly and with a lot of idealism, that if only these countries would open their doors to private enterprise and private investments, all capitalists would rush in and they of course would do the job. I think this is a very dangerous myth and a few figures, I think, should be enough to demolish it." (Tibor Mende, "Southeast Asia and Japan" in *Bulletin of the International House of Japan, Inc.*, No. 3, Winter, 1959, p. 25.)

[2] Chapter 19.

[3] Cf. Table 13–10. The estimates in the table are not very reliable, however.

10 *Public Grants and Credits*

With so little private capital forthcoming, the main burden of helping the South Asian countries meet their dire needs for imports over and above what their stagnating export returns could finance has fallen on foreign governments, and until the post-Stalin era exclusively on the Western governments, especially the United States. As a result, capital from public sources has been flowing to South Asia in increasing amounts. This inflow greatly exceeds any private capital inflow previously recorded. To a small but increasing extent this public capital assistance has been handled multilaterally through inter-governmental organizations, particularly the World Bank and its affiliates, but for the most part it has taken the form of bilateral grants and loans. This constitutes a new departure in international financial relations.

Broadly speaking, three main periods may be distinguished in the post-war era as far as direction, source, quantity, and type of capital movements are concerned.

The immediate post-war period was one of turbulence throughout much of South Asia. The destruction following the withdrawal of the Japanese from Southeast Asia was very severe and especially so in Burma and Indonesia. In Indonesia and Indo-China the Dutch and French tried to reassert their authority by force of arms. In all the countries of Southeast Asia, except Thailand, the situation was aggravated by internal rebellions associated with the liquidation of colonial rule. As the factions in these countries strove for political supremacy amid fighting and widespread distress, economic collapse seemed imminent. Thus most of the capital moving into Southeast Asia was of a military nature or directed toward immediate consumption needs. At that time the former colonial powers were also confronted with serious economic problems at home following the war; they were scarcely in a position to assist their former dependencies effectively, let alone to embark upon large-scale developmental or reconstruction programs in Southeast Asia. Only the United States was in a position to give much assistance to the region. But the United States was preoccupied with European recovery and, aside from the Philippines, provided little in the way of economic aid. In contrast to Southeast Asia, the territories of the Indian subcontinent and Ceylon not only were spared severe wartime destruction, but had built up large foreign exchange reserves as a result of favorable trade balances during the war. This area was not to be spared unrest, however. The partition of Pakistan and India brought a serious refugee problem, bitterness, and general economic and political turbulence.

In the second period, extending roughly from 1950 to 1955 or 1956, concern with South Asia in the United States was translated into a growing volume of U. S. grants and loans to this region, as Western Europe showed signs of rapid economic recovery. Most of the funds went to countries still threatened with political and economic collapse. The reserve balances of India and Pakistan dwindled as they tried to push development and feed their rapidly growing population. They developed serious foreign exchange difficulties – which, toward the end of the period, were only partly alleviated by U. S. assistance. Meanwhile those Southeast Asian countries which had achieved a semblance of stability and order benefitted from rapidly rising export earnings, especially during the Korean boom. Malaya in particular built up large foreign exchange holdings.

The third period, from about the middle of the 1950's, is characterized not only by an acceleration of U. S. interest in and assistance to South Asia, but also by the appearance of new suppliers of foreign grants and loans. Western European recovery permitted an enlarged flow of capital to South Asia, and the Communist countries began to provide credits in increasing amounts. In the early 1960's South Asia received a capital flow on a scale never before achieved. At the same time, however, the needs of the region became greater than ever before and the specific forms, conditions, and direction of capital flows to the region made them qualitatively less potentially stimulating than the capital movements prior to the First World War and the 1920's, as we shall discover below. While there was a general tendency for the capital inflow to underdeveloped countries to slow down in the first half of the 1960's, South Asia tended to fare a little better than the average; the future, however, is uncertain, as we shall see (Section 16).

These are the main general features of post-war public capital movements as they relate to South Asia. In the remaining pages of this section we shall examine them in more detail and analyze their causes and their implications for developmental prospects in the region.

In the period 1945–50 capital inflow to South Asia was relatively small and limited mainly to inter-governmental grants or credits to the countries most unsettled by the war. United States economic aid "in the two and one-half years after World War II was a response to wartime damage and dislocation. Its principal goal was to provide relief to severely depressed civilian consumption, and it typically took the form of consumer goods and raw materials for local processing into consumer goods."[1] The bulk of this assistance went to the Philippines; it bypassed most of the countries of major interest to this study. French outlays in Indo-China were large[2] but, like those of the Dutch in Indonesia, were concentrated on military operations designed to quell rebellions. British assistance went to Burma and Malaya, while the release of sterling balances helped finance the rising imports into Pakistan, India, and Ceylon. Loans to South Asia from the International Monetary Fund and the International Bank for Recon-

[1] Charles Wolf, Jr., *Foreign Aid: Theory and Practice in Southern Asia*, Princeton University Press, Princeton, N. J., 1960, p. 27.

[2] Approximately $475 million annually between 1948 and 1950. (*Ibid.*, p. 37.)

struction and Development were relatively small through 1949 (about $144 million) and went entirely to India. Leaving aside the war expenditures of France and Holland and the large-scale aid the United States gave to the Philippines, the early period may be characterized as one of sporadic, *ad hoc* financial assistance designed essentially to prevent economic and political collapse. Oriented strictly toward immediate needs as seen by the donor countries, it did not involve either long-term commitments or carefully thought-out plans for subsequent development. Important as it was in coping with emergency situations in some of the countries following the war, it was inadequate in quantity and defective in quality as far as developmental needs were concerned. The first period was in a real sense transitional.

The period 1950–55 witnessed the start of foreign governmental financial assistance programs unprecedented in the history of international capital movements. The scene was completely dominated by the economic assistance rendered by the United States government, whose interest in South Asia suddenly blossomed under the influence of the cold war. Furthermore, the United States abandoned any idea of multilateral action and adopted a national foreign policy whose major instrumentality was bilateral economic and military aid. The growing threat of Communist penetration in South Asia amid continuing guerrilla warfare in several of the countries, Communist success in China, and the Korean war impelled the United States to consider South Asia a region of prime significance. As a result, South Asia was no longer to be bypassed. As Table 13–12 indicates, total U. S. grant and loan commitments to the South Asian countries in the period 1951–55 exceeded $2 billion, a sum not much below total U. S. net capital outflows to all countries during any comparable time span in the 1920's. Financial assistance from other countries was relatively small during this period, though it increased toward the end. The contribution made by the inter-governmental agencies was also quite meager (Table 13–13). Indeed, from the end of the Second World War through the fiscal year 1958 the United States alone supplied over 80 percent of the greatly enlarged total of grants and net credits to South Asia.

In the meantime, however, the need for capital inflows had expanded dramatically in most South Asian countries. Attempts to spur economic growth after independence, sluggish export earnings, an accelerating rate of population growth, and the insignificance of foreign private investments, all combined to create a vast discrepancy between import needs and actual foreign exchange receipts. Dwindling foreign exchange reserves highlighted the increasing need for foreign capital. Indian gold and foreign exchange holdings fell from $1,975 million at the end of 1951 to only $624 million by the end of the first quarter of 1962.[1] The Indian Planning Commission stated that the "Third Plan commences with a level of [foreign

[1] International Monetary Fund, *International Financial Statistics,* Vol. XV, June, 1962, p. 22.

Table 13–12

UNITED STATES GOVERNMENT ECONOMIC AND TECHNICAL ASSISTANCE COMMITMENTS, 1951–64
(*Millions of dollars*)

Country	*1951–55 fiscal years*					*1956–60 fiscal years*				*1961–64 fiscal years*					
	Total	*AID and predecessor programs*	*P.L. 480*	*Ex.-Im. Bank loans*	*Other*	*Total*	*AID and predecessor programs*	*P.L. 480*	*Ex.-Im. Bank loans*	*Total*	*AID and predecessor programs*	*P.L. 480*	*Ex.-Im. Bank loans*	*Peace Corps*	*Total 7/1/50 through 6/30/64*
Pakistan	297	137	93		67	1,039	659	373	7	1,406	793	548	63	2	2,742
India	825	275	360		190	1,732	512	1,054	166	3,186	1,399	1,582	204	1	5,743
Indonesia	227	30	97	100		190	70	56	64	264	78	186			681
Burma	42	20	22			54	33	21		26	18	8			122
S. Vietnam	160[a]	160				1,242	1,173	69		748	573	175			2,150
Philippines	338	108		26	204	295	166	40	89	189	23	58	106	2	822
Thailand	81	77	2	2		179	162	3	14	126	90		35	1	386
Ceylon						69	23	46		28	6	22			97
Malaya						22	20	2		6	2	2		2	28
Other[b]	74	74				513	505	8		769	524	243		2	1,356
	2,044	881	574	128	461	5,335	3,323	1,672	340	6,748	3,506	2,824	408	10	14,127

Source: The Colombo Plan, For Co-operative Economic Development, Fifth through Thirteenth, Her Majesty's Stationery Office, London, 1957–64.

[a] Estimated.

[b] Other includes Laos, Cambodia, Nepal, Singapore, Sarawak, and North Borneo as well as "regional assistance" in the amount of $134 million in the latest period. It also includes Afghanistan and Korea from the year each joined the Colombo Plan, 1963 and 1962 respectively.

Table 13–13

NET INTERNATIONAL ECONOMIC ASSISTANCE, 1954–58
(*Millions of dollars*)

	Bilateral												*Multilateral*		*Total*	
	Australia		*Canada*		*U. K.*		*U. S.*		*Other*		*Total Bilateral*					
Country	G	L	G	L	G	L	G	L	G	L	G	L	G	L	G	L
Pakistan	14.2	–	45.1	–	2.1	20.2	336.6	34.3	3.9	–	401.9	54.5	8.6	38.8	410.5	93.3
India	13.7	–	53.9	16.8	2.0	–8.6	292.7	–74.6	8.1	–	370.4	–66.4	19.7	197.7	390.1	126.3
Indonesia	4.9	–	0.6	–6.3	0.1	–	39.8	33.8	1.6	–22.1	47.0	5.4	9.0	–	56.0	5.4
Burma	1.4	–	0.8	–	0.4	–	4.9	0.1	9.6	21.0	17.1	21.1	7.1	6.2	24.2	27.3
S. Vietnam	1.0	–	0.2	–	–	–	794.2	35.2			795.4	35.2	1.1	–	796.5	35.2
Philippines	0.2	–	–	–	0.2	–	109.4	–0.8			109.8	–0.8	4.4	2.4	114.2	1.6
Thailand	0.3	–	–	–	0.1	–	94.3	11.8			94.7	11.8	4.6	17.3	99.3	29.1
Ceylon	4.7	–	12.8	–	0.4	–	20.1	1.4	1.9	–	39.9	1.4	3.1	11.5	43.0	12.9
Malaya	1.0	–	0.7	–	28.4	3.1	1.0	–	0.2	–	31.3	3.1	1.1	–	32.4	3.1
Laos	0.6	–	0.1	–	–	–	152.7	–	–	–	153.4	–	0.8	–	154.2	–
Cambodia	0.5	–	0.2	–	–	–	121.6	–	–	–	122.3	–	1.8	–	124.1	–
South Korea	–	–	0.8	–	–	–	1,260.8	–	–	–	1,261.6	–	111.7	–	1,373.3	–
Total	42.5	–	115.2	10.5	33.7	14.7	3,228.1	41.2	25.3	–1.1	3,444.8	65.3	173.0	268.9	3,617.8	334.2

G = Grants L = Loans

Source: U. N., *Statistical Yearbook 1959*, pp. 421–426.

Note: Contributions from France totalling $77.3 million relate to development and to Cambodia, Laos and South Vietnam. Grants from the United States amounting to $60.2 million went to these three countries as well. The above data exclude $60.0 million transferred from the United Kingdom to the Far Eastern Territories War Damage Compensation Scheme.

exchange] reserves that cannot bear any significant further decline."[1] Nevertheless, by December of 1965 reserves stood at $599 million, and even this low figure was considerably above that prevailing at the end of 1964. The official foreign exchange and gold holdings of the Philippines declined about 70 percent between the end of 1951 and early 1962, but they rose steadily thereafter and at the end of 1965 were only about 20 percent lower than in 1951. Ceylon's official holdings at the end of 1965 were less than half of what they were at the end of 1952, while Pakistan's official holdings were about 60 percent of their 1952 level. Burma's official holdings of gold and foreign exchange fell about 11 percent between the same dates. On the other hand, the reserves of Thailand and Malaya roughly doubled over this period.[2] In general, the neediest countries and those putting forth the most substantial developmental efforts have been the ones seriously affected by continuing balance of payments difficulties, especially since the end of the Korean boom. Exchange difficulties have not developed in direct proportion to the widening gap between imports and exports, because drawings from the International Monetary Fund have relieved the situation, as has the increase in the inflow of public capital. Exchange difficulties have represented danger signals and have served to alert foreign governments to South Asia's urgent need for capital.

In the third period the United States continued to provide the major part of the increasing flow of official funds made available to South Asian countries. Indeed, by the 1964 fiscal year the total grant and credit commitments of the United States to the countries shown in Table 13–12 had risen to almost $2 billion, or more than four times the annual average for the early years of the 1950's. As late as 1960, 88 percent of all the public donations and 60 percent of all the public capital going to South Asia emanated from the United States. The allocation of United States aid changed sharply, however. Pakistan, India, and South Vietnam received most of the increased funds available. The other countries in the region were largely bypassed, either because of increasing political friction with the United States (Burma, Indonesia) or because they were better off and better able to obtain private capital (Malaya, the Philippines, and Thailand). In short, the neediest countries of the region, except for Burma and Indonesia, were the main foci of the rapid expansion of the United States commitments. If we examine actual *net* official financial flows from all countries in Tables 13–14 and 13–15, a somewhat similar picture emerges.

Some important changes also took place in the commitments involved in the movement of public capital to the South Asian countries. In the period from 1951 through 1955, almost 100 percent were in the form of grants,

[1] India, Government of, Planning Commission, *Third Five Year Plan Draft Report,* May, 1961, Part I, p. VI–24.

[2] Data from I.M.F., *International Financial Statistics.*

Table 13–14

NET INFLOW OF CAPITAL FROM NON-COMMUNIST COUNTRIES, 1951–55 AND 1956–59
(*Millions of dollars per annum*)

					Net Long-Term Capital					
	Total		Net Official Donations		Total		Official and Banking		Private	
Country	1951–55 (1)	1956–59 (2)	1951–55 (3)	1956–59 (4)	1951–55 (5)	1956–59 (6)	1951–55 (7)	1956–59 (8)	1951–55 (9)	1956–59 (10)
Pakistan	20	122	33	84	–12	38	–17	34	5	4
India	70	223	34	62	37	161	46	181	–9	–20
Indonesia[a]	–13	60	5	57	–18	3	–20	7	2	–4
Burma	–12	38	4	23	–15	14	–14	12	–1	2
Philippines	61	79	21	38	40	41	2	2	38	39
Thailand	–	–	6	32	–	–	5	4	–	–
Ceylon	2	–1	2	8	1	–9	7	–3	–6	–6

Source: U. N., *International Flow of Long-Term Capital and Official Donations 1951–1959*, New York, 1961, Table 8, pp. 18–19.

[a] Private capital includes both long-term and short-term capital.

Table 13–15

NET INFLOW OF OFFICIAL CAPITAL, 1951–64
(*Millions of U. S. dollars*)

Country	*1951–55* (*annual average*) (1)	*1956–59* (*annual average*) (2)	*1959* (3)	*1960* (4)	*1961* (5)	*1962* (6)	*1963* (7)	*1964* (8)
Pakistan	15	118	176	224 (253)	192 (264)	318 (397)	501	518
India	79	243	455	710 (782)	693 (662)	710 (742)	978	1230
Indonesia	–15	64	139	162 (61)	365 (133)	110 (151)	116	85
Burma	–11	36	38	31	3	32	...	...
S. Vietnam	...	...	179	187 (192)	163 (173)	172 (184)	227	246
Philippines	23	40	68	54	–1 (23)	18 (35)	30	94
Thailand	...	...	41	29 (50)	26 (42)	38 (56)	46	46
Ceylon	8	5	29	16	8	16	...	...
Malaya	...	...	27	2	18	13	...	...

Source: Columns 1 through 6 from U. N., *International Flow of Long-Term Capital and Official Donations* for the years 1951–59, 1959–61 and 1960–62, after excluding net private capital inflows. Columns 7 and 8 and the figures in brackets for columns 4, 5 and 6 exclude capital movements from Communist countries. Data from O.E.C.D., *The Flow of Financial Resources to Less Developed Countries, 1956–63*, Paris, 1964, p. 44, and O.E.C.D., *Development Assistance Efforts and Policies, 1965 Review*, Paris, 1965.

whereas barely 50 percent were in this form in the years 1960–62.[1] But this change-over has been accompanied in recent years by a shift toward lower interest rates and longer maturities, mainly because of recognition of South Asia's growing debt servicing problem (see Section 16). The creation of the International Development Association in 1960 furthered the principle of soft loans, although not all of the Western countries have accepted this approach to the problem.[2] In 1963 roughly two-thirds of all U. S. loan commitments had repayment periods of forty years or more and interest charges of less than one percent.[3] Other lending countries have begun to follow the United States lead, but at some distance.

The Communist countries began furnishing capital to underdeveloped countries in 1954 and the trend since then has generally been upward. In the beginning the Soviet Union was almost the only Communist country to offer grants and credits to underdeveloped nations. It still accounts for over 60 percent of such offerings; China accounts for about 13 percent, Czechoslovakia for 10 percent, and Poland for 6 percent. The cumulative total of commitments from all Communist countries to all underdeveloped countries from 1954 through 1964 is estimated at over $6 billion, although actual disbursements amounted to less than one-third of that sum;[4] in 1964 alone, the total may have reached $1.2 billion. These commitments were heavily concentrated in a few countries. It appears that through 1964 India received over $1,000 million and Indonesia almost $800 million, while Pakistan, Burma, Cambodia, and Ceylon received around $130, $90, $50, and $80 million, respectively.[5]

Most of the loans made by the Communist countries are repayable over eight to fifteen years, beginning one year after the completion of the project for which the money has been borrowed or, if the purpose of the loan is to finance the purchase of machinery and equipment, one year after the latter has been delivered. The interest rates are around 2½ percent; payments of both principal and interest are allowed to be made in the debtor country's own currency. Over the period from 1954 through 1962 Communist commitments were about one-third as large as United States commitments in

[1] United Nations, *International Flow of Long-Term Capital and Official Donations 1960–1962,* New York, 1964, pp. 17–18.

[2] For a detailed discussion, see James H. Weaver, *The International Development Association,* Praeger, Special Studies in International Economics and Development, New York, 1965.

[3] U. N., *International Flow of Long-Term Capital and Official Donations 1961–1965,* New York, 1966, p. 18.

[4] The long delay in the utilization of credits is largely explained by the fact that most of the credits committed have been for large-scale installations requiring a great deal of preparatory work.

[5] United Nations, *World Economic Survey 1965,* Part I, roneod, E/4187/Add. 4, New York, May 5, 1966, pp. 4f.; cf. U. N., *International Flow of Long-Term Capital and Official Donations,* various years.

the case of India, and double United States commitments in the case of Burma and Indonesia; the two were roughly equal as far as Ceylon was concerned. Adding credits and grants from the Western and the Communist countries, it is probably fair to assume that during the first half of the 1960's the South Asian countries received non-private net capital inflows at an average annual rate of over $1.5 billion, and that the current annual rates were running in excess of $2.2 billion.

The evidence presented in this section should be used with great caution, and interpreted as providing merely the raw material for plausible inferences about broad trends and the general order of magnitudes. Not only are the estimates for credits and grants from the Communist countries extremely weak, but the statistics relating to public capital flows from Western countries are also shaky.[1] Under "aid" or "assistance" several countries include strictly commercial loans, often on short terms, along with grants and loans of the "soft" variety; also, the distinction between economic and military assistance is often a very tenuous one. The published data refer sometimes to actual disbursements and sometimes to new commitments, and both disbursements and commitments may be figured on a net (that is, with interest and principal repayments deducted) or gross basis. For the most part, these various categories are not kept clearly separated in the statistical presentations.

11 *The Quality of the Public Capital Flow and Technical Assistance*

The preceding sections have shown that South Asia remains heavily reliant on bilateral governmental grants and loans. As already indicated, these have been forthcoming in amounts that more than offset the dwindling private capital inflows. Although small in comparison with either the needs of the recipients or the capabilities of the richer countries, the inflow of capital to South Asia in these altered forms far exceeds anything the region ever received in the past. The main reason for this is that South Asia has become politically important to the larger powers at the same time that internal instability and other factors have created a climate unfavorable to private foreign investment. The two are not unrelated. Indeed, a close causal connection exists between the internal difficulties that frighten off private foreign investors and the rise in bilateral governmental grants and loans. Foreign governments provide economic assistance in order to pre-

[1] A comparison of the figures in Tables 13–14 and 13–15 reveals inconsistencies.
Table 13–15 indicates net capital inflows as reported by two different sources. The figures in brackets exclude inflows from Communist countries, yet for Pakistan, India, and Indonesia they are not regularly lower than the figures that include such inflows. Even the figures for South Vietnam, Thailand, and the Philippines, which have not had any capital inflow from the Communist countries, show little consistency.

vent friendly countries from foundering or more neutral governments from becoming aligned too closely with another of the large power blocs. The greater the internal instability or frequency of crises of various sorts, the greater the apparent need for external support and the smaller the likelihood that such support will be forthcoming from private sources.[1]

These facts, which account for the post-war pattern of capital movements, render such capital assistance less potentially stimulating to economic development in South Asia. In the first place, the specific placement of the financial assistance is not uniquely related to economic considerations. During 1954–58, for example, Laos and South Vietnam received from the United States grants and loans almost equal in total to those received by India and Pakistan. South Korea alone received more aid (designated economic) during this period than India, Pakistan, the Philippines, Burma, and Ceylon combined.[2] In general, however, the developmental efforts of South Vietnam, Laos, and South Korea scarcely warranted assistance of such magnitude; India, whose population is more than ten times that of these three countries together, was making considerably greater developmental efforts. As Golay points out, "the distribution of [United States] aid appropriations seems to reflect strategic and political considerations rather than economic considerations."[3]

A second fact, closely related to the first, is that much of the economic assistance has strings attached. Aside from political overtones, serious enough in themselves, which partially dictate which countries receive the grants or loans, the grants and loans themselves are often made for specified purposes, for example, to provide showcases for the assisting country. Frequently, the beneficiaries of foreign aid are required to spend any monies received in the donor country or to ship any needed materials in its vessels. As most of the rich Western countries, for various reasons but mainly because of their inability to preserve an internal monetary balance, have experienced foreign exchange difficulties, the practice of "tying" the capital outflow to underdeveloped countries has become increasingly common.

[1] Not least in India one often hears the suggestion that financial crises may not be entirely bad, as they induce the Western countries to come forth with assistance. ". . . it seems very unlikely that in the absence of foreign exchange difficulties, we would have got foreign assistance to the extent that we did. This does not mean that we should continue to live recklessly, hoping to be rescued by the charity of others, but it is certainly a plea of not being afraid of taking well thought out and calculated risks, despite the advice of orthodox pundits to the contrary." (Man Mohan Singh, "Balance of Payments and Economic Growth," *Problems in the Third Plan: A Critical Miscellany*, Government of India, New Delhi, 1961, p. 127.)

[2] United Nations, Department of Economic and Social Affairs, *Statistical Yearbook 1959*, New York, 1960, pp. 424–426. If military assistance were included, the discrepancy would be far greater.

[3] F. H. Golay, *The Philippines: Public Policy and National Economic Development*, Cornell University Press, Ithaca, N. Y., 1961, p. 125.

By the period 1961–63, about two-thirds of gross bilateral assistance was contractually tied or limited in other ways. The proportion of commodity expenditures financed by the United States Agency for International Development has risen from less than one half in 1961 to over 90 per cent in 1964/65. . . . In the Federal Republic of Germany, there was an increase in the proportion of tied assistance from 10 per cent in 1962 to somewhat less than 50 per cent in 1964.[1]

There are no separate estimates for South Asia, but there is no reason to assume that the practice of tying grants and loans is less prevalent where this region is concerned. Such restrictions prevent the most efficient utilization of foreign capital by the recipient countries[2] and are in sharp contrast to earlier practice. British loans during the nineteenth century were not tied. "The borrowers could freely use them to buy from foreign countries as well as from Britain . . . the fact that the borrower was free to go elsewhere was a protection against exploitation and a help to the development of multilateral trade."[3] Likewise, "So-called tied loans . . . were rare in the American experience."[4]

Foreign assistance on a bilateral basis with a large element of political motivation tends in addition to be uncertain and subject to unilateral increase or decrease on short notice. In contrast to most private investment, it has an excessively short-run bias. A speech by a prime minister critical of, say, United States or Soviet policy may result in large reductions in "economic" assistance. Pursuit of strongly anti-American policies may, on the contrary, be rewarded with enlarged credits by the Soviet Union, while the pursuit of anti-Communist policies may call forth more American dollars. A regime that threatens to collapse and fall into Communist hands can extract large amounts of U. S. funds. Unstable governments in particular can exert a disproportionately large influence on the allocation of foreign aid. It is thus no accident that Laos and South Korea have received even non-military U. S. assistance in unduly large amounts while Indonesia has accumulated substantial credit commitments from the Soviet Union and, until recently, China as well. The deliberate precipitation of an economic and political crisis is often rewarded by an enlarged grant, the greater part of which may find its way into the pockets of those precipitating the crisis. In this fashion some foreign aid simply feeds corruption and maintains inefficiency.[5] In the interest of "stability," several corrupt governments in

[1] United Nations Conference on Trade and Development, *Report,* Part I, roneod, TB/B/82/Add. 2, July 2, 1966, p. 120.

[2] In a study of certain projects with which Pakistan was involved it was found that "prices for products purchased with tied funds averaged about 50 per cent higher than competitive prices for comparable goods" and that "tied development finance raises the average price of procurement for Pakistan by about 12 per cent." (*Ibid.,* quoting Manbub Ul Haq, *Tied Credits: A Quantitative Analysis,* International Economic Association, Washington, D. C., 1965, pp. 2–4.)

[3] Salter, *Foreign Investment,* p. 7.

[4] U. S., *The United States in the World Economy,* p. 157.

[5] Chapter 20, Sections 3 and 6.

South Asia have received substantial foreign assistance. These facts of life make it very difficult for South Asians to undertake those economic and political reforms essential for stimulating growth and weeding out favoritism and bribery. Any pressure for internal reforms the donor country might apply can easily be thwarted by the threat of collapse, the very thing the foreign aid was designed to prevent.

It is clear, then, that the present system of bilateral aid has a strong tendency toward what from an economic point of view can only be construed as misallocation. It is impossible to say how much of the "economic" assistance to South Asia is misplaced, but that much of it is wasted or inhibits essential reforms cannot be doubted. For all these reasons, bilateral foreign aid provides a slender reed on which to base long-term economic growth. Unless it can be effectively purged of allocative and other shortcomings, relatively few positive results can be expected. Thus, while the quantity of foreign exchange made available to South Asia has risen sharply, it is not an unmixed blessing. From an economic point of view much of the public capital flowing into the region is doubtless inferior in quality to the private capital that flowed in earlier, and this fact partly offsets the increase in quantity. Aid dictated by the interests of the participants in the cold war often does not significantly contribute to an accelerated rate of economic growth.

This suggests that, unless changes are made in the nature of bilateral grants or loans, or there is some immediate prospect of renewed private foreign investment, greater reliance should be placed on loans from international agencies where the political element is less pronounced, though not, of course, entirely lacking. As has been suggested: "This form of aid is of great importance in introducing . . . [the] co-operative principle and having a certain air of being above the battle politically . . ."[1] However, today such assistance constitutes only about 10–13 percent of the annual total received by South Asia.[2] Without some rather drastic changes in national policies, multilateral assistance will continue to play a relatively minor role in the near future, though it may have a strategic significance beyond its quantitative impact. Eugene Black, the former President of the World Bank, in an address in Washington in 1962, made a comparison between bilateral and multilateral loans that deserves quotation at some length:

> Are we likely to get the best results if these funds are supplied on a bilateral basis — direct from one government to another — or should they be channeled through, and administered by a multilateral agency? . . . I do believe that the

[1] M. M. Bayne, "Economic Aid to Asian Countries," *Australia's Neighbours,* May–June, 1961, p. 4.

[2] *Ibid.*

emphasis should and can be changed, away from bilateral and toward multilateral aid. Bilateral aid is usually – and unfortunately, increasingly – tied to purchases of the giver's products. However well intentioned a lending government, it is vulnerable to pressure from its own commercial interests to help finance the sale of particular goods for projects abroad, whether the projects themselves are well justified or not. And, however sensible the government of the recipient country, it may have difficulty in resisting offers of finance, even for low-priority projects and on terms that often are not suited either to the circumstances of the country or the requirements of the project.

My most serious criticism of bilateral aid programs, however, is their susceptibility to political influences, whether overt or otherwise. At its worst, aid is offered or exacted as a price in political bargaining that takes no account of the actual economic requirements of the recipients. But even at best, there is always the risk that political influences may misdirect development aid, since they may bring in considerations that are irrelevant to the real needs. I have known cases where, as a result, a splendid new sports stadium has been built, while the highway system remains primitive; or where the national airport has acquired a strikingly modern terminal building, while parched but fertile land is left without irrigation. Economic priorities are inevitably confused when economic objectivity is lost – and economic objectivity is not easy when aid is influenced by political ends. Moreover, the problem goes deeper than the simple waste of a given amount of money. Aid directed to a government that is unwilling to meet the real needs of a country has a pernicious consequence. The most obvious result of some of the bilateral lending of the past decade has been to make it possible for countries to put off undertaking needed reforms; because well-meant but ill-judged offers of aid have been forthcoming, governments have been able to postpone such essential but disagreeable tasks as the overhaul of systems of taxation or essential currency reforms.[1]

Another aspect of foreign aid merits some mention in the present context even though it does not involve pecuniary flows. This is the "gift" of technical experts from the developed countries. There is some reason to believe that, as in the case of capital flows, while the quantity of such assistance to South Asia has risen, the quality may have deteriorated. In the colonial period, young men went out to the region and spent the greater part of their lives there as administrators, organizers, planners, engineers, and so on; hence they became experts in South Asian problems in a very real sense. Those now going to the region tend to stay only a few years at the most and seldom become intimately involved. Moreover, the acute shortage of engineers, physicists, and doctors in the developed countries means that often only second- or third-rate people, those who can be spared, leave their jobs to embark on a technical assistance mission. In

[1] International Bank for Reconstruction and Development, *Address* of Eugene R. Black, President, to the Boards of Governors of the World Bank, the International Finance Corporation and the International Development Association, in Washington, D. C., September 18, 1962, p. 8.

the social sciences, and economics especially, those willing to remain for relatively long periods of time are, as Dudley Seers puts it, "often people who have not succeeded in finding satisfactory niches at home."[1]

Furthermore, even highly trained and capable people are apt to arrive equipped primarily with a Western conceptual apparatus, which is largely irrelevant to South Asia and, indeed, misleading. Certainly the typical scholarly training does not prepare economists for the task and "in some ways makes it more difficult. What usually happens is that the model the economist consciously or unconsciously uses turns out to be the sort of model suitable for a developed economy."[2] Indeed, we have frequently heard competent economic theorists in the West praise development models of underdeveloped countries because they were "mathematically elegant." There is, of course, nothing wrong with elegance, but too often elegance is a substitute for relevance; it becomes an intellectual pastime diverting attention from the realities of underdevelopment. This is a theme emphasized in several chapters of this book and particularly in the Prologue and Appendices 2 and 3. This "common mistake of transference," as Seers calls it, can be dangerously misleading if it eventuates in policy or, less seriously, a waste of effort leading to yet another report conveniently filed and forgotten. In both cases it serves as an excuse for not grappling with the often very serious inhibitions and obstacles to development that are peculiar to the underdeveloped countries of the region. Thus the increase in the number of technical experts going to South Asia is not an unmixed blessing.

Another aspect of this topic concerns a serious psychological and social problem that, for reasons of diplomacy and discretion, has not been given enough attention. Usually the experts come from rich countries with high standards of living. These experts, even if they are not of the highest caliber, must be offered very much higher remuneration than persons in comparable posts in the underdeveloped country concerned can even dream of; moreover, special privileges such as exemption from custom duties are negotiated for their comfort. As a result, the experts, particularly those stationed in the capitals, are often estranged from the people of the country and have strained personal relations with the persons with whom they are supposed to work. This detracts from their usefulness and creates tension. The situation becomes more complex as the work of the expert is a gift. The writer has observed how governments and officials in South Asia take it as a matter of course that they will have to pay a Western expert according to his market rate when they are buying his services; they feel

[1] "Why Visiting Economists Fail," *Journal of Political Economy*, University of Chicago, Vol. LXX, No. 4, August, 1962, p. 327. Seers' article is one of the few to have pin-pointed and examined the quality of economic advice rendered by "experts" to underdeveloped economies. It discusses in detail some of the points made here.

[2] *Ibid.*, p. 329.

differently about his compensation when his services are offered gratis.[1] Experts from Communist countries, most of whom are engaged on special projects or, in any case, in work connected with inter-governmental trade and credit agreements, are less likely to run up against that type of problem, as the business aspect of their presence is stressed even when their services are a grant. Also, they come from less affluent societies and are under strict instructions to organize their life and work in such a way as to avoid creating difficulties; if they are engaged on a relatively big project they often live by themselves in a compound.

12 *A Résumé of Past Trends and Some Lessons for the Future*

The foregoing analysis of trends in the level, composition, and direction of exports, imports, and capital movements has revealed several tendencies significant enough to be worth recapitulating briefly.

First, the need and, to a lesser extent, actual demand for imports have increased faster than the rate of increase in exports. This tendency for imports to outdistance exports creates constant pressure on and concern for foreign exchange balances, necessitates import regulations, and generally reduces the scope for policy, as it virtually compels industrialization to take the form of import substitution (Section 17 below). Secondly, there has been no apparent reduction in the degree of reliance even on a few key exportable commodities, except slightly in India and Pakistan. Thirdly, there is an increasing reliance on Western countries both as a source of imports and a market for exports. These last two tendencies increase the difficulties of rapid economic development, since the growth prospects for the key South Asian export products, especially in Western markets, do not appear very bright (Section 13 below). That is, further economic growth in the West will not lead to an equivalent expansion in purchases of most of the primary South Asian commodities. Not only do the underdeveloped countries in the region appear to have too many eggs in one basket; the basket itself may be unsuitable for accelerated growth. The increasing significance of the Western countries in South Asia's trade has been accompanied by a relative decline in trade within the region, which, in any event, was never very important. At a time when many countries of

[1] Part of the problem is referred to in guarded terms in a recent U. N. report:
"The whole operation [of adjusting the foreign expert to his task] is . . . a highly personal one and the relationships involved often very delicate. They are almost inevitably complicated by the fact that standards of remuneration applicable to a temporary expatriate who has been persuaded to interrupt his career in order to undertake the mission in question are likely to differ considerably from those of his local counterpart and of other local personnel with whom he has to work and associate." (U. N., *World Economic Survey 1965*, Part I, Chapter 3, roneod, E/4187/Add. 3, New York, June 3, 1966, p. 33.)

the world are combining into trading blocs, the failure of the South Asian countries to form a similar kind of association may expose them to systematic discrimination. By limiting the size of the market it may also keep the size of plants and enterprises below the optimum for efficiency.[1] Furthermore, the attempts at national self-sufficiency in the individual countries are often inconsistent with comparative advantages and tend to retard increases in productivity (Section 17).

All of these broad tendencies reduce the policy flexibility of the South Asian countries and keep them excessively dependent on the health of particular industries in a few major countries of the West. The obvious implication is that diversification of exports in both a commodity and directional sense would increase the scope for maneuver and provide a degree of flexibility more conducive to long-run growth. The potentialities for such a policy are discussed in Sections 14–15. The point here, however, is that the basic trends have successively reduced the scope for development policies, and the fact that South Asia's freedom of action is now limited will in turn make a reversal of these trends more difficult in the future and, in any case, impossible of accomplishment without more radical government intervention than in the past.

Finally, both the quantity and quality of capital inflows to South Asia have changed significantly. The amount of capital available to the region has risen dramatically in response to an even more rapid increase in capital requirements. It is difficult to assess the quality of these accelerated capital inflows. On the one hand, the project-oriented and tied nature of much of the bilateral governmental lending (which today makes up the bulk of the international capital flowing to South Asia), and its heavy political motivation, reduce the potential economic stimulus of the larger aggregate. On the other hand, the current emphasis on investments in social overhead capital and the large amount of aid in the form of grants and soft loans are favorable factors.

If the trends of the past few decades have not been very beneficial to South Asia (except more recently for capital movements), future prospects seem even less promising. The critical factor is, of course, the acceleration of the rate of population increase. Even if fertility can be reduced substantially by the spread of birth control among the masses, this will invariably take time; the "braking distance" will be the longer because of the youthfulness of the South Asian populations. In any case, the labor force will continue to increase rapidly throughout any planning period now envisaged, as the workers of the future are already born or will soon be born.[2] The die is cast for at least a generation to come. All of the South Asian countries must prepare to give work to, and support, a vastly greater

[1] However, see Section 15, p. 656, footnote 1, for a critique of the notion of optimal plant size.

[2] Chapter 27, particularly Section 13.

number of people. Unless something very fundamental is done to increase output, especially of food, the situation may become explosive. Hence, a basic problem is to stimulate productivity. Without far more vigorous economic growth a viable economic system is not to be expected, particularly on the Indian subcontinent, in Burma, and in Indonesia.

With the overwhelming need to raise total output sharply, and faster than the population increases, export prospects become vitally important, especially since South Asia's growing indebtedness and increasing burden of debt service will steadily reduce the ratio of net to gross capital inflows (Section 16 below). Already, of course, regardless of the export prospects on the demand side, the population growth has heightened domestic food needs and hence reduced the exportable surpluses in some countries and the potentialities of developmental policies in all. Several of the countries, especially India and Pakistan, are desperately trying to maintain their developmental efforts against this increasingly unfavorable background. In the last few years India and Pakistan have become more than ever dependent on foreign assistance, not only to buy the goods needed for development but also to feed their people. In India, the border conflict with China and the worsening relations with Pakistan have radically increased the outlays for defense. The mounting needs for imports of developmental goods, basic foodstuffs, and even military equipment, in conjunction with a deteriorating balance of payments situation, make the possibility of rapid economic advance very doubtful. Burma and, of course, Indonesia are worse off than India and Pakistan. Even Ceylon has had increasing financial problems during the 1960's. Malaya is in a much better position, having not only abundant foreign exchange reserves but a credit rating good enough to permit it to borrow on commercial terms in order to finance developmental imports. Malaya also has more flexibility because its imports are not nearly so pared down to essentials as those of India and Pakistan. The other countries of the region are in an intermediate position in these respects between India and Pakistan on the one hand and Malaya on the other. But these other countries, and Malaya itself, are approaching the situation of India and Pakistan, at a pace depending upon the rate at which their populations are growing and their balance of payments trends. Without substantially greater dynamism than they have shown up to now, all will sooner or later experience difficulties comparable to India's and Pakistan's.

Offsetting these unfavorable trends to some extent has been a growing awareness in the rest of the world of the assistance needs of the South Asian countries. But until a more appropriate mechanism is devised and accepted to channel external assistance on a larger scale and a long-term basis to those countries whose needs and efforts most warrant it, such assistance will remain insufficient, short run, *ad hoc,* and subject to radical shifts dictated by the political situation of the moment. As a basis for sustainable economic growth, the present international provisions for making grants and loans are inadequate. Even assuming an increase in gross capital inflow, the greater part of the increasing debt service and the rising need for developmental imports during the next decade must be financed by export proceeds. We turn now to examination of the outlook for exports.

13 *Prospects for Traditional Exports*

Two projections of exports from South Asia for 1975 prepared by research secretariats of the United Nations[1] make the assumptions that between 1954–56 and 1975 U. S. gross national product will increase by 80 percent,[2] Japanese G.N.P. by 130 percent, and the G.N.P. of Western Europe by 100 percent. On these assumptions, and allowing for no adverse movements in the terms of trade, primary exports of South Asia are expected to increase at rates substantially below the growth rates in the West and Japan.

The outlook differs among the countries of the region as indicated in Table 13–16, where the latest projections are summarized. Thus the combined demand of the industrial countries of the West and Japan is expected

[1] *Economic Survey of Europe in 1957;* and *Economic Survey of Asia and the Far East, 1959,* Chapter 5.

[2] This is a conservative estimate, however. A more recent estimate, and in our view a more realistic one, calls for a 116 percent increase between 1954–56 and 1975. See Arnold B. Barach, *U.S.A. and Its Economic Future,* Macmillan, New York, 1964.

Table 13–16

PROJECTIONS OF DEMAND FOR PRIMARY EXPORTS IN 1975, BY DESTINATION

(*Index of volume; 1954–56 = 100*)

Country/Destination	*Western Europe*	*North America*	*Japan*	*Total industrial countries*
Pakistan	128	150	162	136
India	143	152	276	155
Indonesia	161	175	289	175
Burma	156	263	146	153
South Vietnam	174	160	130	169
Philippines	104	134	252	140
Thailand	122	154	148	147
Ceylon	133	160	182	141
Fed. of Malaya and Singapore	173	147	251	179

Source: U. N., *Economic Survey of Asia and the Far East, 1959,* p. 91, Table 38.

Table 13–17

PROJECTIONS OF INCREASE IN EXPORTS BETWEEN 1960 AND 1980
(*Value in millions of dollars; index of volume: 1960 = 100*)

	Share of 1960 exports used as basis for predictions		*1980 (Low estimate)*		*1980 (High estimate)*	
Country	*Percent of total 1960 exports*	*Value*	*Value*	*Volume*	*Value*	*Volume*
Pakistan	70	238	242	102	369	155
India	48	618	795	129	987	160
Indonesia	87	744	1,242	167	1,748	235
Burma	84	179	166	93	434	242
South Vietnam	92	66	73	111	139	211
Philippines	77	406	617	152	689	170
Thailand	72	257	281	109	563	219
Ceylon	89	329	437	133	536	163
Fed. of Malaya and Singapore	63	690	898	130	1,268	184

Source: U. N., *Economic Bulletin for Asia and the Far East,* December, 1963, Table 13, p. 19.

to rise by only 55 percent over the 1954–56 level so far as India's traditional exports are concerned; in the case of Burma's exports, the figure is 53 percent, and in the case of Pakistan's a mere 36 percent. Only Malaya-Singapore (79 percent) and Indonesia (75 percent) can expect to find markets for their traditional exports expanding at a rate approaching that of economic growth in the Western countries, and this more hopeful outlook is largely due to the over-riding importance of rubber in their export trade. The outlook for Indonesia can no longer be expected to be so favorable because of persistent internal political and economic instability. For South Vietnam no forecast is possible.

More generally, recent experience indicates that these projections may be on the optimistic side. In 1963, projections were made of the South Asian countries' exports to the world between 1960 and 1980 (Table 13–17). If we average the high and low projections in this series it appears that in the case of India, Pakistan, and Malaya the growth rates are substantially below those forecast in the earlier series that covered exports to the countries of Western Europe, North America, and Japan in the period 1954–56 to 1975. The growth rates projected for Burma, Indonesia, the Philippines, and Thailand are substantially higher. It is difficult, however, to assess the validity of these later projections.[1] Unless the downward trend

[1] The coverage of exports used as a basis for prediction in Table 13–17 is far from uniform. It is high for the small countries that rely on a few primary exports; also for

in economic activity in Burma and Indonesia can be decisively reversed, these countries have little prospect of achieving the degree of export dynamism suggested by Table 13–17. In any event, only in the case of Indonesia does the expected rise in volume of exports exceed the probable growth of population. Moreover, it has been predicted that "growth in exports will lag considerably behind the postulated rate of growth in GNP during 1960–80."[1] Thus, as was noted previously, the stimulating effects of a rapidly rising export demand such as that experienced by the now developed economies of the West during their initial period of industrialization are precluded for South Asia. Instead of exports increasing in comparison with gross national product, that proportion is expected to decline further. Even more significant, exports will continue to decline relative to import needs, thus creating an ever-widening gap. Consequently, policy alternatives will be restricted and greater capital inflows will be needed merely to ensure the present unsatisfactory development.

Past trends in world trade tend to support these rather gloomy forecasts. Nurkse has pointed out that "recent studies have provided evidence that world demand for the poorer countries' exports has tended to rise much less than in proportion to the production and incomes of the advanced countries."[2] The analysis of export trends to date in Section 5 confirms this view.[3] Thus the over-all outlook for exports of primary products is far from optimistic. The relatively downward trend since the end of the First World War, to which we referred in Section 5, is likely to continue, and may accelerate. If the key exports of the region are examined, similar conclusions emerge.

In the case of *rice* we have already noted the adverse impact of population growth on exportable surpluses in the exporting countries. Demand has been affected by attempts at self-sufficiency in the rice deficit countries of the region. The success of these efforts is a matter of record in Ceylon where domestic production of milled rice as a percentage of total consumption rose from 28 in 1909–13 to 50 in 1953–54; in Indonesia and Malaya the rise over the same period was from 86 to 90 and from 15 to 53 percent, respectively.[4] In addition, gifts of surplus food from North America and rising commercial wheat imports have made inroads on South Asia's de-

Burma, which exports mainly rice; and for Indonesia, which exports mainly rubber, petroleum, tin, and vegetable oils. The coverage is lowest for India, as India's exports are fairly diversified and include many manufactured goods.

[1] U. N., *Economic Bulletin for Asia and the Far East,* December, 1963, p. 21.

[2] Ragnar Nurkse, *Lectures on Economic Development,* Faculty of Economics, Istanbul University, and Faculty of Political Science, Ankara University, 1957.

[3] See also GATT, *Trends in International Trade,* 1958.

[4] P. Lamartine Yates, *Forty Years of Foreign Trade,* Allen & Unwin Ltd., London, 1959, pp. 92–93.

mand for commercial rice imports. Self-sufficiency policies in rice deficit countries will undoubtedly persist, so rice exports in the area will be subject to continual downward pressure (see below in Section 17).

China may provide an outlet in the future, though it has been suggested that exports to China "are unlikely to exceed those needed to cover a shortage arising from a bad harvest, or a temporary shortfall in production behind rising demand."[1] Even this element of demand is liable to bypass the South Asian rice surplus countries, as the recent Chinese wheat purchases from Canada suggest. There is, of course, the opposite possibility that China may succeed in increasing its yields so much that it will be able to export a fraction of its food production – and even a small fraction would be enough to adversely affect Burma, Thailand, and South Vietnam. Recent reports from China suggest, however, that such a prospect is at the moment remote indeed. Moreover, China committed much of its future agricultural output to the Soviet Union in exchange for industrial goods according to the Sino-Soviet trade agreement of 1959,[2] though since the Sino-Soviet rift it is possible that these commitments will not be fully honored or that such commitments will not vitally affect China's freedom of action in the future.

The future for *rubber* exports is brighter, even though the share of natural rubber in world demand for all rubber (including synthetic) will diminish if past trends are any indication. By 1960, synthetic rubber producers provided about one-half of all the rubber consumed in the world and much more than half of that consumed in the United States and Canada; between 1960 and 1965 the consumption of synthetic rubber increased more than three times as fast as that of natural rubber.[3] The key factor here is the price and quality of natural as compared with synthetic rubber. One report estimated that "manufacturers preferred natural rubber for 27 percent of their products . . . Synthetic . . . for 38 percent. . . . For the remaining 35 percent the choice depended almost entirely on relative price."[4] There seems little doubt that natural rubber prices will have to continue to decline,[5] if natural rubber is to maintain its competitive position in the face of continuing technical improvements in synthetic rubber and the fact that manufacturers of this commodity have experienced a

[1] U. N., *Economic Survey of Asia and the Far East, 1959,* p. 100.

[2] Alec Nove and Desmond Donnelly, *Trade with Communist Countries,* Hutchinson & Co., London, 1960, pp. 110–111.

[3] UNCTAD, *Report,* Part I, roneod, TD/B/82/Add. 1, July 20, 1966, p. 35.

[4] Quoted in Lennox A. Mills, *Malaya: A Political and Economic Appraisal,* University of Minnesota Press, Minneapolis, 1958, p. 162. Recent quality improvements in synthetic rubber have decreased the manufacturer's preference for natural rubber and increased his interest in price.

[5] United Nations Conference, *Synthetics and Their Effects on International Trade,* pp. 17–46. Natural rubber prices (RSS. 1, New York) declined from 38.57 cents per pound in 1952 to 26.76 cents per pound in 1963. (*Ibid.,* p. 34.)

sharp rise in capacity, and possibly a fall in production costs. Indeed, the Malayan Second Five Year Plan assumed a decline in rubber prices that might more than offset the anticipated volume increase.[1] The main problem on the supply side is that of replacing older trees with newer, improved varieties. This is a lengthy, costly, and difficult task, especially for the small holdings, but recent trends in Malaya indicate a substantial improvement in yields due to replanting.[2] Ceylon has also engaged in replanting, while Indonesia's rubber plantations have in general been left to decay.

Tea is the most stable of the major export items of South Asia in rate of growth of world demand. When exports have lagged behind production in the exporting countries, the gap has been partly closed by increases in internal demand.[3] The effect of the emergence of alternative suppliers in Africa has been offset, at least temporarily, by the low levels of green tea exports from China and Japan, so that the share of India and Ceylon in world exports increased from 76 percent in 1956 to 78 percent in 1959.[4] Competition from African sellers has not made a major dent in the tea market so far, and the market in future years will in the best case continue to be marked by stable prices and slow but steady growth in volume. The possible re-emergence of China as an exporting country cannot be ignored, of course, nor can the effect of the E.E.C. discrimination in favor of the former African dependencies.

The successful rehabilitation of its *sugar* plantations after the war put the Philippines back in the market, and it now has a larger share of the total than in the pre-war period. In a much stratified market, the Philippines' marketing arrangements with the United States have made its receipts more stable than those of other exporters.[5] Against the background of an upward trend in world sugar consumption,[6] sugar exports from the Philippines will probably continue to expand. India's exports of sugar rose from negligible amounts in 1958–60, averaging only about 55,000 tons, to over 480,000 tons – about half the Philippine export volume – in 1963. Furthermore, price quotations for Indian and Philippine sugar have risen since 1958.[7]

The increased use of synthetic fabrics, the emergence of new suppliers, the protectionist policy of the United States, and a low rate of increase in

[1] Federation of Malaya, *Second Five-Year Plan 1961–1965*, Government Printer, Kuala Lumpur, 1961, pp. 64–65.

[2] *Ibid.*, pp. 5 and 17. Important advances are also under way in processing and marketing; cf. P. W. Allen, "Malaysian Natural Rubber Looks to 1970," *International Trade Forum*, Vol. II, No. 2, June, 1966, pp. 28ff.

[3] United Nations, *Commodity Survey 1958*, New York, 1959, p. 95.

[4] *Economic Weekly*, January 14, 1961, p. 45.

[5] U. N., *Economic Survey of Asia and the Far East, 1959*, p. 29.

[6] F.A.O., *State of Food and Agriculture 1960*, Rome, 1960, p. 79.

[7] See U. N., *Economic Bulletin for Asia and the Far East*, June, 1964, Tables 10 and 14 at pp. 89 and 93.

world demand for wearing apparel are the four major causes of stagnation in *raw cotton* exports from India and Pakistan.[1] The declines in price and volume of raw cotton exports will probably continue since none of these factors show signs of decreasing in importance.

Although cotton exports cannot be expanded easily, cotton-producing countries in South Asia have used raw cotton to manufacture domestic textiles to replace imports of cotton fabrics. Exports of *cotton textiles* have not grown, however, at least in India, the main regional exporter. Increased synthetic production in the United States and other Western countries, higher quality exports from Japan, and protectionist policies everywhere have led to a decline in Indian textile exports since 1951. Intraregional trade in textiles has decreased substantially as all the South Asian countries want to be self-sufficient at least in these goods.[2] The prospects for exports of inferior fabrics are thus not bright. Exports of higher quality textiles might increase, but only if a new technology is applied and aggressive marketing policies are adopted (see the next section).

The story of *jute* production is one of oversupply in a shrinking market. National policies in India have emphasized the planting of jute crops for the established industry in Calcutta, which formerly received its raw material from what is now East Pakistan. Meanwhile Pakistan has built factories. Partition of India and Pakistan and continued rivalry have thus induced policies leading to excess capacity in both countries. At the same time, the world consumption of jute has expanded little over the past five decades.[3] Substitutes are taking the place of jute in packing. In the United States, paper has been replacing jute as a sacking material since 1940.[4] More recently the processing of a rival plant, kenaf, which produces a similar fibre, has been improved to the point where some observers claim that it is now commercially competitive with jute. It has even been suggested that kenaf poses a serious threat to India and Pakistan. Exports of *jute manufactures* have also declined, though not as much as exports of raw jute. In particular, the use of jute for linoleum carpets and as backing for floor coverings restored world trade in jute goods so that by 1957–58 it was close to the 1937 total.[5] However, since 1952, there has been a "continuation of the substitution process away from jute" and, even as to backing for floor coverings, the "substitution has, on balance, been ad-

[1] For an outline of these factors, see Yates, *Forty Years of Foreign Trade,* p. 109; U. N., *Economic Survey of Asia and the Far East, 1959,* p. 61; and F.A.O., *State of Food and Agriculture 1960,* p. 91.

[2] U. N., *Economic Survey of Asia and the Far East, 1959,* p. 42.

[3] Surendra J. Patel, "Export Prospects and Economic Growth: India, A Case Study," 1959, mimeographed, p. 6.

[4] U. N., *Economic Survey of Asia and the Far East, 1960,* p. 72.

[5] *Monthly Bulletin of Agricultural Economics and Statistics,* F.A.O., Rome, Vol. IX, No. 12, December, 1960, p. 3.

verse to the use of jute." "The ratio of jute consumption to linoleum production will probably continue to decline."[1] The prospects for exports of jute manufactures do not seem, therefore, to be particularly bright.

Details of recent developments with respect to *tin* are given in Appendix 15. A growing shortage of supply relative to demand forced prices to a thirteen-year high in mid-1964. As a result, export earnings from tin for Indonesia and Malaya have risen sharply – some three to four times – since 1958. Production has increased less, and there is concern regarding the exhaustion of presently exploited tin resources and the possibility of technical substitution. But, for the time being at least, the South Asian tin producers can look forward to a seller's market. One set of projections suggests that the value of tin exports from the ECAFE region will exhibit a "moderate" increase of some 52 percent between 1960 and 1980.[2]

These brief comments on specific commodities confirm that the South Asia countries will be hard pressed to increase their exports of traditional products to the West and Japan, except in the case of rubber and, to a lesser extent, tea and tin, and even here they face certain handicaps. World tea demand will not expand vigorously, and optimism about accelerated exports from India and Ceylon is tempered by the fact that they already supply the greater part of world demand. The future of rubber exports from Malaya and Indonesia depends largely on how successful these countries are in rehabilitating their plantations and lowering prices. Thus far the situation in Indonesia is not promising despite the high potential not only for rubber but also for oil. The outlook for the sale of traditional products to the industrialized West and Japan thus seems reasonably promising only for Malaya, which is already better off than the other countries of South Asia. Thus, if a substantial rise in export income is needed to finance essential imports, the South Asian nations must concentrate their efforts on diversifying their exports and finding alternative markets.

14 *Diversification*

The South Asian countries might diversify their export list by adding to it items in three categories: new primary products, services, and manufactured goods. The resource base of these countries does not appear adequate to generate substantial supplies of new materials, even should they meet with a rising demand in foreign markets. A few countries may be able to sell more non-ferrous metals and forest products,[3] but the region as a

[1] *Ibid.*, pp. 2, 10, and 11.

[2] U. N., *Economic Bulletin for Asia and the Far East*, December, 1963, p. 15.

[3] See Table 11–6.

whole undoubtedly lacks sufficient resources to contribute significantly to over-all supplies of these items. Moreover, demand expansion is offset in part by the saving of raw materials which technological change makes possible. When account is also taken of the much larger apparent reserves of most raw materials in other areas (Africa, South America, Canada, etc.), this avenue of diversification hardly seems likely to hold much promise for South Asia. New discoveries are possible, of course, but it would be foolhardy to place much reliance on such uncertain prospects.

As for services, it is believed that "although some service items [tourism; procurement by foreign governments for civil or military aid missions] may expand in the next twenty years, as a group they are unlikely to raise by very much the import capacity of the primary exporting countries of the region."[1] Other services, such as transport and insurance, will continue to be furnished mainly by the already industrialized and commercialized countries. Little significant increase can be expected in foreign use of services now provided by the South Asian countries.

Consequently, manufactured commodities offer the main prospect for diversification. But with the exception of a few products, such as ceiling fans and sewing machines from India, cricket balls from Pakistan, and, of course, textiles, no South Asian country has been able to make major inroads into the markets for manufactured products in the industrialized countries.[2] There are both natural and artificial reasons for this state of affairs. In the first place there is the relatively poor raw material base, which, though not an absolute barrier to greater industrialization, represents an important constraint when labor is not efficient, wages are low, and capital is not abundant.[3] More fundamental is the difficulty of penetrating markets firmly held by enterprises that have built up trade connections, achieved external and internal economies on the basis of a wide and diversified industrial foundation, built up research departments for continuous improvement of products and rationalization of production, and organized marketing facilities through which they are kept aware of their customers' needs and how these are changing. Taking foreign markets away from those accustomed to supply them is difficult enough for the best equipped enterprises. For enterprises in underdeveloped countries the difficulties are compounded by a shortage of efficient managerial and laboring personnel, a lack of the capital and business acumen so frequently associated with advanced techniques, and a lack of experience in standardized, high-quality mass production. In some lines, cheap labor should

[1] U. N., *Economic Survey of Asia and the Far East, 1959*, p. 97.

[2] Indeed, South Asia's share in total world exports of manufactured goods is very small – less than 3 percent in 1960. Yet the region contains about 30 percent of world population and produces perhaps 10 percent of world income. (U. N., *Economic Bulletin for Asia and the Far East,* December, 1963, p. 31.)

[3] Chapter 11, Section 7.

give these countries a cost advantage. Unfortunately, however, the inefficiency of both labor and management and the absence of specialized ancillary facilities in the region tend to raise the cost per unit of output, and so to negate, in part at least, the low wage scales per unit of time.

This combination of circumstances means that easy advance in the direction of manufactured exports is not to be expected. Any substantial shift in export composition from traditional, primary materials to manufactured commodities would require a higher level of economic development than has yet been achieved. Also relevant is a most important inhibition on the part of the industrialists. The import restrictions which most South Asian countries have been forced to adopt because of their foreign exchange difficulties blunt incentives to produce commodities for export; by insulating the internal market from foreign competition they make it possible for even high-cost producers to do a profitable business at home, as we shall see in Section 17.

The development of export industries in the now developed countries occurred at a time when competition was not nearly so overwhelming. Today, even if it were more feasible than it is for the underdeveloped countries of South Asia to expand their production of manufactured goods for export, they would face the prospect of protectionism if their products adversely affected existing industries in foreign markets. The "cheap-labor" argument, however erroneous in general, is a powerful political weapon that is invoked whenever a domestic industry senses rising competitive pressures from an underdeveloped, low-wage country.[1] The import restrictions on textiles, bicycles, watches, and the like in the United States and other Western countries attest to the success with which lobbies wield this weapon even in rich countries dedicated to assisting the underdeveloped regions of the world. Reinforcing discrimination of this kind is the rise of regional trading blocs in Europe, to which we have already referred. Such economic cooperation and integration stimulates trade within the blocs at the expense of outsiders.

Thus the South Asian countries find themselves in a dilemma: A rise in export proceeds is essential to finance the imports they need, and manufactured products constitute the only area wherein exports might have much chance to grow. The achievement of viable and dynamic economic

[1] ". . . one path of relief for the thickly populated developing countries is to export labour-intensive manufactured goods such as textiles to the advanced countries where they come into competition with the old established but frequently less efficient industries of the advanced countries. This is where the 'cost' of helping the underdeveloped countries simply by letting the principle of comparative costs take its course may hit the advanced countries in a concentrated way in the declining sectors of their economy. This is likely to arouse more opposition than general propositions to increase aid, and may put the altruism of the advanced countries to a severe test." (H. Myint, *The Economics of the Developing Countries*, Hutchinson & Co., London, 1964, p. 183.)

systems therefore rests largely on the ability of these countries to increase exports of manufactured goods. Yet a branching out in this direction would encounter all the obstacles and inhibitions we have enumerated. This means that if the rich countries want the countries of South Asia to succeed, they will have to go out of their way not only to remove artificial restrictions against South Asian manufactured goods but also to create markets in their own country for such products and to guarantee long-run freedom from import restrictions. Such a policy would have only beneficial results for the rich countries, as those industries – mainly labor intensive – where the South Asian countries could compete should logically be declining anyway. As for policy within South Asia, the governments concerned are trying to interest businessmen in producing manufactured goods for export by offering them tax advantages or subsidies,[1] but these policies are meeting with relatively little success since the opposing forces are very strong. Nothing effective can be accomplished along these lines unless the developed countries deliberately make room for manufactures from South Asia. It is difficult to overestimate the importance of such measures to the South Asian economies. At the same time, the difficulties of implementing them should not be underestimated; they will require of the wealthier nations a greater degree of understanding in their approach to the underdeveloped countries and a greater willingness to resist powerful domestic pressures for short-run protective measures than they have hitherto shown. There can be no assurance that appropriate steps will be taken in time.[2]

Politically it is far easier for the rich Western countries to provide the underdeveloped countries with grants and credits that enable their own commercial interests to increase their exports than it is for them to permit a volume of imports that may adversely affect some branch of domestic industry. Resistance to the idea of open importing is all the more likely when the industry in question (e.g., textiles) or the whole economy (e.g., the United States during the late 1950's and Great Britain continually) is relatively stagnant. This is one reason why dynamic growth in the already

[1] See, for example, Chapter 3, "Export Promotion Measures and the Fourth Five Year Plan," India, Government of, Ministry of Commerce, *Report 1964–65,* New Delhi, 1965, pp. 14ff.

[2] Further analysis along these lines and practical policy proposals will be found in United Nations, Economic Commission for Europe, *Economic Survey of Europe in 1960,* Geneva, 1961, Chapter V. These proposals were taken up at the United Nations Conference on Trade and Development in 1964 and by UNCTAD. Harry G. Johnson recently remarked, perhaps a little too pessimistically, that "The process would be politically unpopular on both sides. The developed countries would have to devise policies for the planned contraction or extermination of established protected industries. The less developed countries would have to give up their aspirations for industrial self-sufficiency. But it would contribute both to increased efficiency in the utilization of the world's human and material resources, and to the economic development of the less developed world." (Harry G. Johnson, "Trade Preferences and Developing Countries," *Lloyds Bank Review,* April, 1966, p. 18.)

industrialized countries is so important for South Asia and why stagnation accentuates the preference for financial assistance to the underdeveloped countries. Yet an increase in manufactured exports is potentially more stimulating to an underdeveloped economy than bilateral foreign grants and loans, which suffer from great uncertainty and other shortcomings discussed in Section 11 above. Financial support is essential, but an increase and diversification of exports is even more so.

15 *Alternative Markets*

Three major alternative markets provide some scope for the South Asian countries to increase their trade with areas other than the West and Japan. These are: the Communist countries; the countries in South Asia itself; and the underdeveloped countries in Latin America, Africa, and West Asia.

Communist countries have tended to seek national or bloc independence in raw materials, partly to save foreign exchange but mainly for ideological, political, and strategic reasons. This has caused a decline in South Asian exports to these countries. Except for natural rubber and to an extent sugar, the "centrally planned economies have greatly increased their self-sufficiency in primary materials since before the war, and in many cases, their imports have declined absolutely."[1] Also, the embargo on exports to China imposed by the United States and pressed on the "free world" – though subject to change and not always obeyed – has precluded for the time being diversion of some tin and rubber in that direction. However, the conclusion that "the existence of alternative markets for primary products in the centrally planned economies is unlikely to make any real difference to the export prospects of the primary producing countries of the region"[2] may be premature. We noted in Section 6 that South Asia's trade with the Soviet Union and the other East European Communist countries has accelerated in recent years. With its high rate of growth of heavy-goods output and its generally rapid over-all growth, the Soviet Union could soon be pressing its key natural resources to the limit. Although diminishing returns will doubtless be offset by technological advances and capital deepening, this process itself creates enormous demands for industrial raw materials. It may well be that there is in the Soviet Union "both a growing scarcity and increasing cost of exploiting natural resources."[3] If comparative advantage is shifting in favor of capital goods, it follows that the U.S.S.R., and the other Communist countries in Eastern

[1] U. N., *Economic Survey of Asia and the Far East, 1959*, p. 99. For details see U. N., *World Economic Survey 1958*, Part I, Chapter 4, and later surveys.

[2] U. N., *Economic Survey of Asia and the Far East, 1959*, p. 100.

[3] Michael Sapir, *The New Role of the Soviets in the World Economy*, Supplementary Paper of the Committee for Economic Development, New York, April, 1958, p. 27.

Europe as well, could emerge as large-scale exporters of industrial goods, particularly of capital equipment, to the underdeveloped countries, taking in return primary or traditional products. Thus their trade offensive with respect to the less developed regions of the world, which has received so much attention since Stalin's death in 1953, may have less of an exclusively political motivation than American writers tend to assume. It may be grounded in economic developments. Mutually beneficial trade on a considerably larger scale between the Communist countries and South Asia would therefore seem to be a distinct possibility.

The Soviet Union and the East European Communist countries constitute an even greater potential market for consumer goods. Consumption expenditures have risen sharply in the Soviet Union since 1950. Indeed, "consumption has shared fully in the high and sustained rate of over-all growth," and the rapid growth of the consumer goods sector is not likely to be reversed.[1] A wide "range of foodstuffs, clothing and other . . . [consumer] goods are imported already. It is true that these come largely from within the bloc, but there is no ideological principle to prevent their being bought from other countries . . . Thus the potentialities for expansion are there . . ."[2] In particular, the excess capacity in the Indian and Pakistan textile industries, coupled with the low priority hitherto assigned to clothing in the U.S.S.R., might provide the basis for a substantial and mutually profitable exchange.[3] Other traditional and non-traditional consumer goods might also fit into the emerging pattern. In addition, as the Soviet Union continues its economic development, its exportable surpluses may be expected to rise; sale of these will necessitate imports, many of which could come from South Asia.

All of this is largely speculative but not inconsistent with present tendencies. Much, of course, depends on how the Communist countries visualize their own interests. At present they appear to see both political and economic advantages in stepping up their trade with some South Asian countries, notably India and, at least until recently, Indonesia, and in giving them long-term credits. As a leading Soviet economist said in 1957: "The most important form of economic cooperation of the U.S.S.R. with other powers, including the countries which are poorly developed in re-

[1] Joseph A. Kershaw, "Directions for Future Growth of the Soviet Economy," in Nicolas Spulber, ed., *Study of the Soviet Economy*, Indiana University Publications, Russian and East European Series, Vol. 25, Bloomington, Ind., 1961, pp. 12–13.

[2] Nove and Donnelly, *Trade with Communist Countries*, pp. 49–50.

[3] It is difficult to explain – except by the heavy inertia of bureaucracy, not least in foreign trade – why the Soviet Union, which needs to import from India because it has agreed that its loans may be repaid in rupees, has not bought more textiles from India, which has substantial capacity in this field.

gard to economic relationships, is foreign trade."[1] The 1965 *World Economic Survey* devotes much space to new tendencies in the approach of the Communist countries to their credit and trade policies in relation to underdeveloped countries,[2] and points out that there has recently been put forward the suggestion that the problem of long-term loans to underdeveloped countries be considered in the broader framework of extended economic cooperation in production and trade. Cooperation in this respect would be a condition for increasing the amount of such loans, which is generally advanced as the intention. "According to these views it is far more important in the long run to create conditions enabling the developing countries to increase their export earnings . . . than merely providing them with foreign loans." A "productive cooperation" is envisaged, leading to "the establishment of [new] export industries in the developing countries, designed to create complementarity of economies and based on specialization and partial division of labour between the contracting parties. . . . The centrally planned countries have indicated their readiness to adopt their development plans so as to import a stated proportion of the output of industries built under these agreements. . . . The centrally planned economies are also prepared to assist the developing countries in the promotion of exports to Third countries."

If these thoughts could be translated into practical policies, we would see a new contrast in the relations of the Communist countries and the Western countries with underdeveloped countries. The Communist countries would seek to expand their imports of manufactured products from the underdeveloped countries since that would help the latter to repay their loans. The Western countries often act as if they give grants and loans in order to avoid having to open up their markets to the products of underdeveloped countries, particularly manufactures. On this particular point the Communist countries undoubtedly have logic and reason on their side.[3] It is not yet known whether the Communist countries will implement

[1] V. Alkhimov, "Cooperation Between the U.S.S.R. and Economically Underdeveloped Countries," *Voprosi Ekonomiki,* No. 6, June, 1957, quoted in United States, Department of State, *Sino-Soviet Economic Offensive in the Less Developed Countries,* Publication 6632, Government Printing Office, Washington, D. C., May, 1958, p. 31.

[2] U. N., *World Economic Survey 1965,* Part I, Chapter IV, roneod, E/4187/Add. 4, May 5, 1966, pp. 26ff.

[3] "Critics of American trade policy have been pointing out for years that it makes no sense to restrict U. S. imports from countries which the United States is helping with free grants and other forms of foreign aid. From the business interests affected, however, one often hears the argument that the United States should help these countries precisely by means of governmental grants *instead of* by admitting imports which have bad effects on local employment conditions and possibly also on domestic income distribution. But this argument, which sounds curiously like a variant of the compensation principle in trade and welfare theory, leads to an awkward question. What are the receiving countries to do with the resources put at their disposal? If, first, their exportable primary products face a low rate of expansion in external demand and if,

this new policy to a greater extent than is already implied by their agreeing that payments of principal and interest due them can be made in the debtor countries' currency.

Trade among the countries of South Asia provides another potential path of market expansion. Yet, as noted above, past trends have been away from such a development. Given the frictions within the area and the other conditions referred to in Section 6, the immediate prospects for significant increases in intra-regional trade appear slim. Failure of exports to the developed economies to grow rapidly requires that emphasis be placed on both import substitution and alternative markets; but, as we have seen, import substitution is easiest in precisely those lines which other countries in South Asia have already developed and thus acts as a kind of "beggar-thy-neighbor" policy for the region as a whole. This has most obviously occurred in the production of such traditional commodities as rice and textiles. In regard to rubber and some other products that are only produced in certain of the South Asian countries, intra-regional trade has developed without organized efforts toward intra-regional cooperation.

When it comes to new manufacturing industries, import substitution as applied to a single country often runs up against the problem of the internal market being too small in lines where significant economies of scale are realizable.[1] In economic terms, therefore, this dilemma logically implies that import substitution be conceived along lines extending beyond

---

secondly, their exports of manufactured goods encounter obstacles, there remains only a third possible opening: output expansion for home consumption." (Ragnar Nurkse, *Patterns of Trade and Development,* Wiksell Lecture, Almqvist & Wiksell, Stockholm, 1959, p. 41.)

[1] In the frequent assertion that in underdeveloped countries, particularly the smaller ones, the limited markets are major obstacles to accelerated economic growth, there is implicit the notion of an optimal plant size, a concept that is both elusive and excessively static. In the first place, the size of the market is difficult to construe with any degree of precision. A market depends not only on the number of people and their disposable incomes, but also on their willingness to purchase a particular commodity. One cannot, therefore, logically speak of markets being restricted in general, as is so often done; the industry and commodity must be specified. The size of the market depends also on such factors as the price and quality of the particular product. The market has, in addition, a time dimension; it may either widen or narrow, depending on a host of factors – some within the range of discretion of the particular producers and others determined by external developments. Thus, from the demand point of view, the quantities of any particular product that can be sold in a given period of time are subject to many changing factors. Even on the cost side there are serious ambiguities. The technique that would result in minimum per unit costs depends not only on the product but also on relative factor prices and how they are changing. For the underdeveloped economy the optimal technique will not necessarily be the most recent one used in an advanced economy. Nor will the optimal plant size (however measured!) inevitably be so large. There may be several optima, or "near optima," some of them much smaller. As has been suggested, "the scope for developing new technological innovations, by modification and combination of various alternatives, is considerably broader than was the case when the original technological changes were

national boundaries – a policy of *regional* import substitution coupled with specialization in certain goods, especially manufactured goods, by particular countries is clearly suggested. More and more this has become the focus of attention as export proceeds stubbornly lag behind developmental needs and as import substitution as now practiced gives rise to high-cost production (Section 17). Over time the economic pressures will mount if exports to other parts of the world cannot be greatly expanded; hence, the desirability of closer regional economic integration or cooperation will grow.

These points have been made with increasing emphasis by the Secretariat of the U. N. Economic Commission for Asia and the Far East.[1] There are some signs that the South Asian countries are coming to recognize the need for cooperation, although as late as 1955 they refused even to admit the desirability of adjusting national plans in the interests of regional specialization. The sessions of the Commission for Asia and the Far East from 1960 on have shown considerable progress, though mainly on the ideological level.[2] A large number of Secretariat studies and reports of meetings, sometimes at the ministerial level, have been produced. The Mekong project, the Asian Highway scheme, and geological mapping projects also attest to the growing spirit of cooperation. But aside from such isolated and specific projects, nothing has as yet been accomplished in regard to the wider problem of regional integration.

The difficulty is that an attempt to increase intra-regional trade in South Asia must entail much more than lowering tariffs and other trade barriers. Among developed countries of the West this may suffice, since the price mechanism will lead to a higher degree of specialization and greater econ-

---

developed." (C. Wolf and S. C. Sufrin, *Capital Formation and Foreign Investment in Underdeveloped Areas,* Syracuse University Press, Syracuse, N. Y., 1955, p. 40.)

This is not to deny that the sales potential of some commodities in some of the South Asian countries may be less than is required to permit reasonably efficient production at prices that yield a return considered to be in some sense "satisfactory" or perhaps even "optimal." This is particularly true of steel, cement, newsprint, and also a large number of manufactured products not in the field of heavy industry. Nor should the foregoing be viewed as inconsistent with certain gains to be reaped through some form of closer economic cooperation. We are simply pointing out that blanket and generalized assertions about the narrowness of markets cannot be rooted in reality. There is no substitute for a detailed study of productive techniques for particular products in the light of actual or anticipated factor costs and potential demand in the various countries. See also Chapter 14, Section 6.

[1] For an early statement of the rationale for regional cooperation see *Economic Bulletin for Asia and the Far East,* Vol. XLL, No. 3, December, 1961, pp. 52–76 and pp. 80–82. A comparable rationale underlies the Latin American Free Trade Association and the Central American Common Market. For details see United Nations, Department of Economic and Social Affairs, *Multilateral Economic Co-operation in Latin America,* New York, 1962.

[2] See Chapter 14 of Wightman's *Toward Economic Cooperation in Asia* for a detailed discussion of the slow and tortuous process by which the South Asian countries have been led to adopt positions conducive to a higher degree of mutual cooperation.

omies of scale more or less automatically once the obstructions to trade are reduced, and since the countries are all so highly developed that they have little need to defend themselves against each other. In South Asia, the market mechanism works much too ineffectively to ensure an automatic development toward greater over-all efficiency through regional specialization. In particular, the risk is obvious that the new and successful ventures would become the province of the bigger and industrially more developed countries, in the first place India, while the other countries get only the negative backwash effect. Thus, in addition to a reduction of trade barriers behind a common tariff wall, there is need of joint planning to decide formally which countries should specialize in particular product lines.[1] In the words of a United Nations publication, "the market can be expanded not by liberalizing but rather by organizing. . . . if a new and more rational pattern of intra-regional division of labour is to be developed, this will have to be designed consciously through negotiations and agreements, rather than emerging spontaneously as a result of the price mechanism of free trade."[2]

By this approach the frequently alleged lack of complementarity among the countries of the region, which is supposed to stand in the way of closer economic cooperation, can be offset. Indeed, even though the countries are more competitive than complementary in their present economic structures, it is everywhere the aim to change the existing pattern of production. In short, complementarity is precisely what is to be created and shaped by whatever form of cooperation emerges. But the creation of complementarity requires a high degree of joint planning to determine what country should have what industry. In this joint planning the present pattern of import restrictions, licenses, and exchange rates would have to be restructured and coordinated with over-all goals if the gains from a higher level of intra-regional trade are to be reaped. A mutually beneficial expansion of trade and output cannot be generated merely by eliminating trade barriers among the countries.[3] It should be added that there is already a need for joint deliberation and planning simply so that the region can protect itself against the discriminatory trade policies (actual or poten-

[1] Ceylon's development plan recognizes this fact. See *The Ten-Year Plan,* p. 33.

[2] "Approaches to Regional Harmonization of National Development Plans in Asia and the Far East," U. N., *Economic Bulletin for Asia and the Far East,* Vol. XV, No. 3, December, 1964, p. 39.

[3] Roy Harrod, commenting on the Seminar on Asian Trade held in Karachi in December, 1961, reports in this context that "A certain idea seemed to take shape during the sessions, first conveyed in the expression 'investment oriented regionalism' and then in the expression 'agreed specialization.' The basic idea here was that the advantages of a larger market should be secured, not *ex post* by some tariff manipulation, but *ex ante* by some previous agreement about the directions into which investment should be channeled in each separate country." (Roy Harrod, "Economic Development and Asian Regional Cooperation," *Pakistan Development Review,* Vol. 2, No. 1, Spring, 1962, p. 14.)

tial) of regional blocs elsewhere. Common trade policies relating to imports from members of other trading blocs could augment South Asia's bargaining power.

There need not, however, be a multilateral agreement – which, at the present time, would be very difficult to obtain. Beneficial results could be achieved through a series of bilateral arrangements, provided they led to an improved division of labor. For example, Ceylon might reserve the right to establish a large-scale tire industry to supply both itself and India in exchange for giving India the right to supply the market for machine tools. Ceylon has the rubber and India the basis of a large machine tool industry. Benjamin Higgins has pointed out similar possibilities so far as Indonesia and the Philippines are concerned.[1] Much scope exists for such advantageous cooperation in agriculture as well, especially between food surplus and food deficit countries. This implies that even attempts at self-sufficiency in food need to be subordinated to the larger goal of enhanced progress through cooperation.

That substantial potential exists in both manufacturing industry and agriculture is undeniable, but the implications for national planning need to be faced. Joint planning and a breaking away from the narrow nationalism of present planning in the region are essential in order to achieve an acceptable distribution of the gains from cooperation and to compensate for the lack of an appropriate market mechanism. Aside from the problems involved in creating a political climate of solidarity in a region marked by many deeply rooted animosities, there are difficulties of a more technical character. We have already referred to the necessity of preventing the larger and industrially more advanced countries from overwhelming the smaller and less industrially developed countries. If the more powerful countries are given to understand that they cannot dominate any proceedings designed to give substance to the idea of regional cooperation, their interest in such proceedings will decline. But unless this is clearly established, the weaker countries cannot be expected to let down their guard. Positive results cannot, of course, be expected, except after hard bargaining. Furthermore, the bargaining cannot be restricted to the subject of establishing new industries. This implies that it may easily deteriorate into a debate on whether it is better to create larger markets for already established industries that are poorly located and thus costly, or to dismantle them and start from scratch in a new location. Whatever the decision, some party is going to suffer what is, or appears to be, a loss. This particu-

[1] "Regional planning among countries in Asia and Africa is long overdue. Industrialization is not tantamount to every country's endeavouring to produce everything, and some integration of national plans to avoid costly overlapping is surely desirable. For example, both countries might benefit if Indonesia leaves iron and steel production to the Philippines, while the Philippines stays out of rubber and aluminum, and does not expand its petroleum refining capacity." (Benjamin Higgins, *Economic Development*, Norton, New York, 1959, p. 561.)

lar difficulty is unfortunately apt to increase with every year that passes as individual countries proceed to develop import substitutes. A third technical difficulty is that the several countries are not equally advanced in their national planning, and it is national plans that need to be coordinated. All these special difficulties emerge from the fact that economic integration in South Asia must be "organized," attained by joint planning.

Under these conditions it is not so surprising that little has as yet resulted from the lively discussion about regional integration in South Asia. With fair certainty it can be predicted that whatever progress there may be will be restricted to special agreements involving only two or a few countries. But the strivings have so much to recommend them that they will probably not be given up. Furthermore, they will be stimulated by the rise of trading blocs in the rest of the world. The notion of countervailing power is not uniquely related to groups within a nation; the countries of South Asia may be driven toward a closer economic association by the trends in world trade and the emerging pattern of international economic relations.

The third set of alternative markets, the other underdeveloped countries outside the region, also represents a possible source of mutually advantageous trade. Not much can be anticipated in this direction, however. Indeed, as production of primary products grows in Africa and Latin America, increasing competitive pressures will be put on some important South Asian exports, notably tea, tin, cocoanuts, and rubber. Since the underdeveloped countries as a group are short of the very items each so desperately needs, there is little chance that trade among them will increase significantly. Such a development would again require joint planning, which with remote countries is especially difficult to achieve. Moreover, the great distances involved mean that transport costs are high, particularly for goods whose value is low in relation to their bulk.

Nevertheless, the same logic impelling the countries within South Asia into closer economic cooperation should apply equally well to all underdeveloped countries:[1] a kind of "poor countries' common market for cheap goods" has a certain logical basis. Without closer economic ties on a formal and carefully planned basis, however, the underdeveloped countries of the world are more apt to compete with one another in attempting to expand exports to the richer countries. The possibility that they will trade more extensively among themselves appears negligible; on balance, therefore, they are likely to hinder rather than promote each other's growth. This prospect in itself provides a reason for attempting to achieve a higher degree of cooperation that takes cognizance of each country's needs, perhaps

[1] India's Second Five Year Plan stresses the desirability of cooperative trading arrangements for "the entire underdeveloped region of Asia and Africa." (India, Government of, Planning Commission, *Second Five Year Plan,* New Delhi, 1956, p. 19.)

along the lines suggested by the Afro-Asian Organization for Economic Cooperation and later followed up at the U. N. Conference on Trade and Development and in UNCTAD.

Taking all of the foregoing together, export prospects for the South Asian countries do not appear promising. Not only is the future for exports of traditional commodities to the West and Japan somewhat bleak, but diversification of either products or markets appears to have only limited potentialities. Developments within the Communist world may offset these gloomy prospects to some extent, but this possibility should not be overestimated, especially in view of the very small share of South Asian trade presently accounted for by the Communist countries in Europe and Asia. Considerable scope exists for mutually beneficial intra-regional economic cooperation. This has received increasing attention in recent years, but there is little prospect that significant progress will be made in the near future.

16 *Inflow of Capital*

The prospect of foreign private long-term lending increasing significantly is negligible. The forces that brought about the collapse of the international capital market are still operating as far as South Asia is concerned. Direct private investment in some of the countries of the region has apparently tended to rise over the past few years, although the volume is still relatively very small and progress has been erratic. Those countries having large potential markets (like Pakistan and India, which though poor are populous, or smaller but richer Malaya, Thailand, and the Philippines) and a seemingly more stable political situation (again like Pakistan, India, Malaya, Thailand, and the Philippines) should be capable of attracting private capital in larger amounts.[1] There are some reasons for expecting the apparent though slight and hesitant improvement evident in recent years to continue, although not very rapidly or far. But if political or economic disturbances should occur, even such improvements could be scared off.

Behind the direct investments that have taken place or are planned is a growing realization among Western businesses that import restrictions are here to stay[2] and may spread and stiffen. What makes it profitable for

[1] For India, see Reserve Bank of India, *Report of the Central Board of Directors for the year ended June 30, 1960*, Bombay, August, 1960, p. 13. Malaya anticipated a slight rise in such investment during the "second plan period." See *Second Five-Year Plan 1961–1965*, p. 62. For more recent data see U. S. Department of Commerce, *Survey of Current Business*, September, 1965, pp. 23–29.

[2] Appendix 8, Part I.

foreign firms to establish themselves within the domestic market is not so much the money to be made from the direct investments themselves as certain "by-products" less easy to control or tax. These include such things as selling equipment and semi-manufactured products for the new factory, sometimes at "salted" prices.[1] With an established foothold and numerous contacts with officials, there are also greater opportunities to pass through the licensing walls and sell other products. From the viewpoint of indigenous businessmen, going into partnership with a foreign concern makes it easier to obtain permission from the licensing authorities to establish a new enterprise, since this involves no further depletion of the already low foreign exchange reserves. This kind of investment accords with the South Asian countries' urge to speed up industrialization. Also, there is a growing recognition in South Asia that foreign participation in industrial ventures has other advantages than saving foreign exchange; in particular it leads to an inflow of valuable managerial and engineering personnel and technical know-how. The South Asian governments want generally to have assurances from foreign capitalists that any enterprises with which they are connected will employ indigenous personnel, particularly in the higher posts. They also want to have a hand in determining the branch of industry in which foreigners invest, and the location of their enterprises. Once these matters have been negotiated, they are prepared to offer various guarantees and even special inducements, particularly in regard to taxation.[2] No-

[1] "For intra-company transactions . . . the profit of any one subsidiary may be sacrificed in the interest of a unit more favourably situated from the point of view of the whole concern." (*World Economic Survey 1965*, Part I, Chapter 2, roneod, E/4187/Add. 2, May 6, 1966, p. 29.)

[2] Early in the game the Draft Outline to India's First Five Year Plan saw the advantages in foreign direct investment and outlined a policy that is now fairly common in the region.

"From the point of view of industrial development, it would be best if foreign investments in the country take the form of equity capital.

"By providing the necessary incentive to foreign investors, this form of capital would facilitate the flow of capital goods and bring in industrial know-how, technical personnel and business experience and organisation which would all be useful. The inflow of capital in this form, however, needs, besides the prospects of a fairly good return, certain assurances in regard to equality of treatment, facilities for transfer of profits, compensation in case of nationalisation, etc. These have been expressly provided under the policy announced in April 1949. The main features of this policy are:

"(a) no discrimination would be made between foreign and Indian undertakings in the application of general industrial policy;

"(b) reasonable facilities, consistent with foreign exchange position, would be given for the remittance of profits and repatriation of capital; and

"(c) in case of nationalisation, fair and equitable compensation would be paid.

"Since investment of foreign capital also necessitates the utilisation of indigenous resources, which are limited, it is desirable that such investment should take place in certain specific fields. Broadly, it might be stated that foreign investment should be permitted in spheres where new lines of production are to be developed or where special types of experience and technical skill are required or where the volume of domestic production is small in relation to the domestic demand and the indigenous industry is not likely to expand at a sufficiently rapid pace. The system of joint enter-

where in South Asia, however, is there an unreserved eagerness to welcome foreign investments. P. S. Lokanathan, who is certainly not an unalloyed and suspicious Indian nationalist, wrote in a book review:

Foreign investment is costly. Costs have been inflated in a number of ways, of which the excessive mark up of prices of the machinery and equipment imported [by foreign firms] and the excessive charges for know-how, patents and the like are only two. Other disquieting features are the reluctance to transmit knowledge, skills, processes and the rest to their Indian partners; the preference to turnkey jobs; the restrictions imposed on exports of products manufactured in India with collaboration arrangements; the tight hold the foreign firms have on policies and operations despite the growing degree of Indianisation; the prevention of manufacture of standardised items through each foreign firm bringing its own brand of machinery and plant, resulting in unstandardised parts and components and too many and too varied types of equipment; their reluctance to earn foreign exchange, but readiness to drain away the limited foreign exchange resources and a number of other similar features. Cumulatively, were it not that the evidence cited is too strong to be dismissed, one would think that the author is biased against all foreign investment in this country. . . . The result has been that foreign investments have had a relatively easy time. They have been able to fix the prices for their products produced in India from 50% to 100% higher than those prevalent in their home countries. The profits earned by foreign investments have also been very much higher. Altogether the time is ripe for a review of the working of foreign investments in India from the point of view of efficiency, economy and contribution to industrial development and of the collaborative arrangements which have often imposed constraints on the budget of research, know-how and skills and on increasing the exports. The need for India to become more self-reliant and to use the foreign loans and aids in a more effective way has indeed become imperative with the changing moods of the donor countries.[1]

In the Western countries there is a brisk demand for capital and highly profitable investment opportunities. Therefore, in view of the economic and political instability in South Asia and the likelihood that the forces described in this and other chapters of our study will continue to prevent vigorous economic development in the larger part of the region, it cannot

prises under which a number of foreign concerns have established new industries in the country in collaboration with Indian businessmen appears to be suitable for securing the employment of equity capital. Agreements for such joint participation between foreign and Indian concerns should be subject to the approval of the Government. The share of national capital in joint enterprises, the facilities for the training of Indians, the disclosure of patented processes to Indian associates, etc., are matters in respect of which no hard and fast rules need be prescribed." (India, Government of, Planning Commission, *The First Five Year Plan – A Draft Outline,* New Delhi, July, 1951, pp. 159–160.) On tax exemptions, see Appendix 8, Section 9.

[1] *Economic Journal,* Vol. LXXVI, No. 304, December, 1966, pp. 923ff. Lokanathan was agreeing with views expressed by M. Kidron in *Foreign Investments in India,* Oxford University Press, London, 1965.

be expected that private direct investment will be much more significant in the future than it has been in the recent past.

We have seen that insofar as the widening gap between rapidly rising import needs and stagnating export returns in the major countries of South Asia has been filled at all, it has been filled by an inflow of public capital in the form of grants and credits of much greater magnitude than the private capital inflows of any earlier period. As we pointed out in Section 10, this inflow of public capital continued to swell through the first half of the 1960's. The particular beneficiaries were Pakistan and India, which were the two largest and poorest countries and also the countries that took planning most seriously.[1] However, these countries were warned that a continued inflow from the West, unconditionally given and increasing in scale, was not to be taken for granted when "aid" and negotiations about further commitments were postponed because of the September war in which they engaged each other in combat.[2] Decisions as to the size and the terms of further commitments are still in abeyance at the beginning of 1966.

Meanwhile the more general issue of financial assistance to underdeveloped countries has reached a state of acute crisis, which is reflected in all the intergovernmental organizations concerned with this matter. The tendency of population increases to outrun increases in food production is apparent in Latin America, Africa, and West Asia as well as in South Asia.[3] Partly because of the sluggish growth of their agricultural production and, in many instances, the continued deterioration in their trading position, the underdeveloped countries have been making slower progress toward viability in recent years.[4] Against this background it is disquieting to note that the flow of public grants and loans to all underdeveloped countries, which rose rapidly in the second half of the 1950's, has levelled off since 1961; private long-term investments have shown large year-to-year fluctuation but have tended to decrease. On the average the ratio of the total outflow of public and private capital to the national income of the rich countries has decreased from 0.87 to 0.66 percent.[5]

The situation is the more serious because of what the President of the World Bank, George D. Woods, has called the "debt explosion."[6] The rap-

[1] Chapter 15, Sections 7 and 8.

[2] Chapter 6, Section 8.

[3] F.A.O., *The State of Food and Agriculture 1965*. Cf. Chapter 26, Section 2.

[4] UNCTAD, *Report,* Part I, Chapter II, "Growth of Developing Countries," roneod, TD/B/82/Add. 1, July 20, 1966, pp. 6ff.

[5] *Ibid.,* Part II, Chapter IV, roneod, TD/B/82/Add. 2, July 20, 1966, pp. 103ff.; cf. U. N., *International Flow of Long-Term Capital and Official Donations 1961–1965,* and U. N., *World Economic Survey 1965,* Part I, roneod, E/4187, May 20, 1966, and E/4187/Add. 2, May 6, 1966.

[6] "In 1956, the outstanding international debt of the low-income countries, stemming from public sources or carrying governmental guarantees, was estimated at just

idly increasing debts of underdeveloped countries imply, among other things, that debt service is becoming an increasing burden,[1] absorbing a growing portion of their export earnings and so decreasing the net value of the new grants and loans they receive. Another high official of the World Bank, S. Aldewereld, explains the consequences of the developing countries' indebtedness,[2] and concludes: ". . . if gross aid should remain approximately stable, as it has for the past four or five years, the amount of net aid would decline sharply." It would indeed "drop to zero within 15 to 20 years." This development, he adds, had not been foreseen.[3] Putting it the other way around, even to maintain the present level of net capital inflow, let alone increase it, annual gross commitments would have to rise sharply and with increasing speed, and this would have to happen while the "credit worthiness" of the receiving countries in terms of their balance of payments prospects is declining and their debts are mounting.

In the paper quoted above Woods asks for "a marked change of outlook" on the part of the rich countries, a preparedness for a "major and irrevocable decision about development assistance," that would make "more aid available to the developing countries and on better terms." And he warns against "cases of default," pointing out that "the harm done by defaults is much deeper than statistics can indicate; it is truly incalculable."[4]

Concerning first the need for a substantial increase in the flow of public funds to the underdeveloped countries, serious doubt must be expressed that this need will be met. Because of the inability of the Western countries to preserve internal balance between aggregate demand and supply for other reasons, all of them have come to feel apprehensive about their for-

under $10 billion. In 1964, it reached an estimated $33 billion. Because of rising interest rates and the accumulation of short-term debt, the amount of money needed each year to service this debt climbed even faster. From 1956 to 1964, it rose over four times, from $800 million to $3.5 billion." (George D. Woods, "The Development Decade in the Balance," *Foreign Affairs*, January, 1966, p. 211.)

[1] About the problem of the rising burden of debt service, see International Bank for Reconstruction and Development, *Economic Growth and External Debt*, Vols. I and II, roneod, March 12, 1964; and UNCTAD, *Report*, Part II, pp. 112ff.

[2] "In the mid-1950s service on foreign debt absorbed less than 4 percent of the export earnings of the developing countries. By 1964 this figure had risen to 12 percent, and for a number of important countries it was almost twice as high. . . . In the mid-1950s the gross flow of capital, public and private, to the developing countries was roughly $7.5 billion per year and the net flow after deducting annual debt service payments was more than $6.0 billion. . . . The gross flow had increased [in 1964] to $12.0 billion (most of the increase occurring in the late fifties) but the net flow had already declined slightly to about $6.0 billion as a result of the increase in annual debt service plus returns on direct private investments. The decline is more dramatic if the population increase is taken into account and the figures are expressed on a per capita basis." (S. Aldewereld, *The External Debt of the Developing Countries*, Address to the Political Economy Association, Uppsala, May 4, 1966, pp. 7, 9–10.)

[3] *Ibid.*, pp. 5 and 16.

[4] "The Development Decade in the Balance," p. 215 and p. 212.

eign exchange balances. This provides them with an excuse, or occasionally more than an excuse, for not letting the outflow of capital grow very greatly, if at all.[1] Also, there are many indications that popular opinion in the rich Western countries might not support a move to increase substantially the assistance given to underdeveloped countries.[2] The slow rate of development in underdeveloped countries – though partly a result of the slowing down of the capital inflow – is often cited as a reason for not speeding up that inflow. In this connection it is ominous that the largest contributor to South Asia, the United States, has shown no signs that it plans to increase its contribution, except for the food aid given under P.L. 480.

As for the terms on which assistance is given, it is, of course, evident that a substantial change-over from loans to grants would help to stem the rise in the debts and debt service charges of the underdeveloped nations. But the trend has been, and is, in the opposite direction.[3] A capital advance, destined to be paid back "sometime," has more chance of being approved by a Congress or a Parliament concerned with "fiscal integrity" or "sound" finance in the traditional sense than does a simple "give-away." Aside from these homely attitudes regarding the respective merits of grants and loans, many legislators take the view that the need to repay will induce a more careful employment of funds for development needs. With the "debt explosion," however, there must be a growing awareness that South Asia cannot realistically be expected to repay all the credits it receives. This fact should serve to support the efforts that are under way to make loans to the region softer, in regard both to interest rates and to the time allowed for amortizing the principal (Section 10).

There is every reason to expect that the inflow of public capital from the West will differ considerably among South Asian countries. Malaya and Thailand may continue to be less in need of a big inflow of public capital than most of the other countries; Burma may prefer to remain isolated and may continue to pursue policies that make the Western countries uninterested in aiding her; the Philippines enjoys "special relations" with the United States; Indonesia under a new authoritarian regime leaning to the right may be better qualified than it was under the Sukarno troika to receive financial assistance from the West, and will certainly need it very badly; in the successor states to French Indo-China anything may happen. Pakistan and India, as well as Ceylon, will be pressing for the largest pos-

[1] At the same time it gives them a motive for keeping aid funds tied to national exports; see Section 11 and below.

[2] Gunnar Myrdal, *The McDougall Memorial Lecture,* Address given at the opening of the Thirteenth Conference of the Food and Agriculture Organization of the United Nations, November, 1965, C65/Lim/3 Rev. 1, roneod, Rome, 1965.

[3] U. N., *International Flow of Long-Term Capital and Official Donations 1961–1965,* pp. 18–19. See Section 10 above.

sible financial support for their new five year plans. How much they will get is anybody's guess. The one thing certain is that the volume of public capital the South Asian countries receive will be determined within the framework of financial relations between underdeveloped countries in general and the rich Western countries in particular. This is why we stressed that framework.

Especially is this true for the two biggest countries, Pakistan and India, which have based all their plans on the assumption of a continued, very large capital inflow from the West. Realistically viewed, this inflow must also continue to grow for an undetermined time in the future, although that fact is usually played down or denied. The foreign public debts of both countries rose between the end of 1955 and 1962, Pakistan's from $147 million to $829 million and India's from $310 million to $2,936 million; the average annual rates of growth were 28 and 38 percent respectively.[1] Between 1956 and 1963 Pakistan's service payments increased from $21.1 million to $58.1 million, while those of India increased from $12.2 million to $238.0 million.[2] In 1962, debt service amounted to 7 percent of Pakistan's total export returns and 9 percent of India's.[3] The figures for 1962 and 1963 are already far out of date. The rapid acceleration of the rise in debt service payments and what this means in terms of the underdeveloped countries' need for capital may be illustrated by the following quotation:

> During India's third Five-Year Plan period, which ended March 31, 1966, aid disbursements by the India consortium plus the East bloc and other countries totalled approximately $4.3 billion (excluding United States shipments of grains and other agricultural commodities under United States Public Law 480). In the same period debt service payments to the aid-givers were $1.2 billion, leaving net aid disbursements of $3.1 billion. If in the coming five-year period the same amount of gross aid were to be disbursed, namely $4.3 billion, and this aid were to be made available on present average terms, debt service would then be about $2.6 billion, thus reducing net aid available to finance imports to $1.7 billion or by 45%. Expressed another way, gross aid disbursements would need to be increased by one-third, or from $4.3 billion to $5.7 billion to maintain net aid disbursements at the same $3.1 billion level.[4]

Considering the general climate for financial assistance to underdeveloped countries, it would seem that new loan commitments to countries like Pakistan and India large enough to counterbalance the rising burden of debt service are unlikely to be forthcoming; the substantial rise in net inflow of capital needed by these countries does not seem indicated.

In regard to the "quality" of the capital inflow (Section 11), it seems

[1] I.B.R.D., *Economic Growth and External Debt*, Vol. II, p. 6.

[2] *Ibid.*, Table 8, p. 14a.

[3] *Ibid.*, Vol. I, Table 6, p. 30.

[4] S. Aldewereld, *The External Debt of the Developing Countries*, p. 16.

likely that future credits will be tied to deliveries from the creditor countries to at least the same extent as at present. In 1965, 92 percent of the financial assistance provided by the United States was tied, as compared with 79 percent in 1963 and 47 percent in 1959.[1] With the prospect of disturbing political development in the region, it is difficult to believe that "aid" activity, particularly as carried out by the United States, will be any less influenced by political considerations than in the past.

But the pressures exerted by the United States and other Western countries will not only be of a "political" type. They may increasingly come to be economic in nature, in which case they may sometimes have a wholesome effect on planning. If the economic situation tightens, and particularly if the food situation worsens, the Western countries may find it necessary to formulate stiffer conditions for their assistance. They may demand that vigorous attempts be made to raise yields in agriculture, and it may increasingly come to be understood that land reform is among the means to be employed. Also, they may insist that more effective efforts be made to spread birth control. That the Western governments will continue to give massive public financial assistance, perhaps on an increasing scale, while leaving national planning almost exclusively to the aid-receiving countries themselves, seems highly improbable. A good deal of "advice" has, of course, always been given out, often monitored through the World Bank and its missions, but now there will probably be more of it. When the United States increased its food aid to India very considerably late in 1965, it stipulated changes to be made in India's agricultural policy. Such directives will often be resented, as they have previously been, and it is of supreme importance that they be carefully thought out in terms of the receiving country's interest; up to now, this has not always been the case.

So far we have been thinking mainly of the inflow of public capital from the West. As we mentioned in Section 10, a considerable amount of capital has come from the Communist countries. In Section 10 we pointed out that these countries are now considering incorporating the idea of "productive cooperation" into their aid programs. The aim would be to negotiate long-term agreements, which would ensure that underdeveloped countries use their credits to create export industries. The Communist countries clearly recognize that giving credits to underdeveloped countries outside their own group involves a sacrifice, as so much is needed at home. But they have made explicit their belief that such credits should be given in increasing amounts.[2] The nature and size of the future credit flow from Communist countries are as difficult to foresee as the nature and size of the future capital inflow from the West. A fair guess would be that credits will be

[1] U. N., *World Economic Survey 1965,* Part I, Chapter 3, roneod, E/4187/Add. 3, June 3, 1966, Table 3–2, p. 13.

[2] *Ibid.,* Chapter 4, pp. 22ff.

given to some countries, particularly to India, on the same terms as heretofore, while the new system of "productive cooperation" is considered further and, perhaps, tested out in individual cases.

17 *Import Substitution*

In the preceding sections we came to the following conclusions:

(a) exports of traditional commodities will not expand rapidly;
(b) branching out into manufactured exports is so beset with problems that easy or significant advance within the next five to ten years is unlikely;
(c) alteration of the direction of exports is not only difficult in itself but has no great potential, at least in the immediate future;
(d) foreseeable capital inflows will not be adequate in either quantity or quality to fill the gap between import needs and export earnings.

If these general conclusions are valid for South Asia as a whole – and, with considerable differences in emphasis, valid for the several countries – only two policies are left that can close the exchange gap: import substitution and curtailment of non-essential imports. Everywhere in the region import substitution is hailed as the main avenue to industrialization, which is generally considered to be the essential condition for development.[1] Although it is very difficult to reach out in the export market, there is a home market that can provide the demand basis for the growth of industry. Cutting off imports from abroad not only saves foreign exchange but builds a protective wall behind which industrialization can take place. A program to develop substitutes for imports by building up new manufacturing industries involves, however, the purchase of plants and machinery and often equipment to provide power, transportation, and other public utilities, and most of these items have a high import content. Therefore, the immediate impact of an import substitution policy is often to increase the demand for imports and put greater pressure on the balance of payments, even though later savings of foreign exchange can be expected. If the balance of payments situation is already serious and foreign exchange reserves are depleted, this represents a limitation on the import substitution policy.

Before we proceed further in our analysis, it should be stressed that in South Asia import substitution is less a free policy choice than a necessity. If industrialization is the goal, it has to be directed to the home market since export expansion in the field of manufacturing industry meets with such great difficulties (Section 14). Moreover, in most of South Asia im-

[1] Chapter 24, Section 1.

port restrictions have been necessitated by exchange difficulties. They come first and unasked for, even if they then can result in import substitution. Malaya, Thailand, and until recently Ceylon, have had a relatively favorable exchange situation and have traditionally preserved considerable freedom with respect to imports. If these countries decide to embark on import substitution in order to push industrialization, this will be to a considerable extent a free policy choice. Pakistan and India, at the other extreme, have for many years severely restricted or prohibited practically all imports, except imports of essential consumer goods, mainly food, and development goods; there import substitution is less a matter of choice than necessity. With the rapid population growth and the generally gloomy trade balance prospects facing all the South Asian countries, with the possible exception of Malaya, it is probable that the need to apply import restrictions as severe as those of Pakistan and India will become general, particularly if more countries push their industrialization drives. A trend toward less stringent import restrictions in South Asia is not foreseen.

The fact that in countries like Pakistan and India import restrictions came first, necessitated by the exchange situation, has important consequences for the resulting import substitution. The protection of home industry has had another purpose than to direct development. It therefore is "unplanned" and, indeed, strongest in the case of the least essential goods, the import of which is most severely cut down. All along the line it tends to be "unnecessarily high" and to create "too high" profits, that is, profits higher than are needed to stimulate enterprise.[1] Quite aside from the effects on distribution, this tends to foster high-cost production. Industrialists who are provided with a cozy, overprotected domestic market will shun, to a greater extent than would otherwise be the case, the vicissitudes of the far more demanding international market. If the South Asian governments want to effect savings in foreign exchange, they must direct import substitution as much as possible toward the production of essential goods that are still imported. The possibility of making further import substitution has been a main reason why India, with its more sufficient raw material base, has concentrated its development efforts on heavy industry.[2] As the governments are usually unable, or unwilling, to decrease the "too high" profitability of import substitution in the less essential fields — by internal excess taxes and other means — they are compelled to resort to a large variety of direct controls in order to divert resources into directions other than those which profit considerations would dictate; exports of manufactured goods have to be stimulated by subsidies in various forms.

[1] Chapter 19, Sections 6 and 7; Appendix 8, Part I.

[2] Chapter 24, Section 3.

These problems and the serious consequences they have for efficiency and honesty in administration and business are analyzed in Chapters 19 and 20 and Appendix 8, Part I.

The import substitution policy as propounded and discussed in South Asia has focussed mainly on manufacturing industry. This is in line with the belief that industrialization is the engine of development.[1] However, increasing food production in the food deficit countries is now coming to be regarded as the area where import substitution is most desirable and urgently needed. Malaya, Ceylon, and even Indonesia have traditionally relied on large imports of food, which they have paid for with foreign exchange derived from their plantation crops. In recent years the first two of these countries, and to a lesser extent Indonesia, have managed to increase their food production substantially (Section 13). Pakistan and India, which used to be nearly self-sufficient in food and at one time even had an export surplus, have failed to expand their food production enough to satisfy the needs of their rapidly growing populations. In both countries serious food crises have been averted only by increased deliveries without exchange requirements from American surpluses under P.L. 480. Belatedly, a rapid rise in agricultural production has acquired top priority in their planning.

We shall discuss this subject in Chapter 26. In the present context only one major conclusion from our analysis of the agricultural situation needs to be emphasized, namely, that yields cannot be raised substantially merely by making investments in fertilizers, irrigation, seeds, agricultural extension work of various types, and so on. It is necessary to change the relation between the cultivator and the land so that investments and harder work are worthwhile and possible. Land reform measures have not been, and are not now, effectively implemented, because they lack political backing. Also, they are invariably time consuming. There is therefore a clear danger that this crucially important import substitution will not proceed fast enough to prevent the pending food crisis from worsening.

Finally, we should stress that the South Asian countries' efforts at import substitution, if they are not coordinated in such a way as to provide a more rational labor division within the region, are likely to damage the cause of regional integration, which has received a general endorsement from all of the South Asian governments (Section 15). As we pointed out, it is often easiest to develop substitutes for imports such as the food and textiles that come from neighboring countries. But even in regard to new industries national import substitution is likely to prevail without any re-

[1] Chapter 24, Section 1.

gional coordination. When all the countries want to have steel mills, the possibility of developing an export market in the region for the country that can produce the cheapest steel is eliminated.

There is no easy solution to any of the problems mentioned in this chapter. All avenues of policy are severely circumscribed, and each has significant and often adverse repercussions on other aspects of policy. Import substitution, in particular, is no shortcut to engendering development. This, of course, is one of the several dilemmas that weigh most heavily on those countries which are poorest and most in need of raising output per head, and which harbor the bulk of the region's population. There is a certain desperation in India's and Pakistan's attempts at development in the very difficult climate of the 1960's, and it is far from certain that they will succeed in their purpose. Clearly, these countries face a fundamentally more difficult task in trying to achieve what is glibly referred to as a "take-off into sustained growth" than any of the now developed countries of the West faced a century or more ago. This is the thesis of Chapter 14, to which we now turn.

Chapter 14

DIFFERENCES IN INITIAL CONDITIONS

In our analysis we often resort to comparisons, either explicit or implicit, between the underdeveloped South Asian countries and the highly developed Western countries. Such comparisons are valid and relevant inasmuch as the differences between the two groups of countries are, on the whole, much greater than the differences within the groups.

Two types of comparisons can be made, both of which are important: Present conditions in South Asia can be compared either with present conditions in the Western countries or with conditions in the Western countries on the eve of their rapid economic development, particularly their industrialization. In this concluding chapter of Part Three on economic realities in South Asia, we shall concentrate on the second type; that is to say, we shall attempt to spell out the main differences in "initial conditions" for economic development between the South Asian countries and the developed Western countries. This type of comparison has been considered relevant to the problem of formulating economic policy in South Asia. The countries of the region recognize that they are underdeveloped and should develop: their plans all are built on a desire for modernization, especially industrialization, and it is natural to believe that they could learn a great deal from the experience of the developed countries.

The general conclusion we shall reach is that the differences in initial conditions are extremely significant and that they regularly work to the disadvantage of the underdeveloped countries in South Asia. Furthermore, the differences are in many instances of such a nature as to prohibit a pattern of growth analogous to that experienced by the developed Western countries. It is important to take note of the newness of the development problems confronting the countries of South Asia today – and most other underdeveloped countries – because of the tendency to overlook their uniqueness that is inherent in the biases common in research and prevalent also in planning and, generally, in public discussion. These biases are discussed in the Prologue (Sections 3–6), and we shall come back to them often in later chapters.

1 *The Problem*

In the modern approach to the economic problems of the South Asian countries, the two types of comparisons are logically related to each other by the assumption, either stated or implied, that the present differences represent a time lag in development. This was not the assumption when, in pre-war and pre-independence times, "backward regions" was the term used to signify what are now referred to as "underdeveloped countries," or even as "developing countries."[1] The change in approach is related not only to the greater awareness of, and concern for, the economic problems of underdeveloped countries but also to the optimistic biases just referred to. The modern approach is widely rationalized in the theory of "stages of growth" with the implied assumption that there is a predetermined sequence of stages. Although by no means new, this theory was usually extended in earlier times only to the Western world and some countries on its fringe, and not to "backward" areas like South Asia – except by a few radical thinkers like Marx. We have noted throughout this study how often modern Western economists have taken over theories from Marx, usually without crediting him with them. Sometimes they are unaware of their intellectual debt, and sometimes they deny it exists and call themselves non-"Marxists."[2]

The concept of a time lag implies that in the history of the West there was a period – somewhat differently located on the time axis for the several countries – when conditions were essentially "comparable" to those that now exist in South Asia – again with individual variations among countries. The concept of a time lag also implies that it is possible to postulate a fairly uniform development for countries, which in turn implies that

[1] Appendix 1.

[2] "The country that is more developed industrially only shows, to the less developed, the image of its own future," wrote Marx in the Preface to *Das Kapital.* (Karl Marx, *Capital,* translated by Samuel Moore and Edward Aveling, edited by Frederick Engels, Allen & Unwin Ltd., Woking, 1957, p. xvii.)

the entire set of conditions relevant for development move together with a degree of internal harmony. Differences in development are believed to have a "dimensional," not a "qualitative," character. When applied to a single South Asian country or the region, the concept of a time lag implies, finally, that the present world environment, if not identical to what it was in the Western countries in the period of comparison, is at least not so much less favorable as to block or seriously hamper its development.

The logical weakness in this theory is at once apparent when we try to determine more precisely the appropriate period of comparison, that is, the period in history when the Western countries were underdeveloped in the same sense that the South Asian countries are underdeveloped today, and after which they, successively, began to develop. One thing is certain: at the beginning of what we recognize as the industrial revolution – or, more precisely, their industrial revolutions – the Western countries had behind them many years – in some cases centuries – of social, political, and also incipient economic development;[1] in a number of ways they were already much more favorably situated for further development than South Asia is today. In many respects, therefore, the period of comparison should be fixed centuries before the industrial revolutions in the West. In other respects conditions in South Asia are comparable to those in Western countries at any time in recent history. And in still some other respects conditions in the South Asian countries are more comparable to those existing now in the West, or at least at periods much later in the Western development process.[2] Efforts to define the time of "take-off" in the Western countries assume a basic similarity among them in initial conditions and in the process of development – an assumption that is open to question. Be that as it may, to use this Western concept of a "take-off" and

[1] The point is succinctly made by Simon Kuznets: "If the 'earlier situations' in the presently developed countries that could be viewed as examples of underdevelopment existed three centuries ago or possibly even earlier, it follows that these older units of the European community must have had a long period of development and rise before the coming of the economic and technological revolutions. It also follows that when the recent rapid pulse of economic growth began, the countries now in the forefront probably were also among the advanced units of that time." (Simon Kuznets, "Underdeveloped Countries and the Pre-Industrial Phase in the Advanced Countries: An Attempt at Comparison," U. N., *Proceedings of the World Population Conference,* 1954, Papers: Vol. V, Meeting 26, New York, 1955, pp. 952–954.)

[2] These modern characteristics have been pressing themselves upon the region. They reflect the impact of the whole modernization movement, on everything from ideologies and political institutions to industries. How disparate conditions are is suggested by Kuznets when he writes that birth rates in the underdeveloped countries, compared with Europe's in pre-industrial times, "may be said to reflect the lower economic level of many of the currently underdeveloped countries as over against that of older European units in their pre-industrial phase. On the other hand, their lower death rates may be said to reflect the more recent date for which we observe them in the underdeveloped countries of today – mortality thus mirroring the advantages of the technological advance made since the pre-industrial phase of the now developed countries." (Kuznets, "Underdeveloped Countries and the Pre-Industrial Phase," p. 965.)

attempt to locate on an assumed general development axis the "stage" at which any South Asia country now is, is to do violence to the facts.[1]

When in the ensuing discussion we leave the period of comparison in the history of the Western countries vague, we do so intentionally. Realism and logic preclude the determinateness aimed at in the theory of stages of growth. In some instances – as in regard to climate or population increase – this indeterminateness presents no problem, as the differences in conditions are very largely independent of time. In other cases we shall have to establish the period of comparison in a specific context. Particularly because of the change in world environment and the "qualitative" as well as "dimensional" character of the differences, we shall, however, be skeptical about our inferences. And we shall not put them in the quantitative form of a model, since to do so would give them what in this study we often refer to as unwarranted precision. One major set of differences between the South Asian countries today and the developed Western countries in the past will not be touched on in this chapter, except incidentally; namely, differences in policies and in the ideological outlook that influences policies. Part Four will be devoted to an intensive analysis of this important complex of problems. The present chapter will be restricted to those conditions that policy is designed to change or that it must at least take into consideration.[2] Since most of these "initial conditions" are examined in detail in earlier or later chapters, we shall aim here at a synoptic treatment. In a sense, then, this chapter is one presenting conclusions from our study, placed in the middle of the book instead of at the end and dealing with a set of conditions that excludes for the most part ideologies and policies.

2 *Some Constants or Quasi-Constants: Natural Resources and Climate*

There are some differences between South Asia and the Western world that are constant or quasi-constant in time. To this group belongs, first of all, the natural resource endowment.

In Chapter 11 we pointed out that, so far as we now know, South Asia as a region is poorly endowed with resources. Only India is known to have both coal and iron ore in sufficient quantity to provide a basis for heavy

[1] It is a procedure associated with the common biases analyzed in the Prologue (Sections 3–6) and, in particular, with the tendency to analyze South Asian problems in Western terms and to underestimate differences; logically, it is based on metaphysical preconceptions of the teleological variety. On the theory of "stages" see Appendix 2, Section 3.

[2] Conditions under 1–5 in Appendix 2, Section 5.

industry. Scattered deposits of many metals and minerals have been found throughout the area but they do not seem to be large; thus far they have not been very intensively exploited. There does not seem to be much oil anywhere in the region except in Indonesia. Land resources, by and large, are poor, either because they were so to begin with or because they have been damaged by overcrowding and the climate (see below). Ceylon, however, possesses excellent though limited land for the cultivation of tea, cocoanuts, and rubber, and Malaya and Indonesia also have excellent land, less limited in extent, for the growing of rubber trees. Large forested areas, not yet fully utilized, remain in Malaya, Thailand, Burma, Ceylon, and the Philippines.[1]

The fact that some countries without abundant natural resources have succeeded in creating a flourishing industry, mainly by importing raw materials — notably Switzerland, Denmark, and Japan — does not necessarily mean that South Asia could readily do the same. The difficulties in relying on imported raw materials are greatest at the beginning of industrialization, and are probably more severe for late-comers. Once a country is further along in the development process, the costs of such imports can be borne more easily, for then capital investment and consequently relative capital cost, and particularly wage rates, have reached levels sufficiently high that raw material costs constitute a much smaller portion of total production costs.

Of course, large areas of South Asia have not been thoroughly surveyed. It is for this reason that we characterize the endowment of natural resources as a quasi-constant factor. Through systematic efforts, hidden resources may come to light, but it seems improbable that most of the countries will ever equal the average Western country in raw materials.

Climate, insofar as it affects the productiveness of resources, might be treated as an aspect of the natural resource endowment. But as it also affects the productivity of labor, it is more accurately treated as a separate set of conditions. Although we have little knowledge of its precise implications for development, climate constitutes another major difference between South Asia and the Western world that is a constant or quasi-constant in time. The South Asian countries are situated in the tropical or arid subtropical zones — as, indeed, are almost all the underdeveloped countries of the world. It is a fact that all successful industrialization in modern times, including that of Japan and the Soviet Union, has taken place in the temperate zones; in China, too, industrialization has been attempted mostly in the northern provinces. This cannot be entirely an accident of history but must have to do with some special handicaps, directly or indirectly

[1] Chapter 11, Section 7.

related to climate, faced by countries in the tropical and subtropical zones.[1] It should also be noted that almost all Western countries initiated economic development and industrialization from a base of self-sufficiency in food, and sometimes a surplus; generally speaking, an agricultural revolution preceded their industrial revolution. Although the agricultural sector in South Asian countries is very large in terms of the labor attached to it, yields are mostly so low that the region as a whole has become a deficit area in foodstuffs, and is in large part becoming more so. Again this contrast suggests the importance of climate to development, for extremes of temperature and rainfall have obvious effects on the productivity of both labor and land in agriculture.

It needs to be explained, therefore, why the climatic factor is almost entirely neglected in the literature on development problems in South Asia and in the underdeveloped countries generally,[2] why there is so little specialized research on the economic effects of climate and the possibilities for their amelioration, and why the development plans of these countries are almost entirely silent on this subject.

This present-day lack of interest in climatic conditions is in sharp contrast to the thinking about underdevelopment in pre-independence times. Among the stereotyped opinions then elaborated to explain the poverty of the underdeveloped countries – more specifically, the lack of drive, enterprise, and efficiency of their peoples – were theories that all this was attributable to the unbearable climate and its effects on soils, crops, animals, and people, and on the pattern of civilization in general. These popular theories were regularly reflected in the pre-war scientific literature and

[1] In refutation of the argument that climate is important in development it is often pointed out that great civilizations sprang up in tropical areas in ancient times and lasted for centuries. How this was possible and how it can be reconciled with the generalization in the text lies outside our analysis in this book, which is restricted to modern times. Probably, however, these ancient civilizations differed in fundamental ways from modern ones; also, they often grew up in smaller regions favored by exceptional climatic conditions; soil erosion and deforestation had not proceeded so far, and so on.

[2] Of the several general texts available, G. M. Meier and R. E. Baldwin, *Economic Development: Theory, History, Policy* (Wiley, New York, 1957) has no reference at all to climate, nor has W. W. Rostow, *The Stages of Economic Growth* (Cambridge University Press, London, 1960) or A. O. Hirschman, *The Strategy of Economic Development* (Yale University Press, New Haven, 1958). W. A. Lewis devotes about six pages at various places in *Theory of Economic Growth* (Allen and Unwin, London, 1955) to very general points about climate – in a book of 450 pages. Benjamin Higgins in *Economic Development* (Norton, New York, 1959), a work of over 770 pages, provides a very interesting condensed discussion of the climatic factor, but one entirely directed toward criticism of geographic determinism (pp. 265–274) and giving no attention to climate as a complex of conditions for production. W. E. Moore's *Industrialization and Labor* (Cornell University Press, Ithaca, 1951) provides a standard discussion of socio-economic problems of labor efficiency in "developing" countries but is totally without mention of climate. The best selections of readings – Amar Agarwala and Sampat Singh, eds., *Economics of Underdeveloped Areas* (Oxford University Press, London, Bombay, 1959) and L. W. Shannon, ed., *Underdeveloped Areas* (Harper, New York, 1957) – contain only the most perfunctory mention of climate.

were often supported by statistics.[1] There is a tendency in this pre-war literature, represented by Ellsworth Huntington's *Civilization and Climate*,[2] toward pessimistic geographical determinism. As popularized, it was a doctrine consonant with the vague beliefs in the racial inferiority of the colonial peoples.[3] In any case this pessimism supported the common view, badly needed as a rationalization of Western colonial policy, that little could be done to improve the productivity of the colonies and the life of the colonial peoples. That this interest in the climatic conditions, and especially the glib popular theories concerning their effects, served opportunistic ends should not, of course, be taken to mean that these conditions are unimportant or even that all the observations made in the pre-independence era were incorrect. Yet the reaction to this type of thinking has been so complete that, as we have pointed out, climate is no longer discussed as an important factor in economic development.[4]

We observed early in the book that the post-war approach to economic development problems in South Asia has been in the nature of a protest movement on the part of the intellectuals to which Westerners, both in public discussion and in scientific literature, have deferred for reasons of both sympathy and diplomacy.[5] The treatment of climatic conditions is typical of this new, opposite bias. Indeed, it is an extreme example of the effects of this all-pervasive bias. For, although research, planning, and public discussion that are based on Western concepts, theories, and models tend systematically to bypass the complications arising from attitudes, institutions, and modes and levels of living, the relevance of these to prob-

[1] Chapter 21, Sections 6 and 7.

[2] 3rd ed., Yale University Press, New Haven, 1924.

[3] This view is occasionally expressed even in works written after the Second World War.

"But there is something lacking, some mental or spiritual attribute which has in the past weakened in the races of India the powers of cohesion, of citizenship, of corporate resistance to outside influences. There is in the Urdu language a word 'ghabhrana,' which has no exact English equivalent, but which may be approximately translated as 'to fall into a state of mental confusion.' It is significant that the principal language of northern India should include this word. It is an indication that this state of mind is sufficiently common, this lack of mental stamina so universal a feature of everyday life as to require a special word to describe it.

"What then is the reason for this peculiar mentality? To anyone who has lived and worked for many years in India and with Indians, there is a very simple answer to this question, too simple perhaps to be wholly satisfying. It is the environment and particularly the climate in which the people of India live and have lived for countless generations." (Sir William Kerr Tytler, *Afghanistan, A Study of Political Developments in Central and Southern Asia,* 2nd ed., Oxford University Press, London, 1953, p. 289.)

[4] There are, however, signs of renewed interest on the part of geographers, at least, in problems of underdevelopment as related to environment, an interest that is free of any naive environmental determinism. See, for example, Norton Ginsburg, ed., *Essays on Geography and Economic Development*, Department of Geography, University of Chicago, Research Paper No. 62, Chicago, 1960.

[5] Prologue, Sections 4 and 6. For an elaboration of this point, see Chapter 21, Section 7.

lems of development is at least "accounted for" by interspersed reservations and qualifications and by the habitual admission that development is a "human" problem. Climatic conditions, on the other hand, are either ignored or casually dismissed as being of little or no importance.[1]

There can be only one scientific attitude: to shun easy and obviously incorrect generalizations about climatic conditions and their economic effects and to make these the subject of empirical study. Such research is especially important in view of the fact that climatic conditions are only quasi-constants. It is possible, in some small measure, to alter the climate; more important, the effects of climate on the productivity of land, capital, and labor can be changed in many ways, and both production and consumption can be better adapted to the climate. It is, indeed, altogether wasteful to attempt to plan economic development in the South Asian countries without taking climatic conditions into consideration. There is here a vast, unexplored field for economic and social engineering, requiring close cooperation between the natural and the social sciences. In Appendix 10 we have tried to outline its scope, without pretending to do more than scratch the surface. Almost any generalization about climatic conditions must for the time being be uncertain or merely suggestive. One difficulty should be emphasized: the effects of climate can rarely be isolated from the effects of other conditions. Some of these, like the levels of nutrition and health, and, to some degree, all other conditions as well, are causally related to climatic conditions. But, as we have said, all conditions tend to be causally interrelated.[2] The main reason for the difficulty in arriving at well-founded generalizations about the effects of climate is simply that little empirical research has been devoted to study in this field.

Nevertheless, it is possible to say that the extremes of heat and humidity in South Asia seem to contribute to deterioration of the soil and of many kinds of material goods; to be partly responsible for the low productivity of certain crops, forests, and animals; and not only to cause discomfort but also to impair health and efficiency. Almost all of these unfavorable effects can be in large part avoided or counteracted by planned policies. It is true, of course, that to overcome the difficulties – and occasionally turn them into advantages – would require expenditures, and sometimes very high expenditures, often of the investment type. And since capital and all other

[1] From the many examples available we need cite only two:

"Climate . . . is a convenient bogeyman to be blamed for psychological difficulties whose real origin is much more personal." (D. H. K. Lee, *Climate and Economic Development in the Tropics,* Harper, New York, 1957, p. 104.)

"Because economic growth is currently most rapid in the temperate zones, it is fashionable to assert that economic growth requires a temperate climate, but the association between growth and temperate climates is a very recent phenomenon in human history." . . . "The climate hypothesis also does not take us very far." (Lewis, *Theory of Economic Growth,* pp. 53, 416.)

[2] Appendix 2, Section 5.

real cost elements such as administration are scarce, climatic conditions impose serious obstacles to development and constitute an important difference in initial conditions between South Asia and the Western world.

3 *Population*

The basic facts in regard to population will be analyzed in detail in Part Six of this book; some of the pertinent historical data have been dealt with in Chapter 10 (Section 5). In the present discussion, which is simply intended to catalogue the main differences in initial conditions, only a few of the generalizations that are substantiated in these other chapters need be set forth.

In pre-industrial times the secular trend of population growth in Western Europe had been comparatively slow, though it rose somewhat as the industrialization phase was approached. By contrast, the population of all the South Asian countries has been increasing over a very long period, though not as rapidly as today. As a result, those of the South Asian countries that contain most of the region's population now start out with a considerably higher man/land ratio than did the European countries, at the same time that their supply of industrial natural resources, as we have noted, is inferior to Europe's. This disproportion of population and resources in itself puts South Asia at a considerable disadvantage in regard to development prospects. To this must be added the effects of the population explosion, which in recent years has raised the average rate of population increase in the region to well above 2 percent a year and in some of the countries to 3 percent or even higher. Moreover, the rate of population increase is still rising.

A spontaneous spread of birth control practices is not in prospect; indeed, in the Western countries it took place on a large scale only when they had reached a much higher level of development, characterized by higher living levels and more rational attitudes. And even in those South Asian countries where dissemination of birth control information among the masses is accepted government policy, the policy measures taken have nowhere had substantial effects. Because of the youthfulness of the South Asian populations, the inhibitions and obstacles encountered, and the administrative difficulties, a continued rapid, even a more rapid, increase in the population, and especially in the labor force, can be expected for a considerable time to come.

The present population density and the prospective population trend thus constitute a very important difference in initial situation. The South Asian countries, none of which has as yet experienced a rapid economic development and some of which are stagnating or retrogressing, have and will continue to have an annual rate of natural increase in population and in the labor force double, or more than double, that in the countries of Western Europe when they were already well on their way to rapid development.[1] Europe, moreover, had an escape hatch for its increasing population in emigration to the New World: Western Europe would now have almost 100 million more inhabitants if there had been no emigration and if other vital factors had remained the same. No such possibilities of escape exist for South Asia. Even such migrations within the region as could lead to a more favorable allocation of labor force to land and other resources are virtually excluded as between countries and are possible within countries only to a rather limited extent and usually at very high cost.[2]

By any criterion these population trends present a serious impediment to development prospects in South Asia[3] and constitute one of the principal differences in initial situation.

4 *International Trade and Capital Movements*

It is commonly recognized that expansion of export outlets played a crucial role in the early period of development in all the now highly developed Western countries. In Dennis Robertson's phrase, international trade was the "engine of growth."[4] As far back as 1890, Alfred Marshall had concluded that "the causes which determine the economic progress of nations belong to the study of international trade."[5]

Rising exports – and imports – characterized not only the early spurts of rapid development but its successful continuation in all the now developed Western countries. In the nineteenth century, as one country after another had its industrial revolution – which for those in the New World and some others included the production of primary products for the export market – international trade increased faster than the sum total of gross national products in the several countries. There was mutual stimulation in this process for which foreign trade was the main vehicle. "Growth through trade" aptly describes much of the economic progress of the nineteenth century.

[1] In the United States, the rate of natural population increase was much higher. Similarly the other "younger" developed economies of the New World – Canada, New Zealand, and Australia – had growth rates higher than those of Western Europe. However, the experiences of these countries, where population increased also through immigration from already developed countries, are for this and many other reasons hardly relevant to South Asia.

[2] Chapter 27, Section 16; Appendix 11; and Chapter 26, Section 6.

[3] Chapter 28, Part I.

[4] Dennis Robertson, "The Future of International Trade," *Essays in Monetary Theory*, King & Staples Ltd., London, 1940, p. 214.

[5] Alfred Marshall, *Principles of Economics*, 8th ed., Macmillan, London, 1920, p. 270.

South Asia was not unaffected by this movement. As we observed in Chapter 10, there was a period when all South Asian countries, in some degree, experienced a pattern of development that corresponded rather closely to the early development spurts in the West. The introduction of plantation agriculture, mining, and, in a few colonies, forestry, and the rise of commercial rice production in Burma and Thailand, could not have taken place without the opening up of export markets. The fact that at first this external demand stimulated the production and export of only a few products was not extraordinary at that period, nor would this alone have precluded a later, more balanced and diffused economic growth. But, for reasons mentioned in Section 8 of Chapter 10, this development was largely abortive in South Asia. The initial spurts in production for export did not trigger a cumulative process of development in other sectors. Even when, as in plantation agriculture and mining, the colonial enterprises were of an "industrial" kind and were complemented by the creation of ports, railroads, and financial and commercial institutions, they did not produce much in the way of spread effects but remained enclaves amid backwardness and stagnation. Enterprise and investment were merely bubbles on the surface; they filtered down hardly at all to stimulate indigenous entrepreneurial activity.

In any event, the epoch of rapidly growing export markets has ended — except perhaps for Malaya where rubber may still be subject to an increase in demand if it can compete with artificial rubber in the world market,[1] and possibly also Indonesia if internal order and efficient government could be achieved. Generally speaking, the South Asian countries have in recent decades seen the demand for their exports shrink relative to the development of world trade. Their terms of trade have not deteriorated sharply, but this is because the increase in their production of export products has been slow, and is thus not a source of much satisfaction. The outlook for their export earnings is not bright.

The forces responsible for the unfortunate trading position of the South Asian countries have been analyzed in Chapter 13; in the present chapter we have already touched on one of these forces. The accelerating rate of population increase, in conjunction with the slow rise of agricultural production, has decreased the ability of these countries to export foodstuffs, or increased their need to import them, with the result that the region as a whole is now a food deficit area. More important, however, have been the changes in the demand for their exports. Rapid and all-around technological development has decreased the demand for these in the Western countries by raising agricultural productivity at home, by providing industrial substitutes for some important imports, by permitting substantial cut-backs in the amount of raw materials used, and by inducing a

[1] This is a precarious assumption, as scientific and technological advances will almost certainly lower the costs of production of artificial rubber. See Chapter 13, Section 13.

switch in demand from goods requiring large amounts of imported raw materials to those whose raw material content constitutes a small part of their value. Furthermore, with the exception of rubber, most goods traditionally exported by South Asia have a low income elasticity of demand and almost none are products the demand for which is rapidly rising as a result of economic development in the developed countries; discriminatory tariffs – which rise in line with the stage of processing – hamper the development of export industries. The export of manufactured products from South Asia is not very significant and is concentrated on a few cheap, low-quality goods for which the world market is not expanding; many of these exports meet rising protective walls. The increase in the volume of international trade since the end of the Second World War has been mainly in other industrial products, and in trade between the developed countries. We have seen also that there are serious hindrances to efforts by the underdeveloped countries in South Asia to basically improve their export situation through diversification of their products and markets. Rigidity and lack of adaptability are two characteristics of economic underdevelopment. Above all, the possibility of building up a manufacturing industry that could successfully compete on the world market is severely limited by the markedly superior conditions under which the entrenched industries in the developed countries operate – the advanced skills and other external economies, the heavy investments in research, and the ever more rapidly accelerating technology.

The whole climate for development through trade has also changed fundamentally since the nineteenth century, which, seen in historical perspective, we now know to have been an era of unequalled freedom of international trade. The Western countries that led in the development process, all small in population, stood out like islands in an ocean of backward peoples. Having the field of international trade virtually to themselves, they could and did exploit the resources and peoples in the huge backward areas of the world and kept them politically and economically dependent. Now that these large areas are trying to emerge from political and economic dependency, they cannot simply repeat the development process of the developed countries. While being a late-comer in the nineteenth century was not a disadvantage but often quite the opposite, it is in the twentieth century a serious disadvantage. As the South Asian countries do not enjoy the stimulation from rising demand for their exports at a time when their import needs are increasing, they are forced to direct their development efforts toward something hitherto untried–import substitution. Protectionism played its role in many of the now developed Western countries, but all of them, unlike the South Asian countries today, had access to growing export markets. There is no historical example in the Western world of economic development based on a policy of self-sufficiency and import substitution.

The development of the Soviet Union since the end of the 1920's is somewhat similar to the South Asian situation, at least insofar as the Soviet Union did not utilize international trade as the engine of growth. Had it attempted to do so, it would probably have run into political and economic difficulties, especially after the onset of the Great Depression in the Western countries. Instead, it instituted state control of all foreign economic relations and central planning of a much more exacting type than any South Asian country has contemplated. Moreover, the Soviet Union started from a higher level of industrial and pre-industrial development, was better endowed with natural resources, was initially a food surplus country, and had not the climatic handicaps of the South Asian countries.

One dilemma inherent in the attempt to industrialize by means of import substitution, to which the South Asian countries are forced, is that the initiation of new industries requires large imports of capital goods, and often continuing imports of spare parts, raw materials, and semi-manufactured goods; the building up of ancillary industries to make the countries independent of these other and continuing import needs will again create a need to import capital goods. Even if the final result should be a saving of foreign exchange, the initial effect is invariably to increase import needs, usually for a not inconsiderable period. This augments the tendency toward a negative balance of payments already inherent in the lagging export demands and the increased food needs consequent upon the population explosion. This gap between import needs and export possibilities has been widening and is bound to widen further. While the obvious remedy is capital inflow to cover the deficits and enable the South Asian countries to import essentials for consumption and the capital goods necessary in furthering import substitution, the deterioration in their trading position is itself likely to decrease the availability of foreign capital.

Although it is true that Britain and Japan, for example, managed to develop with few or no capital imports, foreign capital played a major role in the development of most other countries. The relationship to the trading position was very close. The early spurt in exports and the outlook for rising exports created, at home and abroad, a confidence in future growth that enabled these countries to borrow from abroad, often to the extent that a major result of the initial increase in their exports was the possibility of a still greater increase in their imports. Although the initial change was an increase in exports, their balance of trade could then become negative. It was through this mechanism, whereby the expansion of export outlets made possible large-scale borrowing abroad, that the development spurts could gather momentum and permit the increase in foreign trade to exceed the growth in national product for a long time. The capital movements flowed mainly between the Western countries—those that developed early and the late-comers—but some also flowed to the underdeveloped South

Asian countries during that early period when their export production was rising rapidly. Ragnar Nurkse has commented on these capital movements and the change in recent times:

> The 19th century pattern of development in outlying areas was geared to export markets for primary staples. This mechanism of growth transmission is now at a comparatively low gear. Nor is this all. Conditions in the trade field have some influence on international investment. The vigorous expansion of demand for primary commodities induced a massive flow of private capital to peripheral areas in the past. Conversely, the lag observed at the present time in the export trade of most of the less developed countries provides a simple explanation for the lack of incentive for private foreign investment.[1]

Even had the international capital market remained intact, the deterioration in their trading position and, in particular, the contraction in the demand for their export products would have made it almost impossible at the present time for the South Asian countries to rely on foreign capital in their development efforts. This situation therefore constitutes a difference in initial conditions to the great disadvantage of these countries.

In fact, however, the old competitive international private capital market, particularly for long-term capital at fixed interest rates, has almost disappeared. After a brief revival in the years following the First World War, the crisis in international payments, culminating in 1929, resulted in the almost total extinction of that market, which had earlier furnished developing countries with long-term credit at very low interest rates—sometimes less than half the rate of interest that the World Bank, working with guarantees from the governments of the rich countries, today charges for its loans (which in view of the need for guarantees cannot be considered loans on commercial terms). As long as the South Asian countries were colonies and their money and banking systems were integrated with those of the metropolitan countries, even they had benefitted from this easy access to cheap foreign capital. Behind the virtual collapse of the international private capital market lie many fundamental changes in international relations. It is certain that in the Western countries the tendencies toward autarkic policies have been much stronger in the financial than in the trade field. Through the exigencies of wars and business crises, states have become much less inhibited by the taboos of liberalism than before the First World War, and they are especially likely to interfere in foreign exchange and payments relations. The unstable international political situation has discouraged private loans to foreign countries. And the political and economic uncertainties in newly independent countries such as those of South Asia have weakened confidence that obligations to foreign capitalists will always be honored.

While long-term private lending to South Asian countries has almost

[1] Ragnar Nurkse, *Patterns of Trade and Development*, Almqvist & Wiksell, Stockholm, 1959, p. 27.

disappeared, there is some direct investment in the region, but on a very small scale since opportunities for enclave enterprises in oil and other dynamic extractive industries are rather limited. In addition to the discouraging effects of bleak export prospects, foreign businessmen are wary of nationalization and other policies that could lower the profitability of investments.

A new element in the situation, however, has been the flow of capital in the form of grants and loans from foreign governments and intergovernmental agencies. Such aid has been virtually a necessity because of the deteriorating trading position, the widening gap between exports and imports, the demise of the international private capital market, and the actual or assumed uncongenial climate for direct investment in South Asia. While most of the Marshall Plan aid to Europe was given in the form of grants, the tendency at present is to favor loans. Insofar as payments of interest and amortization are expected, increasing burdens are placed on the payment balances of the South Asian countries in future years. Particularly in view of their unfavorable export prospects, the limits to what many of them can borrow in this way are being reached.

These problems are dealt with in detail in Chapter 13. Here we need only recognize that the closely interrelated developments in trade and in capital movements must be regarded as a difference in initial conditions that is very much to the disadvantage of the South Asian countries.

Approaching the subject imaginatively, and assuming the same type of human solidarity with respect to the underdeveloped countries in South Asia as has developed within the individual rich democratic welfare states of the West – as well as in the Communist countries – it is not difficult to frame policies that could counteract the disadvantageous commercial and financial conditions under which South Asia now labors. In the field of trade, the developed Western countries could not only initiate effective international action to stabilize their imports of primary products; they could give the South Asian countries preferential treatment in a number of ways. South Asian products, both primary and manufactured, could be granted freer entry to Western markets. The Western countries could take measures to reduce domestic production in fields where the South Asian countries have the best chance of becoming competitive; they could even subsidize imports from these countries. In the field of finance, they could make much more capital available to the South Asian countries as grants or loans with low or no interest rates and extended repayment provisions.

Substantial changes of this type in the trade and financial policies of the developed countries are not to be expected within the foreseeable future. But the *ability* to offset some of the most serious disadvantages of the South Asian countries in trade and in capital movements clearly exists. It can be done if the developed countries are willing to make the attempt against strong internal opposition.

5 *Economic Levels, Social Structure, and Attitudes*

Heroic efforts have been made to compare levels of income per head in South Asian countries today with those in the Western countries in pre-industrial times.[1] But comparison of these aggregates between different regions in different historical eras raises formidable problems. Quite apart from the difficulty of defining a time period in the Western countries appropriate for this type of comparison and the unsatisfactory primary data, it is difficult to see how any index could have much meaning. As, presumably, the differences between the two regions not only are large but point in different directions for different items of "income," and as the climatic, economic, social, and cultural settings are so dissimilar whatever period of comparison is chosen, it is more revealing to compare modes and levels of living and working in specific respects. Even such specific, and therefore more realistic, comparisons can yield only vague and tentative conclusions about the relative levels of welfare. Logically viewed, an overall index figure must be regarded as unwarranted precision.[2]

Our very broad impression, supported by the above-mentioned studies and by everything else we know, is that on the Indian subcontinent the masses live in worse poverty than did those in the Western European countries at any time during several centuries before the industrial revolution. In Malaya, on the other hand, the economic level even of the bulk of the population may be as high as and possibly higher than it was in Western European countries even in late pre-industrial times. The other South Asian countries would fall somewhere between these two extremes.

But what significance do income levels have for development prospects? When references are made in the literature to income differences in time and space, it is usually assumed that the level of income has a direct bearing on a country's ability to support the savings needed for those investments considered to be crucial for development. However, this savings-centered approach to the problem of economic development is highly questionable for several reasons, which we touch on in many contexts in this book. First, savings and investment do not play the exclusive role for development assumed in most economic writings on the problems of South Asia; this is one point where the approach is clearly influenced by modern, Western preconceptions. Attitudes and institutions are more important in the region — even, incidentally, in determining savings ratios — than are levels of income *per se*. Second, what is saved out of income,

[1] Phyllis Deane, "The Industrial Revolution and Economic Growth," *Economic Development and Cultural Change,* Vol. V, No. 2, January, 1957. Simon Kuznets has presented a series of essays entitled "Quantitative Aspects of the Economic Growth of Nations" in *ibid.,* Vols. V through XI. See also his "Essays in the Quantitative Study of Economic Growth" in Vol. IX, April, 1961.

[2] Chapter 11, Section 1.

whether it is high or low, depends very much on the direction and effectiveness of government policy. And finally, low income levels probably hamper development more by keeping down consumption than savings, because inferior living conditions, particularly poor nutrition, reduce labor input and efficiency.[1] Strangely, this point is overlooked in most comments concerning the effect of low income levels in South Asia.

The emphasis on the low levels of income of the South Asian masses, the strained comparison with Western levels of income at an earlier period, and the Western approach to income, savings, and investment in South Asia, all represent attempts to apply an over-simplified and narrow formula to what in reality is an intricate complex of social, economic, and even political conditions that impede development. But even if we reject the savings-centered approach, and remain skeptical of the inter-regional comparison involved, it is true that the great poverty in South Asia, particularly in those countries containing the bulk of its population, is itself a major barrier to development. Moreover, the present and foreseeable increase in population noted in Section 3 must there lead to a decline in the already low levels of living unless resolute development policies are pursued. This worsening trend implies a difference in initial conditions, detrimental to all the South Asian countries, that is fairly independent of the period in Western history chosen for comparison.

We have still less information that would enable us to judge whether economic inequality today is greater in South Asia than in the Western countries in pre-industrial times. It is probable, however, that on the Indian subcontinent social inequality is more pervasive and more detrimental to free competition, in the wider sense of the term, than anywhere in the Western world in recent centuries. As both economic and social inequality in our conception[2] hinders economic progress, this would put India and Pakistan, at least, at a disadvantage in initial conditions compared with Western Europe, again fairly independent of the comparison period. This judgment would be less true of the other South Asian countries.

We are thus led to the major question of whether in South Asia today the complex of political, social, and economic institutions and the attitudes underlying and deriving from these institutions represent greater inhibitions and obstacles to development than did those in the Western world in earlier times. In accordance with our approach to the development problem,[3] these conditions in South Asia enter into our discussion in almost every chapter. We have not, of course, been able to investigate the Western countries in the same way, least of all for periods preceding their industrialization. A more definitive study of the difference in initial conditions

[1] Appendix 2, Section 21.
[2] Chapter 16, Section 3.
[3] Prologue, Section 8.

in these respects would have to take account of many more things than can be suggested in the few cursory remarks to which we must here confine ourselves. On the whole, our research and observations incline us to the belief that attitudes and institutions in the South Asian countries are less favorable than were those in the now developed Western countries at the start of their industrial revolutions or in the centuries before. Like this statement, the illustrations below are in terms of the general pattern.

In regard to political institutions, one obvious difference is that the Western countries were independent and mostly had become consolidated nation-states, able to pursue national policies, well before their industrial revolutions. For centuries the feudal structure of society had been gradually breaking down, and even in medieval Europe, the free cities were strongholds of non-feudal attitudes and practices in industry and commerce. The Western countries formed a small world of similar culture within which people and ideas circulated rather freely. In this world, before the industrial revolution, rationalism was fostered and traditionalism weakened as the Renaissance, the Reformation, and the Enlightenment, successively, revolutionized concepts and valuations. Modern scientific thought developed in the Western countries, and modern technology was early introduced in their agriculture and industries. The great discoveries and the colonization of the non-European world had helped pave the way; they changed attitudes and institutions in the European countries more than in the territories colonized, except where the latter were sparsely populated, as in the New World.

By contrast, the South Asian countries have only recently become independent and have yet to become consolidated nation-states capable of pursuing national policies effectively. All of them have a Westernized educated class and an intellectual elite that understands and has assimilated the scientific spirit of the Western world. These educated Asians, however, are more a "part of the intellectual life of the cosmopolitan world than they are of their indigenous cultures."[1] They are the vehicle for impulses to change, but these impulses, since they are not indigenous as in the West but emanate from a totally different culture, encounter substantial resistance. Furthermore, change has to be rapid in South Asia instead of building up slowly as in the Western countries.[2] The necessity for speed is accentuated by the population explosion, which itself strengthens the resistance to change as, in a stagnant society, it tends to depress living levels and increase social and economic inequality. And so these new nations — as we shall illustrate when we get to Part Four on ideologies — are from the start attempting to apply, or pretending to apply, policies, and adopt institutions, that have been maturing gradually in the Western countries:

[1] H. L. Keenleyside, "Obstacles and Means in International Development," *International Development Review,* Vol. II, No. 1, 1960, p. 21.

[2] Section 9, the last section in this chapter, will enlarge on this point.

planning, political democracy, economic and social equality – in short, the whole apparatus of the modern democratic welfare state. Alien as they are to the attitudes and institutions pervading poor, traditionalist, and stagnant societies, these reforms often remain on paper, and inherited patterns of life and work persist.

Similarly with economic modernization. Only India and the Philippines have the nucleus of a national entrepreneurial class; Pakistan's smaller group of entrepreneurs consists mainly of refugee-immigrants from India. In all the other countries industry and business had been almost entirely in the hands of European, Chinese, and Indian minority groups. Efforts to encourage enterprise among the indigenous majority have been less successful in promoting development than discriminatory measures against foreign enterprises, stimulated by independence, have been in retarding it.

Obviously, South Asia is attempting to close a yawning gap in attitudes and institutions. In this as in other respects, those Western countries that, in their day, were also late-comers to industrialization were in a more advantageous position. First of all, they were not as late as South Asia. Secondly, the speed of change was not as great then as now. Finally, if among the Western countries technology had been advancing unevenly, attitudes and institutions had been advancing on a broad front; by the time the late-comers began to catch up industrially, their educational level, for example, was higher than England's had been at a similar level of economic development. The South Asian countries, however, have been losing ground for a long time. Everything they have to try to catch up with is moving ahead faster all the time. This fateful dilemma will be the subject of Section 9.

6 *The Availability of Modern Technology*

The differences in initial conditions accounted for so far all make the problem of economic development more difficult for the nations of South Asia than it once was for the now developed economies of the West. There is, however, one important difference that would seem, at least in part, to counterbalance these difficulties: technology has advanced far beyond its level in the nineteenth century or before. The South Asian countries need not go through a slow, painful process of experimentation; today, as Mason puts it, "a highly productive technology . . . is available for the borrowing." Mason notes that "if this technological heritage were not available, economic growth in the underdeveloped world would undoubtedly be even slower than . . . it promises to be."[1]

Of course, more than simple borrowing is involved. The technology has

[1] Edward S. Mason, *Economic Planning in Underdeveloped Areas: Government and Business*, Fordham University Press, New York, 1958, pp. 14, 47.

to be adapted to South Asian conditions. Moreover, the introduction of any new production process inevitably necessitates a period of learning, and a longer and more intense one if its users have not been instrumental in its creation. Despite these obvious caveats, the availability of a more efficient technology is clearly an advantage. Learning and modifying an existing technique must be less costly than developing a new one. As Mason points out: ". . . the underdeveloped countries . . . could hardly be at an absolute disadvantage, as compared with the initiators of industrial development, since they always have the alternative of devising techniques themselves, as their predecessors in development have done."[1]

The advantage of having an accumulation of technological knowledge to draw on was evident in the unprecedented rapidity of industrialization and general economic development in those Western countries that were latest to enter the development phase. South Asian planners are conscious of this fact of history and prone to see it wistfully as a sign of the future.[2] But it does not follow from past experience that the availability of a greater amount of technological knowledge necessarily works to the advantage of the late-comer nowadays. All writers on this subject – including Mason – set down a number of qualifications that tend to reduce this advantage. Unfortunately, in the absence of empirical studies of the relevant facts it is impossible to be more than tentative about the significance of such qualifications.

One main category concerns the nature of modern technology compared with that applied by the now developed countries in their early spurts of industrialization. For one thing, it is usually held that technological development has greatly increased the optimal size of plants or firms. With advanced techniques, the volume of output required to achieve minimum costs – or costs close to the minimum – will therefore often be in excess of what a limited domestic market can absorb. This creates a special hardship for those countries of South Asia – not always the smallest in population[3] – that have a particularly small aggregate monetized demand, actual and potential. The size of the domestic market is the more important because of the absence of regional cooperation and the generally unpromising outlook for manufactured exports: the South Asian countries are thereby forced to direct their industrialization efforts toward import substitution. It has been suggested that "the scope for developing new technological innovations, by modification and combination of various alterna-

[1] *Ibid.*, p. 85, f.n. 13.

[2] For example: "Countries which start later on their industrial career have some advantage in that they have, in the main, to take over and apply techniques that have been worked successfully in more advanced countries." (India, Government of, Planning Commission, *Second Five Year Plan*, New Delhi, 1956, p. 6.)

[3] This should be remembered when comparing countries like Malaya, Ceylon, and the Philippines with India or Pakistan.

tives, is considerably broader than was the case when the original technological changes were developed."[1] But such innovations require enterprise, fresh thinking, and a considerable effort of research, all of which are scarce in the underdeveloped countries (see below). Sometimes, on the other hand, the technique of the smaller optimal size – or the smaller size that is not very much more costly – may be simply a less modern one than is now used in the advanced countries under the pressure of labor scarcity. It has often been suggested, therefore, that the underdeveloped countries could with great advantage buy second-hand equipment; though obsolescent in the advanced countries, it would be more efficient than present techniques in the underdeveloped countries. The purchase of such equipment would not only reduce the initial investment but in many cases would also permit smaller plants.[2] However, acceptance of anything but the most up-to-date meets both with strong inhibitions and with other and more substantial difficulties in the underdeveloped countries.

In our opinion, the adverse economic impact of limited domestic markets tends to be overemphasized in the literature. At least, the impact is different in different industries, and is often greater in heavy than in light industry. But much more detailed research is needed before one can gauge the true significance of market size for the optimum size of plant or enterprise. Not enough relevant information is available to warrant the blanket assertions so many writers make, and sometimes embellish by mathematical models based on abstract assumptions not tested in regard to their relevance and realism.

Another aspect of modern technology usually thought to add to the difficulties of its adaptation in South Asia is its requirement of large initial investments. Since present-day technology is mainly a product of economies that have a scarcity of labor and a relative abundance of capital, it tends to be labor-saving and capital-intensive. Much of it may therefore be beyond the means of the very poor, capital-starved economies in the region. In any case, the necessity of large capital investments may severely limit the scope and rate of their industrialization. But the sweeping assumption often encountered, that modern technology has become more capital-intensive than in the earlier phases of Western industrialization, is another proposition that requires more specific evidence and is certainly not valid in every instance. Many branches of industry using modern technology are capital-saving in the important sense of consuming less capital per unit of output. Neither is it universally true that modern technology requires larger units of capital initially, especially in light industry. Again, as in the case of optimal size, intelligent adaptation to the different factor propor-

[1] C. Wolf and S. C. Sufrin, *Capital Formation and Foreign Investment in Underdeveloped Areas,* Syracuse University Press, Syracuse, 1955, p. 40.

[2] United Nations, *Report of Expert Group on Second-Hand Equipment for Developing Countries,* December 7–22, 1965, New York, 1966.

tions and other conditions in South Asia might enable modern technology to be utilized in such a way that less, rather than more, capital is required. The usual broad generalization seems, therefore, to be hazardous and somewhat misleading. Nevertheless, technology today may and probably does entail more investment in transport and power than in earlier periods. If so, and if these magnitudes are somehow allocated to new industries, then new production techniques can be said to require a heavier initial investment. Even this generalization must be tentative, however, for much of the early industrial development in England involved canal building, which at the time represented a substantial investment; and the countries of Western Europe and the New World that industrialized later had to invest in railways.

One can be more certain that there are tremendous external economies for an industrial enterprise growing up in an already developed industrial surrounding. Conversely, there is great difficulty in starting even one industry without the support of that surrounding. As Everett Hagen points out:

> . . . every Western industry depends for its efficiency on other industries. It assumes the ready availability of materials, components, and tools. It depends also on auxiliary enterprises which can provide technical, financial, and managerial services on demand; on a complex network of communication and transportation facilities; and on an intricate system of business practices. A Western economy is a technical (and cultural) complex, not a set of isolated pieces of technology. In an underdeveloped society the auxiliary industries are missing and the framework of business practices is different. One piece cannot be detached from the complex and used efficiently elsewhere without skillful adaptation.[1]

This interconnection of the economic system makes the beginning stages of industrialization much more difficult today, particularly when shortages of capital, enterprise, and skills set narrow limits to the scope of the industrialization efforts.

The shortage of skills, indeed, represents a third main difficulty for the underdeveloped countries of South Asia in advancing to a higher technological level. The use of modern technology calls for a certain minimum supply of various skills that are generally lacking in the region. Not only is a somewhat more skilled labor force needed, but a greater number of technicians and managers as well. Achievement of the requisite skill levels of all kinds necessitates substantial efforts in education, using the word to include a widespread attack on illiteracy, academic study in science, and much for-the-job and on-the-job training. Managerial and engineering skills, in particular, can be perfected only after actual working experience.

[1] Everett E. Hagen, *On the Theory of Social Change, How Economic Growth Begins*, The Dorsey Press, Cambridge, 1962, p. 31.

Also, the possibility of adapting modern technology to the smaller plant size and lower capital intensity often appropriate in South Asia rests on the availability of engineers and managers in sufficient number to explore and experiment with modifications of all kinds. If imagination and enterprise are wanting, the South Asian countries may settle for adopting the techniques of the advanced countries without making adjustments to their conditions, and the difficulties already mentioned would then be more valid and relevant. Thus limitations of their domestic markets will pose a greater problem if managerial and engineering skills are scarce. Larger plants and firms may, indeed, provide a means of economizing these types of rare skills. For the same reason, these countries may be compelled to use more capital-intensive techniques than would *per se* be economic; in the same way lack of a skilled work force may induce more capital-intensive production techniques. Obviously, too, without trained managers, engineers, and workers it is impossible to strive for the optimal complex of industries and auxiliary enterprises. It can be said, therefore, that *the lack of skills is a fundamental hindrance to progress.*

There can be little doubt that the educational level of management, technical personnel, and workers now considered minimal for successful operation of a modern industrial establishment is substantially higher than it was in the early period of Western industrialization. Most of the technical innovations of the late eighteenth and nineteenth centuries were mechanical inventions whereas today and increasingly they grow out of discoveries concerning the structure of matter and energy, chemical processes, metallurgy, and so on. In the early phase of the industrial revolution it was the entrepreneurs themselves, in textiles and other industries, who had to make the machines needed for their factories. They were capable of doing this because the new machinery "involved no principles that an intelligent merchant could not grasp. Indeed, much of the mechanical invention of these years was simply the result of the harnessing of the traditional skills of clockmakers, millwrights, blacksmiths, and the like to the needs of the entrepreneur."[1] Or, in the words of Mason, "the early developments in industrial technology were undertaken not by men of science who discovered the practical application of general principles but by skilled artisans and thinkers working in the eighteenth-century equivalent of the twentieth-century garage."[2] Successful adoption and adaptation of present-day technology requires a much greater knowledge of general science. The connection between science and technology (to be discussed in Section 9) is probably closer now than ever before in history. An economy whose

[1] Charles Wilson, "Technology and Industrial Organization," in Charles Singer, E. J. Holmyard, A. R. Hall, and Trevor I. Williams, eds., *A History of Technology,* Vol. V. *The Late Nineteenth Century c1850 to c1900,* The Clarendon Press, Oxford, 1958, pp. 799–800.

[2] *Economic Planning in Underdeveloped Areas,* p. 32.

work force is largely unskilled and illiterate and whose managerial and engineering talent is in short supply is therefore severely handicapped.

7 *In Regard to Agriculture*

Industrialization is unquestionably of crucial importance for long-range development, but the more immediate problem in the South Asian countries is agriculture. It contains the vast majority of the labor force and must absorb most of the increase in the labor force for decades to come, even if industrialization should proceed at a faster rate than at present.[1] The problem of using modern technology in agriculture is altogether different from that of its utilization in industry. In industry, it is feasible and may be advantageous to set up a new plant basically along Western lines; in fact, industrialization implies that many such plants are established, selected, and coordinated so as to form a complex containing as many external economies as possible. Modern technology in Western agriculture, however, has been directed toward raising yields, while the labor force engaged has been rapidly and steadily declining. Technological development in this pattern simply does not fit South Asian conditions.

Apart from the institutional barriers that would stand in the way – much more so than in industry since the modern industrial sector is new – the application of this pattern on a large scale in South Asian agriculture would rob the labor force imprisoned there of its meager livelihood. Generally, most land is cultivated; if more can be cultivated this is costly and there is usually labor pressing to use it following more or less the old pattern of labor intensity. The proportions of land and labor are thus in the main given, and on the whole changing in a way to increase the need for a much bigger labor input per unit of cultivated area. The improvement of productivity in agriculture has to adjust to these existing and foreseeable factor proportions, as well as to the fixed institutional conditions that limit technical advance in various ways. In consequence, the larger part of modern agricultural technology is unadaptable to South Asian conditions, and a new technology has to be devised, as we explain in Chapter 26.

A second reason why adoption of modern agricultural technology from advanced countries is not very practical is that this technology is based on research directed, quite understandably, at a kind of agriculture that operates under climatic and soil conditions different from those in South Asia – except insofar as it relates to plantation culture, which has been of direct economic concern to investors in the Western countries. Some specific techniques, such as artificial insemination and new methods of preventing plant diseases, are applicable, but even these often have to be radically

[1] Chapter 24, Sections 5 and 6.

adjusted to local conditions. The institutions in the region that are working on basic or applied research in agriculture — or in forestry — are far too few and ineffective to have had any major impact. Moreover, like economic research, their work is too much under the spell of Western science and technology. Often their ambition is to produce results more in line with the Western tradition than with the needs of their own countries. In Section 8 we shall have something to say about the kind of research that is needed.

The improvement of agricultural productivity requires not only research but also vigorous public policies. It may be noted in passing that this is only one of many ways in which the effort to advance production techniques in the South Asian countries tends to induce the state to become much more involved in development than was true in the Western countries in their early phase of development. This problem will be discussed in the next chapter.

8 *Criticism of the Static Approach*

Despite the reservations we have noted as to the difficulties of adapting modern technology to South Asian conditions, the availability of this technology, and the scientific knowledge on which it is based, should constitute a net advantage in initial conditions. The qualifications mentioned above refer essentially to the differences between modern technology and the technology applied when the now developed countries were beginning to industrialize. They should not obliterate the fact — which in itself should constitute a difference in initial conditions favorable to the underdeveloped countries in South Asia — that individual entrepreneurs and states now have access to scientific and technological knowledge vastly superior to that accessible to the Western countries during their pre-industrial phase of development.

But this whole approach to the problem is, in a sense, static. The important thing is not that science and technology have achieved a much higher level, which South Asia can try to approach by adoption and adaptation, but that they are continually and rapidly moving toward ever higher levels. This dynamic quality of technological change may seem to be adequately acknowledged by occasional assertions that the problem "is not merely one of introducing some degree of improvement in techniques; it is a matter of raising the *rate* of technological progress."[1] It is frequently added that a high rate of technological progress in the South Asian countries will require far more advanced research facilities than were needed in the Western countries in the early phases of their industrialization; and

[1] Higgins, *Economic Development*, p. 185.

also higher levels of education generally and more rational and enterprising attitudes, particularly among administrators and business entrepreneurs. This thinking is then rationalized in demands for a more scientific outlook and the emergence of a "scientific man" or an "industrial man."

The trust in further scientific and technological progress has been the basis for the optimism implied in the planning ideology, which we shall scrutinize in the next chapter. This optimism regarding the role of science and technology in economic development in South Asia has often been given pathetic expression by intellectual and political leaders in the region, including Jawaharlal Nehru; and the hopes expressed have been endorsed unreservedly by Western statesmen. Nor have Western economists been eager to dampen such expectations, except occasionally by the type of qualifications we noted in Section 6 above. No one, surprisingly enough, has pointed out the importance of the world environment within which the advances in enterprise, the innovations, and research in the South Asian countries must take place. In the developed countries, with huge resources at their disposal, science and technology are now progressing at an ever faster pace. This activity is naturally directed toward the interests and industries of the developed countries themselves. Only to a very minor, almost infinitesimal, extent does it have bearing on problems of direct importance to South Asia.[1]

What is, almost inexplicably, concealed in economic writings is the obvious fact that *scientific and technological advance in the West has had, and is having, an impact on the South Asian countries that is very detrimental to their development prospects*: only in regard to specific problems is this negative impact registered and analyzed. The general point that technological development continually creates new or increased impediments to economic development in South Asia is regularly missed. This is another example of the working of the optimistic bias we noted in the Prologue (Sections 4–6), common to Western economists and their South Asian colleagues.[2]

The deterioration of the trading position of the South Asian countries since soon after the First World War, which we discussed in Section 4, is

[1] There are, of course, exceptions such as the growing concern for water scarcity that has led certain Western nations to invest heavily in research on desalination of sea water. If efficient means to use sea water were developed, the arid regions of, say, West Pakistan might be rendered productive.

[2] The truth is glimpsed more often by the philosopher-historian than by the economist. Thus Panikkar, referring to the negative impact of technology, writes: "Briefly it may be stated . . . that the world is on the doorstep of a great transformation which will make the gap between the scientifically advanced and the scientifically backward nations deeper and wider; making the latter more than ever dependent for all essential things on the more powerful nations." (K. M. Panikkar, *Afro-Asian States and Their Problems*, Allen & Unwin Ltd., London, 1959, p. 80.) The only fault with Panikkar's statement is that this impact is not new, but dates far back. Like the widening gap, the process has been going on for a century or more.

thus in large part due to scientific and technological advances in the developed countries, which have made possible the rapid rise in agricultural productivity there, substantial reductions in the use of raw materials imported from South Asia for industrial production, and the substitution of synthetic products for other imported raw materials. Similarly, the population explosion in South Asia has been due to advances in medical science and technology that have lowered mortality rates. Since the development of science and technology is rapidly proceeding, not abating, its detrimental impact on the economies of South Asia can be expected to continue. As by far the greater part of all research is carried on in the developed countries and is financed by their governments, their foundations, universities, and industries, it would be unreasonable not to expect the research efforts to be directed to their advantage. Moreover, it would be contrary to our belief in progress, the very spirit of our civilization, to argue that, as a protection to underdeveloped countries, these advances should be stopped or their results should not be used.[1] We will continue to raise agricultural productivity, make savings in the use of raw materials, and develop substitute products; we may, for instance, as the report of a committee of the U. S. Congress suggests, produce synthetically at some not too distant time not only coffee but also tea and cocoa. And to prevent and cure disease and prevent untimely deaths, and to do this ever more effectively in the underdeveloped countries as well, is an even more intrinsic part of the ethos of our civilization. These efforts will continue, though they accelerate the population increase in a region like South Asia and build up ever greater impediments to economic progress.

Although restriction of scientific and technological advance is out of the question, its unfortunate impact could be counteracted by deliberately increasing research activity and directing it toward problems the solution of which would be in the interest of the underdeveloped countries. This would imply aid of another type by the developed countries, and aid on a larger scale than anything previously done or now contemplated in the way of technical assistance. In agriculture there are vast needs for scientific and technological research. Studies are needed, for example, about the attributes of soils in various tropical areas and their reaction to diverse

[1] This was stressed in the Secretary General's report to the United Nations Conference on Trade and Development in 1964, though with a reservation: "In no circumstances could we seriously entertain the thought of restraining technological advances. That does not mean, however, that it is advisable to encourage types of research which should not, for the time being, enjoy any priority whatsoever, as, for instance, research into substitutes for coffee. Moreover, in some cases, the transition might be made easier for the producing countries if minimum proportions were established in the use of the natural product, just as minimums are fixed in some cases in the use of certain national primary products in relation to imported commodities." (*Proceedings of the United Nations Conference on Trade and Development,* Vol. II, New York, 1965, p. 25.)

patterns of rainfall; about drainage, irrigation, and fertilizers; about improved seeds and animal stocks, cropping patterns, the use of agricultural implements, the prevention of plant and animal diseases, the storage of perishable products. Localized and intensive study of such problems in the temperate zones has made possible dramatic increases in yields of land and animals with steadily decreasing inputs of labor. It is no exaggeration to say that the efforts to raise agricultural productivity in South Asia by extension services and other means have so far been based on very limited knowledge of the fundamental facts regarding the physical, social, and economic conditions peculiar to the region. Much more research should also go into planning irrigation schemes and the use of energy from wind and even the sun and tides. In industry there is the whole problem, referred to in Section 6, of adjusting plants, machines, tools, and materials to the climatic and other conditions in South Asia, including consideration of the relative proportions of labor of various kinds and other factors of production. In the population field the problem, of course, is primarily one of improving contraceptive techniques and extending the practice of birth control in order to bring births into some kind of balance with deaths.

In all these respects – except perhaps the last – very little has as yet been accomplished. What is needed is clearly much more research systematically directed toward solving the problems of the underdeveloped countries. Some of this research could be carried on in the underdeveloped countries themselves, but hardly on a scale that would even come close to balancing the detrimental effects of the scientific and technological development in the advanced countries without considerable outside assistance in the form of research personnel and funds. Unless the research effort is very large and in the right direction, *the dynamics of technological progress will work to the ever greater disadvantage of the underdeveloped countries, increasing their difficulties and decreasing their development potential.*

9 *The Acceleration of Technological Advance and the Quickening Pace of History*

The true significance of the foregoing observations can only be grasped when we realize that technological advance, now proceeding so rapidly in the developed countries, can be expected to proceed ever faster in the future. In a sense, the most fundamental difference in initial conditions between the South Asian countries today and the Western countries in any period of their pre-industrial phase is the difference in the pace of history. A telescoping of change has become the only alternative not only to continued stagnation but to regression. In the final analysis, this situation is a result of the high levels of economic development now achieved by the developed countries and the accelerating speed with which they continue to develop.

Change was not rapid in the beginning of Western development prior to industrialization. It is, indeed, difficult to overestimate the importance of gradualness in the early development of the Western countries where "economic development" originated. All the major "revolutions" of the West — religious, intellectual, geographic, and even political (the emergence of consolidated nation-states) — occurred long before the industrial revolution, and they proceeded slowly, thereby permitting a relatively smooth adaptation of all relationships in society. Thus Western Europe had several centuries in which to become accustomed to, and prepare for, change. It is as if the "coefficient of changeability,"[1] starting at a low point in the Middle Ages, rose and then continued to rise at an ever faster rate. And so the ideas of change, adaptability, and mobility were gradually accepted as a way of life, until Westerners became accustomed to the kind of "permanent industrial revolution" in which they live today.

It is generally recognized that progress in science and technology was a result of and, at the same time, a driving force in this gradual development. From the viewpoint of the economist and the economic historian, the improvement of the methods of production was of primary importance. The industrial revolution was understood to have required a number of "inventions" of new production methods — over and above the changes in social and economic conditions, among which were the advances in rationality and in scientific knowledge that made the inventions possible and, even more important, led to their application and widespread use. During the nineteenth century, when economics took shape as a science, and before the speed of technological change had become so pronounced, it was natural for economists to lean toward the view that the great and radical inventions had already been made and that only "improvements" remained to be added. This is the impression that comes to mind on looking backward and discovering how often a large number of improvements branched out from earlier innovations; with hindsight, these appear to be consequential, indeed radical, technological breakthroughs. Although nineteenth century economists produced very little explicit discussion of technological advance — less than their forerunners from Adam Smith's time — this was the usual implicit assumption. It was this way of looking at things that made it natural to assume that there would be no alteration "in the state of the arts." This assumption permeates classical and neo-classical economic analysis. We see it reflected today in the regular type of quasi-static analysis of the underdeveloped countries' problem of adopting the modern powerful technology of the advanced countries (Section 6). The assumption also fits the common bias of assigning to savings and investment the

[1] The term is Gerschenkron's. (A. Gerschenkron, *Economic Backwardness in Historical Perspective*, Harvard University Press, Cambridge, 1962, Chapter 3.)

crucial and almost exclusive rôle in economic development; it still dominates planning and most economic analysis of the development problem.

But this view of technological advance should now be excluded by our experience of living in a society where technological advance is so very rapid and is, in fact, constantly accelerating. More and more it becomes an almost automatic process driving development forward. The reality of the situation is blurred by saying that we are living through a new industrial revolution. Whatever measure we apply, the Western world has had many "industrial revolutions" since the first, each following more closely upon the preceding one. Indeed, we have good reason to expect that the great technological breakthroughs are yet to come. One element in this process, pointed out in Section 6, is that scientific research is playing an ever larger and more direct role in technological advance. This advance is increasingly characterized by systematic and coordinated innovations, founded on newly acquired scientific knowledge often of the basic type, while the role of invention as such is decreasing. J. P. Corbett has described this transformation:

> Of course, this new cooperation between theory and practice was, at first, extremely loose and unsystematic. The practical problems of navigation were indeed a powerful stimulus no less to astronomical enquiry than to the improvement of clocks. Even in the absence of such precise connexions, there was, no doubt, throughout the early period, a constant vague pressure of science and production on each other. At the very least they can be said to have flourished in the same climate of opinion. Yet such a crucial invention of the early industrial revolution as the steam engine was developed very slowly by practical engineers, on the basis of general mechanical knowledge, but without any rigorous scientific analysis; and much the same appears to have been generally true of the other inventions of that period. With the nineteenth century, however, the pace began to change. The old and influential but still very loose connexion between science and production began to be much more effective and direct. Over an ever widening field the achievements of research paved the way for production, and the problems of production called successfully upon research. Thus electrical generators were in economic use within a few decades of the fundamental work of Faraday which made them possible in theory. In our day, finally, this cooperation between the producer and the theorist has reached a very high level of efficiency.[1]

This increasingly close relation between science and technology has certainly been a major cause of the acceleration of technological advance. It also gives us reason to expect the curve to be of the exponential variety. Without wanting to press the analogy too far — as we are not in a position to define either knowledge or the increase of knowledge in terms permitting quantitative measurement — it is reasonable to assume that the growth in scientific knowledge is proportional to the sum of knowledge previously

[1] J. P. Corbett, *Europe and the Social Order*, A. W. Sythoff, Leyden, 1959, p. 20.

acquired. Knowledge should thus grow at a compound rate of interest, and technology should advance along a parallel, or more steeply rising, line.[1]

Taking as given the civilization within which it takes place, the accelerating growth of scientific and technological knowledge becomes a force, speeding up and bending the course of history in a way that is largely outside our control. Even in the field of armaments and war preparations, where the mutual interests in control are immense, the difficulties of carrying it out in practice loom so large that few are optimistic. In other fields a slowing down of the practical application of science and technology in production and consumption is not even desired. It could not be, given the spirit of our civilization and the competitive co-existence of nations and political blocs under which we live. The effects on our societies of this force for change, however, are beyond our perception. Historians and philosophers themselves have generally shied away from attempting to analyze in more specific terms its implications for the sort of society we will be living in. However, the speeding up of history is clearly visible even if we do not perceive its direction.

Until now, the modern democratic welfare states of the West have been able to contain the dynamics of scientific and technological change without bursting. This is undoubtedly due to two facts: first, from the beginning that kind of change was indigenous to these countries; secondly, it had a slow beginning over many centuries, during which it only gradually gathered its present explosive momentum. Society has adjusted to it; at least it has succeeded in doing so up to now. As for Russia, it was part of Europe and always had scholars and technicians active in the development of science and technology. The Soviet state has directed its planning so that it has its full share in scientific and technological advance, and even leads the march in one field after another. It has the resources to do this, and by means of its political system can allocate them effectively for this purpose.

The underdeveloped countries cannot possibly realize their aspirations in the same way, except in very limited, indeed insignificant, fields. Modern science and technology is to them a force emanating almost entirely from outside. And these countries are not afforded the opportunity for gradualness in development that typified the now developed countries. Technological advance is experienced as a shock administered by external forces. Meanwhile scientific and technological advance in the developed world has had, and continues to have, the detrimental effects on their de-

[1] William Ogburn was probably the first social scientist to think systematically along this line. In support of his view he pointed to the fact that new knowledge tends to develop simultaneously through the work of many researchers in different places. See William F. Ogburn, *Social Change*, The Viking Press, New York, 1928.

velopment prospects that we pointed out in Section 8. The foreseeable acceleration of this advance makes it probable that these effects will be increasingly detrimental.

There is little the South Asian countries can themselves do to prevent this. And we have assumed that any restriction on these advances, in order to protect the underdeveloped countries, is excluded. The only possible "control" is a positive one, through massive research directed toward solving the problems of the South Asian countries. At present, making this possibility explicit – as its realization on such a scale is not in sight – is only to underline the additional difficulties that the increasingly rapid technological development in the developed countries is bound to create in South Asia.

Even apart from this consequence of the dynamism of technological advance, the adoption and adaptation of modern technology in South Asia is very difficult, as we pointed out in Section 6. In colonial times, attempts to do it mostly resulted only in the creation of enclaves that left the larger part of the economy stagnant. A danger facing the independent governments in South Asia today is that their development efforts will have a similar effect: small islands of more or less modernized industrial production may be created, while the larger part of the economy remains backward. We shall return to this problem in Chapter 24; the special difficulties facing a modernization policy in the large sector of agriculture will be studied in Chapter 26.

The need is for telescoping changes, for having them take place faster than they ever did in the early development of the Western countries, faster even than they are now taking place in those countries. But the long stagnation in the underdeveloped countries has solidified institutions and attitudes, and hardened resistance to change in all strata of their population. The onslaught of modernization from outside, without the gradual transition experienced by the Western countries and in the presence of a population explosion, leads to a situation where elements of modernism are sprinkled through a society in which many conditions have remained almost the same for centuries. As Nehru said of India: "Our country at the present moment is a very mixed country. Almost every century is represented in India: from the stone age in which some tribals live, you may say, to the middle of the twentieth century. We have atomic energy and we use also cow dung."[1] To take the optimistic view that these spurts of modernism are "growing points" or provide a "base for further advance" is to assume a number of things: that the hampering effects of the population explosion at home and of the ever more rapid technological advance in the developed countries can be overcome, and that the spread effects within the South Asian countries themselves can be made to operate with much greater effectiveness than they have done up to now.

[1] R. K. Karanjia, *The Mind of Mr. Nehru,* Allen & Unwin Ltd., London, 1960, p. 38.

It is evident that these things will not come about by a process of "natural" evolution, and this constitutes the case for radical state policies. The aim of planning is to engender by state intervention development *in spite of* the greater difficulties we have noted throughout this chapter. What is attempted through planning is something entirely different from the mainly self-propelled economic development of the Western countries a hundred or two hundred years ago. Their development came about through a process of industrialization that was kept moving by the widely scattered activities of individual entrepreneurs bent on utilizing individual new techniques, as they became available, for their own profit. The emergence of the ideology of state planning for development thus itself constitutes a difference in initial conditions, to which we shall devote the next chapter.